Comparative Government and Politics

An Introduction

6th Edition

Rod Hague
and
Martin Harrop

First edition 1982
Second edition 1987
Third edition 1992
Fourth edition 1998
Fifth edition 2001
Sixth edition 2004

Published by
PALGRAVE MACMILLAN
Houndmills, Basingstoke, Hampshire RG21 6XS and
175 Fifth Avenue, New York, N.Y. 10010
Companies and representatives throughout the world

PALGRAVE MACMILLAN is the new global academic imprint of
St. Martin's Press LLC Scholarly and Reference Division and
Palgrave Publishers Ltd (formerly Macmillan Press Ltd).

ISBN 1–4039–1314–5 hardcover
ISBN 1–4039–1315–3 paperback

This book is printed on paper suitable for recycling and made
from fully managed and sustained forest sources

A catalogue record for this book is available from the British Library.

10 9 8 7 6 5 4 3 2
12 11 10 09 08 07 06 05 04

Printed in Great Britain by
J. W. Arrowsmith Ltd, Bristol

Summary of Contents

Contents

List of illustrative material

Debates

Profiles

50 years of

Boxes

A full list of boxes is provided in the Appendix.

Preface

This edition retains the purpose of its predecessors: to provide a wide-ranging, contemporary and clearly written introductory text for courses in comparative politics, and for other introductory courses in politics and political science. We have retained the framework and chapter division used in the previous edition but we have added 14 new sections and subsections addressing current developments in the subject and the literature. We have also rewritten many existing sections and revised the entire book to provide more recent examples and references; to enhance clarity; and to take account of suggestions from readers and our own evolving appreciation of the subject matter.

It might be helpful to outline the thinking behind the new sections. In Part I, we have added 'Nations and states' to the opening chapter, seeking to distinguish more sharply between two concepts that can no longer be presented as a compound 'nation-state'. We have restructured Chapter 2 to present the state in a more historical and global context, with new sections on 'How the state emerged', 'The Western state' and 'The post-colonial state'. We hope the changes here blend this chapter's global themes more successfully with the book's comparative approach, as recommended by Haynes (2003). Chapter 3 on authoritarian rule includes extended coverage of contemporary authoritarian regimes with a particular focus (in the light of increased interest since 9/11) on 'The Arab and Muslim worlds'. We have also added 'China in transition' not least to show that authoritarianism is not just a feature of Islamic societies. The material on China, in this section and elsewhere, also reflects the country's growing importance in the world economy.

In Part II, the chapter on political culture now includes a section on 'Political trust and social capital' as well as an introduction to cultural aspects of the relationship between 'Islam and the West'. Within the political communication chapter, we have extended the material on media impact through 'Reinforcement, agenda-setting and framing'. And the participation chapter now covers 'Social movements'.

The decline in formal political participation in contemporary democracies is an issue that interests students – and rightly so. This theme features more significantly in Part III, with 'Turnout' and a debate topic on compulsory voting added to the chapter on elections and voters. Falling party membership and its implications are carried though to the updated chapter on parties which now covers both 'Party membership and finance' and 'Selecting candidates and leaders'.

We have also strengthened Part IV on the struc-

BOX P.1

New sections and subsections in this edition

Chapter 1 Politics and government
Nations and states

Chapter 2 The state in a global context
How the state emerged
The Western state
The post-colonial state

Chapter 4 Authoritarian rule
The Arab and Muslim worlds
China in transition

Chapter 6 Political culture
Political trust and social capital
Islam and the West

Chapter 7 Political communication
Reinforcement, agenda-setting and framing

Chapter 8 Political participation
Social movements

Chapter 9 Elections and voters
Turnout

Chapter 11 Political parties
Selecting candidates and leaders
Party membership and finance

Chapter 15 The political executive
Presidential government: Brazil

tures of government, aware that what should be the core of the book was in danger of sliding towards its periphery. In particular, we have added a subsection on presidentialism in Brazil to the chapter on the executive, enabling us to broaden the discussion of presidential government beyond the United States. Our classroom experience is that student interest in President Lula da Silva can be carried though to a broader appreciation of the diversity in presidential systems. To reflect recent research on the parliamentary executive, we have also rewritten 'Minority and coalition government'.

We continue in this edition to use as the organizing framework within each chapter a three-part division of states into established democracies, new democracies and authoritarian states (see Boxes 3.1 and 4.1). Given that most new democracies have now survived for a number of years, we have in this edition placed our discussion of them immediately after the section on established democracies. This strikes us as a more intuitive sequence.

BOX P.2
Key features of the website http://www.palgrave.com/ politics/hague

▸ An extra comparative political economy chapter
▸ Hague and Harrop's Guide to Comparative Politics on the internet
▸ A searchable bibliography for each chapter
▸ Chapter summaries
▸ Essay questions and reading.

We invite you to visit our website. It supports this book specifically and your access to it is free and unrestricted. A major new feature for this edition is an entirely new chapter – only available on the website – on comparative political economy.

We would like to thank our publisher Steven Kennedy and his reviewers for their constructive advice; Keith Povey and Glynis Harris for their copy-editing skills; and Tim Flower of Florida International University for advising us on recent changes to the decree powers of the Brazilian president. We would also like to acknowledge a more general debt to the thousands of political scientists who provided the findings and insights on which this edition, in particular, is based. Without their effort, this book could not exist.

In all its manifestations, this book has now sold well over 100,000 copies. We are grateful for the support reflected in this figure and also for the corrections and suggestions provided by the many teachers and students around the world who use the book. We continue to welcome all feedback, not least because some errors of fact or interpretation are bound to have crept into this new edition. Please contact Martin Harrop at

School of Geography, Politics and Sociology
University of Newcastle
Newcastle upon Tyne
England
NE1 7RU

e-mail Martin.Harrop@newcastle.ac.uk

Rod Hague
Martin Harrop

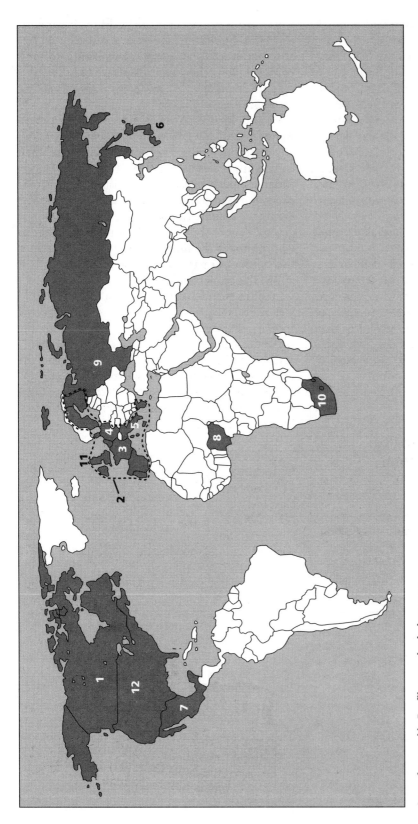

Areas featured in Profiles are shaded on map

Map of the World

Part I
FOUNDATIONS

In this part we set out the foundations of comparative government and politics. Chapter 1 outlines the key concepts of the subject while Chapter 2 focuses in more detail on the state: its emergence, character and alleged crisis. The subsequent chapters discuss the two main ways of organizing power in the state: democracy (Chapter 3) and authoritarian rule (Chapter 4). In Chapter 5, we conclude the part by discussing the comparative approach used in the book.

Chapter 1

Politics and government

In this book we examine the organization of politics in countries around the world. We focus on how nations solve the core political problem of making collective decisions. But we cannot jump straight into these issues. For just as what astronomers 'see' in the sky depends on the type of telescope through which they peer, so too does any interpretation of politics depend on the concepts through which we approach the topic. Indeed, in politics it often seems as though everyone has their own telescope – and claims that their own instrument is best!

In politics, major concepts remain at the forefront of discussion in a way that does not normally apply to more scientific disciplines. Political analysis is far more than mere opinion; yet even so, conclusions vary with the analyst rather more than is comfortable for those who advocate a strictly scientific approach to the subject. Comparative politics, based on a range of countries, is especially suited to the task of revealing contrasting perspectives on our subject matter. So in this chapter we discuss some central concepts of the discipline, not so much to establish 'correct' definitions as to introduce our own interpretations.

Politics

To start at the beginning: what is politics? We can easily list, and agree on, some examples of political activity. When the American president and Congress start their annual tussle over the federal budget, they are clearly engaged in politics. When terrorists crashed hijacked planes into the World Trade Center and the Pentagon in 2001, their acts were patently political. The heartland of politics, as represented by such examples, is clear. However, the boundaries of the political are less precise. When one country invades another, is it engaged in politics or merely in war? Would politics occur if resources were unlimited? Is politics restricted to governments or can it also be found in families, universities and even seminar groups?

A crisp definition of politics – one which fits just those things we instinctively call 'political' – is impossible. Politics is a term with varied uses and nuances. Perhaps the nearest we can come to a capsule statement is this: politics is the activity by which groups reach binding collective decisions through attempting to reconcile differences among their members. Four significant points inhere in this definition (Miller, 1991):

▸ Politics is a *collective activity*, involving people who accept a common membership or at least acknowledge a shared fate. Robinson Crusoe could not practise politics.
▸ Politics presumes an initial *diversity of views*, about goals or means or both. Were we in agreement all the time, politics would be redundant.
▸ Politics involves *reconciling such differences* through discussion and persuasion. Communication is therefore central to politics.
▸ Political decisions become *authoritative policy* for a group, binding members to agreements that are implemented by force if necessary. Politics scarcely exists if decisions are reached solely by violence, but force, or its threat, underpins the execution of policy.

The necessity of politics arises from the collective character of human life. We live in groups that must reach collective decisions about sharing resources, about relating to other groups and about planning for the future. A family discussing where to take its vacation, a country deciding whether to go to war, the world seeking to limit the damage caused by pollution – all are examples of groups seeking to reach decisions which affect all their members. As social creatures, politics is part of our fate: we have no choice but to practise it.

Indeed, the Greek philosopher Aristotle (384–322 BC) argued that 'man is by nature a political animal' (1962 edn, p. 28). By this he meant not just that politics is unavoidable but also that it is the essential human activity, the feature which most sharply separates us from other species. For Aristotle, people can only express their nature as reasoning, virtuous beings through participating in a political community. Politics is what we are for.

Of course, members of a group rarely agree, at least initially, on what plan of action to follow. Even if there is agreement over goals, there may still be a skirmish over means. Yet a decision must be reached, one way or the other, and once made it will commit all the members of the group. Thus politics consists in procedures for allowing a range of views to be expressed and then combined into an overall decision. As Shively (2002, p. 11) points out,

> political action may be interpreted as a way to work out rationally the best common solution to a common problem – or at least a way to work out a reasonable common solution. That is, politics consists of public choice.

By debating the options, the quality of the final choice should improve as the participants to the discussion become both better informed and more committed to the agreed course of action. In other words, good politics yields policy which is both well-designed and well-executed.

But the members of a group share some interests but not others. A collective decision will typically engage both common and conflicting interests. Deciding to expand higher education is one thing; working out who should pay for it is quite another. A decision will affect all, and may even benefit all, but not everyone will gain equally.

Most often a course of action will produce both winners and losers.

Here we arrive at what is the essence of the subject: politics is about reaching decisions which impinge on both the shared and the competing interests of the group's members. Indeed some authors *define* political situations as those in which the participants mix common and competing interests. 'Pure conflict is war', wrote Laver (1983, p. 1). 'Pure cooperation is true love. Politics is a mixture of both.'

So one aim of politics is compromise: to reach an agreement acceptable to all even if the first choice of none. Thus, Crick (2000, p. 21) defines politics as the 'activity by which differing interests within a given unit of rule are conciliated by giving them a share in power in proportion to their importance to the welfare and the survival of their community'. Crick's definition is somewhat idealistic; it seems to dismiss the possibility of politics occurring at all in dictatorships. But he is surely right to stress that politics involves (if not exclusively) negotiation, bargaining and compromise. And the venue for such discussions is government.

Government

Groups must not only reach decisions on their common affairs, they must also work out how their decisions are to be agreed and implemented. Small groups can often reach agreement by informal discussion, without needing to develop special procedures for decision-making. And their agreements can be self-executing: those who make the decision put it into practice themselves. However, these simple mechanisms are impractical for large groups, which must develop special institutions for making and enforcing collective decisions. By definition, these bodies form the government – the arena within which political issues are resolved.

Once government reaches a decision, it must be put into effect. In Easton's famous definition (1965a and b), 'politics is the authoritative allocation of values'. Values are allocated through implementing decisions, not just by making them. Taxes must be raised as well as set; wars must be fought and not merely declared. Here we encounter the harder edge of politics. Public authority – ultimately, force – is used to implement collective decisions. If you break the rules, the government may put you in prison; at any rate, it is the only body with the authority to do so. The words 'politics' and 'police', it is well worth noting, come from the same root.

Further, your government has not explicitly asked you whether you would like to abide by its laws, pay its taxes or die in its wars. You may have played no part in shaping the laws of your country but you are still expected to abide by them. And even if you leave one country, you will be subject to the government of another. From government there is no escape. You cannot – in the contemporary world – choose a life without government.

> **Definition**
> A **government** consists of institutions responsible for making collective decisions for society. More narrowly, government refers to the top political level within such institutions.

In popular use, 'the government' refers just to the highest level of political appointments: to presidents, prime ministers and cabinet members. But in a broader sense government consists of all organizations charged with reaching and implementing decisions for the community. Thus by our definition public servants, judges and the police all form part of the government, even though such people are not usually appointed by political methods such as election. In this broad sense, government provides the landscape of institutions within which we experience public authority.

Given the special authority of government, why should individuals ever agree to cede their autonomy to such a body? One argument for government, much favoured by contemporary economists, is the efficiency gained by establishing a standard way of reaching and enforcing decisions. If every decision had to be preceded by a separate agreement on how to reach and apply it, politics would be tiresome indeed. Efficiency gains mean that people who disagree on what should be done can nonetheless agree on a mechanism for resolving their disagreement.

In addition, government offers the benefits of security and predictability (Peters, 1999). In a well-governed society, citizens expect laws to be durable, or at least not to be changed arbitrarily; they know that rules apply to other people as well as to themselves; and they have grounds for expecting that decisions will be enforced fairly. In these ways, government serves as an escape hatch from the gloomy state of nature envisaged by the English philosopher, Thomas Hobbes (1588–1679):

> Hereby it is manifest, that during the time men live without a common power to keep them all in awe, they are in that condition which is called war; and such a war, as is of every man, against every man.
>
> (Hobbes, 1651, p. 100)

Without government, Hobbes continued, the life of man is 'solitary, poor, nasty, brutish and short'. Only when government overcomes the war of all against all, can society – including industry, science and culture – flourish. Thus government creates a framework of settled order within which endeavours such as a free market and a welfare state can emerge.

Once government is established, it may of course have unforeseen consequences. The danger of Hobbes's common power is that it will abuse its own authority, creating more problems than it solves. As one of Hobbes's critics pointed out, there is no profit in avoiding the dangers of foxes if the outcome is simply to be devoured by lions (Locke, 1690). This point is one on which the 130 million people murdered by their own government during the lethal twentieth century would doubtless agree, were they in a position to comment.

Further, even when a government does secure internal peace, it may simply turn its attention to external war. The twentieth century was an era of warfare states as well as welfare states. Government, then, is a two-faced, high-risk enterprise, offering the rewards of peace but also the danger of intensified conflict. Our aim in studying government should be to work out how to control Hobbes' common power while also securing its benefits.

Governance

An old word enjoying renewed popularity, governance refers to the activity, process or quality of governing. The term directs our attention away from the institutions and powers of government towards the task of public regulation, a function which government may share with other actors. Because governance is more abstract than government, denoting an activity rather than an institution, we need here to clarify its meaning and to explore why the term has become more common in political analysis.

As Pierre and Peters (2000, p. 7) say, governance is 'a notoriously slippery concept'. In essence, the word encourages us to focus on the wide range of actors involved in regulating modern societies. Depending on the particular sector, these actors might include employers, trade unions, the judiciary, professional employees, journalists and even academics. In areas such as health care or education, these expert participants form a specialist network which delivers substantial self-regulation. Because professions such as medicine and law do not take kindly to instructions from government, political institutions such as the executive and the legislature are just particular actors in these networks and by no means always the commanding players; hence the need for the broader term.

Understood as the task of managing complex societies, governance involves the coordination of both public and private sector bodies; it is the ability to get things done without the capacity to command that they are done (Rhodes, 1996). Governance implies persuasion exerted through a network, rather than direct control over a hierarchy.

The term grew in popularity in the final two decades of the twentieth century as Western democracies lost some confidence in the ability of their governments to directly manage economic production and welfare provision. As a result, more emphasis was placed on government as a regulator (e.g. of telecommunications networks) rather than as a provider (e.g. through a state-owned telephone company).

Governance is also the preferred term when examining the activity and effectiveness of government, rather than just the institutions themselves. In this context, governance refers to what governments do and to how well they do it. For example, many international agencies suggest that 'effective governance' is crucial to economic development in new democracies. Thus, the World Bank (1997, p. 1) argued in an influential report that 'the state is central to economic and social development, not as a direct provider of growth but as a partner, catalyst and facilitator'. The focus here is on government policies, activities and achievements, not its internal organization or its direct provision of goods and services.

> **Definition**
> **Governance** denotes the activity of making collective decisions, a task in which government institutions may not play a leading, or even any, role. In international relations, for example, no world government exists to resolve problems but many issues are resolved by negotiation – a case of governance without government.

And it is the field of international relations which offers the best examples of governance. The reason is clear: there is no world government, no institution making enforceable decisions for the world as a whole. Even so, many aspects of global relations are regulated by agreement. One example is the internet, a massive network of linked computers beyond the control of any one government. Yet standards for connecting computers and data to the internet are agreed, mainly by private actors. Thus we can speak of the governance, but not the government, of cyber-space (Hall and Biersteker, 2002).

Similarly, international institutions have emerged to formulate rules in many other areas: for instance, the World Trade Organization (WTO) works to reduce trade barriers between its member states. However, such bodies are certainly not governments; they have limited powers, especially in enforcement, and they lack a police force to enforce their will. Indeed, the WTO reaches decisions – when it does so at all – by the cumbersome method of consensus.

So the emerging pattern, in international and perhaps also in national politics, is rules without rulers, order without orders, governing without government. In a word: governance (Rosenau, 1992).

The state and sovereignty

The state is now the dominant principle of political organization on the world's landmass. The main exceptions are a few remaining colonies (such as Britain's Gibraltar) and territories currently administered by the United Nations (such as Bosnia). In addition, some territories are voluntarily subject to partial external control – for example, Puerto Rico is affiliated with the United States – while others claim substantial autonomy within a larger state – for instance, Hong Kong and Tibet within China. But leaving such anomalies to one side, the world is parcelled up into separate states which, through mutual recognition, form the international system (Krasner, 2001).

The state is a unique institution, standing above all other organizations in society. The state can legitimately use force to enforce its will and citizens must accept its authority as long as they continue to live within its borders. As Edelman (1964, p. 1) writes,

> the state benefits and it threatens. Now it is 'us' and often it is 'them'. It is an abstraction, but in its name men are jailed, or made rich on defense contracts, or killed in wars.

The state is more than its government. The term denotes the ensemble formed by combining government, population and territory. It is the state that claims a monopoly of authorized force, providing a mandate which government then puts into effect. To bring out the distinction between state and government, note that all countries have someone who serves as head of state but that this person is not usually head of the government. European monarchs are examples: they symbolize the state but leave prime ministers to control the levers of power. In short, the state defines the political community of which government is the executive branch.

A central feature of the state is its capacity to regulate the legitimate use of force within its boundaries. In describing states as 'bodies of armed men', the Russian revolutionary Vladimir Lenin (1870–1924) articulated this link between the state and violence. But although the state can and does employ coercion, it is far more than a mere band of hoodlums. Because the state is based in a fixed territory, it has a long-term incentive to increase the wealth of its people and therefore of itself. To use Olson's phrases (2000), states are 'stationary bandits' rather than 'roving bandits' and they behave better as a result.

> **Definition**
> The **state** is a political community formed by a territorial population which is subject to one government. A **country** usually refers to a state's territory and population, rather than its government. In international law, a state's **territory** extends to its airspace, continental shelf and territorial waters.

Most importantly, the state claims not just the capacity but also the right to employ force. As the German sociologist Max Weber (1864-1920) noted, the exclusive feature of the state is its integration of force with authority. As Weber wrote, 'a state is a human community that (successfully) claims the monopoly of the legitimate use of physical force within a given territory' (Gerth and Mills, 1948, p. 78). Any state must successfully uphold its claim to regulate the authorized use of coercion within its domain. When the state's monopoly of legitimate force is threatened, as in a civil war, its existence is at stake. While the conflict continues, there is no legitimate authority. Contrary to Lenin, a body of armed men is not a state because the law of the gun is no law at all.

Much of the theoretical justification for the state is provided by the idea of sovereignty. In describing the state, we must therefore unpack this related notion. As defined by the French philosopher Jean Bodin (1529–96), sovereignty refers to the untrammelled and undivided power to make laws. Echoing Hobbes, the English jurist William Blackstone (1723–80) argued that 'there is and must be in every state a supreme, irresistible, absolute and uncontrolled authority, in which the right of sovereignty resides'.

The word 'sovereign' originally meant the one seated above. So the sovereign body is the one institution within a country which is not subject to higher authority – and that body is, by definition, the state. As Bodin wrote, the sovereign can 'give laws unto all and every one of the subjects and receive none from them'. By consecrating central authority in this way, the legal concept of sovereignty contributed powerfully to the development of the European state.

Sovereignty originally developed in Europe to justify the attempt by monarchs to consolidate control over unruly kingdoms. Indeed, the British monarch is still known as the 'sovereign'. But as democracy gained ground, so too did the belief that elected parliaments acting on behalf of the people are the true source of sovereignty. The means of acquiring sovereignty evolved although the need for Blackstone's 'supreme authority', wherever located, remained unquestioned in Britain and France.

Beyond Europe, however, the notion of sovereignty remained weaker. In the federal 'United States', for instance, political authority is shared between the central and state governments, all operating under a constitution made by 'we, the people' and enforced by the Supreme Court. In these circumstances, the idea of sovereignty is diluted and so too is the concept of the state itself.

> *Definition*
> **Sovereignty** refers to the ultimate source of authority in society. The sovereign is the highest and final decision-maker within a community. Sovereignty is a legal title which is possessed in its entirety or not at all; a state cannot be partly sovereign. **Internal sovereignty** refers to law-making power within a territory. **External sovereignty** describes international recognition of the sovereign's jurisdiction over its territory. The phrase 'the sovereign state' reflects both dimensions.

Contemporary discussions of sovereignty distinguish between internal and external aspects. The law-making body within the state possesses internal sovereignty: the right to make and enforce laws applying within its territory. By contrast, external sovereignty is the recognition in international law that a state possesses authority over a territory. By implication, the state is answerable for that jurisdiction in international law. External sovereignty is important because it allows a state to claim the right both to regulate affairs within its boundaries and to participate as an accepted

member of the international system. In this way, the development of the international system has strengthened the authority of states in the domestic sphere; indeed, internal and external sovereignty represent two sides of a single coin.

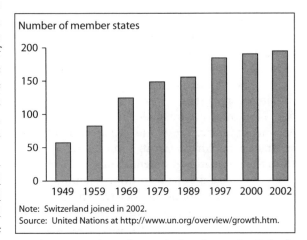

Note: Switzerland joined in 2002.
Source: United Nations at http://www.un.org/overview/growth.htm.

Figure 1.1 Number of states belonging to the United Nations, 1949–2002

Nations and nationalism

A nation is more easily recognized than defined. We all know that France is a nation but we find it harder to specify what characteristics justify this designation. A single language, for example, is often taken as evidence of a common nationality and many countries share a name with their language, France among them. But in France, as in some other states, nation-builders created a shared language, rather than the other way round. After the revolution of 1789, the country's centralizing elite insisted that only French should be taught in schools, thus overwhelming traditional dialects. A common language is as much an achievement as a condition of nationhood.

In any case, a single language is not necessary for a shared nationality. Switzerland, for instance, is indisputably a single nation even though French, German and Italian are spoken within its borders. Similarly, of the many countries in which English is the leading language, only one comprises the English nation. In truth, seeking to identify a nation using any single marker, whether language, history or ethnicity, is fruitless. Nations are imagined communities and a nation is often viewed as any group which upholds a claim to be regarded as such (Anderson, 1983).

In two ways, though, we can be a little more precise. First, nations are peoples with homelands. As Eley and Suny (1996, p. 10) put it, a nation – like a state – implies 'a claim on a particular piece of real estate'. Here the origin of the word 'nation' is relevant: it derives from a Latin term meaning place of birth. This link between nation and place is one factor distinguishing a nation from an ethnic group or tribe. Where a tribe can up sticks and move home, a nation remains tethered to its motherland, changing shape mainly through expansion and contraction.

Second, when a group claims to be a nation, it asserts a right to self-determination within its homeland. The group uses or invents a shared culture to justify its claim to political autonomy. It is this assertion of self-rule that gives the idea of a nation its political character. A group united by a common language, history or ethnicity becomes a nation by achieving or seeking control over its own destiny, whether through independence or devolution. In short, nations 'are spatially concentrated and culturally distinct groups attempting to attain political self-determination' (Hechter, 2000, p. 14).

Some examples will clarify these points. To describe French-speaking Canadians as a separate nation, as opposed to a linguistic community, indicates a demand for autonomy if not independence for this group. In a similar way, to refer to the indigenous people of the Americas as Indian nations, as opposed to tribes, also implies a claim to self-determination. Note that French Canadians and American Indians are also linked to particular areas, thereby satisfying the territorial condition of national status.

Definition
A **nation** is defined by Guibernau (1999, p. 14) as 'a human group conscious of forming a community, sharing a common culture, attached to a clearly demarcated territory, having a common past and a common project for the future and claiming the right to rule itself'.

So much for what a nation is. The next question, far more difficult, is: why do nations exist? When and why did they come into being? Here debate centres on whether nations should be seen as ancient or modern (Motyl, 2002). On the one hand, nations are sometimes viewed as creatures of antiquity, emerging from the primeval soup of past times. Smith (1998), for instance, points out that several large ethnic groups ('nations'?) are indeed of distant origin. Examples include the Jews and the Chinese. This position is the 'primordial' view of nations, meaning 'existing from the beginning'.

On the other hand, a modernist approach links nations to more recent ideas of self-determination. From this perspective, nations are made rather than found. They may indeed draw on ancient cultures but their core lies in justifying self-government amid a world of states. Nations, after all, assert statehood and states themselves are products of modernity (Mann, 1995).

In addition, a national identity serves broader modern functions. It unites people who do not know each other but who nonetheless find themselves yoked together under common rulers and markets (Gellner, 1983). It was, for example, only after the creation of the USA following the Philadelphia convention of 1787 that an American identity emerged to supplement loyalty to the 13 founding states. The American nation followed the founding of the central government.

As in white, male America, national loyalties glued large populations together under a veneer of equality. According to Anderson (1983, p. 49), this integration was itself made possible by the modern development of literacy and mass communication using a single national language:

> The convergence of capitalism and print technology on the diversity of human language created the possibility of a new form of imagined community which set the stage for the modern nation.

Certainly, many nations have been constructed in the course of recent struggles. In the nineteenth and especially the twentieth centuries, many colonial peoples marched to independence under the banner of national liberation. Often, these freedom-claiming 'nations' were as artificial as the boundaries originally imposed by colonial rulers. In a process of nationalism from above, the leaders of independence movements sought to construct national identities on extremely insecure foundations. Even so, the constructions served their immediate purpose: nationalism did indeed prove to be the grave-digger of empires (Tivey, 1981). Dating the precise origin of nations is impossible but their starring role surely lies in modern times.

> *Definition*
> **Nationalism,** the key ideology of the twentieth century, is the doctrine that nations are entitled to self-determination. Gellner (1983, p. 1) writes that nationalism 'is primarily a political principle, which holds that the political and national units should be congruent'. The significance of nationalism is that it offers one answer to a question beyond the reach of democracy: who are 'the people' who are to govern themselves?

Even more than nations themselves, nationalism is a doctrine of modernity. Like some other 'isms', nationalism emerged in the nineteenth century to flourish in the twentieth. But unlike some other ideologies, the principle of nationalism is reassuringly straightforward. It is simply the doctrine that nations do have a right to determine their own destiny – to govern themselves. The British philosopher John Stuart Mill (1806–73) was an early advocate of this position. He argued that 'where the sentiment of nationality exists in any force there is a *prima facie* case for uniting all the members of the nationality under the same government, and a government to themselves apart' (Mill, 1861, p. 392).

This principle of national self-determination proved to be highly influential in the twentieth century. It provided a justification for redrawing the map of Europe with the final collapse of the Austro-Hungarian Empire in 1918. The United Nations Covenant on Civil and Political Rights (UNHCHR, 1966) offered further support to the principle of national self-government:

> all peoples have the right to self-determination. By virtue of that right they freely determine their political status and pursue their economic, social and cultural rights.

Nations and states

National identities are a potent political force yet the aspirations of nationalism have not been fully achieved. Mill's hope that each nation should form its own state remains unfulfilled. Indeed, to understand contemporary politics, we must examine the various ways in which nations and states can combine. Box 1.1 sets out four situations. The first two rows in the box describe types of state (nation-state, multinational state) while the latter two rows denote additional possibilities for national groups (stateless nation, diaspora).

The first and most straightforward category is the traditional *nation-state*. Here each country contains only the people belonging to its nation. The French Revolution of 1789 established the idea that the state should articulate the interests and rights of citizenry bound together by a shared

---

BOX 1.1
Nations and states

Description	Type of	Definition	Example
Nation-state	State	A state with its own nation	Iceland
Multinational state	State	A state with more than one nation	Scotland and Wales in the United Kingdom
Stateless nation	Nation	A nation which lacks its own state and whose people are spread across several countries	Palestinians, the Kurds
Diaspora	Nation	A nation dispersed beyond a home state	Jews

national identity. In today's world, an example of a pure nation-state is Iceland – a small country whose population shares such a well-documented descent that its birth records provide a perfect laboratory for genetic research. Despite being Mill's favoured option, the traditional nation-state is less dominant today. Nearly 3 per cent of the world's population now live outside the country of their birth and, in consequence, many states have significant national minorities (IOM, 2003).

Even though such figures encouraged Anderson (1996) to pronounce the 'crisis of the hyphen', the nation-state is probably still an appropriate term when discussing the many countries in which one nationality remains dominant, politically and numerically. In France, Germany and Israel, for example, the state remains rooted in the soil of a strong national identity despite the presence of significant minorities – Algerians and Moroccans in France, Turks in Germany and Palestinians in Israel (Smooha, 2002). In essence, these countries remain nation-states, even if they lack the ethnic homogeneity of Iceland.

The second category in Box 1.1 is the *multinational state*. In this form, more than one nation is fundamental to a country's politics and assimilation to a dominant nationality is not a realistic option. Britain, for instance, is divided between English, Welsh, Scottish and Irish nationals; Canada between English- and French-speakers; and Belgium between Dutch- and French-speakers. As these examples demonstrate, multinational states can achieve internal peace and political stability.

But there are, of course, other cases where national divisions within a country have led to conflict. For instance, Balkan states such as Bosnia and Croatia experienced vicious conflicts between Croat, Muslim and Serbian national groups in the1990s. A key issue in comparative politics is to identify the governing arrangements which contribute most to political stability in multinational states.

One device available here is to separate citizenship from nationality. This distinction is subtle but increasingly important. Citizenship refers to the rights and obligations flowing from membership of a state; it represents a political and legal status which can, in principle, be shared by people with different national identities. In this way, citizenship can offer a protective roof under which different nationalities can live together.

> ### Definition
> A **citizen** is a person accorded the legal rights and duties flowing from membership of a state. In contrast to subjects, citizens are related to the state as equals and their rights are set out in law. Reflecting the traditions of ancient Greece and Rome, citizens possess the right and perhaps the obligation to participate in the affairs of their republic, including waging its wars (Heater, 1999).

For example, many immigrants from the Indian subcontinent who have become citizens of the United Kingdom think of themselves as British citizens but as Indian or Pakistani, rather than English, nationals. In a similar way, citizens of the European Union can now vote in local and European elections when resident in a member state other than that of their home nationality (Day and Shaw, 2002).

The 'nation of nations' in the United States achieves a similar blend through a different route. 'Hyphenated Americans' – immigrants who retain their traditional national loyalty while also embracing the citizenship and credo of their new homeland – are a familiar category in the USA. Such illustrations show how the capacity to acquire citizenship, without imposing a specific national identity, can be a flexible technique of integration within multinational states.

This book centres on states, whether nation-states or multinational in character. But there is a danger in this state-centred approach: namely, that we ignore how nations can cut across state boundaries. Our third category, the *stateless nation*, refers to just such a situation. Here a nation lacks a home state of its own. The Kurds, for example, have inhabited a mountainous region of Asia for over 4,000 years and their national identity is well-established. But the emergence of modern state frontiers has not proved kind to the Kurds. The national homeland of Kurdistan is now divided between Iran, Iraq, Syria and Turkey, with little immediate prospect of a Kurdish nation-state.

The Palestinians are an equally tragic instance of a stateless nation. After the postwar creation of Israel, the Palestinians became an uprooted Arab people, living mainly in refugee camps not just in traditional areas of Palestine but also in other Arab countries such as Jordan. However, a sense of national identity has developed among the Palestinians, paralleling a growing demand for statehood. The prospects of their claim succeeding seem greater than for the Kurds (Telhami, 2001).

Our final category is the *diaspora*. This term refers to a group which retains its national identity despite being widely distributed beyond its home country. The Jews are the leading case. Since its creation in 1949, the modern state of Israel has served as a Jewish homeland. However, the Jewish diaspora is widely spread, with only a minority of the world's Jews living in Israel itself. The Chinese diaspora, encompassing economically significant minorities in Malaysia, Thailand and other Asian countries, is another important example (Luce and Sevastopulo, 2003).

In Islamic theory, the Muslim world – known as *Dar al-Islam* – also forms a single entity which extends far beyond the religion's Arabian homeland. But Islam is not so much a diaspora centred on Saudi Arabia as a religion which transcends states. This transnational ethos may have been a background factor permitting the mobilization of radical Muslims from a range of countries into international terrorist organizations (Mandaville, 2003).

Using modern communications and transport, the members of a diaspora can keep in touch with their homeland, illustrating the feasibility of what Anderson (1998) calls long-distance nationalism. With increased mobility, these cross-border communities are growing in importance, diluting the traditional concept of the nation-state.

Power

Power is the currency of politics. Just as money permits the efficient flow of goods and services through an economy, so power enables collective decisions to be made and enforced. Without power, a government would be as useless as a car without an engine. Power is the tool that enables rulers both to serve and to exploit their subjects.

Some authors define politics in terms of power. For Hay (2002, p. 3), politics is 'concerned with the distribution, exercise and consequences of power'. On such accounts, politics is found not just in government but also in the workplace, the family, the university and indeed in any other arena in which power is exerted. Such a view is probably too catholic; those who study politics are primarily interested in the flow of power in and around the state. Morgenthau's definition of politics (1966, p. 63) as concerned with the nature of power 'with special emphasis on the power of the state' perhaps comes closer to the mark. But all are agreed that power is central to politics. How then should power be defined and measured?

One indicator of power is simply the ability of a community to achieve its aspirations. In this sense, describing the United States as a powerful country simply means that it has the capacity to achieve its objectives. Notice that the emphasis here is on power *to* rather than power *over* – on the capacity to achieve goals, rather than to exercise control over other countries or people (Box 1.2).

BOX 1.2
The language of power

Power	The production of intended effects
Power *to*	The ability to achieve one's goals
Power *over*	The ability to overcome opposition
Incentive-shaping	Exerting power through the use of inducements and threats
Preference-shaping	Exerting influence through persuasion and control of the climate of opinion

---

This 'power to' approach is associated with the American sociologist Talcott Parsons (1967). He interpreted power as the capacity of a government to draw on the obligations of its citizens so as to achieve collective purposes such as law and order and protection of the environment. From this perspective, political systems resemble energy sources: the more power they deliver, the better. After all, the more powerful the government, the more effective it should be at achieving the goals of the community. For Parsons, political power is a collective resource rather than an attribute of individuals.

The German-born political theorist Hannah Arendt (1906–75) made a similar point in defining power as 'not just the ability to act but the ability to act in concert' (1966, p. 44). A group whose members are willing to act together possesses more horsepower – an enhanced capacity to achieve its goals – than does a group dominated by suspicion and conflict. Thus Arendt viewed power and violence as enemies rather than siblings: 'power and violence are opposites; where the one rules, the other is absent. Violence can destroy power; it is utterly incapable of creating it' (1966, p. 56).

This view of power has exerted some influence but remains incomplete. Power, like politics, has a harder edge. Politics is more than a technical task of implementing a vision shared by a whole society. It is also an arena of conflict over which goals to pursue. Politics is substantially a matter of whose vision triumphs, a point that must be reflected in any definition of power. From this perspective, power consists of the ability to get one's way, to impose one's opinions, to overcome opposition. The underlying view of power here assumes conflict rather than consensus. In Dahl's famous definition (1957), power is a matter of getting people to do what they would not otherwise have done. Dahl's definition is neutral as to means; power is equated with influence, however exerted.

Of course, power and influence can be exerted by a variety of methods. One form is incentive-shaping: that is, altering the incentives confronting those subject to power. This can include the threat of punishment for disobedience or the promise of reward for acceding to a request. In either case, A seeks to alter the context within which B acts rather than B's overall political views. American presidents, for example, spend a significant amount of time on such activities. They threaten, bribe and cajole overseas leaders, wealthy corporations, leading members of Congress and anyone else who can help them achieve their goals. Indeed, their success in office depends in part on the skill with which they shape the incentives facing other political actors.

But power can also be exerted by shaping preferences rather than incentives. Here A's effort goes into shaping what B wants to achieve rather than the context within which B behaves. For example, an American president may seek to persuade the Secretary-General of the United Nations that the USA's intervention in another country's affairs is morally justified. Here power shades into influence, exerted through persuasion by discussion and debate.

On a wider scale, preference-shaping can taking the form of controlling the overall climate of opinion within which preferences are formed. Here influence arises from agenda-setting: that is, controlling what issues are addressed and how they are interpreted. For example, George W. Bush sought to convince his public that the invasion of Iraq in 2003 was a response to a threat to American security; this battle for public opinion proved to be more prolonged and more difficult than the initial invasion itself. On a smaller scale, parents exert influence over their children by shaping the way they see the world, not just by directly giving them incentives to behave in a particular way.

Awareness of this point led Lukes (1974) to conclude that A exerts power over B when A affects B in a manner contrary to B's interests, even if B is unaware of the damage caused. So, the manager of a nuclear power plant that leaks radioactivity into the surrounding community has exercised power over the residents, even if the population is unaware of the contamination. The difficulty here resides in specifying what a person's 'true' interests are, a challenging task once we move beyond physical well-being.

Even so, we must accept that controlling people's knowledge and attitudes is the most efficient way to control them. As the French philosopher Michel Foucault (1977) reminded us, supplying the framework within which an issue is approached is a potent form of control.

Authority

Authority is a broader notion than power. Where power is the capacity to act, authority is the right to do so. Authority gives the holder the right to exercise power, just as owning property offers the right to decide how that property is used.

Authority exists when subordinates acknowledge the right of superiors to give orders. So a general may exercise power over enemy soldiers but he does not have authority over them; this is restricted to his own forces.

When writers such as Parsons and Arendt argue that power is a collective resource, they mean that power is most effective when converted into authority. Yet authority is more than voluntary compliance. To acknowledge the authority of rulers does not mean you agree with their decisions; it means only that you accept their right to make decisions and your own duty to obey. Relationships of authority are still hierarchical.

Definition
Authority is the right to rule. Strictly, authority is the right to act, rather than the power to do so. However, authority creates its own power so long as people accept that the authority figure has the right to make decisions.

The German sociologist Max Weber (1922) provided a path-breaking analysis of the bases of authority. He distinguished three ways of validating political power (see Box 1.3).

The first type is by reference to the sanctity of *tradition*. This authority is based on 'piety for what actually, allegedly or presumably has always existed' (Weber, 1923, p. 296). Traditional rulers do not need to justify their authority; rather, obedience is demanded as part of the natural order. For example, monarchs rule because they always have done so; to demand any further justification would itself challenge traditional legitimacy – and would meet a firm response. Traditional authority is usually an extension of patriarchy: that is, the authority of the father or the eldest male. Weber offers several examples of paternal relationships:

> patriarchy means the authority of the father, the husband, the senior of the house, the elder sibling over the members of the household; the rule of the master and patron over the bondsmen, serfs, and freed men; of the lord over the domestic servants and household officials, of the prince over house- and court-officials.
> (Weber, 1923, p. 296)

BOX 1.3
Weber's classification of authority

Type	Basis	Illustration
Traditional	Custom and the established way of doing things	Monarchy
Charismatic	Intense commitment to the leader and his message	Many revolutionary leaders
Legal–rational	Rules and procedures; the office, not the person	Bureaucracy

---

While such illustrations may seem old-fashioned, in reality traditional authority remains the model for many political relationships, especially in non-democratic countries. In the Middle East, for example, 'government has been personal, and both civil and military bureaucracies have been little more than extensions of the leader' (Bill and Springborg, 2000, p. 152). The leader takes care of his followers and so on down the chain. These relationships are presented as familial but in practice they are based on inequality: the strong look after the weak in exchange for their loyalty. When entire political systems operate on the principle of traditional, patriarchal authority, they are termed 'patrimonial'.

Charismatic authority is Weber's second form of authority. Here leaders are obeyed because they inspire their followers, who credit their heroes with exceptional and even supernatural qualities. Where traditional authority is based on the past, charismatic authority spurns history. The charismatic leader looks forward, convincing followers that the promised land is within reach. A key point here is that, contrary to popular use, charisma is not for Weber an intrinsic quality of a leader. Rather, charisma refers to how followers perceive such figures: as inspirational, heroic and unique. So there is little point in searching for personal qualities that distinguish charismatic from ordinary leaders; rather, the issue is the political conditions which bring forth a demand for charismatic leadership.

Generally, charismatic leaders emerge in times of crisis and upheaval. Jesus Christ, Mahatma Gandhi, Martin Luther King, Adolf Hitler and Ayatollah Khomeini are illustrations. Khomeini, for instance, was a Muslim cleric and exiled hero who returned in triumph to take over the government of Iran following the revolutionary overthrow of the Shah in 1979.

Charismatic authority is short-lived unless it can be transferred to a permanent office or institution. 'It is the fate of charisma', wrote Weber (1922, p. 129), 'to recede with the development of permanent institutional structures.' This process is called the routinization of charisma. For example, Ayatollah Khomeini succeeded in establishing a theocratic regime (system of government) in Iran, dominated by the Islamic clergy, which outlasted the Ayatollah's death in 1989. But as memories of the regime's founder recede, so younger generations increasingly question the political authority of religious leaders. Authority in the Iranian theocracy is not fully routinized.

The third and final base for authority in Weber's scheme is called *legal–rational*. Here obedience is owed to principles rather than to people. The result is government based on rules, not traditional or charismatic leaders. Legal–rational authority inheres in a role or a position, not a specific person.

Indeed, a major virtue of legal–rational authority is that it limits the abuse of power. Because it derives from the office rather than the person, we can speak of officials 'going beyond their authority'. Setting out the extent of an office-holder's authority reveals its limits and so provides the opportunity for redress.

In this way, legal–rational authority is a foundation of individual rights. Weber believed legal-rational authority was becoming predominant in the modern world and certainly it has become the dominant form in established democracies. Indeed Weber's homeland of Germany is the best example of a *Rechtsstaat,* an entire state based on law.

Legitimacy

We must introduce one final concept in this chapter: legitimacy. This notion is a close cousin of authority but there is a significant difference in the context in which the terms are used. Legitimacy is normally used in discussing an entire system of government, whereas authority often refers to a specific position. When the authority of a government is widely accepted by those subject to it, we describe it as legitimate. Thus we speak of the authority of an official but the legitimacy of a regime.

Although the word legitimacy comes from the Latin *legitimare*, meaning to declare lawful, legitimacy is much more than mere legality. Legality is a technical matter. It denotes whether a rule was made correctly – that is, following regular procedures. By contrast, legitimacy is a political question. It refers to whether people accept the validity either of a specific law or, more generally, of the entire political system.

> ### Definition
> A **legitimate** system of government is one based on authority: that is, those subject to its rule recognize its right to make decisions.

Regulations can be legal without being legitimate. For example, the majority black population in white-run South Africa considered the country's apartheid laws to be illegitimate, even though these regulations were made according to the country's then racist constitution. The same could be said of many laws passed by communist states: properly passed and even obeyed but not accepted as legitimate by the people.

While legality is a topic for lawyers, political scientists are more interested in legitimacy: in how a regime gains and sometime loses public faith in its right to rule. Legitimacy is judged in the court of public opinion, not in a court of law.

Legitimacy is a crucial concept in understanding both the stability and the effectiveness of governments. In a famous analysis, Lipset (1960, p. 77) argued that 'legitimacy involves the capacity of the political system to engender and maintain the belief that the existing political systems are the most appropriate ones for the society'. How exactly political systems succeed, and sometimes fail, in creating a perception of their own appropriateness is the subject of Chapter 6.

Key reading

> **Next step:** *Shively (2002) is a clear and wide-ranging introduction to politics.*

Crick (2000) is a lively and argumentative examination of the nature of politics. On specific topics, governance is covered by R. Rhodes (1996) and Pierre and Peters (2000). For the state, Hall and Ikenberry (1989) and Poggi (1990) are good starting points while van Creveld (1999) traces the state's rise and alleged fall. Hinsley (1986), Hoffman (1998) and Krasner (1999) survey sovereignty from historical, sociological and international perspectives respectively. For nations, see Smith (1998) and Guibernau (1999). Nationalism is examined by Breuilly (1993) and Hechter (2000) while Heater (1999) introduces citizenship. See Kennedy and Roudometof (2002) for diasporas. On power, see Poggi (2001); Haugaard (2002b) is an annotated collection. Watt (1982) introduces authority while Lipset (1960) provides the classic account of legitimacy.

Chapter 2

The state in a global context

Although we now take for granted the division of the world into states, we should not assume that the state always was the dominant principle of political organization, nor that it always will be. There was a world before states and, as advocates of globalization tirelessly point out, there may be a world after them too (Guéhenno, 1995).

Before the state, formal government consisted, in the main, of kingdoms, empires and cities. Some of these units were substantial by any standards. For example, the ancient Chinese empire 'proved capable of ruling a population that eventually grew into the hundreds of millions over a period of millennia – albeit control was not always complete and tended to be punctuated by recurring periods of rebellion' (van Creveld, 1999, p. 36). Ancient history quickly disposes of the idea that all modern states are larger and more stable than every traditional political system.

Nor does the contemporary democratic state hold a patent on self-government by free citizens. Democratic ideas emerged in the classical cities of Athens and Rome, several centuries before the birth of Christ, and have merely been recovered and adapted to modern conditions.

Yet the modern state remains a unique political form, distinct from all preceding political systems. Melleuish (2002, p. 335) argues that 'the development of the modern state can be compared to the invention of the alphabet. It only happened once but once it had occurred it changed the nature of human existence for ever.'

Today's states possess the sovereign authority to rule a specific territory though their own specialized institutions. States form an abstract entity with a special legal status, a notion which contrasts with more personal rule by traditional kings and emperors. The modern idea of the state developed in Europe between the sixteenth and eighteenth centuries. Indeed, the use of the word 'state' as a political term only came into common use in Europe towards the end of this period (Dyson, 1980, p. 26).

In this chapter, we portray some of the historical and contemporary forces shaping the state. Our aim is to present the state not just as an abstract idea but also as a force that has moulded, and is in turn shaped by, the modern world. We begin by reviewing the emergence, growth and partial retreat of the state in its Western heartland. We then examine the export of the state from its European home to the rest of the world through colonialism. With this historical context set, we turn to two contemporary challenges facing the state: international organizations and the world economy.

How the state emerged

The state emerged from the embers of medieval Europe (c.1000–c.1500). In the Middle Ages, European governance had been dominated by two institutions, the Roman Church and feudalism, which together left no room for monarchies to develop into sovereign states.

The Church formed a powerful transnational authority placed above mere monarchs. Kings within the Christian commonwealth were considered to be secular agents of the Church's higher authority (Figgis, 1960). So strong were these external limits on monarchs that some authors who believe that global forces are constraining today's rulers describe this process as 'the new medievalism' (Slaughter, 1997).

Further, within their nominal territories, kings were further constrained by feudal noblemen who exerted extensive authority over men of lower rank. In this decentralized national setting, the king frequently learned that he needed his noblemen rather more than they needed him (Strayer, 1965).

The problem before us, then, is to explain how modern states emerged from this dual configuration of church and feudalism. How did European states shake off these medieval restraints to become the defining political units of the modern world?

War and reformation

If any single force was responsible for the transition to the modern state, that factor was war. As Tilly (1975, p. 42) writes, 'war made the state, and the state made war'. The introduction of gunpowder in the fourteenth century transformed military scale and tactics, as organized infantry and artillery replaced the knight on horseback. The result was an aggressive, competitive and expensive arms race. Between the fifteenth and eighteenth centuries, military manpower in France and England grew almost tenfold (Opello and Rosow, 1999, p. 50).

New technology required fresh thinking from rulers. Kings needed administrators to recruit, train, equip and pay for large standing armies. Reflecting these new benefits of scale, units of rule increased in size. The number of independent political units in Europe fell from around 500 in 1500 to just 25 by 1800, as a medieval architecture of principalities, duchies and bishoprics gave way to a more recognizable framework of larger countries (Tilly, 1975, p. 24). (Note, however, that two major European states, Germany and Italy, did not unify until the second half of the nineteenth century.)

With the growth of bureaucracy, local patterns of administration and justice became more uniform. Rulers began to establish formal diplomatic relations with their counterparts abroad, a core feature of the contemporary state system. The outcome was the more centralized monarchies which developed in England, France and Spain in the sixteenth century and which flourished in the seventeenth century. In France, for instance, Louis XIV of France (r.1643–1715) became known as the Sun King: the monarch around whom the realm revolved.

Just as war-making weakened the feudal pillar of the medieval framework, so the Reformation destroyed its transnational religious foundations. From around 1520, Protestant reformers led by Martin Luther condemned what they saw as the corruption and privileges of the organized Church. Their reform movement exerted profound political consequences, shattering the Christian commonwealth as war developed between Protestant and Catholic rulers, notably in the Thirty Years' War (1618–48) in German-speaking Europe.

This conflict was finally ended by the Peace of Westphalia (1648), an important if occasionally overstated chapter in the book of the state (Osiander, 2001). Westphalia is considered pivotal because it permitted rulers themselves to regulate the public exercise of religion within their kingdoms, thus rendering secular authority superior to religious edict. The medieval idea of the Church as a transnational religious authority, superior to secular rule, fell apart. The threat posed by Westphalia to papal supremacy doubtless explains the vigour of Pope Innocent X's criticisms: 'null, void, iniquitous, unjust, damnable, reprobate, inane, empty of meaning and effect for all time' (van Creveld, 1999, p. 82).

Sovereignty, contract and consent

As central authority developed in Europe, so did the need for its theoretical justification. The crucial innovation here was sovereignty, as later tamed by the notions of contract and consent. The French philosopher Jean Bodin (1529–96) made a crucial contribution to this centralizing ideology. He argued that within society a single authority should possess the untrammelled and undivided power to make laws. In Bodin's view, the sovereign – literally, the one seated above – should be responsible for legislation, war and peace, appointments, judicial appeals and the currency. Such concentrated authority is clearly far removed from the decentralized medieval framework of Christendom and feudalism.

The English philosopher Thomas Hobbes (1588–1679) drove the argument forward. He shared Bodin's belief in the need for a powerful sovereign. Without such a body to enforce the peace, suggested Hobbes, life would be impoverished indeed. But where Bodin's sovereign still derived his authority from God, Hobbes's analysis was firmly secular. Hobbes located the sovereign's authority in a contract between rational individuals seeking protection from each other's mischief. If the sovereign failed to deliver social order, people would no longer be under an obligation to obey. In this way, the sovereign serves the people, no longer the other way round, and religion becomes entirely a matter of inner conviction.

So, if Bodin was post-medieval in his thinking, Hobbes represents the first of the moderns. As Skinner (1978, p. 349) puts it, 'by the seventeenth century, we may be said to enter the modern world: the modern theory of the state remains to be constructed, but its foundations are complete'.

The vision of a government made by and for the governed was developed by John Locke (1632–1704), an English philosopher whose thinking shaped one influential interpretation of the Western state: namely, the liberal vision underpinning the American revolution. Locke argued that citizens possess natural rights to life, liberty and property. These rights must be protected by rulers governing through law. Citizens consent to obey the laws of the land, if only by tacit means such as accepting the protection which law provides. But citizens can withdraw their consent, and institute new magistrates, should rulers violate the natural rights of the citizens.

As if to mark the transition from traditional kingdoms to modern states, Locke further insisted that political rulers are not just benevolent father-figures caring for a notional household. Rather, political relationships are based on contract and consent. In Locke's writing, we see a modern account of the liberal state, with society placed before government and sovereignty limited by popular consent.

These ideas of sovereignty, contract and consent were reflected, in contrasting ways, in the two most momentous and tangible affirmations of modernity: the American and French revolutions. The American Revolution, in which the colonists established their independence from Britain and went on to create the United States, gave substance to Locke's liberal interpretation of the state.

Thus, the Declaration of Independence (1776) boldly declared that governments derive 'their just authority from the consent of the governed' while the American constitution (drafted 1787) famously begins, 'We, the people of the United States'.

However, it was the French Revolution (1789) that made the most ambitious and radical attempt to reinterpret sovereignty in democratic terms. Finer (1997, p. 1516) has no doubt as to the revolution's significance, describing it as 'the most important single event in the entire history of government'.

In essence, the French mapped out the contours of modern democracy. Where the American federal government remained strictly limited in its authority, the French revolutionaries regarded a centralized, unitary state as the sovereign expression of a nation consisting of citizens with equal rights. As national identity joined forces with the state in this way, so sovereignty – once the device used by monarchs to establish their supremacy over popes and princes – was reinterpreted for a new democratic age. These principles were expressed in the Declaration of the Rights of Man and the Citizen, a document which served as preamble to the constitution of 1791 and which Finer describes as 'the blueprint of virtually all modern states' (Box 2.1).

The Western state

With the French Revolution, the theoretical underpinnings of the Western democratic state were, in essence, complete. The detailed construction work was completed in the nineteenth and the first three quarters of the twentieth centuries, supported by growing nationalist sentiment. Only late in the twentieth century, and in the twenty-first, did the state begin to contract.

Expansion

Externally, the cage of the state became more precise during the nineteenth century, especially in Europe. Borders slowly turned into barriers as precise maps marked out defined frontiers. Lawyers established that a state's territory should

---

BOX 2.1

Declaration of the Rights and Duties of Man and the Citizen (France, 1789), Articles 1–6

1. Men are born and remain free and equal in rights. Social distinctions may be based only on considerations of the common good.
2. The aim of every political institution is the preservation of the natural and imprescriptible rights of man. These rights are liberty, property, security and resistance to oppression.
3. The source of all sovereignty lies essentially in the Nation. No corporation or individual may exercise any authority that does not expressly emanate from it.
4. Liberty is the capacity to do anything that does not harm others. Hence the only limitations on the individual's exercise of his natural rights are those which ensure the enjoyment of these same rights to other members of society. These limits can be established only by legislation.
5. The law is entitled to forbid only those actions which are harmful to society. Nothing not forbidden by legislation may be prohibited and no one may be compelled to do what the law does not ordain.
6. Law is the expression of the general will. All citizens have a right to participate in shaping it either in person, or through their representatives. It must be the same for all, whether it punishes or protects.

Source: Article 6 above is an extract. For the concept of the general will mentioned in that clause, see Rousseau (1762). For the Declaration's full text, see Finer (1997, p. 1538) or http://www.elysee.fr/ang/instit.

Internally, government functions began to expand. Many tasks we now take for granted as public responsibilities only emerged in the nineteenth century. These included policing, elementary education, gathering statistics and factory regulation.

For most of the twentieth century, Western states bore ever deeper into their societies (Box 2.2). Once again, this expansion was fuelled by the demands of war. The First (1914–18) and Second (1939–45) World Wars were total conflicts, demanding unparalleled mobilization of citizens, economies and societies. These campaigns were fought by massive forces equipped with the industrial weapons of tanks, planes and bombs. Such conflicts were extraordinarily expensive. As a result, tax revenues as a proportion of national product almost doubled in Western states between 1930 and 1945 (Steinmo, 2003, p. 213). The twentieth century was an era of war and therefore a century of the state.

Yet the onset of peace in 1945 did not initially lead to a corresponding reduction in the role of the state. Rather, Western governments sought to apply their enhanced administrative skills to domestic requirements, taking responsibility for managing the overall economy with the aim of securing full employment. In Europe, the warfare state gave way to the welfare state, with governments accepting direct responsibility for protecting their citizens from the scourges of illness, unemployment and old age (Flora and Heidenheimer, 1981). In this way, the state led a postwar settlement which integrated full employment and public welfare with an economy in which the private sector continued to play a substantial part.

extend into the sea by the reach of a cannonball and, later, above its land to the flying height of a hot-air balloon (Palan, 2002). Reflecting this new concern with state boundaries, passports were introduced in Europe during the First World War. To travel across frontiers became a rite of passage, involving the formal permission of state officials as expressed by a stamp in a passport. Such documents remained necessary for overseas travel at least until some member states of the European Union abolished mutual border controls in 1990 (Anderson, 1997).

Contraction

The expansion of the state proved to be expensive and ultimately unaffordable. By 1975, the proportion of national income which West European countries devoted to public social expenditure reached 30 per cent, a tenfold increase compared to 1900 (Pierson, 1998). With social democratic governments redistributing income in the name of greater equality, the top rate of income tax in Western countries reached an inhibiting 63 per cent by the mid-1970s (Steinmo, 2003, p. 221).

BOX 2.2
Aspects of the growth of the Western state, 1789–1975

Aspect	Definition	Examples
Centralization	The centralization of power over a specified territory	Law enforcement, border controls
Standardization	Greater uniformity within society	Common language, standard weights and measures, consistent time zones
Force	Strengthened monopoly of legitimate force	National police force
Mobilization	Increased capacity to extract resources from society	Taxation, conscription
Differentiation	State institutions and employees are increasingly distinct from society	The idea of 'public service'
Functions	Growth in the state's tasks and its intervention in society	War-making, welfare provision
Size	Expansion of the state's budget and personnel	Growth of public sector

Source: Adapted from Clarke (1995), Table 1, p. 12.

As public employment continued to expand, so financial pressures mounted. Following the oil crises of the 1970s, speculation even began to emerge about whether governments might go bankrupt. Rather like the empires of old, no sooner had the Western state reached its full extent than it began to look overstretched.

In consequence, the final decades of the twentieth century witnessed some retreat of the state, particularly in English-speaking countries where the conservative agenda linked with Ronald Reagan (American president, 1980–88) and Margaret Thatcher (British prime minister, 1979–90) gained ground. State-owned industries were sold, welfare provision was trimmed and the state increasingly sought to supply public services indirectly, using private contractors. Significantly, military demands were for once consistent with a diminished state: spending on the armed forces declined after the end of the Cold War.

To be sure, the retreat of the state was less pronounced in continental Europe than in the Anglo-American world. Even in the English-speaking democracies, only time will tell whether the state's role has evolved – from producer to regulator – rather than declined. But as the violent twentieth century approached its unusually peaceful end,

some commentators discerned a fundamental shift in the approach of the state. Rather than waging war and providing welfare, the state began to focus on meeting the challenges of an increasingly open world economy. Just as medieval kings had plied their restricted trade in the transnational framework of Christendom, so modern governments, it was alleged, had fallen victim to a new master: globalization (Cerny, 1990).

The post-colonial state

The state was born in Europe and then exported to the rest of the world by colonial powers, notably Britain, France and Spain. As Opello and Rosow (1999, p. 161) write, 'it is impossible to understand the development of modern states without taking into account the way European states constructed an interconnected global order by means of conquest, trade, religious conversion and diplomacy'. Of all Europe's exports, the state is perhaps the most important.

Most states in the world (including, of course, the USA) are former colonies. Countries without a history as a colony, leaving aside the ex-colonial powers themselves, are few and far between: they include Japan and Thailand in Asia, Ethiopia in Africa and Iran in the Middle East. In addition, a few former empires – notably Russia and China – have redefined themselves as states to fit the demands of the current state-based international system (Oksenberg, 2001).

While the state form may have been successfully exported from Europe, its substance has rarely followed. In many post-colonial countries, the state has been superimposed on traditional ethnic, regional and religious divisions. Often, the state becomes a prize for which the traditional leaders of such groups compete, resulting in a lack of autonomy for the state from social interests. In these circumstances, the state is more a resource to be fought over than an actor in the fight. Government institutions are fragmented and the state as a whole lacks the coherence and drive of its European forebears. This contrasting role of the state is the key political contrast between European and post-colonial countries.

How then did colonies emerge into statehood? Described by Crawford (2002) as the largest single change in world politics over the last five hundred years, this process took place in four waves spread over two centuries (Box 2.3). The retreat from empire by European powers after 1945 was certainly the largest of these waves but by no means the only one.

The *first* wave of decolonization occurred early in the nineteenth century, in the Spanish and Portuguese territories of Latin America. Prompted by the American and French revolutions, these early wars of independence resulted in 15 new sovereign states. But these early battles for self-determination had been initiated by a white economic elite in the colony's capital. The wealth of this class derived from stringent control of large indigenous populations extracting commodities for export.

In Latin America, the outcome of independence was not a Western-style constitutional state legitimized by a contract between citizens and subject to their consent. Rather, the result was continued economic exploitation of native workforces within deeply unequal societies governed by autocrats lacking direct control over the interior (McCreery, 2002). These authoritarian traditions remain significant in Latin America today, even though most such countries have now embraced formal democracy.

The *second* and perhaps neglected wave of post-colonial statehood emerged in Europe and the

---

BOX 2.3
States from empires: waves of decolonization

Wave of decolonization	Main imperial powers	Main locations of colonies and imperial territories	Approximate number of new states created by decolonization	Examples of newly independent states
1810-38	Spain, Portugal	Latin America	15	Argentina, Brazil
After the 1914–18 war	Ottoman, Austro-Hungarian and Russian empires	Europe (beyond its Western core), Middle East	12	Austria, Finland, Poland, Turkey
1944–84	UK, France, Belgium, Portugal	Mainly Africa, Asia and the Caribbean	94	Algeria, Angola, Congo, India, Jamaica
1991	Russia	Soviet Union republics (East Europe, Central Asia)	15	Kazakhstan, Latvia, Ukraine*

* See Table 4.1 (p. 54) for a full list
Sources: Adapted from Derbyshire and Derbyshire (1999) and Opello and Rosow (1999).

Middle East with the final collapse of the multinational and religiously diverse Austro-Hungarian, Ottoman and Russian empires around the end of the First World War. The principle of national self-determination, espoused by American President Woodrow Wilson and reflected by nationalist sentiment within the imperial territories themselves, played a key role in redrawing the map of Europe.

Thus, the Austro-Hungarian Empire dissolved into five separate states: Austria, Hungary, Poland, Czechoslovakia and Yugoslavia. Turkey, the historic core of the Ottoman Empire, became a sovereign state in 1923. Ottoman territories in the Middle East, including Iraq and Palestine, were placed under British or French control under mandates from the new League of Nations. The Russian Revolution of 1917 provided an opportunity for Finland, Estonia, Georgia, Latvia, Lithuania and Ukraine to achieve at least temporary independence.

With the exception of Turkey, however, the outcome was rarely strong and stable statehood. Most of these new states were multinational in composition; Czechoslovakia, for example, combined Czechs and Slovaks. National identities overwhelmed the limited history of independent statehood. Eventually, most of these countries were incorporated into Hitler's Germany or the Soviet Union (Batt, 2003). It was only with the collapse of communism in the 1990s and the entry of many of these post-colonial countries into the European Union in 2004 that independent statehood seemed finally to be assured.

The *third* and largest wave of state creation occurred after 1945, with the retreat from empire by European states diminished by war. The exemplar was Indian independence, achieved in 1947; many other colonies, in Africa, Asia, the Middle East (including Iraq again) and the Caribbean, followed suit. This wave of decolonization grew into a veritable tsunami. Over 90 new independent states were created between 1944 and 1984, around half the world's current total (Derbyshire and Derbyshire, 1999). As a result, about one in two of the world's countries have existed as independent states for less than a century.

It is in this group of states that the colonial legacy is most pronounced, with ethnic groups strengthened by imperial classification battling to control the resources of the government. Once the contest is won, the dominant group or individual sees the state as a mine to be exploited. The victor distributes resources to its supporters, often copying the coercive ruling style of the departing power. The result is governance far removed from that found in Western states (Werbner and Ranger, 1996).

The *fourth* and final wave of state formation occurred in the final decade of the twentieth century, with the collapse of communism. The Baltic states, and a dozen soviet satellites in East Europe such as Hungary, Poland and Romania, achieved effective independence with the dissolution of the communist bloc previously dominated by the Soviet Union. In addition, the Soviet Union itself – in effect, a Russian empire – dissolved into 15 successor states, including the Ukraine, Uzbekistan and of course Russia itself (Table 4.1, p. 54).

The experience of these new post-communist states has been mixed. In the Baltic region, states such as Lithuania have gained economic and political stability from their proximity to the European Union. However, central Asian republics such as Uzbekistan show a more typical post-colonial pattern: small size, ethnic division, pre-industrial economies and autocratic rule. In the successor states to the Soviet Union, these problems are generally reinforced by the absence of any pre-colonial experience as an independent state (White *et al.*, 2003).

Overall, then, the contrasts between West European parent states and their post-colonial progeny are deep-rooted. Post-colonial states rarely possess the hard edge which their European forebears acquired during their own long and violent development. This contrast can be seen in the treatment of borders. While European states were keen to mark off their own frontiers, they invented borders for their colonies which bore little relation to natural or social features. For instance, almost half the boundaries of African states today contain at least one straight section and many national borders are treated with indifference by government and people alike. Some are completely unguarded, hardly the sign of a state concerned to demonstrate its sovereignty over a defined territory. Sovereignty remains important as a title of statehood, securing international recognition and access

Profile THE WORLD

Population: 63 bn (2003 estimate), increasing by about 1.2 per cent per year.

Population composition: Asian 58 per cent; African 12 per cent; European 10 per cent; North American 5 per cent.

Life expectancy: 64 years (male 62; female 70).

Literacy: 77 per cent (male 83 per cent; female, 71 per cent).

HIV/Aids infection: 40 million, increasing by about 5 million per year.

Gross world product (GWP): about $49 trillion, increasing by 2.7 per cent in 2002.

Composition of GWP: agriculture 4 per cent, industry 32 per cent, services 64 per cent.

Language: Mandarin 17 per cent; English 6 per cent; Hindu 6 per cent; Spanish 6 per cent.

Religion: Christian 33 per cent (including Catholic 17 per cent); Muslim 20 per cent; No religion 15 per cent; Hindu 13 per cent.

Unemployment: in the developing world about 30 per cent unemployed or underemployed; in the developed world typically 4 per cent–12 per cent unemployment.

Inequality: the richest 20 per cent receive about 80 per cent of the world's income; the poorest 20 per cent receive about 2 per cent of the world's income.

Environment: Depletion of minerals, forests, soil, wetlands, animal and plant species and ozone layer. Global warming producing adverse changes to the climate.

Number of states: 1972 – 150; 2002 – 192.

Number of democracies: 1988 – 66; 1993 – 99; 1998 – 117; 2002 – 121.

Number of free countries: 1988 – 58; 1998 – 81; 2002 – 89 (covering 46 per cent of the population).

Following the Second World War, the planet underwent a sequence of political changes lasting into the final decade of the twentieth century. First, with decolonization, a world of empires gave way to a world of states. Second, many of these newly independent countries experienced military coups as the army seized power, often with the implicit or explicit support of a superpower. Third, the collapse of communism, and thus the end of the Cold War, created more authentic independence for former client states of the Soviet Union, leaving the USA as the world's only superpower. Finally, the retreat of the generals and of ruling communist parties led to a remarkable flowering of freedom and democracy in many countries.

But even in the early years of the twenty-first century it would be simplistic to imagine that the globe now consists of free, democratic, sovereign and peaceful states. The Arab and Muslim worlds remain enclaves of economic stagnation under authoritarian rulers, fuelling historically grounded resentment against the West and underpining terrorism within and beyond the region.

China, the world's most populous country, remains under the direction of a political if no longer communist elite even as it emerges as a global economic force. Many smaller post-colonial countries, particularly in Africa, combine impoverishment with weak government control over society, creating conditions for ethnic conflict both within and across state boundaries.

Even the countries of the developed world are becoming caught in a web of connections between and beyond states that challenge traditional ideas of sovereignty. A huge expansion of international commerce in the second half of the twentieth century forced even the wealthiest countries to pay more attention to international competition and multinational corporations. As the Cold War ended, most countries formed regional trade associations with their neighbours while the oldest states of all developed the European Union, a unique amalgam of intergovernmental and federal principles.

There can be little doubt that such connections between states will need to deepen if the world is to overcome American indifference to the global environmental problems, including global warming, which will surely move up the political agenda as the twenty-first century unfolds.

Sources: CIA World Factbook, http://www.cia.gov/cia/publications/factbook; Freedom House, http://www.freedomhouse.org.; *Financial Times*, 28 November 2003.

Note: Most figures are estimates for 2002 or 2003; some are for earlier years.

Further reading: Kennedy (1994), Lechner and Boli (2003), Meadows (1994).

to aid, while deterring some invaders (Sørensen, 2004, p. 117). But the title's significance rests largely in its symbolic value.

Internally, too, the rulers of many post-colonial states – particularly in Africa – find that their penetration through their territory is limited. Control may not extend far beyond the capital, with government outposts falling under the influence of local strongmen. The state is not so much a coherent actor as an arena in which groups and individuals jostle for control over particular ministries and local offices (Migdal, 2001). The authority of political rulers is sometimes subject to further competition from criminal gangs such as drug cartels in Colombia or vigilante groups in Africa. In view of such difficulties, Englebert (2002) suggests that in Africa territorial restructuring may be needed to bring about long-term and sustainable development.

Certainly, post-colonial states possess economic as well as political problems. Most are not just young but also small and poor, with unbalanced economies overdependent on the export price of a single commodity. While a few such states possess a rich endowment of natural resources, even this apparent advantage can turn into a resource curse as politicians compete to control commodities such as oil and minerals so as to obtain resources to distribute as patronage, thus unbalancing development (Luong and Weinthal, 2001).

So the capacity, autonomy and stability of most post-colonial governments are more restricted than in Western Europe, where states drew on previous traditions of central authority to develop as sophisticated taxing, war-making and welfare machines. The contrasts with Europe are too great to justify the easy prediction that post-colonial states will in due course develop along European lines. As far as the state is concerned, Latouche's (1996) 'Westernization of the world' may be limited to form rather than substance.

The state and international organizations

No state is an island entire unto itself. The first wave of states originated in the requirement to raise men and taxes for foreign wars; later waves emerged from the end of empires; and contemporary states continue to be buffeted by international and global winds. So, as Krasner (1999, p. 13) reminds us, 'globalization is not new, challenges to the authority of the state are not new, transnational flows are not new'.

But the nature and complexity of the external challenges confronting states have altered. Where medieval rulers in Europe had to contend with the Christian commonwealth, their equivalents today must respond to a range of newer forces. These include:

▶ regional bodies such as the European Union
▶ intergovernmental organizations such as the International Monetary Fund
▶ multinational corporations such as Microsoft
▶ international terrorist groups such as al-Qaeda
▶ a massive growth of international trade in goods and currencies in the second half of the twentieth century.

In the remainder of this chapter, we examine how the international and global context impinges on the operation of contemporary states, focusing on two key areas: international organizations and the global economy. In both areas, we will see how these transnational forces bear far more heavily on post-colonial developing countries than on the developed states of the West.

Definition
Waters (2000) defines **globalization** as 'a process in which the constraints of geography on social and cultural arrangements recede and in which people become increasingly aware that they are receding'.

Intergovernmental organizations

The majority of established states belong to most of the 250 or so intergovernmental organizations (IGOs) which now populate the international environment (Figure 2.1). These include the multiple agencies of the United Nations system, such as the International Labour Organization and the World Health Organization (WHO). At the very least, belonging to so many IGOs complicates the task of governance for states. They must arrange to pay their subscriptions, attend meetings, identify their national interests, consult with domestic interest groups, initiate some proposals, respond to others and implement agreements. Such activities dilute the distinction between domestic and foreign policy and give an international dimension to many, perhaps most, government activities.

Source: Data from the Union of International Organizations at http://www.uia.org/statistics/ using the series for conventional organizations.

Figure 2.1 Number of intergovermental organizations, 1909–97

What, though, is the broader impact of IGOs? Have they acquired some of the policy-making role of national governments or do they just express the interests and values of the most powerful states?

One perspective on IGOs is that they have become important political actors, exerting significant influence over their member governments, including those in the developed world. After all, setting up an IGO creates a body with its own employees and agenda. IGOs may be created by states – indeed, they may be the state 'gone global' – but, like children, they grow up to develop their own interests and perspectives.

For developing countries in particular, the policies of such bodies as the International Monetary Fund impinge directly on domestic policies. For instance, when the SARS virus began to spread from China in 2003, intervention by the World Health Organization soon led China to revise its initial evasiveness about the illness. An authoritarian government found it could not adopt the same indifference to the international community as it practised with its own people.

> **Definition**
> **Intergovernmental organizations** (IGOs) are bodies whose members include states. IGOs are established by treaty and usually operate by consent, with a permanent secretariat. They include single purpose entities such as the International Telecommunications Union (established 1875), regional organizations such as the European Union and universal bodies such as the United Nations.
> **International non-governmental organizations** (usually called NGOs) are private institutions with members or groups drawn from more than one country. Examples are the International Red Cross, Greenpeace and the Catholic Church.

Furthermore, even though most IGOs lack an enforcement mechanism, most states do comply with IGO decisions. The mechanisms of IGO governance – conferences, discussions, treaties and pronouncements – are characteristic of modern politics; they are an appropriate response to global problems by an international community lacking a world government. IGOs may be less visible than states, and they certainly lack the legitimacy of direct election, but these points hardly justify the conclusion that IGOs are politically tame. In times of peace, the IGO network spins a web of constraints around even the strongest states.

There is, though, a more critical reading of IGOs: namely, that they are mere decoration designed to conceal the continued pursuit of national self-interest, particularly by the one remaining superpower. For example, when President George W. Bush failed to achieve a second UN resolution authorizing military intervention in Iraq in 2003, his decision was simple: invade anyway. Operating under the United Nations brand, as President Bush did during the Gulf War in 1991, would have been useful but was not deemed essential. Thus, sceptics of IGO influence allege that IGOs do not govern states; at most, dominant states govern through IGOs. As a rule, strong states comply with IGO recommendations because they only commit themselves to what they are already doing (Downs *et al.*, 1996).

So a state-centred position is that leading countries remain dominant, only agreeing in IGOs to what is in their national interest. At most, IGOs are arenas through which states influence each other, and through which stronger states exert authority over their weaker brethren.

BOX 2.4

Some key acronyms in the global order

EMU	European Monetary Union
EU	European Union
FTA	Free trade association
IGO	Intergovernmental organization
IMF	International Monetary Fund
MNC	Multinational corporation
NAFTA	North American Free Trade Association
NATO	North Atlantic Treaty Organization
NGO	Non-governmental organization
SARS	Severe acute respiratory syndrome
UN	United Nations
WHO	World Health Organization
WTO	World Trade Organization

While sceptics are surely correct to suggest that strong states retain most of their traditional autonomy, it is also the case that IGOs return specific benefits to their members, enhancing their ability to achieve shared goals:

▶ Membership of universal organizations, especially the UN, confirms to all and sundry that national rulers have acquired statehood and sovereignty.
▶ IGOs help to endorse unpopular policies, providing national governments with both a conscience and a scapegoat: 'of course, we don't want to close your steel mill but the European Union insists on it'.
▶ IGOs perform useful functions. Everyone gains from a world telephone network and from safer nuclear power.

Whether or not IGOs exert power over states, they have certainly affected the balance of forces within them. Specifically, IGOs tend to fragment national policy-making. In part this is because a club-like spirit often develops among ministers in 'their' IGO. For instance, finance ministers – never popular at home – are among friends at meetings of bodies such as the International Monetary Fund. In this way IGOs lessen the fragile cohesion of national executives and perhaps even contribute to the emergence of a transnational political elite (Sklair, 2003). As a Dutch minister of agriculture said about the European Union,

> In the Dutch Council of Ministers I met the ministers from the departments, and I had to defend the farmers' interest against other interests, but in the European Council of Ministers [an EU body] I met only other ministers of agriculture, and we all agreed on the importance of agriculture.
>
> (Andeweg and Galen, 2002, p. 169)

Given that IGOs tends to fragment national political systems, we must ask which governing institutions gain, and which lose, from interdependence. Among the winners are the executive and the bureaucracy (Box 2.5). These bodies provide the representatives who attend IGO meetings and conduct negotiations; they therefore occupy pole position. Protective interest groups also benefit, since they provide their government with the information and expertise it needs to formulate a sensible negotiating position.

BOX 2.5

The impact of IGOs on national politics: winners and losers

Winners	Losers
Executive	Legislature
Bureaucracy	Parties
Judiciary	
Protective interest groups	

The judiciary is also growing in significance as a result of IGO activity, partly because some influential IGOs such as the World Trade Organization adopt a highly judicial style, issuing judgements on the basis of reviewing cases. In addition, national judges are increasingly willing to use international agreements to strike down the policies of their home government.

As for losers, the most significant is surely the legislature, which may only learn of an international agreement after the government has signed up to it. In some countries, Australia for one, international treaties are an executive preserve, enabling government to bypass the assembly by signing treaties on proposals opposed by parliament.

Political parties, too, seem to have lost ground under pressure from IGOs. Like assemblies, their natural habitat is the state, not the international conference. While party groupings have developed in the EU, these are loose groupings lacking the cohesion and drive of national parties.

Regional organizations

Regional bodies are a specific form of IGO in which neighbouring governments join together for common purposes, most often trade. These agreements have multiplied in number and significance since the end of the Cold War as countries which once sheltered under the skirts of a superpower have turned to their neighbours to find a response to international economic pressures.

So what can a focus on regional organizations add to our understanding of the relationship between IGOs and states? Most regional associations are simple free trade areas, with little prospect of institutional development. Their purpose is to secure gains from trade for their members without compromising political sovereignty. For that reason, their political impact is likely to be unplanned and indirect.

The North American Free Trade Association (NAFTA) is an example. Over a 15-year period beginning in 1994, NAFTA seeks to eliminate trade tariffs between two developed states, the USA and Canada, and a developing economy, Mexico. Even though the agreement does not compromise traditional ideas of sovereignty, its establishment was controversial. American unions feared that free trade with Mexico would cause a migration of jobs to low-cost assembly sites on the Mexican side of the border. In a famous phrase, the independent politician Ross Perot referred to the 'great sucking sound' of jobs being pulled down to Mexico. When even simple free trade areas create such debate, attempts at formal political integration between neighbouring countries are likely to be impossible in most circumstances.

Even the European Union, undoubtedly the most developed example of regional integration in the modern world, illustrates the problems of deepening integration. The effort to establish a common currency among some member states, though ultimately successful, is one illustration. German citizens in particular judged that the introduction of the euro in 2002 provided an opportunity for businesses to put up prices, a perception that no doubt reflected traditional national pride in the Deutschmark. As always, the specific, short-term costs of change proved more visible than the general, long-term benefit.

Just as IGOs are often conceived as an outgrowth of state power, so regional integration in particular flourishes on the foundation provided by strong and stable states. The cornerstone of regional integration is established democracies capable of making, implementing and sustaining agreements with other countries. States make regions at least as much as regions limit states. As Hurrell (1995, p. 354) puts it,

> It is no coincidence that the most elaborate examples of regionalism have occurred in regions where state structures remain relatively strong and where the legitimacy of both frontiers and regimes is not widely called into question.

The European Union is a good example: stable democracies have come together, pooling some sovereignty, to create a regional body with unique powers. The regional organization with the most elaborate institutions was constructed on the continent which invented statehood.

By contrast, when a country faces severe internal tensions, it is unlikely to be able to build regional alignments. For example, the post-soviet republics which formed the Commonwealth of Independent States in 1991 were so preoccupied with domestic difficulties that they had little spare capacity to develop their association in any meaningful way.

Like other IGOs, most regional organizations lack the legitimacy that only direct election can provide. In contrast to established democracies, they suffer from a 'democratic deficit' which limits their legitimacy and even their visibility to national populations (Dahl, 1999). Thus the European Union may prove to be a false model for the rest of the world. Certainly, it seems unlikely that the turn to economic regions in today's world will result in political federations of the type established in the USA in the eighteenth century. As NAFTA shows, moving towards a free trade zone does not require political integration. Regional free trade agreements need only limited supporting organization.

50 YEARS OF THE EUROPEAN UNION

The European Union is the world's most developed example of regional integration. It represents a deliberate attempt by European politicians to bring peace to a continent with a long history of war. From modest beginnings in the 1950s, the Union has developed its institutions, acquired considerable policy-making authority, reduced national barriers to trade, established a new currency and broadened its membership.

1951 Treaty of Paris signed by France, West Germany, Italy, Belgium, the Netherlands and Luxembourg. This set up the European Coal and Steel Commission (ECSC) which included a supranational High Authority.

1957 The ECSC members sign the Treaty of Rome, establishing the European Economic Community (EEC) and Euratom.

1965 The Merger Treaty combines the ECSC, EEC and Euratom.

1973 Britain, Denmark and Ireland join the EEC.

1979 The European Monetary System (EMS) is agreed, linking currencies to the European Currency Unit (ECU). First direct Europe-wide elections to the European Parliament held.

1981 Greece joins the EEC.

1986 Spain and Portugal join the EEC. Signing of the Single European Act, to streamline decision-making and set up a single market by 1992.

1992 Treaty of Maastricht launches provisions for Economic and Monetary Union (EMU) and replaces the EEC with the European Union (EU) from 1993.

1994 Austria, Finland and Sweden join the EU.

1997 Treaty of Amsterdam agrees to extend the Union's role in justice and home affairs and to enhance the authority of the European Parliament.

1999 Launch of European Monetary Union (EMU), irrevocably linking 11 (now 12) national currencies to the euro. The euro is launched as a virtual currency.

2000 Treaty of Nice agrees on institutional reforms to prepare for enlargement, including a reallocation of member states' voting power and a reduction in the issues requiring unanimity.

2002 National currencies are withdrawn within the eurozone.

2003 Cyprus, the Czech Republic, Estonia, Hungary, Latvia, Lithuania, Malta, Poland, Slovakia and Slovenia sign an accession treaty to join the EU in 2004.

2003 Publication of a draft constitution for Europe.

Note: Nomenclature of the 'European Union' has varied over time, reflecting institutional and constitutional developments. For a map, see p. 173.

Non-governmental organizations

As private and unofficial bodies lacking the status offered by a membership of governments, we might expect international non-governmental organizations (NGOs) to exert less influence on domestic politics than IGOs. This conclusion is probably justified, at least for the more powerful states. However NGO impact on post-colonial countries can be considerable. Leading NGOs such as the Red Cross and Médecins Sans Frontières can apply substantial pressure in countries where the international community is already engaged in supplying services as a result of civil war or humanitarian crisis (Adams, 2003).

In such conditions, NGOs have become important actors as executors of IGO, especially United Nations, policy. By the mid-1990s, over 10 per cent of all public development aid was distributed through NGOs, compared to less than 1 per cent in 1970 (Weiss and Gordenker, 1996). About 10 super-NGOs, including CARE, Save the Children and Oxfam, dominate the distribution of aid in complex emergencies.

In acting as UN subcontractors, NGOs can in some ways substitute for government. For instance, NGOs coordinated primary education in northern Sri Lanka after civil war started there in 1987. As a channel for distributing aid and implementing associated policy, NGOs possess clear attractions to outside donors: they are more efficient and less corrupt than many domestic governments and they are also more sensitive to local political conditions than are military forces.

All this gives NGOs considerable clout in the least developed countries on which aid is concentrated. Fernando and Heston (1997, p. 8) go so far as to suggest that 'NGO activity presents the most serious challenge to the imperatives of statehood in the realms of territorial integrity, security, autonomy and revenue'. Furthermore, the number of NGOs has continued to expand over the last 20 years whereas the number of IGOs has fallen (Figure 2.1, p. 26).

The state in the global economy

While international organizations can provide a concrete challenge to state authority, the global economy is a more abstract, but no less important, influence on national governments. The 'global economy' is a convenient phrase to describe the growing trend for economic activity to operate between countries (e.g. international trade) and even beyond them (e.g. currency trading). Particularly in the second half of the twentieth century, international trade grew apace while production and especially finance broke free of national restraints. Has the global economy now escaped state control, reducing political sovereignty to a redundant fiction?

As with other aspects of the global environment, the impact of an interdependent economy varies between the economically developed Western states and the less developed, mainly post-colonial countries. The global economy presents states in the developed world with a reasonably favourable balance of opportunities and threats. But the least developed countries remain in a dependent position, surviving by exporting basic foodstuffs or minerals in competition with other equally poor states. We will therefore assess the global economy's impact on the developed and developing worlds separately, beginning with the affluent West.

Developed countries

Perhaps the main influence of today's open trading world on developed states in the West has been to modify their policy agendas. International competition remorselessly exposed economic weaknesses that could be disguised in an era of national markets and state-owned monopolies. From the 1980s, rulers in many developed states placed greater emphasis on economic competitiveness (Cerny, 1990). In a process of competitive deregulation, public ownership has now been reduced by privatization; budget deficits have been cut back; corporate and individual tax rates have been reduced; and opaque share-trading and corporate reporting requirements have been modified in line with international (in practice, mainly American) standards.

Two key channels through which external economic forces exert influence in developed states are multinational corporations (MNCs) and global financial flows. Consider MNCs. The

DEBATE

STATE SOVEREIGNTY OR HUMANITARIAN INTERVENTION?

'The time of absolute exclusive sovereignty has passed; its theory was never matched by reality.' (Boutros Boutros-Ghali, speaking in 1992 when Secretary-General of the United Nations)

The history of the international system has been based on non-intervention in sovereign states. International law, for example, makes little reference to how states should organize themselves internally (Rich, 2001). This tradition was reinforced during the Cold War by the division of much of the world into two opposed armed camps. But the collapse of communism opened up new possibilities for intervention. So is the international community now justified in intervening in another state's affairs – by force if necessary – to reduce acute human suffering? Is saving strangers now a practical possibility?

The case for

All governments should reduce human suffering when they are able to do so. Whether that suffering occurs inside or beyond a state's boundaries is irrelevant; the value of a human life is the same everywhere. This view is far from new: in the seventeenth century, the Dutch jurist Hugo Grotius (1583–1645) had argued that sovereignty was not the highest law.

Hoffman (1995, p. 35) is among those who has reinforced this opinion: 'the state that claims sovereignty deserves respect only as long as it protects the basic rights of its citizens. When it violates them, the state's claim to sovereignty falls.' Oxfam adopts a similar position: 'we do not accept that the principle of sovereignty should block the protection of basic rights, including the right to emergency relief and safety' (Harriss, 1995, p. 3). Sovereignty, it is argued, does not entitle a state to decline humanitarian aid, since the result is added suffering for the people who are the state's tangible expression. Also, when the state has failed, as several have done in Africa, arguably there is no sovereignty left to violate.

The case against

By itself, ethics makes poor politics. At issue is not the principle of intervention but its likelihood of success. There is simply no world force capable of providing effective humanitarian intervention. Instead, an inter-national consensus has to be built behind intervention on each occasion and such agreements soon disintegrate when problems arise in the field.

Somalia is an example (Mayall, 1996, p. 9). When television images of starvation generated a public demand for the international community to do something, the UN authorized military intervention to support the distribution of aid. The project was a disaster. An inadequate number of troops was despatched in 1992 after a long delay to carry out an unfamiliar mission with insufficient local knowledge in a hostile situation. After a local warlord killed 20 Pakistani soldiers serving with the UN, and a captured American pilot was paraded in public, the United States decided to bring the boys back home. The entire UN mission folded in 1995.

Although the American-led invasion of Iraq in 2003 lacked clear UN backing, this intervention also confirmed the dangers inherent in such projects. Saddam Hussein was efficiently removed from power but the invading troops then found themselves immersed in challenging peacekeeping duties for which they had not been trained.

Assessment

If the principle of intervention is accepted, the next steps will be practical. Will powerful states ever permit the emergence of a global military force? Should intervention be subcontracted to regional bodies, as with NATO's air-strikes into Bosnia to enforce the 1995 Dayton Peace Agreement? In addition, the international community will need to work out under what conditions intervention is justified. For example, van Eijk (1997) suggests that any humanitarian intervention must pass seven specific tests: (1) human rights must be threatened, (2) no alternative solution is available, (3) intervention must receive wide international support, (4) intervention must be justified to the UN in advance, (5) the extent of intervention must be minimized, (6) intervention must be able to make a constructive contribution and (7) intervention must last no longer than is required.

Further reading: Holzgrefe and Keohane (2003), Owen (2002), Wheeler (2002).

balance between MNCs and governments raises, in modern form, the age-old question of the relationship between economic and political power. In its current form, the logic governing this relationship is simple: capital is mobile, labour less so and states not at all. Companies can move – or just threaten to move – their factories and technology between countries. But states, by definition, are anchored to their territory.

However, compared to the vulnerable states of the developing world, the relationship between Western governments and MNCs is balanced. MNCs must sell their products in the affluent and sophisticated markets of the developed world. Aware of their attractions, host governments can strike a deal. For instance, they may require local factories of the MNC to buy a certain share of their resources from domestic suppliers. In addition, states can join together in an alliance such as the European Union to create a larger market which gives the member states, acting together, more bargaining power with MNCs. As with many relationships, each side needs the other.

International financial flows are the second major way in which markets constrain policymaking in developed countries. Governments fund their debt by borrowing, often from overseas. The less confidence financial markets possess in a country's government or economy, the higher the rate of interest they will demand for lending to that country. This relationship is sustained through rating agencies, such as Standard and Poor's, which evaluate the creditworthiness of countries as well as companies.

In similar fashion, a country's currency will decline in value if dealers in foreign exchange lose confidence in its government. Because the weight of money in the financial market is far greater than that in the vaults of central banks, central banks are unable to stem such losses. The outcome may be an unwanted devaluation for those governments that seek to maintain a fixed exchange rate.

A final effect of economic globalization on the developed world has been to increase economic inequality within borders, both at individual and regional level. Unskilled workers in developed countries face downward pressure on incomes from the low-wage economies of the developing world, notably China. However, firms are willing

to pay more to recruit and retain managers – whatever their nationality – who can increase corporate profitability. Partly as a result of these forces, economic inequality within Britain at the end of the twentieth century was greater than at the start.

Globalization also increases inequality across regions within states. Core regions possess the location and skills needed to prosper from increases in trade. In particular, financial centres such as the City of London and Wall Street march to the drum of the global economy, partly delinking from their national homeland (Sassen, 2002). But peripheral regions, rather like individuals lacking relevant skills, find themselves trapped in a cycle of decline. Eventually, we may find that the categories 'rich' and 'poor' apply less to countries than to sectors and regions within them, producing massive new problems of political management for national governments.

Developing countries

Most developing countries find themselves in a more exposed position in relation to external economic forces. For better or worse, the impact of the global economy is far greater than on developed states. Partly, this weakness arises from the dependence of many developing countries on a single product: for example, Nigeria's exports consist overwhelmingly of oil. Alternatively, a developing country may depend on a single market for its exports: for instance, most of Mexico's exports go to the USA.

Many commentators suggest that through such concentrated trade patterns the economies of the least developed countries are locked into dependence on rich countries. The result is unbalanced development. Dependency theorists argue therefore that what has emerged is not a neutral global economy but rather a new form of economic colonialism in which the developed world shapes the structure of client economies in the developing world. This is not development but rather what Frank (1969, p. 16) called 'the development of underdevelopment'.

The IGOs which have emerged to regulate the global economy according to the liberal principle of free trade are particularly influential in vulnerable developing economies (Box 2.6). The ability of IGOs to grant or withhold loans gives them an oversight role over the least solvent states which amounts to veto power. A crucial test of the skill of the leaders of such countries is their ability to negotiate not just with these economic IGOs but increasingly with sources of private capital from overseas.

BOX 2.6
Intergovernmental organizations and the world economy

IGO	Full title	Function
IMF	International Monetary Fund	To promote international monetary stability and cooperation
IBRD	International Bank for Reconstruction and Development ('World Bank')	To promote economic recovery and development
WTO	World Trade Organization	To supervise and promote international trade

Note: The WTO was founded in 1995 to replace GATT (General Agreement on Tariffs and Trade) which, like the IMF and the World Bank, had been established at Bretton Woods (Jackson, 1998).

Consider, by way of example, the impact of the World Trade Organization (WTO). Its function is to provide a way of resolving trade conflicts between member states and to seek further reductions in tariffs and other barriers to trade. In practice, this means that member states gain preferential access to each other's markets. With most countries requiring access to lucrative North American and European markets, membership of WTO is highly desirable. But in order to join, as Russia wants to do, states must meet specific conditions. In essence, the price to governments of entering the global economy is to open their domestic market. Thus the WTO has leverage not just over its 146 members but also over the 50 or so states which have yet to join.

The weaker the finances of a developing country, the more leverage international agencies can exert. IGO impact has been particularly strong in those countries most affected by the 1980s debt crisis, a problem which arose when Western banks increased lending to developing countries which then failed to meet repayments. Many of the least developed states remain in massive debt. As late as 1995, the developing world as a whole owed $1.5 trillion; interest payments stood at $232 billion per year. Like any other debtor, the least developed states were unable to bargain about the terms of any further financial aid.

Bodies such as the World Bank and the IMF are generally willing to provide additional support but this debt restructuring is conditional on domestic economic reform, often including privatization, lower trade tariffs and more transparency in allocating government contracts. For example, the international community (led by the IMF and Japan) offered a $16 billion loan to the Thai government in 1997. The conditions attached to the loan were extensive and specific, including:

▶ halving the country's trade deficit
▶ balancing the budget
▶ speeding up privatization
▶ allowing foreign ownership of banks
▶ floating the currency.

Definition
Conditionality is the practice of attaching strings to aid. Political conditionality might include a requirement to legalize opposition and hold competitive elections. Economic conditionality often takes the form of a specified **structural adjustment programme**, typically involving privatizing state companies, introducing more competition and opening domestic markets to overseas companies.

Governments which build domestic political support by using the economy to reward their supporters find the injunction to reduce their control striking at the heart of their power. In effect, the international agencies require such countries to restructure their politics as well as their economy. Mahathir bin Mohamad, Malaysia's Prime Minister from 1981 to 2003, was skilled at exploiting this dependence for domestic political purposes. He likened the international political economy to 'a jungle of ferocious beasts', claiming that the IMF was willing 'to subvert our economy' in order to prove the validity of its own theories.

Attacks by developing countries on such bodies as the WTO have not gone unsupported by groups in the developed world. To date, the most prominent example of a backlash was the 'battle in Seattle' in 1999, when a WTO conference was marked by violent protests outside the conference hall. Over 5,000 anti-globalization protestors marched through the streets and over 500 were arrested as police in riot gear fired tear-gas and plastic bullets. The activists included union members, environmentalists, students and indigenous people. The conference itself ended in acrimony, with many developing countries objecting to what was seen as an American attempt to impose its own agenda.

Seattle demonstrates that, even more than the EU, IGOs such as the WTO suffer from a democratic deficit which limits their scope. Four years after Seattle, a two-pronged attack by developing countries and NGOs was able to exploit this weakness, leading to the failure of WTO trade talks. In Cancún, Mexico, in 2003, the USA and especially the EU came under attack for continuing to subsidize their own farmers, thus discriminating against agricultural exports from the developing world. Since WTO agreements require consensus, delegates from poorer states were able to prevent an agreement. Cancún provides tentative evidence of a modification in the balance of power between IGOs and developing countries.

But of course it is not just IGOs which impose conditionalities on vulnerable countries. Since the end of the Cold War, individual states – including established democracies such as the UK – have subjected bilateral aid to specific conditions. Donor governments which turned a blind eye to the internal politics of developing countries are now willing to attach conditions to aid, strings which may take the form of pressure for political change.

For example, sanctions may be imposed on countries with poor human rights records (such as China) or corrupt governments (Kenya). States which have invaded other countries (Iran), which sponsor international terrorism (Syria), which are ruled by undemocratic means (Libya) or which are still under communist control (North Korea, Cuba) find themselves isolated from, or entirely without influence within, the international system.

Thus dominant countries can directly affect the political situation confronting national leaders in poorly regarded developing states. The worst cases become pariah states, kept out of the international community altogether.

Key reading

> **Next step:** *Opello and Rusow (1999) is a wide-ranging but accessible historical introduction to the state.*

Van Creveld (1999) and Pierson (2004) also examines the rise of the state but the most monumental history of government, sparkling with insight, is Finer (1997). Turning to the contemporary position of the state, both Sørensen (2004) and Paul (2004) examine its alleged transformation in a global era. On globalization itself, Waters (2000) offers a clear introduction while Lechner and Boli (2003) is a wide-ranging reader. On international organizations, Diehl (2001) is a useful introduction, while Boli and Thomas (1999) examine non-governmental organizations specifically. Holzgrefe and Keohane (2003) cover the many dilemmas of humanitarian intervention while Chatterjee and Scheid (2003) focus on the ethical dimension. On regionalism, Breslin *et al.* (2002) blends theory with cases; see also Hettne (1999). On international political economy, Stubbs and Underhill (1999) is a helpful edited collection. Strange (1994) and the more sceptical Hirst and Thompson (1999), have each generated considerable debate on the autonomy of states in a global economy.

Chapter 3

Democracy

We live in an era of democracy; for the first time in history, most people in the world live under tolerably democratic rule. This upsurge in democracy reflects the transformation of the world's political landscape in the final quarter of the twentieth century. Over this short period, the number of democracies more than doubled. Democracy expanded beyond its core of Western Europe and former settler colonies to embrace Southern Europe (for example Spain), Eastern Europe (for example Hungary), Latin America (for example Brazil), more of Asia (for example Taiwan) and parts of Africa (for example South Africa).

This shift to democracy, while important in itself, will also have international ramifications. It is likely to contribute to peace and prosperity since democracies rarely go to war with each other and are more likely to form trade agreements than are non-democracies (Huth and Allee, 2003). The terrorists who attacked the United States on September 11, 2001, we should note, originated from authoritarian rather than democratic countries.

As democracy continues to spread, so it becomes more varied (Box 3.1). Understanding the forms taken by democracy in today's world is therefore a central task for comparative politics. In this chapter, we examine the established democracies of Europe and its settler colonies, with their emphasis on representative and limited government. We then discuss the newer democracies emerging from the ashes of communist and military rule. Finally, we assess those awkward semi-democratic regimes – Russia is an example – that straddle the border between democratic and authoritarian rule. But to begin we must explore the origins of democracy itself. And that task must take us back to the fifth century BC to the world's most influential example of self-government: ancient Athens.

BOX 3.1
Forms of democracy

Form	Definition
Direct democracy	The citizens themselves assemble to debate and decide on collective issues
Representative democracy	Citizens elect politicians to reach collective decisions on their behalf, with the governing parties held to account at the next election.
Liberal democracy	The scope of democracy is limited by constitutional protection of individual rights, including freedom of assembly, property, religion and speech
New democracy	A democracy in which an authoritarian legacy continues to influence political action and debate. Democracy is not the only game in town
Established democracy	A consolidated democracy which provides an accepted framework for political competition. The outcome of free elections is accepted by the losers as well as the winners
Semi-democracy	An illiberal democracy in which elected presidents do not respect individual rights, or in which elected governments form a façade behind which traditional rulers continue to exercise effective power

Direct democracy

Democracy is a form of government offering a workable solution to the fundamental political problem of reaching collective decisions by peaceful means. But it is also an ideal and an aspiration. So we cannot understand democracy simply by looking at contemporary examples. Judged against the democratic ideal, even the most secure 'democracies' are found wanting. Indeed, the tension between high ideals and prosaic reality has itself become part of the democratic condition (Dahl, 2000).

So what, then, is the core principle of democracy? The essential idea is self-rule: the word itself comes from the Greek *demokratia,* meaning rule (*kratos*) by the people (*demos*). Thus democracy in its literal and richest sense refers not to the election of the rulers by the ruled but to the denial of any separation between the two. The model democracy is a form of self-government in which all adult citizens participate in shaping collective decisions in an environment of equality and open deliberation. In a direct democracy, state and society become one.

The birthplace of democracy is ancient Athens. Between 461 and 322 BC, Athens was the leading *polis* (city-community, often translated as city-state) in ancient Greece. *Poleis* were small independent political systems, typically containing an urban core and a rural hinterland. Athens, one of the larger examples, held only about 40,000 citizens. Especially in the earlier and more radical decades of the period, the Athenian *polis* operated on the democratic principle summarized by Aristotle as 'each to rule and be ruled in turn' (see Box 3.2). This principle applied across all the institutions of government within the city-community. All citizens could attend meetings of the assembly, serve on the governing council and sit on citizens' juries. Because ancient Athens continues to provide the archetypal example of direct democracy, we will look at its operation in more detail (Figure 3.1).

History has judged there to be no more potent symbol of direct democracy than the Ekklesia (People's Assembly) at Athens. Any citizen aged at least 20 could attend assembly sessions and there address his peers; meetings were of citizens, not their representatives. The assembly met around 40 times a year to settle issues put before it, including the recurring issues of war and peace which were central to the prospects and prosperity of the *polis*. In Aristotle's phrase, the assembly was 'supreme over all causes' (1962 edn, p. 237); it was the sovereign body, unconstrained by a formal constitution or even, in the early decades, by written laws.

But the assembly did not exhaust the avenues of participation in the Athenian democracy. Administrative functions were the responsibility of an executive council consisting of 500 citizens aged over 30, chosen by lot to serve for a one-year period. Through this device of rotation, the council exemplified the principle of direct democracy: government by, and not just for, the citizens. Hansen (1991, p. 249) suggests that about one in three citizens could expect to serve on the council at some stage in their life, an astonishing feat of self-government entirely without counterpart in modern democracies.

A highly political legal system provided the final leg of Athens's complex democracy. Juries of several hundred people, again selected randomly from a panel of volunteers, considered lawsuits which citizens could – and frequently did – bring

---

BOX 3.2

Aristotle's characterization of democracy

▸ All to rule over each and each in his turn over all.
▸ Appointment to all offices, except those requiring experience and skill, by lot.
▸ No property qualification for office-holding, or only a very low one.
▸ Tenure of office should be brief and no man should hold the same office twice (except military positions).
▸ Juries selected from all citizens should judge all major causes.
▸ The assembly should be supreme over all causes.
▸ Those attending the assembly and serving as jurors and magistrates should be paid for their services.

Source: Aristotle, *The Politics*, Book VI.

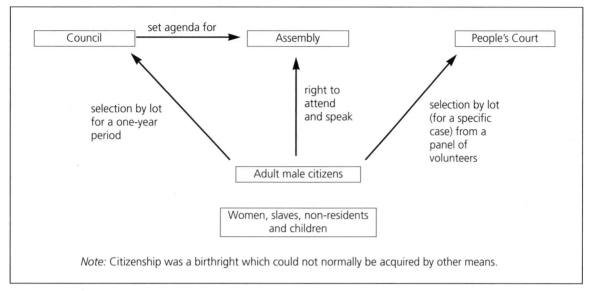

Figure 3.1 The direct democracy of ancient Athens

against those considered to have acted against the true interests of the *polis*. The courts functioned as an arena of accountability through which top figures (including generals) could be brought to book.

Thus the scope of the Athenian democracy was extraordinarily wide, providing an all-encompassing political framework within which citizens were expected to develop their true qualities. For the Athenians, politics was intrinsically an amateur activity, to be undertaken by all citizens to develop both themselves and the broader community.

Of course, we should not blind ourselves to serious flaws in Athens's little democracy:

▸ Citizenship was restricted to a small elite: it was a birthright of males whose parents were themselves citizens. Most adults – including women, slaves and foreign residents – were excluded. Women played no significant public role and critics allege that slavery was the platform which allowed citizens time to devote to public affairs (Finley, 1985).
▸ Participation was not in practice as extensive as the Athenians liked to claim. Most citizens were absent from most assembly meetings even after the introduction of a payment for attendance.
▸ Athenian democracy was hardly an exercise in

lean government. A modern management consultant would conclude that the system was a time-consuming, expensive and over-complex method of governing a small society. Its applicability to a modern world in which people are committed to paid work, and the affluence resulting therefrom, is questionable.
▸ The principle of self-government did not always lead to decisive and coherent policy. Indeed, the lack of a permanent bureaucracy eventually contributed to a period of ineffective government, leading to the fall of the Athenian republic after defeat in war.

Perhaps Athenian democracy was a dead-end in that it could only function on an intimate scale which precluded expansion and proved inherently vulnerable to predators. As Finer (1997, p. 368) observes, 'the *polis* was doomed politically if it expanded and doomed to conquest if it did not. It had to succumb and it did.' Yet for over 100 years, the Athenian democratic experiment survived and prospered. It provided a settled formula for rule and enabled Athens to build a leading position in the complex politics of the Greek world. Athens proves that direct democracy is, in some conditions, an achievable goal.

Certainly, Finer (1997, p. 371) was correct in acknowledging the Athenian contribution to

Western politics: 'the Greeks invented two of the most potent political features of our present age: they invented the very idea of citizen – as opposed to subject – and they invented democracy'.

Representative and liberal democracy

The contrasts between the classical democracy of ancient Athens and the modern democracies of today's world are clear. Most obviously, citizenship is no longer an elite status but has been extended to the vast majority of the adult population. But two other contrasts are equally important.

First, today's democracies are representative rather than direct. The democratic principle has transmuted from self-government to elected government. This transformation can be seen in the contrasting treatment of elections offered by ancients and moderns. The Greeks viewed elections as an instrument of aristocracy: a device for selecting qualified people for technical tasks which required an unfortunate departure from self-government. However, as the phrase 'representative democracy' shows, the modern world regards elections as an expression rather than a denial of democracy.

Second, modern democracy is based on a liberal philosophy in which the state's scope is restricted by the constitution. This limit is based on a distinction between public and private that would have been unacceptable in classical Athens where citizens who lived an entirely private life were dismissed as *idiotes*. Today's democracies are liberal democracies and it is the constitution as much as the legislature that is 'supreme over all causes'.

In this section, we examine how these modern concepts of representation and liberalism were grafted on to the original democratic idea so as to deliver a new hybrid. The requirement for this new form was clear. In contrast to the little democracy of Athens, any modern version of democracy must be compatible with the much larger states found in today's world.

In reinventing democracy for the modern era, the key breakthrough was to modify traditional ideas of representation. In itself, the idea of leaders representing their community in a wider assembly was nothing new. In Europe, for example, medieval monarchs had summoned leaders of the various estates of the realm – lords, commoners and representatives of the cities – to help them with their tasks of raising revenues and fighting wars. But unlike the Athenian assembly, the members of these royal advisory assemblies were summoned or self-appointed, not elected. They were not elected by those they represented, nor would they have deigned to have been so.

Indeed, representation was still viewed as a desirable brake on democracy. Thus James Madison, an architect of the American constitution, judged that representation served to 'refine and enlarge the public views, by passing them through the medium of a chosen body of citizens, whose wisdom may best discern the true interest of their country' (Madison, 1787, p. 45). At this stage, then, representation was still a device for limiting 'pure democracy'.

But in the nineteenth century, stimulated by the French Revolution of 1789 and by the diffusion of power brought about by mass literacy and industrialization, the notion of turning assemblies into representative bodies elected from a wide franchise rapidly gained ground. One of the first authors to graft representation on to democracy was the British-born pamphleteer and international revolutionary Tom Paine. In his *Rights of Man* (first published in 1791 or 1792), Paine wrote:

The original simple democracy . . . is incapable of extension, not from its principle, but from the inconvenience of its form. Simple democracy was society governing itself without the aid of secondary means. By ingrafting representation upon democracy, we arrive at a system of government capable of embracing and confederating all the various interests and every extent of territory and population.

(Paine, 1984 edn, p. 180)

Scalability has certainly proved to be a key strength of representative democracy. The conventional wisdom in ancient Athens was that the upper limit for a republic was the number of people who could gather together to hear a speaker. However, modern representative government allows massive populations (such as 1.05 billion Indians and 290 million Americans) to exercise some popular control over their rulers. And there is no upper limit. In theory, the entire world could become one giant representative system. Adapting Tom Paine's phrase, representative government has proved to be a highly convenient form.

As ever, intellectuals were on hand to secure the transition of representative democracy from an inherent contradiction to a workable system of rule. Prominent among them was Joseph Schumpeter (1883–1965), an Austrian-born economist who became an academic in the United States.

Schumpeter (1943, p. 269) conceived of democracy as nothing more than party competition: 'democracy means only that the people have the opportunity of refusing or accepting the men who are to rule them'. He wanted to limit the contribution of ordinary voters because of his jaded view of their political capacity: 'the typical citizen drops down to a lower level of mental performance as soon as he enters the political field. He argues and analyzes in a way that he would recognize as infantile within the sphere of his real interests. He becomes a primitive again.'

Reflecting this jaundiced view of the public, Schumpeter argued that elections should not be construed as a device through which voters elect representatives to carry out their will; rather, the role of elections is simply to produce a government. From this perspective, the elector becomes a political accessory, restricted to selecting from broad packages of policies and leaders prepared by rival parties. Representative democracy is merely a way of deciding who shall decide:

> The deciding of issues by the electorate [is made] secondary to the election of the men who are to do the deciding. To put it differently, we now take the view that the role of the people is to produce a government . . . And we define the democratic method as that institutional arrangement for arriving at political decisions in which individuals acquire the power to decide by means of a competitive struggle for the people's vote.
> (Schumpeter, 1943, p. 270)

These ideas represent a considerable thinning of the democratic ideal envisaged in classical Athens. But that is not all. The second distinctive feature of modern democracy, its liberal character, contributes a further qualification to strict rule by the people. Like representative democracy, liberal democracy is a compromise: it seeks to integrate the authority of democratic governments with limits on the scope of their action.

The central feature of liberal democracy is limited government. The goal is to secure individual freedom, including freedom from unwarranted demands by government itself. The object is defensive: to protect the population from its rulers and minorities from the danger of majority tyranny (Held, 1996). Liberal democracy is a settlement between individual liberty and collective organization which reflects the key issues involved in its emergence. These issues include the desire to entrench religious freedom, to protect against the recurrence of tyranny and to secure the rights of property against the mob. All these elements were central to the design of the American system of government, the most liberal (and perhaps the least democratic) of all the democracies.

In place of the all-encompassing scope of the Athenian *polis,* liberal democracies are governments of laws rather than men. Even elected rulers are subject to constitutions that almost always include a statement of individual rights. In theory, citizens can use domestic and international courts to uphold their rights when the government becomes overbearing. In this way, a liberal democracy is democracy disarmed.

Both the representative and liberal elements of modern democracy dilute the original principle of self-rule. We find in contemporary democracies a form of rule in which decision-making is the responsibility of governments rather than the governed and in which the public sphere is limited by protecting the rights of citizens in general and of property-owners in particular. The watering down is considerable but the outcome is a flexible and scalable political system which is coming to dominate the world.

Waves of democratization

How then were these principles of representative and liberal democracy implemented in the transition to democracy? When and how did modern established democracies emerge? As with the phases of decolonization discussed in the last chapter, so too did democracies emerge in a series of distinct waves (Box 3.3). As defined by Huntington (1991, p. 15),

> A wave of democratization is a group of transitions from nondemocratic to democratic regimes that occur within a specified period of time and that significantly outnumber transitions in the opposite direction during that period . . . Three waves of democratization have occurred in the modern world.

The first modern democracies emerged in the 'first long wave of democratization' between 1828 and 1926. During this *first wave* nearly 30 countries established at least minimally democratic national institutions, including Argentina, Australia, Britain, Canada, France, Germany, the Netherlands, New Zealand, the Scandinavian countries and the United States. Some of these fledgling democracies were later overthrown by fascist, communist or military dictatorships during Huntington's 'first reverse wave' from 1922 to 1942.

However, democracy did consolidate in the earliest nineteenth-century democratizations, including the United States and the United Kingdom. We will examine these two transitions of the first wave in more detail, not least because the USA remains the leading example of liberal democracy while Britain usefully illustrates representative democracy.

The emergence of democracy in the United States was rapid but it was a transition nonetheless. The founders had thought of political leadership in non-democratic terms, as the duty of a disinterested, leisured gentry. However, the idea that citizens could only be represented fairly by those of their own sort quickly gained ground, supported by the egalitarian spirit of a frontier society. The suffrage quickly extended to nearly all white males. But some groups had to wait until the twentieth century for the full franchise. Women were not offered the vote on the same terms as men until 1919 and the black franchise was not fully realised until the Voting Rights Act of 1965 (Dahl, 2001).

Today, the USA gives us the clearest picture of a *liberal* democracy in which limited government is entrenched by design. The Founding Fathers wanted, above all, to prevent dictatorship, including tyranny by the majority. To prevent any government – and especially elected ones – from acquiring too much power, the constitution set up an elaborate system of checks and balances between the institutions of government (Figure 3.2). Because power is so fragmented, the danger of any particular faction manipulating public authority for private ends is much reduced. Power checks power to the point where it is often difficult for the government to achieve even needed reforms. The constitution placed government under law before government by all the people. In this way, the liberal dimension of America's

---

BOX 3.3
Huntington's three waves of democratization

Wave	Period	Examples
First	1828–1926	Britain, France, USA
Second	1943–62	India, Israel, Japan, West Germany
Third	1974–91	Southern and Eastern Europe, Latin America, parts of Africa

Note: The first wave was partly reversed between 1922 and 1942 (for example, in Austria, Germany and Italy) and the second wave similarly between 1958 and 1975 (for example, in much of Latin America and post-colonial Africa). A return to authoritarian rule after a democratic interlude is termed backsliding.

Source: Huntington (1991). For some criticisms of the wave approach, see Grugel (2002), pp. 32–7.

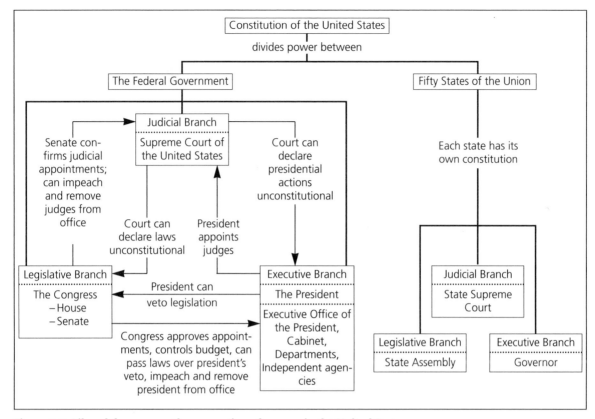

Figure 3.2 Liberal democracy: the separation of powers in the United States

democracy emerged victorious over its representative aspect. Only during periods of external threat, including post-9/11, do individual liberties come under threat (Lyon, 2003).

In Britain, by contrast, the outcome of the democratic transition was a less liberal but more representative form of government. By the eighteenth century, the power of the monarch had been checked by the authority of parliament. However, the rights of the individual citizen were never stated as clearly as in the USA. The widening of the suffrage also occurred more gradually in the United Kingdom, with each step easing the fears of the propertied classes about the dangers of further reform (Table 3.1). As the House of Commons acquired democratic legitimacy, so both the monarchy and the non-elected House of Lords retreated into the background. As in the United States, the implementation of democratic procedures in Britain continued well into the twentieth century

but the battle of principle was fought and won in the nineteenth.

Yet if the USA emphasizes liberal democracy, Britain gives priority to its representative element. Where American democracy diffuses power across institutions, British democracy emphasizes the sovereignty of parliament. Representation operates through parties that retain tight control over their own members of the House of Commons. A single governing party wields extensive powers until the voters offer their verdict at the next election. Except for the government's sense of self-restraint, the institutions that limit executive power in the United States – including a codified constitution, the separation of powers and federalism – are absent. Instead the electoral rules normally ensure a secure majority of seats to the winning party. In reality, the hallowed sovereignty of parliament is leased to the party in office.

Far more than the United States, Britain exemplifies Schumpeter's model of representative democracy as an electoral competition between organised parties. 'We are the masters now', trumpeted a Labour MP after his party's triumph in the British election of 1945; similar thoughts must have occurred to many Labour MPs after their party's equally emphatic victory in 1997. From a comparative perspective, a governing party in Britain is still given an exceptionally free hand.

Despite these contrasts between Britain and the USA, both countries are of course examples of consolidated democracies emerging during the first nineteenth-century wave of democratization. Huntington's *second wave* of democratization began in the Second World War and continued until the 1960s. Like the first wave, some of the new democracies created at this time did not con-solidate. For example, elected rulers in several Latin American states were quickly overthrown by military coups. But established democracies did emerge after 1945 from the ashes of defeated dic-tatorships, not just in West Germany but also in Austria, Japan and Italy. These postwar democra-cies were introduced by the victorious allies, led by the USA and usually acting with the support of domestic partners. Yet despite their partly imposed character, these second-wave democracies did establish firm roots, helped by an economic recovery itself nourished by American aid. During this postwar wave, democracy also consolidated in the new state of Israel and the former British Dominion of India.

Second-wave democracies differed in character from their predecessors. Their liberal traditions were somewhat weaker as representation through parties proved to be the stronger suit. Parties had gone unmentioned in the American constitution but by the time of the second wave they had emerged as the leading democratic instrument. Indeed, Germany's Basic Law (1949) codifies their role: 'the political parties shall take part in forming the democratic will of the people'. In several second-wave democracies, the importance of party was confirmed by the emergence of a single party which dominated national politics for a gen-eration: Congress in India, the Christian Democrats in Italy, the LDP in Japan and Labour in Israel.

The *third wave* of democratization, finally,

Table 3.1 The British electorate as a percentage of the adult population, 1831–1931

Year	Electorate (per cent of population aged 20+)
1831	4.4
1832	First Reform Act
1832	7.1
1864	9.0
1867	Second Reform Act
1868	16.4
1883	18.0
1884	Third Reform Act
1886	28.5
1914	30.0
1918	Vote extended to women over 30
1921	74.0
1928	Equal Franchise Act
1931	97.0

Note: In 1969, the voting age was reduced from 21 to 18.

Source: Adapted from Dahl (1998), fig. 2.

began in 1974 and continued until 1991. Its main and highly diverse elements were:

▶ the end of right-wing dictatorships in Southern Europe (Greece, Portugal and Spain) in the 1970s
▶ the retreat of the generals´ in much of Latin America in the 1980s
▶ the collapse of communism in the Soviet Union and Eastern Europe at the end of the 1980s.

This third wave has transformed the global polit-ical landscape: the predominance of democratic forms in today's world itself places added pressure on those non-democratic regimes that survive.

Within the third wave, it is only the Southern European group that provides consistently secure cases of democratic consolidation, aided by mem-bership of the European Union and economic development. Elsewhere, in Eastern Europe and Latin America, many third-wave democracies have not yet fully consolidated, if indeed they are ever to do so at all. The category of new democracy – as also of semi-democracy – remains central to understanding these uncertain regimes. We will explore this theme further by examining in more detail the political and economic challenges facing these new democracies.

New democracies

Just as the first wave of modern democracies represented a severe dilution of the Athenian vision of self-rule, so too many new democracies of the third wave are developing a further compromise with their own authoritarian histories. Certainly, the distinctions between most new democracies and the early modern democracies such as the United States and the United Kingdom remain important. In this section, we review the challenges facing these new additions to the democratic family.

To be sure, many new democracies do seem to have consolidated by one crucial test: a peaceful transfer of power through elections. For example, the South Korean presidential election of 1997 witnessed the first peaceful transfer of power to the centre-left in that country's history. Similarly, Herbst (2001) notes that by 1999 a dozen African states had experienced at least one change of government through the ballot box. Peaceful transfers have also become almost routine in Eastern Europe and parts of Latin America.

Yet even when elections have succeeded in the delicate task of replacing a governing elite, most new democracies remain distinctive; the question is not whether they will consolidate but what exactly they are consolidating into. The difficulties facing new democracies can be grouped into two clusters: the political problems associated with an illiberal inheritance and the economic problems caused by the combination of limited development and extreme inequality.

The political challenge

Consider first the political challenges facing new democracies of the third wave. Reflecting an authoritarian legacy, liberal ideas often remain weak. As Luckham and White (1996b, p. 7) point out, the development of democracy requires more than just competitive elections. It also requires the enforcement of legal restraint on state power, pro-

tection of civil rights, the establishment of relatively uncorrupt and effective bureaucracies, and the imposition of democratic control over potentially authoritarian forces such as the military and the security services.

Definition
A democracy has **consolidated** when it provides an accepted framework for political competition. As President Havel noted in Czechoslovakia after communism's collapse, democratic consolidation requires more than creating appropriate institutions: 'we have done away with totalitarianism but we have yet to win democracy'. The standard definition comes from Przeworski (1991, p. 26):

Democracy is consolidated when under given political and economic conditions a particular system of institutions becomes the only game in town and when no-one can imagine acting outside the democratic institutions.

To the extent that democratic consolidation requires substituting a government of laws for one of men, the task is still incomplete in new democracies. The inheritance from the old regime continues to limit progress. After all, ruling communist parties and military councils had brooked no interference from the judiciary and paid no heed to constitutions, including statements of human rights. The agencies of repression – the military, the intelligence services and the police – were as strong as the mechanisms of representation were weak. However well-intentioned the new rulers may be, constructing a *liberal* democracy from an authoritarian history is a greater challenge than the blank canvas facing the framers of the United States constitution, designing a new state where none of any significance had previously existed.

Take, for example, the post-military democracies of Latin America. Here the generals still possess considerable prestige deriving from their historical role as providers of order to unstable societies. This status is sometimes reflected in a guaranteed budget, seats in the legislature and virtual exemption from civil law. Even in the civil arena, justice in much of Latin America remains underdeveloped. Lower courts are often inefficient and corrupt and many cases do not arrive there because the police are themselves corrupt or because ordinary people regard the courtroom as the prerogative of the wealthy. In urban slums, the concept of individual rights does not apply, no matter what fine words appear in the constitution.

In post-communist states, too, any national traditions of rule by law were dulled by the totalitarian experience. Ruling communist parties were above the law and public officials continue to regard their position as an opportunity to obtain private advantage. The combination of an inadequate legal framework with systematic evasion and inadequate enforcement of those laws that do exist is a difficult base from which to consolidate liberal democracy.

In Africa, the problems differ. Far from achieving communist levels of penetration though society, the limited incision of the African state into its territory limits the impact of a transition from authoritarian to democratic rule. For African peasants, as for Latin American slum-dwellers, regime transitions in the capital city must seem remote indeed.

So in many new democracies, the tradition of power revolving around individuals – whether communist party bosses, the arrogant generals and landowners of Latin America or the 'big men' of African politics – tends to subvert attempts to consolidate the democratic framework.

The economic challenge

The economic difficulties confronting new democracies of the third wave are even more obvious than the political challenges. These problems consist of a combination of poverty and inequality, exacerbated by severe economic decline in the early years of the new democracy. Even in many of the larger and more developed new democracies, living standards remain well below Western levels. In the USA, gross domestic product (GDP) per head had reached $36,300 by 2002; in the new democracy of neighbouring Mexico, the equivalent figure was just $9,000 and 40 per cent of the population lived in poverty. European contrasts are equally stark: German GDP per head is almost double the figure for post-communist countries such as the Czech Republic and Hungary.

Relative poverty goes hand in hand with greater inequality. Many new democracies retain a large agricultural sector, where sharp contrasts continue between a rich, powerful elite and a poorly educated, and often powerless, population. Conflicts between landowners and dependent peasants are endemic in much of Latin America, for instance. As Vanhanen (1997) notes, such conditions favour neither the diffusion of power resources nor the development of mutual toleration and compromise which foster democratic consolidation.

Further, the ex-communist states in Eastern Europe suffered enormous economic dislocation in the transition from the old order. As planned economies began to be dismantled in tandem with democratization, unemployment soared. Throughout the post-communist world, the 1990s was a decade of deep economic decline in which the real suffering of the many was exacerbated by the ostentatious affluence of a few. Only in the opening years of the twenty-first century did economic growth return to most post-communist democracies, with Central and Eastern Europe as a whole now growing at a faster rate, albeit from a lower base, than in the Western part of the continent.

Lower levels of affluence in new democracies are important partly because a long research tradition claims that economic well-being is the key to democratic consolidation. In *Political Man* (1960, pp. 48–9), Lipset famously concluded that 'the more well-to-do a nation, the greater the chances that it will sustain democracy'. Lipset demonstrated that stable democracies scored highest on such measures as income per person, literacy and the proportion of the population living in cities. Following Aristotle, Lipset believed that a large middle class opposed to extremism was conducive to democracy.

More recent research confirms the correlation between affluence and stable democracy, even though there are exceptions such as poor but democratic India. Marks and Diamond (1992, p. 110) seem to be fully justified in describing the connection between affluence and democracy as 'one of the most powerful and stable relationships in the study of comparative national development'.

Crucially, the economic and political weaknesses of new democracies are linked. The absence of a

Profile **MEXICO**

Population: 105m.
Gross domestic product per head: $9,000. Mexico is the world's ninth largest economy.
Form of government: a federal and presidential republic.
Legislature: the 500 members of the Chamber of Deputies are elected for a single three-year period and the 128 members of the Senate for a six-year tenure.
Executive: the president, directly elected for a non-renewable six-year term, heads both the state and the government, choosing the members of the Cabinet.
Judiciary: headed by the Supreme Court of Justice, the judicial system mixes American constitutional principles with the civil law tradition. In practice, both judicial independence and police enforcement of law have been weak.
Electoral system: 300 members of the Chamber represent single-member districts, the other 200 are elected by the list system of proportional representation. The Senate also operates a mixed electoral system.
Party system: dominated by the Institutional Revolutionary Party (PRI) until the 1990s. Other major parties are the conservative National Action Party (PAN), which formed part of Fox's Alliance for Change in the 2000 elections, and the left-wing Revolutionary Democratic Party (PRD).

'Yes, it can be done,' shouted the crowds in Mexico City as they celebrated the downfall of the PRI after the presidential election of 2000. After 70 years in power, the PRI not only lost a presidential election for the first time but also no longer controlled either house of the national legislature. The world's oldest ruling party had suffered an historic reverse, defeated by a centre-right coalition led by Vicente Fox. This peaceful transfer of power decisively confirmed Mexico's status as a new democracy. For students of comparative politics, Mexico offers a remarkably successful example of democratization.

The PRI had been founded in 1929 in the decade following the radical Mexican revolution. Gradually, however, socialist principles were diluted as the PRI established a classic semi-democracy based on patronage networks. The PRI distributed favours while repressing opposition and manipulating election results. In the 1950s and 1960s, the PRI seemed to have discovered the perfect recipe for a stable dictatorship. However, three problems recurred:

▸ continuing poverty for those excluded from the PRI network, reflected in periodic revolts
▸ increasing opposition from the expanding urban middle class created by economic growth
▸ occasional economic crises when the PRI placed its political objectives before sound economic policy.

With the political effectiveness of the PRI machine decaying, Carlos Salinas (President, 1988–94) initiated economic reforms, including privatizing major firms and opening the economy to international competition, not least through NAFTA. In contrast to the Soviet Union, where Gorbachev had initiated political reform before restructuring the economy, liberalization in Mexico preceded political change. As the PRI lost direct control of economic resources, so its powers of patronage declined and voters became free to support opposition parties, especially in the cities. Independent trade unions began to form outside the enveloping embrace of the PRI.

But the PRI also introduced political changes that served to enliven a moribund opposition. By the 1990s, the PRI no longer felt able to manipulate election results. In 1997, it lost its majority in the Chamber of Deputies after relatively fair elections. The decisive election in 2000 was overseen by an independent election commission. So the PRI's fall was partly self-induced: its leaders recognized that the tools needed to guarantee their party's continued grip on power were hindering the country's further development.

Mexico's gradual moves to democracy seem to have avoided what Baer (1993, p. 64) described as 'the dilemma of all reforms from above, particularly in ageing regimes: how to avoid unleashing a revolution from below'. But it remains to be seen how far, and at what speed, democracy will consolidate in Mexico. The PRI remains a significant force, controlling half the country's 32 states. Mexico's continuing problems – peasant revolts and urban squalor, drugs and crime, corrupt judges and incompetent police – mean that it remains premature to place the country in the same political category as the USA and Canada, its NAFTA partners.

Further reading: Camp (2002), Cornelius and Weldon (2004), Craske (2001), Levy and Bruhn (2001).

liberal political framework itself inhibits economic advance. Weak legal systems restrict economic development because corporations lack confidence that commercial disputes can be resolved fairly and promptly through the courts. Close personal connections develop between politicians in need of money and well-placed business executives who value political influence. These semi-corrupt networks preclude the development of a clear framework for market regulation. Dominant firms with political protection can see off competitive threats, preventing the development of a level playing field in which the most efficient companies can prosper. Scared off by corrupt and slow-moving bureaucrats, foreign investors are inclined to go elsewhere, especially as population and market size are relatively small in new democracies. As a result, both economic and democratic development wither, held back by the incomplete penetration of liberal ideas and institutions.

The challenge of timing

We should mention one final factor affecting the consolidation of third-wave democracies: the timing of their transition. To be born into a world which is already democratic is a mixed blessing. On the one hand, it increases the pressures on new democracies to consolidate too quickly. Populations value not just democracy but the affluence they sense goes with it; and they demand both now. On the other hand, an international environment supportive of democracy – and even more so since 9/11 – is beneficial to democratic consolidation. To understand new democracies, it is helpful to explore the challenge of timing in more detail.

The first wave democracies were not so much adopting a new political order as inventing it. As we saw in discussing the United Kingdom, innovation was a leisurely, even evolutionary, process of adapting old ideas to large states. By contrast, third-wave democracies were delivered into a world where democratic ideas were already becoming predominant. As a result, they are expected to mimic established examples without the economic resources and gradual maturation which helped the countries of the first wave. Both domestic and international audiences expect the

process of developing democracy to be collapsed into a decade or two. The result is rushed rather than leisurely democratization. In the first wave, democracy could be an outcome but in the third wave it has to be an intention. As Hollifield and Jillson (2000, p. 11) suggest,

> The latest transitions to democracy have occurred with dizzying speed, giving the societies involved little time to prepare for the leap to representative government. Whereas democracies in Western Europe, the United States and the former British dominions had a gestation period of one or two centuries, in the third wave democratization has come virtually overnight. This has led to a great deal of improvisation and many setbacks.

At the same time, democracies of the third wave have one clear advantage over their predecessors: a favourable global and regional context. Leading actors such as the United States and the European Union, and sympathetic institutions such as the World Bank, began to promote democracy once the Cold War ended. This support began even before September 11 gave the USA a further reason to promote democracy in the authoritarian Middle East.

Often, a favourable regional context also eased transition. Greece, Portugal and Spain – and more recently post-communist Poland, Hungary and the Czech Republic – undoubtedly benefited from their position close to the heartland of European democracy. In a similar way, Mexico's transition from semi-democracy surely owes something to its trading links with the USA, consolidated through NAFTA. Indeed Diamond (1997, p. 39) suggests that 'the greatest regional force for democratic consolidation in the Americas may well be the move towards regional free trade'.

Semi-democracy

The final concept to explore in this chapter is that of semi-democracy. This term lacks the theoretical purity of either democratic or authoritarian rule; its task is more descriptive. Semi-democracy denotes forms of government which, in practice, blend both democratic and authoritarian elements. In a semi-democracy, democratic legitimacy is not wholly lacking; rather, it is acquired and exploited in dubious ways and often remains contested. As in Asian states such as Singapore and Malaysia, the dominant leaders use ethnic diversity, fear of political instability or the demand for economic development as reasons for departing from the liberal aspects of established democracies.

In a world dominated by democratic ideology, semi-democracy is a more likely outcome than a return to authoritarianism for those new democracies that do not consolidate. This hybrid is not new but it is becoming more prevalent. Carothers (2002, p. 18) observes that 'what is often thought of as an uneasy, precarious middle ground between democracy and dictatorship is actually the most common political condition in countries of the developing and postcommunist worlds'.

Definition

A **semi-democracy** blends democratic and authoritarian elements in stable combination. Although rulers are elected, they govern with little respect for individual rights and often harass opposition or even non-official groups. By contrast, a **new democracy** is one that has not yet had time to consolidate; that is, democracy has not become the 'only game in town'. In practice, new democracies and semi-democracies show similar characteristics but a new democracy is transitional while a semi-democracy is not. Assuming a new democracy does not slide back into authoritarian rule, it will develop into either an established democracy or a semi-democracy.

The crucial point is that we should not think of democracy and authoritarianism as sole and incompatible ways of organizing government. Rather, each principle can provide pockets of power that can coexist, sometimes indefinitely, within the one political system; once set, semi-democracy is a strong amalgam. Crouch (1996, p. vii), for instance, shows how Malaysia's 'repressive–responsive' regime combines democratic and authoritarian features in a manner that 'provides the foundation for a remarkably stable political order'.

Similarly, Borón (1998, p. 43) refers to the

'faulty democracies' of Latin America in which rulers, once elected, govern in an authoritarian style, showing little concern for mass poverty or legal niceties. In these conditions, suggests Borón, democracy 'endures but does not consolidate'.

The notion of semi-democracy also captures the political reality of many states in sub-Saharan Africa. As Herbst (2001, p. 359) writes, 'it is wrong to conclude that African states are travelling between democracy and authoritarianism simply because a majority of them belong to neither category. Rather, the current condition of African states could well prevail for decades'.

In understanding the operating methods of semi-democracies, it is useful to distinguish two variants. In the *first* type, an elected party or leader sets the framework for political competition, governing in an illiberal fashion. O'Donnell (1994, p. 59) describes this format: 'whoever wins election to the presidency is thereby entitled to govern as he or she sees fit, constrained only by the hard facts of existing power relations and by a constitutionally limited term of office.'

Russia's super-presidential system is an example. The president not only takes the lead in seeking to impose solutions to national problems but more significantly is expected to do so. Boris Yeltsin (President 1991–2000) ruled in a highly personal way which inhibited the development of government institutions. Yeltsin's successor, Vladimir Putin, is an equally tough political operator. In many African countries, too, 'presidents have an inordinate amount of power invested in them and little in the way of institutional provisions to check that power' (May, 2000, p. 176).

One way in which these democratic despots acquire at least some legitimacy is through semi-competitive elections. They use control over money, jobs, contracts, pensions, public housing, the media, the police, the electoral system and the courts to deliver success, usually without any need to manipulate the election count. Egypt and Tunisia are examples of countries where elections have long been semi-competitive.

Note, however, that such methods are often combined with effective governance and a favourable disposition towards a dominant ruler or party. For example, Singapore's People's Action Party may manipulate elections in its favour but it

DEBATE
'ASIAN DEMOCRACY'

Many Asian leaders reject aspects of the Western democratic tradition. They claim to be building a distinctive form of 'Asian democracy'. For example, the rulers of Malaysia and Singapore explicitly reject the Western interpretation of liberal democracy based on individual rights. They favour an approach that gives more weight to Asian values, including respect for authority, avoiding public conflict and accepting the primacy of the group. Democracy is defined in almost familial terms, with the elected leader adopting a paternal style. The state leads society, and democracy therefore depends less on the independent groups and associations which provide the foundation for Western democracy.

The institutional consequences of 'Asian democracy' include a subservient media and judiciary. In addition, the police and security forces become more aggressive in their approach to criminals and dissenters. But is there really a distinctive form of democracy in Asia or is democracy a universal principle?

The case for
The attempt to develop non-Western models of democracy derives in part from the natural cynicism of former subjects to their colonial masters. Asian leaders reject what they see as imperialist attempts to universalize Western democracy. Dr Mahathir, when Prime Minister of Malaysia, condemned Western democracies 'where political leaders are afraid to do what is right, where the people and their leaders live in fear of the free media which they so loudly proclaim as inviolable'. A former foreign minister of Vietnam exposed Western hypocrisy more bluntly: 'Human rights? I learnt about human rights when the French tortured me as a teenager' Thompson (2001, p. 160). Further, the Asian model has delivered economic growth by allowing leaders to focus on long-term modernization free from electoral pressures. Thus Prime Minister Goh of Singapore suggests that

> our government acts more like a trustee. As a custodian of the people's welfare, it exercises independent judgement on what is in the long-term economic interests of the people and acts on that basis. Government policy is not dictated by opinion polls or referenda (Wang, 2002, p. v).

The case against
Critics allege that 'Asian democracy' is simply an excuse for failing to move beyond semi-democracy. Putzel (1997, p. 253) roundly declares that 'claims for "indigenous forms of democracy" appear to be no more than justifications for authoritarian rule'. And Brzezinski (1997, p. 5) suggests that 'the "Asian values" doctrine is nothing but a rationalization for a certain phase of historical development'. By this he means that through accidents of history Western societies have more experience with protecting individual freedom. Asia, Brzezinski suggests, is still playing catch-up, both economically and politically. And resolving the financial crisis that engulfed East Asia in 1997 required most countries in the region to somewhat reduce state intervention in the economy, yielding a rather more liberal form of democracy. Finally, a Western human rights activist argues that democracy and human rights are inherently universal:

> There is nothing special about torturing the Asian way. Rape is not something that is done an Asian way. Rape is rape, torture is torture and human rights are human rights.
>
> (Vatikiotis, 1995, p. 98)

Assessment
The debate on Asian democracy can not be resolved easily. It mixes ideology and colonial memories in an explosive combination. But three points are clear. First, Asia has never been a single category. China is still authoritarian, Indonesia largely so, Singapore is a semi-democracy and Japan is an established democracy. Second, rather than referring to 'Asian' democracy, it might be more useful to consider the kind of democracy best suited to economic development. The 'Asian' approach may be more effective in countries which are still growing their industrial capacity even if the Western model is more appropriate for developed economies. Third, the liberal form of democracy found in the West reflects a long-term project to tame the power of secular and religious rulers. If Asia is to 'catch up', it will take generations to do so.

Further reading: Bell *et al.* (1995), Diamond and Plattner (2001), Thompson (2001).

has also ruled with competence. Similarly, President Putin's willingness to pull all the levers of power available to him has not dented his support among the Russian public; it may indeed have endeared him to them.

Once elected, semi-democratic presidents rule the roost and the assembly and the judiciary are cowed into insignificance. Ordinary 'citizens' may have a vote and their rights are tolerably secure when the interests of the regime are not at stake. But citizens are sensitive to the sound of gunfire. They know when to lie low. With good reason, this form of semi-democracy is sometimes called illiberal or electoral democracy (O'Donnell, 1996).

In a semi-democracy based on a dominant party or individual, power is concentrated in a few hands. But there is a *second* form of semi-democracy in which elected rulers have too little rather than too much power. Here elected rulers are puppets rather than despots. In this version, 'power is shifted to the military, bureaucracy or top business groups' (Case, 1996, p. 439). Like weak monarchs surrounded by powerful noblemen in medieval Europe, these elected politicians must continue to govern alongside military, ethnic, religious and regional leaders determined to maintain their established privileges.

When the president is merely a frontman, the outcome is an unconsolidated democracy in which elections are established but do not function as definitive statements of who should exercise final decision-making power. In Thailand, Turkey and Pakistan, for example, the military stands as a guardian of the nation, exerting a 'silent veto' over civilian decisions (Gills *et al.*, 1993, pp. 21–8). Such semi-democracies are sometimes called supervised or even façade democracies.

Some post-soviet republics, including central Asian republics such as Kyrgyzstan and Uzbekistan, exemplify this pattern of limited authority for elected politicians (Fairbanks, 2001). Real power comes from patronage and from deals with regional and ethnic power brokers or even with criminal gangs. In this type of semi-democracy ('disguised authoritarianism' might be more accurate), power gives the capacity to take elected office but elected office does not add much power. In these circumstances, the president is merely the mouthpiece of a dominant and corrupt elite, and

elections are just plebiscites to confirm the elite's choice of top leader. Democracy fails because presidents are impotent rather than despots.

The ways of semi-democracy are a sobering reminder to those who take a naive view of the triumph of democracy. Simplistic counts of the number of democracies tell only part of the story. As quantity has increased, quality has fallen. Why is it, then, that so many new democracies turn out, on closer inspection, to be only semi-democratic? There are two answers, the optimist's and the pessimist's.

The optimist's view is that semi-democracy is merely transitional, a temporary staging post in the world's pilgrimage from authoritarian rule to established democracy. This scenario possesses a certain plausibility. After all, nearly all Western democracies passed through a stage in which the contest for power became open and legitimate, a phase which preceded the introduction of universal suffrage. Even in the United States, democracy took decades to establish.

But it is prudent to consider a more pessimistic account of semi-democracy: that it is a stable method of governing poor and unequal societies, particularly now that blatant dictatorship has become less acceptable. When poverty coincides with extreme inequality, and when ethnic divisions are strong, the prospects of creating a democratic community of equals are slender indeed. Further, semi-democracy is usually sufficient for the ruling elite to meet the conditions of aid set by the World Bank, the IMF and donor governments. While these international bodies may welcome democracy, in practice they give higher priority to economic reform.

The heart of the matter is perhaps that semi-democracy is a tacit, but stable, compromise between domestic elites and international organizations. For such reasons, Case (1996, p. 464) concludes that semi-democracy is not 'a mere way station on the road to further democracy'.

Key reading

> **Next step:** *Dahl* et al. *(2003) is a wide-ranging collection on the nature, conditions, procedures and impact of democracy.*

Dahl (1989, 1998) offers lucid accounts of democracy. The 1989 book is more advanced, the 1998 volume more introductory. Other overall assessments include Arblaster (2002) and Held (1996). Democratization has spawned an outstanding literature: Huntington (1991) and O'Donnell *et al.* (1986) are influential, while Pridham (1995) is a collection of classic articles. Also on democratization, Grugel (2002) provides an introductory overview while Diamond (1999) focuses on consolidation. Carothers (2002) discusses the end of the transition paradigm as countries enter a seemingly permanent grey zone of semi-democracy. For democracy in the developing world, see Haynes (2001); for Islam and democracy, Diamond *et al.* (2003) and for democracy after communism, Diamond and Plattner (2002). Gill and Marwick (2000) review Russia's stillborn democracy. Agüero and Stark (1998) remains an excellent survey of post-transition Latin America.

Chapter 4

Authoritarian rule

Brooker (2000, p. 1) writes that 'non-democratic government, whether by elders, chiefs, monarchs, aristocrats, empires, military regimes or one-party states, has been the norm for most of human history'. As late as 1981, Perlmutter (p. xi) could still claim that 'the twentieth century is the age of political authoritarianism'. Certainly that brutal century will be remembered more for the dictatorships it spawned – including Hitler's Germany, Stalin's Russia, Mao's China and Pol Pot's Cambodia – than for the democratic transitions at its close.

But studying non-democracies remain far more than an historical exercise. Authoritarian rulers may be under more pressure as democratization spreads but the species is far from extinct. Indeed, September 11, 2001 brought non-democratic regimes into sharper focus. Most of the terrorists involved in the attacks on the United States, including Osama bin Laden, were nationals of Saudi Arabia, a leading example of an authoritarian Islamic state. More generally, the Arab world contains a high proportion of the world's stock of both authoritarian governments and oil.

Other non-democratic regimes are also of international significance. In China, for instance, a nominally communist ruling elite continues to govern a quarter of the world's population and a rapidly expanding economy. China's distinctive combination of authoritarian politics with a partly free economy has acquired global significance particularly since China joined the World Trade Organization in 2001.

We begin by examining authoritarian rule in the traditional style, a form common to non-democratic rulers past and present, before turning to the new forms of authoritarianism which emerged in the twentieth century, namely communist, fascist and military rule (Box 4.1). We then consider contemporary authoritarianism in the Arab and Muslim worlds and we conclude with an examination of China.

Traditional authoritarian rule

Traditional authoritarianism is a distinct form of non-democratic rule in which authority is owed to the ruler himself rather than to a more abstract entity such as a communist or fascist party. The people are subjects, not citizens, and the ruler is constrained neither by law nor by competitive election. Nonetheless, the ruler is expected to take responsibility for his people, just as a father should look after his children, in a format known as patrimonial rule. The abstract idea of a state linking rulers and citizens is missing, as are such modern notions as constitutions, rights, the separation of powers and the rule of law. Rather, the law (if it exists at all) expresses the wishes of the ruler.

> *Definition*
> Weber's notion of **patrimonial rule** is based on the personal authority of a leading male who rules as if he were the head of a large family. As a father-figure, the ruler claims to care for his dependants but at the same time his dominant position affirms a relationship of inequality. Patrimonial rule is traditional – patrimony literally means an inheritance from one's father – but remains common in authoritarian regimes today (Gerth and Mills, 1948).

The major forms of traditional rule were chiefdoms and monarchies, though these sometimes extended to larger empires such as Imperial China, Mesopotamia and the Aztecs (van Creveld, 1999). With the rise of the modern state, traditional rule

Form	Definition
Authoritarian rule	(1) Any form of non-democratic rule. (2) Those non-democratic regimes which, unlike totalitarian states, do not seek to transform society and the people in it
Traditional authoritarian rule	Allegiance is owed to an individual ruler who often claims a religious mandate passed down through family succession. The chief, monarch or president rules his subjects as if he were the head of an extended family
Communist states	Political systems in which the communist party monopolized power, leading to an all-encompassing bureaucratic state. In theory, the object was to implement Marx's vision of a classless society; in practice, the party sought to protect its position through social control
Fascism	An anti-liberal doctrine that glorified the nation and advocated a warrior state, led by an all-powerful leader, to whom the masses would show passionate commitment and submission. Advocated by Mussolini in Italy and, supplemented by Aryan racism, the basis for National Socialism in Nazi Germany
Military rule	Government by the military, often ruling through a junta comprising the leader from each branch of the forces. Half the countries in Africa were under military control as late as 1987

has become less common. However, presidents governing in the traditional style are still common in Africa and the Arabian Gulf.

Whether chief, monarch, emperor or president, the authority of the traditional ruler is technically unlimited. The leader's authority is typically based on religion, as with the divine right of kings in pre-modern Europe and the mandate of heaven claimed by Chinese emperors. Succession is often based on heredity, maintaining the fictional descent from God, but in practice is often acquired through usurpation. Succession can be either to the eldest son or (as with many ruling families in the Middle East) to the eldest capable relative. The latter method is less clear-cut, inviting short-term conflict.

However, even when an outsider does become ruler, the method of governing often continues unchanged. Thus, traditional authoritarian rule can provide a settled political framework, especially for static agricultural societies with little need of government.

For all their theoretical authority, the power of most traditional non-democratic leaders is neither unlimited nor arbitrary. For one thing, rulers who claim divine authority must ration those actions contradicting the religious code. More important, in the absence of an extended bureaucracy, rapid transport and modern communications, rulers lack direct means of controlling their subjects. They are forced to administer their kingdoms and empires indirectly, calling on the services of local leaders. Kings, and emperors even more so, have little choice but to govern by making deals with provincial notables.

Finer (1997, p. 38) suggests that palace politics is the characteristic mode of traditional authoritarianism. Befitting the personal character of authoritarian governance, in palace politics the officers of state are nothing more than servants of the ruler. Thus, the Keeper of the King's Purse and Minister of Finance are one and the same. Because allegiance is owed to the ruler rather than to rules, palace politics is based on personal relationships. Finer's examples of pure 'palace-type political systems' include ancient Egypt, the Roman empire and some eighteenth-century absolute rulers in Europe, such as the court of Louis XIV in France.

While palace politics can provide stable governance, the danger of traditional authoritarian rule is that it becomes insular and introverted; too much politics and not enough government. Further, the court constitutes a tax on society: money comes in from the authority of officials to grant licences and take bribes. This intensely political economy discourages economic development and is increasingly unpopular with international agencies. With good reason, traditional authoritarian leaders rightly regard not just democracy, but also development and the agencies which promote it, with suspicion.

Communist, fascist and military rule

The twentieth century raised the political stakes. Unlike their traditional counterparts, modern dictators could exploit the political power of an extended state, the economic resources of the Industrial Revolution and the communications facilities of national media. These developments permitted unprecedented mobilization and control of mass populations. Authoritarian leaders were no longer just masters of their palace; their decisions now impinged directly on ordinary people. In extreme cases such as Stalin's Russia and Hitler's Germany, the result was the systematic murder of millions. So although much traditional rule continued in the twentieth century, our focus in this section will be on that century's new cast of dictators: communist, fascist and military leaders.

Both communist and fascist rulers claimed to be seeking a reconstruction of human nature and society. Communist states notionally aimed for a classless utopia while fascist rulers sought to renew the nation's strength through submission to a dominant leader. These bombastic declarations were not always matched by political reality but even so, such bold aspirations were far removed from the traditional authoritarian regime, with its overriding commitment to maintaining the ruler's position. Certainly, a distinctive feature of communist and fascist regimes was what Perlmutter (1981, p. xi) terms the 'conspicuous political innovations' of twentieth-century authoritarianism, namely:

> the unopposed single party, the party-state, political police, the politburo [top party committee], revolutionary command councils, storm troops, political youth movements, cadres and gulags, propaganda machinery and concentration camps.

> **Definition**
>
> A **totalitarian** regime aims for total penetration of society in an attempt, at least in theory, to transform it. As defined by Linz (2000, p. 4), a totalitarian system is 'a regime form for completely organizing political life and society'. During the Cold War, communist and fascist states were bracketed as totalitarian, a connection which served to link communist regimes with disgraced fascism (Gleason, 1995).

Below, we will outline communist and fascist rule before turning to the large number of military governments – usually authoritarian rather than totalitarian – which ruled many developing countries for part of the second half of the twentieth century.

Communist states

The 1917 October Revolution in Russia was a decisive event of the twentieth century. It signalled the international advent of a regime, an ideology and a revolutionary movement which sought to overthrow the capitalist democracies of the West. Although communism failed to become a governing force in the affluent West, communist power did expand dramatically in Eastern Europe and Asia. The Union of Soviet Socialist Republics (USSR) – effectively a new Russian empire – was formed in 1924, extending from the Ukraine in the west to the central Asian republic of Kazakhstan in the east (Table 4.1 and Map 4.1). By area, the USSR became the largest country in the world.

After 1945, Eastern European countries such as Poland and Romania became satellite territories of this new empire. In Asia, the Chinese revolution of 1949 established an additional if distinctive communist state. During the Cold War, several developing countries such as Benin and the Congo also declared a nominal Marxist allegiance. Until the decisive collapse of the communist order in the late 1980s and early 1990s, regimes claiming Marxist inspiration ruled more than 1.5 billion people: about one in three of the world's population.

In seeking to understand communist rule, we should note the sharp contrasts between ideology

Table 4.1 Post-communist states in Eastern Europe and the former Soviet Union

State	Population estimate, 2003 (million)	Gross domestic product per head, 2002	Ethnic groups comprising over 10% of the population, 2002 (listed by size of group)
Eastern European states formerly under the control of the Soviet Union			
Albania	3.6	$4,500	Albanian
Bosnia and Herzegovina	4.0	$1,900	Bosniak, Serb, Croat
Bulgaria	7.5+	$6,600	Bulgarian, Turk
Croatia	4.4	$8,800	Croat
Czech Republic*	10.2+	$15,300	Czech, Moravian
Hungary*	10.0+	$13,300	Hungarian
Macedonia, Former Yugoslav Republic of	2.1	$5,000	Macedonian, Albanian
Poland*	38.6	$9,500	Polish
Romania	22.4	$7,400	Romanian
Serbia and Montenegro	10.7	$2,370	Serb, Albanian
Slovakia*	5.4	$12,000	Slovak, Hungarian
Slovenia*	1.9	$18,000	Slovene
States formed from the Soviet Union			
Armenia	3.3+	$3,800	Armenian
Azerbaijan	7.8	$3,500	Azeri
Belarus	10.3+	$8,200	Belarusian, Russian
Estonia*	1.4+	$10,900	Estonian, Russian
Georgia	4.9+	$3,100	Georgian
Kazakhstan	16.8	$6,300	Kazakh, Russian
Kyrgyzstan	4.9	$2,800	Kyrgyz, Russian, Uzbek
Latvia*	2.3+	$8,300	Latvian, Russian
Lithuania*	3.6+	$8,400	Lithuanian
Moldova	4.4	$2,500	Ukrainian, Russian, Moldovan/Romanian
Russia	144.5+	$9,300	Russian
Tajikistan	6.9	$1,250	Tajik, Uzbek
Turkmenistan	4.8	$5,500	Turkmen
Ukraine	48.0+	$4,500	Ukrainian, Russian
Uzbekistan	26.0	$2,500	Uzbek

* Joined the European Union in 2004.
+ Falling population.

Source: CIA World Factbook at http://www.cia.gov/cia/publications/factbook.

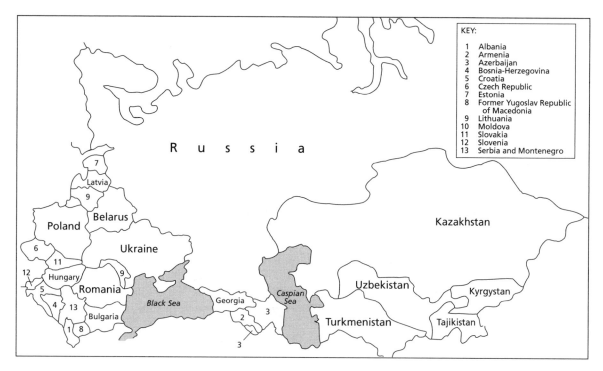

Map 4.1 Post-communist Eastern Europe and Central Asia

and practice. In his theoretical writings, Karl Marx (1818–83) had envisaged an equal, classless and stateless utopia in which goods would be distributed from each according to their ability to each according to their need. In *The Communist Manifesto* (1848, p. 244), Marx and Engels claimed that 'in place of the old bourgeois society, with its classes and class antagonisms, we shall have an association, in which the free development of each is the free development of all'. In the transition to this utopia, Marx suggested that the state would be converted 'from an organ superior to society to one completely subordinate to it'.

Practical revolutionaries, though, faced a more immediate problem: how to overthrow the existing capitalist order. Here Vladimir Lenin (1870–1924), the Russian revolutionary, made a pivotal contribution. He argued that the communist party should serve as a vanguard organization, leading the workers into political activity that would further enhance their revolutionary consciousness. By assuming the party possessed a deeper understanding of the true interests of the working class than did the workers themselves,

Lenin provided the crucial rationale for the monopoly position which communist parties created once in power. In this way, the dictatorship of the party supplanted Marx's utopian dreams.

In power, ruling communist parties dominated society. Lenin's view that the workers must be forced to be free simply resulted in no freedom whatever. Communist regimes were strongly authoritarian, brooking no opposition, stage-managing elections, acting above the law, rewriting constitutions, determining all major appointments to the government, controlling the media and spying on their populations. Far from disappearing as anticipated by Marx, the state under the party's tutelage became an enveloping presence. Economies were brought under public control as part of the push to industrialize; the elaborate five-year plans produced in the Soviet Union were undoubtedly the most ambitious, detailed and comprehensive attempts at economic planning the world has ever seen. The party controlled and the state implemented.

This new form of party-state snuffed out independent organizations, creating a social wasteland of distrust in which true political beliefs could only be expressed safely within the family (and sometimes not even there). Not only was active opposition suppressed but explicit support – in the form of attendance at demonstrations, party-led meetings and elections – was required. This insistence on active if ritual support was one factor distinguishing totalitarian from merely authoritarian regimes.

As communist states retreat into history, we should be careful to avoid stereotyping their characteristics. Communist regimes varied among themselves and also over time. In parts of Eastern Europe, for example Poland, local communist leaders governed with a lighter touch than in the communist heartland of the Soviet Union. China followed an even more independent path, with the triumph of the communist revolution in 1949 owing as much to nationalism as to Marxism, and resulting from the efforts of the army as well as the party (Selden, 1995).

Similarly, communist states grew less totalitarian as they matured. Once the initial thrust to industrialize had been achieved, many such regimes settled into the routines of middle age. The Soviet Union is a striking example. During the 1930s, under Stalin's brutal dictatorship, Russia had achieved forced industrialization and the collective ownership of agriculture. But after the tyrant's death in 1953, a programme of 'de-Stalinization' quickly emerged. Nikita Khrushchev, the new party secretary, famously denounced Stalin in his secret speech to the party elite in 1956. Terror ceased to be a routine political tactic and the Soviet Union came to offer a more predictable environment to its citizens.

Yet far from stabilizing the party's control, the attempt to transform communist rule into more rational and orderly governance eventually proved its undoing. State-led planning achieved speedy industrialization but proved incapable of delivering the advanced products and services found in the West. 'Advanced socialism' proved to be a contradiction in terms. Communism reached its dead end. The party lost its mission and continued to rule only because it had done so in the past. In such circumstances, reform was always likely to escalate into revolution.

When Mikhail Gorbachev became General Secretary of the Soviet Communist Party in 1985, his intention was modernization but the outcome was dissolution. In Eastern Europe, communist rule fell apart in 1989 once the new Russian leader made it clear that the USSR would no longer intervene militarily to protect the puppet rulers of its satellite states. The following year, the Soviet Union itself dissolved into 15 constituent republics (Table 4.1). In Russia, by far the most important of these republics, the Communist Party was outlawed, a humiliating fate for what had been the most powerful party on earth.

Even where nominally communist rule still survives, as in China, Vietnam and Laos, most economic development now occurs outside the state sector. In the twenty-first century, communism's major significance lies in its legacy for successor regimes. As a system of rule and a method of economic organization, communism is finished. It was the future that didn't work.

Fascist states

Fascism was the twentieth century's second remarkable contribution to authoritarian rule. Located at the extreme right rather than the far left of the ideological spectrum, fascist regimes nonetheless sought – like communist states – to dominate the societies they ruled. But fascist regimes were rarer and less stable than their communist equivalents. Although we can still observe the consequences of communism in the twenty-first century, fascism's challenge was confined to the period bordered by the two world wars.

Fascism began with the emergence of revolutionary groups (*fascia*) in Italy during the First World War (1914–18). As a serious force, it ended with the defeat of Germany in 1945. Fascist elements continued to be found in Spain under General Franco and even Portugal under Salazar, two dictators whose right-wing rule continued well into the 1960s. But these were conservative authoritarian regimes rooted in the army and the church; they sought merely to recover traditional national glories rather than to build a new and self-consciously modern order (Linz, 2000). Similarly, the right-wing anti-immigrant parties found in contemporary Europe do not embrace all

DEBATE

AUTHORITARIAN RULE AS A RECIPE FOR ECONOMIC DEVELOPMENT

Can authoritarian rule be defended as an effective method for economic development? If so, we will have a powerful critique of democracy's claims to be universally the best form of government since we would nearly all prefer to eat under a dictator than to starve in a democracy. In addition, we could reasonably anticipate that democracy is unlikely to consolidate in poor countries over the long term if the cost is slower economic development.

The case for

Sørensen (1997a, p. 65) points out that 'in the twentieth century there was no case of successful economic development without comprehensive political action involving enormous state intervention in the economy'. The reason is clear: industrialization requires massive investment in infrastructure such as transport, communications and education; initially, these can only be funded by the state. And authoritarian rulers can generate the surplus needed for investment precisely because they can resist short-term pressures for immediate consumption. Simply put, they can kick-start development because they can ignore the squeals of those whose consumption is initially held down.

Consider some examples. The communist revolution in Russia initiated a remarkably rapid transformation from a rural to an industrial society. Similarly, the Chinese economy has grown under communism at twice the rate achieved by democratic India. Between 1960 and 1985, authoritarian Indonesia, Singapore and South Korea were among the fastest-growing economies in the world. In parts of Latin America, too, technocrats operating under more or less authoritarian governments succeeded in the final decades of the century in imposing coherent economic policy on unruly societies. Even some military rulers have initiated worthwhile modernization: for example, the land reforms introduced by General Abdel Nasser (President of Egypt, 1956–70) mean that nearly all Egyptians now have access to safe water, an accomplishment as yet unmatched by India.

The case against

A few non-democratic regimes may initiate economic development but the vast majority do not. Many traditional rulers, such as the ruling families in the Middle East, continue to resist modernization. Other dictators, for example Nigeria's military 'lootocrats', set back economic development by decades. An overall assessment by Przeworski et al. (2000) concludes that there is no 'cruel choice' to be made between democracy and development. If industrialization really does require forgoing immediate consumption, rulers should attempt to persuade the people of the need for sacrifice, not impose dictatorial solutions. Besides, even if non-democratic rule can lead to industrialization, that point does not excuse the abuses of power and human rights which are an inherent danger of authoritarian regimes. For example, China's path of communist modernization involved the brutality of the Great Leap Forward, in which around 40 million people died between 1958 and 1963 as a result of a bungled experiment in forced collectivization. Who is prepared to say – indeed, who is entitled to say – that economic growth is justified at such a massive human price?

Assessment

Perhaps economic development in the twentieth century could only be achieved by a stable authoritarian elite capable both of extracting resources for investment and of providing state leadership for emerging private industries. But in the twenty-first century, globalization has given developing countries access to new sources of capital through multinational corporations, overseas banks and the World Bank. To access these resources, developing countries benefit from convincing lenders that their economy is market-based and that their politics takes the form of a tolerably liberal democracy. The twentieth century may prove to have been the pinnacle of 'the developmental state' led by authoritarian rulers; in the new century, markets and democracy may belong together in developing as well as developed countries.

Further reading: Przeworski et al. (2000), Robinson and White (1998), Sørensen (1997a).

aspects of the interwar ideology. Even though these protest parties are frequently condemned as fascist, their essential character is post-fascist (Ignati, 1992).

Even in its interwar heyday, fascist regimes were rare on the ground. Mussolini's leadership of Italy, lasting from 1922 until *il duce* was deposed in 1943, is the main example. However even this dictatorship was fascist more by bombastic declaration than by institutional reality. In Hitler's Germany, the Nazi party espoused an ideology that certainly included fascist principles. However, these elements were blended with crude Aryan racism to form the compound known as national socialism.

Yet the fascist worldview cannot be ignored; it represents an important nationalist response to the rise of communism. Its significance for the twentieth century – and for six million European Jews in particular – was profound.

What, then, was the doctrine expressed by the classic fascist regimes? Fascism was an extreme glorification of the nation, often defined in racial terms. The notional purpose was to create an all-embracing nation to which the masses would show passionate commitment and submission. An autocratic ruler and a single party would personify the state. State and nation would become one.

Fascism lacked the theoretical sophistication of communism; it offered an ideological impulse more than a coherent plan. It sought to use the power of the state, as revealed by the First World War, to revive the countries defeated in that conflict. Religion, liberalism, parliamentary democracy and even capitalism were condemned as weak distractions from the key task of national revival. Fascists claimed that a strong, self-sufficient, warlike nation could mobilize the population more effectively – and in a more modern way – than any other type of regime. 'Everything in the state: nothing against the state: nothing outside the state', said Mussolini. Fascism, not liberalism, was the defence which proud nations should adopt against the communist threat. In short, fascism was the twentieth-century doctrine of nationalism taken to extremes (Griffin, 2004).

In power, fascist regimes governed very differently from ruling communist parties, even though both forms are often grouped under the totalitarian label. Certainly, fascist rulers were com-mitted to mobilizing the population in an organized effort at national rebirth, just as communist regimes claimed to be constructing a classless society. And both ideologies gave primacy to politics: nothing could compete with the authority bestowed on the supreme fascist leader, just as ruling communist parties dominated their own societies.

But fascism lacked the organized character of communist rule. It favoured the risky 'leader principle' in which governance depended on a single individual rather than a well-developed party. Hitler, for one, never showed much interest in administration, preferring to leave his underlings to fight their own bureaucratic battles (Kershaw, 2000). Mature communist states often ran on auto-pilot, with an anonymous party functionary in charge, but fascism – a doctrine of constant movement and change – never developed comparable routines of rule.

Fascist parties were essentially personal vehicles through which the leader managed his rise to power; unlike communist parties, they lost significance once the state was won. In power, neither Mussolini nor even Hitler achieved the domination of society found under communism. Mussolini proved incapable of abolishing even the Italian monarchy while Hitler preferred to exploit rather than nationalize German industry. For all its impact on the twentieth century, fascist practice often seemed to present politics as theatre: marches, demonstrations, symbols and speeches. It was no surprise that fascism's collapse in 1945 preceded that of its better-organized communist bogeyman.

Military rule

Military rule is our final form of twentieth-century authoritarian government. Most military regimes lacked the ideological underpinnings of communism or even fascism; indeed, they typically lacked any theoretical justification at all. Nonetheless, military government was an important aspect of twentieth-century government. As Pinkney (1990, p. 7) writes,

the involvement of soldiers in politics is not new, and can be traced back at least as far as

Roman times. The phenomenon of military government, in the sense of a government drawn mainly from the army and using the army as its main power base, is much newer and belongs essentially to the last 50 years.

The contrasts between military regimes, on the one hand, and communism and fascism, on the other, are acute. Most military coups came later in the century, between the 1960s and 1980s, and, more significantly, they occurred in post-colonial countries in Latin America, Africa and parts of Asia where the state had not achieved the penetration found in Europe. While fascism and communism sought to exploit the power of the modern state, many military coups (especially in smaller African countries) were made possible precisely because the state remained simple and underdeveloped. An ambitious general just needed a few tanks, driven by a handful of discontented officers, to seize the presidential palace and the single radio station.

Yet because the post-colonial state's penetration through society remained limited, life outside the capital would continue unchanged after the coup. Lacking the economic resources and governance tools of modern states, most military rulers were modest in their policy aspirations. The state in uniform lacked the grand objectives of both communist and fascist regimes; in some cases, the aim of the generals was little more than to steal public money. Military government was always authoritarian and sometimes brutal, not least during Latin America's phase of repressive army rule from the mid-1960s to the mid-1970s. But, reflecting the societies in which the military came to power, army rule was rarely totalitarian.

> **Definition**
> A **military coup** is a seizure of political power by the armed forces or sections thereof. The term conjures up images of a violent, secretive and unwelcome capture of power against the opposition of civilian rulers. In fact, many coups replaced one military regime with another, involved little if any loss of life and were more or less invited by the previous rulers.

In many of the post-colonial countries created in the 1950s and 1960s, generals soon seized power from civilian rulers – and then from other generals. Sub-Saharan Africa is the major arena. Here, 68 coups occurred between 1963 and 1987 (Magyar, 1992). But military takeover was not restricted to new states. In Latin America, where colonies had gained independence in the nineteenth century, only Mexico and Costa Rica were immune from military government in the postwar period. Military governments became far more numerous than communist and fascist regimes combined.

> **Definition**
> The **Cold War** refers to the competition between the United States and the Soviet Union which lasted from the late 1940s to the Soviet Union's collapse in 1991. The Cold War reached a high intensity of confrontation, particularly before détente began in the late 1960s. Its end was an event of the first magnitude, releasing the waves of globalization, regionalization, nationalism and democratization which characterize the twenty-first century.

Why did military coups cluster in the decades following the Second World War? As with other aspects of politics during this era, the Cold War was a crucial factor. In this period, the United States and the Soviet Union were more concerned with the global chessboard than with how post-colonial countries were governed internally. Each superpower sought allies and did not enquire closely into the background, civilian or military, of a country's rulers. Thus, governing generals could survive through the political, economic and military backing of a superpower even though they might lack support in their own country. Simple contagion, in which a coup in one country was emulated by its neighbours, was another influence.

Inclusionary and exclusionary regimes represented the two extremes of military rule (Remmer, 1989). In the former, the military leaders sought to build a base of support among the political class – and even, on occasion, in the wider population – often by exploiting the population's respect for a strong leader. Civilian politicians were represented in a cabinet and the bureaucracy continued to make important decisions.

The modernizing regime of Colonel Juan Perón in Argentina was an example. Perón came to power in a coup in 1943, serving as president between 1946 and 1955 and again in 1973–74. He undertook a populist programme of state-led industrialization based on a strong trade union movement and a commitment to social welfare for the urban working class. This Peronist amalgam, based on a distinctively Catholic commitment to both order and reform, continues to influence Argentinian politics (Norden, 1996).

But most military governments were exclusionary rather than inclusionary. In classic authoritarian fashion, the generals sought to prevent popular participation so as to entrench their own position. Opposition was always monitored and suppressed as necessary. Consider General Pinochet's bloody rule of Chile between 1973 and 1989. Pinochet eliminated all potential sources of popular opposition. He exterminated, exiled or imprisoned thousands of labour leaders and left-wing politicians, concentrating power in the hands of his ruling military clique (Drake and Jaksic, 1989).

The standard institutional form of an exclusionary military regime was the junta (council), a small group made up of the leader of each branch of the armed forces. In Chile, Pinochet himself acted as chief executive while a classic four-man junta representing the army, navy, air force and national police took over legislative tasks.

Just as military governments prospered during the Cold War, so they shrivelled after its close. As Wiseman (1996, p. 4) writes, 'authoritarian African political leaders [such as the generals] were more strongly placed to resist the pressures of African democrats when they could turn to outside pressures to help them stay in power'. By

the 1990s, these rulers could no longer rely on their sponsoring superpower; instead, conditionality ruled the roost. Aid and technical assistance flowed to civilian regimes that adopted democratic forms and offered at least some protection to civil rights. International bodies such as the World Bank stipulated market-based economic policies that did not sit comfortably with military rule.

Just as contagion had accelerated the diffusion of military coups in the 1960s and 1970s, so also did it encourage generals to return to their bases in the 1980s and 1990s. In Latin America, even before the Cold War ended, and later in most of Africa, the military withdrew from formal rule, transforming the pattern of government around the world. The last Latin American generals were back in their barracks by 1993 and any coups since then have been sporadic affairs confined to smaller countries in the region (Figure 4.1).

For now at least, military governments – like communist states – are known mainly for their impact on successor regimes. So we conclude this section by examining the difficult legacy of military rule for contemporary civilian leaders. The main problem is that long periods of army rule led to an interweaving of civilian and military power. In many Latin American countries, senior officers had become accustomed to such privileges as

▶ guaranteed seats in the cabinet
▶ a high level of military expenditure
▶ sole control of the security agencies
▶ personal profit from defence contracts
▶ exemption from civilian justice.

The ending of military government did not mean an end to these resources. Indeed, some of these privileges were entrenched before military rulers could be persuaded to relinquish their occupancy of the state.

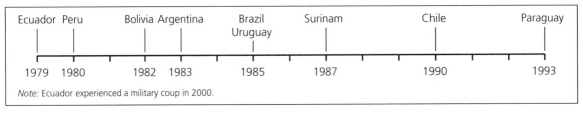

Note: Ecuador experienced a military coup in 2000.

Figure 4.1 The ending of military rule in Latin America

Profile **NIGERIA**

Population: 134m, the tenth largest in the world (HIV/Aids, 6 per cent).
Gross domestic product per head: about $345 but with marked inequality.
Main groups: Hausa-Fulani (29 per cent) in the north, Yoruba (21 per cent) in the southwest and Ibo (18 per cent) in the southeast.
Religions: Muslim 50 per cent, Christian 40 per cent, traditional religions about 10 per cent. Nigeria has the fifth largest Muslim population in the world.
Form of government: a presidential republic. Civilian rule was reintroduced in 1999 following 15 years of military rule.
Territorial basis of power: federal, with the number of provinces increasing from 12 in 1967 to 37 in 2003.

In April 2003, Olusegun Obasanjo was reelected civilian president of Nigeria in elections considered to have been only partly rigged. Hardly an inspiring summation, we might think, except that this was the first time since independence that two successive elections had occurred without an intervening period of military rule (even in 2003, the two leading candidates were former military heads of state). Nigeria illustrates many of the difficulties faced by countries with an authoritarian history in consolidating democracy.

Under General Sani Abacha, the country's military ruler from 1993, governance had been corrupt, sordid and self-serving. Nigerians called the regime a lootocracy because it consisted of stealing public assets for personal benefit. After the general's death in 1998 – popularly known as God's coup – his wife was caught fleeing to Saudi Arabia with 38 suitcases full of foreign currency. A son was intercepted carrying the considerable sum of $100m in cash. Later governments have devoted considerable effort to securing the return of these monies from deposit accounts in the City of London.

The transition to civilian rule under Obasanjo was remarkably smooth, raising hopes that Nigeria would begin the road to recovery after decades of authoritarian misrule. Yet so far the results have been limited, demonstrating not just the long-term damage inflicted by the military but also the deeper problems facing many African states. Apart from an expanding mobile telephone system, Nigeria's economy remains in poor condition. In the oil-producing Niger Delta, wealthy executives employed by multinational companies extract the vital commodity while local people subsist in squalor amid a degraded environment. The government's foreign debt remains an imposing $30bn, denting its international credibility.

The infrastructure which might permit rapid economic recovery has also decayed. Electricity is irregular while endemic corruption scares off many foreign investors; Nigeria is probably the most corrupt country in the world. The civil service is massively overstaffed, with many illiterates appointed to posts requiring documents to be processed. Inefficiency is rife: over $5bn of public money has been invested in a steel mill that has not yet produced any steel. Military equipment is in a chronic condition: the navy has more admirals than seaworthy ships. In a major oil-producing country, petrol is sometimes rationed.

Ethnic and religious conflict, superimposed on provinces operating in a federal framework, holds back post-military recovery. The central government became an arena for conflict between regions and between ethnic groups, leading to civil war in 1967. Even today, divisions between Hausa-Fulani, Yoruba and Ibos are entrenched. Because a gain for one group is defined as a loss by the others, the national interest is subordinated to conflicts between North and South and between Muslims and Christians. These divisions, leading to around 10,000 deaths in Obasanjo's first administration, have intensified with the introduction of traditional Islamic law to some northern states.

The transition from authoritarian rule has thrown Nigeria's continuing difficulties into sharper relief. An aimless continuation of the status quo is perhaps the most likely prognosis but neither national disintegration, nor even another phase of military rule, can be ruled out. Partly free elections notwithstanding, Nigeria seems to be incapable of developing into a consolidated, united democracy.

Further reading: Holman and Wallis (2000), Maier (2002), Momoh and Adejumobi (2002).

Chile illustrates the difficulties of full disengagement. Before returning power to civilians in 1980, General Pinochet ensured that the new constitution secured military autonomy. The armed forces were granted exemption from prosecution in civilian courts and retained their position as guarantors of the 'institutional order' and 'national security'. Similarly, Ecuador's armed forces were guaranteed 15 per cent of the country's oil revenues until 2010. Such conditional transitions, characteristic of Latin America, helped the shift to, but weakened the depth of, the post-military regime. They signal the continued perception of the military as a source of order for the nation and they leave a difficult bequest for new democracies (Pion-Berlin, 2001).

The Arab and Muslim worlds

In the twenty-first century, authoritarian regimes form a more diverse group than ever before; no longer are their ranks dominated by military governments and communist party states. Instead, we are presented with a varied collection including Chinese Communist Party leaders, Pakistani generals, Iranian clerics, Saudi princes and assorted authoritarian presidents in some of the smaller states of Central Asia, Africa and Latin America. These rulers have little in common beyond their rejection of Western democracy. It is tempting to dismiss this ragged band as twentieth-century leftovers, soon to fall victim to an American-inspired embrace of democracy and capitalism. But such a judgement is certainly premature, involving a risky bet on yet another wave of democratization.

In this section, we will focus on the authoritarian regimes of the Arab and Muslim worlds, the main enclaves of non-democracy today. These two categories overlap but not completely. The *Arab* world is centred on the Arabian peninsula and North Africa. It includes Algeria, Egypt, Libya, Iraq, Morocco, Saudi Arabia and Syria. There is no established democracy in Arab countries.

Muslim countries – those with an Islamic majority – include the Arab heartland but extend beyond it. For example, Indonesia, Pakistan and Turkey are populous Islamic but non-Arab countries. Again, most but not all Muslim countries are

Table 4.2 Islam and democracy, 2001

Is the government elected by democratic means?	Countries with an Islamic majority	Non-Islamic countries
Yes	11	110
No	36	35
(Total number of countries)	(47)	(145)

Source: Adapted from Karatnycky (2002).

authoritarian, with democracy confined to part of the Islamic periphery, notably Turkey (Map 4.2).

Table 4.2 shows the strong statistical relationship between Islam and non-democratic rule. It demonstrates not only that Islamic democracies are rare but also that Muslim countries comprise one in two of the world's authoritarian regimes.

With their massive oil reserves, the Arab and Muslim worlds have always attracted interest from Western commentators. But this attention was of course magnified by 9/11 and the resulting American-led invasions of Afghanistan and Iraq. Suddenly, the authoritarian governments of the Arab and Muslim worlds became a focus of Western interest, with some American policy-makers beginning to seek ways of promoting both democracy and market economies in a region characterized by poor governance and low growth.

Why have Arab and Muslim countries resisted the waves of democratization which have lapped against the shores of other authoritarian states? There can be little doubt that Islam and democracy are difficult bedfellows. In Islam – unlike Christianity – religious and secular authority are combined rather than separated. Religious values suffuse politics, limiting the space for an independent political will expressed through democratic means. Just as Islam dominates culture, so religious figures take the lead in guiding politics. Yayla (2002, p. 3), for example, concludes that 'in all Islamic countries decision-making is over-centralized, power-sharing mechanisms are very few, civil society is extremely weak and the spontaneous forces of society are strictly limited'.

Certainly, the form taken by Islam varies across time and space. Contemporary Turkey demonstrates that tolerably democratic politics can be achieved in an Islamic society. But even in Turkey the combination has been difficult to sustain. At times, Turkey's army has intervened to maintain the secular vision of the country's modern founder, Kemal Atatürk (Altunisik and Kavli, 2003). Elsewhere in the Muslim world, Islamic traditions have hindered the spread of democracy.

But we should also recognize the West's historical role in shaping the political environment within the contemporary Arab and Muslim worlds. At least until 9/11, most Western powers had shown little interest in democracy promotion. Instead, Western influence has worked in three main ways against the establishment of democracy in the East.

First, the Middle East consists of what are, in effect, post-colonial states. As elsewhere, Europe imposed the state form on areas that had previously been organized differently – mainly as provinces of the Turkish Ottoman Empire. With the collapse of this Empire after the First World War, the British and the French became effective masters of the region. Operating under a mandate from the League of Nations, Western powers ruled in colonial style, creating arbitrary state boundaries, new administrative centres and a forceful bureaucracy more concerned with internal security than social development. The absence of an indigenous state tradition and the post-colonial legacy combined to inhibit the development of stable democracies in the region.

Second, the Middle East has proved to be a fulcrum of world politics where forms of government have historically taken second place to superpower strategy. 'For the last two centuries,' as Brown (1984, p. 3) observes, 'the Middle East has been more consistently and more thoroughly ensnared in great power politics than any other part of the non-western world.' The region's oil reserves, and the continuing conflict over Israel, have certainly engaged Western attention. But when its strategic interests were at stake, the West – and especially the USA – showed little concern about the internal organization of Arab states.

For example, the United States was content to build a relationship with the authoritarian rulers of oil-rich Saudi Arabia, even though the presence of America troops between 1991 and 2003 in a country containing the holy Islamic cities of Mecca and Medina fuelled resentment throughout the Muslim world. Strategic calculation has dominated the West's approach to the Middle East, as President George W. Bush acknowledged in a speech to the National Endowment for Democracy in November 2003:

> sixty years of Western nations excusing and accommodating the lack of freedom in the Middle East did nothing to make us safe – because stability cannot be purchased at the expense of liberty.

Third, the contemporary vigour of Islam, particularly in its fundamentalist forms, is in part a reaction against Western preeminence. As the economic, scientific and military superiority of the West has become apparent, so radical and explicitly anti-Western variants of Islam have gained ground. Some Muslims take refuge in the era long gone when Islamic civilization was indeed more advanced than the West, concluding that their task is to restore this pure culture against its external desecration. Once Islamic voices articulate this anti-Western turn, the task of importing democracy from its European and American heartlands becomes even more challenging.

With these points in mind, let us review three varied examples of authoritarian rule in Islamic countries: Saudi Arabia, Iran and Pakistan (Map 4.2). Saudi Arabia is at the centre of the Arab world while Iran and Pakistan are major examples of non-Arab Muslim countries.

Saudi Arabia

Saudi Arabia, possessed of the world's largest oil reserves, is of particular interest as a major source of both personnel and funding for anti-Western terrorism. The country also exemplifies authoritarian rule in the region, with the government led by the cautious and conservative Saud family. Advocates of Wahhabism, the dominant and puritanical strain of Islam found in the kingdom, have been particularly active in promoting Islam internationally.

Saudi Arabia's political style reflects the influence of King Abdul Aziz Ibn Saud. He led the Saudi state from its inception in 1902 until his death in 1953. In true patrimonial style, Ibn Saud ran his kingdom as a gigantic personal household, using marriage as a vital political tactic. In total, he took 300 wives drawn from all the powerful families in the state. The king was in a position to control the political and personal fortunes of all the leading figures, and did so. The carrot was used more than the stick but the ruler's monopoly of both devices enabled him to combine rewards for supporters with ruthlessness towards opponents (Kostiner and Teitelbaum, 2000).

Like most authoritarian rulers, Ibn Saud was more concerned with protecting his position than developing his kingdom. Politics came before policy. Such developments as education (or more recently television and the internet) are always perceived as a threat by traditional rulers. Their main concern, after all, is to maintain the population's dependence on their own control of wealth and patronage. While American colonists raised the cry, 'no taxation without representation', the oil-inspired deal the Saudi king offered to his people was rather different: 'no taxation, therefore no representation'.

Slowly, however, social pressures in Saudi Arabia have begun to build. A predominantly young population, limited by inadequate education, has begun to experience unemployment even in a country which is still the world's largest oil exporter. Internal surveillance is extensive, the media practise self-censorship, male domination is virtually complete and political parties are banned. In such a controlled environment, society beyond the ageing ruling family consists largely of the mosque, meaning that radical Islamic movements provide one of the few outlets for expression which is formally separate from the state:

> The religious opposition groups are the only ones that have regular meeting places where they can assemble and have at their disposal a network not fully subject to the state. The more oppressive the regime, the more it helps the fundamentalists by giving them a virtual monopoly of opposition.
>
> (Lewis, 2003, p. 102)

Given the long-term alliance between Saudi's ruling family and the United States, verbal and physical assaults on the West by youthful members of such movements also represent implicit cri-

tiques of Saudi Arabia's own autocratic rulers (Niblock, 2003). But Islamic terrorists have also sought to strike at Saudi Arabia itself. One of al-Qaeda's earliest attacks, in 1995, was against the Saudi National Guard; more recently, compounds for foreigners have been targeted.

So the country is in an awkward position as both a source for and a victim of terrorist activity. With even the USA now beginning to look more critically at the country's funding of radical Islamic groups beyond its borders, the foundations of the House of Saud are beginning to shake, if not crumble.

Iran

Iran (formerly Persia) is our second example of authoritarian rule in an Islamic society. Although the Iranian population is predominantly Persian rather than Arab, the main contrast with Saudi Arabia – and with other Muslim countries – lies in the direct political role played by Iran's religious leaders. Whereas in Saudi Arabia, the royal family and the Wahhabis coexist uneasily, Iran exemplifies that rarest form of authoritarian rule: theocracy. The country illustrates with exceptional clarity the close relationship in Islam between church and state. However, even in Iran the political authority of the clerics (ayatollahs and mullahs) remains contested; indeed, increasingly so.

Definition

A **theocracy** is government by religious leaders. Although Christianity separates political and religious roles, clerics play a direct political role in some other religions. In ancient Israel, for example, God's laws were expounded and applied by holy men. The regime established in Iran after the overthrow of the Shah in 1979 is a more recent example of theocratic rule.

Iran's theocracy was a child of the 1979 revolution, the last great insurrection of the twentieth century. In this revolution, Ayatollah Khomeini, a 76-year-old cleric committed to Islamic fundamentalism, overthrew the Shah of Iran. The Shah, an absolute monarch whose family had ruled the country since 1926, had supported Western-style economic development. In reaction the revolu-

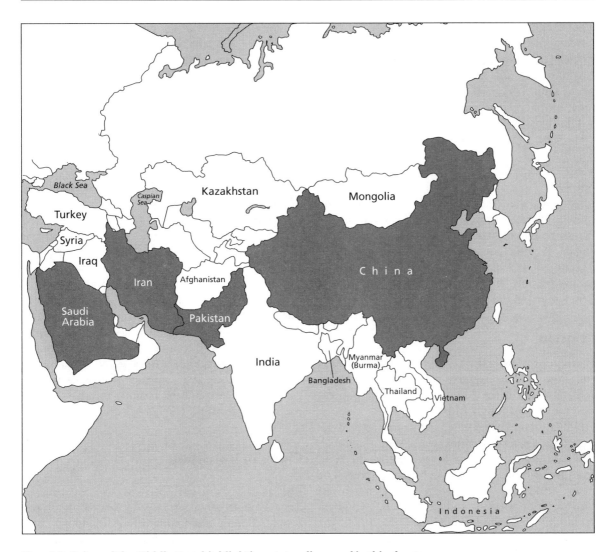

Map 4.2 Asia and the Middle East, highlighting states discussed in this chapter

tionaries advocated a traditional Islamic republic free from foreign domination. 'Neither East nor West' became the slogan. In power, the ayatollahs created a unique Islamic state in which they governed directly rather than by overseeing secular rulers.

Iran's post-revolutionary constitution did incorporate a directly elected presidency and assembly. Yet the real power lay with the clerics, expressed in part through a 12-member Council of Guardians which certifies that all bills and candidates conform with Islamic law. In strictly enforcing traditional, male-dominated Islamic codes, the aya-

tollahs permeated society in a manner reminiscent of totalitarian regimes. The Interior Ministry still makes extensive use of informants while the state employs arbitrary arrests and even assassination as a form of control through terror. These are classic signs of totalitarianism.

But as with many radical Islamic movements, Iran's revolution was backward-looking, seeking to recreate the religion's former glories. Rule by ayatollahs has not delivered economic growth, even in a country with considerable oil reserves, and Iran's politics has turned into a lengthy battle between the now traditional clerics and liberal reformers.

The liberals are led by Mohammad Khatami, a moderate advocate of Islamic democracy who was first elected president in 1997. In a country where two-thirds of the population are under 25, it seems unlikely that religious leaders will be able to resist further reform indefinitely (Schirazi, 1998).

This division between an authoritarian establishment and a young population is also found in Saudi Arabia and other Islamic countries. But the battle of generations and outlook is waged more openly in Iran than elsewhere, with the young relying on the internet, satellite television and mobile phones to circumvent official censorship. Although no counter-revolution to 1979 is guaranteed, how the conflict of generations is resolved in Iran will, in time, resonate through the Muslim world, possibly providing the opening for a more democratic politics throughout the region.

Pakistan

Pakistan provides our final case of non-democratic rule in an Islamic country. Pakistan is located in Asia rather than the Middle East but its population is overwhelmingly Muslim.

Unlike Iran, which has a long history as a sovereign state, Pakistan is more typically post-colonial. The country was created by the British in 1947 from the Muslim provinces of colonial India. The name 'Pakistan' is taken from the northwest provinces of British India: *P*unjab, *A*fhghan, *K*ashmir, *S*indh and Baluchi*stan*. In 1971, the country's separate eastern wing broke away to form independent Bangladesh.

In some ways, contemporary Pakistan is a curiously old-fashioned example of authoritarian government. For one thing, it provides a rare contemporary instance of military rule. Throughout its post-colonial history, military and civilian rule have oscillated in what is a large, poor, unequal and virtually feudal state lacking the oil wealth of Saudi Arabia and Iran. The current government, led by General Pervez Musharraf, is the fourth military regime since Pakistan was created from the partition of India in 1947. It dates from a coup in 1999 which followed several years of ineffective civilian rule, including a setback in the long-running conflict with India over Kashmir.

Together with the bureaucracy, Pakistan's army has long seen itself as the guardian of the national interest – and the common weal is indeed a concept remote from the workings of civilian politics in the country. Money has become the core political currency, with allegiances simply bought and sold. In these circumstances, it is neither difficult nor even implausible for the army to present itself as national guardian. Pakistan provides a continuing example of a political system in which the military supervises domestic politics, exerting a silent veto even when civilian rulers are nominally in charge (Constable, 2001).

In addition, President Musharraf has courted American support to bolster his own political position, a tactic associated with authoritarian rulers during the Cold War. Musharraf did not oppose the American invasion of Afghanistan. In consequence, America has so far had little choice but to acknowledge Pakistan's military regime (and its nuclear weapons), again in a manner reminiscent of Cold War realities. As the United States continues its attack on terrorism and its causes, it remains to be seen whether Pakistan's ruling general can continue to balance internal Islamic pressures against his dependence on the USA.

China in transition

Just as the Arab and Muslim worlds attracted more Western attention after 11 September, so the People's Republic of China (PRC) has drawn more Western interest with its emergence at the start of the twenty-first century as a powerful force in the global economy. China's population, estimated at 1.28 bn and growing at 0.6 per cent per year, is already the world's largest. Its increasingly open economy has grown fourfold since 1978 and is likely to become the world's largest in the first half of the century. The country is the world's fourth largest exporter, with particular strengths in assembly and manufacturing, resulting in massive reserves of American dollars ('China lends while America spends'). China's massive trade surplus with the USA attracts increasing criticism from American labour unions. Already a regional power, the country is destined to become a world force – perhaps *the* world force – over the course of the present century (Kennedy, 1993). The world is learning the truth of Napoleon's observation: 'when China wakes, she will wake the world'.

Contemporary China is now rediscovering historic strengths. As Manion (2004, p. 422) points out,

> imperial China was the longest-lasting major system of government in world history, enduring as a centralized state for more than two millennia until the fall of the Qing, the last dynasty, in 1911.

This period established an authoritarian tradition in which the emperor governed through an elaborate social hierarchy, supported by a small bureaucratic elite, all rationalized by the Confucian philosophy of harmony and piety. Democracy has played little role in Chinese governance, past or present, a fact which may have important if unpredictable consequences for the world as the country engages with a mainly democratic external environment.

The seizure of power by the Chinese Communist Party (CCP) in 1949, following nearly four decades of internal upheaval, reinforced the authoritarian traditions established under the emperors. Initially, the CCP followed the Soviet model of industrialization and collectivization of agriculture. However, from the late 1950s Mao Zedong followed an increasingly independent strategy in which politics took priority, culminating in the Cultural Revolution (1966–77) which reduced the country to near anarchy. It was only in 1978, two years after Mao's death, that the current era of economic modernization began. All these developments, including the contemporary commitment to economic growth, have been initiated from the top and have reflected the internal politics of the party.

Contemporary China is of particular interest to students of authoritarian regimes. Together with Vietnam, it has helped to define a distinctive transition in which ruling communist parties loosen their control of the economy while retaining a dominant political position. The key question facing China's ruling party is whether its political monopoly can be sustained as the economy continues to grow. The answer may be that since China is still a developing economy, there remains room for a dominant party to oversee economic growth. As with communist Europe, the decisive

moment may not arrive until the party comes to be seen as a brake on further development.

So far, at least, Mao's successors have shown considerable skill in giving priority to economic growth while maintaining the party's leadership of society. Reformers have reduced the state's role in direct economic production while creating a somewhat more predictable legal environment for transactions that are not politically sensitive. Reformist propaganda slogans have included 'to get rich is glorious' and even 'some get rich first', astonishing contrasts to the theme of 'politics in command' adopted during Mao's Great Leap Forward of 1958.

China's political system is no longer communist in any traditional sense. With the acceptance of private wealth, the country has become one of the most unequal in Asia (Saich, 2004). Successful businessmen are officially labelled model workers and awarded May Day medals. At the party's congress in 2002, an entrepreneur even won a seat on the party's central committee. However, governance remains deeply authoritarian. The Communist Party is above the law because the party still makes the law. Its members occupy many leading posts in the public sector, reflecting the traditional communist theory that the party should guide the state.

The key reform has been the reduction of central control from Beijing, rather than the introduction of markets. As a result, local state officials have gained a strong role in economic development through licensing and regulation. On the ground, informal networks of power-holders determine 'who gets rich first'. These alliances are composed of well-placed and increasingly well-heeled men in the party, the bureaucracy and the army. So far, China's transformation has involved the decentralization of economic, and to some extent political, power more than a shift towards a Western market economy operating within the rule of law. China is situated somewhere between Marx and the market, an unusual political economy with distinctly Chinese characteristics.

True, a growing number of thriving companies operate outside the inefficient and overmanned state sector. However, even supposedly private companies operate in a context where local political influence is crucial (Dittmer and Gore, 2001). Overseas companies arrive in China expecting to find a clear distinction between public and private spheres; they quickly discover that the two sectors remain interwoven in the country's socialist market economy. As ever in China, informal political connections (*guanxi*) remain important for economic success.

China's rulers are aware of the tensions induced by decentralization. One problem unleashed by the loosening of central political control has been an explosion of corruption at lower levels. In the new environment, public employees are quick to recognize that their position can be turned to their own advantage. In one port city, a smuggling racket responsible for about 10 per cent of China's total imports of gasoline was found to include the deputy mayor, the head of customs and over 100 other officials, six of whom were sentenced to death after the scheme was uncovered (Gong, 2002).

While the central party elite is concerned about corruption, its policy often seems to consist of little more than exemplary punishment for the few cases that happen to come to light. Some officials even blame the problem on foreigners: 'you can't open the door without letting in a few flies'. But such glib assertions merely increase suspicion. Wang (2002, p. 3) notes that 'the continuing invocation of socialist values in an increasingly capitalist society has only deepened cynicism, allowing neither socialist nor capitalist values to gain a firm foothold'. Here, perhaps, is one of the party's major dilemmas: it can only attract members by offering opportunities to acquire resources but the dubious manner in which these are obtained increases the distance between party and society.

An additional difficulty is the growing contrast between the richer coastal regions and the poorer internal provinces, a division which potentially threatens the survival of the state itself. In the 1990s, mechanization and the introduction of the profit motive resulted in the loss of about six million jobs per year from the countryside. The resulting movement of the rural unemployed to the cities created an impoverished floating population of about 200m migrants seeking work, a resentful group which will be further enraged if the many remaining state-owned enterprises (SOEs) are shut down. The danger of unrest arising from reducing the public sector too rapidly is one reason why China's rulers must steer a delicate middle course, reforming at a socially acceptable rate.

In theory, China's long-delayed entry into the World Trade Organization in 2001 should encourage further moves towards a genuine market economy. The entry agreement, after all, required the government to protect private property rights, separate government from enterprise, limit bureaucratic corruption and reduce the role of the military in business (Fensmith, 2001).

Yet the withering away of the party, and the reduction of the state to the role of umpire, are still far distant. China's entry to the WTO took 16 years to negotiate and will doubtless take even longer to implement. In any case, the idea of 'politics in command' is entrenched in Chinese history; the country's rulers have traditionally acted as guardians of stability in what is a fragmented but dynamic country. China's continuing political experiment is of worldwide significance but the final outcome – if there is to be one – is most unlikely to be a Western-style liberal democracy in which a market economy operates under the rule of law.

Key reading

> **Next step:** *Linz (2000) is an influential and insightful guide to authoritarian rule.*

Brooker (2000) is a wide-ranging source on non-democracy. Classic works on totalitarianism include Arendt (1966) and Friedrich and Brzezinski (1965); Gleason (1995) is a more recent review. For fascism, see Griffin (2004) and, for communist states, Harding (1984). Kershaw and Lewin (1997) compare these two forms of dictatorship. For twentieth-century authoritarianism, see Perlmutter (1981 and 1997). Jackson and Rosberg (1982) remains the key account of personal rule in Africa, while Chebabi and Linz (1998) examine sultanistic regimes. On military governments, see Finer (1962) and for Africa specifically, Keih and Ogaba (2003). For military disengagement, consider Howe (2001) for Africa, Cottey *et al.* (2001) for Eastern Europe and Silva (2001) for Latin America. Owen (2000) offers a useful background on Middle Eastern politics while Lewis (2002 and 2003) places Islamic politics in the context of September 11. On China, Saich (2004) is a reliable guide.

Chapter 5

The comparative approach

The goal of comparative politics is to encompass the major political similarities and differences between countries. The task is to understand the mixture of constants and variability which characterizes the world's governments, bearing in mind the global, regional and national contexts within which they operate. Given this definition of comparative *politics,* the comparative *approach* is simply the family of strategies and techniques which advances understanding within this field.

Grander definitions are of course available. The comparative approach can with justification be regarded as the master strategy for drawing inferences about causation in any area of study. After all, experiments and statistical analysis designed to uncover relationships of cause and effect must involve a comparison between observations, whether of individuals, social groups or countries. All investigations of cause and effect are by nature comparative.

But most political research has more modest ambitions than the systematic analysis of causes and effects. In the main, the challenge is to describe and to interpret rather than to explain in a traditional scientific sense. For example, identifying cross-national trends in electoral reform or political participation is itself a worthwhile exercise, involving the ability both to immerse ourselves in the politics of particular countries and to identify broader trends. Nor is there anything limited about such generalized description: there is much sense in King *et al.*'s observation (1994, p. 44) that 'good description is better than bad explanation'.

We proceed in this chapter from the general to the specific. We begin by outlining the strengths of comparison by asking the simple question, 'why compare?' We then turn to some pitfalls of comparative research. We follow by discussing different levels or units of comparison – institutions, societies and states – and conclude by outlining the major techniques used in the field: case studies, focused comparisons and statistical analysis.

Why compare?

To begin, we will raise the obvious question: what is to be gained by comparing politics in different countries? Why *comparative* politics? The answer is that a comparative approach broadens our understanding of the political world, leading to improved classifications and giving potential for explanation and even prediction (Box 5.1). We discuss each of these virtues in turn.

The *first* strength of a comparative approach is straightforward: it enables us to find out more about the places we know least about. This point was well-stated by our predecessor Munro. In 1925 he described the purpose of his book on foreign governments as aiding 'the comprehension of daily news from abroad' (p. 4). This ability to interpret overseas events grows in importance as

---

BOX 5.1
The advantages of comparison

- ▸ Learning about other governments broadens our understanding, casting fresh light on our home nation.
- ▸ Comparison improves our classifications of political processes.
- ▸ Comparison enables us to test hypotheses about politics.
- ▸ Comparison gives us some potential for prediction and control.

the world becomes more interdependent. No one today can afford the insular attitude of Mr Podsnap in Dickens's *Our Mutual Friend*: 'Foreigners do as they do, sir, and that is the end of it.' In any case, Munro was perhaps a shade modest in stating his purpose. Even when the focus is on just one overseas country, an implicit comparison with the home country provides much of the background.

Understanding foreign governments not only helps to interpret new developments, it also helps with practical political relationships. For instance, British ministers have a poor track record in negotiations with their European partners partly because they assume that the aggressive tone they adopt in the Commons chamber will also work in EU meeting rooms. Their assumption is incorrect, showing ignorance of the consensual political style found in many continental democracies. What works at home often fails in an away fixture.

Similarly, American students frequently puzzle at how the British parliamentary system can deliver stable government when the prime minister, unlike their own president, is constantly at the mercy of a vote of confidence in the Commons. Because American parties are so decentralized, the tendency is to underestimate the powers of a governing party in Britain.

Conversely, British students are so accustomed to the importance of party that they experience difficulty in understanding why Congress and the White House continue to quarrel even when the same party controls both institutions. The general point here is well-made by Dogan and Pelassy (1990): through comparison, we discover our own ethnocentrism and the means of overcoming it.

A *second* advantage of comparison is that it improves our classifications of politics. For instance, we can group constitutions into written and unwritten types, and electoral systems into proportional and non-proportional formulae. We can then search for the factors which incline countries to one form rather than the other. Similarly, once we classify executives into presidential and parliamentary systems, we can look at the consequences of each. Classification is inherently comparative and it turns what is a constant within a single country into a variable between them,

thereby providing the raw material from which explanatory ventures can be launched.

The potential for explanation is the *third* advantage of a comparative approach. Comparative researchers seek to understand a variety of political systems not just for its own sake but also to formulate and test hypotheses about politics. Comparative analysis enables us to develop and scrutinize such questions as: do first-past-the-post electoral systems always produce a two-party system? Are two-chambered assemblies only found under federalism? Are revolutions most likely to occur after defeat in war?

As these questions illustrate, an hypothesis is a relationship posited between two or more factors or variables: for example, between electoral and party systems, or between war and revolution. Confirmed hypotheses are valuable nor just for their own sake but because they are essential for explaining the particular.

Consider, for example, one specific question: why did a major socialist party never emerge in the United States? An obvious answer is because the USA was built on, and retains, a strongly individualistic culture. This explanation may seem to be particular but in fact it is quite general. It implies that other countries with similar values would also lack a strong socialist party. It also suggests that countries with a more collective outlook will be more likely to support a party of the left. These comparative hypotheses would need to be confirmed by looking at a range of countries before we could claim a full understanding of our original question about the USA. So explaining the particular calls forth the general; only theories explain cases.

Generalizations, once validated, have potential for prediction. Here we come to our *fourth* and final reason for studying politics comparatively. The ability to predict is not only a sign of systematic knowledge but it also gives us some base for drawing lessons across countries. So, if we find that proportional representation (PR) does indeed lead to coalition government, we can reasonably predict at least one effect of introducing PR to countries such as Canada which still use the plurality method. Equally, if we know that subcontracting the provision of public services to private agencies raises the quality of delivery in one country, we can advise governments elsewhere that here is an idea at least worth considering. Or authoritarian rulers might look to China for clues on how non-democratic rulers can reduce their control over the economy while retaining their own hold on political power.

In this way, lesson-drawing provides some capacity to anticipate and even to shape the future (Rose, 2004). This function of comparative politics was nicely stated by Bryce (1921, p. iv):

Many years ago, when schemes of political reform were being copiously discussed in England, it occurred to me that something might be done to provide a solid basis for judgment by examining a certain number of popular governments in their actual working, comparing them with one another, and setting forth the various merits and demerits of each.

The risks of comparison

Any approach brings its own dangers and the breadth inherent in comparative politics brings its own risks (Box 5.2). Again, we can proceed by examining these pitfalls one by one.

Knowledge requirements

By definition, any comparative study involves more than one country. A statistical analysis, such as an examination of the relationship between economic development and democracy, may draw on information from every country in the world. Clearly, the knowledge requirements for research in comparative politics can be substantial. One common solution is to form a team of researchers, each expert in at least one of the countries included in the study. In this way, knowledge deficits can be reduced.

Fortunately, the idea that knowledge requirements increase directly with the number of cases is a misunderstanding, albeit an understandable one. In comparative research, the focus should be on the comparison as much as the countries. Breadth is at least as valuable as depth; indeed detail can often distract from the larger picture.

For example, discussing the general trend

BOX 5.2
The difficulties of comparison

▸ By definition, comparative research demands knowledge of more than one political system.
▸ The 'same' phenomenon can mean different things in different countries, creating difficulties in comparing like with like.
▸ Globalization means that countries cannot be regarded as independent of each other, thus reducing the effective number of cases available for testing theories.
▸ The countries selected for study may be an unrepresentative sample, limiting the significance of the findings.
▸ Any pair of countries will differ in many ways, meaning we can never achieve the experimenter's dream of holding all factors constant apart from the one whose effects we wish to test.

---

towards proportional representation does not call for in-depth knowledge of the electoral system in every country in the study. Similarly, we can draw conclusions about democratization in Latin America without understanding the intricacies of the transition in every case. And those who debate the relative merits of presidential and parliamentary government cannot possibly read all that has been written about the operation of the executive in every country where these forms of government have been tried.

The task in comparative politics is not to know all there is to know. Rather, the skill is to use specialist knowledge so as to produce new and more general observations. What matters is knowing what needs to be known – and being able to find it out.

Understanding meaning

In comparing politics across countries, we should remember that the meaning of an action depends on the conventions of the country concerned. When British MPs vote against their party in the House of Commons, their acts are far more significant than when American legislators do the 'same' thing in the less partisan Senate. To take another illustration, many observers from democratic countries were shocked by the apparent indifference with which military coups used to be greeted in developing countries. They failed to recognize that coups had become a regular and fairly peaceful mechanism for the circulation of elites. In a sense, coups had become the functional equivalent of elections in the West and should have been compared accordingly.

Students of comparative politics must therefore be capable of understanding how politics is viewed in different countries. Rather than assuming that all politicians are motivated by, say, rational self-interest, researchers must recognize that political acts can mean different things in different places at different times. For example, is politics in a particular country based on class, race or religion? The answer can only be discovered by understanding how people in that country construct and interpret their political world. As Green (2002a, p. 6) puts it, 'actors have identities, world-views and cognitive frames, informed by culture, that shape perceptions and interests'.

For some authors, interpreting how politics is constructed or interpreted in a particular country is no mere preliminary to a comparative project; rather, it is the stuff of comparative research itself. For instance, do politicians in a particular country view globalization as a danger to be resisted (a view many French politicians claim to support) or as a spur to essential domestic reform (as with Margaret Thatcher's administration in the United Kingdom). From this perspective, there is no phenomenon of globalization independent of the ideas political actors hold about it (Hay, 2002, p. 204).

> **Definition**
> Different institutions are **functionally equivalent** when they fulfil the same role within the political system. For instance, legislative committees, an independent media and opposition parties can each serve as scrutineers of government, holding the actions of the executive to account. Thus a comparative study of this topic might need to compare different mechanisms of scrutiny across the selected countries (Myers and O'Connor, 1998).

The implication of this interpretive approach is that we should be wary of starting comparative projects with excessively scientific pretensions. Our first task – some would say our main task – is to understand politics from the viewpoint of participants in the countries concerned.

> **Definition**
> An **interpretive** approach to politics emphasizes the importance of grasping the ideas which political actors themselves hold about their activity. The assumption is that political reality does not exist independently of people's ideas; rather, political discourse in a particular country largely defines that 'reality' (Bevir and Rhodes, 2002).

This problem of the meaning and significance of action is particularly important in politics because the activity is partly conducted through coded language (Ch.7). Were the people who attacked the World Trade Centre and the Pentagon murderers, martyrs or both? Were American civil rights activists also black militants? Were active members of the Irish Republican Army terrorists or freedom-fighters? How such actors are described reflects existing political opinions, raising doubts about whether we can find, or should seek, a neutral language for interpreting our subject matter.

Globalization

Globalization poses a considerable challenge to comparative politics, understood as the comparison of separate states. Although 191 'independent' countries belonged to the United Nations by 2002, in reality far fewer cases are available to the student of comparative politics. Countries learn from, copy, compete with, influence and even invade each other in a constant process of interaction. Even the states which provide the units of our subject did not develop separately; rather, the idea of statehood diffused outwards from its proving ground in Europe. As Dogan and Pelassy (1990, p. 1) say, 'there is no nation without other nations'. The major transitions of world history – industrialization, colonialism, decolonization, democratization – unfolded on a world stage. In that sense we have one global system rather than a world of independent states. Green (2002a, p. 5) puts the point well when he says it is 'as if national polities are in fact cells of a larger entity with a life all its own'. The implication is that we should study this larger organism rather than its individual cells.

Specific institutional forms also reflect diffusion. The communist model was often imposed by force of Soviet arms, the presidential system in Latin America was imported from the United States and the ombudsman was a device copied from Sweden. The development of international organizations, from the United Nations to the European Union, also creates a newer layer of governance to which all states must react.

Why do connections between states constitute a pitfall for students of comparative politics? The answer is provided by Tilly (1997): comparative politics traditionally presumes distinct and separate units of comparison, most often states, which can be treated as if they are independent of each other. That assumption was always a simplification but in an interdependent and even global world such a presumption has become positively misleading. More technically, treating countries as independent artificially inflates the sample size in statistical analysis, resulting in exaggerated confidence in the significance of the results obtained.

How students of comparative politics will react to the issue of globalization is a story still to unfold. It is one thing to agree with Jackson and Nexon (2002, p. 89) that it is 'difficult to clearly differentiate between the subject areas of comparative politics and international relations'. However, it is quite another to propose a merger between these two distinct fields, each with its own history and body of knowledge. How global processes interact with state forms is clearly an important theme for both disciplines. But this relationship flows in both directions: states shape the world at least as much as the world reshapes states.

Nor should we forget the continuing fact that states remains the fundamental unit of rule in all developed nations and most post-colonial countries. The state's unique capacities – to shape identities, regulate societies, raise taxes and wage wars – remain unmatched and largely unthreatened.

Selection bias

We turn now to a more technical difficulty in comparative politics which nonetheless has impli-

cations for all those who practise the art. In general form, selection bias arises when the choice of what to study, or even of how to study it, produces unrepresentative results. This risk inheres in any study covering only a few countries.

The danger often emerges as an unintended result of haphazard selection. For example, we choose to study those countries which speak the same language, or which have good exchange schemes, or in which we feel safe. As a result, large, powerful countries are studied more intensively than small, powerless ones.

One result is that the findings of comparative politics are weighted toward established democracies, a rare form of government in the expanse of human history. A virtue of designs covering a large number of countries is that they reduce the risk of selection bias. Indeed, if the study covers all current countries, selection bias disappears – at least so long as generalization is restricted to the contemporary world.

But, alas, the problem may just resurface in another form, through an unrepresentative selection of variables rather than countries. The difficulty here is best approached through an example. Much statistical research in comparative politics relies on existing data collected by governments and international bodies with different interests from our own. But the priorities of these organizations tend to be financial, economic, social and political – in that order. So financial and economic variables may receive more attention than they justify, and politics runs the risk of being treated as a branch of economics.

For instance, a large body of research examines the relationship between economic conditions and government popularity as reported in opinion polls (Norpoth, 1996). This work has produced worthwhile findings but its sheer quantity reflects the availability of regular statistics about economic trends more than the intrinsic significance of the topic for comparative politics.

A final important form of selection bias comes from examining only positive cases, thus eliminating all variation in the phenomenon we seek to explain. Because this is a common, noteworthy and avoidable mistake, it deserves careful consideration. King *et al.* (1994, p. 129) explain the problem:

The literature is full of work that makes the mistake of failing to let the dependent variable vary; for example, research that tries to explain the outbreak of wars with studies only of wars, the onset of revolutions with studies only of revolutions, or patterns of voter turnout with interviews only of nonvoters.

When only positive cases of a phenomenon are studied, comparison is avoided and the conclusions become limited. Comparison is needed to give variation, so that we can then consider what distinguishes times of war from times of peace, periods of revolution from periods of stability and abstainers from voters.

Skocpol's (1979) study of revolutions in France, Russia and China illustrates the difficulty. Her research design allowed her to identify the features common to her revolutions, such as the declining international and domestic effectiveness of the old regime. However, she was unable to say how often a failing regime was followed by a revolution. By selecting on the dependent variable, she was restricted to positive cases. As a result, she was unable to assess how far government ineffectiveness covaried with revolutions.

Definition
Selection on the dependent variable occurs when only similar (usually positive) cases of a phenomenon are selected. By eliminating variation, there is no contrast left to explain; we are left with variables that do not vary. For example, a study of countries which have democratized successfully tells us nothing about the conditions of successful democratization. Those conditions can only be identified through a comparison with failed transitions.

Note: the **dependent variable** is simply the phenomenon we seek to explain – for example, whether democratization succeeds or fails.

History plays a trick on us by selecting on the dependent variable through evolution. For instance, in our discussion of the origins of the modern European state, we noted that the emergence of states flowed from the requirement for monarchs to mobilize men and materials for war.

However this point tells us nothing about how many monarchs failed in the task, with the result that their proto-states disappeared into the wastebin of history (Przeworski, 1995, p. 19). Similarly, we are often told that democracy is triumphant in the world today but few pause to ask how many democracies were lost en route (Linz and Stepan, 1978). Survivorship bias creates a danger of drawing false conclusions by treating those that complete the journey as representative of those that started out, ignoring the casualties on the way.

Too many variables, too few countries

This is a major problem for those who conceive of comparative politics as analogous to the experimenter's laboratory, in which researchers patiently seek to isolate the impact of a single variable. Even with 191 sovereign states, it is impossible to find a country which is identical to another in all respects except for that factor (say, the electoral system) whose effects we wish to detect. For this reason, political comparison can never be as precise as the experiments conducted in the natural scientist's laboratory. We just do not have enough countries to go round, a difficulty termed the 'small-N' problem ('N' is the statistician's term for 'number of cases').

To make the same point from another angle, we will never be able to test all the possible explanations of a political difference between countries. For example, several plausible reasons can be invoked to 'explain' why Britain and the USA were two of the countries most sympathetic to introducing the ethos of the private sector into the running of public services during the 1990s. Perhaps the strength of these reforms reflected the right-wing ideology of Prime Minister Thatcher and President Reagan. Or perhaps the public sector in these English-speaking countries was vulnerable to reform because – unlike several democracies in continental Europe – its structure was not protected by the constitution.

Here we have two potential explanations for Anglo-American distinctiveness, one based on ideology and the other on the constitution. Both interpretations are broadly consistent with the facts. But we have no way of isolating which one of the two is decisive. Ideally, we would want to

---

BOX 5.3
Levels of analysis in comparative politics

Level	Definition	Examples
Institution-centred	The organizations of government and the relationships between them	The balance between president and Congress in the USA
Society-centred	How social factors influence individual behaviour in politics	The impact of education on voting behaviour
State-centred	How the priorities of the state impinge on society	Building the welfare state; regulating for economic competitiveness

---

discover whether the public sector had been reformed in those crucial countries where just one of the two factors applied. But at this point we typically discover that there are no such countries; we just run out of cases.

In such circumstances, we can of course resort to asking hypothetical 'what if' questions. For example, would public sector reform have progressed in Britain and the USA even without the right-wing leadership of Thatcher and Reagan? Such counterfactuals are a useful sharpening tool when cases run short and Tetlock and Belkin (1996) have developed useful guidelines for judging the plausibility of any particular counterfactual. But by definition such thought experiments can never be tested against the acid test of reality.

Comparing institutions, societies and states

When we engage in comparative politics, what is it that we compare? In one sense, the answer is obvious: comparative politics adopts the country, rather than regions, intergovernmental organizations or indeed the entire world, as its core unit. But even a country focus leaves us with a choice between three different levels of analysis: the institutions of government, the social context of politics and the state as a whole (Box 5.3). Nor are decisions about the appropriate emphasis merely technical; in fact, the recent history of comparative politics is a story of shifts in the favoured

level. So as we examine each of these three traditions of enquiry, we will also be covering the intellectual development of the subject.

Comparing institutions

The study of governing institutions will always be a central activity of political science. As Rhodes (1995, p. 43) writes,

If there is any subject matter at all that political scientists can claim exclusively for their own, a subject matter that does not require acquisition of the analytical tools of sister fields and that sustains their claim to autonomous existence, it is of course, formal political structures.

Because virtually all countries possess an executive, legislature and judiciary, such institutions are natural units for comparative politics.

But how exactly should an 'institution' be understood? Usually, the term refers to the major organizations of national government, particularly those defined in the constitution. But the concept also radiates outwards in two directions. The first extension is to other governing organizations which may have a less secure constitutional basis, such as the bureaucracy and local government. And the second extension is to other important political organizations which are not formally part of the government, notably political parties.

However, as we move away from the heartland of constitutionally mandated structures, so the term 'organization' tends to supplant the word 'institution'. Implicitly, therefore, an emphasis on institutions in political analysis affirms the origins of political studies in constitutional studies and the unique character of those organizations charged with the task of governance.

> **Definition**
> An **institution** is a well-established body, often with public status, whose members interact on the basis of the specific roles they perform within the organization. In the study of politics, the core meaning of an institution is an organ of government mandated by the constitution. **Institutionalization** is the process by which such organizations become entrenched by acquiring the capacity to shape the behaviour of their members.

The starting point of institutional analysis is that roles matter more than the people who occupy them. It is this assumption that enables us to discuss presidencies rather than presidents, legislatures rather than legislators and the judiciary rather than judges (Ridley, 1975). Put differently, the capacity of institutions to affect the behaviour of their members means that politics, like other social sciences, is more than a branch of psychology. In one sense, institutions are little more than accepted rules for interaction between their members. But institutions can also be conceived as possessing a history, culture and memory of their own, frequently embodying founding values and traditions and often simply growing 'like coral reefs through slow accretion' (Sait, 1938, p. 18). They often possess legal personality, acquiring their own rights and duties under law.

The value of institutions in political affairs lies in their capacity to make long-term commitments which are more credible than those of any single employee, thus building up trust. For example, because governments are less likely than their employees to go bankrupt, they can normally borrow money at lower rates than are available to individual civil servants. Similarly, a government can make credible promises to repay its debt over a period of generations, a commitment that would be beyond the reach of an individual debtor. So in and beyond politics, institutions help to glue society together, extending the bounds of what

would be possible for individuals acting alone (Johnson, 2001).

An institutional approach implies that organizations do indeed shape behaviour. Employees acquire interests such as defending their organization against outsiders and ensuring their own personal progress within the structure. Crucially, institutions define interests. As March and Olsen (1984, p. 738) conclude in their influential restatement of the institutional approach:

> The bureaucratic agency, the legislative committee and the appellate court are arenas for contending social forces but they are also collections of standard operating procedures and structures that define and defend interests. They are political actors in their own right.

Further, institutions bring forth activity which takes place simply because it is expected, not because it has any deeper political motive. When a legislative committee holds hearings on a topic, it may be more concerned to be seen to be doing its job than to probe the topic itself. Much political action is best understood by reference to its appropriateness within the organization, an objective that is separate from the institution's ostensible purpose.

Similarly, when a president visits an area devastated by floods, he is not necessarily seeking to direct relief operations or to achieve any purpose other than to be seen to be performing his duty of showing concern. In itself, the tour achieves the goal of meeting expectations arising from the actor's institutional position.

> **Definition**
> The **logic of appropriateness** refers to actions which members of an institution take to conform to its norms. For example, a head of state will perform ceremonial duties because it is an official obligation. By contrast, the **logic of consequences** denotes behaviour directed at achieving an individual goal such as promotion or reelection. March and Olsen (1996) point out that much behaviour within institutions is governed by appropriateness rather than consequences.

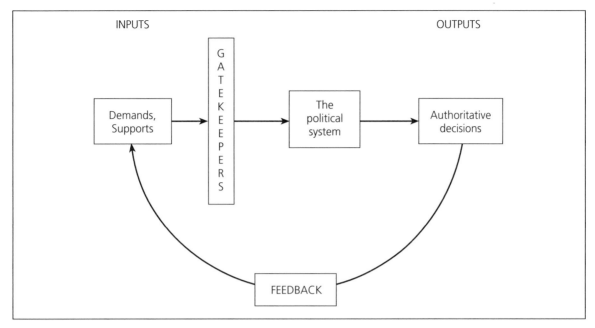

INPUTS   OUTPUTS

G
A
T
E
K
E
Demands,   E   The   Authoritative
Supports   P   political   decisions
                E   system
                R
                S

FEEDBACK

Figure 5.1 Easton's model of the political system

This emphasis within the institutional framework on the symbolic or ritual aspect of political behaviour contrasts with the view of politicians and bureaucrats as rational, instrumental actors who define their own goals independently of the organization they represent. Institutions are far more than the theatre within which a political actor performs; they also shape the script (Peters, 1999).

Comparing societies

In the 1960s and 1970s, however, the focus of comparative politics moved away from the institutional level. Decolonization spawned many new nations in which the formal structures of government proved fragile. The failure of newly designed democratic institutions to take root in former colonies led naturally to a concern with the social foundations of democracy. Institutions seemed irrelevant to the question, 'why did democracy consolidate in the West but not in post-colonial Africa?' Nor were the forms of government of particular importance in communist states where the ruling party was the real wielder of power; in practice, 'governing' institutions served the party.

In addition, the Second World War had stimulated new developments in social science techniques (e.g. opinion surveys) which younger scholars were keen to apply to politics. So the qualitative study of institutions lost prominence as researchers used the comparative method in a search for quantitative generalizations about political attitudes and behaviour.

In this shift to a more society-centred approach, Easton's systems model of the political system led the way (1965a and b). Although few political scientists explicitly use Easton's framework today, his work still forms part of the vocabulary of political analysis. In particular, 'the political system' has become a widely used phrase.

Easton conceived of politics in terms of its relationship with the wider society (Figure 5.1). His political system consists of all those institutions and processes involved in the 'authoritative allocation of values' for society. Specifically, the political system takes inputs from society, consisting of demands for particular policies and expressions of support. The political system then converts these inputs into outputs – that is, into enforceable policies and decisions. These outputs then feed back to society so as to affect the next cycle of inputs.

For instance, trade unions may demand and win legislation achieving improved health insurance for their members. In operation, however, this policy may add to employers' costs, leading their representatives to request tax relief from the government.

Inputs from society do not automatically reach the decision-makers. Rather, inputs are regulated by gatekeepers, such as parties and interest groups, which can bias the system in favour of certain demands and against others. In office, a left-wing party may listen more to the trade unions while a right-wing administration might only hear the employer's voice. In essence, however, Easton's model views the political system as a mechanism for converting demands from society into concrete policies. The real driver is the inputs rather than the institutions. Indeed, the institutions of government are reduced to little more than a 'black box' in an abstract diagram. In practice, Easton's model also proved to be too static, premised on the achievement of equilibrium between inputs and outputs. It offered little insight into political change.

Definition

Behaviouralism was a school of thought in political science which emphasized the study of individuals rather than institutions. The focus was on voters rather than elections, legislators rather than legislatures and judges rather than the judiciary. The aim was to use statistical techniques to discover scientific generalizations about individual political attitudes and behaviour.

Society-centred analyses formed part of the behavioural revolution in politics, an approach which offers a useful contrast with institutional analysis. The central tenet of behaviouralists was that 'the root is man' rather than institutions (Eulau, 1963). People are more than badges of the institution they work for; they possess and indeed will always create some freedom to define their own role. The higher the position in an organization, the more flexibility the occupant possesses. Those at the very top can even reshape the institution itself.

Organizations were not ignored altogether but the study of assemblies, for instance, moved away

from formal aspects (e.g. the procedures by which a bill becomes a law) towards legislative behaviour. Thus, researchers investigated the social backgrounds of representatives, their individual voting records and how they defined their own roles within the institution (Wahlke *et al.*, 1962). In the study of the judiciary, too, scholars began to take judges rather than courts as their level of analysis, using statistical techniques to assess how the social background and political ideology of justices shaped their decisions (Schubert, 1972).

The disregard of institutions by much society-centred analysis of the 1960s now seems extreme but its effect in broadening horizons represents a permanent and positive legacy for comparative politics. Note, for example, that the parts of this book examining the relationship between society and politics take up more space than the sections dealing with government institutions. One legacy of society-centred analysis, and of the behavioural movement that went with it, is that comparative government is now irreversibly embedded in comparative politics.

Comparing states

In the 1980s, attention once more returned to the state. 'Bringing the state back in' became a stirring rallying-cry in comparative politics (Evans *et al.*, 1985). Partly, this shift reflected a belated recognition that the state is the single central concern of political study. In addition, statistical and behavioural studies had run out of steam, becoming increasingly technical and failing to engage with political change.

Yet the new focus on the state represented more than a return to descriptive studies of government institutions. Rather, the state as a whole, rather than its specific manifestations, became the level of analysis. The focus lay not so much on institutional detail but on the state as an active agent, shaping and reshaping society. Thus the state presents an additional level of analysis in comparative politics, distinct from both institutions and individuals.

Where society-centred analysis saw the state as embedded in society, the state-centred approach saw society as part of a configuration defined largely by the state itself. The state acts autonomously and is not just imprisoned by social forces. In particular, the state is seen as using its administrative capacity and monopoly of legitimate force to bring about fundamental social changes. For example, Skocpol (1979) showed how successful revolutionaries such as the Russian Bolsheviks and Iranian mullahs used their control of the state to produce total transformations of society.

But examples are not confined just to post-revolutionary situations. Throughout the world, states have played a large role in the shift to an industrial economy, most recently in Asian countries such as Japan and Singapore. Such large-scale transformations require a public effort going beyond the work of a particular institution or ministry. States have also led the introduction of mass education and welfare states, achievements that are again misread if they are attributed simply to specific departments of state.

State-centred analysts suggest that the uses to which public power has been put by those charged with its exercise cannot be understood by the routine analysis of specific institutions. Rather, the state itself must provide the unit of analysis. The interests of the state can be identified and analysed without declining into institutional detail, just as a country's 'national interest' is a useful guide to its foreign policy even though that policy is in practice the work of many hands.

Thus Marxists, for example, suggest that the state performs underlying functions in supporting capitalism which run deeper than the manifest purpose of any particular element within it. Burnham (1982, p. 75) illustrates this perspective:

Any state fulfils three basic functions. First, it defends the basic needs and interests of those who control the means of production within the society in question. Closely associated with this is the second function of the state: achieving legitimacy for itself and ensuring social harmony. Finally, no state can survive if it cannot adequately defend itself, and the dominant powers in the economy and society, from external attack.

When we do use states as our unit of analysis, it soon becomes clear that their powers (if not their functions) are a variable rather than a constant. For example, in communist countries, the state was an overarching influence, pervading virtually all aspects of life. In established democracies, the state is less dominant though even here a contrast is sometimes drawn between strong states such as France and Japan whose rulers are expected to lead society and weaker states such as the USA where the government is more a servant of society (Dyson, 1980). In much of the developing world, the state is less important still; its writ may not run far beyond the capital city and a few other towns. These contrasts in state power would again be obscured if we concentrated solely on comparing government institutions.

Techniques of comparison

This section turns from strategy to techniques. Comparative politics offers a wide repertoire of techniques and here we examine three major methods: case studies, focused comparisons and statistical analysis (Box 5.4). These devices range from intensive scrutiny of one country (case studies) or a small number (focused comparisons) to systematic analysis of variables drawn from a larger number of countries (statistical analysis).

Case studies

A case is an instance of a more general category. To conduct a case study is therefore to investigate something with significance beyond its own boundaries. For instance, lawyers study cases which are taken to illustrate a wider legal principle. Physicians study a case of a particular ailment because they want to learn how to treat similar instances in the future. So a project turns into a case study only when it becomes clear what the study is a case *of*.

As Scarrow (1969, p. 7) points out, case studies make a contribution to general knowledge of politics if 'the analysis is made within a comparative perspective which mandates that the description of the particular be cast in terms of broadly analytic constructs'. In other words, a single case should offer a detailed illustration of a theme of wider interest. For instance, we could take the United

---

BOX 5.4
Major techniques in comparative politics

	Number of cases	Case- or variable-centred?	Strategy
Case studies	One	Case	Intensive study of a single instance with wider significance
Focused comparisons	A few	Case	Qualitative comparison of a few instances
Statistical analysis	Many	Variable	Quantitative assessment of the impact of variables

---

States as an example of presidential government, Canada as an illustration of federalism or Sweden's Social Democrats as an example of a dominant party. Thus cases can be deliberately chosen as examples of broader phenomena.

Because case studies locate their findings in a wider context, they are a tool of comparative politics, even though only one example is examined. In that sense, comparative politics resembles anthropology, a discipline where case studies of particular communities have nonetheless cumulated into a body of general knowledge (Peters, 1998, p. 61).

In the absence of overarching theory, case studies are the building blocks from which we construct our understanding of the political world (Yin, 2003). We usually proceed by comparing cases rather than by making deductions from first principles. In consequence, much comparative political analysis takes the form not of relating cases to abstract theory, but simply of drawing analogies between the cases themselves. For instance: how did the process of state-building differ between post-colonial states of the twentieth century and the states of early modern Europe? What are the similarities and differences between the Russian and Chinese revolutions?

Reflecting this pragmatic approach, Khong (1992) suggests that much political reasoning, especially in foreign policy, is by analogy. Decision-makers and analysts look for earlier crises which resemble the current one, so that lessons can be learned and errors avoided. This strategy reflects common sense but runs the risk of over-weighting history. Just because democracy failed in Latin America in the 1960s, we should not conclude that it will do so again in the changed circumstances of the twenty-first century. Just because the United States lost the war in Vietnam, we should not infer that America cannot win other wars on foreign soil. The art of comparing cases is to be as sensitive to differences as to similarities; and the contrasting location of the cases in time is often a major distinguishing feature.

In practice, case studies are multi-method, using the range of techniques in the political scientist's toolkit. This kit includes: reading the academic literature, examining secondary documents (for example newspapers), searching for primary material (for example unpublished reports) and ideally conducting interviews with participants and other observers in the country under scrutiny. In other words, scholars of cases engage in 'soaking and poking, marinating themselves in minutiae' (King et al., 1994, p. 38). Case studies aim to provide a description which is both rounded and detailed, a goal which the anthropologist Clifford Geertz (1973) famously defined as 'thick description'. They blend well with the current emphasis on interpretive explanation in politics.

By definition, all case studies possess broader significance but this added value can be acquired in various ways. Box 5.5 outlines four types of case study. A case can be useful either because it is representative – a typical, standard example of a wider category – or because it is prototypical, deviant or archetypal.

Of these designs, the *representative case* is the

BOX 5.5
Some types of case study

Type	Definition	Example
Representative case	Typical of the category	Finland: coalition government
Prototypical case	Expected to become typical	USA: a pioneering democracy
Deviant case	The exception to the rule	India: democracy in a poor country
Archetypal case	Creates the category	USA: presidential government

Further reading: Yin (2003), Gomm and Hammersley (2000).

---

most common. It is the workhorse of case study designs, as useful as it is undramatic. Often researchers will use their own country as a representative case. For example, researchers may be interested in female political participation throughout the democratic world but choose to study the phenomenon in their own country in detail. The home country is the research site but the hope is that the results will contribute to a broader, cross-national debate. Of course, no country is exactly like any other but a collection of representative case studies will provide the raw material for later distillation.

By contrast, a *prototypical case* is chosen not because it is representative but because it is expected to become so. As Rose (1991, p. 459) puts it, 'their present is our future'. Studying an early example can help us to understand a phenomenon which is growing in significance elsewhere.

In the nineteenth century, for instance, the French scholar Alexis de Tocqueville (1835, Ch. 1) studied America because of his interest in the new politics of democracy. He wrote, 'my wish has been to find there [in the USA] instruction by which we [in Europe] may ourselves profit'. De Tocqueville regarded the United States as a harbinger of democracy and a potential guide to Europe's own future.

More recently, Carey (1996) examined the term limits on the tenure of Costa Rican legislators in order to identify the possible effects of introducing similar limits to state assemblies in the USA. Like de Tocqueville before him, Carey realized that pro-

totypical case studies offer opportunities for lesson-drawing. Rather than speculate about the possible effects of term limits in the United States, relevant evidence could be gathered from an early adopter. In this way, later adopters can learn from the experience of the innovator (Rogers, 1971).

The purpose of a *deviant case* study is very different. It deliberately seeks out the exceptional and the untypical, rather than the norm: for instance, the countries which remain communist, or which are still governed by the military, or which seem to be immune from democratizing trends. Deviant cases are often used to tidy up our understanding of exceptions and anomalies. We might ask why India is an exception to the thesis that democracy presupposes prosperity. Or we could seek to explain one of Switzerland's several anomalies: why did such a small country adopt a federal architecture?

Normal science, suggests Kuhn (1970), proceeds in exactly this way, with researchers seeking to show how apparent paradoxes can be resolved within a dominant intellectual tradition. Deviant cases always attract interest and, by providing a contrast with the norm, can help our understanding of typical examples. But since the exceptional is always more exotic than the typical, the danger of over-studying deviant cases is that comparative politics turns into a collection of curios.

Reflecting the tendency for comparative politics to move from cases to theory, rather than vice versa, some of the most important examples in comparative politics are best conceived as *archetypal cases*, our final form of case study. The idea here is that an archetypal case generates the category of which it is then taken, in a somewhat circular way, as representative.

Take the French Revolution. This episode altered the whole concept of revolution, reconstructing the idea as a progressive, modernizing force. In this way, the French Revolution made possible all the modern revolutions which followed. In similar fashion, the American presidency does far more than illustrate the presidential system of government; it is the model which influenced all later attempts to create similar systems, notably in Latin America.

Focused comparisons

Focused comparisons fall between case studies and statistical analysis. They are 'small N' studies concentrating on the intensive comparison of an aspect of politics in a small number of countries. Most often, the number of countries is either two, a paired or binary comparison, or three, a triangular comparison. The emphasis is on the comparison at least as much as on the cases; otherwise, the design would be a multiple case study. Countries are normally selected to introduce variation into the dependent variable, thus overcoming an inherent limit of the single case study.

To illustrate the technique, consider two examples of the strategy, each using paired comparison. First, Kudrle and Marmor (1981) compared the growth of social security programmes in the United States and Canada. They sought to understand Canada's higher levels of spending and programme development, concluding that the elements of left-wing ideology and conservative paternalism found there were the key contrasts with the USA.

Second, a classic study by Heclo (1974) compared the origins of unemployment insurance, old age pensions and earnings-related supplementary pensions in Britain and Sweden. In both countries, Heclo concluded, the bureaucracy was the main agency of policy formulation. In contrast to Kudrle and Marmor, and indeed to many focused comparisons, Heclo's project was unusual in seeking to explain a similarity rather than a difference between the countries examined.

Focused comparisons such as these have proved to be the success story of comparative politics in recent decades (Collier, 1991). Like case studies, they remain sensitive to the details of particular countries and policies but in addition they demand the intellectual discipline inherent in the comparative enterprise. That is, the dimensions of comparison must be addressed, similarities and differences identified and some effort made to account for the contrasts observed.

Also, focused comparisons remain sensitive to history. Indeed, the format works particularly well when – as with Heclo – a few countries are compared over time, examining how they vary in their response to common problems such as the transition to democracy. If it is difficult to produce a poor case study, it is virtually impossible to deliver an uninteresting report using focused comparison.

How should countries be selected for a focused comparison? A common strategy is to select countries which, although differing on the factor under study, are otherwise similar. This is a 'most similar' design. With this approach, we seek to compare countries which are as similar as possible in, say, their history, culture and political institutions, so that we can clearly rule out such common factors as explanations for the particular difference of interest to us. For instance, Kudrle and Marmor's study (1981) sought to explain the contrasts in social security programmes between Canada and the United States, two countries which are similar in many other ways. Or we might seek to explain why Britain managed a more peaceful transition to democracy than Germany, comparing two large countries which share a European heritage.

However, even with a most similar design many factors will remain as possible explanations for an observed difference and usually there will be no decisive way of testing between them. The problem of too many variables and too few countries cannot be sidestepped; in practice, the value of a focused comparison lies in the journey rather than the destination.

A 'most different' design takes a contrasting approach. Here, the object is to test a relationship by discovering whether it can be observed in a range of different countries. If so, our confidence that the relationship is real, and not due to both factors depending on an unmeasured third variable, will increase (Peters, 1998).

For example, Rothstein (2002) examines the evolution of social and political trust in two contrasting democracies, Sweden and the United States, assuming that any trends shared between these two very different countries should also be observable in other democracies. In a similar way, if we were to find that the plurality method of election were associated with a two-party system in the diverse group of countries employing that method – including Canada, India and the United Kingdom – our confidence in the robustness of this relationship would increase. A most different design is the basis of much statistical research, to which we now turn.

Definition

A **most similar** design takes similar countries for comparison on the assumption, as Lipset (1990, p. xiii) puts it, that 'the more similar the units being compared, the more possible it should be to isolate the factors responsible for differences between them'. By contrast, the **most different** design seeks to show the robustness of a relationship by demonstrating its validity across diverse settings (Przeworski and Teune, 1970).

Statistical analysis

Far from being unrelated, statistics and politics are linked by origin. The word 'statistics' originally meant the science dealing with facts about the state. The growth of statistics formed part of the rise of the state itself, particularly through the development of the census as a basis for taxing property and people (Fransmyr *et al.*, 1990). In comparative politics, statistical research is less common than in the behavioural era but it remains a significant and worthwhile strand.

In contrast to the techniques reviewed so far, the statistical approach is based on variables rather than cases. Specifically, the object is to explore the covariation between variables. Some of these factors are usually measured on a quantitative scale (such as percentages) but it is also possible to draw up tables based on qualitative variables (for example, whether a country employs parliamentary or presidential government).

In such analyses, one variable is dependent –

that which we seek to explain. The others are independent or explanatory – those factors which we believe may influence the dependent variable (Box 5.6). Examples of such work in comparative politics include tests of the following hypotheses:

▸ the more educated a population, the higher its proportion of post-materialists
▸ the higher a person's social status, the greater his or her participation in politics
▸ the more affluent a country, the more likely it is to be an established democracy
▸ presidential government is more like to be overthrown than is parliamentary government.

To illustrate the statistical approach, consider an example. Figure 5.2 is a scatterplot showing the relationship between the number of members in a national assembly (the dependent variable) and a country's population (the independent variable). Such a plot displays all the information about

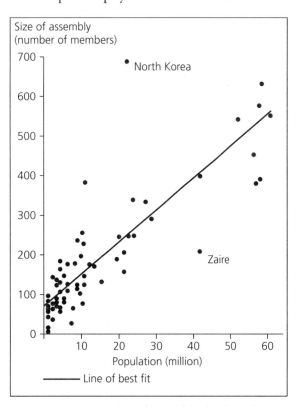

Figure 5.2 Population and assembly size from fig. 14.1 (p. 248), showing the line of best fit and highlighting two outliers

---

BOX 5.6
Dependent, intervening and independent variables

Type of variable	Definition	Example
Dependent variable	The factor we seek to explain	Party voted for
Independent variable	The factor believed to influence the dependent variable	Social class
Intervening variable	A factor through which the independent variable influences the dependent variable	Attitudes to party policy

---

these two factors for the countries surveyed. Clearly, the larger the population, the larger the assembly.

However, the content of the graph can be summarized more precisely. This is achieved by calculating a regression line: that is, the line giving the best fit to the data. This line, also shown in the figure, is defined by a formula linking the variables. Given such an equation, we can use the population of any particular country to predict its assembly size; indeed, these predictions can easily be made from the regression line using a ruler.

A regression equation allows us to identify deviant cases, known as outliers in statistics. The greater the difference between the predicted and the actual assembly size for a given legislature, the greater the need for additional explanation, thus providing a link to case analysis. In our example, North Korea's Supreme People's Assembly is far larger than would be expected for a country with a population of just 23 million. How can we account for this outlier? Many communist states adopted large assemblies as a way of reducing any threat they might pose to the party's power. Such an interpretation would provide a plausible starting point for further investigation.

Statistical methodology can provide precise summaries of large amounts of data using standard techniques whose use can be checked by other researchers. But the approach carries two main risks. The first is that a strong correlation between two variables may arise simply because both depend on a third, unmeasured factor. For example, the relationship between proportional representation (PR) and multi-party systems might arise because both factors emerge in divided societies, not because PR itself increases the number of parties. Or minority ethnic status might be correlated with low turnout simply because ethnic minorities are concentrated among the low-voting poor.

In principle, the solution to spurious correlation is simple: include all relevant variables in the analysis, for statistical techniques can effectively control for such problems. In practice, not all the relevant variables will be known and spurious correlation is a continuing danger. However, even a spurious correlation may be a useful if risky basis for prediction.

Second, even if a relationship is genuine, the direction of causation remains to be established. Suppose we find that democracies have higher rates of economic growth than authoritarian regimes. We still face a problem of interpretation. Does the correlation arise because democracies facilitate economic growth or because a high rate of growth fosters a stable democracy? A case can be made either way and by itself a correlation will not provide the answer.

But not all statistical work is concerned with estimating the impact of one factor on another. In new areas, simple counts provide a useful beginning. As Miller (1995) points out, asking the plain question 'how many of them are there?' is well worthwhile. For instance: how many federations are there? How many Arab states are democratic? What was the probability that an authoritarian regime in 1980 had become democratic by 2000? Such questions must be answered if we are to achieve our objective of comprehending the variability of the political world. Just as straightforward case studies often contribute more to comparative politics than elaborate attempts at theory-testing, so simple counting often offers more than sophisticated statistical analysis. As Peters (1998, p. 191) wisely says, 'statistical analysis may not be everything but it is certainly something'.

Key reading

> **Next step:** *Peters (1998) is a thorough and judicious discussion of the comparative method.*

Dogan and Pelassy (1990) is a challenging account of the comparative approach, more philosophical than Peters but insightful even so.

For general overviews, Lijphart (1971), Keman (1993) and Mair (1996) are all worth reading. Landman (2003) usefully combines issues of method with detailed examples. King *et al.*, (1994) contribute much to comparative research strategy. Green (2002b) examines the interpretive approach to comparative politics. For the institutional approach, see Peters (1999) and Lowndes (2002). For the state-centred approach, see Evans *et al.*, (2003). Yin (2003) is the standard source on case studies. For focused comparisons, see Ragin (1994a) and Ragin *et al.* (1996). Pennings *et al.* (1999) look at statistical methods in the context of comparative politics. We should also mention Wiarda (2004), an extensive and expensive edited collection covering approaches to comparative politics.

Part II
POLITICS AND SOCIETY

The relationship between politics and society has always preoccupied political thinkers. Government does not operate in isolation, unaffected by the society of which it forms part. This part locates politics in a broader social framework. Chapter 6 looks at the attitudes of people toward government, Chapter 7 discusses communication flows between politics and society while Chapter 8 examines how and whether people take part in politics.

Chapter **6**

Political culture

The assault on the United States on September 11, 2001 killed more people than any other single terrorist attack in history. So it is natural to ask what caused these events. And what motivated the terrorists to sacrifice their own lives in the process? Such questions are simple but the answers, of course, will be complex, involving many factors and disciplines.

Still, we would probably want to begin with the political culture of the terrorists and of others in their network. Political culture is, after all, 'the sum of the fundamental values, sentiments and knowledge that give form and substance to political processes' (Pye, 1995, p. 965). So the starting point would be to describe the 'values, sentiments and knowledge' of the terrorists, beginning perhaps with their perceptions of the United States, which gave form and substance to their attack. In this way, political culture would help us to identify the first link in a long chain of causation.

The events of 9/11 also show the importance of studying political culture comparatively. A full understanding of those events must surely involve comparing the cultures of Islam and Christianity, East and West and – perhaps above all – the dispossessed and the powerful. But before we can proceed to a discussion of what Huntington (1996) claims is a 'clash of civilizations', we must explore how political culture has been treated in traditional political science. Here, the focus has been on how values, sentiments and knowledge influence politics within rather than between states. In examining political culture within established democracies, we begin with Almond and Verba's classic account before turning to ideas that have attracted more recent attention: trust, social capital and postmaterialism.

The civic culture

The classic study of political culture and democracy is Almond and Verba's *The Civic Culture* (1963). Based on surveys conducted during 1959–60 in the USA, Britain, West Germany, Italy and also Mexico, this landmark investigation sought to identify the political culture within which a liberal democracy is most likely to develop and consolidate. Their study provides a helpful introduction to the topic.

Almond and Verba's argument is based on a distinction between three pure types of political culture: the parochial, subject and participant. In a *parochial* political culture, first of all, citizens are only indistinctly aware of the existence of central government, as with remote tribes whose existence is seemingly unaffected by national decisions made by the central government. Parochial cultures have been rare in established democracies but elements can be found in isolated rural communities or in the growing number of inner city areas where government is remote from people's lives.

In a *subject* political culture, second, citizens see themselves not as participants in the political process but as subjects of the government, as with people living under a dictatorship. Although we may not associate subject cultures with democracies, subject attitudes may be growing among young people, many of whom remain distant from politics even though they recognize government's impact on their lives.

The third and most familiar type is the *participant* political culture. Here, citizens believe both that they can contribute to the system and that they are affected by it.

It would be natural to assume that people with participant attitudes are the model citizens of a stable democracy. But the interest of Almond and Verba's study rests precisely in their rejection of such a proposition. Rather, the authors propose that democracy will prove most stable in societies blending different cultures in a particular mix they termed the 'civic culture' (Figure 6.1). The ideal conditions for democracy, they suggest, emerge when subject and parochial attitudes provide ballast to an essentially participant culture.

In this civic culture, many citizens are active in politics but the passive minority, whether parochials, subjects or both, provides stability to the system. Further, the participants are not so involved as to refuse to accept decisions with which they disagree. Thus the civic culture resolves the tension within democracy between popular control and effective governance: it allows for citizen influence while retaining flexibility for the governing elite.

Armed with this theory, Almond and Verba set out to discover through opinion surveys which countries in their study came closest to their model of the civil culture. Britain, and to a lesser extent the United States, scored highest. In both countries citizens felt they could influence the government but often chose not to do so, thus giving the government its required agility. By contrast, the political cultures of West Germany, Italy and Mexico all deviated in various ways from the authors' prescription.

Like most original works, Almond and Verba's study attracted considerable scrutiny (Barry, 1988). Critics alleged that attempting to portray a national political culture was as vague an undertaking as investigating national character. Perhaps the research should have focused more on subcultures of race and class within the societies examined. Nor did the authors offer a detailed account of the origins of political culture. It is possible, after all, that citizens believe they can influence government just because they can actually do so, a point that would suggest political culture reflects as much as it influences government. Nor did the authors focus on the evolution of political culture, a theme which – as we will see – has characterized much later discussion in this area.

Political trust and social capital

Times move on. In the decades following Almond and Verba's study, many established democracies hit turbulent waters: Vietnam and student activism in the 1960s, the oil crisis of the 1970s, the anti-nuclear and ecology movements of the 1980s, privatization and cutbacks to the welfare state in the 1990s, terrorism in the 2000s.

As Almond and Verba (1980) noted in an initial update, such events left their mark on Western political cultures. More recent research in the area has therefore focused on whether established democracies have suffered a decline in political and social trust. And the answer, in general, is that they have, although the fall focuses on the public's confidence in the performance of democratic institutions rather than on the principle of democracy itself.

For example, Norris (1999, p. 20) concludes that overall public confidence in such institutions as parliament, the civil service and the armed forces declined between 1981 and 1991 in each of the 17 countries she examined. Today's disillusioned democrats, as Norris calls them, may be cynical but they remain committed to democracy's ideals:

democratic values now command widespread acceptance as an ideal, but at the same time citizens have often become more critical of the workings of the core institutions of representative democracy.

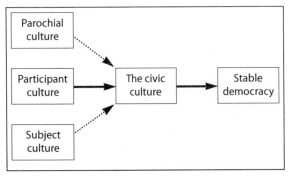

Figure 6.1 Almond and Verba's theory of the civic culture

The United States clearly illustrates the decline of trust in government. In 1964, three-quarters of Americans said that they trusted the federal government 'to do the right thing'; by 1994, at the bottom of the cycle, only a quarter did so (Figure 6.2). As Wuthnow (2002, p. 59) points out, much of this decline was brought about by specific events such as the Vietnam War and Watergate, with partial recoveries during periods of peace and prosperity. Thus, trust recovered somewhat as the economy and stock market boomed in the late 1990s. Despite the intelligence failings exposed by September 11, faith in government received a massive short-term boost following the attacks as Americans rallied round the flag (Brewer et al., 2003). But contemporary faith in national government remains well below the levels recorded in the late 1950s, when Almond and Verba issued their positive appraisal of America's civic culture.

The long-term trend in political trust slopes down in other democracies too. In the UK, for example, trust in government fell from 47 per cent in 1987 to 28 per cent in 2001 (Bromley and Curtice, 2002). So both the American and the British 'civic cultures' have witnessed a shift towards more sceptical and instrumental attitudes to politics since Almond and Verba's study.

When we probe in more detail into these broad trends, the picture becomes more negative. Surveys from a number of European democracies suggest that the public places more trust in the institutions of law and order, such as the military and the police, than in the agencies of representation such as parties. As Table 6.1 shows, political parties come bottom of the confidence league in all the countries examined. So public support for core functions of the state remains generally high but those mechanisms which provide democratic control over rulers are rated poorly. This pattern confirms the public's jaundiced view of democratic performance.

What are the consequences of falling confidence in political institutions? This question has preoccupied Putnam (2002) who suggests that a culture of trust oils the wheels of collective action, enabling projects to be initiated which would not be feasible in a society where mutual suspicion prevailed. Declining faith in government is therefore a form of political deflation, reducing the capacity of the political system to achieve shared goals.

In an influential study using Italy as his laboratory, Putnam (1993) attempted to test these ideas to show how a supportive social environment directly enhances the performance of a political system. In their original work, Almond and Verba had portrayed Italy as a country whose people felt uninvolved in, and alienated from, politics. At the time, Italy showed strong elements of the subject and parochial cultures. Putnam revisits Italy's

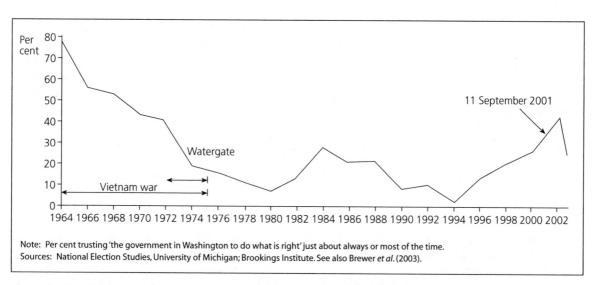

Note: Per cent trusting 'the government in Washington to do what is right' just about always or most of the time.
Sources: National Election Studies, University of Michigan; Brookings Institute. See also Brewer et al. (2003).

Figure 6.2 Americans' trust in the 'government in Washington', 1964–2002

Table 6.1 Confidence in political institutions, 2001

	France	Germany	Sweden	United Kingdom
High confidence (greater than 50%)	Civil service, Police, Military, Media	Police	Police, Courts	Military, Police
Low confidence (30–49%)	Courts, Parliament	Courts, Military, Parliament	Military, Parliament, Civil service	Courts, Civil service, Parliament
Very low confidence (below 30%)	Parties	Civil service, Media, Parties	Media, Parties	Media, Parties

Note: Ranking is based on the proportion of the sample expressing confidence in the institution. Institutions within each cell are ranked by confidence level.

Source: Data from Inoguchi (2002, Table 9.4b).

political culture, paying more attention to diversity within the country. He demonstrates how cultural variations within Italy influenced the effectiveness of the 20 new regional governments created in the 1970s. Similar in structure and formal powers, these governments nonetheless varied greatly in performance. Some (such as Emilia-Romagna in the North) proved stable and effective, capable of making and implementing innovative policies. Others (such as Calabria in the South) achieved little. What, asks Putnam, explains these contrasts?

Definition

Social capital refers to a culture of trust and cooperation which makes collective action possible and effective. As Putnam (2002) says, it is the ability of a community to 'develop the "I" into the "we"'. A political culture with a fund of social capital enables a community to build political institutions with a capacity to solve collective problems. **Bonding** social capital is sustained by networks of people drawn from similar backgrounds while **bridging** social capital brings together dissimilar types.

Putnam finds his answer in political culture. He argues that the most successful regions have a positive political culture: a tradition of trust and cooperation which results in high levels of social capital. By contrast, the least effective governments are found in regions lacking any tradition of collaboration and equality. In such circumstances, supplies of social capital run low and governments can achieve little.

But where does social capital itself come from? How does a community establish a foundation of mutual trust? Like Almond and Verba before him, Putnam's answer is historical. Somewhat controversially, he attributes the uneven distribution of social capital in modern Italy to events deep within each area's history (Morlino, 1995). The more effective governments in the north draw on a tradition of communal self-government dating from the twelfth century. The least successful administrations in the south are burdened with a long history of feudal, foreign, bureaucratic and authoritarian rule. Thus, Putnam's analysis illustrates how political culture can be used as the device through which the past is taken to influence the present.

The idea of social capital extends the idea of

trust beyond its political domain into the wider field of social relationships. Putnam suggests that the declining faith of Americans in their government is matched by a corresponding social change: namely, a fall in trust in other people. In the United States, those who give a positive response to the survey question 'Generally speaking, would you say that most people can be trusted?' declined from 46 per cent in 1972 to 34 per cent in 1994 (Wuthnow, 2002, p. 71). Such findings have led to extensive debate about the danger of social capital disintegrating in the USA.

But there is little evidence suggesting that the decline in social trust in the United States is matched in other democracies. In a study of public opinion in the member states of the European Union, Newton (1999, p. 175) found 'no evidence of a general decline in social trust. On the contrary, nine of the EU twelve show higher levels of trust in 1993 than 1976.' In Sweden, two in three people say they trust others, notwithstanding the assassination of the country's prime minister in 1986 and its foreign minister in 2003. The equivalent figure for trust in the USA, overall a more violent country than Sweden, is far lower (Rothstein, 2002, p. 320).

Within Europe, only Britain has shared the American pattern of a marked decline in interpersonal trust. The populations of both countries, it may be significant to note, are heavy viewers of television, a behaviour which reduces social contact and communication.

Nor do the connections between social and political trust seem to be strong. Newton found that 'the correlations between trust in people and trust in government are so small that they can be ignored'. Rothstein's study of Sweden (2002, p. 321) also found only 'a weak correlation' between these concepts. Certainly, declining faith in government is an important trend in the democratic world. But social trust, and with it social capital, appears to be a separate issue.

Postmaterialism

One factor which helps to account for developments in political culture, at both mass and elite level, is postmaterialism. Along with the themes of political trust and social capital, this notion illustrates how political scientists have sought to incorporate change into their understanding of political culture.

From the late 1940s to the early 1970s, the Western world witnessed a period of unprecedented economic growth. 'You've never had it so good' became a cliché that summarized the experience of the postwar generation. This era – long before 9/11 and the wars resulting from it – was also a period of relative international peace. A cohort grew up with no experience of world war. In addition, the newly instituted welfare state offered increased security to many Western populations against the scourges of illness and unemployment.

According to Inglehart (1971, 1997), this unique combination of affluence, peace and security led to a silent revolution in Western political cultures. He suggests that the emphasis on economic achievement as the main priority is making way for an emphasis on the quality of life:

in a major part of the world, the disciplined, self-denying and achievement-oriented norms of industrial society are giving way to the choices over lifestyle which characterize post-industrial economies (Inglehart, 1997, p. 28).

From the 1960s, a new generation of postmaterialists emerged: young, well-educated people with concerns centred on lifestyle issues such as ecology, nuclear disarmament and feminism. Where prewar generations had valued order, security and fixed rules in such areas as religion and sexual morality, postmaterialists take political and religious authority for granted. They give priority to self-expression and flexible rules. Postmaterialists are elite-challenging advocates of the new politics rather than elite-sustaining foot soldiers in the old party battles. They are more attracted to single-issue groups than to the broader packages offered by political parties. A loaf of bread does not satisfy postmaterialists; it must also be wholemeal, organic and preferably hand-baked!

Based on extensive survey evidence, Inglehart shows that the more affluent a democracy, the higher the proportion of postmaterialists within its

Profile **GERMANY**

Population: 82m.
Gross domestic product per head: $26,600 (much lower in former East Germany).
Form of government: a constitutional and parliamentary federal republic.
Legislature: the 603-member Bundestag is the lower house. The smaller and weaker upper house, the Bundesrat, represents the 16 federal *Länder* (states).
Executive: the Chancellor leads a cabinet of between 16 and 22 minis-

ters. A President serves as ceremonial head of state.
Judiciary: Germany is a state based on law. The Federal Constitutional Court has proved to be highly influential as an arbiter of the constitution and, externally, as the model of a constitutional (rather than an American-style supreme) court.
Electoral system: the Bundestag is elected through an influential additional member system which has now been adopted in over 20 countries

(p. 148). Members of the Bundesrat are nominated by the *Länder*; hence, the Bundesrat is never dissolved.
Party system: the leading parties are the SPD (Social Democrats) and the CDU (Christian Democrats). Traditionally, these have governed in coalition with the smaller FDP (Free Democrats). However, the Greens joined a coalition with the SPD in 1998, a coalition which was renewed after the 2002 election.

The Federal Republic of Germany boasts the third largest economy in the world. Its skilled employees, based in capital-intensive factories, produce manufactured goods for sale at premium prices throughout the world. Germany's exports have exceeded its imports each year since 1955 and the country's 'economic miracle' supports extensive public services; both contributed to the growth in the legitimacy of the Federal Republic founded in 1949 on the ashes of Hitler's Third Reich. Only in the later 1990s, as unemployment passed the four million mark, and the costs of reunification began to mount, did the German economic model and its generous welfare system begin to experience stress.

Germany has been a leading player in the development of the European Union. Its political commitment to a united Europe is entrenched in its constitution and Germany has been willing to support its objectives with hard cash. Because Germany naturally views European developments through the lens of its own system of government, the country's political institutions are of continental significance.

Seeking to avoid the political instability of the Weimar Republic (1919–33), which had contributed to the Nazi seizure of power, the framers of the postwar constitution made the chancellor the key figure in the new republic. The chancellor determines government policy, appoints cabinet ministers, heads a staff of 500 and can only be removed from office when parliament also demonstrates a majority for a named successor. Within a parliamentary framework, Germany offers a distinctive form of 'chancellor democracy'.

Most of the republic's six chancellors have been strong figures, further enhancing the status of the office. For example, Helmut Kohl (Chancellor, 1982–98) was the dominant force behind the rapid but peaceful unification of Germany following the dramatic opening of the Berlin Wall in 1990. Though unification has proved costly for the Western provinces, and required massive restructuring in the former German Democratic Republic, the result is the largest country in Western Europe – and a state which is strategically positioned at the heart of the European continent.

For students of political culture, the country's postwar history shows how the legitimacy of a political system can flow from successful economic performance. Between 1959 and 1988 the proportion of Germans expressing pride in their political institutions increased from 7 to 51 per cent. Over a similar period, support for a multiparty system grew from 53 to 92 per cent. This success story has not been repeated so easily in the former East Germany, and some recent reductions in welfare have dented the previously cosy compact between the government and its citizens in the Western provinces. Even so, the emergence of a supportive public in the Federal Republic since 1949 offers hope to other transitional countries seeking to build a democratic culture on an authoritarian history.

Further reading: Conradt (2001), Helms (2000), Schmidt (2003).

borders. The United States was in the vanguard. In the early 1970s, American postmaterialists were concentrated among yuppies – young, upwardly mobile urban professionals, especially those in the wealthiest state of all, California. Three decades later, this baby-boom generation retains a relatively progressive outlook despite its unparalleled affluence.

In Europe postmaterialism came first to, and made deepest inroads in, the wealthiest democracies such as Denmark, the Netherlands and West Germany. The affluent Scandinavian countries (except Norway) also proved receptive to these values (Knutsen, 1990). Postmaterialism remains less common in poorer democracies with lower levels of education: for example, Greece.

Definition
Postmaterialism is a commitment to radical quality of life issues (such as the environment) which can emerge, especially among the educated young, from a foundation of personal security and material affluence. Postmaterialists participate extensively in politics but they are inclined to join elite-challenging promotional groups rather than traditional political parties (Inglehart, 1997).

If other things remain equal, postmaterial values will become more prominent. When Inglehart began his studies in 1970–71, materialists outnumbered postmaterialists by about four to one in many Western countries. But by 2000 the two groups were much more even in size, a major transformation in political culture. Population replacement will continue to work its effect. As Inglehart (1999, p. 247) notes, 'as the younger birth cohorts replace the older more materialist cohorts, we should observe a shift towards the postmaterial orientation'.

The unerring expansion of education gives postmaterialism a further boost. Experience of higher education is the best single predictor of a postmaterial outlook. Indeed 'postmaterialism' can be largely understood as the liberal outlook induced by degree-level education, especially in the arts and social sciences. Such values are then sustained through careers in professions where knowledge, rather than capital or management authority, is

key (Farnen and Meloen, 2000). The march of higher education, and the changing structure of the workforce, may be more important mechanisms of cultural change than the factors Inglehart emphasizes, namely peace and affluence.

Although postmaterialism is normally interpreted as a value shift among the population, its most important effects may be on political elites. Inglehart's infantry are an active, opinion-leading group and already his shock troops have moved into positions of power, securing a platform from which their values can directly affect government decisions.

For instance, the 1960s generation retained touches of radicalism even as it secured the seductive trappings of office. Thus, Bill Clinton (born 1946, the first president to be born after the war) offered a more liberal agenda to the American people than did his predecessor in the White House, George Bush (born 1924). These two men belonged to different parties, to be sure, but they also represented contrasting generations. A similar claim can be made about Britain by comparing Tony Blair (born 1953) with his predecessor John Major (born 1943).

However, the political success of George W. Bush (born, like Clinton, in 1946) reminds us that postmaterialism may not carry all before it. In the short and medium term, direct political developments exert more influence over the cultural mood than long-term forces such as postmaterialism.

Political culture in new democracies

In new democracies, political culture offers less support to the system of government than is the case in established democracies. In part, this weakness derives from mere unfamiliarity with a new order. New rulers lack the authority which accrues naturally to a regime with a record of success. At the same time, they must confront the excessive expectations initiated by the overthrow of the old rulers; public opinion may expect too much, too quickly and above all too easily. In addition, the inheritance from the old regime is likely to be a cynical and suspicious attitude to politics, and a culture which is more parochial than participant.

The communist legacy, in particular, is far removed from Almond and Verba's civic culture.

Since new democracies lack a reservoir of goodwill built up over generations, attitudes to the political system depend more on current performance. A new democracy which literally delivers the goods will engender supportive attitudes capable of sustaining it in the future. As Diamond and Lipset (1995, p. 751) write, 'for the long-run success of democracy, there is no alternative to economic stability and progress'.

Two examples of successful democratic consolidation, Germany and Spain, confirm this point. West Germany's success in translating its economic miracle of the 1950s and 1960s into favourable attitudes to its new democracy was testament to the power of economic performance to reshape political culture (see the profile on p. 94).

In a similar if less dramatic way, the consolidation of Spain's new democracy in the final quarter of the twentieth century owed much to economic development which had been inhibited – though not prevented – under the authoritarian rule of General Franco. Economic and political liberalization marched hand in hand. So in both Germany and Spain, strong economic performance contributed to the consolidation of a democratic culture.

Compared to these success stories, post-communist and post-colonial regimes have experienced more difficulty in delivering the performance needed to strengthen democratic commitment. Consider the post-communist countries. In the giddy moment of revolution in 1989, expectations ran away with themselves. With a measure of freedom achieved, the people expected affluence to follow, seemingly unaware of the magnitude of change needed to transform an inefficient state-run economy into a vibrant free market. Anticipating effortless wealth, many in East Europe simply encountered long-term unemployment. As de Tocqueville noted long ago (1856), dashed expectations are politically more damaging than outright fatalism.

Initial reserves of goodwill were soon running short as factories closed, infrastructure decayed and the welfare safety net provided by communism disappeared. Far from delivering affluence, the new democracies seemed to deliver insecurity and poverty to many, and illicit wealth only to a few. As one frustrated politician said, 'When people had security, they wanted freedom; now they have freedom, they want security.'

By the first decade of the twenty-first century, however, post-communist states had clearly diverged in the development of their political cultures. Most East European countries, for example Poland, had witnessed considerable economic recovery after the initial meltdown of the early and mid-1990s. Total production at last exceeded levels achieved under communism. The population began to learn that over the longer term, democracy could deliver an improved standard of living for most, if not all, the people. Prospective membership of the European Union offered a further stimulus to embracing a democratic culture.

In post-communist Asia, however, political leaders saw no reason to imitate Western models. Primitive pre-industrial economies declined rather than developed and authoritarian rule seemed the surest guarantee of political stability. In any case, even the pre-communist heritage simply offered weak foundations on which to build a democracy; Tismaneanu (1995) describes the political cultures of the Asian republics, such as Kazakhstan and Uzbekistan, as 'antidemocratic, anti-liberal and ethnocentric'. With Russia and China as powerful neighbours, regional politics in Asia were also less favourable to constructing a democratic culture than was the case in East Europe. In such circumstances, it would have required an astonishing economic transformation to induce a democratic orientation in either the political elite or the general population. Such agricultural societies may need a generation of industrialization, quite possibly state-led, before a democratic culture can emerge.

Political culture in authoritarian states

In the mature democracies of the West, political culture contributes to the stability of government, offering broad support to those charged with the task of ruling. Authoritarian rulers, by contrast, face characteristic problems arising from their unwillingness to confront the challenge of the ballot box. Lacking the legitimacy which flows from free election, such rulers must find other ways of responding to the political culture of the societies they govern. Broadly speaking, their options are threefold: to ignore, to manipulate or to seek to transform the existing political culture. Each approach merits separate discussion even though in practice non-democratic rulers often combine these strategies.

Ignoring political culture

Disregarding the political culture of the wider society is the tactic favoured by most authoritarian governments. Military rulers, for example, ride to power on a tank and show little concern for the niceties of political culture. Their task is to protect their own back against challengers seeking to supplant them. Far from seeking to draw support from the wider culture, military rulers typically seek to isolate the mass population from engagement with government, thus shrinking the political arena.

In extreme cases, tyrants (civil or military) demand the submission of the populace, not its support. Yet it is a tribute to the power of political culture that such repressive survival strategies rarely succeed over the long term. In practice, naked power only prospers when wrapped in legitimacy's clothes.

Manipulating political culture

The second approach is to exploit the political culture by selectively emphasizing its authoritarian elements. This strategy can be more effective over the long term. As Eckstein (1998a) remarks, an authoritarian government which is congruent with cultural values may prove to be more stable than a democratic regime which remains unnourished by the wider culture.

For instance, traditions of deference, and of personal allegiance to powerful individuals, are a cultural resource which many leaders in Asia and Latin America have exploited to the full to sustain their power. Loyalty to the national leader is presented as a natural outgrowth either of the submission of the landless peasant to the powerful landowner or of the unforced obedience of the

child to its parent. The ruler is father and/or chief patron to the nation, providing security and stability but not democratic accountability.

In pre-democratic Mexico, for example, scholars suggested that 'underlying values were fundamentally authoritarian in the sense that Mexican children learned in the family to accept the authority of their fathers and they later transferred this acceptance of authority to political leaders, including the president' (Turner, 1995, p. 209).

Seeking to transform political culture

The most interesting approach to political culture in non-democratic regimes is to seek to reshape the country's values. By definition, totalitarian regimes sought to transform the political values of their subjects. In Hitler's Germany, for instance, all textbooks had to conform to Nazi ideology and pupils were trained in arithmetic using examples based on 'the Jewish question'.

But it was communist regimes which made the most systematic and long-lasting effort at transforming political culture. Their starting point was that the state must restructure the way people think and behave. As Meyer (1983, p. 6) comments, communist revolutions were originally intended as cultural revolutions. Through education and persuasion, the aim was to create a new communist personality which would flourish in a classless, atheist society, free of the poisons inhaled under capitalism.

Take the Soviet Union and China as examples. In both countries the post-revolutionary communist rulers sought to increase mass participation in politics. Mass campaigns ensured that everyone became involved in politics. Yet the anticipated transformation of political culture never came about. Eventually, mass participation took on a purely ritual form, based on passive obedience to power rather than active commitment to communism. Fear created citizens who outwardly conformed but in reality adopted strategies designed to ensure their own survival: two persons in one body.

So communist reconstructions of political culture rarely succeeded in transforming might into right. Instead, they often strengthened critical attitudes to politics and depleted social capital by creating a social environment in which no one could be trusted. This negative climate continues to hold back the development of participatory cultures in post-communist countries.

Elite political culture

Although the impact of mass political culture on political stability has been debated widely, the significance of elite political culture has been addressed less often. Yet in countries with a parochial or subject political culture, elite political culture is primary. Even where mass attitudes to politics are well-developed, as in consolidated democracies, it is still the views of the elite which exert the most direct effect on political decisions. As Verba (1987, p. 7) writes, the values of political leaders can be expected to have both 'coherence and consequences'. Political leaders have, for example, proved central to recent democratic transitions. In this section, we examine elite political culture, again focusing on its consequences for political stability.

Elite culture is far more than a representative fragment of the values of the wider society. Throughout the world the ideas of elites are distinct from, though they overlap with, the national political culture. For example, leaders in democracies generally take a more liberal line on social and moral issues. Stouffer's (1966) famous survey of American attitudes to freedom of speech, conducted in 1954, confirmed this point. Stouffer showed that most community leaders maintained their belief in free speech for atheists, socialists and communists at a time when the public's attitudes were much less tolerant. By the 1980s, surveys revealed a striking increase in the American public's support for free speech (Weissberg, 1998). Nonetheless, it was crucial to the cause of free speech in the United States during the 1950s that a majority of the political elite resisted the strong pressure from Senator Joe McCarthy's populist anti-communist witch-hunt (Fried, 1990).

In a similar way, many leaders of post-communist countries accept the need for a thorough transition to a market economy even while mass culture continues to find reassurance in the equality of poverty practised under communism.

> **Definition**
> **Elite political culture** consists of the beliefs, attitudes and ideas about politics held by those who are closest to the centres of political power. The values of elites are more explicit, systematic and consequential than are those of the population at large.

One reason for the liberal and sophisticated outlook of political leaders is their education; in most democracies, politics has become virtually a graduate profession. The experience of higher education nurtures an optimistic view of human nature, strengthens humanitarian values and encourages a belief in the ability of politicians to solve social problems (Farnen and Meloen, 2000). Indeed the contrast between the values of the educated elite and the least educated section of the population is itself a source of tension in many political cultures.

In assessing the impact of elite political culture on stability, three dimensions are crucial:

▶ Does the elite have faith in its own right to rule?
▶ Does the elite accept the notion of a national interest, separate from individual and group ambitions?
▶ Do all members of the elite accept the rules of the game, especially those governing the transfer of power? (see Figure 6.3.)

The first and perhaps most vital component here is the rulers' belief in their own right to rule. The revolutions of 1989 in Eastern Europe dramatically illustrate how a collapse of confidence among the rulers themselves can enforce a change of regime. As Schöpflin (1990) points out,

> an authoritarian elite sustains itself in power not just through force and the threat of force but, more importantly, because it has some vision of the future by which it can justify itself to itself. No regime can survive long without some concept of purpose.

In the initial phase of industrialization, communist rulers in the Soviet Union and Eastern Europe

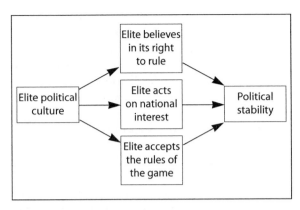

Figure 6.3 How elite political culture affects political stability

in concluding that 'an elite culture links all of the different historical apparitions of expert rule' on the continent. Rule by experts provided an instance where the technical, depoliticized views of an educated elite came to dominate the political agenda.

> *Definition*
> **Technocracy** is rule by experts, a temporary form of rule that sometimes emerges after a period of poor governance. The term implies rule by specialists with expertise in non-political subjects, often economics and engineering. The word itself was coined by William Smyth, an engineer based in California, who founded Technocracy, Inc. in 1919. Today, a **technocrat** denotes a specialist with a job or outlook that is technical rather than political.

had good reason to believe their new planned economies were producing results. But by the late 1980s progress had given way to decline: industrial planning had reached a dead end. As any remaining support from intellectuals faded, so party officials began to doubt their own legitimacy. In the end, communist rule was toppled so easily because it had already become enfeebled. Communist rulers were aware that they had become a barrier to, rather than a source of, progress. Elite values had ceased to underpin the system of government. By contrast, economic growth continues apace in contemporary China, sustaining the elite's confidence in its own legitimacy.

A more recent example of elite political culture sustaining non- or semi-democratic government is rule by experts. Latin America provides the best recent instances of this technocratic culture. The 'techno-boys' were a cohort of European- or American-trained graduates (mainly in economics or engineering) who influenced economic policy-making in much of the continent, notably Chile, in the final decades of the twentieth century. While communist rulers were losing faith in their right to rule, the techno-boys possessed every confidence in the validity of their own prescriptions.

When supported by a strong political leader, these specialists were able to impose harsh monetary remedies on countries where financial discipline had often taken second place to political requirements. Because the authority of these specialists derived in part from their self-belief, Centeno and Silva (1998, p. 3) were surely justified

The second aspect of elite political culture lies in its approach to the national interest. At issue here is the attitude of rulers to the government posts they hold. Is public service seen as just that – a way of serving the national interest? Some national bureaucracies, from France to Pakistan, have seen themselves as guardians of the nation even to the point of protecting their country from 'mere politicians'. Latin America's technocrats are again an example: they assumed that their assessment of the country's long-term economic interests should take priority over the preferences of specific social groups.

More often in the developing world, the state is seen by its ruling elite as a seam of scarce resources to be mined for the benefit of the rulers, their families, their constituents and members of their ethnic group. This approach predominates where economic resources are scarce and – just as important – where state institutions are weak. Both factors apply to many post-colonial countries. In post-communist countries, too, officials who survived the collapse of the old order often gained personally from acquiring public assets through corrupt privatizations.

It would of course be naive to suppose that politicians anywhere are guided solely by the national interest. However, at a minimum, elite values should not condone self-interested behaviour which threatens the collective interest. When exposed, corruption should generate criticism, not a mere shrug of the shoulders.

The third dimension of elite political culture, and one with obvious implications for political stability, is the attitudes which politicians hold to the rules of the game. A range of possibilities exists here. Is elite competition absolute, as in divided countries such as Northern Ireland where gains to one side (Protestant or Catholic) were traditionally viewed as losses by the other? Alternatively, is strong party conflict moderated by agreement on the rules of the competition, as in mainland Britain, thus rendering political stability consistent with vigorous political debate?

The consequences of these attitudes to the political game are highly significant. As an example of unmoderated conflict, consider America's Watergate scandal (1972–73), during which President Nixon's Republican supporters engaged in illegal acts such as break-ins and phone-taps against their Democratic opponents. This unhappy episode reflected the President's own stark view of politics: 'us' against 'them'. Nixon was willing to dispense with the normal rules to ensure that his enemies 'got what they deserved'. In the USA, of course, most politicians do support the rules of the game as set out in the country's constitution. If Nixon's attitudes predominated among America's elite, its democracy would be far less stable.

When party or group leaders are willing to compromise to allow the expression of other interests and values, the prospects for political stability improve. In a classic analysis, Lijphart (1977) suggested that just such an accommodating attitude prevailed among group leaders in divided societies such as Austria and the Netherlands in the 1950s and 1960s. Then, religion still strongly divided these countries, with considerable physical separation between the various communities. In the Netherlands, for example, the Catholics, Protestant and secular communities formed separate subcultures or 'pillars'. The issue was how these pillars could be integrated to form a stable democratic culture.

Crucially, the leaders of each pillar accepted the right of each group to a fair share of state resources. The leaders privately agreed among themselves, and in private, on how to slice the national pie. However, each group then controlled the distribution of its own resources; so that Catholics, for example, might give higher priority to welfare while socialists allocated more money to education. In this way, a culture of accommodation among the elite allowed separate and even hostile communities to live together within the one state. Today, religious divisions have softened but compromise remains a key theme in Dutch political culture.

Elite accommodation as a formula for managing divided but separate communities is still relevant today, particularly in post-conflict situations where distrust between subcultures remains high. For example, the device might have value in Sri Lanka following its long period of fighting between the Sinhalese majority and the minority Tamils. Elite compromise offers a form of informal federalism, casting light on the key issue of how hostile communities can learn to live together even when the foundations are too insecure to support the elaborate architecture of formal federation.

Political socialization

Political socialization is the means by which political culture is transmitted across the generations. It is a universal process. All societies must find a way of passing on the skills needed for people to perform political roles, varying from voting at an election to governing the country. The key point about socialization is that it is largely an uncontrolled and uncontrollable process. No matter how much rulers try, they find themselves unable to dominate either its process or content. By its nature, therefore, socialization serves to replicate the status quo. As a result, political culture becomes a stabilizing force, providing a major barrier against planned change.

> *Definition*
> **Political socialization** is the process through which we learn about politics. It concerns the acquisition of emotions, identities and skills as well as information. Its main dimensions are what people learn (content), when they learn it (timing and sequence) and from whom (agents).

Learning a political culture is very different from acquiring formal knowledge of politics as obtained, say, from this book. Political socialization is a more diffuse, indirect and unplanned process. It involves the development of political emotions and identities (what is my country? my religion? my party?) as well as the acquisition of information. Political socialization takes place through a variety of institutions – the family, peer group and workplace – and is as much influenced by the context of communication as its content. For example, children's attitudes toward politics are influenced by their experience of authority at home and at school at least as much as by the preachings of parents and teachers.

Most studies of political socialization are based on the primacy model. This holds that basic political loyalties are formed when young. Childhood learning is 'deep learning' because it provides a framework for interpreting further information acquired in adulthood. Core political identities are developed in early childhood, when the family is the critical influence on the child. In late childhood, these attachments are supplemented by a marked increase in information. The main effect of adolescence is to refine the child's conceptual understanding, building on information already obtained.

These three stages of socialization – early childhood, late childhood and adolescence – prepare the child for political participation in adult political life (Figure 6.4). Adult experiences modify but rarely transform the outlook secured when young.

Some authors use Asian cultures to illustrate the centrality of childhood to political socialization.

The argument advanced is that strong family traditions encourage a group-centred style of adult politics in which deference to authority places a leading role. For instance, Pye (1985) suggests that

> the cornerstone of powerbuilding in the Asian cultures is loyalty to a collectivity. Out of the need to belong, to submerge one's self in a group identity, is power formed in Asian cultures.

But what is the origin of this need to belong and conform? Pye suggests that the answer lies in the experience of childhood. The Asian child, perhaps more than elsewhere, finds unconditional love and attention from the family. As a result, the child respects and does not question parental authority, leading to similar deference to political rulers later in life. This acceptance of benevolent leadership (or perhaps more accurately a reluctance to express open dissent) is supposedly characteristic of 'Asian democracy'.

Although most research on political socialization has focused on children, we must remember that the process is lifelong; basic political outlooks mature in response to events and experience, and political learning does not stop at childhood's end (Conover and Searing, 1994). Indeed we can contrast the primacy model with an alternative recency model. This is the idea that current information carries more weight just because it is contemporary. What we see on television today matters more than

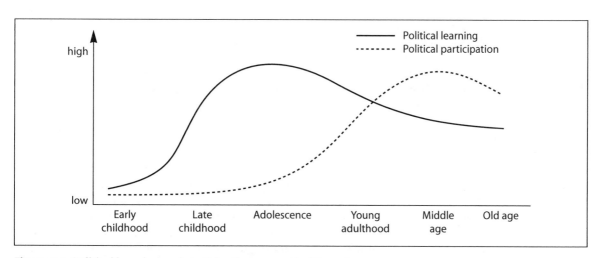

Figure 6.4 Political learning and participation across the life cycle

submerged childhood memories; in other words, adult reality packs more punch than childhood myths. In the eighteenth century, Montesquieu (1748) observed that

> we receive three educations: one from our parents, another from our teachers, and a third from the world. The third contradicts all the first two teach us.

The recency approach undoubtedly carries some plausibility. Adult experiences of such major events as war or depression surely leave their mark, helping to shape the political outlook of a generation. There can be no doubt, for example, that September 11, 2001 coloured the approach of American politicians to subsequent foreign policy decisions, just as the scars of Vietnam discouraged the previous generation of leaders from military adventures. But crises such as 9/11 are exceptional. Routine events come and go but most often they are viewed through – rather than overriding – established perspectives, notably those acquired during childhood.

Islam and the West

To conclude our discussion, we examine the value of political culture in understanding the relationship between Islam and the West. Such a comparison has acquired added significance since 9/11 but also possesses two further advantages. First, it takes us beyond the state towards a more global perspective. Second, the comparison raises the topic of religion, a dimension of culture that we have not so far addressed. To what extent, then, should the current division between the Muslim and the Western worlds be viewed as a conflict of political cultures?

Huntington (1996) is the main proponent of the proposition that the division between Islam and the West is cultural or, to use his term, civilizational. Huntington's view derives from a broader analysis, published before September 11, 2001, in which he suggests that cultures based on civilizations rather than countries will become the leading source of conflict in the twenty-first century.

According to Huntington, the old base of inter-national conflict between the communist Soviet Union and the free market United States is exhausted. But the end of the cold war, he suggests, does not mean the end of cultural divisions. Rather the focus will shift from a battle of ideologies to a clash of civilizations, an irreducible division between the world's major cultures, including Islam and the West (Box 6.1). Since such groupings are supranational, Huntington (1996, p. 20) implies that political culture has escaped its national moorings to embrace wider but still competing identities:

> A civilization-based world order is emerging: societies sharing cultural affinities cooperate with each other; efforts to shift societies from one civilization to another are unsuccessful; and countries group themselves around the lead or core states of their civilization.

Between the contradictory worldviews of these civilizations, suggests Huntington, there is little common ground or room for compromise. As globalization proceeds, interaction and friction will intensify, producing a high potential for conflict. He notes, for example, how cultural kinship influences the choice of sides in recent wars: 'in the Yugoslav conflicts, Russia provided diplomatic support to the Serbs . . . not for reasons of ideology or power politics or economic interest but because of cultural kinship' (1996, p. 28). Huntington is also sceptical of pragmatic efforts to switch civilizations, suggesting that the reason Australia failed to reinvent itself as an Asian country was simply that it's not.

In discussing the specific relationship between Islam and Christianity, Huntington draws on these civilizational themes. The transnational character of civilizations is indeed exemplified by these religions, each of which pre-dates the emergence of states. Thus, in medieval Europe, Christendom stood above kingdoms in the political hierarchy. Similarly, contemporary Muslim countries form an Islamic domain in which a shared religious commitment transcends national divisions.

Although the origins of the conflict between Islam and the West may lie in religion, Huntington argues that the contemporary division is cultural or civilizational rather than religious.

The clash of civilizations?

Huntington defines civilizations as the broadest cultural entities in the world; they are 'cultures writ large'. He divides the world into six or seven major civilizations:

1. Western
2. Japanese
3. Islamic
4. Hindu
5. Slavic–Orthodox
6. Latin American
7. (possibly) African

Such divisions pose special problems for torn countries located on the fault-lines between civilizations. Mexico (situated between the West and Latin America) and Turkey (on the border between the West and Islam) are examples of such split countries.

With the Islamic world falling ever further behind the West in science, technology and wealth, it is no longer the West's Christian foundations, but rather its secular character as exemplified by American materialism, which has become the target of Islamic criticism.

As would be expected for a civilizational divide, differences in socialization underpin and perpetuate these cultural differences. Western education is avowedly secular, allowing schooling to concentrate on scientific knowledge and technical training. But in many Muslim countries, literal instruction in the Koran (Islam's holy text) remains a major theme of education, ill-preparing young people – male as well as female – for the modern world.

The upshot is that Huntington (1996, p. 217) portrays Islam and the West as civilizations locked in permanent and seemingly unavoidable conflict:

The underlying problem of the West is Islam, a different civilization whose people are convinced of the superiority of their culture and are obsessed with the inferiority of their power. The problem for Islam is the West, a different civilization whose people are convinced of the universality of their culture and who believe that their superior,

if declining, power imposes on them the obligation to extend that culture throughout the world.

Although Huntington's analysis is clear and straightforward, its sweeping character also provides its weakness. Indeed, the widespread criticism of his discussion helps to identify the limits of political culture as a tool for political analysis. Huntington's work is pitched at an extremely general level, showing insufficient sensitivity to variations within civilizations. Just as Almond and Verba underplayed subcultures within the countries they surveyed, so Huntington discounts variation within civilizations across space and time.

Stepan (2001, p. 234) is surely closer to the mark when he interprets Islam as 'multivocal', capable of varying its voice across place and time. In similar fashion, Feldman (2000) describes Islam as a 'mobile idea'. Thus, both Turkey and Saudi Arabia are Muslim countries but Turkey's state is secular and largely democratic whereas Saudi Arabia is an authoritarian regime leading a society dominated by a severe form of Islam. The reaction to September 11 confirms Islam's multivocal character: the hijackers undoubtedly drew on one anti-Western dialect within Islam but most Muslims, like most Christians, regarded the attacks as morally unjustified (Saikal, 2003, p. 17).

So, like any other dimension of political culture, such as America's commitment to freedom or the French idea of equality, Islam is a resource which can be used and developed in innumerable ways according to political circumstances to which Huntington devotes insufficient attention. In political analysis, we should avoid an 'essentialist' reading of Islam focused on its inherent characteristics which assumes all believers speak with one voice (Lane and Ersson, 2002, p. 158).

Over time, too, the nature of Islam, and its relationship with the West, has varied. The potential for conflict with the West may be inherent but this potential often remains latent. Saikal (2003, p. 24) writes that 'since the advent of Islam in the early seventh century, relations between its domain and the largely Christian West have been marked by long periods of peaceful coexistence but also by many instances of tension, hostility and mutual recrimination'. As long as civilizations are conceived as static, it is difficult to account for variability in the relationship between them. Huntington's expansive claim that the West's problem is 'not Islamic fundamentalism but Islam' does indeed involve a breathtaking dismissal of entire centuries:

> The causes of this ongoing pattern of conflict [between Island and the West] lie not in transitory phenomena such as twelfth century Christian passion or twentieth century Muslim fundamentalism. They flow from the nature of the two religions and the civilizations based on them.
>
> (Huntington, 1996, p. 210)

Rather than regarding Muslim fundamentalism as 'a transitory phenomenon', we should seek to locate its emergence in the events of the twentieth century, an approach which takes us away from political culture towards more specific themes in political history. Brzezinski's list (2002, p. 18), for instance, would probably be acceptable to many:

> Arab political emotions have been shaped by the region's encounter with French and British colonialism, by the defeat of the Arab effort to prevent the existence of Israel and by the subsequent American support for Israel and its treatment of the Palestinians, as well as by the direct injection of American power into the region.

So political culture (or equivalent terms such as civilization) can only take us so far. Culture identifies the general climate but fails to offer specific forecasts. As Roy (1994, p. viii) observes, 'culture is never directly explanatory and in fact conceals all that is rupture and history: the importation of new types of states, the birth of new social classes and the advent of contemporary ideologies'. By itself, terms such as 'political culture' and 'civilization' are blanket explanations, offering wide coverage but also obscuring the intricate detail underneath.

Key reading

> **Next step:** *Pharr and Putnam (2000) is an important comparative study of political culture in established democracies, focusing on increasing dissatisfaction with the performance of government.*

Norris (1999a) is a useful supplement to Pharr and Putnam while Crothers and Lockhart (2002) is a wide-ranging reader on the concept of political culture. Almond and Verba (1963, 1980) remain a useful starting point; see also Lane and Ersson (2002). For social capital, see Putnam (1993); Putnam (2002) is an interesting comparative attempt to apply the concept beyond the United States. The key source on postmaterialism is Inglehart (1971, 1990, 1997). On political culture in post-communist Europe, Pollack *et al.* (2003) is an extensive, survey-based collection. Haynes (1998) is an accessible introduction to religion and politics; Madeley (2003) is a comprehensive reader on the topic. Huntington (1993, 1996) is the main source on the clash of civilizations but see also more grounded works such as Saikal (2003) or even, perhaps, Lewis (2003).

Chapter 7

Political communication

Society, and with it politics, is created, sustained and modified through communication. Without a continuous exchange of information, attitudes and values, neither society nor politics would be possible. As Williams (1962, p. 11) writes, 'What we call society is not only a network of political and economic arrangements, but also a process of learning and communication.' In similar vein, Habermas (1978) suggests that democracy can best be understood as a form of communication in which citizens inform, educate and become reconciled to each other in the process of reaching collective agreements. For Habermas, as for many others, democracy *is* a form of political communication.

Because communication is central to politics, the ability to control its content, style and flow is a crucial if indirect source of power. The willingness of people to listen to what their leader has to say is perhaps the ruler's most important resource. Getting issues on to the agenda, and keeping them there, is a necessary objective for any politician seeking radical change. The additional ability to frame issues – to determine how they are discussed – adds further influence since, as Foucault (1977) remarks, those who define situations thereby control them.

The main business of politicians is communication; their task is to signal their agendas, policies and strategies to other players of the political game. Indeed, in public affairs words often speak louder than actions. For example, statements by America's Federal Reserve Board and its chairman Alan Greenspan seem to be at least as influential in determining expectations of interest rates in the money market as the Board's decisions on what the current rate should be (Beattie, 2003). The signals are as important as the actions they foreshadow.

Even when politicians do act, their actions convey meanings that transform their behaviour into communication. When President Truman authorized atom bombs to be dropped on Hiroshima and Nagasaki in August 1945 he was also indicating to Japanese opponents his willingness to continue using these new weapons of mass destruction on civilian populations. The Japanese got the message and quickly surrendered. In short, political activity is invariably a form of communication and the analyst's first task is always to interpret ('decode') the message so that its underlying themes ('subtexts') become apparent.

Once the message itself is understood, the traditional 'transmission model' offers a useful guide to research (Figure 7.1). This account interprets communication as consisting of who says what to whom, through which media and with what effects. The model distinguishes five aspects to any communication: a sender (who?), a message (what?), a channel (how?), a receiver (to whom?), and a presumed impact (with what effects?). For example, a local party (the sender) might distribute a leaflet (the channel) advocating voting at a forthcoming election (the message) to its own supporters (the receivers), with the result that turnout increases (impact).

This simple account is often criticized as one-directional – that is, it fails to recognize that most communication involves continuing interaction

Sender $\Rightarrow$ Message $\Rightarrow$ Channel $\Rightarrow$ Receiver $\Rightarrow$ Impact

Figure 7.1 The transmission model of political communication

between the participants. The model also pays limited attention to the multiple meanings embedded in most political communication. Yet despite these weaknesses the transmission model does break down the process of communication into its component parts. In this way, it assists research.

Development of the mass media

To understand contemporary trends in the communications media, we must begin by placing the mass media in a historical context. This task is a political assignment since the expansion of mass communication was intimately linked to the growth of the state, especially in the nineteenth and twentieth centuries. A history of politics must also be, in part, a history of communication.

Two preliminary points should be made. First, the impact of each new medium, from writing through printing to television, has generated more controversy than consensus. The impossibility of isolating pure media effects means there is more sense in asking in what ways, rather than to what extent, specific media have altered politics.

Second, we must beware of technological determinism. Technical advances are rarely the sole explanation of innovations in communication. Typically, new media have emerged in response to a recognized social need. For instance, the telegraph, the telephone and the internet were each consciously developed to improve communication across distance. If communication technologies have transformed the social and political world, it is because society has been in search of change (Williams, 1989).

Table 7.1 outlines the major developments in the history of the media. The first innovation shown there, namely writing, was the most important of all. Ong (1982) argues that the invention of writing in the early civilizations of the Near East in the fifth millennium before Christ changed everything. He suggests that 'by separating the knower from the known', writing permitted the development of abstract concepts, objectivity and the accumulation of detailed knowledge.

Certainly, the long-term political impact of writing has been profound. It permitted the record-keeping which is a foundation of the modern state; without writing, states could not have penetrated society to the extent that they did. Writing also made possible the transmission of both information and values over large distances, as with the spread of Christianity through monasteries and church schools in early Europe (Mann, 1986, p. 335).

However, the bridge to the era of modern communication was provided not by writing itself but rather by Gutenberg's fifteenth-century invention of printing to paper using movable type. This innovation enabled written knowledge to reach a wider market.

Yet it was not so much the invention of writing and printing, but rather the later extension of literacy to the wider population, which marked off the current era of both communication and states. Mass literacy in a common language was central to the successful development of contemporary states, facilitating administration of large areas and encouraging the development of a shared national identity. By the end of the eighteenth century, 'signing literacy' had reached about 80 per cent in innovative Sweden. Other European countries, and New England, achieved mass literacy in the nineteenth century, following the introduction of compulsory primary education. Mass literacy was a function, an achievement and an affirmation of the modern state, just as it remains an aspiration for many countries in the developing world today.

In particular, widespread literacy in a shared language made possible the popularization of newspapers, the key development in political communication during the nineteenth and early twentieth centuries. Originally, newspapers had been small-circulation party journals containing lengthy editorials and dreary reports of politicians' speeches (Dooley and Baron, 2001). But advances in printing (e.g. the steam press) and distribution (e.g. the railway) opened up the prospect of populist and profitable papers funded by advertising. By growing away from their party roots, papers became not just more popular but also, paradoxically, more central to politics.

In compact countries with national distribution, such as Britain and Japan, newspapers built enormous circulations which largely continue to this day. Newspaper owners became powerful political figures. In interwar Britain, for example, four

Table 7.1 The development of communication media

Date	Development
Fifth millennium BC	Writing systems develop in the earliest urban civilizations of the Near East, notably Phoenicia.
About 750 BC	The first modern alphabet, based on sounds rather than symbols, emerges in Greece.
1450 AD	In Mainz, Johannes Gutenberg invents printing with movable metal type. Book production is aided by new techniques for the mass manufacture of paper.
Nineteenth century	Compulsory primary education introduced, and mass literacy achieved, in Western states.
	The telegraph – a way of sending information across wires using electric signals – permits international dissemination of news, decisions and instructions (e.g. by the British empire to its colonies).
Later nineteenth century and early twentieth century	Popular newspapers emerge, often with mass circulation. New railway networks allow national distribution.
1930s	Radio's golden age. For the first time, politicians broadcast directly into electors' homes.
1950s–1960s	Television becomes the most popular, and usually the most trusted medium in Western countries. Election campaigns are soon fought on, and not just reported by, television. Entertainment programmes from the USA are widely exported, contributing to the diffusion of American values.
1970s–1980s	The television audience begins to fragment, with an increase in the number and commercialization of channels; distribution by cable and satellite; and widespread use of video.
1990s	Internet access reaches more affluent and educated groups in Western societies, representing a further opening of international communication. Emergence of mobile telephony.
2000s	The internet reaches the mass population in Western societies. Broadband facilitates distribution of streaming media such as television, films, radio and telephone. Mobile telephony becomes standard in the West but China becomes the world's largest single market for mobile phones.

newspaper barons – Lords Beaverbrook, Rothermere, Camrose and Kemsley – owned newspapers with a total circulation of over 13 million, amounting to one in every two daily papers sold. The press barons were committed to the circulation of their papers more than to the parties they supported; under competitive pressure, they reduced the political coverage in their publications. But they were also willing to use their organs to advocate favoured and often idiosyncratic causes, such as Rothermere's Anti-Waste Campaign. Stanley Baldwin, a prime minister of the time, described these papers as

> engines of propaganda for the constantly changing policies, desires, personal wishes and personal desires of [their owners] . . . What the proprietorships of these papers is aiming at is power and power without responsibility – the prerogative of the harlot throughout the ages.
>
> [Curran and Seaton, 2003, p.64]

For better or worse, control over the means of mass communication had become, as it remains, a major political resource.

Definition

Mass media refers to methods of communication that can reach a large and potentially unlimited number of people simultaneously. Television and newspapers are the most important examples; others are posters, radio, books, magazines and cinema. An email to a friend is personal, not mass, communication, but sending a message to all members of an email list is mass communication.

Although newspapers remain important channels of political communication, in the twentieth century their role was of course supplanted by a new dominant medium: broadcasting. Cinema newsreels, radio and then television enabled communication with the mass public to take place in a new form: spoken rather than written, personal rather than abstract and, on occasion, live rather than reported. Oral communication reasserted itself, though now in a form which could escape the confines of the small group.

Significantly, the two major ideologies founded in the twentieth century – communism and fascism – consciously sought to mobilize popular support through exploiting broadcasting. In these brave new worlds of total and totally controlled communication, mass media would be used to create people with the knowledge and attitudes specified by the political elite. Such visions proved to be fanciful but the broadcast media, like newspapers earlier, did serve as agents of national integration. In most countries, a small number of national channels initially dominated the airwaves, providing a shared experience for a dispersed population of everything from national events to popular entertainment.

The political impact of broadcasting was immediate. Politicians had to acquire new communications techniques. A public speech to a live audience encouraged expansive words and dramatic gestures but a quieter tone was needed for transmission direct to the living room. The task was to converse with the unseen listener and viewer rather than to deliver a speech to a visible audience gathered together in one place. The art was to talk to the millions as though they were individuals.

President Franklin Roosevelt's 'fireside chats', broadcast live by radio to the American population in the 1930s, exemplified this new, informal approach. The impact of Roosevelt's somewhat folksy idiom was undeniable. He talked not so much to the citizens but as a citizen and was rewarded with his country's trust. In this way, broadcasting transformed not just the reach but also the tone of political communication (Barber, 1992).

The media: contemporary trends

In the first decade of the twenty-first century, the three major trends in communications are commercialization, fragmentation and globalization (Box 7.1). The combined political effect of these developments is to reduce national political control over broadcasting, permitting consumers either to choose their own political programming or increasingly to escape from politics altogether. If the mass media performed a nation-building function in the twentieth century, their emerging impact in the new century is to splinter the traditional national audience, fragmenting the shared experience induced by twentieth-century broadcasting and perhaps contributing thereby to declining political participation.

BOX 7.1
Contemporary trends in mass communication

Trend	Definition
Commercialization	The decline of public broadcasting and the rise of for-profit media
Fragmentation	The increased range of channels and an enhanced ability to consume programmes on demand (e.g. videos)
Globalization	Improved access to overseas events and media in the global village

POLITICAL COMMUNICATION 109

Commercialization

Communication is increasingly treated as the important business it has become. The American Federal Communications Commission estimates that worldwide revenues from the mass media exceeded $1 trillion per year by the start of the 1990s; the figure rises each year (Tracey, 1998, p. 8). Commercialization also allows new media moguls, such as Rupert Murdoch, to build transnational broadcasting networks, achieving on a global scale the prominence which the newspaper barons of the nineteenth century had acquired at national level.

In the Americas, Canada excepted, broadcasting had always been commercially led but in Western Europe commercialization has been a disputed political development. The first television stations in Europe had been national and publicly owned. The British Broadcasting Corporation (BBC) was a notable example. Such stations were controlled by public supervisory boards; were funded by a special licence fee; and adopted a public service ethos which aimed to educate and inform, rather than merely to entertain. However in the 1970s and 1980s new commercial channels were introduced and advertising was added to many public stations (though not to the BBC's main channels).

These developments threatened previously cosy links between parties and broadcasters and represented a shift to conceiving the viewer in less political terms, as a consumer rather than a citizen. In this increasingly commercial environment, Tracey (1998) claims that public service broadcasting has become nothing more than 'a corpse on leave from its grave'. Even the BBC has become more commercial, establishing numerous specialist channels and creating one of the world's most successful websites.

In *Rich Media, Poor Democracies*, McChesney (1999) argues that commercialization shrinks the public space in which political issues are discussed. Channels in search of profit will devote little time to serious politics. What coverage there is will be infotainment – information as entertainment. Profit-seeking media have no incentive to supply public goods such as an informed citizenry and a high electoral turnout, traditional concerns of public media. For those who view democracy as a

form of collective debate, engaging most of the citizenry in matters of common concern, media commercialization is a challenge indeed.

Against which, commercial broadcasters can reply that it is preferable to reach a mass audience with limited but stimulating political coverage than it is to offer extensive but dull political programming which, in reality, only reaches the small minority who are already strongly interested in public affairs (Norris, 2000).

Fragmentation

Consumers are increasingly able to watch, listen to and read what they want, rather than what they are given. Long gone are the days when American viewers were restricted to the three large networks (ABC, CBS and NBC) and when British viewers could choose only between the public BBC and the commercial ITV. Distribution of programmes by cable and satellite allows viewers to receive a greater range of content, local and overseas as well as national. The advent of video recorders in the 1980s introduced another distribution channel: the local video store. The internet allows interested citi-

---

Table 7.2 Countries in which a majority of people use the internet, 2002/03

Internet penetration	Countries
70% or higher	Sweden (76%)
60–69%	Hong Kong (67%), Australia (64%), Netherlands (64%), USA (63%), Denmark (60%)
50–59%	Switzerland (59%), UK (58%), South Korea (56%), Singapore (55%), New Zealand (55%), Germany (54%), Canada (53%), Finland (51%), Norway (51%)

Note: The ten countries with the most internet users are, in order, USA, China, Japan, Germany, UK, South Korea, France, Italy, Canada and India.

Source: Data from Internetworldstats at http://www.internetworld-stats.com.

zens to access newspapers, radio and television from anywhere in the world (Table 7.2). Unlicensed pirate stations further complicate the picture (Soley, 1998), as does the emergence of mobile telephones and email as channels of communication. The combined result of these developments is a more splintered audience. During the 1990s, for instance, the audience share of the big three American television networks dropped by a third.

The political implications of this shift from broadcasting to narrowcasting are substantial. The media cease to be agents of national integration. Instead, they function to bring together groups with narrow interests, both within and across countries. Freedom of speech – including the freedom to express racist and sexist views – emerges by default, due to the practical impossibility of regulating the babble of sounds emerging from diverse media and often delivered over the internet. Governments and politicians encounter more difficulty in reaching a mass audience when the audience can defend itself through remote controls and sophisticated video recorders. The electorate becomes harder to reach, forcing political parties to adopt a greater range and sophistication of marketing strategies, including the use of personalized techniques such as direct mail.

In this more fragmented environment, politicians will have to communicate in a manner, and at a time, of the voters' choosing. They will have to continue their migration from television news to higher-rated talkshows. The sound-bite, never unimportant, will become even more vital as politicians learn to articulate their agenda in a 30-second commercial. In short, just as the balance within the media industry has shifted from public service to private profit, so the emphasis within political communication will move from parties to voters. Politicians rode the emergence of broadcasting with considerable success in the twentieth century but they are finding the going tougher in the new millennium.

Globalization

In the global village, the world has been compressed into a television screen. In 1776 the English reaction to the American Declaration of Independence took 50 days to filter back to the United States. In 1950 the British response to the outbreak of the Korean War was broadcast in America in 24 hours. In 2003 British and American viewers watched broadcasts of the Iraq War at the same time. We now take for granted the almost immediate transmission of newsworthy events around the world.

Further, access to mass media is no longer a preserve of the developed world. Around half of the population in developing countries now have access to television; there are already more sets in China than in the USA. Even in poor areas of Indian cities, entrepreneurial 'cable wallahs' have put a single satellite dish on to a roof and then illicitly strung wires round the neighbourhood, charging affordable fees to local residents. Where TV ownership remains low, as in Africa, many villages possess a shared radio (Thomas, 2003). The ability to receive, if not transmit, information is becoming global at a faster rate than is the case for many other goods and services.

Even wars have become, in part, battles of communication. During the conflict in Kosovo in 1999, television stations worldwide were supplied by NATO with video footage of high-tech weapons hitting specified objectives. At the same time, Serbia offered pictures of civilians 'taken out' by missiles destroying wrong targets. In the Iraq war of 2003, reporters were embedded in the coalition's military units, distributing live and occasionally dramatic coverage to viewers throughout the world (Iraq excepted).

The prime impact of the global village has been to encourage more open and informed societies. It is now harder than ever for governments to isolate their populations from international developments. Even communist states found it difficult to jam foreign radio broadcasts aimed at their people. Discussing the collapse of communist states, Eberle (1990, pp. 194–5) claimed that 'the changes in Eastern Europe and the Soviet Union were as much the triumph of communication as the failure of communism'.

Recent technological developments also facilitate underground opposition to authoritarian regimes. A small group with a fax machine and internet access now has the potential to draw the world's attention to political abuses, providing source material for alert journalists. Burma's military

DEBATE
THE POLITICAL SIGNIFICANCE OF THE INTERNET

By the twenty-first century, the internet had become one of the most talked-about communications channels, not just because of its explosive growth but also because it permits the dissemination of any kind of data: images, music, speech, text and video. But what will be the long-term significance of the internet for politics?

The case for

The internet has spread more rapidly than previous innovations such as radio and television (Table 7.3) Already, internet access has become routine in the developed world, at least among the young and better-educated. By 2002/03, a majority of the population in 15 countries had used the internet (Table 7.2).

The internet goes further than any previous medium in overcoming distance, paying scant regard to national boundaries. During the war in Kosovo in 1999, for instance, it was as easy for users to access the views of the Yugoslav, American or British governments – or of all three. Thus the web weakens the hold of states over their populations and fragments political communication, allowing specialized communities to exchange information and ideas in a manner which overwhelms national boundaries.

State censorship will become impractical; national libel laws carry little sway on the internet frontier. If a government wants its economy to benefit from global e-commerce, it must pay the political price of allowing its citizens access to the net. Governments may be unable to tax e-commerce on electronic services offered across borders; the internet will bring about the final triumph of business over politics. And the regulation of the internet itself will remain in the hands of technical committees rather than states, a leading case of governance without governments.

The case against

The long-term political impact of the internet is exaggerated. Users can surf the world, but how many Americans, in particular, will do so, given the predominance of American sites? In any case the sites receiving most hits are those from governments, corporations and institutions which are already best-known. In that sense, the internet is a secondary or reinforcing medium.

Nor can a computer network overcome differences of language; secondary nets for languages other than English are recreating rather than bypassing linguistic divisions. And for all the talk of electronic democracy, official referendums by internet are nowhere to be found. Note, too, that in the past, newspapers, radio and television all improved coverage of far-off affairs but none succeeded in displacing the state; why should the technical act of linking computers together be any different?

Table 7.3 Time taken for new media to reach 50 million households in the USA

Medium	Years
Radio	38
Television	13
Cable	10
Internet	5*

*estimate for 1995–2000.

Source: Data from *Financial Times*, 28 July 2000, citing Morgan Stanley Dean Witter.

Assessment

Firm judgements are premature. The lesson of previous innovations is that projections of their impact proved to be wildly inaccurate. Some people thought radio would change the world; others said the telephone would never catch on. But two points are clear. First, technology does not determine content. The messages which travel round the internet will reflect forces beyond the net itself. Second, access to the internet requires a telecommunications infrastructure which barely exists in many developing countries. At the end of the twentieth century, most people in the world had never made a telephone call, let alone surfed the net, and wireless telephony offered the most immediate prospect for improving interactive communication in developing countries.

Further reading: Hall and Biersteker (2002), Norris (1999b), Sunstein (2001).

rulers, China's communist government and Saudi Arabia's ruling families have all suffered from overseas groups in this way.

Internet communication also allows extremist organizations to communicate beyond national boundaries. Groups seeking suicide bombers can ask for volunteers from across the world. Also, odd links emerge between remarkably disparate groups: for instance, Western anti-Semites and Islamic fundamentalists opposed to Israel. In the era of the internet, neither dictatorial nor democratic governments can control global information flows.

The media in established democracies

The media possess a natural vitality in consolidated democracies, where freedom of expression is legally protected. In this section, we examine the political game played between journalists and politicians in established democracies. We then discuss the distinct character of the two main media, television and newspapers, before turning to the vexed question of the media's impact on voting behaviour.

The media game

The relationship between politicians and journalists is increasingly central to the character of elite politics in modern, communication-rich democracies. Recognizing the influence of the media, governments and parties make enormous efforts to influence coverage. Governing parties, in particular, devote considerable attention to informing, cultivating and seeking to manipulate the journalists whose reports achieve national coverage. The humble government press office, now populated by highly paid spin doctors, has never been more important.

Consider the media game played between government (say, a White House spokesperson) and journalists (say, a White House correspondent). This contest is classically political, mixing shared and competing objectives. The government needs coverage and the media must fill its space, creating a shared interest in news. But the government seeks favourable coverage while journalists are after

a big story, objectives that are rarely consistent since, as every reporter knows, good news rarely makes the headlines. The game is further complicated by competition among journalists themselves, giving the administration leverage it can exploit by placing stories with compliant correspondents.

But as with so many political relationships, the game of government–media relations is repeated each day, allowing long-term norms of acceptable behaviour to develop. A spokesperson who gives out misleading information, or no information at all on a significant topic, will lose credibility. So briefers accept that over the long run it pays to be accurate and even-handed in distributing information; the facts must be correct if rarely complete. Equally, competition among journalists reduces as they learn to hunt as a pack. Correspondents know that their key task is to avoid missing the story that everyone else has. Obtaining exclusives is an optional extra.

Thus, in practice, stable routines develop which reduce the game of government–media relations to a few well-understood ground rules. The outcome is not so much collusion as contained competition; sometimes, not even that. Feeding off each other, journalists and politicians find themselves locked in a permanent if occasionally uncomfortable embrace.

Definition

Spin doctor is a critical term applied to public relations experts working for politicians. The spin doctor's job is to encourage favourable media coverage for a party or its leader. The term derives from the spins applied by baseball pitchers and was first applied to politics in 1977 by the novelist Saul Bellow. Although the phrase itself is new, public relations has always been important in politics. Nor should we overestimate the impact of spin. Indeed, public relations can become counterproductive when it becomes its own story, a problem which afflicted Tony Blair's Labour government in Britain (Bayley, 1998).

Of course, the government invariably has a head start over opposition parties in media presentation. Statements by presidents and prime ministers are always more newsworthy than those made by their political opponents. Journalists have no option but to cover a prime ministerial press release, even if they are fully aware of the party-political motives underlying its timing. Many a prime minister has arranged a prestigious overseas trip in the run-up to an election, keen to exploit the domestic impact of a handshake with the American president. Coverage of opposition parties is inevitably a lower priority for the media (Rudd and Hayward, 2001).

Television and newspapers

In nearly all established democracies, television has become the preeminent mass medium. Television is a visual, credible and easily digested format which reaches almost every household, providing the main source of political information. In election campaigns, for instance, the television studio has become the main site of battle. The party gladiators participate through appearing on interviews, debates and talk shows; merely appearing on television confirms some status and recognition on candidates. Ordinary voters consume the election, if at all, through watching television. Local party activists, once the assault troops of the campaign, have become mere skirmishers. In short, television has ceased to cover the campaign, it has become the campaign.

Of course, the political significance of television goes far beyond elections. Much larger, if still declining, numbers watch the evening newscasts

---

BOX 7.2
Some tests used by journalists to determine newsworthiness

▸ Will the story have a strong impact on our audience?
▸ Does the story involve violence? ('if it bleeds, it leads')
▸ Is the story current and novel?
▸ Does the story involve well-known people?
▸ Is the story relevant to our audience?

Source: Adapted from Graber (1997), pp. 106–8, based on studies in the USA.

---

and it is here, in deciding what to cover and what to leave out, that television exerts most influence (Box 7.2). Through their assumptions about newsworthiness, editors resolve their daily dilemma of reducing a day's worth of world events to less than 30 minutes on the evening news.

Because news programmes focus on the exceptional, their content is invariably an unrepresentative sample of events. For example, policy fiascos receive more attention than policy successes. Similarly, corruption is a story but integrity is not. Necessarily, television is a distorting mirror on the world. The more compressed news coverage becomes, the less accurate the TV lens must be.

Despite the primacy of television, it would be wrong to discount the political significance of the second mass medium, newspapers. Even today, quality newspapers possess an authority springing from their longevity. More important, perhaps, the press remain free of the tight regulation still applied to national broadcasters. In nearly all democracies, newspapers are freer with comment than is television. In an age when broadcasters dominate the provision of instant news, the more relaxed daily schedule of the press allows print columnists to offer interpretation and evaluation.

Television tells us what happened; at their best, newspapers can place events in context. Broadcast news can only cover one story at a time whereas newspapers can be scanned for items of interest and can be read at the user's convenience. Newspapers offer a luxury which television can rarely afford: space for reflection. For such reasons, quality newspapers remain the trade press of politics, read avidly by politicians themselves.

In many if not all democracies, newspaper circulations remain large. In Japan, Britain and Scandinavia, most adults still read a daily newspaper. In Japan, unusually, the public still relies more on the national press than on television for its information and some studies there indicate that Japanese newspapers exert more influence over the electorate's agenda (Feldman, 1993, p. 24).

In Britain and Scandinavia, newspapers retain at least some loyalties to the parties from which they originally emerged. When a national British paper switches its party support, as the best-selling *Sun* did to Labour in 1997, the shift commands attention elsewhere in the media, illustrating how newspapers remain significant political players in their own right.

Furthermore, newspapers also influence television's agenda: a story appearing on TV's evening news often begins life in the morning paper. And when an elector sees a story covered both on television and in the press, the combined impact exceeds that of either medium considered alone. In countries with a lively press tradition, newspapers retain a political significance greatly in excess of their circulation.

Reinforcement, agenda-setting and framing

What is the media's impact on those exposed to it? By virtue of its general nature, this question remains without an agreed answer. Even so, it is worthwhile examining how scholars have thought about media effects and the mechanisms through which such effects are achieved.

In the 1950s, before television became preeminent, the reinforcement thesis held sway (Klapper, 1960). The argument here was that party loyalties were transmitted through the family and that, once developed, such identities acted as a political

sunscreen protecting people from the harmful effects of propaganda (Box 7.3). People saw what they wanted to see and remembered what they wanted to recall. In Britain, for example, many Labour supporters read left-wing papers while most Conservatives bought a paper close to their own outlook. Given such self-selection, the most the press could do was to reinforce their readers' existing dispositions.

The reinforcement theory proved its value half a century ago and even today many studies of media impact find only limited effects (Gavin and Sanders, 2003). Even so, reinforcement is surely too limited as an account of media effects today. Party loyalties are now weaker, and television more pervasive, than in the 1950s. For this reason, the agenda-setting view of media impact has gained ground.

The agenda-setting perspective contends that the media (and television in particular) influence what we think about, though not necessarily what we think. The media write certain items on to the agenda and by implication they keep other issues out of the public's gaze. As Lazarsfeld and Merton (1948) put the point, 'to the extent that the mass media have influenced their audiences, it has stemmed not only from what is said but more significantly from what is not said'.

BOX 7.3
Media effects: reinforcement, agenda-setting and framing

Concept	Definition	Comment
Reinforcement	The media strengthen existing opinions	People read newspapers which support their existing outlook (selective exposure). In addition, people interpret information to render it consistent with their opinions (selective interpretation) and forget information that runs counter to their beliefs (selective recall)
Agenda-setting	The media influence what we think and talk about	The compressed nature of television news means its coverage is highly selective. Reported events are widely discussed by the public but non-reported events lose all visibility
Framing	How an event is narrated as a coherent story highlights particular features of it	A frame focuses on particular aspects of a problem, its origins, remedies and evaluation. It encourages viewers and readers to portray the topic in a similar way

In an election campaign, for example, television directs our attention to the candidates and to the race for victory; by contrast, the issues are often of secondary concern. Walter Lippman's (1922) view of the press is applicable to the media generally: 'it is like a beam of a searchlight that moves restlessly about, bringing one episode and then another out of the darkness and into vision'.

The frame of a story – the way in which reports construct a coherent narrative about the events – can also make a difference, especially when repeated. Are immigrants presented as a stimulus to the economy or as a threat to society? Is a war portrayed critically (Vietnam in its later stages) or positively (Iraq in the invasion phase)? Is a convicted criminal confronting the death penalty facing his just deserts or cruel and unusual punishment? As the concept of a 'story' suggests, the journalist must translate the event covered into an organized narrative which connects with the viewer or reader (Entman, 1993).

So the journalist's words, as much as the camera operator's images, help to frame the story, providing a narrative which encourages a particular reaction from the viewer. In turn, the frame may exert a priming effect, encouraging the viewer to articulate opinions which might otherwise have gone unexpressed (Norris *et al.*, 2003).

The media in new democracies

An assessment of the position of the media in new democracies depends heavily on the point of comparison. When we draw a contrast with the preceding regime, media independence seems to be a hallmark of the new order. As communist and military rulers depart, so censorship gives way to a multitude of new publications, peddling everything from news to pornography. Old people are bemused, just as the young are amused, but everyone can see that the climate has changed. Indeed, an increasing spirit of media adventure is one of the first cracks to appear in pre-democratic structures; journalists are quick to sense their opportunity when authoritarian rule begins to crumble.

Yet even after several years in a new democracy, the position of the media usually remains weaker than in established democracies. Judged by the standards of most consolidated democracies, media autonomy remains limited. Governing parties continue to exert influence over broadcasting media while political entrepreneurs use ownership of newspapers to maximize their influence. Far from becoming the fourth estate, the media in many new democracies are pawns in a political game played above their heads.

Russia is an example of a post-communist semi-democracy where pressures on the media, from powerful business people as well as politicians, remain intense. This influence derives precisely from the centrality of television to political communication in Russia. As in many poor countries, broadcasting is the main way of reaching a large, dispersed and impoverished population for whom free television has more appeal than paid-for papers. The television audience in Russia for nightly news programmes is substantial indeed, matching that in the United States for the Super Bowl (Zassoursky, 2002).

For good reason, then, Moscow's power-holders compete intensely for control of a pluralistic, but far from independent, television system. In this ruthless game, politicians in government still hold the upper hand. Over 100 laws refer to the mass media, giving rulers legal scope to close down any particular channel they deem to be unfriendly. And the public television stations – ORT and RTR – still experience direct political interference.

But in contrast to the communist period, the Russian government no longer monopolizes the media. Politicians on the make will seek to acquire their own newspapers and broadcast channels and then to exploit them in building their political base. The leading Russian banks also own many private television stations, which dutifully propagate their masters' interests.

In such a context, self-censorship – the voice in the editor's head which asks 'am I taking a risk in publishing this story?' – remains rife. The Russian experience demonstrates that lack of direct government control does not guarantee freedom for the media; indeed, Russia comes close to the bottom in expert rankings of press freedom (Table 7.4). Vladimir Putin's success in the presidential election of 2000 owed much to his control of public television, whose news broadcasts in the final days

Table 7.4 Countries ranked by press freedom, 2001/02

Top 13:

1=	Finland, Iceland, Netherlands, Norway
5	Canada
6	Ireland
7=	Denmark, Germany, Portugal, Sweden
11	France
12=	Australia, Belgium

Selected others:

17	USA
21	UK
26	Japan
39	South Korea
54	Brazil
76	Mexico
99	Turkey
121	Russia
125	Saudi Arabia
138	China

Note: Based on a survey of 139 countries using national experts. The criteria of press freedom include a supportive legal environment, no attacks on journalists and media organizations, and the possibility of redress when such assaults occur. The USA is ranked only 17th mainly because journalists who refuse to reveal their sources can be prosecuted.

Source: Data from Reporters without Borders at http://www.rsf.fr.

of the campaign portrayed his opponents as sympathetic to gays and Jews. However, even the president was unable to suppress the surge of media criticism that followed an explosion abroad a Russian submarine, with the loss of all 118 lives on board, a few months later. While Putin's election demonstrates beyond doubt that the Russian media are subject to political influence that can alter election outcomes, the *Kursk* disaster showed that such control is markedly less complete than in the communist period.

In post-communist Europe, journalistic standards remain low, reflecting decades in which reporters appointed by the communist party just reproduced party platitudes. Easy editorializing still takes priority over the hard graft of news-gathering. There is little tradition of media scrutiny of rulers to carry over from the pre-communist era. In some countries, media freedom amounts to little more than an opportunity for journalists to bribe public figures. In impoverished Romania, for instance, newspapers threaten unfavourable coverage of politicians unless they are paid hush money.

Entrenching the freedom of the media to investigate and criticize public conduct is inevitably a gradual affair in new democracies, requiring government restraint, media professionalism and independent courts. Despite a rhetorical commitment to free speech, the impulse of many leaders is still to manipulate and even control (Milton, 2000).

Public opinion

Especially in democracies, politics is a battle for influence over the important but imprecise terrain of public opinion. Governments, parties and interest groups jostle to influence public opinion, seeking to persuade the public to adopt their agenda, their frame of reference and their policy preferences. Yet the notion of public opinion itself remains somewhat opaque. One approach is highly pragmatic: public opinion is simply what the public thinks about a given issue, nothing more and nothing less. This down-to-earth view was reflected in the definition offered by Sir Robert Peel, twice prime minister of Britain in the nineteenth century. He referred to public opinion as 'that great compound of folly, weakness, prejudice, wrong feeling, right feeling, obstinacy and newspaper paragraphs' (Green, 1994, p. 213).

A second view of public opinion is more ambitious, linking the idea of a 'public' to the views of an informed community which shares basic political principles. Lippman (1922) illustrates this more refined approach. He writes that 'a body of men are politically capable of public opinion only so far as they are agreed upon the ends and aims of government and upon the principles by which those ends shall be attained'. Here public opinion is interpreted as the considered will of a cohesive group. This perspective derives from the model of a self-governing republic and treats public opinion as far more than an opinion poll finding. Rather, public opinion acquires moral weight and any minorities within the wider community should normally accept the public's verdict.

Definition
Public opinion can simply refer to (1) 'the range of views on some controversial issue held by some significant portion of the population' (Qualter, 1991). More ambitiously, the term can denote (2) the informed judgement of a community on an issue of common concern, where that judgement is formed in the context of shared political goals.

In democracies, public opinion extends to virtually the entire adult population. Nearly all adults can vote, their views are represented in frequent opinion polls and politicians facing reelection have an incentive to study the findings. Even in democracies, however, a minority underclass exists which rarely votes, lives in no-go areas for pollsters and does not follow politics at all. In authoritarian regimes, of course, national politics engages far fewer people and public opinion shrinks.

Given that public opinion is an important element of democratic politics, how exactly does it exert its influence? In a sense public opinion pervades all policy-making. It forms the environment within which politicians work. Thus public opinion sits in on many government meetings even though it is never minuted as a member. In such discussions public opinion usually performs one of two roles, acting either as a prompt or as a veto. 'Public opinion demands we do something about traffic congestion' is an example of the former; 'public opinion would never accept restrictions on car use' illustrates the latter. So as Qualter (1991, p. 511) writes, 'while public opinion does not govern, it may set limits on what governments do'.

Yet public opinion is never all-powerful, even in liberal democracies. Four factors limit its influence:

▶ The impact of public opinion declines as issues become more detailed. Voters are concerned with goals rather than means; with objectives rather than policies. 'What policies politicians follow is their business; what they accomplish is the voters' business' (Fiorina, 1981). A few important objectives preoccupy the public but most policies are routine and uncontroversial. In detailed policy-making, expert and organized

opinion matters more than public opinion.
▶ The public is often ill-informed, and this, too, limits its impact. Most Americans, for example, are unable to name their members of Congress. Similar findings from other democracies confirm the ignorance of large sections of the public, especially on remote issues involving foreign policy. Limited knowledge is another reason why public opinion functions more often, and more appropriately, as an agenda-setter than as a policy-maker.
▶ Public opinion can evade trade-offs but governments cannot (though they sometimes try). The public may want both lower taxes and increased public spending but rulers must make a choice. Further, the risks associated with a policy are poorly assessed by the public but require close attention from decision-makers (Weissberg, 2002).
▶ Politicians respond to their perceptions of public opinion but these interpretations can be inaccurate, derived as they are from the distorting lens of interest groups and the selective telescope of the media. Politicians typically respond to mobilized opinion rather than to public opinion (Herbst, 1998).

So even in the most democratic of countries, government by public opinion remains a distant dream or nightmare. Even so, the idea of public opinion has gained further currency as opinion polls, citizen juries and focus groups have developed to study it. Indeed there are few areas in politics where a concept is so closely linked to how it is measured. In modern democracies, public opinion is both measured by, and partly composed of, reports of investigations into its content (Box 7.4).

Consider opinion polls, and sample surveys, the most accurate method of identifying what people profess. Although the public itself remains resolutely sceptical of samples, their accuracy is now well-attested, at least in predicting election outcomes. In the United States, the average error in predicting the major parties' share of the vote at postwar national elections has been around 1.5 per cent. This accuracy is impressive even if not always sufficient for the television networks to pick the right winner on election night. Precision is similar in other democracies. Counter-intuitive it may be,

BOX 7.4
Measuring public opinion

▸ An **opinion poll** is a series of questions asked in a standard way of a systematic sample of the population. The term usually refers to short surveys on topical issues for the media. Polls are usually conducted face to face or by telephone (Mann and Orren, 1992).

▸ A **sample survey** is conducted using similar methods as opinion polls but involves a more detailed questionnaire, often conducted for government or for academic researchers (Broughton, 1995).

▸ In a **deliberative opinion poll**, or **citizens' jury**, people are briefed by, and can question, experts and politicians on a given topic before opinions are measured. The technique seeks to measure what public opinion would be if the public were fully informed on the issue (Fishkin, 1991).

▸ A **focus group** is a moderated discussion among a small group of respondents on a particular topic. A focus group is a qualitative device used to explore the thinking and emotions lying behind people's attitudes. It is an open-ended technique that has found favour with party strategists (Greenbaum, 1998).

but 1,000 people carefully selected for an opinion poll can accurately represent the whole population.

A well-chosen sample will certainly provide a more reliable guide to public opinion than the self-selected readers who answer write-in polls in magazines; the listeners who call radio discussion shows; or the voters who contact their representative about their pet topic. In fact, a major virtue of opinion polls is that they capture the views of the many bored and uninterested electors who would otherwise be left out of the debate.

Opinion polls contribute to the democratic process in three ways. First, they bring into the public realm the voices of people who would otherwise go unheard. They are the only form of participation, apart from the ballot box itself, in which all count for one and none for more than one. Second, polls are based on direct contact between interviewers and the public; they get behind the group leaders who claim to speak 'on

behalf of our members'. Third, polls enable politicians to keep in touch with the popular mood and they give some insight into the reasons for election results. In these ways, opinion polls oil the wheels of democracy.

Yet it would be wrong to overstate the value of opinion polls in defining the 'mood of the people'. Like students taking a test, interviewees in a survey are answering questions set elsewhere. Polls are commissioned not by ordinary people but by party officials and journalists in the capital city. As a result, people may never have thought about a topic before they are invited to answer questions on it. They may give an opinion when they have none or they may agree to a statement because it is the easiest thing to do ('yea-saying').

For these reasons, Ginsberg (1986) suggests that elites use polls to 'pacify or domesticate opinion' by reducing citizens to passive respondents who voice opinions in response to a narrow range of topics selected by the elite itself. Certainly, one danger of opinion polls is that they construct, and even shape, public opinion at the same time as they measure it.

Because opinion polls do not give respondents a chance to discuss the issue before expressing their views, the technique is criticized by those who favour more ambitious interpretations of public opinion. When public opinion is defined as community judgement of an issue against the standard of the common interest, opinion polls are found wanting. Where, ask the critics, is the equivalent of the vigorous debate which preceded the moment of decision in the Athenian assembly? To be useful, it is argued, public opinion must have been shaped in the press of collective discussion, not simply measured through individual questionnaires.

Building on this richer view of public opinion, scholars have developed the idea of a deliberative opinion poll or citizen jury (Fishkin, 1991). This technique involves exposing a smaller sample of electors to a range of viewpoints on a selected topic, perhaps through presentations by experts and politicians. With awareness of the problem established in this way, the group proceeds to a discussion and a judgement. Opinion is only measured when the issues have been thoroughly aired. As Fishkin (1991, p. 1) explains, an ordinary opinion poll models what the public thinks, given how little it knows. A deliberative opinion poll models what the public would think, if it had a more adequate chance to think about the questions at issue.

Deliberative polling can therefore be used to anticipate how opinion might develop on new issues. It is also particularly useful on issues with a large technical content, for example nuclear energy or genetic testing. Though not widely used, citizens' juries are an ingenious attempt to overcome the problem of ill-informed replies which bedevils conventional opinion polls.

A focus group, finally, is similar in some ways to a deliberative poll. In a focus group, a researcher gathers together a small group of people – normally eight to ten – for a general discussion of a topic in which they share an interest. Examples might include lapsed Democrats, young nonvoters or college drop-outs. The idea is to explore the perspectives through which the participants view the issue, sometimes for its own sake and sometimes in preparation for drafting a questionnaire on the same topic.

The advantage of a focus group is that it stimulates those involved to react to each other's thoughts, thus providing richer information than can be obtained through opinion polls and sample surveys. But the findings are qualitative rather than quantitative and may be unrepresentative of the wider population (Greenbaum, 1998).

The media in authoritarian states

If democracy thrives on the flow of information, authoritarian rulers survive by limiting free expression, leading to journalism which is subdued even when it is not subservient. Far from acting as the fourth estate, casting its searchlight into the darker corners of government activity, the media in authoritarian states defer to political power. Lack of resources within the media sector usually increases vulnerability to pressure. Official television stations and subsidized newspapers reproduce the regime's line while critical journalists are harassed and the entire media sector develops an instinct for self-preservation through self-censorship.

In her study of sub-Saharan Africa before the wave of liberalization in the 1990s, Bourgault (1995, p. 180) identified several means used by authoritarian leaders to limit independent journalism. These included:

▶ broad libel laws
▶ states of emergency
▶ licensing of publications and journalists
▶ heavy taxation of printing equipment
▶ a requirement to post bonds before new publications can launch
▶ restricted access to newsprint
▶ the threat of losing government advertising

Sub-Saharan Africa also demonstrates the lack of resources which holds back the development of the media sector – and authoritarian states are most often found in relatively poor countries. A shortage of resources limits journalistic initiative and increases vulnerability to pressure; impoverished journalists may even be reduced to publishing favourable stories in exchange for money.

Pressures from authoritarian leaders on the media are by no means restricted to Africa. In post-communist central Asia, journalists continue to practise the delicate art of coexisting with non-democratic rulers. Large parts of the media, including news agencies and printing presses, often remain in state hands, giving the authorities direct leverage. The state also typically retains ownership of a leading television channel. Foley (1999) reports that

from Kazakhstan to Kyrgyzstan and Tajikistan to Belarus and Ukraine, the story is a dismal one: tax laws are used for financial harassment; a body of laws forbids insults of those in high places; compulsory registration of the media is common. In Azerbaijan, as in Belarus, one-man rule leaves little room for press freedom.

The justification for restricting the freedom of the media typically refers to an overriding national need such as social stability, nation-building or economic development. A free press, like a competitive party system, is presented as a recipe for squabbling and disharmony. Many of these 'justifications' for controlling the media may just be excuses for continuing non-democratic rule. Even so, we should not assume that the Western idea of a free press has universal appeal. Islamic states, in particular, stress the media's role in affirming religious values and social norms. A free press is seen as an excuse for licence; why, the question is asked, should we import Western, and particularly American, ideas of freedom if the result is just scandal-mongering and pornography? In some Muslim societies, the result is what Mernissi (1993, p. 68) terms 'TV Islam', a strange brew of dull religious programming and inoffensive American movies.

As with other aspects of politics, totalitarian states developed a rather more sophisticated approach to their dominance of the media. Mass communication was expected to play its part in the transformation of political culture. The media were therefore brought under tighter control than in authoritarian systems. Unrelenting penetration of mass communication into everyday life was a core component of the totalitarian system. 'It is the absolute right of the state to supervise the formation of public opinion', said Joseph Goebbels, Hitler's Minister of Propaganda.

It is significant however that neither communist nor fascist regimes regarded the media, by themselves, as a sufficient means of ideological control. Communist states supplemented mass propaganda with direct agitation in places where people gathered together; fascist regimes valued direct control through public meetings rather than impersonal broadcasts through the media.

In communist states, the dual dimensions of political communication were propaganda and agitation. Propaganda explained the party's mission and instructed both the elite and the masses in the teachings of Marx, Engels and Lenin. To achieve their propaganda objectives, ruling communist parties developed an elaborate media network with radio, posters, cinema and television all reinforcing each other. Even art had to become 'socialist art', playing its part in the revolution of hearts and minds. Communist societies were short of many things but propaganda was not one of them.

Where propaganda operated through the media, agitation operated at local level. Agitation sought to mobilize the masses behind specific policies such as increased production. The party sought to place an agitator in each factory, farm and military unit. Together, propaganda and agitation dominated the flow of information; their combined effect would be all the greater because, in the nature of a total regime, no dissenting voices were permitted.

> *Definition*
> **Propaganda** is communication intended to promote a particular cause by changing attitudes and behaviour; today, the term also implies the absence of a balanced perspective. The word is religious in origin: in the seventeenth century, the Catholic Church established a College of Propaganda to propagate the faith. Propaganda was an important feature of communication in totalitarian regimes but it has also been important to democracies in times of war.

The communist experience offers an important real-life experiment of the attempt to use the media as a tool for influencing the public. What, then, was the impact of such propaganda? It seems to have helped with agenda-setting by disguising local problems such as accidents, poverty or pollution which could be hidden from people in other parts of the country. It may also have scored some success in highlighting achievements such as industrialization. And, just as advertising by parties in democracies is often aimed at their own activists, so communist propaganda may have helped party members to keep the faith.

But the communist experience also revealed the limits of media power. A cynical public was not easily fooled. Grandiose statements about national progress were too often contradicted by the grim realities of daily life under communism. While official reports on Western cities showed images of drunks and beggars in shop doorways, the viewers would gawp at the unimaginable luxuries on display in the shop windows.

In any case, as communist states became inert, so propaganda became empty ritual. Eventually, the main function of propaganda became that of showing the population that the party still ruled; whether the propaganda was convincing almost ceased to matter. Propaganda became less a mechanism of conversion and more a symbol of

---

BOX 7.5
Limiting the damage: China and the internet

As an example of how authoritarian governments seek to limit media freedom, consider the following rules introduced by the Chinese government in 2000 to regulate internet content providers. Website providers in China are required:

▶ to obtain government approval before cooperating with businesses overseas
▶ to avoid content that subverts state power or harms the country's reputation
▶ to avoid content that supports banned cults
▶ to record the content of their site
▶ to record all website visitors for 60 days
▶ to hand over records to the police on demand.

Even so, internet access is expanding rapidly in China, allowing a sophisticated minority to circumvent the party's attempt to restrict full information to its own elite.

Source: Adapted from *Financial Times*, 3 October 2000.

---

of language. Although the regime is keen to promote e-commerce, internet users who search for 'inappropriate' topics such as democracy or Tibetan independence will find their access to search engines withdrawn. The excuse offered is that the authorities are merely protecting Chinese people from unwholesome Western influence.

Key reading

Next step: *Norris (2000) offers an interesting comparative account of the media's role in Western democracies.*

Communication may be central to politics but the definitive contemporary treatment of the topic is still to be written. Williams's short but influential study (1962) is still relevant to students of politics. Mann's history of power (1986) includes considerable material on communication. However, most modern studies focus on the media rather than communication generally. Gunther and Mughan (2000) offer a comparative collection; see also Bennett and Entman (2001) and Street (2001). On the USA, Graber (1997) is an authoritative text while Barber (1992) provides a lucid history. Norris *et al.* (2003) compare the frames used in media coverage of 9/11 with earlier terrorist incidents. On public opinion, Glynn *et al.* (1998) is a wide-ranging collection while Manza *et al.* (2002) examine the impact of polls on policy. Fishkin (1991) looks at citizen juries. Away from the West, McCargo (2002) examines the media in Asia and Bourgault (1995) discusses sub-Saharan Africa. Milton (2000) is an overview of the media in post-communist states.

control. Like the drizzle, nothing could be done about it so it was ignored.

It is noteworthy, however, that the remaining states with a nominal communist allegiance have kept close control over the means of mass communication. In China, access to information has traditionally been provided on a need-to-know basis. The country's rulers remain keen to limit dissenting voices even as the party's tolerance of non-political debate increases (Box 7.5). For instance, critics refer to the Great Firewall of China, a phrase that describes the state's attempts to control internet use beyond the natural barrier

Chapter 8

Political participation

An environmentalist lying in front of workers constructing a new road, a citizen contacting a legislator about a missing social security cheque, a terrorist plotting a suicidal assault on a despised regime – all are examples of individual participation in politics. This chapter examines general citizen involvement in politics; we reserve participation through elections for the next chapter.

Patterns of participation differ greatly between democratic and authoritarian governments (Box 8.1). In established democracies, voluntary participation is the norm. People can choose whether to get involved (for example by voting or abstaining) and how to do so (for example by joining a party or signing petitions). The main exception to the voluntary nature of participation is compulsory voting, found in a few democracies such as Australia and Belgium.

In authoritarian regimes, by contrast, participation is diminished in quality if not quantity. Most non-democratic rulers hang a 'keep out' sign over the political sphere, often limiting formal participation by ordinary people to rigged elections. Only in totalitarian regimes did non-democratic rulers seek to mobilize the people behind the regime's effort to transform society, whether towards a communist or fascist ideal.

In this chapter, we examine political participation in democratic and non-democratic settings before turning to the less orthodox forms of participation represented by violence, terror and revolution.

Participation in established democracies

The most striking fact about political participation in established democracies is how far it falls short of a participatory ideal. Voting in national elec-

---

BOX 8.1
Patterns of political participation, by type of regime

Regime type	Amount of participation	Character of participation	Purpose of participation
Democratic	Moderate but declining	Mainly voluntary	To influence who decides and what decisions are reached
Authoritarian	Low	Manipulated	To protect rulers' power and to offer a democratic façade
Totalitarian	High	Regimented	*In theory:* to transform society *In practice:* to demonstrate rulers' power

tions is normally the only activity in which a majority of citizens engages. Throughout the democratic world anything beyond voting is the preserve of a minority of activists. These participants are outnumbered by the apathetics: people who neither vote nor even follow politics through the media. With turnout and party membership falling in most democracies, even the traditional activists seem to be reducing their involvement in formal politics (Mair and van Biezen, 2001).

In a renowned analysis, Milbrath and Goel (1977, p. 11) divided the American population into three groups, a classification which has since been applied to participation in other democracies. These categories were:

- a few *gladiators* (around 5–7 per cent of the population) who fight the political battle
- a large group of *spectators* (about 60 per cent) who watch the contest but rarely participate beyond voting
- a substantial number of *apathetics* (about one-third) who are withdrawn from politics.

Milbrath's labels were based on an analogy with Roman contests at which a few gladiators performed for the mass of spectators but some apathetics did not even watch the show (Figure 8.1).

> **Definition**
> **Political participation** is activity by individuals formally intended to influence who governs or the decisions taken by those who do so. Citizens can be classified both by the extent of their political involvement (e.g. gladiators, spectators and apathetics) and by the form their engagement takes (e.g. conventional, unconventional or both).

In every country, political gladiators are far from a cross-section of society. In most democracies, participation is greatest among well-educated, middle-class, middle-aged white men. Furthermore the highest layers of political involvement show the greatest skew. As Putnam (1976, p. 33) put it,

The 'law of increasing disproportion' seems to apply to nearly every political system; no matter how we measure political and social status, the higher the level of political authority, the greater the representation for high-status social groups.

What explains this bias in participation towards upper social groups? Two factors seem to be particularly influential: political resources and political interest.

Consider, first, the question of resources. People in high-status groups are equipped with such political assets as education, money, status and communication skills. Education gives access to information and, we trust, strengthens the ability to interpret it. Money buys the luxury of time for political activity. High status provides the opportunity to obtain a respectful hearing. And communication skills such as the ability to speak in public help in presenting one's views persuasively. Added together, these resources provide a tool-kit for effective political intervention.

Second, high-status individuals are more likely to be interested in politics. They possess the motive as well as the means to become involved. No longer preoccupied with the daily struggle, they can take satisfaction from engagement in collective activity (Inglehart, 1997). The wealthy are also more likely to be brought up in a family, and to attend a school, where an interest in current affairs is encouraged. So upper social groups show an interest in politics and can afford to put these concerns into practice.

We can apply this dual framework – of political resources and political interest – to the problem of why women are still under-represented at higher political levels. In 2000, women made up just 14 per cent of the world's legislators, double the

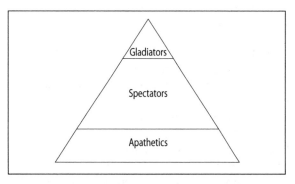

Figure 8.1 Patterns of participation in democracies

figure 25 years earlier but a large under-representation (Table 8.1). There is no doubt that, as a group, women still possess fewer political resources than men. Across the world, they have less formal education (even though this difference has reversed among the young in many established democracies). Further, interest in formal politics is sometimes limited by childbearing and home-making responsibilities.

In addition to these underlying factors, male preeminence in politics tends to be self-perpetuating. Some women lack the confidence needed to throw themselves into the hurly-burly of formal, male-led politics while many still face the high hurdle of discrimination from sexist male politicians. These gatekeepers claim that women are unsuited to politics – and then use the scarcity of women in high office to prove their point (Burns *et al.*, 2001).

Institutional factors, some of which are rather easy to modify, also help to explain female under-representation. Three such features are:

▸ *The electoral system.* Women do best under the party list version of proportional representation, a method that allows party officials to select a gender-balanced set of candidates. Scandinavia is a prominent example (Table 8.1).
▸ *Quotas.* These ensure women make up a specified proportion of a party's candidates or, more radically, of its elected representatives. In Norway, for example, the leading parties introduced quotas as early as 1973.
▸ *Turnover of legislators.* Low turnover, as in the United States Congress, creates a recruitment bottleneck which enables men, once elected, to remain in post for decades.

Definition
Political exclusion refers to those people who are effectively excluded from participation in collective decision-making because they occupy a marginal position in society. Migrant workers, prisoners, drug addicts and those who do not speak the native language are examples of groups confronting this difficulty.

The emphasis of research on political participation is on explaining what distinguishes the gladia-tors from the spectators. But what about the apathetics, the people who do not participate at all? This group raises the emerging problem of political exclusion. The apathetics in effect exclude themselves – or perhaps are excluded – from the normal means by which citizens collectively shape their society (Verba *et al.*, 1995).

A typical non-participant might be an unemployed young man with no qualifications, inhabiting a high-crime inner-city neighbourhood, often from a minority culture and perhaps not even speaking the dominant language. Usually such people are not registered to vote, often they do not watch the news on television and rarely do they read a national newspaper. Their political activity, if any, is often irregular and spasmodic, as with riots.

Just as higher social groups possess both the resources and the interest to overparticipate, so a shortage of resources and lack of interest in the remote goings-on of national politics explain the underparticipation of those near the bottom of increasingly unequal Western societies. The emergence of a two-tier political system, characterized by a majority which votes at national elections and a non-participating underclass, is a growing challenge to the assumption of political equality on which democracy is based.

Participation in new democracies

The participation challenge facing new democracies is considerable. The transition from authoritarian rule requires the population to learn new styles of political participation: votes must be cast, parties organized and leaders recruited to political office. Cynicism must give way to a measure of engagement. Creating democratic institutions is a short-term constitutional task but embedding the habit of voluntary participation is a long-term necessity.

Consider, for example, post-communist democracies. The old style of regimented participation quickly disintegrated as communism fell apart, partly in response to dramatic street protests in the capital cities. Once new and nominally democratic institutions had been created, the task was to consolidate the new order by developing structured

Table 8.1 Female representation in national legislatures, 1950s–2000s

	Year of female suffrage	Current electoral system*	Female representation in the legislature (%)#		Change (most recent election minus 1950s average)
			Average in the 1950s	Most recent election	
Sweden	1919	List PR	12	45	+33
Denmark	1915	List PR	8	38	+30
Finland	1906	List PR	13	38	+25
Netherlands	1919	List PR	8	37	+29
Norway	1913	List PR	5	36	+31
Germany	1918	Mixed	8	32	+24
New Zealand	1893	Mixed	4	28	+24
Australia	1902	AV	0.2	25	+25
Canada	1917	Plurality	1	21	+20
United Kingdom	1918	Plurality	3	18	+15
USA	1920	Plurality	3	14	+11
Ireland	1918	STV	3	13	+10
France	1944	Majority	4	12	+8
Italy	1945	Mixed	6	12	+6

* For definitions of electoral systems, see p. 148 (AV, alternative vote; PR, proportional representation; STV, single transferable vote).

\# In bicameral assemblies, figures are for the lower house. The most recent election is as at 2003 .

Sources: Inter-Parliamentary Union (2000), http://www.ipu.org; McAllister and Studlar (2002).

forms of voluntary participation through parties, elections and interest groups.

This task has proved to be demanding. The populations of many Eastern European states had experienced regimented participation under communist rule and seen mass participation on television during its collapse. But this outburst of engagement did not last long. Once the communists were ousted, participation soon began to decline, reflecting the communist legacy of political cynicism among large sections of the public. In Czechoslovakia, Illner (1998, p. 75) notes that 'more active participation was reduced again after the short period of post-1989 exhilaration and the traditionally detached attitudes of the population towards public involvement were continued'. In many countries traditions of paternalism and elite arrogance reestablished themselves.

Reflecting both communist and pre-communist influences, many more people express an interest in politics than actually take part. This discrepancy is especially marked in Russia. Two-thirds of

Russians say they regularly or sometimes discuss national problems but fewer than one in five believe they can influence public decisions. Disengagement seems to reflect not so much lack of interest as lack of belief in the ability to make a difference (Remington, 2004, p. 385). So a stable system of voluntary participation requires the relationship between state and society to be completely recast, a task requiring far greater skill than merely chopping up the rotting timbers of the communist state.

The problem is to build a 'civil society' regulated by law but remaining separate from the state. Such a society provides opportunities for people to participate in collective activities that are neither pro-state nor anti-state but simply non-state. But developing such social capital is a conspicuous challenge in countries emerging from communism. Under communist rule, civil society had been demobilized. It had been stood down so that the rulers could directly control the individual: 'everyone was supposed to be the same – working

DEBATE
BOWLING ALONE

'Americans of all ages, all stations in life, and all types of disposition are forever forming associations ... Thus the most democratic country in the world now is that in which men have in our time carried to the highest perfection the art of pursuing in common the objects of common desires' (de Tocqueville, 1835, p. 513)

In influential publications, Putnam (1993, 2000) questions whether de Tocqueville's thesis about the United States still applies. Putnam claims that 'something has happened in America in the past two or three decades to diminish social engagement and civic connectedness', with damaging consequences for the quality of politics. He suggests that Americans now spend more time watching *Friends* than making them. Is Putnam right? If so, does his thesis also apply to other democracies?

The case for
Putnam marshals considerable evidence from the USA to illustrate his theme. For instance, between the 1960s and the end of the 1980s:

▸ voter turnout declined by nearly a quarter (and by rather more among young electors)
▸ the proportion of Americans claiming to have attended a public meeting 'in the last year' fell by more than a third
▸ the proportion of people engaged in regular volunteer work dropped by a sixth
▸ the proportion agreeing with the survey statement 'most people can be trusted' fell from a half to a third.

Putnam believes that the significance of these findings lies in their implications for social capital (see p. 92). Face-to-face communication nurtures commitment to the common good; allows networks to develop from which new projects can emerge; permits individuals to develop their skills, knowledge and understanding; and generally encourages the give-and-take which is a hallmark of democracy. What kind of 'democracy' awaits, he asks, if most people are now 'bowling alone'?

The case against
All arguments that 'things are not what they were' are suspect. Golden ages are more often tricks of memory than historical realities. Even in the 1950s, commentators were bemoaning the rise of the 'lonely crowd', 'mass society' and the 'inner-directed personality' (Riesman, 1950). It is much more likely that social activity has changed its form rather than its extent. As Putnam (2002) himself recognizes, some types of group, such as crime-watch groups, health clubs, support groups (e.g. of crime victims) and public interest groups have expanded.

With the advent of mobile phones, email and the internet, people can associate with like-minded individuals elsewhere in the country rather than face to face. As a result, they depend less on old-fashioned neighbours. There is no reason to suppose that this change reflects any loss of 'social capital'. Indeed, the ability to join, benefit from and then leave specific, instrumental and short-term networks in response to changing individual needs may increase the 'efficiency' of social relationships compared to an era when people relied on a few neighbours.

Assessment
Even if social participation is declining in the USA, it is difficult to see what can be done to reverse the trend. Any political implications need political solutions. If America is to solve its turnout problem, for instance, the solution surely lies in improved registration procedures, not in persuading people to invite their neighbours to a barbecue. Further, the long-run effects of 9/11 are as yet unclear. On the one hand, the attacks may encourage families to retreat further into the safety of their own home, diminishing social participation. On the other hand, the immediate effect seemed to be a rush of civic engagement, citizen surveillance and support for the government. At least in the short term, these factors reduced the extent to which Americans could be said to be 'bowling alone'.

Further reading: Pharr and Putnam (2001), Putnam (1993, 2000, 2002).

for the state, on a salary, on a leash' (Goban-Klas and Sasinka-Klas, 1992). Creating a participatory civil society from the communist inheritance is a difficult and continuing task.

Definition

Civil society consists of those groups which are 'above' the personal realm of the family but 'beneath' the state. The term covers public organizations such as labour unions, interest groups and, on some definitions, recreational bodies. However, firms are usually excluded because they are not voluntary bodies emerging from society. Italians say that if the state is represented by the *palazzo* (the palace), civil society is found in the streets of the *piazza* (the square). By contrast, totalitarian regimes contain only rulers and ruled, a **civic deficit** which leaves a difficult challenge for post-totalitarian rulers.

Despite the absence of a communist legacy, the story is similar in many of the African countries seeking to nurture new avenues of participation following the retreat of the generals in the 1980s. Again, the act of overthrowing the old order did stimulate significant mass participation, at least in major cities, providing echoes of the original struggle for independence in the 1950s and 1960s. As Wiseman (1995, p. 5) writes,

the prodemocracy movements of most African states in the late 1980s represented a remarkable coming-together of political participation by a range of social groups. Prominent among them were church leaders and professional associations of lawyers, journalists, students and medical staff.

Yet the difficulties of entrenching voluntary participation in Africa remain substantial. The core problem of poverty narrows horizons while illiteracy provides a barrier to voluntary participation. Further, the national government in many African states has limited functions and weak penetration outside the capital. The political culture remains strongly parochial. Such participation as emerges, at least beyond voting, is directed towards informal politics in ethnic groups and contained through patron–client networks. These factors all suggest that voluntary participation in the new African democracies is unlikely to match even the undemanding levels of consolidated democracies.

Social movements

In 1996, 325,000 Belgians, 3 per cent of the country's population, marched through Brussels in a peaceful protest against an inadequate public investigation into a sexually motivated child murder. This White March (white was worn as a symbol of purity) was an example of a social movement, a form of participation that has come to mount a significant challenge to the 'official' political system in established democracies.

Social movements (also called popular movements) consist of people from outside the mainstream who come together to seek a common objective though an unorthodox challenge to the existing political order. The White March was a typical movement in that many participants considered themselves to be conventional citizens who would not ordinarily take an active part in politics. Their protest was both political and anti-political. Social movements espouse a political style which distances them from established channels, thereby questioning the legitimacy as well as the decisions of the government. The members of social movements adopt nonconformist forms of participation such as demonstrations, sit-ins, boycotts and political strikes. Some such acts may be illegal but, in contrast to other criminal behaviour, the actors' motives are political.

Definition

Social movements are defined by Tarrow (1998, p. 4) as 'collective challenges by people with common purposes and solidarity in sustained interaction with elites, opponents and authorities'. They are political entities with a coating of anti-politics. Rather like protest parties, movements can emerge and disappear at speed, a feature which distances them from the more static concept of civil society.

We can contrast social movements with both interest groups and political parties (Box 8.2). Like parties whose origins lie outside the legisla-

Profile RUSSIA

Population: 145m (and falling).
Gross domestic product per head: $9,300.
Form of government: federation of 21 autonomous republics.
Executive: formally semi-presidential but with a strong presidency. The prime minister heads the Council of Ministers and succeeds the president if needed (no vice-president).

Assembly: the Duma (lower house) contains 450 members elected by an additional member system. The Federal Council (upper house) contains two members from each of 89 geographical units.
Judicial branch: based on civil law. Headed by a Constitutional Court and, for civil and administrative cases, a Supreme Court. Substantial lawlessness.

Natural resources: massive reserves of oil, gas, coal, timber and minerals. Russia is the world's second largest exporter of oil.
Environment: extensive pollution, deforestation and contamination (including local radioactivity).

Russia is a vast country with an imperial and authoritarian past. It is a place full of problems, potential and paradoxes. By area Russia is the largest country in the world, almost twice the size of the United States. The population includes numerous minorities, with 36 national groups containing more than 100,000 people. Russia's rulers have in the past been autocratic empire-builders, basing their imperial expansion on control of a serf society and (until the communist era) a rural economy. Thus Russia's experience with communist dictatorship represented a culmination of a familiar authoritarian pattern. Internationally, the Union of Soviet Socialist Republics (USSR, 1922–91), encompassing 15 European and Asian republics, formed what amounted to a Russian empire.

Of all the post-communist countries, Russia raises the most interesting questions about the relationship between participation and democracy. For many observers a country with Russia's autocratic past cannot expect to develop the voluntary participation underpinning established democracies. The country's history has bequeathed a political culture based on a fatalistic acceptance of strong personal leadership. Russian critics of a competitive party system cite the saying, 'a child with six nannies is sure to lose an eye'. This desire for a single powerful leader was, it is claimed, reinforced by the economic decline and ethnic divisions of the early post-communist years. Eckstein (1998b, p. 377), for example, suggests that

> It would be harder to think of a less likely case for successful democratization than Russia. Support for the idea of democracy is at best tenuous and instrumental, it has no strong roots in an accustomed central political culture and the social context is inhospitable to it in almost all respects.

Yet this assessment may be too gloomy. In any large country, attitudes to politics are neither simple nor uniform. Among younger generations, and in the Moscow region, support for democracy is firmer. The desire for effective government in post-communist Russia may be a short-term response to social breakdown, not an indicator of deep-seated authoritarianism. Russia's past may be non-democratic but this does not prevent its educated population learning from established democracies elsewhere. Further, by the mid-1990s Russia had succeeded in holding a series of reasonably free elections to both the presidency and the Duma. Since then, a return to economic growth has led to some consolidation of the post-communist order.

Whatever the future may hold for post-communist Russia, it is surely too fatalistic to claim that an authoritarian past rules out the possibility of building democracy in Russia. The real question, perhaps, is just how democratic Russia's 'democracy' will prove to be.

Vladimir Putin, president since Boris Yeltsin's sudden resignation in 1999, has governed in ruthless style, exploiting his influence over the media and arresting powerful businessmen who might threaten his position. Putin is popular and effective but it is doubtful whether his rule is subject to the limits associated with a fully constitutional democracy.

Further reading: Eckstein (1998b), Petro (1995), Remington (2004), Rose and Munro (2002).

BOX 8.2
Comparing social movements, political parties and interest groups

Political goals, structure and means	Social movements	Protective interest groups	Political parties
Seek to influence the government?	Yes	Yes	Yes
Seek to become the government?	No	No	Yes
Focus on a single issue?	Yes	Yes	No
Formally organized, led and funded?	No	Yes	Yes
Tactics used	Unconventional	Conventional	Conventional

Further reading: Zilliacus (2001). On protective interest groups, see p. 168.

ture, movements emerge from society to challenge the political establishment where their voice is unheard. But movements are also more loosely organized, typically lacking the precise membership, subscriptions and leadership of both parties and interest groups.

Like interest groups, social movements typically focus on a single issue: for example, nuclear disarmament, feminism or the environment. Again like interest groups, social movements do not seek state power; rather they seek to influence government, usually by claiming their voice has previously been ignored. But where protective interest groups seek precise regulatory objectives, movements are more diffuse, often seeking to articulate a common identity, as with gay pride. Social movements therefore share the explicitly political focus of parties. However, unlike parties movements do not seek to craft distinct interests into an overall package; rather, they claim the moral high ground in one specific area.

Social movements are sometimes described as 'new social movements' or as practising 'new politics'. Yet in truth there is little that is new here. Single-issue protest movements must surely be as old as politics itself. Many contemporary politicians (and your authors) were schooled in the successful anti-apartheid and anti-Vietnam protests of the 1960s and 1970s. In the 1950s, an earlier generation (but not your authors) wrote about the threat to political stability posed by mass movements such as the Nazis. Kornhauser (1959), for instance, argued that mass movements were based on people at the margins of society, including unemployed intellectuals, isolated workers and the peripheral middle class.

Delving further into the past yields more examples: for example, the anti-slavery, suffragette and temperance movements. In Sweden, the late nineteenth century has been labelled the age of associations since this was the era when numerous *folkrörelser* (popular mass movements) emerged, initially to challenge the state. Examples include the farmers' movement, the temperance movement and the free churches. Rothstein (2002, p. 299) suggests that if any organizations could be said to be the owner of Sweden's extensive stock of social capital, it is the *folkrörelser*.

However, some features of the contemporary environment certainly encourage social movements to flower on a national or even global scale. One such factor is the ease of direct communication among sympathizers. Take the movement in Britain in 2000 against the country's high tax on petrol (Joyce, 2002). A diverse network of British farmers and road hauliers blocked petrol refineries in a coordinated series of protests, quickly creating a national fuel crisis. This movement made a sharp impact on both public opinion and the government. Its capacity to expand so rapidly, albeit building on foundations previously established, owed much to mobile (cell) phones. A contemporary newspaper report suggested that in this protest mobile phones played a key part. The organisers ran an informal but effective 'bush telegraph'. Anyone they contacted had the numbers of a dozen supporters. And they would each have a dozen more. A single call could mobilise hundreds of people within an hour

(Doherty *et al.*, 2003, p. 8).

In addition, global communication renders international coordination perfectly feasible. Compared to parties or interest groups, social movements cross borders with relative ease. The best example here is surely the protest in February 2003 against the American-led war in Iraq. Over a single weekend, an estimated six million people took part in demonstrations in 600 or so cities throughout the world (Table 8.2.). The ability of social movements to mushroom in this way – even without any central organization or leader – confirms their capacity to articulate authentic public concern at a transnational level. Social movements are a form of participation that is well-suited to a more global world.

Established democracies hold no monopoly over social movements. In the 1970s and 1980s, they also became a significant feature in many authoritarian and developing states. In contrast to Western democracies, however, these movements in developing countries have been the territory of the poor, as people facing acute problems of daily life collaborate to improve their living conditions in a hostile political environment. The urban poor organizing soup kitchens, the inhabitants of shanty towns lobbying for land reform, groups of mothers pressing for information on their sons who 'disappeared' under military rule – all were examples of this blossoming of popular political activity.

It is natural to imagine that the existence of poverty and oppression will provide an encouraging environment for the collective self-organization practised by social movements. But in practice the daily struggle for survival can leave little time, energy and resources for politics of any kind. In reality, a policy entrepreneur, often external to the community concerned, frequently emerges to mobilize the downtrodden and to bring their concerns into public focus. The policy entrepreneur's task is to create social capital by developing resourcefulness among people lacking formal political experience.

Definition

A **policy entrepreneur** is a person or group with the 'appropriate political experience, vision and resources to help a particular constituency' (Zirakzadeh, 1997, p. 12). When such skills are lacking, human suffering is unlikely by itself to generate a sustained movement for its amelioration.

Table 8.2 The ten largest demonstrations against the Iraq War, by city, 15–16 February 2003

City	Estimated number of protestors
Rome	As many as 3,000,000
Barcelona	1,300,000
London	1,000,000
Madrid	600,000
Berlin	500,000
Paris	200,000
Sydney	200,000
Damascus	As many as 200,000
Melbourne	160,000
New York	100,000

Note: Figures are estimates reported in the *Financial Times*, 17 February 2003. Protests in smaller countries included Amsterdam (70,000 participants), Oslo (60,000) and Stockholm (35,000). To compare with the first Gulf War of 1991, see Koopmans (1999).

The entrepreneur's role can be played by organizations or individuals. In Latin America under military rule, development agencies and radical priests in the Catholic Church encouraged the development of local movements as they sought to carve political space for themselves by asserting their identity as indigenous peoples, gays, feminists and environmentalists. Here, external organizations played an influential part.

But an inspirational individual can also serve as catalyst. For example, the contribution of Cesar Chavez proved decisive in the attempt to unionize seasonal migrant farm-workers in California during the 1960s. Previously, these poorly paid fruit-pickers, including many illegal immigrants from Mexico, had been cowed by vigilante groups acting with the implicit approval of local police. Chavez succeeded in enlisting financial and legal support from outside bodies such as churches, universities and the liberal wing of the Democratic Party. Exploiting media interest, he led a successful national boycott of California grapes, eventually forcing the farm owners into concessions. In a fashion characteristic of many movements, Chavez created a cross-class coalition in which those with resources were mobilized to help those without (Jenkins, 1983).

Two cautionary points are necessary in assessing the overall significance of social movements. First, in the developing world, many community-based movements have lacked the desire or the means to engage with national politics. A culture of anti-politics – also found in many post-communist countries – limits the movements' wider impact. Indeed the democratic transition has taken some wind from their sails. In Uruguay, for example, 'democracy brought, by a curious twist, the disappearance of many grass-roots movements that had been active during the years of dictatorship' (Canel, 1992, p. 290). Movements rise and fall but parties and interest groups remain.

Second, we must beware of exaggerating the contrast between social movements and orthodox politics. At one level, of course, the whole rationale of the movements is to threaten the dominance of existing elites. They provide a 'people's challenge' to the iron triangles of government, protective interest groups and mainstream parties. Yet beneath the surface the distinction is muddied. Kornhauser's fears notwithstanding, social movements seem to have extended the repertoire of participation more than they have endangered political stability (Ibarra, 2003). For example, the Swedish *folkrörelser* have long collaborated with the state, functioning as schools of democracy for citizens (Rothstein, 2002, p. 296).

In general, the unconventional activists of the era of protest in the West during the 1960s resembled the orthodox activists of an earlier era. In the main, they were well-educated, articulate young people from middle-class backgrounds. And more than a few leaders of the new politics are switching to orthodox politics as they age; many a protest activist of the 1960s had turned into a party leader by the century's end. Prominent examples include Joschka Fischer, Germany's foreign minister since 1998, and Peter Hain, a minister in Tony Blair's government in Britain. For all the stylistic contrast between politics old and new, one function of the movements has been to provide a training ground for future national leaders. Conversely, protest activism has entered the mainstream; it is no longer confined to younger generations (Norris, 2002).

Participation in authoritarian states

In contrast to democratic governments, authoritarian rulers seek either to limit genuine participation in politics or, in the case of totalitarian states, to direct it through tightly controlled channels. In either case, the object is to minimize any threat which unregimented participation might pose to the regime. But even in non-democracies, the limits and nature of participation are often subject to an implicit dialogue as activists test the boundaries of the acceptable. Further, as societies governed by authoritarian rulers grow more complex, so rulers often come to realize that responding to popular pressure on non-sensitive issues can enhance political stability.

Patron–client networks

The main technique for controlling participation in authoritarian states is the patron–client network. Clientelism, as this practice is often called, is a form of political involvement which differs from both voluntary participation in liberal democracies and the regimented routines of totalitarian states. Although patron–client relationships are found in all political systems, the developing world (and especially authoritarian regimes within it) offers the fullest expression of such relationships. In many developing countries, networks of patrons and clients are not just the main instrument for bringing ordinary people into contact with formal politics but also the central organizing structure of politics itself. These networks are the functional equivalent of institutions in established democracies, integrating people through well-understood practices.

So what exactly are patron–client relationships? They are informal hierarchies fuelled by exchanges between a high-status 'patron' and 'clients' of lower status. The colloquial phrase 'big man/small boy' conveys the nature of the interaction. Patrons are landlords, employers, party leaders, government ministers or most often ethnic leaders. Lacking resources of their own, clients gather round their patron for protection and security. Political patrons control the votes of their clients and persuade them to attend meetings, join organizations or simply follow their patron around in a deferential manner. In Sri Lanka, for instance, patrons with access to the resources of the state largely decide how ordinary people vote (Jayanntha, 1991).

Definition
Clientelism is a term used to describe politics substantially based on patron–client relationships. These relationships are often traditional and personal, as in the protection provided to tenants by landowners in developing countries. But they can also be more instrumental, as with the resources which dominant parties in American cities provided to new immigrants in exchange for their vote. Where clientelism is common, it pervades the political culture, affirming the inequality from which it springs.

In return for their clients' unqualified support, patrons offer access to jobs, contracts, subsidies, physical protection and even a guarantee of food in hard times. In other words, they provide security for poor people who, lacking organized protection through collective insurance or the rule of law, are in a vulnerable position. Patrons can then exploit their local power-base to strike deals with ministers in the national government, offering the support of their clients in exchange for a share of the government's resources. In this way, patronage networks grow and decline according to their patron's skill, just as more orthodox businesses rise and fall with the quality of their management.

The patron's power, and its inhibiting effect on democracy, is nicely illustrated in this quotation from Egypt's President Abdul Nasser, interviewed in 1957 when he was still a reforming leader (Owen, 1993):

We were supposed to have a democratic system between 1923 and 1953. But what good was this democracy to our people? You have seen the landowners driving the peasants to the polling booths. There they would vote according to the instructions of their masters. I want the peasants to be able to say 'yes' and 'no' without this in any way affecting their livelihood and daily bread. This in my view is the basis for freedom and democracy.

Participation through patronage is a device which appeals particularly in authoritarian settings because it links elite and mass, centre and periphery, in a context of inequality. Although inequality provides the soil in which patronage networks flourish, they still act as a political glue, binding the 'highest of the high' with the 'lowest of the low' through membership of a patron's network.

Military governments

The military governments which populated large sections of the developing world in the second half of the twentieth century provide useful examples of participation – or more commonly non-participation – in authoritarian polities. As one might expect, most military governments adopted what Remmer (1989) calls an exclusionary approach to popular participation. These regimes discouraged mass involvement in politics because they feared its consequences for their own position.

Chile between 1973 and 1989, under General Pinochet, was an extreme but revealing case. Pinochet sought not just to govern without popular involvement but to suppress all potential sources of popular opposition. He exterminated, exiled or imprisoned thousands of labour leaders and left-wing politicians, concentrating power in the hands of his own military clique. Pinochet himself acted as chief executive while a four-man junta representing the army, navy, air force and national police performed legislative functions.

As with juntas elsewhere, the purpose was to monitor political participation so as to identify threats to the military's position, for example from students or organized workers. By such means, ordinary citizens were persuaded to keep their heads down and to steer clear of any engagement with military might.

However, not all military regimes were as brutal as Chile's. More interesting, perhaps, are the few which adopted Remmer's inclusionary approach to participation. Some military leaders did attempt to build a base of support among the political class, and even on occasion among the wider population. The usual approach here was to seek to exploit the population's respect for a strong leader. Such inclusionary regimes were often organized on presidential lines, based around a dominant ruler committed to national development and a strong country.

The modernizing regime of Abdel Nasser in Egypt was such a case. Nasser was an army colonel who led a coup in 1952, became president in 1956 and remained in post until his death in 1970. He sought to broaden his political appeal beyond the military, though as a result his regime became presidential and bureaucratic, rather than narrowly military. However, even in Nasser's Egypt (as in contemporary China) any political competition was confined to elite groups. As Lesch (2003, p. 589) says,

The government demobilized and depoliticized the public. The regime offered access to jobs, socioeconomic equity and national independence: in return, the public was expected to be politically quiescent.

So even those military leaders who initially sought to mobilize the population behind their reform agenda often found that participation declined over time, resulting in the more limited and controlled engagement characteristic of authoritarian regimes.

Totalitarian governments

It is when we turn to totalitarian governments that we find the most ambitious attempts to develop mass participation in non-democratic systems. In communist and fascist states, participation was both more extensive and more regimented than in democracies. This profile of participation – high in quantity, low in quality – was a central feature of totalitarian rule.

For the classic case, we must look back to communist states, particularly in their earliest and most vigorous decades. At first glance, participation left established democracies in the shade. Under communism, citizen activity certainly outscored the level found in today's democracies. Ordinary people sat on comradely courts, administered elections, joined para-police organizations and served on people's committees covering local matters. This apparatus of participation derived from the Marxist idea that all power at every level of government should be vested in soviets (councils) of workers and peasants.

> **Definition**
> **Regimented participation** is elite-controlled involvement in politics designed to express popular support for the notional attempt by the rulers to build a new society. Its purpose is to mobilize the masses behind the regime, not to influence the personnel or policies of the government. Regimented participation was characteristic of totalitarian regimes.

However, the calibre of participation in communist states did not match its extent. To ensure that mass engagement always strengthened the party's grip, party members guided all popular participation. At regular meetings of women's federations, trade unions and youth groups, party activists would explain policy to the people. But communication flowed only from top to bottom. So the members of such groups eventually behaved the way they were treated: as passive recipients rather than active participants. Because the party controlled participation so tightly, cynicism soon replaced idealism. Only careerist die-hards were prepared to invest their full energy in the charade.

Eventually, some ruling parties did allow more participation but only in areas that did not threaten their monopoly of power. Especially in Eastern Europe, industrial managers were given more say in policy-making as political participation became more authentic on local, specific and economic matters. But these modest reforms were not matched in national politics. Because no real channels existed for airing grievances, people were left with two choices: either to shut up and get on with life or to express their views outside the system. For all the notional participation, communist governments chose to ignore popular indifference to their rule.

The trajectory of participation in communist China illustrates some of these themes. In the early decades of the People's Republic, participation through accepted channels was required as a way of demonstrating active support for the Communist Party's goals. The question was not whether citizens participated but to what extent. In particular, Mao Zedong developed the doctrine of the 'mass line' by which party officials were expected to learn from the people while retaining tight control over policy formation.

But Mao became dissatisfied with the caution of the political elite emerging from this party-led framework. In 1966, he launched the Cultural Revolution, encouraging the masses to turn on corrupt power-holders within the party, the workplace or the family. Even harmless intellectuals found themselves condemned as 'the stinking ninth category'. The outcome was an orgy of uncontrolled participation, including violent score-settling, which threatened the social fabric and caused permanent damage to the party's reputation.

Following this exceptional episode, political participation developed along the more predictable lines associated with most authoritarian regimes. After Mao, the leadership gave priority to economic reform over political purity, discouraging any form of participation which might threaten growth. Political passivity became acceptable. More recently, the party has opened some social space in which sponsored groups in areas such as education and the environment can operate with relative freedom.

However, channels for explicit opposition to party rule remain closed. Memories remain of the Tiananmen Square massacre of 1989, when the army's tanks turned on pro-democracy demonstrators in Beijing. Local protests – against corruption, unemployment, illegal levies or non-payment of wages or pensions – continue but outside the framework of accepted political activity. These demonstrations have not been directed against national rulers but they provide one more headache for the country's hard-pressed rulers in Beijing.

Political violence and terror

The forms of participation we have examined so far operate within a peaceful framework. Even when social movements engage in illegal acts, their protests remain largely civil. Yet when orthodox politics leaves conflicts unresolved, and sometimes even when it does not, the outcome can be violence – by the state against its own people, by citizens seeking to change government policy or by one social group against another. To appreciate the full repertoire of activities falling under the heading of political participation, we must also consider the role of violence in politics.

> *Definition*
> **Political violence** consists of 'those physically injurious acts directed at persons or property which are intended to further or oppose governmental decisions and public policies' (LaPalombara, 1974, p. 379). **Political terror,** a subcategory of political violence, occurs when such acts are aimed at striking fear into a wider population. Both violence and terror can be committed by as well as against the state. **Genocide,** in which the state is again usually implicated, is the deliberate extermination of a large proportion of a people, nation, race or ethnic group.

The events of September 11, 2001 brought violence and terror into focus (Lutz and Lutz, 2004). The assaults on New York and Washington were unprecedented in the number and range of national origins of the victims but they built on a tradition of political violence (Table 8.3). The World Trade Center had first come under attack from Islamic terrorists in 1994 when a bomb in the Center's car park killed six people. Further, the dangers posed by al-Qaeda were well-recognized: early in 2001, 40 CIA officers were working on the bin Laden case (US Congress, 2002). And, of course, such activity did not cease on 9/11. The following year, bombs in the Indonesian resort of Bali killed 202 people, including many Australian tourists. Attacks have also taken place in other countries, notably Saudi Arabia, Spain and Turkey. So while September 11 was certainly a bolt, it can hardly be said to have come from the blue. Understanding September 11 requires, among

Table 8.3 World Trade Center fatalities by nationality, September 11, 2001

Nationality	Number killed
United States	2106
United Kingdom	53
India	34
Dominican Republic	25
Jamaica	21
Japan	20
China	18
Colombia	18
Canada	16
Germany	16
Other	290

Note: Based on over 90 per cent of the death toll of over 2,800 from around 80 countries, including those on the planes. Deaths at the Pentagon and from the hijacked plane which crashed in Pennsylvania are not shown. For an analysis of global responses to terrorism, see Buckley and Fawn (2003).

Source: Data from New York City Health Department, 18 April 2002.

other things, placing that case of terrorism in a comparative context.

Political violence is as ancient as politics itself. Many terms used today in describing terrorism derive from these earliest cases. For example, the Zealots were political activists who resisted Roman rule in Palestine. In the era of the Crusades, the Assassins (literally, hashish-eaters) were a Muslim sect who believed their religious duty was to hunt down Christians. The Thugs were religiously motivated bandits in central and northern India.

The central point about political violence (including 9/11) is that it must be viewed through the conventional lenses of political analysis, not through a distorting filter that 'explains' violence solely as the product of irrational fanaticism. As Clausewitz said of war, violence is 'a continuation of politics by other means'. The threat and use of force is a way of raising the stakes; it extends but rarely replaces conventional politics. Most political violence is neither random nor uncontrolled but tactical. When farmers block a road, or when the secret police beat up a student activist, or even when terrorists blow up a plane, the act carries a deliberate political signal. Even when so-called

'uncontrolled' violence erupts between ethnic groups, the disturbances are usually initiated – though not carried out – by political leaders.

Campaigns of terror exemplify the use of violence for tactical political ends. By creating a climate of fear, such terrorist acts are intended to coerce a wider target into submitting to its aims. To take an influential example, the Reign of Terror unleashed throughout France after 1789 was a deliberate policy of the Jacobin revolutionaries. As Davies (1996, p. 706) notes,

> The Terror was not confined to the destruction of the revolution's active opponents. It was designed to create such an atmosphere of fear and uncertainty that the very thought of opposition would be paralysed. It produced a climate of spies, informers and unlimited suspicion.

It is precisely this desire to influence the wider political atmosphere which converts casual brutality into political terror. Paradoxically, 'random' violence is a systematic technique for inducing anxiety among a broader population, a goal achieved by exploiting the oxygen of publicity. In that sense, the assault on the United States on 9/11 was supremely effective. Watching the collapse of the Trade Center towers, television viewers throughout the Western world said, and were intended to say, 'there but for fortune go you or I'. From a political and economic perspective, the impact of September 11 lay less in the events themselves, severe though these were, than in the inevitable reaction to them. These included an immediate slump in air travel, the cost of additional security measures, America's invasion of Afghanistan and secondary terrorism such as the anthrax spores sent through the post to addresses in the United States.

In the aftermath of 2001, it is natural to interpret terror as a tactic employed by non-state actors *against* the state. But again such a conclusion would be too narrow. Terrorism can also be sponsored *by* states against other states, as with Iran, Libya and Syria or as seen in the indirect support offered by Afghanistan and Saudi Arabia to the 9/11 terrorists.

Most important of all, states can terrorize their own people. A vital lesson of the twentieth century is that the state is in a unique position to exploit political violence for its own ends. As the monopolist of authorized coercion, states are well-positioned to intimidate their citizens, and over the course of the twentieth century many did so. Precisely because political violence is an organized technique, its practice increased with the growth of the state in the last century. Rummel (1997) estimates that between 1900 and 1987, almost 130 million people were killed by the very institution intended to provide peace, law and order (Table 8.4).

To demonstrate the link between violence and government, consider the extreme case of genocide. A well-organized state and a population accustomed to obedience can make the systematic destruction of an ethnic group entirely feasible. The Nazi genocide of the Jews is of course the best-known example but it is neither the only case nor the most recent. The central African state of Rwanda is a more contemporary example. There, in a few weeks in 1994, most of the minority Tutsi, and some Hutu considered to be sympathizers, were butchered. In total, about 800 000 people, or one in ten of the population, were massacred.

We can use three particular features of the Rwandan tragedy to illustrate broader characteristics of genocide: its planned character, long development and dependence on the state. First, the butchery was far from a spontaneous outburst of ethnic hatred. Although Hutu peasants dutifully implemented the killings, the orders came from government and military leaders who told the peasants to 'clear the bush' and 'pull up the roots' (i.e. kill women and children too).

Second, the Rwandan case illustrates the deep-seated origins of genocide. In Rwanda, the traditional balance between Tutsi and Hutu had been distorted by Belgian colonialists, contributing to mass slaughters of Hutu in 1972 and 1988, and initiating the dynamic that culminated in 1994.

Third, an effective system of local rule, also inherited from the colonial era, provided the administrative means to implement genocide. In the end, the Tutsi could not escape with their lives because they could not escape from the state (Mamdani, 2001).

The cultural residue of officially sanctioned mass murder can be profound, with the emergence of traumatized, broken societies such as Cambodia (2 million dead, 1975–79). How, then, can populations be protected against this threat from the very body that is supposed to protect them? Rummel (1997) suggests that democracy is the key. He notes that democracies rarely fight each other and hardly ever kill their own people. In a democracy, the ballot replaces the bullet; it is absolute power which creates the conditions for democide. Thus, the transition to democracy in the final decades of the twentieth century may reduce state-sponsored political violence and render the twenty-first century a time of relative peace in comparison with the barbarities of preceding decades.

Rummel's point may also apply to the form of terror against the state practised by organizations such as al-Qaeda. Were the authoritarian regimes of the Middle East to be replaced by prosperous democracies, terrorist organizations would surely find the ground beneath them becoming infertile.

Table 8.4 The ten most lethal governments, 1900–87

Country	Years	Rate* (%)	Total killed
Cambodia	1975–79	8.2	2,000,000
Turkey	1919–23	2.6	703,000
Yugoslavia	1941–45	2.5	655,000
Poland	1945–48	2.0	1,585,000
Turkey	1909–18	1.0	1,752,000
Czechoslovakia	1945–48	0.5	197,000
Mexico	1900–20	0.4	1,417,000
USSR	1917–87	0.4	54,769,000
Cambodia	1979–87	0.4	230,000
Uganda	1971–79	0.3	300,000
World	1900–87	0.2	129,909,000

* Per cent of its population that a regime murders each year, on average.

Note: Murderous governments after 1987 include Armenia, Azerbaijan, Burundi, Bosnia, Croatia, Iran, Iraq, Rwanda and Somalia.

Source: Rummel (1997).

Revolution

Occasionally, political violence extends to the governing framework itself as the entire political order becomes a matter for dispute. When the existing structure of power is overthrown, leading to a long-term reconstruction of the political, social and economic order, we can speak of a revolution. Such episodes are rare but pivotal, inducing broad and deep alterations in society. The major instances – France, America, Russia, China, Iran – have substantially defined the modern world. We therefore conclude this chapter with an assessment of the nature and causes of revolutions, focusing in particular on France and Russia.

Although changes of the magnitude needed to qualify as a revolution usually require violence, it is debatable whether violence should be built into the definition of the term. The question here is whether a 'peaceful revolution' is a contradiction in terms. On the one hand, we can certainly make a case for the possibility of revolutions without violence. After all, the ancient world used the term 'revolution' just to refer to a circulation in the ruling group, howsoever induced. To 'revolve' is literally to move round, and in this traditional sense there was no necessary link between revolution and disorder.

Recent experience confirms that major political changes can occur without large-scale violence. The collapse of communism in Eastern Europe in 1989, leading to the fall of the Soviet Union in 1991, was a major reform initiated by peaceful means, with Czechoslovakia's Velvet Revolution a particular case in point. Yet 1989 surely qualifies as a year of revolutions when such efforts are measured by their impact rather than by the violence of their birth.

Definition
Skocpol (1979, p. 4) defines **revolutions** as 'rapid, basic transformations of a society's state and class structures; and they are accompanied and in part carried through by class-based revolts from below'. Goldstone (1991, p. 37) suggests revolutions consist of three overlapping stages: first, state breakdown; second, the ensuing struggle for power; and third, a radical reconstruction of the state.

On the other hand, the contemporary use of the term 'revolution' still connotes transformation through violence, a change in meaning which reflects the experience of the modern world. After the seminal French Revolution of 1789, the world needed a special term to capture dramatic, seismic shifts in the social and political order; and 'revolution' in the modern sense was born (Lachmann, 1997).

Social psychological and structural theories

The twentieth century vastly increased the world's stock of revolutions (Box 8.3), stimulating a search for general theories of these events. Here we will consider two such accounts: first the social psychological account associated with Gurr; and, second, Skocpol's structural interpretation.

The social psychological theory focuses on individual motivations rather than social groups. It seeks to answer such questions as: What inspires people to participate in revolutionary activity? Why do some people sometimes feel so strongly about politics that they are willing to give time, energy and ultimately their lives to achieve change?

In his study of the French Revolution, de

BOX 8.3
A century of revolutions

Country	Year	Outcome
Mexico	1910	A populist revolution leading to rule by the Institutional Revolutionary Party (PRI) which continued until 2000
Russia	1917	The world's first communist state, lasting until 1990
Turkey	1922	A secular nation-state built amid the ruins of the Ottoman Empire
China	1949	The People's Republic of China, led by a party which is now communist only in name
Iran	1979	An Islamic theocracy led by Ayatollah Khomeini. Religious rulers are now under pressure from more liberal reformers

Tocqueville (1856) noted that grievances patiently endured become intolerable once a brighter future becomes possible. As part of the movement towards a more scientific approach to political analysis in the 1960s, Gurr (1980) sought to develop de Tocqueville's insight.

Gurr argued that relative deprivation was the key to revolutions. For Gurr, political instability only results from deprivation when combined with a belief that conditions are worse than they could and should be. What matters is not absolute deprivation, a condition which often breeds resigned passivity, but relative deprivation: a sense that rewards fall below expectations or entitlement. The point of comparison can vary, of course. Deprivation may be relative to past times, to an abstract standard of justice, or to the rewards accruing to other groups serving as points of reference. But comparison of some kind is integral to the idea of relative deprivation.

When relative deprivation is widespread, suggest Gurr, instability can result. But Gurr is a little more specific. The most explosive situation, he argues, arises when a period of improvement is followed by a decline in the ability of the regime to meet rising demands. Such a situation creates a dangerous gap between expectations of continued improvement and the reality of decline. These conditions produce a revolutionary gap between expectations and achievement (Figure 8.2).

Davies (1962) sums up the implications of this psychological approach: 'revolutions are most likely to occur when a prolonged period of economic and social development is followed by a short period of sharp reversal'. This hypothesis is known as the J-curve theory, with the top of the 'J' indicating an abrupt halt to a previous period of rapid growth.

The contribution of this social psychological approach lies in demonstrating that how people perceive their condition is more important than the actual condition itself. Relative deprivation is certainly a background factor in many revolutions. Peasant frustrations, in particular, were involved in the French, Russian and Chinese examples. Note, however, that by citing actual revolutions, we are restricting our attention to positive cases (p. 73). Relative deprivation may often be extensive without signalling uprisings of any kind. Its status

is more likely to be that of a necessary rather than a sufficient condition of revolution.

> *Definition*
> **Relative deprivation** arises when people believe they are receiving less (value capability) than they feel they are entitled to (value expectations). Relative deprivation breeds a sense of resentment which contributes to political discontent. By contrast, **absolute deprivation** often leads to a struggle for survival and, as a result, political passivity. As the Russian revolutionary Trotsky (1932/3, p. 103) wrote, 'the mere existence of privations is not enough to cause an insurrection; if it were, the masses would always be in revolt'.

Also, although the social psychological account provides some insight into the conditions of political instability and violence, it seems incapable of explaining revolutionary progress and outcomes. Whose discontent matters? How and why do uprisings turn into revolutions? How is discontent channelled into organized opposition movements? Why is such opposition usually suppressed but sometimes not? Because relative deprivation has no answer to these important questions, it is better regarded as a theory of political violence in general rather than of revolutions in particular.

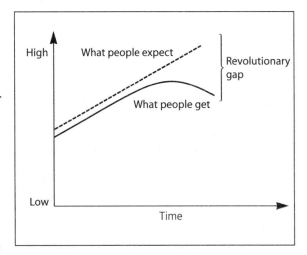

Figure 8.2 The J-curve theory of revolutions

Note: 'What people expect' and 'What people get' refers to expectations of government.

Given the limitations of the psychological approach, in the 1970s the study of revolutions turned away from broad psychological theories and returned to a more fine-grained historical examination. Skocpol's (1979) influential discussion of the French, Russian and Chinese revolutions represented a culmination of this more political structural approach.

For Skocpol, the causes of revolutions cannot be found in the motives of the participants. What matters are the structural conditions: that is, the relationships between groups within a state and, equally important, between states. The background to revolution, suggests Skocpol, is provided by a regime that is weak internationally and ineffective domestically. The classic revolutions occurred when well-organized revolutionaries succeeded in exploiting peasant frustration with an old order which had lost its capacity to compete with more developed international competitors. With the landed aristocracy resisting economic modernization, and offering only limited support to the imperial ambitions of the regime, the old order becomes vulnerable to insurrection:

Caught in cross-pressures between domestic class structures and international exigencies, the autocracies and their centralized administrations and armies broke apart, opening the way for revolutionary transformations spearheaded by revolts from below.

(Skocpol, 1979, p. 47)

Seizing power from a failing regime can be quite straightforward. The real revolution begins as the new rulers develop and impose their vision on society and, in particular, on opposition groups. Revolutions do not stop with the taking of power, as the social psychological theory seemed to imply, but only start at this point. Skocpol tells us much about how discontent is mobilized into political activity and how that activity is turned into a revolutionary transformation. In this way, she brings political, and especially state-centred, analysis back to the study of revolutions.

The French Revolution

Let us conclude by considering the French and Russian revolutions in the context of the social psychological and structural theories we have introduced. Our scrutiny must certainly begin with France in 1789, as this was the defining revolution of modern times. Indeed, it is no exaggeration to say that both the modern concept of revolution and modernity itself were born in France in 1789.

What, then, were the contours of this landmark episode? Before the revolution, France still combined an absolute monarchy with feudalism. Governance was a confused patchwork of local, provincial and royal institutions. However, in the 1780s the stormclouds gathered: the old regime came under pressure as the monarchy became virtually bankrupt. Then, in 1788, a poor grain harvest triggered both peasant revolts and urban discontent. The revolution itself was initiated after the Third Estate of the Estates General, convened in May 1789 for the first time in over 150 years, declared itself to be France's National Assembly.

There followed a half-decade of radical reform in which, amid the enormous violence of the Terror, the old institutions (including the monarchy) were torn down and the foundations of a modern state constructed. After a further period of instability, Napoleon instituted a period of authoritarian rule lasting from 1799 to 1814. Universal male suffrage was not adopted until 1848 and the conflict between radicals and conservatives embedded in the revolution remained important to French political debate for the next two hundred years.

Marx described the revolution as a 'gigantic broom' sweeping away 'all manner of medieval rubbish'. The shockwaves of the events in France certainly reverberated throughout Europe as ruling classes in other countries saw their very existence imperilled. The revolution's mixed outcomes notwithstanding, its progressive character is indisputable:

▶ Politically, the revolution destroyed absolute monarchy based on divine right. It established the future shape of liberal democracy: popular sovereignty, a professional bureaucracy and a liberal philosophy.
▶ Economically, the revolution weakened aristocratic control over the peasantry, helping to create the conditions under which market rela-

tions could spread and capitalism would eventually emerge.

▸ Ideologically, the revolution was strongly secular, fathering individual rights enforceable through codified law. It was also powerfully nationalist: the nation became the transcendent bond, uniting all citizens in patriotic fervour.

What light, then, can the social psychological and structural theories offered by Davies and Skocpol cast on the French Revolution? Davies's concept of relative deprivation certainly helps in understanding the peasant revolts, driven as they were by the conjunction of a failed harvest and a series of failed government policies which had raised but not satisfied popular expectations.

But there seems little doubt that Skocpol's perspective offers deeper insight. The international dimension behind 1789 can be seen in France's generally unsuccessful competition with England in the eighteenth century. The limited domestic effectiveness of the monarchy was then demonstrated by its inability to pay for foreign adventures, resulting in a fiscal crisis that came to a head in the late 1780s. Further, Skocpol's emphasis on the complex dynamics and long-term effects of revolution certainly fits the French experience. The French Revolution became far more than a peasant revolt.

The Russian Revolution

Just as the French Revolution mapped the contours of liberal democracy, so the Russian Revolution of October 1917 established the world's first communist state. It signalled the advent of a regime, an ideology and a revolutionary movement which sought to overthrow Western democracy. The Russian Revolution was a pivotal event of the twentieth century.

The Russian Revolution swept away the ramshackle and decaying empire of the Tsar, just as its French counterpart had destroyed medieval remnants in that country over a century earlier. Although Russia underwent significant state-sponsored industrialization towards the end of the nineteenth century, the political framework remained conservative and autocratic. Under the Tsarist bureaucracy, Russian society had remained

inert. In particular, the mass of poorly educated peasants remained locked in serfdom, dependent on the landowning nobility. Russia was an important imperial power but, domestically, its political, economic and social structures were falling behind its Western competitors.

The country was ripe for revolution and was recognized to be such at the time. But in Russia, unlike France, a dress rehearsal occurred before the revolution proper got under way. An unsuccessful war with Japan stimulated a naval mutiny in 1905, leading to a failed insurrection. The government quickly concluded the war with Japan, freeing loyal troops to suppress what the regime claimed was a 'passing squall' of domestic rebellion.

A decade later, the military disasters of the First World War, and the resulting economic and administrative chaos within Russia, could not be dismissed so easily. By 1917, the capacity of the central government to rule Russia had virtually disintegrated. The Tsarist regime collapsed in March, to be replaced by a weak provisional government. Reflecting Lenin's decisive leadership, the Bolsheviks succeeded in November in replacing this administration, though to say that they seized 'power' would be to understate domestic disorder ('Bolshevik', meaning majority, was the name of a radical faction in the broad Marxist movement).

In Russia, as in France, the revolution was made not by an insurrection but by the transformation of the political order which followed. Even before Lenin ended Russia's involvement in world war in 1918, the country was consumed by civil war lasting until 1921. The decisive outcome was the reestablishment of central authority in the form of a communist dictatorship. The Bolsheviks, despite their democratic and anarchist origins, developed into a communist party wielding a monopoly of power. In this fateful transition, Lenin's notion of the vanguard party – an elite body of revolutionaries which claimed to understand the long-term interests of the working class better than that class itself – provided the crucial rationale.

Why did the first major communist revolution of the twentieth century occur in one of the less-developed links in the capitalist chain? After all, Marx himself had predicted that such events would occur in advanced capitalist countries with an industrial working class, not in largely unmodernized agrarian societies such as Russia. Here, Davies's theory of relative deprivation provides useful service. Although nineteenth-century Russia remained a poor country with a serf economy, the Tsar did institute important reforms between 1860 and 1904, including notional freedom for the serfs, the introduction of a modern legal system, state-sponsored industrialization and general liberalization.

But these reforms served only to induce relative deprivation. Although the peasants were theoretically free, most remained burdened by debt. Many flocked to the expanding cities in fruitless search of a better life. Rapid economic expansion in the final decade of the 1890s, stimulated by industrial development, turned into recession in the first decade of the twentieth century as Western money markets contracted. Expectations raised by political reforms were dashed by the Tsar's inability to push ahead with further, more radical changes. In these ways, reform oscillated with repression in a perfect formula for fostering relative deprivation.

Where Davies is less successful is in explaining why an attempted revolution failed in Russia in 1905 but another succeeded just twelve years later. At this point, Skocpol's emphasis on regime collapse amid international failure comes back into play. With Russia's armies outclassed by the superior equipment and support available to Germany's forces, the Tsar's regime disintegrated from within, leading to a power vacuum which Lenin's Bolsheviks were able to exploit during the summer and autumn of 1917.

Key reading

> **Next step:** *Putnam (2000, 2001) is an interesting assessment of the decline of social participation in the USA, with an eye to its political impact.*

Verba *et al.* (1995) also examine the United States in their major study of participation. For a comparable British investigation see Parry *et al.* (1992). For gender differences specifically, see Burns *et al.* (2001). On social movements, see Tarrow (1998) for a general account, Zirakzadeh (1997) for a comparative study, della Porta *et al.* (1999) for the global context; and Ibarra (2003) and Norris (2002) for the uncertain relationship between movements and orthodox democracy. The literature on participation in post-communist societies is now expanding; on Russia, see Eckstein (1998b). For participation in African transitions, see Bratton and van de Walle (1997, ch. 4). Lutz and Lutz (2004) and Whittaker (2004) examine terrorism while Buckley and Fawn (2003) consider responses to September 11. On revolutions, see Skocpol (1979) for a classic analysis, Foran (1997) for theoretical accounts and Halliday (1999) for the links between revolutions and world politics.

Part III
LINKING SOCIETY AND GOVERNMENT

In this part, we examine the formal mechanisms through which society influences government. We begin with the main linking device in established democracies: elections. We then turn to interest groups, discussing how such associations protect their own turf and, in some cases, promote their vision of the public good. And we conclude with an analysis of political parties, many of which originate in society but which, in power, are charged with directing the state and thereby leading society.

Chapter 9

Elections and voters

As Katz (1997, p. 3) writes, 'elections are the defining institution of modern democracy'. During the brief period of an election campaign, voters are the masters and are seen to be so. To examine the electoral process is therefore to analyse the central device which has made representative democracy a feasible proposition for large countries.

The most obvious function of elections is to provide a competition for office and a means of holding the winners to account. In addition, an election campaign permits a dialogue between voters and candidates, and so between society and state. Like coronations of old, competitive elections also endow the new office-holders with authority, contributing thereby to the effectiveness with which duties can be performed (Ginsberg, 1982).

We should note, however, that not all elections are competitive. Most authoritarian rulers maintain a legislature, and typically employ controlled elections as the means of recruitment to their assemblies. Even these non-competitive elections can provide a measure of legitimacy with the international community, as well as a panel of docile representatives who can safely be permitted to raise harmless grievances emanating from their local area.

But it is competitive elections in a democratic setting that provide the main focus of this chapter. We begin with the neglected issues of the scope and franchise of elections. We then turn to elec-toral systems, voting behaviour, turnout and referendums. The final sections discuss the specific characteristics of elections in new democracies and authoritarian states.

Scope and franchise

An important question to ask about elections in established democracies is how wide is their scope. Which offices are subject to election is almost as important as who has the right to vote. Compare the United States and Britain. The USA is unique in its massive range of elected offices, ranging from the country's president to the local dog-catcher. In total, the USA possesses more than 500,000 elected offices, a figure reflecting a strong tradition of local self-government. Britain would need over 100,000 elected positions to match the American ratio of elected posts to population. Yet in Britain, as in many non-federal democracies in the EU, voting has traditionally been confined to elections for the European and national parliaments and for local councils (however, the Labour government elected in 1997 did introduce elected parliaments to Scotland and Wales). Similarly, Australia has many more elected posts than does New Zealand, even when Australia's larger population is taken in account.

Other things being equal, the greater the number of offices subject to competitive election, the more democratic a political system becomes. However, there are dangers in electionitis. One is voter fatigue, leading to a fall in attention, turnout and the quality of choice. In particular, the least important elections tend to become second-order contests: that is, their outcomes reflect the popularity of national parties even though they do not install a national government. The difficulty with such second-order contests is that they weaken the link between performance in office and the voters' response (Anderson and Ward, 1996).

Many American electors, for example, still vote a straight party ticket for all the offices included on a single ballot. This easy option involves no scrutiny at all of specific contests and can lead to a party winning many extra posts on the coat-tails of a popular candidate for the White House. Similar processes operate in Europe. Elections to the European Parliament become referendums on *national* governments, although their supposed purpose is to elect a member for the *European* Parliament.

The franchise (who can vote) is another important, and rather underemphasized, aspect of elections. Following a reduction in the voting age in the 1960s or 1970s, the franchise in most democracies extends to nearly all citizens aged at least 18. A few countries are now contemplating a further reduction in the voting age to 16.

This wide franchise is fairly recent, particularly for women. Few countries can match Australia and New Zealand where women have been electors since the start of the twentieth century. In some countries, women did not gain the vote on the same terms as men until after 1945, reflecting male recognition of women's contribution to the war effort (Table 8.1).

The main remaining exclusions from suffrage are criminals, the insane and non-citizen residents such as guest workers. Yet in each of these areas there may still be room for further progress. Should the electoral process adopt techniques enabling people with even severe learning difficulties to express preferences? Is denial of the vote really an appropriate response to citizens convicted of a criminal offence?

And how should the franchise respond to international mobility? Should non-citizen residents be granted the vote in the country where they live, work and pay taxes? And should citizens living overseas (not just government employees such as soldiers on foreign service) retain the vote in their country of citizenship? If we answer yes to both questions, migrants would be able to vote in two countries, giving them twice the electoral weight of the stay-at-homes. Such questions illustrate in practical form the difficulties in reconciling states, and elections organized in them, with the demands of a more global world.

Some political systems are adopting a more flexible approach to these contemporary franchise issues. Within the European Union, citizens of country A who reside in country B can vote in local and European, but not national, elections in country B (Day and Shaw, 2002). And since 1975 American citizens living abroad, now numbering over 7 million, retain their vote in federal elections in the USA.

Electoral systems: legislatures

Most controversy about electoral systems centres on the rules for converting votes into seats. Such rules are as important as they are technical. They form the inner workings of democracy, sometimes as little understood by ordinary voters as the engine of a car but just as essential to the operation of the political machine. In this section, we examine the rules for translating votes into seats in parliamentary elections (Box 9.1).

In elections to the legislature, the main question is whether an electoral system ensures that the seats obtained by a party are directly proportional to votes received. Proportional representation (PR) means that a mechanism to achieve this goal is built into the allocation of seats. However, some electoral systems – namely, the plurality and majority methods – are non-proportional. They offer no guarantee that parties will receive the same share of seats as of votes. We examine the older non-proportional formats before turning to PR.

Plurality and majority systems

In non-proportional systems, parties are not rewarded in proportion to the share of the vote they obtain; instead, 'the winner takes all' within each district, whether a Canadian riding, an American district or a British constituency. These systems take one of two forms: plurality or majority.

In the plurality (also called 'first-past-the-post') format, the winning candidate is simply the one who receives most votes in each electoral district. A plurality of votes suffices; a majority is unnecessary. Despite its antiquity and simplicity, the plurality system is rare and becoming rarer. It survives

Profile THE UNITED STATES

Population: 290m.
Gross domestic product per head: $37,600.
Form of government: a presidential, federal republic.
Legislature: the 435-member House of Representatives is the lower house. The 100-member Senate, perhaps the world's most influential upper chamber, contains two directly elected senators from each state.
Executive: the president is supported by a massive apparatus, including the 400-strong White House Office, and the Executive Office of the President, numbering around 2,000. The Cabinet is far less significant than in, say, Britain.
Judiciary: the Supreme Court heads a dual system of federal and state courts. This nine-member body can nullify laws and actions running counter to the constitution. Many political issues are resolved through the court system.
Electoral system: the USA is one of the few countries still employing the plurality method. The president is elected indirectly through an electoral college. A candidate who wins the key states may be elected through this college even if he comes second in the popular vote, as in 2000.
Party system: the Democratic and Republican parties show extraordinary resilience, despite periodic threats from third parties. The survival of the major parties reflects ideological flexibility, an entrenched position in law and the bias of plurality elections against minor parties.

With the end of the Cold War, the United States became the world's one remaining superpower. This unique status is based partly on the country's hard power: a large population, the ability to project military force anywhere and a dynamic economy accounting for a third of the world's total production. Yet America's soft power is also significant. Its leading position in the technology, media and telecommunications sector is underpinned by a strong base in science and university education. Its culture, brand names and language have universal appeal.

Above all, America retains a faith that it is bound to lead, a confidence demonstrated by its robust reaction to 9/11. Military interventions in Afghanistan (2001) and Iraq (2003) confirm that the USA remains willing to use its hard power, even at the risk in the latter case of damage to its reputation (Nye, 2002).

The internal politics of the United States is therefore of vital interest. Ironically, the world's No. 1 operates a political system intended to frustrate decisive policy-making. By constitutional design, power is divided between federal and state governments. The centre is itself fragmented between the executive, legislature and judiciary. American politics is extraordinarily pluralistic; reforms are more easily blocked by interest groups than carried through by the executive.

The president, the only official elected by a national constituency, finds his plans obstructed by a legislature which is among the most powerful and decentralized in the world. Substantial reforms such as the New Deal require a major crisis, such as the Depression, to bring forth that rare consensus which generates rapid reform. Excepting such times of crisis, Washington politics is a ceaseless quest for that small amount of common ground on which all interests can agree. The president may lead the world but the separation of powers mean that in domestic politics he is a supplicant like any other.

Similar paradoxes abound in the American experience with elections:

▶ The United States has over 500,000 elected offices, more than anywhere else, yet turnout is low for most of them, including the presidency.
▶ A premise of equality underlies elections yet Southern blacks were effectively denied the vote until the Voting Rights Act of 1965.
▶ The 'log cabin to White House' ideal is widely accepted but money is increasingly necessary, though not sufficient, for electoral success.
▶ Many states use devices of direct democracy (e.g. the recall of the California governor in 2003) but the constitution does not allow national referendums.
▶ Elections are expected to involve debates between candidates and parties but in many contests advertising by interest groups overwhelms the candidates' voices.
▶ Elections should create legitimacy for the winner but the many confusions of the 2000 presidential election – including the fact that more electors voted for Al Gore than for George W. Bush – hardly contributed to the authority with which the eventual winner entered the White House.

Further reading: McKay (2001b), Wilson and Dilulio (2004)

BOX 9.1
Electoral systems: legislatures

PLURALITY AND MAJORITY SYSTEMS

1. Simple plurality: 'first past the post'
Procedure   Leading candidate elected on first and only ballot.

Where used   Nine countries, including Bangladesh, Canada, India, UK and USA.

2. Absolute majority: alternative vote ('preferential vote')
Procedure   Voters rank candidates. If no candidate wins a majority of first preferences, the bottom candidate is eliminated and his or her votes are redistributed according to second preferences. Repeat until a candidate has a majority.

Where used   Australia.

3. Two-ballot systems
Procedure   If no candidate wins a majority on the first ballot, the leading candidates (usually the top two) face a second, run-off election.

Where used   Mali, Ukraine (1994 only). For the French National Assembly, all candidates winning the support of more than 12.5 per cent of the electorate on the first ballot go through to the second round. The candidate securing most votes wins this additional ballot.

PROPORTIONAL SYSTEMS

4. List system
Procedure   Votes are cast for a party's list of candidates though in many countries the elector can also express support for individual candidates on the list.

Where used   Twenty-nine countries, including Brazil, the Czech Republic, Israel, Netherlands, South Africa and Sweden.

5. Single transferable vote (STV)
Procedure   Voters rank candidates in order of preference. Any candidate needs to achieve a set number of votes (the quota) to be elected. All candidates are elected who exceed this quota on first preferences. Their 'surplus' votes (that is, the number by which they exceeded the quota) are then distributed to the second preferences shown on these ballot papers. When no candidate has reached the quota, the bottom candidate is eliminated and these votes are also transferred. Continue until all seats are filled.

Where used   Ireland, Estonia (1990 only).

MIXED SYSTEMS

6. Mixed member majoritarian (MMM)
Procedure   Some candidates are elected for electoral districts and others through PR. Electors normally have two votes. One is for the district election (which usually uses the plurality method) and the other for a PR contest (usually party list). In MMM, these two tiers are separate, with no mechanism to achieve a proportional result overall.

Where used   Seven countries, including Japan, Russia and Thailand.

7. Mixed member proportional (MMP) or the 'Additional member system' (AMS)
Procedure   As for MMM, except that the two tiers are linked so as to deliver a proportional outcome overall. The party vote determines the number of seats to be won by each party. Elected candidates are drawn first from the party's winners in the district contests, topped up as required by candidates from the party's list.

Where used   Seven countries, including Germany, Italy, Mexico and Venezuela.

Note: The figures for the number of states employing each method are not based on all countries but just on the 58 democracies (lower chamber) examined in LeDuc *et al.* (2002b).

mainly in Britain and British-influenced states such as Canada, various Caribbean islands, India and the United States. However, because India is so populous, around half the world's people living under democratic rule still use first past the post (Lijphart, 1999).

The crucial point about the plurality method is the bonus in seats it offers to the party leading in votes. In the Canadian election of 2000, for example, the Liberals gained a majority of seats on a minority of votes (Table 9.1). To see how this bias operates, consider an example in which just two parties, the Reds and the Blues, compete in every constituency. Suppose the Reds win by one vote in every district. There could not be a closer contest in votes yet the Reds sweep the board in seats. This demonstrates the inherent bias of a method which, within each district, offers everything to the winner and nothing to the losers.

The political significance of this amplifying effect lies in its ability to deliver government by a single majority party. In parliamentary systems with national parties, the plurality method is a giant conjuring trick, pulling the rabbit of majority government out of the hat of a divided society. In Britain as well as Canada, a secure parliamentary majority for the winner is customary even though a majority in the popular vote for a single party is exceptional. This characteristic is decisive for those who consider that the function of an electoral system is to deliver majority government by a single party.

It is, however, important to note that this amplifier works best when major parties compete throughout the country. The British contest between Labour and the Conservatives still fits this bill, enabling the swing of the pendulum to deliver a parliamentary majority first for one party, then for the other. But where parties are more fragmented, as in India, majority government is less likely. In India's increasingly regional party system, plurality elections have not delivered majority government since 1989. The ability of the plurality method to produce majority government is often exaggerated because of a failure to consider how the system works beyond its British homeland. Weakening party loyalties, furthermore, mean that a national competition between just two strong parties is becoming less prevalent.

The capacity of first past the post to produce majority government, at least given national competition between two parties, is often presented as the method's greatest strength. But the plurality system also possesses a remarkable weakness. It offers no guarantee that the party which wins the most votes will secure the largest number of seats in the legislature. It is perfectly possible for a party's votes to be distributed so efficiently that it wins a majority of seats even with fewer votes than its main competitor.

Again, take a hypothetical example. Suppose the Blues pile up massive majorities in their own geographical stronghold while the Reds scrape home with narrow wins throughout the rest of the country. The Reds could well win more seats despite obtaining fewer votes, reflecting the greater efficiency of their vote distribution. This possibility arises because the average number of votes required to win a seat is not constant but varies between parties according to how their votes are distributed across constituencies.

This bizarre situation has arisen twice in postwar British general elections. In February 1974, for example, Labour won four more seats than the Conservatives, and formed a minority administration, even though the Conservatives won over 200,000 more votes. For Lijphart (1999, p. 134), this possibility of 'seat victories for parties that are mere runners-up in vote totals is probably the plurality method's gravest democratic deficit'. If we were designing an electoral system from scratch, we would surely reject a method in which the party with most votes could fail to win most seats.

In addition, the importance of constituency boundaries to the result of plurality elections gives incentives for parties to engage in gerrymandering – deliberate manipulation of boundaries so as to improve the efficiency of a party's vote.

Definition

Gerrymandering is the art of drawing seat boundaries in plurality elections to maximize the **efficiency** (seats-to-votes ratio) of a party's support. The term comes from a constituency designed by Governor Gerry of Massachusetts in 1812. It was so long, narrow and wiggly that it reminded one observer of a salamander – hence gerrymander.

Table 9.1 The Canadian elections of 1993 and 2000

Party	1993		2000	
	Votes (%)	Number of seats	Votes (%)	Number of seats
Liberal	**42**	**177**	**41**	**173**
Conservative	**16**	**2**	12	12
New Democratic Party	7	9	9	13
Reform/Alliance	19	52	26	66
Bloc Québécois	14	54	11	37
Total	(98)	(294)	(99)	(301)

Note: The **bold** entries show the extreme bias against the Conservatives in 1993 and the bias in favour of the Liberals in both elections.. Minor parties not shown.

The plurality system, familiar to us from Britain and the United States, is not the only form of non-proportional representation. There is also a less common but perhaps more democratic version: the majoritarian method. As its name implies, this formula requires a majority of votes for the winning candidate, an outcome normally achieved through a second ballot. If no candidate wins a majority on the first round, an additional ballot is held, usually a run-off between the top two candidates.

Many countries in Western Europe used majority voting before switching to PR early in the twentieth century. The system remains significant in France and its ex-colonies. For democrats, the argument for a majoritarian system is intuitively quite strong: namely, that no candidate should be elected without being shown to be acceptable to a majority of voters or even, where the rules so require, to a majority of electors.

Within the majoritarian category, the alternative vote (AV) is a rather efficient way of achieving a majority outcome in a single ballot within single-member seats. In this system, devised by an American academic in the 1870s, voters rank candidates in order of preference. However, lower preferences only come into play if no candidate gains a majority of first preferences on the first count (see Box 9.1). AV is used for Australia's lower chamber, the House of Representatives. Compared to simple plurality voting, AV takes into account more information

about voters' preferences but it is not necessarily more proportional.

Proportional representation

We move now from non-proportional systems to proportional representation. PR is more recent than non-proportional systems; it emerged in continental Europe towards the end of the nineteenth century, stimulated by the founding of associations dedicated to electoral reform. Even so, PR is now more common than plurality and majority systems; it has been the method of choice for most democratic countries since the early 1920s (Blais and Massicote, 2002, p. 41). PR is the norm in Western and now Eastern Europe. It also predominates in Latin America.

The guiding principle of PR is to represent parties rather than territory. The idea is straightforward and plausible: namely, that parties should be awarded seats in direct proportion to their share of the vote. In a perfectly proportional system, every party would receive the same share of seats as of votes; 40 per cent of the votes would mean 40 per cent of the seats.

Although the mechanics of PR are designed with the principle of proportionality in mind, most 'PR' systems are not perfectly proportional. They usually offer at least some bonus to the largest party, though less than most non-proportional methods, and they also discriminate by design or practice against the smallest parties. For these reasons, it would be wrong to assume that any system labelled 'proportional' must be perfectly so.

A single party rarely wins a majority of seats under PR. Hence majority governments are unusual and coalitions become standard. Because PR usually leads to post-election negotiations in parliament about which parties will form the next government, it is best interpreted as a method of selecting parliaments rather than governments.

How does PR achieve the goal of proportionality? The most common method, by far, is the list system. An elector votes for a slate of the party's candidates rather than for just a single person. The number of votes won by a party determines how many candidates are elected from that party's list. The order in which candidates appear on the list (decided by the party itself) governs which people are elected to represent that party. For example, suppose a party wins 10 per cent of the vote in an election to a 150-seat assembly. That party will be entitled to 15 members, who will be the top 15 candidates on its list.

List systems vary in how much choice they give voters between candidates on a party's list. At one extreme stand the closed party lists used in Portugal, South Africa and Spain. In these countries, voters have no choice over candidates; they simply vote for a party. This gives party officials enormous, and perhaps excessive, control over political recruitment.

However, most list systems do give voters at least some choice between candidates. Switzerland and Luxembourg operate exceptionally open lists in which electors are given the opportunity to vote either for a party's list or for an individual candidate from the list. But most voters spurn the choice; they adopt the simple procedure of voting for a party's entire slate.

List systems require multimember constituencies. Normally, the country is divided into a set of multimember districts and seats are allocated separately within each district. Using constituencies in this way preserves some territorial basis to representation but, in the absence of an additional compensating device, reduces the proportionality of the outcome.

The number of members returned per district is known as the district magnitude. This figure is a critical influence on how proportional PR systems are in practice (Lijphart, 1994). As Farrell (2001, p. 79) observes, 'the basic relationship for all proportional systems is: the larger the constituency size, and hence the larger the district magnitude, the more proportional the result'. For example, Spain is divided into 52 small districts, returning an average of just seven members each. This small magnitude means that a party winning a limited share of the vote may not be entitled to any seats at all. Indeed, in 2000 the Popular Party won a majority of seats with just 44 per cent of the vote, confirming the boost which proportional systems with a small district magnitude give to the leading party.

However, in the Netherlands, Israel and Slovakia, the whole country serves as a single large constituency, extending proportionality even to small parties. The Israeli election of 1999, for example, saw a total of 15 parties winning seats in the 120-member Knesset. By dispensing with smaller electoral districts, such countries eliminate the vaunted link between constituency and representative found in single-member plurality systems.

Definition
District magnitude refers to the number of representatives chosen for each electoral district. Under proportional representation, the more representatives to be elected for a district, the more proportional the electoral system can be. When the entire country serves as a single district, very small parties can win representation in parliament. By contrast, when only three or four members are elected per district, smaller parties often fail to win a seat even with a respectable vote. Thus the 'proportionality' of a PR system is not fixed but varies with its district magnitude.

Most list systems add an explicit threshold of representation below which small parties receive no seats at all, whatever their entitlement under the list formula (Table 9.2). Thresholds, operating at district or national level, help to protect the legislature from extremists. As Kostadinova (2002) observes, 'the threshold is a powerful mechanism for reducing fragmentation in the assembly. It can

Table 9.2 Explicit thresholds of representation in some PR systems

Country	Threshold (minimum share of total vote required to be awarded any list seats)
Turkey	10%
Moldova	6%
Czech Republic, Germany, Poland	5%
Hungary, Norway, Sweden	4%
Denmark	2%

Note: Hungary and Germany use mixed electoral systems. German parties winning three district contests achieve representation in the Bundestag even if they fall below the 5% threshold on the party vote.

Sources: Jasiewicz (2003), LeDuc et al. (2002a).

be and is manipulated by elites to cut off access to parliament for smaller parties.'

Turkey is a case in point. Its demanding threshold of 10 per cent of votes cast was designed by the country's secular rulers to exclude small Islamic parties. However, such a high hurdle can have capricious results. In the 2002 election – won ironically by a party with Islamic origins – over 40 per cent of voters supported a party which did not win any seats in parliament. Here is a striking case of 'PR' delivering a most unproportional, and seemingly unfair, outcome.

Mixed systems

Plurality and PR systems are usually considered alternatives yet a hybrid form has emerged which combines the two. This mixed method seeks the best of both worlds (Shugart and Wattenberg, 2000). It combines the geographical representation of the plurality method with the party representation of PR.

Germany is the source of this ingenious compromise. There, electors have two votes: one for a district candidate and the other for a regional party list. Half the seats in the Bundestag are filled by candidates elected by plurality voting within each electoral district. However, the party list vote is more important because it determines the total number of seats to be awarded to each party within each region. Candidates from the party's list are used to top up its directly elected candidates until the correct – that is, proportional – number of seats is achieved within each region. Should a party win more district seats than its entitlement under the party vote, it retains the extra seats and the Bundestag expands in size. In 2002, the SPD won four excess mandates, as they are called, and the CDU one (Scarrow, 2002a).

Table 9.3 shows how the German electoral system operated in the 2002 election. Note that without the party list component, the Free Democrats would not be represented in the Bundestag at all. Similarly, the Greens would have only one seat, precluding them from achieving their current elevated position as a coalition partner of the SPD in Europe's largest and wealthiest democracy.

Because of the additional members drawn from the party list, Germany's format is often described as an additional member system (AMS). The compromise character of AMS has encouraged other countries, including Italy and New Zealand, to experiment with similar methods, though sometimes varying the balance between district and list members. The system has also been adopted for the Scottish and Welsh assemblies in the UK.

Other countries have introduced the idea of separate district and party list votes but without any top-up device to achieve a proportional outcome overall. Countries using this non-proportional mixed member majoritarian (MMM) system include Japan, Thailand, Russia and several other post-communist countries.

Assessing electoral systems

In assessing electoral systems, an issue arising is the relationship between electoral systems and party systems. This topic remains a matter of controversy. In a classic work, Duverger (1954, p. 217) argued that 'an almost complete correlation is observable' between the plurality method and a two-party system; he suggested that this relationship, based on mechanical and psychological

Table 9.3 How the additional member system works: the German federal election of September 2002

A Party	B Party list vote (%)	C Number (and %) of constituency seats won	D Number of list seats awarded (to bring column E more in line with column B)	E Final number (and %) of seats for each party (C + D)
Social Democrats (SPD)	38.5	171 (57.2%)	80	251 (41.7%)
Christian Democrats/ Christian Social Union (CDU/CSU)	38.5	125 (41.8%)	123	248 (41.1%)
Greens	8.6	1 (0.3%)	54	55 (9.1%)
Free Democrats (FDP)	7.4	0 (–)	47	47 (7.8%)
Party of Democratic Socialism (PDS)	4.0	2 (0.7%)	0	2 (0.3%)
Others	3.0	0 (–)	0	0
Total	100	299 (100%)	304	603 (100%)

Notes:
1. The PDS did not pass the 5% threshold required for the award of seats from its party list.
2. The table shows the national outcome from an allocation of list seats which takes place at regional level.
3. Turnout: 79.1%. Spoilt ballots: 1.2% (party list vote), 1.5% (constituency vote).

Source: Federal Statistical Office at http://www.destatis.de.

effects, approached that of 'a true sociological law'. At the time, Duverger's law seemed to favour the plurality system since PR and its accompanying multiparty systems were still found guilty by their association with unstable coalition governments.

Definition

Duverger (1954) distinguished two effects of electoral systems. The **mechanical** effect arises directly from the rules converting votes into seats. An example is the threshold for representation used in many proportional systems. The **psychological** effect is the impact of the rules on how electors cast their votes. For example, the plurality system used in Britain and the USA discourages electors from supporting minor parties with little realistic chance of victory in the voter's home district.

But in the 1960s a reaction set in against attributing weight to political institutions such as electoral systems. Writers such as Rokkan (1970) adopted a more sociological approach, pointing out that social cleavages had produced multiparty systems in Europe long before PR was adopted early in the twentieth century. Bringing the argument up to date, Jasiewicz (2003, p. 182) makes exactly the same point about post-communist Europe: 'political fragmentation usually preceded the adoption of a PR-based voting system, not vice versa'.

Furthermore, Duverger's law has declined in authority with the emergence of more regional party systems in two countries still using plurality elections: India and Canada. In a recent comparative study, Norris (2004, p. 164) does find that the evidence 'supports Duverger's generalization that plurality electoral systems tend towards party dualism while PR is associated with multipartyism'. However, the observed difference is small. Electoral systems are only one of several influences on the number of parties achieving representation.

Much ink has also been used on a related issue: the question of which is the 'best' electoral system.

In truth there is no such thing; different horses run best on different courses. For example, in countries with intense social divisions such as Northern Ireland, PR will provide at least some representation for parties based on minority groups. In this way, the risk of majority tyranny is reduced.

By contrast, in the context of national competition between two main parties, plurality systems usually result in government by a single victorious party. Each new government can implement its policies without needing to water them down through compromises with coalition partners. This philosophy is seen in the UK, where the losing party is willing to trust its opponents to get on with the task of governing, secure in the knowledge that its own time will come again.

It must be acknowledged, though, that the plurality method can thrust parties in and out of office in an erratic and exaggerated way. Canada is a good example. In 1984, the Conservatives won three-quarters of the seats on just half the vote. Nine years later they were unmade in an astonishing election which reduced their representation to just two seats despite retaining 16 per cent support (Table 9.1).

Whatever their theoretical weaknesses, electoral systems tend to persist once established by a founding election. After all, parties elected to power under one system have no incentive to change to another. Yet although electoral reform is uncommon, it is far from unknown. Japan, Italy and New Zealand each changed their electoral system in the 1990s. All three countries adopted the fashionable additional member system. These countries therefore provide useful case studies of the impact of electoral reform. Over the short term, the effects seemed to be limited:

▶ In Japan, the object was to reduce the significance of money in elections by ending an unusual system that forced candidates from the same party into competition with each other. Yet even today factionalism and corruption continue to inhibit real policy debate (Reed and Thies, 2002).

▶ Reformers in Italy wanted to escape from the unstable coalitions produced by PR. In their place, reformers sought to encourage a small number of large parties that would alternate in power, British-style. Yet the first government produced under Italy's new electoral law lasted just eight months and the parties still rely on regional rather than national support (Katz, 2002).

▶ In New Zealand, the motive was to reduce the unrestrained power of the single-party governments produced by the plurality method. Again, however, the first parliamentary term under the new system was hardly a great success. It was marked by a fractious and unstable coalition involving New Zealand First, a new party dominated by a leader who had been expelled from the larger National Party (Denemark, 2002).

Over the medium term, however, electoral reform in these countries may deliver at least some of the desired benefits. Japanese debate now accepts the weaknesses of factionalism, even if factions themselves remain robust. New Zealand is growing accustomed to coalitions and in 1999 its electorate voted New Zealand First not just out of office but almost out of parliament.

But it is Italy that provides perhaps the best recent example of electoral reform achieving some of its objectives. Although the country continues to be governed by coalitions of regional parties, these groupings now represent broad left- and right-wing traditions and have achieved an alternation in office. As Newell and Bull (2002, p. 26) note,

The Italian election of 2001 resulted in alternation in office between a coalition of the centre-right and an incumbent centre-left government seeking re-election. This was the first time this had happened since the birth of the Italian Republic . . . The election brought to office a pre-constituted coalition with an overall majority.

Electoral systems: presidents

Electoral systems for choosing presidents receive less attention than those for electing legislatures. Yet most countries have an elected president and sometimes, as in the Americas, the occupant has clear executive powers. So this rather neglected subject certainly deserves attention.

In one sense, the rules for electing presidents are straightforward. Unlike seats in parliament, a one-person presidency cannot be shared between parties; the office is indivisible. So PR is impossible and the main choice is between the plurality and the majority method. However, in another sense, presidential electoral systems are more complicated: many, including the USA, are based on indirect election through a special college.

We consider directly elected presidents first. As Figure 9.1 shows, 61 of the 91 directly-elected presidents in the world are chosen by a majority system. The reason, presumably, is that it is more important to confirm majority backing for a single president than for every single member of a legislature. Most majority elections for president use a second ballot of the top two candidates if neither wins a majority of votes in the first round. France, once more, is a leading case.

Plurality contests, in which the candidate with most votes on the first and only round wins, are less common. This technique saves the expense of two ballots but the winner may receive only a small share of the vote when several serious candidates emerge. To take an extreme illustration, General Banzer won the Bolivian election of 1997 with just 20 per cent support, hardly a ringing endorsement for a national chief executive.

A further requirement used in a few presidential elections is to impose a turnout threshold of 50 per cent. If turnout falls below that level, the contest begins anew. Such requirements were common in communist states, where the party could dragoon electors to the polls, but are a dangerous requirement in free elections. In the winter of 2002/03, Serbia and Montenegro each experienced two failed presidential elections.

As Figure 9.1 also shows, almost a third of presidents manage to avoid the perils of direct election altogether. Many of these are chosen via indirect election where a special body (which may itself be elected) supposedly acts as a buffer against the whims of the people.

The United States was once an example. Most of the Founding Fathers opposed direct election of the president, fearing the dangers of democracy.

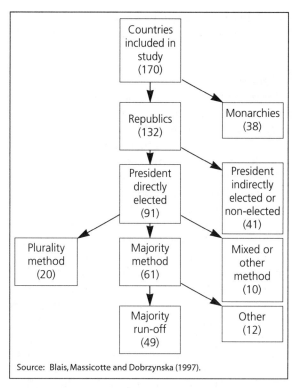

Source: Blais, Massicotte and Dobrzynska (1997).

Figure 9.1 Methods for selecting presidents

After inconclusive debate at the consitutional convention, they eventually settled on a form of indirect election: an electoral college with delegates selected by each state legislature as it saw fit. In choosing the president, the delegates were expected to show wisdom beyond that of ordinary voters. Today, the college survives only as a procedural relic, with nearly all delegates routinely voting for the candidate to which they are pledged.

However, votes for American presidential candidates are still counted by state, with the leading candidate in a state winning all its votes in the college. This federal feature means that a candidate can still gain the White House despite receiving fewer votes than his main opponent. Four presidential elections have led to just such an outcome. In 2000, not only did Al Gore win more votes than Bush, he would also probably have won had the United States employed the majority run-off method. Such an outcome would have resulted from first-round voters for the Green candidate switching to Gore in the run-off. So we still cannot regard the American format for electing presidents as a straight forward example of direct election using the plurality method (Dahl, 2001, p. 81).

> **Definition**
>
> **Indirect election** occurs when office-holders are elected by a body which has itself been chosen by a wider constituency. Indirect election was widely used within communist parties as a device for limiting democratic expression; each level only elected the next level up. The device is also employed in many presidential elections and for upper houses of parliament.

Three other features of presidential elections are worthy of note: the length of the term, the possibility of reelection and the link with other elections. On the first of these points, the presidential term is normally no shorter, and sometimes longer, than for parliament. The longer the term, the easier it is for presidents to adopt a broad perspective free from the immediate burden of reelection. At just four years, the term of office of American presidents is unusually short. The danger is that year one is spent acquiring experience and year four seeking reelection, leaving only the middle period as years of accomplishment.

Second, term limits are often imposed, restricting the incumbent to just one or two periods in office (Box 9.2). The fear is that without such constraints presidents will be able to exploit their unique position to remain in office too long. Thus, the USA introduced a two-term limit after Franklin Roosevelt won four elections in a row between 1932 and 1944. Mexican presidents (like the deputies in parliament) cannot stand for reelection.

As with many institutional fixes, term limits solve one problem at the cost of creating another. Lame-duck presidents lose clout as their term nears its end. For instance, the Korean financial crisis of 1997 coincided with the end of the president's non-renewable six-year tenure, adding to uncertainty. Popular presidents, replete with confidence and experience, may be debarred from office at the peak of their power. Also, presidents subject to term limits sometimes seek to alter the constitution in order to permit their own reelection, a regular source of friction in Latin America.

Third, the timing of presidential elections is also important. When they occur alongside elections to the assembly, the successful candidate is more likely to be drawn from the same party as dominates the legislature. Without threatening the separation of powers, concurrent elections limit the fragmentation of the presidential executive (Jones, 1995a). This thinking lay behind the reduction of the French president's term to five years in 2000, the same tenure as the assembly.

Voting behaviour

Given that voters have a choice, how do they decide who to vote for? Although this is the most intensively studied question in all political science, there is no single answer. As a broad summary, however, since 1945 electors in the established democracies have moved away from group and party voting towards voting on issues, the economy, leaders and party competence. Franklin (1992) describes this process as 'the decline of cleavage politics and the rise of issue voting'.

For two decades after the Second World War, most studies of electoral behaviour disputed the intuitive proposition that voters do 'choose' which party to support. An influential theory of electoral choice, originally developed in the United States in the 1950s, argued that voting was an act of affirmation rather than choice (Campbell *et al.*, 1960). Voting was seen as an expression of a loyalty to a party, a commitment which was both deep-seated and long-lasting. This 'party identification', as it was termed, was acquired initially through one's family and then reinforced through membership of politically uniform social groups (for example, colleagues at work).

In the USA, party attachment was confirmed by the traditional requirement to register as a party supporter to be eligible to vote in its primaries. American electors learned – or were taught – to think of themselves as Democrats, Republicans or, in a minority of cases, as Independents. This view of the American voter as an habitual supporter of a particular party is variously called the socialization, Michigan or party identification model.

In Europe voting expressed loyalty to a social group rather than a party. The act of voting flowed

BOX 9.2
Methods for electing presidents: some examples

Country	Method of election	Term (years)	Reelection permitted?
Argentina	Electoral college	6	After one term out
Brazil	Run-off	5	After one term out
Finland	Plurality	6	Yes
France	Run-off	5*	Yes
Mexico	Plurality	6	No
Russia	Run-off	5	One term out required after two terms served
United States	Electoral college	4	Two-term limit

* Reduced from seven years by constitutional amendment in 2000.

Source: Adapted from Jones (1995b). See also Nurmi and Nurmi (2002).

from one's identification with a particular religion, class or ethnic group. Thus electors thought of themselves as Catholic or Protestant, middle-class or working-class; and they voted for parties which explicitly stood for these interests. In short, social identity anchored party choice. But whether the emphasis was placed on identification with the party (as in the USA) or with the social group (as in Europe), voting was viewed more as a reflex than as a choice. The electoral 'decision' was an ingrained habit.

Definition

Party identification is a long-term attachment to a particular party which anchors voters' interpretations of the remote world of politics. Party identification is often inherited through the family and reinforced by the elector's social milieu. It influences, but is separate from, electoral choice. The stability of party identification was used to explain the continuity of Western party systems in the 1950s and 1960s.

These models of party and group voting had become less useful by the 1960s and 1970s. Those decades witnessed partisan dealignment: that is, the weakening of the ties which once bound voters, social groups and political parties together. Particularly in the third quarter of the century, the

proportion of party identifiers declined in many established democracies (Box 9.3).

What caused this decline in party loyalties? One factor was political: the decay was not uniform but tended to be focused on periods of disillusionment with governing parties. In the USA, for instance, the fall of party identification was sharpest during the period of the Vietnam War and the associated student protests.

Another factor in party dealignment was the declining capacity of social cleavages to fashion electoral choice. In Europe, class and religious identities became less relevant to young, well-educated people living in urban, mobile and more secular societies. Class voting, in fact, declined throughout the democratic world, allowing Dalton (2002, p. 193) to conclude that 'class-based voting . . . currently has limited influence in structuring voting choices'. New divisions, such as that between employees in the public and private sectors, cut across rather than reinforced the traditional class cleavage (Knutsen, 2001). Television – more neutral and leader-centred than the press – also loosened old party loyalties.

The consequences of dealignment are still emerging but will surely be substantial. Much of the democratic world has already witnessed the emergence of new parties with a more radical complexion, such as the Greens, and a decline not just in turnout but also in active participation in campaigns. Electoral volatility has grown, split-ticket voting (where relevant) has increased and more electors are deciding how to vote closer to election day. Also, candidates and leaders seem to have grown in importance relative to the parties they represent (Dalton *et al.*, 2000).

However, in none of these areas have we witnessed a complete transformation. In most democracies, most of the time, most electors still go to the polls to support the same party for which they have always voted. Dealignment, we should remind ourselves, refers to the weakening of existing patterns and not to either their disappearance (non-alignment) or the creation of new links between cleavages and parties (realignment).

Definition

Partisan dealignment refers to the weakening of bonds between (a) electors and parties, and (b) social groups and parties. In most established democracies, such links have declined in strength but they have not disappeared; electorates are dealigning rather than dealigned.

> **BOX 9.3**
> ## Decline in party identification, 1970s–1990s
>
> | Decline over 10% | Decline of 1–10% | No decline |
> | --- | --- | --- |
> | Austria | Australia | Belgium |
> | Canada | Finland | Denmark |
> | France | Japan | |
> | Germany | Netherlands | |
> | Ireland | New Zealand | |
> | Italy | Norway | |
> | Sweden | United Kingdom | |
> | USA | | |
>
> Note: Figures are based on a standard survey question asking people whether they 'think of themselves' as, for example, a Democrat or a Republican. Decline is measured between an initial survey (1967-78, depending on country) and a later survey (1991-98).
>
> Sources: Bentley *et al.*, (2000); Dalton and Wattenberg (2000).

The decay of group and party voting has led political scientists to focus on the question of how voters do now decide. The contemporary emphasis is on four factors: political issues, the economy, party leaders and party image. Fiorina's theory (1981) of retrospective voting captures many of these themes. As developed by Fiorina, retrospective voting means casting one's ballot in response to government performance; his phrase tells us much about the character of contemporary electoral behaviour. Electors do form a general assessment of the government's record and, increasingly, they vote accordingly. A vote is no longer an expression of a lifelong commitment, rather it is becoming a piece of business like any other. The elector asks of the government, 'what have you done for me (and the country) lately?'

Retrospective voting helps to explain why economic conditions, particularly disposable income, unemployment and inflation, seem to have such a consistent impact on the popularity of governments (Dorussen and Taylor, 2002). More voters now proceed on the brutal assumption that governments should be punished for bad times and perhaps also rewarded for economic advance. Especially where a single party forms the government, more voters are happy to judge by results; they are now fairweather friends only (Nadeau *et al.*, 2002). The feel-good factor, however, is not just a matter of objective economic performance; voters' perceptions of the economy are the key battleground and here politicians have some room for manoeuvre.

In this more pragmatic era, electors assess the general competence of parties. Increasingly, they ask not just what a party proposes to do but also how well it will do it. Given that parties are less rooted in ideology and social groups than in the past, their reputation for competence in meeting the unpredictable demands of office becomes a crucial marketing asset. So party image becomes crucial. The skill is to generate trust in one's own side and especially to create doubts about one's opponents. Given volatile and sceptical voters, gaining credibility – or at least more than one's opponents – is the cardinal objective (Bowler and Farrell, 1992).

Turnout

Despite rising levels of education, turnout is falling throughout most of the democratic world. (Table 9.4). In 19 democracies, turnout fell on average by 10 per cent between the 1950s and the 1990s (Wattenberg, 2000). For example:

▸ In the USA, turnout among the adult population declined from 63 per cent in the presidential election of 1960 to 49 per cent in 1996, recovering but modestly to 51 per cent in the close contest of 2000.
▸ Turnout among registered electors at British general elections declined from 78 per cent in 1992 to 59 per cent in 2001, a loss of 7 million voters in just nine years.
▸ In national elections in Switzerland, as in many countries at regional and local contests, abstainers now comprise the majority.

Why has turnout fallen? Precisely because the phenomenon is so widespread, it is difficult to pinpoint its causes. However, there seems little doubt that declining turnout forms part of a wider trend in the democratic world: namely, a growing

Table 9.4 Declining turnout at national elections, 1950s–1990s

Decline over 10%	Decline of 1–10%	No decline
Austria	Australia	Denmark
France	Belgium	Sweden
Japan	Canada	
New Zealand	Finland	
Switzerland	Germany	
United Kingdom	Ireland	
USA	Netherlands	
Norway		

Note: Figures are based on a comparison between the first two elections in the 1950s and the last two elections before 2000. Most of the fall occurred in the late 1980s and the 1990s.

Source: Adapted from Bentley *et al.* (2000) and Wattenberg (2000).

distance between voters, on the one hand, and parties and government, on the other. It is surely no coincidence that turnout has fallen as party dealignment has gathered pace, as party membership has fallen and as the class and religious cleavages which sustained party loyalties in the early postwar decades have decayed.

Franklin (2002, p. 174) links the decline of turnout to the diminishing significance of elections. He suggests that the success of many democracies in establishing welfare states and achieving full employment in the postwar era resolved long-standing conflicts between capital and labour. With class conflict disarmed, electors had fewer incentives to vote on election day. As Franklin writes, 'elections in recent years may show lower turnout for the simple reason that these elections decide issues of lesser importance than elections did in the late 1950s'.

Declining satisfaction with the performance of democratic governments has also played a part (Norris, 1999a). Especially in the 1980s, popular trust in government and parties fell in many democracies, reflecting the growing complexity, internationalization and corruption of governance. Even though mass support for democratic principles remains strong, growing cynicism about government performance has probably led more people to stay away from the polls (Putnam *et al.*, 2000).

Declining turnout does not seem to reflect any decline in political interest. On the contrary, Dalton *et al.* (2000, p. 56) show that with increasing education 'political interest is generally increasing over time'. Rather, electoral participation has been caught up in wider shifts in political behaviour. Younger generations increasingly follow and discuss events as forms of participation in themselves. In addition, because younger cohorts tend to view elections as part of the official political system, participating in them has less appeal than joining informal social movements.

Turnout varies not just over time but also between countries. How then can we explain cross-national difference in turnout? Here a cost–benefit analysis is useful (Downs, 1957). That is, turnout tends to be higher in those countries where the costs or effort of voting are low and the perceived benefits high (Box 9.4). On the cost side, turnout is greater in those countries where voting is permitted through the mail and over the weekend. It is reduced when the citizen is required to take the initiative in registering as an elector with the local administration, as in the USA. On the benefit side, proportional representation enhances voting by ensuring each ballot affects the outcome (Lijphart, 1999). Also, the more importance people attach to an election, the higher the turnout; presidential contests, for example, typically secure a higher ballot than parliamentary contests (Norris, 2003).

At the level of the individual, variations in turnout reflect the pattern found with other forms of political participation. Specifically, high turnout reflects political resources and political interest. Thus, educated, affluent, middle-aged citizens with a strong party identification, and those who belong to a church or a trade union, are particularly prone to vote.

By contrast, abstention is most frequent among poorly educated, unemployed young people who belong to few organizations and who have no party ties. Minorities are particularly likely to abstain. For instance, Hispanics form 10 per cent of the American population but provided only 4 per cent of the voters in the American presidential election of 2000 (Conway, 2001, p. 81).

Referendums

Elections are instruments of representative democracy; the role of the people is only to decide who will decide. By contrast, referendums, and similar devices such as the initiative and the recall, are devices of direct democracy, enabling voters to decide issues themselves. A *referendum* involves a *refer*ence from another body, normally the legislature or the government, to the people for resolution. The device therefore provides a practical counter-example to the common argument that direct democracy is impossible in large states.

Further, technology has opened up the possibility of voting in referendums through convenient electronic devices such as digital television, personal computers and mobile phones (Budge, 1996). Referendum democracy has become tech-

---

BOX 9.4

Features of the electoral system and of individuals which increase turnout

Features of the electoral system	Features of individuals
Compulsory voting	Middle age
Proportional representation	Strong party loyalty
Postal voting permitted	Extensive education
Weekend polling	Attends church
Elections decide who governs*	Belongs to a union
Automatic registration	Higher income

* Examples of elections which do *not* decide who governs are those to the American Congress and the European parliament.

Source: Franklin (2002).

---

nically feasible; the question now is whether it is politically wise.

Referendums vary in their status. Their outcome may be binding, as with constitutional amendments requiring popular approval, or merely consultative, as with Sweden's vote in 1994 on membership of the European Union. A binding referendum will normally be triggered automatically under the constitution whereas a consultative referendum is typically an option for a hesitant government.

In a few countries (now including New Zealand), referendums can also be initiated by citizen petition, a device extending popular influence to the political agenda itself. The initiative, as such citizen-initiated ballots are known, is used widely in Switzerland. It has also been adopted by many Western states in the USA, notably California. For instance, Proposition 13 in 1978 limited property taxes in California, launching a sequence of taxpayers' revolts in Western democracies.

We should note two unusual forms of the initiative. First, Italy uses what has become known as the abrogative referendum. Five regional councils

DEBATE
COMPULSORY VOTING

As turnout declines across most of the democratic world, so attention focuses on potential solutions. Technical fixes, such as putting polling stations in supermarkets and permitting voting by email, may have a role to play. Countries using plurality or majority voting could also boost turnout by introducing proportional representation, in which every vote counts. But has the time come to consider the most radical and effective solution of all: compulsory voting?

The case for
Most citizens acknowledge obligations to the state such as paying taxes, obeying the law and even fighting in war. Why therefore should they not accept what Hill (2002) calls the 'light obligation and undemanding duty' of voting at national elections? Currently, abstainers take a free ride on the backs of the conscientious.

By definition, an election based on a full turnout would be representative of the population and ensure a measure of political equality. It would enhance the authority of the government, a collective benefit. If required to vote, disengaged groups such as the young and ethnic minorities would be drawn into the political process, reducing current divisions.

As with military service, people who object on principle to participating could be exempted. Also, the requirement could merely be to cast a ballot, not necessarily to fill it out (the Australian approach). Alternatively, the ballot could include an 'against all' option, as in Russia. Further, the mere existence of compulsory voting would provide sufficient incentive to participate without any great need to punish non-voters. If compulsory voting can work in Australia, where the fine is a mere $20 if no satisfactory explanation is provided for abstention, it can surely work elsewhere.

The case against
Mandatory voting is a denial of the liberty which forms an essential component of liberal democracy. Requiring people to participate is a sign of an authoritarian regime, not a democracy. Paying taxes and fighting in battle are duties where every little helps, and where numbers matter. However, elections in all

Table 9.5 Turnout in some countries with compulsory voting

Country	Turnout at most recent legislative election (%)	Year of election
Australia	94.9	2001
Belgium	96.3	2003
Turkey	76.9	2002
Brazil	78.5	1998
Greece	75.0	2000
Mexico	57.2	2000

Note: Turnout in the 2002 presidential election in Brazil was 79.5%.

Source: International Institute for Democracy and Electoral Assistance at http://www.idea.int.

democracies still attract more than enough votes to fill the posts. It is unlikely that an increase in turnout would raise the quality of choice; indeed, requiring those with least political interest and knowledge to take part could lead to worse decisions. Furthermore, the law would need to be enforced; otherwise the entire legal system would suffer.

Compulsory voting deals with symptoms rather than causes. It distracts from the real task of attracting people back to the polls of their own volition. In any case, why worry? Perhaps non-voting just reflects contentment with life. Krauthammer (1990) may have been right in claiming that 'low voter turnout means that people see politics as quite marginal to their lives, as neither salvation nor ruin. That is healthy.'

Assessment
Compulsory voting does make a difference: when the Netherlands made voting optional in 1970, turnout fell considerably (Andeweg and Irwin, 2002, p. 74). However, the opposite reform – introducing mandatory voting where it did not previously exist – has not been tried recently. The danger is that it would backfire, increasing political distrust between government and governed. There is surely a case for testing other reforms designed to increase turnout before resorting to compulsion.

Further reading: Franklin (2002), Hill (2002), Katz (1997, pp. 243–5), van Deth (2000).

BOX 9.5

The referendum, initiative and recall

Referendum – a vote of the electorate on an issue of public policy such as a constitutional amendment. The vote may be binding or consultative.

Initiative – a procedure which allows a certain number of citizens (typically around 10 per cent in American states) to initiate a referendum on a given topic.

Recall – allows a certain number of voters to demand a referendum on whether an elected official should be removed from office.

Sources: Bowler *et al.* (1998), Cronin (1989).

---

or 500,000 electors can initiate a popular vote but only on whether to repeal an existing law (Uleri, 2002). So, unlike normal initiatives, the abrogative referendum does not permit the people to raise new issues.

Second, some 15 American states make provision for recall elections. These are ballots on whether an elected official should be removed from office. A ballot is held on a petition from around 25 per cent of the votes cast for the relevant office at the previous election. Originally designed to dismiss corrupt politicians, the recall has rarely been used.

However, a ballot to recall Democratic Governor Gray Davis did take place in California in 2003, following a petition by more than one million registered voters. This recall election allowed numerous Republican candidates (including Arnold Schwarzenegger, the eventual victor) to stand as a potential replacement for Davis without going through the extensive vetting needed to win a party nomination for an ordinary gubernatorial election. This short cut enabled Schwarzenegger to exploit his celebrity status, propelling him into the governorship.

Referendums are growing in popularity. Most referendums held in the twentieth century occurred after 1960 and most democracies held at least one referendum in the final quarter of the century (LeDuc, 2002). Switzerland headed the

list, holding 72 referendums between 1975 and 2000. In 2003, it decided nine referendums at once, on issues ranging from abandoning nuclear power to banning car use on four Sundays each year. However, few countries have made more than occasional use of the device and the USA has held none at all at national level. Despite the tradition of direct democracy in some American states, the constitution makes no provision for national referendums.

What is the contribution of referendums to democracy and governance? How desirable is it to transform citizens into legislators? On the plus side, referendums do seem to increase people's understanding of the issue, their confidence in their own political abilities and their faith in government responsiveness (Bowler and Donovan, 2002). Like elections themselves, referendums provide an education for those who take part in them.

But there are also reasons for caution. By its nature, the referendum treats issues as isolated topics, ignoring the implications for other areas. What would happen, for instance, if the voters decide both to raise teachers' salaries and to lower taxes? Further, voters are often reluctant to embrace change, turning referendums into an instrument of conservatism as much as democracy (Kobach, 1997).

Despite their democratic credentials, the outcome of optional referendums can be influenced by government control of timing. In 1997 the British government only held a referendum in Wales on its devolution proposals after a similar vote in Scotland, where support for devolution was known to be firmer. In 2003, Eastern European countries began a sequence of referendums on joining the EU in Hungary, hoping the result there would influence the outcome in other candidate states where public opinion was more sceptical (in the event, all the accession countries holding referendums voted in favour).

More crudely, rulers can simply ignore the result of a referendum. In 1955, Swedes voted decisively to continue driving on the left; the country now drives on the right. A quarter of a century later, Swedes voted to decommission its nuclear power stations; it took almost twenty years before the first reactor closed. Alternatively, a referendum can be repeated until the desired outcome is obtained. Ireland, for instance, only ratified the Nice Treaty on the European Union in 2002, at the second time of asking.

In addition to these difficulties, referendums can be easily hijacked:

▸ by wealthy companies waging expensive referendum campaigns on issues in which they have an economic interest
▸ by government control over wording as well as timing
▸ by intense minorities seeking reforms to which the majority is indifferent.

So referendums and other instruments of direct decision-making live uneasily in the house of representative democracy. Their main benefit is to provide a double safety valve. First, a referendum allows governments to put an issue to the people when for some reason it is incapable of reaching a decision itself. Like a plumber's drain-rods, referendums resolve blockages. Second, where the initiative and the recall are permitted, aggrieved citizens can use these devices to raise issues and criticisms that might otherwise go unheard.

Elections in new democracies

Nothing seems to mark out a new democracy as clearly as the introduction of free, fair and competitive elections. And the first election following the withdrawal of the dictators is typically a high turnout affair marking the launch of a new regime. The significance of such founding elections lies less in the result than in their capacity to legitimize the new order. Founding elections are both a referendum on, and a celebration of, democracy.

Examples of founding elections include South Africa in 1994 and the first post-communist elections in most of Eastern Europe in 1990. Throughout Africa, founding elections between 1990 and 1994 were marked by exceptionally high turnouts, convincing victories for the winners and, most important, the peaceful ejection of sitting presidents in 11 countries (Bratton, 1998). True democracy seemed to have arrived at last.

> **Definition**
> A **founding election** is the first election following the transition from authoritarian to democratic rule. Such watershed contests are a public affirmation of the new regime; they are normally high-stimulus, high-turnout events. By contrast, **second elections** are normally marked by lower turnout, some disillusionment and, in some cases, the return of electoral malpractice.

However, second and subsequent elections are a more convincing test of successful democratic consolidation. The broad coalitions which brought down the old rulers soon fall apart as the heroes of the struggle – such as Nelson Mandela in South Africa – gradually depart. Popular euphoria gives way to a more realistic assessment of the hard road ahead. In these more chastened circumstances, the question is whether elections in new democracies continue to provide a fair and accepted method of replacing unpopular rulers.

Certainly, elections in some new democracies have acquired the routine character that reflects consolidation of the democratic order. When the election itself ceases to be the issue, and the focus shifts instead to the competing parties, elections have become an institutionalized part of an established democracy. In these circumstances, a decline in turnout may even indicate a maturing democracy. Here, for example, is Levitsky's assessment (2000, p. 56) of the 1999 election in Argentina:

> Perhaps the most striking change was the routine, even boring, character of the election. In short, a central characteristic of the 1999 election was the unprecedented degree to which electoral politics had become routinized.

Although Russia remains no more than a semi-democracy, Sakwa (2000, p. 85) writes in similar vein about its elections in 1999:

> The elections were no longer so much about a change of regime as about a change of leaders within the system. This is no mean achievement and suggests that the Russian political system is beginning to stabilize and mature.

Yet in many other new democracies the quality of elections seemed to decline in second and subsequent contests. Particularly in sub-Saharan Africa, opposition boycotts, manipulation by existing rulers and simple administrative incompetence came to the fore. International monitoring agencies have become increasingly critical of post-founding elections in many African countries. Rather than becoming the only game in town, the nature and significance of elections continue to be contested, suggesting that some new 'democracies' are moving towards semi-democracy rather than an established democracy.

Further, existing rulers seem to have recovered their capacity to secure their own reelection. The prevalence of this outcome suggests – even if it does not prove – electoral manipulation. As Bratton (1998, p. 65) notes, 'in a "big man" political culture, it is unclear whether the re-election of an incumbent constitutes the extension of a leader's legitimacy or the resignation of the electorate to his inevitable dominance'. In an established democracy, leaders have learnt how to lose but, in many new democracies, cunning rulers have quickly mastered the art of winning.

It seems, then, that the consolidation of democracy must be judged against more demanding standards than merely holding regular elections. Such contests are a necessary but not a sufficient condition of democracy. As Rose and Shin (2001, p. 331) point out,

A spectre is haunting contemporary studies of democratization: conventional influences, such as the introduction of free elections, have not (or at least not yet) created political regimes that match the standards of established democracies.

First-wave democracies, such as Britain and the USA, established the rule of law and the principle of executive accountability to the legislature before they extended the vote to the general population. By contrast, many recent democracies introduced elections even though the idea of government under law had still to be accepted. In these circumstances, elections are in danger of being devalued. The risk is that they become an agent of, rather than a choice among, those who wield power.

Elections in authoritarian states

Although we have defined an election as a competition for office, 'elections' in authoritarian regimes do not provide genuine choice. However, only the most extreme dictator dispenses with elections altogether; the appearance of choice must be preserved if only as a useful fiction (Liddle, 1996). In authoritarian systems, elections are often only semi-competitive, with the winner known in advance and electoral malpractice playing its part in delivering the desired result. In totalitarian systems candidates are simply presented to the voters for approval, without even the illusion of choice.

Elections in authoritarian regimes are more often 'made' than 'stolen' (Mackenzie, 1958). In a made or semi-competitive election, the dice of resources, visibility and access to the media are so heavily loaded towards the current rulers that the desired result is manufactured without resort to electoral theft.

Semi-competitive elections mix choice and control in the characteristic fashion of an authoritarian or semi-democratic state. The ruling party uses all the advantages of office, including effective governance and a high-visibility leader, to ensure its reelection. Patronage is the party's key resource; it is used either to reward loyal voters directly, as with cash for votes, or to provide local notables with jobs, contracts, access, influence, status and money in exchange for the votes of their clients. 'A mobile phone for every shepherd', promised the successful candidate for the presidency of the rural Russian republic of Kalmykia in 1993. 'An internet connection for every school in Peru', proclaimed President Fujimori during his reelection campaign in 2000. In poor countries, such promises from incumbents are worth far more to electors than similar statements from opposition candidates whose destiny is defeat.

Rulers also exploit their control over both the media and the administration of the election. Opposition candidates find they are disqualified from standing; that electoral registration is inefficient in their areas of strength; that they are rarely permitted to appear on television; that they are harassed by the police; and that their leaflets and posters are mysteriously lost. The opposition loses heart because it knows its function is always to oppose but never to win.

By contrast, the incumbent president can exploit unique resources. These include unparalleled visibility built over time, easy access to television, the ability to use the state's coffers for the campaign and finally the capacity to call in political credits carefully acquired while in office. Anticipating the president's reelection, all the underlings will seek to help the campaign along, thus amplifying the final victory. Why back losers?

In its heyday, Mexico's Partido Revolucionaria Institucional (PRI) was one of the world's most successful vote-winning machines, providing the classic example of a party-based approach to semi-competitive elections. By winning 11 presidential elections in a row before its historic defeat in 2000, the PRI became a party of the state, giving it unique access to resources which it could pass out through its intricate patronage network. However, in Mexico as in the larger Latin American countries, semi-competitive elections slowly became harder to manage as the electorate become more urban, affluent and educated. With both the domestic media and international observers becoming more critical of blatant corruption, and with privatization reducing the resources under the government's control, the PRI began to fight cleaner elections, creating the conditions for its own defeat in the 2000 presidential contest.

While semi-competitive elections preserve an illusion of choice, elections in totalitarian regimes were more brutal. In communist states, for instance, there was no pretence that the ruling party could be defeated or even opposed through elections. In the Soviet Union, for instance, the official candidate was simply presented to the electorate for ritual endorsement. Soviet elections were grim, ritualistic affairs, irrelevant to the real politics taking place within the party. They were little more than an opportunity for the party's agitators to lecture the population on the party's achievements (Zaslavsky and Brym, 1978).

Contemporary examples of choice-free elections are confined to decaying communist dictatorships. In Cuba, for example, 609 candidates were put up for election to the National Assembly in 2003; there were exactly 609 seats to be filled. The only choice given to voters was whether to support all, some or none of the candidates.

Some communist states did introduce a measure of choice to their elections by allowing a choice of candidates from within the ruling party. These controlled candidate-choice contests were characteristic of communist Eastern Europe in the 1970s and 1980s. Central rulers found candidate-choice elections useful in testing whether local party officials retain the confidence of their communities.

This is one reason for the gradual introduction of such elections to some of China's 930 000 villages since 1987. In addition, elected village committees help to build state capacity in a country where power has traditionally operated on a personal basis. However, even in contemporary China no explicit opposition to the party's policy platform is permitted. As a result, there are few signs of elections in China threatening the party's control.

Key reading

> **Next step:** *LeDuc, Niemi and Norris (2002) is an excellent comparative study of elections and voting, reviewing a wide literature.*

Katz (1997) links elections with broader democratic themes while Ginsberg (1982) remains a stimulating top-down view of competitive elections. On electoral systems, Farrell (2001) is a clear introduction, Shugart and Wattenberg (2000) look at additional member systems specifically and Norris (2003) examines the impact of electoral systems on party systems. Dalton and Wattenberg (2000) is a comparative study of voting trends; see also Broughton (2002) for turnout and Evans (2003) for a UK-based text on voting behaviour. On the United States see Asher (1988b) for presidential elections generally, and Pomper *et al.* (2001) for the 2000 election. For the impact of campaigns, see Farrell and Schmitt-Beck (2002), and for the influence of leaders' personalities specifically, King (2002). On referendums, consider Gallagher and Uleri (1996) and Mendelsohn and Parkin (2001).

Chapter **10**

Interest groups

Interest groups (also called pressure groups) are 'organizations which have some autonomy from government or political parties and which try to influence public policy' (Wilson, 1990b). They presuppose formal organization and thus can be distinguished from social movements. Examples include employers' organizations, trade unions, consumer groups, bodies representing specific industries or professions and campaigning organizations seeking to promote particular causes.

Like political parties, interest groups inhabit the space between society and state, helping to link the two. But where political parties aspire to become the government, interest groups seek just to influence it. Reflecting this narrower focus, interest groups do not fight elections; instead, they typically adopt a pragmatic and often low-key approach in dealing with whatever power structure confronts them.

Although many interest groups go about their work quietly, their activity is nonetheless pervasive in established democracies. Their staff are to be found negotiating with bureaucrats over the details of proposed regulations, pressing their case in legislative committee hearings and seeking to influence media coverage of their position. In authoritarian regimes, however, interests are articulated in a less public, more spasmodic and sometimes more corrupt fashion. Interests are still expressed to government but often through individual firms or powerful individuals rather than through organized interest groups.

There is a puzzle about how interest groups

succeed in developing in the first place. Olson (1968) argued that people have no reason to join interest groups when the fruits of the group's efforts are equally available to non-members. Why should a worker join a union when the wage rise it negotiates goes to all employees? Why should a company pay a fee to join an industry association when the tax subsidies the group negotiates will help all the firms in that sector? Surely it would be more rational to take a free ride on the efforts of others.

However, the fact is that new groups do emerge and grow; the green lobby, for instance, has grown enormously in recent decades. Perhaps this is because members receive the selective benefits of developing their skills and meeting new people as well as contributing to a shared goal which is dear to their hearts (Moe, 1980).

Definition

A **free rider** leaves others to supply **collective goods** – that is, benefits such as unpolluted air that must be supplied to everyone if they are supplied at all. The possibility of free riding creates incentives not to join interest groups such as labour unions that negotiate deals of equal benefit to members and non-members alike: for example, a safer working environment.

From an historical perspective, interest groups developed in a rather predictable way. In the West, they emerged in a series of waves formed by social change (e.g. industrialization) and by the expansion of state activity (e.g. public welfare). Periods of social change raise new problems while an active government gives people more hope of gains from influencing public policy. Box 10.1 summarizes the development of interest groups in one particular example: the United States. Most Western nations have followed a similar course, resulting in the mosaic of independent group activity making up contemporary society.

BOX 10.1
Waves of interest group formation in the United States

Period	Description	Examples
1830–60	Founding of first national organizations	YMCA and many anti-slavery groups
1880–1900	Creation of many business and labour associations, stimulated by industrialization	National Association of Manufacturers, American Federation of Labor
1900–20	Peak period of interest group formation	Chamber of Commerce, American Medical Association
1960–80	Founding of many environmental and public interest groups	National Organization for Women, Common Cause

Source: Adapted from Hrebenar and Scott (1997, pp. 13–15).

The range and influence of modern interest groups raises awkward questions about the distribution of power in democracies. Favoured groups acquire insider status and thus the potential to influence decisions at an early stage. Often interest groups work in tandem with national governments in developing positions for bodies such as the European Union and the World Trade Organization. Despite only representing small minorities, interest groups are deeply entrenched in policy-making, certainly more so than many supposedly 'sovereign' parliaments. Interest group activity creates a system of functional representation operating alongside electoral representation.

Here, then, is an important question to raise about democracies: do interest groups possess power without accountability? Are interest groups, as Lowi (1969) contended, 'a corruption of democratic government'? Or does group access to policy-making simply express the right to organize in defence of specific objectives? In short, do interest groups help or hinder democracy?

Classifying interest groups

When we think of 'interest groups', the bodies which first come to mind are protective groups articulating the material interests of their members: for instance, trade unions, employers' organizations, industry bodies and professional associations of lawyers or physicians. Sometimes called sectional or functional groups, these protective bodies are founded to influence government. They have sanctions to help them achieve their goals. Workers can go on strike; medical practitioners can refuse to cooperate with a new prescription policy. Protective groups seek selective benefits for their members and insider status with relevant government departments (Box 10.2). Because they represent clear occupational interests, protective associations are often the most influential of all interest groups. They are well-established, well-connected and well-resourced.

But protective groups can also be based on local, rather than functional, interests. Thus, geographic groups arise when the interests of people living in the same location are threatened, for instance by a new highway or a hostel for ex-convicts. Because of their negative stance – 'build it anywhere but here' – these geographical bodies are known as NIMBY groups (not in my back yard).

Of course, protective groups are not the only type of organized interest. Indeed, many groups founded since the 1960s are promotional rather than protective. Promotional groups advocate ideas, identities, policies and values. Also called attitude, cause and campaign groups, promotional groups include pro- and anti-abortion groups, organizations combating pornography and ecology groups.

Promotional groups are most significant in

BOX 10.2

Protective and promotional groups

	Protective groups	*Promotional groups*
Aims	A group *of* – defends an interest	A group *for* – promotes a cause
Membership	Closed – membership is restricted	Open – anybody can join
Status	Insider – frequently consulted by government and actively seeks this role	Outsider – not consulted as often by government. Emphasizes public opinion and the media
Benefits	Selective – only group members benefit	Collective – benefits go to both members and non-members
Focus	Mainly national – group aims to influence national government	More international – group may seek to influence bodies such as the EU and global public opinion

---

established democracies, where they are growing in number, significance and recognition by government. Indeed, the increasing influence of promotional groups since the 1960s, especially in the United States, constitutes a major trend in interest group politics. The relative significance of protective and promotional groups reveals much about the nature of politics and policy-making in any particular country. In the United States, significantly, promoting the public interest is largely the responsibility of a legion of private, promotional groups. For example, Common Cause describes itself as 'a nonprofit, non-partisan citizen's lobbying organization promoting open, honest and accountable government' (Gardner, 2000).

The boundary separating protective and promotional groups is not well-defined. For example, because bodies such as the women's movement and the gay lobby seek to influence public opinion, they are often classified as promotional. However, their prime purpose is to promote the interests of specific groups: they are, perhaps, best viewed as protective interests employing promotional means.

Interest groups do not always lobby government directly. Often, they join together in federations or coalitions with other groups to increase their effectiveness. Such bodies are known as peak associations. Examples include the National Association of Manufacturers in the USA and the Confederation of British Industry in the UK (Figure 10.1). The members of these peaks are not

individuals but firms or interest groups representing specific industries. Trade unions respond similarly: Britain's Trades Union Congress (TUC) consists of 69 affiliated unions with 6.7m individual members who do not themselves belong directly to the TUC. America's AFL–CIO is similarly a coalition of individual unions.

Definition

A **peak association** is an organization representing the broad interests of capital or labour to government. Examples from the Netherlands include the VNO–NCW (Association of Dutch Companies–Dutch Association of Christian Employers) and the FNV (Federation of Dutch Trade Unions). The members of peak associations are not individuals but other organizations such as firms, trade associations or labour unions. Peak associations are important components of corporatism.

Peak organizations are particularly important in policy-making. They are generally more attuned to national government than are their members. They have a strong research capacity and talk the language of policy as well as the language of industry. In some states, peaks play an integral role linking government with their own members and, through them, with the wider society. For the peaks to acquire such a position, however, they must achieve some autonomy from, as well as control over, their members. As implied by the fre-

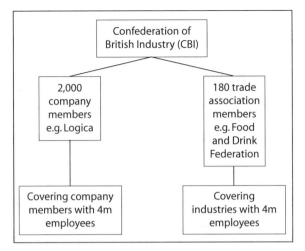

Figure 10.1 A peak association: Britain's CBI

quency with which peak associations label themselves 'federations' or 'confederations', in practice such centralization is often lacking.

The creation of distinct peak associations is largely a phenomenon of protective groups. Among promotional groups, collaboration has so far taken the form of coalitions of existing groups or ad hoc cooperation on specific campaigns. For example, a series of promotional groups might join together to campaign against capital punishment or for writing off third world debt.

Channels of access

How are interests communicated to political decision-makers? What are the channels through

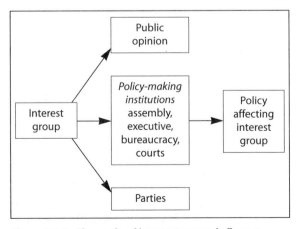

Figure 10.2 Channels of interest group influence

which this process takes place? Figure 10.2 sets out three mechanisms characteristic of established democracies: direct dealings with government, indirect influence through political parties and indirect influence through public opinion. In this section, we will also look at specialist lobbying companies which help to pilot their interest group clients through these varied channels.

Direct discussion with policy-makers

The core business of most interest groups, especially protective ones, is influencing public policy. Most of this activity focuses on the bureaucracy, the legislature and the courts. In established democracies, the *bureaucracy* is the main pressure point. Interest groups follow power and it is in civil servants' offices that detailed decisions are formed. As Matthews (1989, p. 217) comments,

> the bureaucracy's significance is reinforced by its policy-making and policy-implementing roles. Many routine, technical and 'less important' decisions, which are nonetheless of vital concern to interest groups, are actually made by public servants.

Shrewd protective groups focus on the small print because it is difficult for them to control the broad contours of policy, as set by elected politicians. But on matters of detail, most democracies follow a convention of discussion with organized opinion through consultative councils or committees; often the law requires such consultation. After all, the real expertise often lies in the interest group rather than the bureaucracy and, from the minister's viewpoint, an agreement acceptable to all is politically safe.

Consultation is, for example, a key feature of the extraordinarily deliberative character of policy-making in Scandinavia (Blom-Hansen, 2000). Denmark has been termed 'the consulting state' because of the extensive negotiations between the government and the country's 2,000 or so national groups.

Even in France, where the higher bureaucracy traditionally prizes the autonomy of the state, extensive dialogue takes place between civil servants and formally organized interests. This integration is assisted by the role played by the state in organizing the groups themselves. Any association wanting legal rights must register with the state; by 2001, 750,000 had done so. Further, membership of chambers of commerce, agriculture and trade is compulsory for relevant organizations such as firms and farmers. These chambers have acquired semi-public status, helping to implement public policy in consultation with the bureaucracy (Stevens, 2003).

Assemblies are an additional channel through which interests and demands can be voiced. But while the bureaucracy is invariably a crucial arena for groups, the significance of the legislature depends on its political weight. A comparison between the United States and Canada makes the point.

The American Congress (and especially its committees) forms a vital part of the policy process. The separation of powers, the constitutional right 'to petition the government for a redress of grievances', weak party discipline and strong committees combine to create an ideal habitat for lobby operations. Many interest groups have access to individual members of Congress and can arrange to contribute to committee deliberations. Large financial contributions by political action committees (PACs) mean that it can be politically difficult for legislators to spurn group demands (Cigler and Loomis, 2002).

But Congress is a unique case. In most democracies, parliaments are more reactive than proactive; as a result, interest groups treat members of parliament as opinion-leaders rather than decision-makers. For example, party voting is entrenched in the Canadian parliament and lobbyists concentrate their strongest fire on the bureaucracy. As Landes (1995, p. 488) comments on Canada,

interest groups have an acute sense of smell when tracking the scent of power. Interaction with the bureaucracy and not with MPs is the goal of most groups and one reason why interest group activity is not highly visible to the untrained eye.

If interest groups feel ignored in the policy-making process, they may still be able to seek redress through the *courts*. In the European

Union, an interest group that is unsuccessful at home can take its case to the European Court of Justice. In the United States, business corporations routinely subject government statutes and regulations to legal challenge. Class actions are particularly common in America.

> **Definition**
> A **class action** is a legal device initiated by complainants on their behalf and 'for all others so situated'. This mechanism enables legal costs and gains to be shared among a large group and provides a lever by which interest groups can pursue their goals through the courts. The device is commonly used in the USA.

But just as the USA is exceptional in the powers of its legislature, so too does it possess a strong legal culture. Elsewhere, the courts are growing in importance but still as a remedy of last resort. In Australia, for instance, the requirement for litigants to prove their personal interest in the case hinders class actions. When the outcome of a legal case affects only the person initiating it, the policy and financial implications are far less than in a class action covering all those in the same position.

Indirect influence through political parties

Interest groups and parties can overlap since both are devices through which social forces seek to influence government. Britain's labour movement historically regarded its industrial wing (the trade unions) and political wing (the Labour Party) as part of a single movement promoting working-class interests. In a similar way, the environmental movement has spawned both promotional interest groups and green political parties.

But such intimate relationships between groups and parties are the exception. Most interest groups seek to hedge their bets rather than to develop close links with a political party. Loose, pragmatic links between parties and interests are the norm. In the United States, business and organized labour gravitate towards the Republican and Democratic parties respectively but these are partnerships of convenience, not indissoluble marriages. The traditional maxim of the American trade union movement has been to reward its friends and punish its enemies, wherever these are to be found.

American business is equally pragmatic. Despite an ideological affinity with the Republican Party, corporations still contribute heavily to the election coffers of many Democratic members of Congress. Whether representing capital, labour or neither, most interest groups give more to incumbents. They do not waste money on no-hopers, even if these doomed candidates are standing for the 'correct' party.

The theme is similar, if less explicit, in other countries. In Germany, for instance, the powerful Federation of German Industry (BDI) certainly enjoys close links with the conservative Christian Democratic Union. However, it wisely remains on speaking terms with the more left-wing Social Democrats. The rule is that protective interests follow power, not parties.

Indirect influence through the mass media

Press, radio and television provide an additional resource for interest groups. By definition, messages through the media address a popular audience rather than specific decision-makers. Thus the media are a central focus for promotional groups seeking to steer public opinion. Their target is society as much as government.

In addition, promotional groups usually lack both the resources and the access available to protective groups, so free publicity becomes their stock-in-trade. For instance, ecological groups mount high-profile activities, such as seizing an oil rig to prevent it from being sunk, to generate footage shown on television across the world. In contrast to protective groups, promotional groups view the media as sympathetic to their cause (Dalton, 1994).

Traditionally, the media are less important to protective groups with their more specialized and secretive demands. What food manufacturer would go public with a campaign opposing nutritional labels on foods? The confidentiality of the government meeting room is a quieter arena for fighting rearguard actions of this kind; going public is a last resort.

But even protective groups are now seeking to influence the climate of public opinion, especially in political systems where legislatures are important. In the United States, most protective groups have learned that to impress Congress they must first influence the public. Therefore groups follow a dual strategy, going public and going Washington. Interest groups in other democracies are beginning to follow suit. Slowly and uncertainly, protective groups are emerging from the bureaucratic undergrowth into the glare of media publicity.

Lobbyists

The lobby is a term derived from the hall or lobby of Britain's House of Commons. Here people could, and still do, approach members of parliament to plead their cause. Although interest groups are often their own best lobbyists, our focus here is on specialist companies whose job it is to open the doors of government to their clients. These lobbying firms are technicians of influence: hired guns in the business of political communication. And they are growing in number though not necessarily in influence.

The business of lobbying remains highly personal. A legislator is most likely to return a call from a lobbyist if the caller is a former colleague. For this reason, lobbying firms are always on the lookout for former legislators or bureaucrats with a warm contact book. More than most professions, lobbying is about who you know.

Why is lobbying an expanding profession? Three reasons suggest themselves. First, government regulation continues to grow, often impacting directly on companies, interest groups and trade unions. For instance, a decision to permit the sale of a new medicine can be a matter of life and death for the drug company as well as for potential patients. One prosaic task of lobbying firms is to keep a close eye on proposed regulations emanating from legislative committees.

Second, public relations campaigns are becoming increasingly sophisticated, often seeking to influence both the grass roots and the government in one integrated project. Professional advisers come into their own in planning and delivering multifaceted campaigns, which can be too complex for a client to manage directly.

Third, many firms now approach government directly, rather than working through their trade association. Companies find that using a lobbying company to help them contact a government agency or a sympathetic legislator yields quicker results than working through an industry body which has to consider the concerns of all its members. McKay (1997, p. 250) reports that in the United States

> since the 1960s there is overwhelming evidence that individual firms have taken a more active part in public policy-making. Most major corporations now have Washington offices and employ professional lobbyists to advance and protect their interests.

What then is the political impact of lobbying companies? Is it now possible for wealthy interest groups and corporations simply to pay a fee to a lobbying firm to ensure a bill is defeated or a regulation deferred? On the whole, the answer is no. Lobbyists are inclined to exaggerate their own impact for commercial reasons but in reality most can achieve little more than access to relevant politicians and, perhaps, bureaucrats. Lobbyists, like interest groups, tend to cancel each other out. Often, the lobbyist's role is merely to hold the client's hand, helping an inexperienced company to find its way around the corridors of power when the corporation comes to town.

In these ways, professional lobbying firms can contribute to the effectiveness of political communication, focusing the client's message on relevant decision-makers. They can help to ensure that the client's voice is heard but shaping the policy-maker's response to the message is a far greater challenge. Allegations of sleaze notwithstanding, influence can rarely be purchased through a lobbyist but must come, if at all, from the petitioning group itself. And impact depends first and foremost on the intrinsic strength of the case. To the experienced politician, a convincing case direct from the petitioner sings louder than yet another rehearsed presentation from a lobbying firm.

Of course, not everything in the lobby is rosy. Even if a company achieves no more for its client's fee than access to a decision-maker, perhaps that exchange in itself compromises the principle of equality which supposedly underpins democracy. Groups unable to employ lobbyists are not necessarily denied political impact but they do have to operate on a do-it-yourself basis. Further, the widespread perception that influence can be purchased in itself damages the legitimacy of the democratic process.

Iron triangles and issue networks

In the democratic world, many interest groups are in virtually daily contact with government. So the question arises, what is the nature of such relationships? How should they be characterized? This is a core issue in the study of interest groups, bearing on the question of whether groups express or subvert democracy.

Until recent decades, the relationship between interest groups and the state was viewed critically. Within a particular sector, it was alleged, interest group leaders and senior civil servants formed their own small communities. All the members knew each other well, used given names and tried not to upset each other. The participants developed shared working habits and common assumptions about what could be achieved. The actors learned to trust each other and to respect each other's goals and confidences.

Shared interests predominated. For instance, the road-builders and bureaucrats in the transport ministry would seek ever larger highway budgets, fully aware that similar coalitions in other sectors – defence, say, or education – would be seeking to maximize their own funding and autonomy. Business was done behind closed doors to prevent political posturing and to allow a quiet life for all. Insiders were sharply distinguished from outsiders. The golden rule was never to upset the apple cart.

American political scientists used the term 'iron triangle' to describe the particular form taken by the relationship between groups and government in the USA. The three points on the triangle were executive agencies or departments, interest groups and congressional committees (Figure 10.3). Such triangles became an exercise in mutual back-scratching: the *committee* appropriated funds which were spent by the *agency* for the benefit of *interest group* members. Thus, the Department of

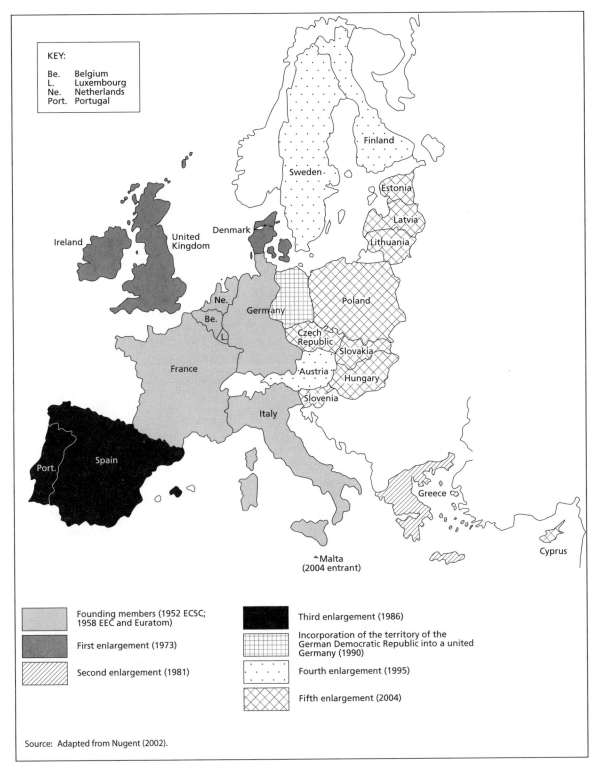

KEY:

Be. Belgium
L. Luxembourg
Ne. Netherlands
Port. Portugal

Finland

Sweden

Estonia

Latvia

Lithuania

Ireland

United Kingdom

Denmark

Ne.

Be.

L.

Germany

Poland

Czech Republic

Slovakia

France

Austria

Hungary

Slovenia

Italy

Port.

Spain

Greece

Cyprus

^Malta
(2004 entrant)

	Founding members (1952 ECSC; 1958 EEC and Euratom)			Third enlargement (1986)
	First enlargement (1973)			Incorporation of the territory of the German Democratic Republic into a united Germany (1990)
	Second enlargement (1981)			Fourth enlargement (1995)
				Fifth enlargement (2004)

Source: Adapted from Nugent (2002).

Map 10.1 The European Union (see also 50 years of the European Union on p. 29)

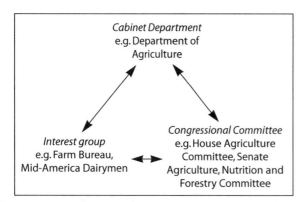

Figure 10.3 Iron triangles: how subgovernments operated in the USA

Agriculture, the relevant committees in Congress and farmers' groups would collude on larger food subsidies. Each point on the triangle benefited. This was a game without losers – except for the taxpayer who rarely knew what was going on.

Iron triangles were also called subgovernments, implying that each triangle formed a mini-government of its own, largely independent of policy-making in other sectors. The effect was to fragment policy-making, deflecting the political aims of the majority party in Congress or even of the president himself (Ripley and Franklin, 1991).

Fortunately, perhaps, these cosy iron triangles and subgovernments have decayed in many democracies. Today, policies are subject to closer scrutiny by the media; new public interest groups protest loudly when they spot the public being taken for a ride; and some legislators are less willing to keep quiet when they see public money being wasted. And as issues become more complex, so more groups are drawn into the policy process, making it harder to stitch together secret deals among a few insiders. In the United States, where this trend has gone furthest, the committee barons who used to dominate Congress have lost much of their power. The iron has gone out of the triangle; now influence over decisions depends on what you know as much as who you know.

Reflecting these trends, the talk now is of 'issue networks'. These refer to the familiar set of organizations involved in policy-making: government departments, interest groups and legislative committees plus expert outsiders. However, an issue

network does not imply a close-knit subgovernment. In an issue network, the impact of an interest group varies from issue to issue, depending on its expertise. As Heclo (1978, p. 102) famously put it,

> the notions of iron triangles and subgovernments presume small circles of participants who have succeeded in becoming largely autonomous. Issue networks, on the other hand, comprise a large number of participants with quite variable degrees of mutual commitment . . . it is almost impossible to say where a network leaves off and its environment begins.

The emergence of issue networks reflects a shift to a more open policy-making style in which back-scratching has become harder to sustain. Clearly, the idea of issue networks enables us to portray policy-making in democracies more positively. A wider range of interests participate in decisions, the bias toward protective groups is reduced, new groups enter the debate and a sound argument carries greater weight. Networks operate in a non-hierarchical way, with resources such as expertise and authority in effect exchanged between the participants.

Definitions

An **issue network** is an open and flexible combination of players who collectively shape policy in a given sector, such as defence or agriculture (Heclo, 1978). Through their deliberations, the members of a network in effect exchange their varying resources such as knowledge (e.g. academic specialists), legitimacy (e.g. elected politicians), control over implementation (e.g. interest groups) and the capacity to draft bills and regulations (e.g. bureaucrats).

Further, epistemic (knowledge-based) communities can often place issues such as acid rain on the policy agenda at an early stage, perhaps countering the conservatism of protective interests. Within these broad communities of expertise, particular coalitions emerge to advocate specific positions (Sabatier and Jenkins-Smith, 1993). The foundation of many issue networks in expert knowledge at least opens up the possibility of more informed policy-making.

Conditions of influence

There is no doubt that some interest groups exert more influence over government than others. In part, no doubt, this difference reflects the varying skill with which groups exploit the opportunities available to them but a deeper explanation must lie in the underlying strength of interest groups themselves. So why are some interest groups more powerful than others? The answer depends on four main features of the group: sanctions, legitimacy, membership and resources.

The ability of a group to invoke *sanctions* is clearly important. A labour union can go on strike, a multinational corporation can take its investments elsewhere, a peak association can withdraw its cooperation with the government in forming policy. As a rule, protective groups (such as industry associations) can bring more sanctions to bear than promotional groups (such as ecology movements).

The degree of *legitimacy* achieved by a particular group is also important. The aphorism 'what is good for General Motors is good for America' expresses the point. Interests enjoying high prestige are most likely to prevail on particular issues. For example, professional groups whose members stand for social respectability can be as militant on occasion, and as restrictive in their practices, as blue-collar trade unions once were. But lawyers and doctors escape the public hostility that unions attract.

Definition

Density of membership refers to the proportion of those eligible to join a group who actually do so. An encompassing membership gives more authority and, in turn, a stronger bargaining position with government. The declining density of trade union membership in the final quarter of the twentieth century undoubtedly weakened labour's bargaining power.

A group's influence also depends on its *membership*. This is a matter of density as well as sheer numbers. The highest penetrations are usually achieved when, as with many professional bodies such as physicians and lawyers, membership is a condition of practice. By contrast, low density reduces influence, especially when an occupation is fragmented among several interest groups. American farmers, for instance, divide between three major organizations with lower total coverage than Britain's National Farmers Union. To be sure, the larger American food producers are politically well-connected but the interests of agriculture as a whole would be better served if all farmers belonged to a single national association.

In the European Union, breadth of membership is especially important for lobbying organizations. Groups which can demonstrate their support from national associations in most member states will receive a more cordial reception from the policy-makers in Brussels.

The organizational *resources* available to an interest group are the final factor affecting its influence. Here as elsewhere, money talks but not always loudly. With an annual budget of $40 million, America's National Rifle Association (NRA) can employ 275 full-time staff. Despite public sympathy, the coalition of gun control groups cannot match the NRA's fire power. Yet even in the USA, poor but skilful campaigners can generate free publicity and wide public sympathy. Ralph Nader's Crusade for Car Safety in the 1960s was an early example. Nader exposed a dangerous design fault in some General Motors models, a flaw that the manufacturer had sought to keep away from the public gaze. In this case, what was good for General Motors was not good for Americans, as Nader proved.

Thus, just as the impact of lobbying firms is often exaggerated, so too is the significance of the money available to an interest group. As a rule, finance is rarely decisive. Consider the NRA once more. It would be naive to suppose that the cause of gun control in the USA is held back solely by the NRA. Two other factors are just as important: (1) the difficulty of passing any legislation opposed by a significant minority within Congress and (2) an ambiguous constitutional reference to the 'right of the people to keep and bear arms'. The NRA has exploited both features but created neither.

In short, all interest groups inherit an endowment of political resources which substantially determines the influence they can exert. External context matters more than internal organisation.

Profile THE EUROPEAN UNION

Population of member states: 454m
Gross domestic product per head:
  Following the 5th enlargement (2004),
  GDP per head fell further below that
  of the USA and Japan.
Form of government: a unique
  regional body in which policy is made
  partly by European Union institutions
  and partly through negotiations
  among the 25 member states.
Executive: the Council of the European
  Union, composed of heads of government, provides political drive. The

powerful European Commission,
divided into 17 directorates, initiates
legislative proposals.
Assembly: the members of the unicameral European Parliament are directly
elected from each country for a five-
year term. The number of MEPs from
each country reflects its population.
Though growing in significance, the
Parliament still lacks full control over
the Commission, the budget and even
legislation.

Judicial branch: the influential European
Court of Justice, composed of one
judge from each member country, has
successfully developed the constitu-
tional underpinnings of federalism.
Members: *Founders:* Belgium, France,
Germany, Italy, Luxembourg,
Netherlands. *1973:* Denmark, Ireland,
United Kingdom. *1981:* Greece. *1986:*
Portugal, Spain. *1995:* Austria, Finland,
Sweden. *2004:* Cyprus, Czech Republic,
Estonia, Hungary, Latvia, Lithuania,
Malta, Poland, Slovakia, Slovenia.

The European Union (EU) is the most developed example of regional integration in the world. Uniquely among regional bodies, the EU has developed institutions resembling the architecture of national governments. It has a parliament and an influential Court of Justice. Proposals for a codified constitution, expressing a commitment for members 'to forge a common destiny' were put forward in 2003. The heart of the EU, however, is the European Commission (an EU body) and the Council of Ministers (an intergovernmental body). The tension between these units – between the EU as a cohesive actor and the EU as an arena for negotiation between member states – is central to its functioning.

The EU's emergence owes much to Europe's history of conflict. After the 1939–45 war, many European leaders set out to create a unified continent within which war would no longer be feasible: a United States of Europe. However, economic factors were also fundamental. European economies needed to be rebuilt after the war and then, to achieve benefits of scale, integrated into a large, single market.

Later members, notably Britain, have emphasized the economic basis of the Union while rejecting the federal vision. Margaret Thatcher (1988) expressed this position well: 'willing and active cooperation between independent sovereign states is the best way to build a successful European Community'. In developing this line, Britain has exploited the continental notion of subsidiarity to argue that decisions should be taken at the lower, national level wherever possible.

Reflecting the European tradition of social partnership, the EU has encouraged interest groups, especially those with a Europe-wide perspective. Over 900 interest groups are listed in the Commission's directory, mostly protective in character. The main peak associations are the Union of Industrial and Employers' Confederation of Europe (UNICE), with 40 employees, and the European Trade Union Federation (ETUC), with 45 staff. There are probably more lobbyists working in Brussels than there are policy-makers employed by the European Commission.

However, many European interest groups possess few resources and they experience difficulty in taking positions acceptable to members drawn from a range of countries. Increasingly, therefore, national interest groups lobby directly in the EU, often working in partnership with their home government. Other lobbying comes from regional and local governments and, increasingly, from individual companies. External bodies, such as Japanese trade associations and American multinationals, are also active.

Most lobbyists focus on the Commission, the nearest equivalent to national executives though without their strong party basis. The Commission is a small body which develops policy across most sectors. It relies even more heavily than national governments on interest groups for information, support and legitimacy.

Further reading: Eising (2003), Greenwood (2003), Hosli et al. (2002), Mazey and Richardson (2001).

Pluralism and corporatism

In this section we consider the wider role of interest groups within the political system. This means broadening the debate beyond specific groups in order to characterize the overall pattern formed by the links between interest groups and the government.

One answer to this question, of course, is that the government stands above the groups. After all, the government, uniquely, is authorized by election and it alone is answerable to parliament and people. In this idealized account, the government forms its policy and interest groups enter the policy cycle only at the stage of implementation. The groups operate within the strategic framework provided by the state. Eising and Cini (2002, p. 171) cite France – the home of popular sovereignty – as an example of a country which aspires to this approach. French political tradition stresses the importance of a collective will, articulated by the state, which is superior to particular interests.

But such accounts, whether of democracies in general or of France in particular, are unrealistic. They understate the role of the groups, and overstate the role of the government, in shaping policy. To accommodate this point, political scientists have developed two broad models of the political role of interest groups: pluralism and corporatism. These two models usefully direct our attention to the contrasts between the pluralistic politics of the United States (see p. 179) and the more corporate politics found in much of continental Europe. So the issue here is to demonstrate two ways in which interest groups can be integrated into the heart of political decision-making.

Definition
Literally 'rule by the many', **pluralism** refers to a political system in which numerous competing interest groups exert strong influence over a responsive government. The state is more umpire than player. However each of these groups concentrates on its own area (for example education or health care) so that no single elite dominates all sectors.

The debate between pluralists and corporatists goes to the heart of a central question in politics:

the relationship between society and the state. Pluralists see society dominating the state; corporatists view the state as leading society. At one level this difference is descriptive, reflecting contrasting assessments of the flow of influence between government and interest groups. But at a deeper level, the debate reflects contrasting views of the proper role of government. Pluralists see the state's task as responding to interests expressed to it. Corporatists, by contrast, favour an organized, integrated society in which the state offers leadership in pursuit of a vision shared with society.

The *pluralist* view dominated early postwar accounts of interest group activity. In this account, politics is seen as a competition between a multitude of freely organized interest groups. These organizations compete for influence over a government that is willing to listen to all the voices it can hear in the political debate. In a pluralist system, the state is largely an arena for competition between interest groups. The governing party is an arbiter, not an initiator. For Bentley (1908), an American pioneer of this approach, 'when the groups are adequately stated, everything is stated. When I say everything, I mean everything.' All kinds of interest have their say before the court of government. Groups compete on a level playing field, with the state showing little bias either towards interests of a particular type or towards specific groups within that type. As new interests and indeed new identities emerge, groups form to represent them. In pluralism, politics is a competitive market with few barriers to entry.

Pluralism brings healthy fragmentation across the range of government activity since most interests are restricted to a single policy sector. Indeed the central tenet of pluralism is that no single elite dominates government. Rather, different interest groups lead the way in each area of policy. Overall, pluralism depicts a wholesome process of dispersed decision-making in which the variety of groups allows government policies to reflect not just economic interests but also social diversity.

The significance of pluralism lies in its implications for our understanding of contemporary democracy. Pluralists accept that, in practice, majority rule is an inaccurate account of how democracies work. Rather, pluralists judge that democracy is, in reality, rule by a series of minorities, each operating in a particular area but subject to the checks and balances of other groups operating in the same sector, with the government as umpire. Furthermore, the strengths of this form of governance are substantial. Dahl (1993, p. 706) summarizes what he sees as the strengths of pluralism, suggesting that groups have

> served to educate citizens in political life, strengthened them in their relations with the state, helped to ensure that no single interest would regularly prevail on all important decisions, and, by providing information, discussion, negotiation and compromise, even helped to make public decisions more rational and more acceptable.

Corporatism provides a contrasting account of the role of interest groups in national politics. Where pluralism was inspired by the United States, corporatism was developed in Europe. In the Middle Ages, a corporation referred not to a profit-making company but to a craft guild with control over recruitment to, and regulation of, its profession. The idea that people should be represented and controlled through such self-regulating occupational bodies remains important to modern corporatism.

How does corporatism conceive the relationship between interest groups and government? The main contrast with pluralism is that where pluralism implies competition between groups, corporatism implies coordination and planning. In conjunction with government, the peak associations representing capital and labour make and implement key policies, thus securing the social order in societies which often have a long history of conflict. This is a top-down approach, requiring a high level of social and political organization, including compulsory membership of firms in employers' organizations and of employees in trade unions.

Though formally accountable to their members, a central role of the peaks in a corporate system is to carry their members with them after agreements have been struck with the government. Issues such as price levels, wage increases, tax rates and pension entitlements are all settled in tripartite discussions among senior politicians, industrialists

and union leaders. Agreements are often then presented as an agreed social pact or social contract between the actors in the social partnership.

Under corporatism, negotiations between the state and recognized groups take an administrative, technical form. Policy-making is depoliticized and electoral representation through parliament becomes less important. Policy is made in private negotiations in government ministries, not in the public debate of the assembly. Corporatism also implies a hierarchy of groups, with the government dealing with the influential peak associations, which then pass decisions on to their members.

Definition

In a democratic context, **corporatism** (often called social partnership in Europe) is a relationship between the state and interest groups in which major decisions on domestic matters emerge from discussion between the government and peak associations representing the major social partners: capital and labour. In return for influence, the partners ensure the compliance of their members. This system is often called liberal or societal corporatism to distinguish it from the state-dominated corporatism of fascism (Schmitter and Lehmbruch, 1979).

So in contrast to pluralism, which emphasizes an upward flow of preferences from group members to their leaders and then on to government, corporatism stresses the downward flow of influence. Politicians govern *with* interest groups and are certainly not governed *by* them. The state retains at least a coordinating role and may even govern *through* interest groups, persuading the peaks to accept necessary reforms.

An example will add some colour to this outline. Just as the United States is taken to exemplify pluralism, so Austria's postwar republic reveals many corporatist features. In common with most countries adopting a corporatist approach, Austria's history is troubled indeed. Civil war in the 1930s was followed by annexation by Nazi Germany and, after 1945, by a further ten years with Russian troops on its soil. Prompted by this history, the country's two blocs – conservative/ Catholic and socialist – eventually agreed to

DEBATE

IS THE USA A PLURALISTIC POLITICAL SYSTEM?

Both as an ideal and as a description of how politics works, pluralism draws on American experience. But can American politics really be presented as an open competition between freely organized interests? Or is the entire decision-making process in the hands of an elite which, in effect, excludes consideration of any policies which would threaten its own values? Is American pluralism reality or myth?

The case for

In the USA, interest group patterns come closer to the pluralist model than anywhere else. As de Tocqueville (1856) wrote, 'in no country in the world has the principle of association been more successfully used, or applied to a greater multitude of objects, than in America'. Petracca (1992, p. 3) makes the point more succinctly: 'American politics is the politics of interests.'

Nowhere else are interest groups so numerous, visible, organized, competitive or successful. Tens of thousands of groups, ranging from Happiness of Motherhood Eternal to the United Autoworkers of America, seek to influence policy at federal, state and local levels. Nor are such groups confined to protective economic interests. Promotional groups are uniquely prominent in the USA with over 500 groups focusing on environmental protection alone.

Washington politics reflects the competitive spirit that is pluralism's hallmark. If one interest group seems to be gaining the upper hand, others will form to counter its influence. Vigorous, independent and competitive media are always willing to listen to new groups with a story to tell. The separation of powers gives interest groups many points of leverage: Congressional committees, executive agencies and the courts. American government is simply too fragmented to be anything more than an umpire of group demands.

The case against

All political systems generate myths and America's is pluralism. In reality, pluralist 'competition' operates within an unquestioned acceptance of broad American values favouring the free market and the pursuit of individual self-interest. The entire political discourse works within a narrow ideological range, shaping and limiting the demands expressed so as to benefit, in particular, corporate USA.

Washington's intricate political games are dominated by middle-aged, middle-class English-speaking graduates, a group which forms only a small minority of an ethnically and linguistically diverse population. In any case, some interest groups are wealthier and better organized than others so that the pluralist ideal of equal representation for all groups is far from reality. And, as the frequency of inner-city disturbances reveals, some interests are left out of the debate altogether. As Schattschneider (1942) claimed, 'the system is skewed, loaded and unbalanced in favour of a fraction of a minority'. Schattschneider's critical conclusion remains valid: some interests are organized into American politics but others are organized out.

Assessment

The danger of the debate is that the word 'pluralism' becomes evaluative rather than descriptive. Those who favour the American way see pluralism; those who are more critical discern a hidden elite.

But one conclusion, at least, seems clear. While overseas observers may interpret American politics as much ado about nothing, that view is not shared by the players themselves. To understand what happens in American politics (as opposed to what overseas observers would like to happen), it is necessary to appreciate the vigorous competition between interest groups, even if this debate does operate within in a limited framework. For the thousands of groups seeking government subsidies for the interests they represent, American politics is a serious business.

Further reading: Cigler and Loomis (2002), Dahl (1961), Mills (1956), Schattschneider (1942).

discard past differences in what proved to be a successful search for compromise.

Austria developed an elaborate corporate system of elaborate and interlocking institutions lasting until the end of the century. The Catholic and socialist parties, representing each bloc, dominated national politics and usually governed in coalition, where careful compromises could be negotiated. Just as important, the peak associations – the ÖGB on the employers' side and the VÖI for labour – were powerful and centralized bodies with high membership density. The leader of these two organizations would agree important decisions affecting the whole economy, with the chancellor (that is, prime minister) acting as chair of the meeting. Furthermore, all working people belonged to one of three statutory chambers of commerce, covering business, labour and agriculture. These chambers provided an additional channel of communication between the state and social interests (Tálos and Kittel, 2002).

In general, corporatism is most likely to take root in countries with recent experience of disorder and in which a strong state meets powerful peak associations with high membership density. The Scandinavian nations and the Netherlands, as well as Austria, fit many of these conditions. Scandinavia exhibits a tradition of compromise and consultation between government and interest groups which some authors argue amounts to Nordic corporatism. Kvavik (1976), for example, interpreted Norway in the 1970s as a 'cooptive polity' in which interest groups were brought into public policy-making and implementation in a distinctly non-pluralist way. Sweden also involves interest groups in a remarkably deliberative process of policy formation.

In the 1980s and 1990s, corporatism came under attack. Even in prosperous Austria, those who felt left out of the system began to voice their protest. The country's extreme right Freedom Party became one of the most successful populist parties in Western Europe, eventually entering government in a remarkable coalition with the conservative People's Party in 2000. This coalition symbolized a thawing of Austria's previously frozen corporate system. The coalition was renewed after 2002, but with the Freedom Party in a weaker position, enabling the leader of the People's Party

---

BOX 10.3
Democracies grouped by the extent of corporatism

Most corporatist
Austria
Denmark
Switzerland
Germany
Finalnd
Belgium
Ireland

Many corporate features
Norway
Sweden
Netherlands

A few corporate features
France
Italy

Least corporatist
Canada
United Kingdom
United States

Source: Adapted from expert assessments in Lijphart and Crepaz (1991).

---

to begin more radical attacks on the country's entrenched corporate traditions.

However, it was in the Anglo-American world, where corporatism had never been more than half-hearted, that the heaviest blows were struck. As early as 1982, Olson had claimed that corporatism was a form of political sclerosis, reflecting the gradual accumulation of power by sectional interests. Corporatism was viewed as inviting excessive state intervention. The carefully crafted corporate consensus between government, capital and labour was held to inhibit the continuous economic changes needed to remain competitive in an increasingly global economy.

Reflecting this intellectual sea change, Margaret Thatcher in Britain, and Ronald Reagan in the United States, launched a political assault in the 1980s on the power of entrenched interests. While such attacks were focused on the privileges of organized labour, some large companies were also affected by more vigorous competition policy, more open markets and a growing emphasis on competitive tendering in the public sector. Structural change, particularly the decline of heavy industry with its strong unions, large companies and powerful trade bodies, accelerated the decay of organized labour, weakening one of the corporate pillars (Addison and Schnabel, 2003).

Writing on Scandinavia, Eriksen (1990) argued that 'the post-corporate state may represent a new order'. But it remains to be seen how far most European countries, with their long history of corporate thinking and the inherent value they place on governing by consensus, have the desire, the ability or indeed the need to change their ways. Blom-Hansen (2000), for one, argues that corporatism is alive and well and living in Scandinavia, albeit in the form of continuing consultation rather than joint decision-making between groups and government. And some countries, including Ireland and the Netherlands, have even developed or revived social partnerships as a route to improved efficiency.

Interest groups in new democracies

The role to be played by interest groups in new democracies remains uncertain, intimately linked to the extent to which democracy itself consolidates. Certainly, the emergence of groups acting independently of the state was integral to the weakening of authoritarian rule. For instance, groups based around the green, peace and women's movements developed in a number of communist states in the 1980s, posing a challenge to party rule by their mere existence as non-party organizations. Eventually, some of these groups became the catalyst of regime change. In Poland, the trade union organization Solidarity (supported by the Roman Catholic Church) emerged in 1980 to assert the interests of Polish workers. Within the decade, it took over the reins of government.

However, groups such as Solidarity were not interest groups in the Western sense; they began as *de facto* opposition groups and then became broad social movements. They sought to replace rather than to influence the communist government. Their historical task was pivotal but short-term

and went far beyond anything of which a narrow interest would have been capable.

In the democratic era, the groups which were the levers of regime change – including environmental and women's groups – have generally declined. Similarly, the churches have paradoxically declined because their position as a 'semi-protected site of opposition' to communist rule is no longer needed in the new, freer order (Fitzmaurice, 1998, p. 174).

As these social movements disappear and some institutional interests decay, so orthodox interest groups, with their detailed and routine demands, should take root in democracy's fresh soil. Ågh (1998, p. 22) suggests that the 'the chief actors of democratic transition are the parties, but those of democratic consolidation are the interest organizations and civil society associations, which provide the fine-tuning and effect the full accomplishment of democratization'.

Yet this is precisely where the uncertainty resides. As yet, interest groups are not consistently developing in new democracies along Western lines, any more than political parties are growing into the mass membership organizations once found in West Europe. Certainly, some of the 'older' new democracies of Southern Europe – notably Spain and Portugal – have moved towards the interest group pattern found in consolidated democracies. Yet even in Spain, Heywood (1995, p. 243) notes that in a context of 'the continuing primacy of the state over civil society', membership of voluntary associations is falling, not rising. Padgett (2000, p. 166) reports that trade union membership has also declined over the brief history of post-communist Europe.

Even in the eastern areas of Germany, now formally part of the highly organized German economy, large firms are preoccupied with direct lobbying and small ones with survival, leaving little space for interest groups representing specific industries or general business values. Padgett concludes that 'nowhere in east/central Europe is even the semblance of a stable, fully functioning interest group system' to be found. Western peak associations and chambers of commerce are weak or non-existent.

A similar story emerges from the post-military democracies of Latin America. Hagopian (1998,

p. 238) considers that the rise of markets means that 'the corporate negotiating channels once open between unions and the state are being rendered obsolete'.

However, the transition to democracy did release some new forces. Many new democracies witnessed a release of traditional social groups rather than interest groups. In the post-communist world, long suppressed groups based on ethnicity and nationality, have proved to be a potent force for (and response to) instability. For example, long-standing national differences brought about the dissolution of Czechoslovakia into the Czech Republic and Slovakia.

In much of Africa, too, group politics in an era of post-military government continues to be based on ethnicity rather than interests generated through the workplace. Many poorer countries lack the complex economy needed to develop interest group patterns found in affluent established democracies. In Botswana, for example, only two organizations – a business association and a conservation group – employ staff to lobby the government (Herbst, 2001). In addition, when such economic resources as are available are parcelled out on ethnic lines, or in any other personal or unregulated way, incentives for orthodox interest groups to develop are limited.

Russia's semi-democracy is, as always, an interesting mixed case. Certainly, the separation between public and private sectors, so central to the organization of interests in the West, has not fully emerged there. Particularly in the early post-communist years, ruthless business executives, corrupt public officials and jumped-up gangsters made deals in a virtually unregulated free-for-all. Individual financiers pulled the strings of their puppets in government but the politics was personal rather than institutional. In such an environment interests were everywhere but interest groups were nowhere. 'Comrade Criminal' was disinclined to join trade associations.

However, the situation may be changing. With economic recovery taking hold at the start of the twenty-first century, some business associations of a Western kind have emerged, even if they have not yet secured political influence. Peregudov (2001, p. 268) even claims that 'in Russia a network of business organizations has been created

and is up and running'. He suggests that this network is capable of adequately representing business interests to the state but it has so far received little attention from President Putin, who continues to reward his business friends and, on occasion, to arrest his enemies.

To assume that new democracies will in due course replicate the group patterns of established democracies places a large bet on both economic development and democratic deepening. Just as many newer democracies led the way in developing media-based rather than mass membership parties, so too do direct links between business owners and government leaders lead us to question whether the Western model of industry-wide trade associations will ever become a potent force in new democracies.

Interest groups in authoritarian states

The role played by interest groups in non-democratic states provides a sharp contrast to their position in established democracies. Authoritarian rulers see freely organized groups as a potential threat to their own power; hence, they seek either to repress such groups or to incorporate them within the power structure. In this section, we will examine the workings of these strategies in authoritarian regimes before turning to the special case of totalitarian states.

In the latter half of the twentieth century, many authoritarian rulers had to confront the challenge posed by the new groups unleashed by economic development. These included labour unions, peasant leagues and educated radicals. How did rulers respond to these new conditions? One strategy was to suppress such groups completely. Where civil liberties were weak and many groups were new, this approach was feasible. For example, a strategy of repression was adopted by many military regimes. Military leaders often had their own fingers in the economic pie, sometimes in tacit collaboration with multinational corporations; the rulers' goal was to maintain a workforce that was both compliant and poorly paid. 'Trouble-makers' seeking to establish labour unions were quickly removed.

On the other hand, authoritarian rulers could

seek to manage the expression of these new interests. That is, they could allow interests to organize but seek to control them, a policy of incorporation rather than exclusion. By enlisting part of the population, particularly its more modern sectors, into officially sponsored associations, rulers hoped to accelerate the push toward modernization. This approach was common in Latin America, where the state licensed, funded and granted a monopoly of representation to favoured groups.

Before the pro-market economic reforms of the 1980s and 1990s, Mexico offered a particular working of this tradition. Its governing system was founded on a strong ruling party (the PRI) which was itself a coalition made up of labour, agrarian and 'popular' sectors (the latter consisting mainly of public employees). Favoured unions and peasant associations gained access to the PRI. Party leaders provided resources such as subsidies and control over jobs to these groups, in exchange for their political support. In effect, Mexico became a giant patron–client network – a form of corporatism for a developing country. For the many people left out of the network, however, life could be hard indeed.

Just as corporatism is decaying in established democracies, so Mexico's system – and many others like it – is also in decline. It was over-regulated, giving so much power to civil servants and PRI-affiliated unions as to deter business investment, especially from overseas. As the market sector expanded, so the patronage available to the PRI diminished. In 1997, an independent National Workers Union emerged to claim that the old mechanisms of state control were exhausted, a point which was confirmed by the PRI's defeat in a presidential election three years later.

The position of interest groups in communist states was even more marginal than in other non-democratic regimes. For most of the communist era, independent interest groups did not exist. Their absence was a deliberate result of communist ideology. Communist states were led by the party, not by society. Groups served the party, not the other way round. Interest articulation by freely organized groups was inconceivable. Communist rulers sought to harness all organizations into transmission belts for party policy. Trade unions, the media, youth groups, professional associations were little more than branches of the party, serving the great cause of communist construction through social transformation.

However, the capacity to articulate interests did increase as communist economies matured. The use of coercion and terror declined as conflict over policy became more visible. Institutional groups such as the military and heavy industry became more important as decisions became more technical. In the 1970s and 1980s, sectional interests began to be openly expressed, particularly in Poland, Hungary and Yugoslavia.

However, one sharp contrast with Western pluralism remained: ruling communist parties tried to restrict interest articulation to safe technical matters. The party continued to crack down vigorously on dissent going beyond these confines. The objectives of the communist state remained beyond criticism. Thus 'socialist pluralism', to the extent that it existed at all, remained far more limited than its Western counterpart.

Even in reforming China, the Western notion of an 'interest group' still carries little meaning. China's Communist Party continues to provide the framework for most formal political activity. 'Mass organizations' such as the All-China Federation of Trade Unions and the Women's Federation are led by party officials and transmit its policy. Saich (2004, p. 206) notes that 'state entities have given birth to many of the new social organizations in China'. These bodies are described in China as GONGOs (government-organized non-governmental organizations).

Private business is intertwined with the state sector and is not represented through traditional industry associations. Too many deals are done 'through the back door' to leave much space for policy-oriented interest groups. 'Rightful resistance' enables citizens to protest to higher authority about lower officials exceeding their legal powers but such appeals operate on an individual rather than a group basis. As Manion (2004, p. 448) concludes, 'for the most part, the function of interest aggregation is monopolized by the communist party'.

In fascist theory, as under communism, the state dominated partial interests. Indeed, the central premise of fascist thought was that the state must lead. But unlike communism, the fascist state

---

BOX 10.4
Examples of social organizations in contemporary China

Organization	Type	Comment
All-China Federation of Trade Unions	Mass organization	A traditional transmission belt for the party
All-China Women's Federation	Mass organization	Traditionally a party-led body, this federation has created some space for autonomous action
China Family Planning Association	Non-governmental organization	Sponsored by the State Family Planning Commission, this association operates at international and local level
Friends of Nature	Non-governmental organization	Led by a well-connected and charismatic figure, Friends of Nature has mobilized student support in defence of habitats threatened by illegal logging

Source: Adapted from Saich (2004), pp. 186–92.

---

sought to mobilize, rather than to destroy, group activity. In particular, it wanted to exploit, rather than take over, private industry. Fascism advocated a corporate relationship between state and industry (Brooker, 2000, p. 156).

The theory was that the economy would be arranged by industrial sector. Within each industry, special corporations (committees or chambers) composed of employers, employees, party and government would plan production, set wages and prices and resolve disputes. In this vertical arrangement, horizontal conflicts between business groups and labour unions would be overcome as both sides learned to serve national goals as defined by the supreme leader. Thus corporatism would secure the national interest by overriding class conflict.

Such a system was formally implemented in Italy in the mid-1930s but in practice the 22 corporations established there were given only token powers. Their impact was minimal. Corporatism was even less significant in Nazi Germany. Indeed, the man charged by Hitler with introducing the format there claimed that after learning of his assignment, 'I did not sleep for several nights on account of the corporate system because I could not make head or tail of it' (O'Sullivan, 1986, p. 133). In practice, industrial

policy took the practical form of ensuring that large privately owned manufacturers met the demands of an expansionist regime. Corporate institutions took second place to the task of serving the Nazi war machine.

Key reading

Next step: *Many of the best studies of interest groups continue to be about the United States; Cigler and Loomis (2002) is an excellent collection.*

Wilson (1990b) is a clear and straightforward introduction to interest groups. Hrebenar and Scott (1997) is a good text on the USA, Eising and Cini (2002) cover Western Europe while M. Smith (1995) is a brief but helpful introduction to Britain. On European corporatism, Berger and Compston (2002) is a useful collection while Arter (1999) and Blom-Hansen (2000) review the relevance of the concept to the Nordic states. Two useful comparative studies are Wilson (2003) on the relationship between business and politics and Thomas (2001) on the links between parties and interest groups. Brown (2001) covers groups, and much else, in post-communist Russia.

Chapter 11

Political parties

'In this book I investigate the workings of democratic government. But it is not institutions which are the object of my research: it is not on political forms, it is on political forces I dwell.' So Ostrogorski (1902) began his pioneering comparison of party organization in Britain and the United States. Ostrogorski was one of the first students of politics to recognize that parties were becoming vital in the new era of democratic politics: 'wherever this life of parties is developed, it focuses the political feelings and the active wills of its citizens'.

Ostrogorski's supposition that parties were growing in importance proved to be fully justified in the twentieth century. In Western Europe, mass parties battled for the votes of enlarged electorates. In communist and fascist states, ruling parties monopolized power in an attempt to reconstruct society. In the developing world, nationalist parties became the vehicle for driving colonial rulers back to their imperial homeland. In all these areas, parties succeeded in drawing millions of people into the national political process, often for the first time. The mass party proved to be the key mobilizing device in the politics of the twentieth century.

In standing between the people and the state, parties continue to perform four main functions:

▶ Ruling parties offer *direction to government,* performing the vital task of steering the ship of state.
▶ Parties function as agents of *political recruitment.* They serve as the major mechanism for preparing and recruiting candidates for the legislature and the executive.
▶ Parties serve as agents of *interest aggregation.* They filter a multitude of specific demands into more manageable packages of proposals. Parties select, reduce and combine policies.
▶ To a declining extent, political parties also serve as a *brand* for their supporters and voters, giving people a lens through which to interpret a complicated political world.

Definition
Sartori (1976, p. 63) defines a **political party** as 'any political group identified by an official label that presents at elections, and is capable of placing through elections candidates for public office'. Unlike interest groups, which seek influence only, serious parties aim to secure the levers of government. In Weber's phrase, parties live 'in a house of power'.

Political parties are complex organizations, operating across domains but with the various levels of the party sharing a common identity and a broadly similar outlook. In the parliamentary democracies of Western Europe, parties are particularly complex; Box 11.1 sets out the elements of a typical major party in that region.

At national level, the main distinction is between the top party leaders (or ministers if the party is in power), the members of the parliamentary party and the officials working at party headquarters. But parties are also represented in other elected domains, including the European Parliament, and both regional and local government. This superstructure is supported at the base by ordinary members, usually organized by area. Clearly, mapping a party's structure, and understanding the relationships between its parts, is itself a significant task.

In Western Europe, parties typically possess a large if declining subscription-based membership,

---

BOX 11.1
Typical elements of a major political party in Western Europe

Element	Description	Level
The party in government (or opposition)	The prime minister and other ministers (or the leadership of non-governing parties)	National
The party in parliament	'Backbench' members of the parliamentary party	National
The party's central organization	Officials at party headquarters	National
The party at regional and local levels	Party members elected to regional and local assemblies; local officials and ordinary party members	Subnational
The party in the European Union	Members of the European Parliament, where representatives of a national party join broader, transnational party groups	Supranational

Source: Adapted from Cotta (2000).

---

a coherent ideology and strong discipline among their members of parliament. By contrast, in North America, party organization is weaker and even more decentralized. Canada as well as the United States lack the European tradition of a large, dues-paying membership. Beyond the legislature, American and Canadian parties are largely devices for organizing elections; they often seem to hibernate between campaigns. Volunteer helpers with campaigns often have no formal links with the party and, in the USA at least, candidates choose parties more than the other way round.

The question for the twenty-first century is whether we are witnessing a crisis of parties and the export to the rest of the democratic world of this North American format of weak, decentralized organizations. The evidence for such a crisis is certainly mounting:

▸ The major parties no longer offer radically different visions of the good society.
▸ Voters' loyalties to party are weakening as traditional social divisions decay.
▸ Party membership is falling and ageing.
▸ Leaders increasingly communicate with electors through television rather than the party.
▸ Party income increasingly depends on state subsidies rather than members' subscriptions.

No longer do parties seem to be energetic agents of society, seeking to bend the state towards their members' interests. Rather, they are in danger of becoming political pensioners, living off past glories and facing an uncertain future. If Ostrogorski were writing today, would he still interpret parties as a 'focus for the active wills' of the citizens?

Party organization

As Panebianco (1988) reminded us, internal organization is a key issue in the study of parties. How is power distributed within the party? What is the relationship between leaders, members and parliamentarians? The answer to these questions, Panebianco claims, must be historical. He places special emphasis on a 'genetic' account of party development, a term he uses to stress the importance of the party's founding moment in dealing out the power cards between the elements of party organization. These 'continue in many ways to condition the life of the organization even decades afterwards'. In this section, we will examine a classification of parties based on their origins before turning to the question of the distribution of power within them.

Types of party organization

Adopting Panebianco's historical approach leads to a threefold distinction between elite, mass and catch-all parties (Box 11.2). *Elite* parties are 'internally created'. They are formed by cliques within an assembly joining together to reflect common concerns and then to fight effective campaigns in an enlarged electorate. The earliest nineteenth-century parties were of this elite type: for example, the Conservative parties of Britain, Canada and Scandinavia. The first American parties, the Federalists and the Jeffersonians, were also loose elite factions, based in Congress and state legislatures. Reflecting this character, elite parties are sometimes called caucus parties, the 'caucus' denoting a closed meeting of the party's members in the legislature.

Mass parties are a later innovation. They originate outside the assembly, in groups seeking representation in the legislature for their interests and goals. The working-class socialist parties that spread across Europe around the turn of the twentieth century epitomized these externally created parties. The German Social Democratic Party (SPD), founded in 1875, is a classic example. Such parties acquired an enormous membership and, in contrast to elite parties, sought to keep their representatives in parliament on a tight rein.

These socialist parties exerted tremendous influence on European party systems in the twentieth century. In particular, they stimulated many elite parties to copy their extra-parliamentary organization. In Germany, again, the Christian Democratic Union (CDU) was created after the Second World War to offer a broadly-based Christian alternative to the SPD. Green parties, too, show features of the mass party, seeking representation for a new social interest. The United States, unusually, never developed substantial mass parties.

The *catch-all* party is a more recent form. Kircheimer (1966) used this phrase to describe the outcome of an evolutionary path followed by many parties, both elite and mass, in response to post-1945 conditions. The catch-all party is a response to a mobilized political system in which governing has become more technical and in which electoral communication takes place through the mass media. Their leaders communicate with the voters through television, bypassing what is still a large membership. Such parties seek to govern in the national interest rather than as representatives of a social group. Catch-all parties seek electoral support wherever they can find it; their purpose is not to represent but to govern.

BOX 11.2
Types of party organization

	Elite party	Mass party	Catch-all party
Emergence:	19th century	1880–1960	After 1945
Origins:	Inside the assembly	Outside the assembly	Developed from existing elite or mass parties
Claim to support:	Traditional status of leaders	Represents a social group	Competence at governing
Membership:	Small, elitist	Large card-carrying membership	Declining, leaders become dominant
Source of income:	Personal contacts	Membership dues	Many sources, including state subsidy
Examples:	19th-century conservative and liberal parties, many post-communist parties	Socialist parties	Many modern Christian and Social Democratic parties in Western Europe

Source: Adapted from Katz and Mair (1995).

The broadening of Christian Democratic parties (such as the CDU in Germany) from religious defence organizations to broader parties of the centre-right is the classic example of the transition to catch-all status. Indeed the German notion of a *Volkspartei* ('people's party') with its support from a wide range of people captures the catch-all idea. The subsequent transformation of several radical socialist parties into leader-dominated social democratic parties, as in Spain and the United Kingdom, is another example of this shift. America's parties, it might be argued, went straight from elite to catch-all status, omitting the mass stage.

Power within the party

Given the complex nature of modern parties, it is natural to ask where authority within them really resides. Of all the elements in Box 11.1, which one really commands the party? The answer is not always clear and the question itself is rather blunt. American parties, in particular, are sometimes seen as empty vessels waiting to be filled by fresh ideas and ambitious office-seekers. The American party is not controlled from any single point; no one pulls the levers, no one rules the party.

Yet much European research on parties does suggest that, in general, authority within the party flows from the top down, with the leaders who represent the party to the public playing a key role. In 1911, the German scholar Roberto Michels (1875–1936) published *Political Parties*, perhaps the most influential work on the distribution of power within parties. Michels argued that even organizations with democratic pretensions become dominated by a ruling clique of leaders and officials. Using Germany's Social Democratic Party (SPD) as a critical case, Michels suggested that leaders develop organizational skills and an interest in their own continuation in power. The ordinary members, aware of their inferior knowledge, accept their own subordination as natural, even in a party such as the SPD with democratic pretensions.

Michels's iron law is that power within parties, as within other organizations, ends up in the hands of the leaders. The law is almost a century old but still possesses considerable validity. Today, it helps to explain why Green parties, with a commitment to internal democracy that at least matches that of Michels's SPD, have seen their leaders acquire more authority as their organizations have matured.

Definition
Michels's **iron law of oligarchy** states that 'who says organization, says oligarchy'. The leaders of organizations, including political parties, develop expert knowledge, specialist skills and a commitment to their own power. Together, these factors ensure that even parties formally committed to democracy become dominated by a ruling elite. (Note: **oligarchy** is rule by and for the few.)

More specifically, in the parliamentary systems of Europe, the party leaders in the legislature are normally the key actors. When their party is in power, they usually provide the ministers of the government, including the prime minister, with all the publicity which flows from such positions. Even in opposition, the legislative leaders are often the party's public face. Perhaps surprisingly, this point applies to mass as much as to elite parties. In a famous study of Britain's Labour Party strongly influenced by Michels, McKenzie (1955, p. 365) argued that authority within the party does and indeed should rest with its parliamentary leadership. McKenzie concluded that, 'whatever the role granted in theory to the extra-parliamentary wings of the [Conservative and Labour] parties, in practice final authority rests in both parties with the parliamentary party in its leadership'.

We should, however, note that the party organization outside the assembly retains some useful power cards. State financial aid normally goes to the party bureaucracy, not to the party in parliament. And only party officials can cope with increasingly technical tasks such as recruiting members and raising funds through mail-shots, or arranging for advertising, briefings and press conferences during election campaigns. The contemporary importance of these tasks is captured in Panebianco's concept (1988) of an electoral–professional party centred around fighting elections through the mass media.

Selecting candidates and leaders

Elite recruitment is a vital and continuing function of parties. Even as parties decline in other ways, they continue to dominate elections to the national legislature from which, in most parliamentary systems, the nation's leaders are drawn. Given that candidates who are nominated for safe districts or who appear near the top of their party's list are virtually guaranteed a place in parliament, it is the selectorate (selectors of candidates), not the electorate, which is the gatekeeper to the house of power. As Schattschneider (1942, p. 46) famously wrote, 'the nature of the nominating convention determines the nature of the party; he who can make the nominations is the owner of the party'. How, then, do the major parties select their candidates and leaders?

Candidates

In choosing candidates for the legislature, parties are conditioned by the electoral system. Under the list form of proportional representation, parties must develop a ranked list of candidates, either at national or more commonly at regional level, to present to the electorate. This task usually involves compromises brokered by party officials between the various factions and interests within the party.

Take the Netherlands as an example. Holland uses national party lists so each party needs to prepare just one list of candidates covering the whole country. In the major parties, a nominating committee begins the selection process, examining applications received either from local branches or directly from individuals. A senior party board then produces the final ordering, with the party leader serving as 'list-puller' – that is, occupying number one position. The board will seek a balance: between incumbents and fresh candidates, and also between genders. In 2002, for instance, the Dutch Labour Party alternated male and female candidates in the first 40 positions on the list.

In a few countries, candidate lists are prepared though a ballot of party members. This procedure is more democratic but, as Michels might have predicted, it causes difficulties of its own. Ballots advantage celebrity over competence, and applicants' wealth over their party experience. In practice, membership ballots are also incompatible with the goal of a balanced list. Significantly, the major Israeli parties introduced ballots of members early in the 1990s but most withdrew the procedure before the 1999 election. The current procedure of selection by committee in the Netherlands also reverses a previous policy of membership ballots.

In the few countries using plurality elections based on local electoral districts, the nomination procedure is naturally more decentralized. Candidates must win selection by local parties keen to guard their autonomy against encroach-

---

BOX 11.3
Selecting candidates for legislative elections

Electoral system used for national elections	How parties select candidates for these elections	Example
Proportional representation (party list)	Party officials (or special party conventions) draw up a ranked list of candidates	Netherlands
Plurality system*	Local parties select the candidate, sometimes drawing from a list prepared by head office	Canada, United Kingdom
Mixed system	The party draws up a list for the PR element and local parties select a candidate for the district contest	Germany

* In the USA, primary elections are held among a party's registered supporters in the area. On electoral systems, see p. 148.

ment from headquarters. In Canada, for instance, constituency parties seek candidates with an attractive local profile, showing little concern for national needs (Carty, 2002). In Britain, selection is also though local associations, drawing on lists of potential candidates approved by party head-quarters. Some democratization has occurred even with local selection, however, with the nomination meeting – previously the preserve of the local management committee – sometimes now open to all local members.

The USA has developed the exceptional device of primary elections to broaden the selection of candidates in a plurality context. Primaries enable a party's supporters in a state to decide its candidates for a subsequent general election. In the absence of a tradition of direct party membership, a 'supporter', in most states, is defined simply and generously as anyone who declares, in advance, an affiliation to that party. Thus primaries extend the power of nomination outwards into the electorate itself. Originally introduced to formalize selection procedures and to weaken the control of corrupt party bosses, primaries are now well-entrenched (Ware, 2002). Yet as with membership ballots, primaries seem to be a mixed blessing. They take control over selection away from the party itself, reducing its cohesion and giving an advantage to better-known and well-financed candidates.

An increasing number of countries operate a mixed electoral system, in which electors vote for both a party list and a district candidate. These circumstances complicate the party's task of selecting candidates. It must both produce a national or regional list and also ensure local selection of constituency nominees. In this situation, individual politicians also face a choice: should they seek election via the party list or through a constituency? Many senior figures ensure they appear on both parts of the ballot, using a high position on the party's list as insurance against restlessness in their home district. In the 1998 election in Germany, most constituency candidates also appeared on their party's list (Roberts, 2002).

Leaders

The method of selecting the party leader and presidential candidate merits special attention. Just as many parties now afford their ordinary members a greater voice in candidate selection, so too has the procedure for selecting the party leader become broader. As Mair (1994) notes, 'more and more parties now seem willing to allow the ordinary members a voice in the selection of party leaders', perhaps to compensate members for their declining role in campaigns increasingly driven through the media. Yet whether this wider selection process yields better results remains distinctly debatable.

The most common way to choose the leader is to use a special party congress or convention (Box 11.4). American parties have long selected their presidential candidates through party conventions but these meetings are no longer the effective site of decision. The real choice is made by voters in the primaries, with the convention itself transformed since the 1970s into a media event for the party and its anointed candidate.

Canada traditionally provided a more typical example of the party congress. From the 1920s, leaders of the major parties were selected (and could be deselected) though special conventions.

BOX 11.4

Selection of party leaders in established democracies

Selection body	Countries in which most major parties use this method	Total number of parties using this method (based on 16 democracies)
Party congress or convention	Finland, Norway, Sweden, USA	37
Rank-and-file members	Belgium	19
Members of the parliamentary party	The Netherlands, New Zealand	17
Party committee	Italy	8

Source: Adapted from Hazan (2002, p. 124).

Delegates were either elected by constituency associations, appointed *ex officio*, or drawn from party groups such as those for young people. But these conventions became large and expensive affairs, with some candidates exerting unforeseen influence over delegate selection. As a result, Canada's parties are experimenting with other methods, including votes by local parties, perhaps running alongside a convention (Young and Cross, 2002).

A ballot of party members is an increasingly popular method of selecting leaders. In Belgium, for example, all the major parties have adopted this approach to choosing their party president. Britain's Liberal Party introduced a membership vote even earlier, in 1975. In some parties, a ballot is integrated with other methods. Thus, the British Conservatives now allow party members to choose between the two leading candidates as selected by vote of members of parliament.

Both conventions and membership ballots require potential leaders to reach large numbers of activists through the media. As Canada's Conservative leader Brian Mulroney said, 'every night I want to be on the 11 o'clock news. It's fine to shake delegates' hands but you can't win them in five minutes. You have to reinforce it' (Davis, 1998, p. 192). These methods therefore simulate the skills the eventual winner will need in a general election campaign.

Selection by the parliamentary party, the remaining widely used technique of selecting the leader, involves a much narrower constituency. This format is of course the traditional method, especially for elite parties with their assembly origins. The device is still used in several countries, including Australia, Denmark and New Zealand. Of course, the ability of potential leaders to instil confidence in their parliamentary peers may say little about their capacity to win a general election fought on television. Even so, colleagues in the assembly will have a close knowledge of the candidates' abilities; they provide an expert constituency for judging the capacity to lead not only the party but also, and importantly, the country.

What members of the parliamentary party give they can also take away. Backbenchers, leaders should always remember, are a potential execution squad. Davis's remark about Australia (1998, p.

195) applies more widely: 'a party leader can be removed from office during a single evening sitting of the parliamentary caucus'.

Membership and finance

In the first decade of the twenty-first century, many parties in established democracies have fewer members but more money than at any time since they became established. This revealing paradox tells us much not just about the changing character of parties but also about their evolving relationship with society and state.

We look first at party membership. Table 11.1 shows the marked and often dramatic decline from the start of the 1960s to the end of the 1990s in the proportion of the population belonging to a political party. Even in Scandinavia, where party systems remain strong, 'since the 1970s and 1980s, membership decline has set in at an unprecedented rate' (Sundberg, 2002, p. 196). In Denmark, to take an extreme example, one in every five people belonged to a party in the 1960s; by the 1990s, the ratio was one in twenty. Across the democratic world, millions of party foot soldiers have simply given up.

Further, the number of members playing an active role in party affairs may be falling, and turnover increasing, with the emergence of credit card members whose participation does not extend beyond automatic renewal of an annual subscription.

Lacking a steady flow of young members, the average age of members has increased. By the late 1990s, the mean age of members of Germany's Christian Democratic Union (CDU), a major European party, had reached 54; fewer than one in twenty members was under 30.

We should locate this recent decline in a longer perspective. If statistics were available for the entire twentieth century, they would probably show a rise in membership in the first part of the century followed by a fall in the final third. The decline is from a peak reached, in many countries, in the 1970s. Perhaps it is the bulge in party membership after the war, rather than the later decline, which requires explanation. Certainly, Putnam's comment (2000, p. 24) about civic engagement in

Table 11.1 Falling party membership in selected European democracies, 1960–99

	Total party membership as a percentage of the electorate			
	Beginning of 1960s	*Beginning of 1980s*	*End of 1990s*	*Decline 1960s–1990s*
Austria	26	22	18	-8
Denmark	21	8	5	-16
Finland	19	13	10	-9
Belgium	8	9	7	-1
Norway	16	14	7	-9
Italy	13	10	4	-9
Netherlands	9	3	3	-6
Germany	3	4	3	0
UK	9	3	2	-7

Sources: Adapted from Mair (1994), table 1.1; Mair and van Biezen (2001), table 1; Sundberg (2002), table 7.10.

the USA applies equally to party membership throughout the democratic world:

It is emphatically not my view that community bonds in the United States have weakened throughout our history – or even throughout the last hundred years. On the contrary, American history is a story of ups and downs in civic engagement, not just downs.

The decline in membership has occurred in tandem with dealignment among electors and surely reflects similar causes. These include the weakening of social cleavages, the loosening of the bond linking trade unions and socialist parties, the decay of local party organization in an era of televised election campaigns, and the appeal of social movements rather than parties to younger generations.

But the consequences of falling membership are more important than their causes. As parties' links with society have weakened, so they have come to depend more on the state for their sustenance. It is this transition from society to the state which explains the paradox of rising or stable revenues for parties in an era of falling membership. State

funding of national parties is now virtually universal in established democracies, providing the main source of party revenue in Austria, Denmark, Finland, Norway and Sweden, and often reducing the incentive to recruit new members. In Germany, 'parties are the self-appointed beneficiaries of extraordinarily generous public subsidies which in recent years have provided on average 20–40 per cent of total party revenues' (Scarrow, 2002a, p. 86). Only in the Netherlands, the UK and the USA do membership contributions still clearly exceed funding from the public purse.

Definition
Cartel parties are leading parties that exploit their dominance of the political market to establish rules of the game, such as public funding, which reinforce their own strong position (Katz and Mair, 1995). In politics, as in business, the danger of such collusion is that it damages the credibility of the participants over the longer term.

Since most state support goes to the leading parties, the effect is to reinforce the status quo. Thus one view of the transition to public funding is that the state and the top levels of major parties are tending to converge into a single, managerial system of rule: the party state. Governing parties in effect authorize subsidies for themselves, a process captured by Katz and Mair's idea (1995) of a party cartel: 'colluding parties become agents of the state and employ its resources to ensure their own survival'. The largest parties become part of the political establishment. Seen as 'them' rather than 'us', parties find that their popular appeal diminishes still further.

The social base

Since most modern parties emerged from outside the assembly to express group interests, they naturally acquired a specific social base which continues to influence their policies and outlook. Western European parties, in particular, retain a foundation in the social structure which gives them not just their historic identity but also a bedrock of electoral support.

These links between parties and social groups usually develop at crucial points of conflict in a country's history. Such moments define new social cleavages (that is, divisions) from which parties emerge and which they then reinforce. Indeed, Lipset and Rokkan (1967) could claim in the 1960s that party systems and social cleavages were largely frozen in a framework of class and religion established forty years earlier. Box 11.5 shows the three main cleavages from which many Western European parties have emerged. As always, the American experience is distinctive.

Definition
The **freezing hypothesis**, advanced by Lipset and Rokkan (1967), was that the party systems and social cleavages of Western Europe in the 1960s reflected those of the 1920s, so that the party alternatives were becoming 'older than the majorities of the national electorates'. Since the 1960s, some thawing of these cleavages has occurred but most major parties have retained a leading position (Mair, 2001).

Since Lipset and Rokkan's analysis, party systems have continued to evolve. In particular, far

right parties have emerged in many Western European countries and prospered in some. France's National Front was a significant and relatively long-lasting example from the final quarter of the twentieth century. In Austria, similarly, the Freedom Party won over a quarter of the vote in 1999 and joined a coalition government. Switzerland's People's Party (SVP) achieved comparable success in national elections in 1999 and 2003. In several other countries, in Europe and beyond, the extreme right succeeded in influencing the agenda of mainstream conservative parties (Minkenberg, 2001).

Such parties blame immigrants, asylum seekers and other minorities for their supporters' sense of insecurity in a changing world. Their social base is remarkably similar, drawing heavily on uneducated and unemployed young men. This constituency is particularly disillusioned with orthodox democracy and, as Lubbers *et al.* (2002, p. 370) report, 'across Europe, the stronger the dissatisfaction with democracy, the larger the support for the extreme right'.

These protest parties can easily flourish in an unsettled society by proffering simple 'solutions' to irreversible changes. However, many have proved to be flash parties whose prospects are held back by inexperienced leaders with a violent or even criminal background. Were the more extreme of these parties to expand to a point where they threatened the existing order, many protest voters would cease to vote for them.

Definition
Protest parties exploit popular resentment against the government or the political system, usually by highlighting specific 'problems' such as high taxes or a permissive immigration or asylum policy. They are often short-lived **flash parties** which fall as quickly as they rise. Their leaders are typically populist but inexperienced, with activists operating on the margins of the law.

Even though no one today would describe party systems as frozen, the plain fact is that in the political market (as in many others) the major players have retained their leading position. Decline does not imply disintegration. Sundberg's assessment of

---

BOX 11.5

Major cleavages in the development of Western European societies and their impact on parties

Stage	Definition	Party cleavages created by this revolution
National revolution	The original construction of the state as a territory governed by a single central authority	▶ Regional parties representing outlying territories vs. parties representing the core region ▶ Catholic parties representing traditional church control vs. secular parties wanting more control by the state
Industrial revolution	The emergence of urban societies based on manufacturing rather than extraction or agriculture	▶ Agrarian parties defending rural interests ▶ Socialist parties representing the new urban working class vs. conservative parties representing employers' interests
Post-industrial 'revolution'	The transition to societies in which education and knowledge replace capital and manufacturing as key resources	▶ Green parties and a shift toward postmaterial values among many 'socialist' parties

Sources: Adapted from Lipset and Rokkan (1967) for the national and industrial revolutions and Inglehart (1997) for the post-industrial 'revolution'. On Green parties in power, see Müller-Rommel and Poguntke (2002).

Scandinavian parties (2002, p. 210) rings true for most democracies:

> Parties in Scandinavia remain the primary actors in the political arena. To be old does not automatically imply that the party as a form of political organization is obsolete. The oldest car makers in the world are more or less the same age as the oldest parties in Scandinavia, yet nobody has questioned the capacity of these companies to renew their models. The same is true for political parties. They have developed their organizations and adapted their policies to a changing environment.

Party systems

To understand the political significance of parties, we must move beyond an examination of them individually. Just as a football game consists of two teams, so a party system consists of interaction between several parties. Parties, like countries, copy, learn from and compete with each other, with innovations in organization, fund-raising and election campaigning spreading across the party system. Similarly, legal regulation of parties – a prominent theme in the United States – applies to all parties. It is a property of the party system as a whole.

> **Definition**
> A **party system** denotes the interaction between the significant political parties. In a democracy, parties respond to each other's initiatives in competitive interplay. The party system also reflects legal regulation applying to all parties.

Like parties themselves, patterns of party competition persist over time, forming part of the operating procedures of democratic politics. We can distinguish the three overlapping formats found in Box 11.6. Note, however, that both dominant and two-party systems are now in decline and that multiparty systems, without a single dominant party, have become the most common configuration in established democracies. The British and American model of two parties engaged in a permanent contest for power may still be influential but it has become rather unusual.

Dominant party systems

Here one party is a constant component of the executive, governing either alone or in coalition. This format was more common in the twentieth century than it is today. A rare contemporary example is the leading position acquired by the African National Congress (ANC) in South Africa. The ANC benefits from memories of its opposition to apartheid, from its strong position among the black majority and from its use of office to reward its own supporters. By contrast, the opposition parties are weak and divided, with a smaller social base.

Sweden provides an additional and unusual example of a party that continues to dominate despite operating in a competitive and well-regulated multiparty system. The Social Democratic Workers' Party (Socialdemokraterna, SAP) has formed all but a handful of governments since the war. Between 1945 and 1998, the party averaged

44 per cent of the vote, the highest rating in Western Europe (Bergman, 2000, p. 193).

SAP occupies a strong historical, sociological and ideological position in Sweden. Historically, it is the country's oldest party, becoming the leading party as early as 1917. Sociologically, the party has benefited from support among both the working class and the large public sector. Ideologically, SAP fills a pivotal ideological position on the centre-left. Unlike South Africa's ANC, the Social Democrats do not benefit from a link to the founding of the nation but the party has succeeded in capturing and reinforcing the population's commitment to public welfare provision. More than most dominant parties, SAP has combined stable leadership with competent governance.

The dominance of the Social Democrats is far from unlimited. SAP rarely secures a majority of votes and it usually lacks a parliamentary majority. Normally, it forms a single-party minority administration, though often relying on parliamentary support from the Left (formerly Communist) Party, the other component of the socialist bloc. Just as Sweden itself is unusual in combining a multiparty system with a tradition of single-party government, so its leading party has so far maintained its dominant position in a genuinely competitive party system.

BOX 11.6
Party systems in democracies

Type	Definition	Examples
Dominant party system	One party is constantly in office, either governing alone or in coalition with other parties	Japan (Liberal Democrats), South Africa (African National Congress), Sweden (Social Democrats)
Two-party system	Two major parties compete to form single-party governments	Great Britain (Conservative and Labour), United States* (Democratic and Republican)
Multiparty system	The assembly is composed of several minority parties, leading to government by coalition or a minority party	Belgium, Netherlands, Scandinavia

* However, divided government means one party can control the presidency while the other has a majority in either or both houses of Congress.

In the long run, dominant parties have tended to fall victim to their own success. The very strength of a dominant party's position means that factions tend to develop within it, leading to an inward-looking perspective, a lack of concern with policy and even corruption. In Japan the conservative LDP (Liberal Democrats), although still the leading political force, illustrates these themes. The LDP did not engage in ballot-rigging or intimidation, devices used by dominant parties in semi-democracies. But the constant tenure in office of the LDP between 1955 and 1993 did create the corrupt meshing of state and party which characterizes such systems. The LDP used state patronage to reinforce its strength, passing out resources such as campaign funds to its candidates through party factions.

Today, the LDP continues as a leading force but governing in coalition with other parties. In public, some LDP leaders – including Prime Minister Koizumi – express commitment to reform and after the 2003 election some analysts claimed to have detected the beginnings of a transition to a two-party system in which the LDP would compete alongside the opposition Democratic Party of Japan.

India provides a clearer example of a diminished 'dominant' party. From independence in 1947, Indian politics was led by the Congress Party, a party which under Mahatma Gandhi had provided the focus of resistance to British colonial rule. To maintain its leading position after independence, the party relied on a patronage pyramid of class and caste alliances to sustain a national organization in a fragmented and religiously divided country. For two decades, Congress proved to be a successful and resilient catch-all party, drawing support from all social groups. But authoritarian rule during Indira Gandhi's State of Emergency from 1975 to 1977 cost Congress dear. The party suffered its first defeat at a national election in 1977 and it now plays second fiddle to the Hindu Bharatiya Janata Party (BJP).

Two-party systems

In a two-party system, two major parties of comparable size compete for electoral support, providing the framework for political competition.

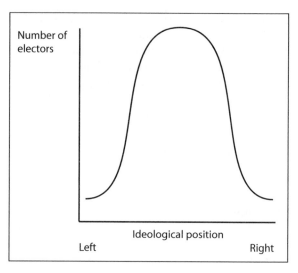

Figure 11.1 A bell-shaped distribution: parties converge at the centre

The remaining parties exert little if any influence on the formation and policies of governments (Sartori, 1976). Neither major party dominates by itself but in combination, they comprise a strong party system.

Today, the United States is the surest example. Although American parties may seem weak by European standards, a two-party system has been a constant feature of American history. The current parties – the Republicans and Democrats – have dominated electoral politics since 1860, assisted by the high hurdle that plurality elections set for minor parties. In addition, winning a presidential election is a political mountain which can only be climbed by major parties capable of assembling a broad national coalition. The United States illustrates how weak parties, lacking the ideological cohesion and mass membership found in Western Europe, can nonetheless make a strong party system.

Britain is also considered to exemplify the two-party pattern. Certainly, the Conservative and Labour parties regularly alternate in office, offering clear accountability to the electorate. However third parties have gained ground; far more so, indeed, than in the United States. In 2001, the centre Liberal Democrats won 52 seats in a parliament of 659 members, the highest proportion for a third party in over 50 years. The

DEBATE
PARTIES AS VOTE-MAXIMIZERS

What are parties for? Their defining feature is to fight elections and many theorists assume, for simplicity, that the sole motive of parties is to maximize their vote. But how realistic is that assumption? Should parties be construed as seeking to influence government policy, rather than just maximizing their electoral support? This question of the fundamental goal of parties has caused controversy among political scientists seeking to construct theories of party competition.

The case for

The classic study of how parties compete is Anthony Downs's *An Economic Theory of Democracy* (1957), one of the most influential works of political science published since 1945. Downs assumes that in a political market, parties act in a rational, self-interested way. He defines a party as 'a team of people seeking to control the governing apparatus by gaining office in a duly constituted election'. To maximize their control over the government, parties seek to maximize their vote, even in a multiparty system:

> The more votes a party wins, the more chance it has to enter a coalition, the more power it receives if it does enter one and the more individuals in it hold office in the government coalition. Hence vote-maximizing is still the basic motive underlying the behaviour of parties. (Downs, 1957, p. 159)

From this assumption, Downs deduces that as long as public opinion forms a symmetrical, bell-shaped distribution around the midpoint of a left–right scale (Figure 11.1 p. 196), parties in a two-party system will converge at the midpoint of the ideological spectrum. A party may start at one extreme but it will move toward the centre because more votes are to be won there than will be lost through its extreme supporters shifting to abstention. Evidence to support this prediction is legion: Bill Clinton and Tony Blair are just two examples of leaders who have won elections by steering their parties to the middle ground. Further, public funding for parties is now often in proportion to their electoral success, giving a further incentive for parties to maximize their vote.

The case against

Critics allege that Downs's vote-maximizing assumption is too extreme. It is often more accurate to see parties as office-seeking, a goal which requires not that votes be maximized but just that a sufficient number be obtained to win. In the United States, for instance, what matters is winning the White House; the magnitude of the victory is secondary. In similar vein, the object of a party in a two-party parliamentary system is surely to win enough seats to form the next government; again, the size of its majority matters far less. For such reasons, Riker (1962, p. 33) distinguishes his position from Downs's as follows:

> Downs assumed that political parties seek to maximize votes. As against this, I shall attempt to show that they seek to maximize only up to the point of subjective certainty of winning.

More radically, parties may be modelled as seeking to influence public policy, rather than to obtain office or to maximize votes. For example, in European countries governed by coalitions (especially Scandinavia), the choice of coalition partners is influenced by agreements over the policies to be followed. More coalitions are formed from parties with a similar ideology than would be the case if parties were motivated solely by the short-run desire for office. Further, if parties followed the goal of power above all else, why would they ever resign from a coalition? One reason why parties are concerned with policy is to reflect the priorities of the members. Activists are often committed to policy as well as power and, unlike company employees, volunteers can walk away if they dislike their party's policy direction. De Swann (1973, p. 88), a leading advocate of this 'policy-influencing' position, suggests that

> Considerations of policy are foremost in the minds of the actors … the parliamentary game is, in fact, about the determination of major government policy.

Assessment

Downs's vote-maximizing model may be simple but that is one of the functions of a model: to simplify. In any case, his assumptions seem to yield reasonable predictions. Müller and Strøm (1999, p.305) find that 'about half of the parties in the 10 Western European countries covered in our case studies used a strategy of vote maximization'. By contrast, only three parties acted as though policy influence were their main objective. Even if specific counter-examples can be found, Downs's model is still a useful yardstick against which actual party behaviour can be measured.

Further reading: Downs (1957), Green and Shapiro (1994), Müller and Strøm (1999).

Profile ITALY

Population: 58m.

Gross domestic product per head: $25,000.

Form of government: parliamentary, with an indirectly elected president who can play a role in government formation.

Legislature: the Chamber of Deputies (630 members) and the Senate (315) are elected simultaneously by popular vote for a maximum of five years. A bill must receive the positive assent of both houses and (as in Australia) the Cabinet is equally responsible to both chambers, producing a strongly bicameral legislature.

Executive: the prime minister formally appoints, but cannot dismiss, the members of the large Cabinet. Coalition requirements limit the PM's choice. An 800-strong Office of the Prime Minister provides support, which has given PMs more influence over the machinery of government.

Judiciary: based on the civil law tradition, Italy has both ordinary and administrative judicial systems. A 15-member Constitutional Court has powers of judicial review.

Electoral system (1994): an additional member system, with three-quarters of both houses elected by simple majority and one-quarter by proportional representation.

Until 1992, Italy was a leading example of a dominant party system. The role of the Christian Democrats (DC) in several ways resembled the position of Japan's LDP. The DC was a leading player in all 47 Italian governments between 1947 and 1992. The DC was a patronage-based, Catholic catch-all party that derived its political strength from serving as a bulwark against Italy's strong communist party. Like the LDP in Japan, the DC slowly colonized the state, with particular ministries becoming the property of specific factions. The party used its control of the state to reward its supporters with jobs and contracts, with little regard for the public purse. This patronage network spun across the country, providing a measure of integration between the affluent North and the backward South. However the DC's rule was based on unstable coalitions with a variety of partners; governments were short-lived and policy development constrained.

Between 1992 and 1994, this party system disintegrated. Still the largest party in 1992, the Christian Democrats had ceased to exist two years later. Its old sparring partner, the communists, had already given up the ghost, largely reforming as the Democratic Party of the Left (PDS) in 1991. Why then did this party-based system collapse? Donovan (1995) suggests that five catalysts initiated the destruction of Europe's oldest ruling elite:

▶ the collapse of communism
▶ the success of the new, regional Northern League in elections in 1990
▶ referendums on electoral reform in the early 1990s which revealed public hostility to the existing order
▶ vivid attacks by Francesco Cossiga (president 1985-92) on the patronage power of the leading parties.
▶ the success of a newly assertive judiciary in exposing political corruption.

Like many other dominant parties, the DC's reliance on patronage also came under pressure from the global economy and, in Italy's case, from EU pressure for a genuine single market.

Although the collapse of the old system was decisive, Italy's new order is only now beginning to deliver more stable government. The election of 1994, the first fought under a new electoral system designed to reduce fragmentation, fell apart after seven months, the victim of traditional coalition infighting. It was replaced by an astonishing crisis government of technocrats containing no parliamentary representatives at all. The next election, in 1996, did produce signs of consolidation. Two major alliances emerged: the centre-left Olive Tree Alliance and the more right-wing Liberty Pole. But it was not until 2001, when Berlusconi's House of Freedom coalition won a majority in both legislative chambers, that stable government seemed to become a serious possibility. However, consolidation of the new order remains somewhat insecure as a result of Berlusconi's own volatile temperament, his controversial ownership of media companies, a continuing debate about constitutional reform, and the strength of the new regional parties.

Whatever the future may bring, Italy's old mass parties have disappeared for ever, replaced by the looser, leader-dominated parties which are characteristic of the new democracies founded in the 1990s. The rapid decline of the DC showed just how vulnerable and outdated its form of dominant party rule had become.

Further reading: Donovan (1995), Newell and Bull (2002), Partridge (1998).

Liberal Democrats have also progressed in local government and, aided by proportional representation, in the new assemblies in Scotland and Wales.

Like dominant parties, the two-party format now appears to be in decline, kept alive only by the ventilator of the plurality electoral method. Duverger's law (1954) says that 'the simple majority single ballot [plurality] system favours the two-party system'. Thus the recent shift away from plurality elections, as in New Zealand and South Africa, has damaged the prospects of two-party systems.

Even where a favourable electoral regime continues, as in Canada, the two-party system has buckled. Traditionally dominated by the Conservatives and Liberals, Canada's Conservatives were reduced to just two seats at the 1993 election. Two regional parties – the Bloc Québécois and the Reform Party – have emerged as the main opposition to the Liberals. Canada's regional fragmentation proved stronger than the integration offered by the national two-party system.

Multiparty systems

In multiparty systems, the legislature comprises several minority parties, resulting in coalitions or, less often, minority government by the leading party. Multiparty systems are a natural consequence of proportional representation, the dominant electoral system in continental Europe and Scandinavia. To judge multiparty systems, a view is therefore needed on the character and functioning of coalitions. How effective are they in delivering sound governance?

Answers to this question have evolved over time, largely in response to national economic performance. In the English-speaking world, coalitions were once held to produce weak and unstable government with confused accountability. If things went wrong, which party or parties in the coalition should be blamed? In some countries, notably Italy, coalitions were slow to form but quick to fall, giving an appearance of continuing political instability. All this is far removed from the concentration of power in a single-party cabinet in Britain or even the focus of responsibility in the United States on the White House. Herbert

Asquith, British prime minister 1908–16, expressed the English-speaking world's suspicion of coalitions when he wrote, 'Nothing is so belittling to the stature of public men, as the atmosphere of a coalition.'

But opinions of coalitions became more positive in the 1960s as the postwar recovery of continental economies took hold. In practice, coalition government did not lead to inconsistent, vacillating policies. In most of Scandinavia, for instance, coalitions were composed of parties with a similar ideological persuasion. Policy was formed by consensus. Coalitions came and went but without threatening continuity of policy. The claim was that the careful, cautious governance induced by multiparty coalitions was well-suited to complex societies with strong social divisions. Coalitions were seen as the anvil of democracy, a forge for manufacturing consensus.

However, the link between coalitions and weak government resurfaced in the 1990s. This reinterpretation reflected the tough 1990s agenda: cutting the government's budget deficit, privatizing state-owned companies and reducing welfare expenditure. The more parties there are in a government, it was now argued, the harder it became to reach agreement on such a reform programme. It was the traditional two-party systems, notably Britain and New Zealand, which pursued the new policies with most energy. Continental Europe, particularly Germany, lagged behind, leading to doubts about whether multiparty systems were sufficiently flexible to produce the rapid policy changes needed to adapt to a global economy. Blondel (1993), for one, argued that

the consensus mode of politics is not well-equipped to lead to long-term strategic action . . . its value appears to lie primarily in its ability to handle deep social cleavages rather than policy development.

Yet several continental countries are cautiously beginning to implement the reform agenda. Confronting rising unemployment, even Germany's Social Democratic/Green coalition advanced modest reform proposals, including limiting increases in health care spending, in 2003. A balanced conclusion is perhaps that coalitions produce continuity of policy which is helpful when the economy is growing naturally, but are slower, though not necessarily less successful in the long run, at reviving economies which have fallen on hard times.

Parties in new democracies

The distinction between established and new democracies is crucial to understanding the varying significance of parties. Parties remain fundamental to the politics and governance of consolidated democracies but their significance is somewhat reduced in the newer post-communist and post-military democracies. In most new democracies, parties lack cohesion, a mass membership and even an ideology. To return to Ostrogorski's distinction, they are often as much a political form as a political force – shells for ambitious politicians rather than disciplined actors in themselves. Certainly, in some new democracies, particularly in Central Europe, parties and party systems are becoming more settled. Even so, it would be a Western conceit to imagine that the future course of party development will follow that of the established democracies.

The soft character of parties in new democracies is illustrated in most post-communist states. As the national movements which initially seized power from the communists began to split, many new parties appeared, representing specialized interests such as peasants and ethnic minorities. Countries in transition from communism were short of many things but they did not lack for parties. However, most of these parties were of the elite type, lacking a mass membership and strong extra-parliamentary structures. Steen's comment (1995, p. 13) about the Baltic countries – Estonia, Latvia and Lithuania – applies more generally to the post-communist world: 'the parties are more like campaigning institutions before elections than permanent institutions propagating ideology'. In that respect, post-communist parties follow the American rather than the Western European model. The contrast with the tight control exerted by their communist predecessors could hardly be sharper.

The failure of parties to penetrate post-commu-

nist societies reflected continuing suspicion of politics and politicians among the population. It remained difficult to enthuse electors who had been denied a political voice during, and often before, the communist era. In addition, newly founded parties did not possess the same incentives to build a mass organization as had confronted European socialist parties a century earlier. Since voting had already extended to virtually the whole population, there was no need for socialist parties to emerge to demand the suffrage for an excluded working class. Parties in the Czech Republic, Poland, Hungary and Slovakia soon obtained state subsidies, eliminating the financial need to build a dues-paying membership. The existence of television provided a channel of communication from the leaders to the electorate, reducing the value of local activists. And the adoption of proportional representation enabled small parties to survive and even prosper, giving little reason for parties to combine into the larger groupings which could develop a coherent programme and present it to the electorate.

> **Definition**
> **Successor party** is the term used to describe the new parties which formed in post-communist states from the old ruling communist parties. The Social Democrats in the Czech Republic and Poland are examples. Several successor parties achieved a remarkable electoral recovery in the mid-1990s. Ideologically, successor parties accepted the end of communism but many did question the speed of transition to a full market economy.

Kitschelt *et al.* (1999, p. 396) even suggest that there may be advantages in the political flexibility of soft party structures:

The absence of sunk costs in large membership organizations enables Eastern European democracies to enjoy the 'advantages of backwardness' and frees its politicians from devoting their energies to fighting armies of party functionaries.

Ironically, the organizational weakness of the new parties allowed the communist successor parties to stage an unpredicted if temporary comeback in several countries. In the early to mid-1990s, successor parties won presidential or parliamentary elections in Poland, Hungary and Russia. The living corpse of communism rose from its uneasy grave, brought back to life in a popular protest against the mass unemployment of the early post-communist period. This political rebirth, surely the most astonishing in the history of parties, owed much to the communists' inheritance of money, property, facilities, people and expertise.

Yet the success of the successor parties itself proved to be temporary, a product of economic decline in the transition from communism. In Eastern European countries where the living standards of the majority finally began to improve, the desire for a return to 'the good old days' weakened, especially among younger generations. In 1997, the Polish successor party was itself voted out of office. In any event, traditional communist rule has gone, born and died in the twentieth century.

Particularly in those countries most influenced by the European Union, there are signs of increasing party stability. In the post-communist world, most parties now fall into one of the seven families shown in Box 11.7. Bear in mind, however, that these groupings are broad and some parties, including many in the Balkans, are driven more by leadership and patronage than by their ideological colour. Post-communist party systems have also become less fragmented as they have matured, often aided by an increase in the voting threshold needed to win representation in parliament. Typically, only one or two new parties achieved seats in the assembly in the second and third post-communist elections.

In any case, we must take care not to judge post-communist parties by an idealized image of party stability in established democracies. Lewis's conclusion (2003, p. 172) about parties in post-communist Europe serves us well: 'many of their characteristics and defects are increasingly evident in Western Europe too, and party development in Central and Eastern Europe certainly appears to be adequate to sustain continuing democratic development'.

BOX 11.7
Party families in post-communist Europe

Party family	Example	Country
Communist successor party	Communist Party of Moravia and Bohemia	Czech Republic
Social Democratic	Social Democratic Party	Czech Republic
Agrarian	United Peasant Party	Poland
Pro-market liberal	National Liberal Party	Romania
Christian Democratic	Christian Democratic Party	Albania
Ethnic	Party of the Hungarian Coalition	Slovakia
Nationalist	Party of Greater Romania	Romania

Source: Adapted from Lewis (2003).

Parties in authoritarian states

Parties are less significant in authoritarian regimes than in democracies. In some cases, authoritarian rulers dispense with parties altogether, claiming they have no value in a country which needs to unite behind its leader. Alternatively, the ruler maintains a system of personal rule behind the façade of a one-party state. As ever, totalitarian regimes are a special case. Especially under communism, parties were the central political instrument through which leaders sought, and sometimes achieved, total control over society. In this section, we will first examine the role of parties in non-totalitarian authoritarian regimes before turning to the communist and fascist experience.

Authoritarian parties

Some authoritarian regimes still get by with no parties at all. These are either pre-party or anti-party states. Pre-party states are most commonly found in the Middle East: for example, Saudi Arabia, Jordan and Kuwait. In these traditional monarchies, a ruling family dominates and parties have yet to emerge or be permitted. Today, pre-party states are rare but internationally important, given their reserves of oil, the conflict with Israel and in some cases their terrorist links.

In the more common anti-party state, existing parties were banned when a new regime took over. For example, newly installed military rulers quickly moved to abolish parties, claiming that the nation could no longer afford the bickering and corruption associated with them.

Many civilian authoritarian rulers have found a single party useful as a disguise for personal rule and as a technique for distributing patronage. In post-independence Africa, for example, the heroes of the nationalist struggle soon put a stop to party competition. With independence achieved, one-party systems were established, with the official party serving as the leader's personal vehicle.

Such parties lacked presence in the countryside, were riven by ethnic and regional divisions, showed little concern with policy and became a device by which the country's hero-founder could parcel out resources. True, the party was one of the few national organizations, and proved useful in recruiting supporters to public office, but the party lacked cohesion, direction and organization. Indeed, when the founder-leader eventually departed, his party would sometimes disappear with him. When a coup overthrew Kwame Nkrumah in Ghana in 1966, his Convention People's Party also collapsed.

Leaving aside communist states, there are few cases of authoritarian rule where the political party, rather than a dominant individual, is the true source of power. One example, on the border between authoritarianism and semi-democracy, is Singapore's People's Action Party (PAP). This party has ruled the island since it achieved independence from Britain in 1959, winning 80 out of 83 seats in the 2001 election. PAP uses the characteristic techniques of a dominant party. Its attitude to the electorate blends threats against hostile localities with benevolence to districts which dutifully return PAP candidates. The party manipulates public opinion by limiting media freedom. It runs smear campaigns against opposition figures, harassing them with lawsuits and tax fraud charges.

But unlike many other authoritarian parties, PAP also provides effective governance. Singapore is a classic example of the Asian developmental state in which tight but paternalistic political control has served as a foundation on which to build a modern trading and export economy. As in communist China, a national commitment to economic development gives the dominant party continued faith in its right to rule.

Ruling parties in authoritarian systems face increasing problems in maintaining their position. International pressures for genuine democratization are growing and election observers are casting a more critical eye over traditional techniques for fiddling the electoral books. Just as important, international pressures to reduce a bloated public sector, stimulated by such bodies as the World Bank, are reducing the supply of patronage on which dominant parties depend to buy political support.

Even ruling parties which have always been sympathetic to the private sector – such as Singapore's PAP – may eventually fall victim to their own economic success. Control by a single party sits uneasily alongside the requirements of an advanced economy. And as Lipset (1960) argued long ago, a wealthy and educated citizenry will eventually become frustrated with the tight control exercised by a single ruling party.

Communist parties

Communist states provide the limiting case of the control that a single ruling party can achieve in a non-democratic environment. The mass party was the key innovation of the twentieth century and the device reached its zenith in the dominance of ruling communist parties over state and society, notably in the Soviet Union (1917–91).

The monopoly position of ruling communist parties was justified by Lenin's notion of the 'vanguard party': the idea that only the party could fully understood the long-term interests of the workingclass. Armed with this doctrine, the Communist Party of the Soviet Union sought to implement its vision of a total transformation of society following the 1917 revolution.

In this as in other communist party states, the party exerted its control through a variety of means. The party acted as a watchdog over society, vetted appointments to all positions of responsibility, controlled the media and carried out agitation and propaganda activities. Initially, hardly any independent groups were permitted and civil society faded, leading to an absence of virtually any associations standing between the family and the state.

As with all totalitarian regimes, coercion, and especially the threat of it, helped communist parties to maintain their control. The secret police were the main instrument of repression, as with the feared NKVD (later KGB) in the Soviet Union. The KGB used a vast network of informers to identify, and then eliminate, 'class enemies' and 'poisonous weeds'. Where this system of social control operated fully, it provided the most systematic penetration of society that any political party anywhere has ever achieved.

Definition
Democratic centralism was a key feature of communist party organization. It was based on two principles. The first was that lower levels must accept decisions made by higher levels (the centralism dimension). The second was that each level was elected by the one immediately beneath, thus forming a pyramid of indirect election (the democratic dimension). But only one person would be nominated for each election; and in reality this candidate was chosen from above. So 'democratic centralism' was centralism without democracy.

Reforms notwithstanding, the Chinese Communist Party (CCP) still illustrates the elaborate internal hierarchy of ruling communist parties, with its base in democratic centralism (Figure 11.2). At the party's base stand 3.5m primary party organizations, found not just in local areas such as villages but also in factories and military units. At the top, at least in theory, is the sovereign National Party Congress, a body of around 2,000 people which meets infrequently and for short periods. In practice, the Congress delegates authority: to its Central Committee and, through that body, to the Politburo (literally, political bureau) and its Standing Committee.

This intricate pyramid allows the half-dozen or so men on the Standing Committee to exert enormous influence over the political direction of the most populous country on earth – in itself, a remarkable political achievement.

The party is massive. In 2000, its membership stood at 63m, comparable to the total population of the United Kingdom. And unlike most parties in the democratic world, the CCP's membership is still growing. Indeed, it has the potential to increase further since the current members are just an elite fraction of the total population and women remain heavily under-represented.

What then accounts for the party's continuing appeal? The answer can hardly be ideology for the party's communist allegiance is now nominal. Indeed, Saich (2004, p. 95) reports that on his travels he has met 'party members who are Maoists, Stalinists, Friedmanites, Shamans, underground Christians, anarchists, and social and liberal democrats'. At local level, many members of the Communist Party are successful capitalists with businesses to run.

Party members are united by ambition rather than ideology. The CCP remains the only academy for the ambitious. Members are prepared to undergo a searching entry procedure, and the continuing obligation to participate in dull party tasks, in order to secure access to resources such as education, travel, information, expenses and automobiles. Above all, members can exploit increasing opportunities – whether legal, corrupt or both – to acquire wealth. Those who are particularly determined will seek out a patron to help them ascend the party hierarchy. Within the party's formal structure, it is personal patron–client networks, not political ideologies or policy differences, that provide the guiding force.

In contrast to many other authoritarian parties, the CCP has sought since the 1990s to strengthen its control over its own members, the government and even public debate. Tighter political control is a response to economic liberalization. Party leaders fear that that the mass unemployment, rural depopulation and increased corruption associated with economic change will diminish the party's standing and eventually limit its political monopoly. Comparative experience suggests they may well be right.

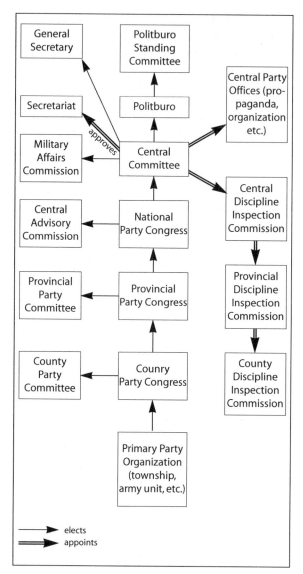

Figure 11.2 Organization of the Chinese Communist Party

Fascist parties

Showing the limits of the concept of totalitarian rule, fascist parties never achieved communist levels of control of either state or society. In large measure, this weakness reflected the cult of the leader (*Führer-prinzip*) within fascism. The fascist party served its leader, not the other way round. For example, the party could not be a site of policy debate because policy was the leader's preserve. Where communist ideology venerated the party as the foundation of progress, fascist thinking was oriented to the leader as the personification of the Italian state or the German people.

The German experience confirms the tangential role of the party within fascist regimes. The rise to power of the Nationalsozialistische Deutsche Arbeiterpartei (NSDAP, Nazi Party) owed much to its leader's opportunistic political skill. Yet once Hitler achieved power in 1933, the party became increasingly marginal. Soldiers, as servants of the state, were even prohibited from joining the party.

The regime focused more on personal loyalty to Hitler, downgrading the party. State officials were made to swear an oath of loyalty to Hitler himself, not to his party. The feared SS (*Schutzstaffel* or 'protection units') may have begun as the Nazi Party's security force but they became Hitler's own henchmen. The NSDAP became primarily a propaganda organization and even this function was eventually taken over by the government's own ministry. As Mommsen (1997, p. 170) writes:

> Many foreign observers, impressed by well-organized mass rallies, took it for granted that the NSDAP exerted an authoritative influence on decision-making; yet, in fact, it was increasingly condemned to political sterility.

Thus the significance of political parties in totalitarian states is not an issue which can be addressed without acknowledging the fundamental contrasts between communist and fascist regimes. Under communism, the political party reached its twentieth-century apogee, with Lenin's notion of the vanguard party rationalizing communist command of both state and society. By contrast, the ruling fascist party occupied a marginal position, becoming the vehicle of a supreme leader in a system that was both personal and state-centred.

Key reading

> **Next step:** *Webb et al. (2002) is an informative collection examining the condition of parties in a range of established democracies.*

Gunther *et al.* (2002), a more thematic collection, helpfully supplements Webb *et al.* (2002). Classic works on parties (and there are many) include Lipset and Rokkan (1967) on the social base, revisited by Karvonen and Kuhnle (2001); Sartori (1976) on party systems; Kircheimer (1966) on the catch-all party; Bartolini and Mair (1990) on the stabilization of European electorates; and Katz and Mair (1995) on cartel parties. Wolinetz (1997) is a reader gathering together work in these areas. On more specific themes, Hazan (2002) examines candidate selection while Davis (1998) discusses leadership selection. Ignazi (2003) considers extreme right parties in Western Europe. Lewis (2003) and Kitschelt *et al.* (1999) cover post-communist parties, van Biezen (2003) looks at new democracies and Brooker (2000) surveys parties in non-democratic regimes.

Part IV
GOVERNMENT AND POLICY

We examine here the key institutions of national government: legislatures, the executive and the bureaucracy. In many political systems, these are the core structures through which policy is shaped and power is exercised. We also analyse territorial politics, reviewing the relationships between central, provincial and local government. In the final chapter we move from the structures of government to a direct focus on the policies that government pursue. But we begin with a chapter on constitutions and the legal framework. Essential foundations of a liberal democracy, constitutions and the judiciary are growing in political significance as more governments come to operate under the rule of law.

Chapter 12

Constitutions and the legal framework

L aw and politics are closely linked. The development of liberal democracy has been an attempt to ensnare absolute rulers in the threads of legal restraint. In the words of A. V. Dicey (1885 p. 27), the nineteenth-century British jurist, the object was to substitute 'a government of laws' for a 'government of men'. Constitutional rule, affording protection for individual rights and a means of resolving disputes between citizens and state, is the major accomplishment of liberal politics. From this perspective, law is not so much separate from politics as an achievement of it.

The academic study of politics began as a branch of law and belatedly these old friends are now renewing their acquaintance. Four factors seem to be involved in this rebirth of interest in the legal dimension of politics:

▶ The late twentieth century witnessed an explosion of constitution-making among postauthoritarian states, with 85 constitutions introduced between 1989 and 1999 (Derbyshire and Derbyshire, 1999).

▶ Several established democracies – including Belgium, Canada, the Netherlands, and Sweden – adopted new constitutions in the final portion of the twentieth century. The European Union followed with a draft constitution in 2003.

▶ Stimulated by the legal character of the European Union and judicial activism in the USA, judges have become more willing to step into the political arena.

▶ The expanding body of international law increasingly impinges on domestic politics, with judges called on to arbitrate between the conflicting claims of supranational and national law.

For such reasons, Shapiro and Stone Sweet (2002, p. 1) suggest that 'it will be increasingly difficult for scholars who do research on government, or governance, to avoid encountering a great deal of law and courts'.

Definition
Constitutional rule (or constitutionalism) is the combination of habits, practices and values which underpin government by law. Constitutions are not self-implementing but depend on the support of the political elite to provide an effective framework for the exercise of power. When constitutionalism is absent, a constitution becomes a mere parchment.

To understand the political role of constitutions we must first introduce the idea of constitutional rule or culture (also called constitutionalism). Constitutional rule is broader than the constitution itself. It refers to a political environment in which the equal rights of individuals are not just stated but also respected. Specifically, rights can be defended through the courts, thus converting a dusty document into a political reality.

In theory, however, constitutional rule can operate without a foundation in a specific constitution: indeed, the United Kingdom is such a case. There, the notion of parliamentary sovereignty historically excluded the possibility of acknowledging a higher, constitutional power. Even so, the freedoms of most citizens are reasonably well-protected by a tradition of rule by law.

Conversely, the mere possession of a written constitution does not guarantee constitutional rule. Parchments depend on people for their implementation. Communist states frequently adopted new constitutions but these statements largely reflected the current objectives of the ruling party. To take a contrasting example, the American constitution did not alter on September 11, 2001, but the rights of many immigrants who found themselves imprisoned for several months without charge suddenly became less certain. As with most other countries facing external threats, constitutionalism temporarily took second place to national security.

Constitutions

We can look at constitutions in two ways. The first reflects their historic role as regulator of the state's power over its citizens. For the Austrian liberal Friedrich Hayek (1960), a constitution was nothing but a device for limiting the power of government. In similar vein, Friedrich (1937) defined a constitution as 'a system of effective, regularized restraints upon government action'. From this perspective, the key feature of a constitution is its statement of individual rights, particularly those held against the state.

Certainly a bill of rights now forms part of nearly all written constitutions (Box 12.1). The first Bill of Rights comprised the ten amendments quickly appended to the American constitution in 1791, covering such liberties as freedom of religion, speech, the press, assembly and the 'right of the people to keep and bear arms'.

Recent constitutions tend to be more ambitious in their statements of rights, often imposing duties on rulers such as fulfilling citizens' social rights to employment and medical care. Several post-communist constitutions have extended the list further, to include the right to a healthy environment. Many scholars argue that the greater the emphasis on rights in a constitution, the more active the judiciary will need to become as it tests government policy against such explicit standards (Shapiro and Stone Sweet, 2002, p. 177).

The second and somewhat neglected role of constitutions is as power maps, defining the structure of government. Constitutions articulate the pathways of power, describing the procedures for making laws and reaching decisions. As Sartori

(1994, p. 198) wisely observes, the defining feature of a constitution is this provision of a frame of government. A constitution without a declaration of rights is still a constitution, whereas a document without a power map is not a constitution. A constitution is therefore a form of political engineering, to be judged like any other construction by how well it survives the test of time. From this perspective, the American version, still standing firm after more than 200 years, is a triumph.

> *Definition*
> A **constitution** sets out the formal structure of the state, specifying the powers and institutions of central government, and its balance with other levels. In addition, constitutions express the rights of citizens and in so doing create limits on and duties for the government.

A traditional distinction contrasts written and unwritten constitutions. Yet no constitution is wholly unwritten; even the 'unwritten' British and New Zealand constitutions contain much statute and common law. A contrast between codified and uncodified systems is more useful. Most constitutions are codified; they are set out in detail within a single document. The flexible constitutions of Britain and New Zealand are unusual in that they are not formalized in this way. Sweden falls in

> **BOX 12.1**
> # The standard format of constitutions
>
> ▸ A *preamble* seeks popular support for the document with a stirring declaration of principle and, sometimes, a statement of the goals of the state.
>
> ▸ An *organizational section* sets out the powers of the institutions of government.
>
> ▸ A *bill of rights* covers individual and perhaps group rights, including access to legal redress, and thereby sets limits on government.
>
> ▸ *Procedures for amendment* define the rules for revising the constitution.
>
> **Further reading:** Duchacek (1991), Maddex (2000).

between the codified and uncodified categories: its constitution comprises four separate Acts passed at different times.

Amendment

Procedures for amendment are an important component of the constitutional architecture. Most constitutions are rigid (or 'entrenched'), thus rendering them more acceptable to the various interests involved in their construction. An entrenched constitution offers the general benefit, much prized by liberals, of predictability for those subject to it. A rigid framework also limits the damage should political opponents obtain power, for unless they can clear the amendment hurdle they too must abide by the values embedded in the settlement.

Definitions
Flexible constitutions can be amended in the same way as ordinary legislation is passed. Britain is one of the few examples. **Rigid constitutions** are entrenched, containing a special amendment procedure. Rigid constitutions are usually **codified** – set out in a single document – as in the United States.

Flexible constitutions, though rare, do offer the advantage of ready adaptability. In New Zealand, this flexibility permitted a recasting of the country's electoral system and government administration in the 1980s and 1990s. In most other countries such radical changes would have required constitutional amendment.

How are constitutions entrenched? This is achieved by setting a higher level and wider spread of support than is required for the passage of ordinary bills. Typically, amendment requires both a two-thirds majority in each house of parliament and additional endorsement by the states in a federation or, in unitary countries, by the people through a referendum (Box 12.2).

The amendment procedure offers clues as to the status of the constitution in relation to the legislature. When modifications cannot be approved by the legislature alone, the constitution stands supreme over parliament (Wheare, 1951). In Australia, for example, amendments must be

---

BOX 12.2
Entrenching the constitution: some examples

Country	Amendments require the approval of
Australia	both houses of parliament, then a referendum achieving majority support (a) overall and (b) in a majority of states
Canada	both houses of parliament and two-thirds of the states containing at least half the population
Germany	a two-thirds majority in both houses of parliament[1]
Spain	a two-thirds majority in both houses of parliament and, if demanded by a tenth of either house, a referendum achieving majority support[2]
Sweden	majority vote by two successive sessions of parliament with an intervening election[3]
USA	a two-thirds majority in both houses of Congress and approval by three-quarters of the states[4]

Notes:
1 The federal, social and democratic character of the German state, and the rights of individuals within it, cannot be amended.
2 'Fundamental' amendments to the Spanish constitution must be followed by an election, ratification by the new parliament and a referendum.
3 Sweden has four fundamental laws which comprise its 'constitution'. These include the Instrument of Government and Freedom of the Press Act.
4 An alternative method, based on a special convention called by the states and by Congress, has not been used.

---

endorsed not just by the national legislature but also by a referendum achieving a double majority – in most states and also in the country as a whole. So far, only eight of 42 questions put to the voters have passed this test.

In a few countries, however, special majorities within the legislature alone are authorized to amend the constitution. In such a situation, the status of the constitution is somewhat reduced. Germany is a partial example: amendments simply require a two-thirds majority in both houses. At the same time, however, the nucleus of the Basic Law –

which sets out core rights – is accorded the ultimate entrenchment. It cannot be amended at all.

Although rigid constitutions may appear to be incapable of coping with change, in practice they are more adaptable than they seem. Judicial interpretation is the key here. The American Supreme Court, for example, has become skilled at adjusting an old document to fit new times, reinterpreting a constitution designed in the eighteenth century for the fresh challenges of later eras. Thus one contrast between rigid and flexible constitutions is that in the former the judiciary manages evolution while in the latter politicians take the lead. In other words, rigid constitutions express a more liberal interpretation of democracy.

Origins

Constitutions are a deliberate creation, designed and built by political architects. As the English political theorist John Stuart Mill (1861) wrote, constitutions 'are the work of men . . . Men did not wake up on a summer morning and find them sprung up.' How then do constitutions come into being? Under what circumstances do societies set about redesigning their political order?

New constitutions typically form part of a fresh start after a period of disruption. Such circumstances include regime change (for example the collapse of communism), reconstruction after defeat in war (Japan after 1945) and the achievement of independence (much of Africa in the 1950s and 1960s). With the collapse of communist and military regimes, the 1980s and 1990s were busy times for constitution-makers: 17 new ones were introduced in Eastern Europe between 1991 and 1995, and over 30 in Africa during the 1990s (Vereshchetin, 1996).

Yet most constitutions experience a difficult birth. Often, they are compromises between political actors who have been in conflict and who continue to distrust each other. An example of such negotiated settlements is South Africa's post-apartheid constitution of 1996. Against an unpromising backdrop of near slavery, this constitution achieved an accommodation between leaders of the white and black communities.

As vehicles of compromise, most constitutions are vague, contradictory and ambiguous. They are fudges and truces, wrapped in fine words (Weaver and Rockman, 1993). As a rule, drafters are more concerned with a short-term political fix than with establishing a resilient structure of government. In principle, everyone agrees with Alexander Hamilton (1788b, p. 439) that constitutions should 'seek merely to regulate the general political interests of the nation'; in practice, they are lengthy documents reflecting an incomplete accommodation between suspicious partners. Some topics are over-elaborated but other issues are left unresolved. The lauded American constitution of 1787, although shorter than most, is no exception. Finer's description (1997, p. 1495) makes the point:

> The constitution was a thing of wrangles and compromises. In its completed state, it was a set of incongruous proposals cobbled together. And furthermore, that is what many of its framers thought.

The danger, then, is that a new constitution will not grant the new rulers sufficient authority. The American constitution, for instance, divides power to the point where its critics allege that the 'government', and specifically the president, is virtually incapable of governing (Cutler, 1980). Far from providing a settled formula for rule, some constitutions do no more than pass the parcel of unresolved political problems to later generations. Too often, political distrust means the new government is hemmed in with restrictions, limiting its effectiveness.

The Italian constitution of 1948 illustrates this point. The hallmark of the Italian constitution is *garantismo*, meaning that all political forces are guaranteed a stake in the political system. Thus the document establishes a strong bicameral assembly and extensive regional autonomy. These checks on power were intended to prevent a recurrence of fascist dictatorship but in practice *garantismo* contributed to ineffective government and ultimately to the collapse of the First Republic in the 1990s.

Judicial review and constitutional courts

Constitutions are no more self-implementing than they are self-made. Some institution must be

Profile **SOUTH AFRICA**

Population: 43m (of whom 20 percent are estimated to be HIV positive or to have Aids).

Gross domestic product per head: $3,167.

Composition:

'Black' 75%
'Indian' 3%
'Coloured' 9%
'White' 13%

Form of government: a democracy with an executive president and entrenched provinces.

Legislature: the National Assembly, the lower house, consists of 400 members elected for a five-year term. The presi-dent cannot dissolve the assembly. The weaker upper house, the National Council of Provinces, contains ten del-egates from each of the nine provinces.

Executive: a president heads both the state and the government, ruling with a cabinet. The National Assembly elects the president after each general election. The president cannot nor-mally be removed while in office.

Judiciary: the 11-member Constitutional Court decides constitu-tional matters and can strike down legislation. Power of appointment rests jointly with the president and a special commission. The Supreme Court of Appeal is the highest court on non-constitutional matters.

Electoral system: the National Assembly is elected by proportional representation. Provincial legislatures appoint members of the National Council.

Party system: the African National Congress (ANC; 266 seats and 66 per cent of the vote in 1999) has domi-nated the post-apartheid republic. It governs in coalition with the mainly Zulu Inkatha Freedom Party (34 seats). The more liberal Democratic Party (38 seats) forms the official opposition.

South Africa's transformation from a militarized state based on apartheid to a more constitutional order based on democracy was one of the most remarkable political transitions of the late twentieth century. The fact that the transition was largely peaceful, defying numerous predictions of an inevitable bloodbath, was the most astonishing fact of all.

Since white settlers came to South Africa in 1652, they had controlled the country by exploiting black labour. After 1945, the system of apartheid (apartness) institu-tionalized these racial divisions. Apartheid defined three races – white, coloured and black – and out-lawed marriage between them. Apartheid's survival into the 1990s showed that governments based on brute power can last a long time. Yet change was eventually induced, by three main factors: the collapse of communism which destroyed the regime's bogeyman; the imposition of sanctions by the EU and the United States; and black opposition which began to encompass armed resistance.

As so often, initial reforms merely stimulated demands for more and faster change. In 1990, ANC leader Nelson Mandela was released from prison after 26 years, symbolizing recognition by the white rulers that the time had come to negotiate their own downfall. Four years later, Mandela became president of a gov-ernment of national unity, including the white-led National Party (NP), after the ANC won the first mul-tiracial elections.

In 1996, agreement was reached on a new constitu-tion that took full effect in 1999. The constitution took two years to negotiate, reflecting hard bargaining between the ANC and the NP. The final 109-page doc-ument reflected the interests of the dominant ANC. It included a bill of rights covering education, housing, water, food, security and human dignity. The NP expressed general support despite reservations that led to its withdrawal from government.

It remains to be seen how South Africa's rainbow nation will be able to reconcile constitutional liberal democracy with the political dominance of the ANC. The ANC's strength in parliament is such that it could by itself virtually achieve the two-thirds majority required to amend the constitution, thus providing an exception to the generalization that fresh constitu-tions normally deny sufficient authority to a new gov-ernment. Further, South Africa remains a minefield of unresolved social problems: crime, inequality, poverty, unemployment and Aids. Yet the country's politics, more than most, should be judged by what preceded it. By that test the achievements of the new South Africa are remarkable indeed.

Further reading: Butler (2004), Deegan (2001), Glaser (2001).

found to enforce the constitution, striking down laws and practices that offend its principles. This review power has fallen to the judiciary. With a capacity to override the decisions and laws produced by democratic governments, unelected judges occupy a unique position both in and above politics. Indeed, India's Supreme Court is even empowered to override amendments to the constitution itself.

Judicial power, furthermore, is only partly limited by the constitution. Inevitably, judicial interpretation varies with the temper of the times. As the American Chief Justice Hughes once remarked, 'we live under a constitution. But the constitution is what the judges say it is.' Shapiro (1964) took this pragmatic view to its extreme, suggesting that the American Supreme Court is a political institution like any other. He regards the Court's function within government as 'basically similar to the city council of Omaha, the Forestry Service and the Strategic Air Command'. Basking in a privileged position, constitutional courts express a liberal conception of politics, restricting the power of even elected rulers. In this way, judicial review both stabilizes and limits democracy.

In reality, judicial power is far from unqualified. For one thing, constitutions themselves do restrict what judges can plausibly say about them. Justices are only unfree masters of the document whose values they defend (Rousseau, 1994). More important, the impact of a court's judgments depends on its status among those who carry out its decisions. After all, a court's only power is its words; the purse and sword belong elsewhere. So courts seeking to protect their own standing must follow a delicate course, paying heed to the climate of opinion without being seen to pander to it. As O'Brien (1993, p. 16) concludes of the American Supreme Court,

> the Court's influence on American life is at once both anti-democratic and counter-majoritarian. Yet that power, which flows from giving meaning to the constitution, truly rests, in Chief Justice White's words, 'solely upon the approval of a free people'.

The function of judicial review can be allocated in two ways (Box 12.3). The first and more tradi-

tional method is for the highest or supreme court in the ordinary judicial system to take on the task of ensuring the constitution is protected. A supreme court rules on constitutional matters just as it has the final say on other questions of law. Australia, Canada, India and the USA are examples of this approach. Because a supreme court heads the judicial system, its currency is legal cases which bubble up from lower courts.

Definition

Smith (1989) defines **judicial review** as 'the power of ordinary or special courts to give authoritative interpretation of the constitution which is binding on all the parties concerned'. This covers three main areas: first, ruling on whether specific laws are constitutional; second, resolving conflict between the state and citizens over basic liberties; and third, resolving conflicts between different institutions or levels of government.

A second and more recent method is to create a special constitutional court, standing apart from the ordinary judicial system. This approach originated with the Austrian constitution of 1920 and is now much favoured in continental Europe. Spain, for example, has both a Constitutional Tribunal to arbitrate on constitutional matters and a separate Supreme Court to oversee national criminal law. South Africa adopts the same division of judicial labour.

In constitutional courts, proceedings are more political and less legal: such courts can typically judge the constitutional validity of a law, or issue an advisory judgment on a bill, without the stimulus of a specific legal case. Where a supreme court is a judicial body ruling on political cases, a constitutional court is more akin to an upper chamber of parliament. Indeed, the Austrian inventor of constitutional courts, Hans Kelsen, argued in 1942 that they should function as a negative legislator, striking down unconstitutional bills but leaving positive legislation to parliament.

We will first examine the supreme court approach, using the United States – the original and most renowned example of judicial review – as an example. America's constitution vests judicial power 'in one Supreme Court, and in such inferior

BOX 12.3
Institutions for judicial review: supreme courts v. constitutional courts

Supreme court	Constitutional court
Relationship to other courts	
Highest court of appeal	A separate body dealing with constitutional issues only
Style	
More judicial (decides cases)	More political (issues judgments)
Recruitment	
Legal expertise plus political approval	Political criteria more important
Normal tenure	
Until retirement	Typically one non-renewable term (six to nine years)
Examples	
Australia, United States	Austria, Germany

1789 as unconstitutional, thereby establishing the principle of judicial review. At the same time, he skilfully avoided offending the administration on the specific issue, which involved the administration's disputed appointment of Marbury to a lower-level judgeship. Honour was satisfied and the Court avoided an immediate controversy.

The Supreme Court favours the doctrine of *stare decisis* (stand by decisions made – that is, stick to precedent) but does sometimes strike out in new directions. This 'inconsistency' has proved to be a source of strength, enabling the Court to adapt the constitution to changes in national mood. For example, after its rearguard struggle against the New Deal in the 1930s, the Court conceded the right of the national government to regulate the economy.

At other times the Court has sought to lead rather than follow. The most important of these initiatives, under the leadership of Chief Justice Warren in the 1950s and 1960s, concerned black civil rights. In its path-breaking and unanimous decision in *Brown v. Topeka* (1954), the Court outlawed racial segregation in schools, dramatically reversing its previous policy that 'separate but equal' facilities for blacks fell within the constitution.

Continental Europe, both West and East, favours constitutional rather than supreme courts. In Western Europe, such courts were adopted after 1945 in, for instance, West Germany, Italy and France (Figure 12.1). They represented a conscious attempt to prevent a revival of dictatorship, whether of the left or the right. Half a century later, the German example provided an influential model for post-communist countries establishing new constitutions.

Just as the USA illustrates the supreme court approach, so Germany exemplifies a successful

Courts as the Congress may from time to time ordain'. Constitutional issues can be raised at any point in the ordinary judicial system, with the Supreme Court selecting for arbitration those cases that it regards as possessing broad significance.

However, it is important to note that the constitution itself does not explicitly specify the Court's role in adjudicating constitutional disputes. Rather, this function was gradually acquired by the justices themselves, with *Marbury* v. *Madison* (1803) proving decisive. In this case, Chief Justice Marshall struck down part of the Judiciary Act of

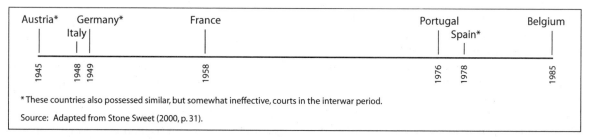

* These countries also possessed similar, but somewhat ineffective, courts in the interwar period.

Source: Adapted from Stone Sweet (2000, p. 31).

Figure 12.1 Establishing constitutional courts in Western Europe

constitutional court. With political power still under a cloud after the Second World War, the new Federal Constitutional Court was charged not just with constitutional review but also with maintaining the constitutional order against groups seeking to overthrow it. It has done just that, banning both communist and neo-Nazi parties in the 1950s. By nurturing Germany's postwar republic, the Court has ensured its high standing with the public. As Conradt (2001, p. 245) writes,

> More than any other postwar institution, the Constitutional Court has enunciated the view that the Federal Republic is a militant democracy whose democratic political parties are the chief instrument for the translation of public opinion into public policy. The court has become a legitimate component of the political system, and its decisions have been accepted and complied with by both winners and losers.

The Court's decisions have also impinged on other areas, including abortion, university reform and party funding. Between 1951 and 1990, the Court judged that 198 federal laws (nearly 5 per cent of the total) contravened the constitution. In framing new bills, German policy-makers anticipate the likely reaction of the Court; partly for this reason, Kommers (1994) argues that its influence is fully the equal of America's Supreme Court.

It would be remiss to conclude this section without considering the European Court of Justice (ECJ). Just as the Federal Constitutional Court in Germany helped to shape the development of a new republic, so too has the ECJ contributed to the strengthening of the European Union. Building on the German tradition of constitutional courts, the ECJ played a central role between the 1960s and 1980s in expanding the EU's legal order. The cumulative impact of its decisions amounted to what Weiler (1994) terms a 'quiet revolution' in converting the Treaty of Rome into what is, in some respects, a constitution for Europe.

The Court's formal purpose is to settle conflicts between the member states of the union, between the organs of the community and between the states and the organs (Nugent, 2003). It consists of one judge appointed from each member state for a renewable six-year term, with broad experi-ence more important than judicial expertise. Cases can be brought before it by member states or the other institutions of the Union. Like national constitutional courts, the ECJ can issue opinions as well as decide cases.

Like many other courts, the ECJ's decisions in its early decades consistently strengthened the authority of central institutions. It insisted that European law applies directly to individuals, takes precedence over national courts and must be enforced by these courts. Even though some members began in the 1990s to question both the Court's procedures and further expansion of its authority, the ECJ remains a major example of judicial influence.

Judicial activism, independence and recruitment

Throughout the Western world, judicial intervention in public policy has grown, marking the shift from government to governance. Judges have become more willing to enter political arenas that would have once been left to elected politicians and national parliaments. For instance:

▶ The Australian High Court under Sir Anthony Mason (Chief Justice, 1987–95) boldly uncovered implied rights in the constitution which had remained undetected by its predecessors.
▶ Even though the Dutch constitution explicitly excludes judicial review, the Supreme Court has produced important case law on issues where parliament was unable to legislate, notably in authorizing euthanasia.
▶ The Israeli Supreme Court has addressed conflicts been secular and orthodox Jews that mainstream politics has been unable to resolve (Hirschl, 2002).

Activism

What explanation can we offer for this significant judicialization of politics? The key seems to lie in the changing nature of politics, rather than developments within the judiciary itself. First, the increasing reliance on regulation as a mode of governing has encouraged intervention by courts. A

50 YEARS OF THE EUROPEAN COURT OF JUSTICE (ECJ)

1952 Court of Justice established as part of the European Coal and Steel Community.

1957 Treaty of Rome: the Court's jurisdiction extends to the new European Economic Community and Euratom treaties.

1963 *Van Gend en Loos*: European laws apply directly to individuals, creating rights and obligations that national courts must implement.

1964 *Costa* v. *Enel*: European law takes priority over national law.

1979 *Cassis de Dijon*: a product sold lawfully in one member state must be accepted for sale in other member states ('mutual recognition').

1987 *Foto-Frost*: national courts cannot invalidate EU measures but must refer their doubts to the ECJ for resolution.

1988 Court of First Instance established to reduce the ECJ's workload and to improve its scrutiny of factual matters.

1992 *Francovich and Bonifaci* v. *Italy*: when member states breach EU law, they must compensate those affected.

1992 Maastricht Treaty clarifies the ECJ's jurisdiction, e.g. to include treaty provisions for closer cooperation between member states but to exclude the Common Foreign and Security Policy.

2003 Publication of draft constitution for Europe.

Further reading: Dehousse (1998), de Burea and Wieler (2002).

---

political decision to deny gay partners the same rights as married couples is open to judicial challenge in a way that a decision to go to war or raise taxes is not. Indeed, Majone (1996, p. 290) argues that 'the progressive judicialization of regulatory proceedings' is how regulation gains legitimacy in the absence of mechanisms of democratic control.

Definition

Judicial activism refers to the willingness of judges to venture beyond narrow legal decisions so as to influence public policy. It is the opposite of **judicial restraint,** a more conservative philosophy which maintains that judges should simply apply the law (including the constitution), irrespective of policy implications and the judges' own values. The two phrases developed in connection with the American Supreme Court but possess wider applicability in an era of judicial politics.

Second, the decay of left-wing ideology has enlarged the judiciary's scope. Socialists were suspicious of judges, believing them to be unelected defenders of property specifically and the status quo as a whole. So in Sweden, for instance, some decline in the strength of social democratic principles has given more room to a traditionally restrained judiciary (Holmstrom, 1995).

Third, international conventions have given judges an extra lever they can use to break free from their traditional shackles. Documents such as the United Nations Universal Declaration of Human Rights (1948) and the European Convention on Human Rights (1950) have given judges a quasi-judicial foundation on which to construct what would once have been viewed as excessively political statements. Within the European Union, of course, national courts are obliged to give precedence to European law, a factor which gives them a stick with which to beat national governments. It is this priority of European over national law that has enabled the Dutch court to overcome the ban on judicial review in its national constitution.

Throughout the democratic world, the expansion of judicial authority has become self-reinforcing. Stone Sweet (2000, p. 55) makes the point: 'as constitutional law expands to more and more policy areas, and as it becomes "thicker" in each domain, so do the grounds for judicialized debate. The process tends to reinforce itself.'

Sensing the growing confidence of judges in addressing broader political issues, interest groups, rights-conscious citizens and even political parties have become more willing to continue their struggles in the judicial arena. With the status of the judiciary remaining high while trust in politicians declines, the willingness of judges to make broadly political decisions seems likely to increase further.

Of course, judicial activism has proceeded further in some democracies than in others. In comparative rankings of judicial activism, the United States always comes top (Figure 12.2). America is founded on a constitutional contract and an army of lawyers will forever quibble over the terms. The USA exhibits all the features contributing to judicial activism. These include: a written constitution, federalism, judicial independence, no separate administrative courts, easy access to the courts, a legal system based on judge-made case law and high esteem for judges.

MOST ACTIVE

United States
Canada
Australia
Germany
Italy
Israel
Japan
France
United Kingdom
Sweden

LEAST ACTIVE

Source: Adapted from Holland (1991, p. 2).

Figure 12.2 Levels of judicial activism in selected democracies

Fewer of these conditions are met in Britain, a country that is one of the few democracies to operate without judicial review. However, even in Britain judicial activism has increased, reflecting European influence. British judges were willing accomplices of the European court as it sought to establish a legal order applicable to all member states. The country's adoption of the European Convention on Human Rights (ECHR) in 1998, and the decay of the royal prerogative which allowed the state to claim to be above the law, also encouraged judicial assertiveness. Proposals for a new Supreme Court to act as a final court of appeal, announced in 2003, may well add to the judiciary's lustre.

Formal statements of rights have also encouraged judicial expansion in other English-speaking countries. Consider Canada and New Zealand. In Canada a Charter of Rights and Freedoms was appended to the constitution in 1982, giving judges a more prominent role in defending individual rights. Canada's court built on the charter to develop a particular interest in protecting the rights of people accused of crimes (Morton, 1995, p. 58). New Zealand introduced a bill of rights in 1990, protecting 'the life and security of the person' and also establishing traditional and previously uncodified democratic and civil rights.

These charters pose a difficulty in countries with a tradition of parliamentary sovereignty, such as New Zealand and the UK. Ingenuity is needed to integrate a bill of rights with the supposed sovereignty of the legislature. How can the authority of parliament be reconciled with the overarching status of rights charters? Fortunately, New Zealand has delivered an ingenious solution. There, the Attorney-General (a cabinet minister who bridges the political and judicial worlds) advises MPs on whether legislative proposals are consistent with basic rights. Technically, at least, parliament retains sole responsibility for adjusting its bills accordingly.

Britain has adopted a similar halfway house in incorporating the ECHR. In theory, the legislature remains supreme but in practice MPs are unlikely to override a judicial opinion that a bill contradicts protected rights. In this way, sovereignty can be simultaneously defended and diluted.

DEBATE
A POLITICAL ROLE FOR THE JUDICIARY?

More than ever before, judges participate in politics, striking down policies and laws deemed to contravene the constitution. But why should the judiciary be permitted to encroach on the authority traditionally accorded to the elected branches of government? Whatever became of democracy – of rule by the people?

The case for
The fundamental argument for judicial authority is a liberal one: that tyranny of the majority is tyranny nonetheless. Subjecting government to the rule of law is a core achievement of Western politics, an accomplishment to be cherished rather than criticized. Dividing power between the legislature, the executive and the judiciary is in practice the only way of containing it.

Of course, interpreting the constitution is bound to cause controversy but an independent judiciary is well-suited to the job of arbiter. Judges are held in higher esteem than politicians and judicial interpretation is likely to be more stable and disinterested than that offered by elected politicians, thus providing more continuity to citizens and businesses alike.

In any case, judicial authority is often exaggerated. Judges review after the event; political initiative remains with the executive. The justices wisely keep away from sensitive areas such as war and taxation. And even an independent judiciary does not escape political influence. Politicians have a say in the appointment of senior justices, the government can always seek to change the constitution if it disagrees with judicial interpretation and in practice the executive retains responsibility for crisis management.

The case against
In a democracy, the people must be sovereign. If a government behaves poorly, the solution lies in the polling booth, not the courtroom. As Bork (2003) argues, societies must be responsible for their own moral judgements and should avoid simply delegating difficult decisions to judges. Historically, judicial authority developed as a device enabling the

wealthy to protect their property in a democratic era and even today the judiciary shows a bias towards defending established interests. This conservative disposition is strengthened by the narrow social and educational background of judges, most of whom are still middle-aged to elderly middle-class white men.

Further, the modern judiciary places increasing reliance on international conventions, a form of contemporary imperialism that enables judges to escape democratic control exercised through national elections. From this perspective, judicial power is a mechanism through which global forces override elected governments.

Even if a mechanism of constitutional arbitration is needed (and Britain has got by well enough by relying on informal conventions), why should judges, with their narrow legal training, be given the job? Why not call upon an upper chamber or that oldest of political institutions – a council of elders – to perform the task?

Assessment
This debate would benefit from fuller appreciation of the constitutional courts that have emerged in many European countries. In the political basis of their appointments, relatively rapid turnover of members and reliance on a political style of operation, constitutional courts operate very differently from traditional supreme courts.

To a degree, constitutional courts have already become the third chamber of politics. Indeed, Shapiro and Stone (1994, p. 405) suggest that 'in the context of executive-dominated legislative processes, the impact of constitutional courts may at times overshadow that of parliaments'. Those who want the judiciary to be kept out of politics are fighting not a losing battle but one that is already lost.

Further reading: Bork (2003), Griffith (1997), Stone Sweet (2002).

Independence and recruitment

Given the growing political authority of the judiciary, the question of maintaining its independence gains in importance. Liberal democracies accept judicial autonomy as fundamental to the rule of law. To achieve this end, security of tenure is protected. In Britain, as in the American federal judiciary, judges hold office for life during 'good behaviour'. Throughout continental Europe the state exerts closer control, reflecting a philosophy that views the judiciary as an agent of the state even if operating autonomously within it. Even so, judges remain secure in their tenure.

How, though, is this security to be achieved? The problem is that if judges are chosen, promoted or dismissed by government, they may become excessively deferential to political authority. In Japan, for example, research suggests that lower-court judges who defer in their judgments to the ruling Liberal Democratic Party are more likely to be given promotion (Ramseyer and Rasmusen, 2001).

Box 12.4 shows the four main solutions. Cooption by other judges offers the surest guarantee of independence but democratic election, as practised in some American states, is more (perhaps excessively?) responsive to popular concerns. The format preferred depends on the weight given to judicial independence, on the one hand, and responsiveness to public opinion or party balance, on the other.

In practice, professional and political criteria can be combined. Judges are often selected by the government from a pool of candidates prepared by a professional body. In South Africa, for instance, the President of the Republic appoints senior judges after consulting a Judicial Services Commission which includes representatives from the legal profession as well as the legislature.

For courts charged with judicial review, selection normally involves a clear political dimension. In the USA, the stature of the Supreme Court is such that appointments to it (nominated by the president but subject to Senate approval) are key decisions. Senate ratification can involve a set-piece battle between presidential friends and foes. In these contests, the judicial experience and legal ability of the nominee may matter less than ideology, partisanship and a clean personal history. Even so, Walter Dellinger, former acting US Solicitor-General, argues that 'the political appointment of judges is an appropriate "democratic moment" before the independence of life tenure sets in' (Peretti, 2001). In European states, members of constitutional courts are usually selected by the assembly. So in both American and Europe, political factors influence court appointments, precluding a sharp distinction between legal and political realms.

But the tenor of judges' decisions cannot always be predicted on appointment. In post, judges con-

---

BOX 12.4
Methods of selecting judges

Method	Example	Comment
Popular election	Some states in the USA	Produces responsiveness to public opinion but at what price in impartiality and competence? May be accompanied by recall procedures
Election by the assembly	Some states in the USA, some Latin American countries	This method was also formally used for senior judges in communist states but in practice the party picked suitable candidates
Appointment by the executive	Britain, Supreme Court judges in the USA (subject to Senate approval)	'Danger' of political appointments though most judges will be appointed by an earlier administration, providing continuity
Cooption by the judiciary	Italy, Turkey	Produces an independent but sometimes unresponsive judiciary

tinue to develop their outlook. The best example is Earl Warren, Chief Justice of the American Supreme Court, 1953–69. Warren, a former Republican governor of California, was appointed by President Dwight Eisenhower but went on to dismay the president with his liberal rulings, notably on school desegregation. Eisenhower was later moved to describe Warren's appointment as 'the biggest damn fool mistake I ever made'.

The crucial point here is tenure. American justices hold office for life, subject only to 'good behaviour', giving time for their own jurisprudence to evolve. By contrast, the constitutional courts of Europe usually limit their judges to one term of seven to nine years. This enforced turnover in Europe reflects the more political environment of an exclusively constitutional court and limits the long-term impact of any one judge.

Administrative law

Where constitutional law sets out the fundamental principles governing the relationship between citizen and state, administrative law covers the rules governing this interaction in detailed settings. If a citizen is in dispute with an agency of government over specific issues such as pensions entitlements, student loans or redundancy payments, resolution is much more likely to be in an administrative court or tribunal than in the regular law courts. Just as the central issue of judicial review is enforcement of the constitution, so the task confronting administrative law is regulation of the bureaucracy.

> **Definition**
> **Administrative law** sets out the principles governing decision-making by public bodies, principally the bureaucracy. For example, America's Administrative Procedure Act, 1946, requires courts to hold unlawful any agency action that is 'arbitrary, capricious, an abuse of discretion, or otherwise not in accordance with law'.

The increase of government activity in the twentieth century led to an expansion of administrative law. Administrative regulation may lack the high-profile political activity of constitutional courts but by subjecting the work of public officials to clear rules they perform a function that is essential to a liberal society. They help to balance the relationship between the state and its citizens.

Typical questions asked in administrative law are:

▶ *competence:* was an official empowered to make a particular decision?
▶ *procedure:* was the decision made in the correct way (e.g. with adequate consultation)?
▶ *fairness:* does the decision accord with natural justice?
▶ *liability:* what should be done if a decision was incorrectly made or led to undesirable results?

Countries can handle the problem of legal regulation of the administration in three ways, with the chosen method reflecting conceptions of the state (Box 12.5). The first solution, common in continental Europe, is to establish a separate system of administrative courts concerned exclusively with legal oversight of the bureaucracy. A *separatist* approach marks out a strong public sphere governed by its own legal principles. This separatist approach speaks directly to the problems arising in public administration but runs the risk of boundary disputes over whether a case should be processed through administrative or ordinary courts.

BOX 12.5
Methods for judicial regulation of the bureaucracy

Method	Definition	Example
Separatist	Special codes and courts	France
Integrationist	Rely on ordinary law and courts	Anglo-American countries
Supervision	A procurator assesses the legality of administrative acts	Russia

Source: Bell (1991).

France is the most influential example of this separatist model. It has developed an elaborate structure of administrative courts, headed by the Conseil d'Etat, founded in 1799 (Figure 12.3). All administrative decisions taken by ministers and their officials are subject to review by the Council, a wide remit which can lead to slow decisions. Nonetheless, by developing its own case law, the Council has established general principles regulating administrative power. The Council's prestige expresses the autonomy of the public realm while also enabling it to check executive power.

The second solution, favoured in Anglo-American countries with a common law tradition, seeks to deny the distinction between public and private law. The idea here, rarely fulfilled in practice, is that the same legal framework should cover public and private transactions alike. For instance, employment in the public sector should be regulated by the same laws as apply to the private sector; no special codes should be necessary. Similarly, ordinary courts should be able to arbitrate disputes between bureaucrats and citizens; no Conseil d'Etat is required. And in the United States, the existing courts do spend a considerable amount of time reviewing rule-making and application by the numerous agencies of the American government.

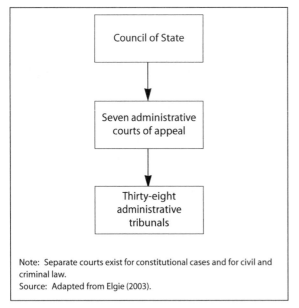

Note: Separate courts exist for constitutional cases and for civil and criminal law.
Source: Adapted from Elgie (2003).

Figure 12.3 Administrative courts in France

One strength of this *integrationist* philosophy is that it prevents boundary disputes and simplifies the judicial system. Above all, the integrationist philosophy affirms a modest aspiration for the public sphere; the state must abide by the same laws as its citizens. However, in reality, special courts are rarely avoided entirely. Thus even the United States has administrative courts dedicated to taxation, military, bankruptcy and patent issues. In any case, special obligations on American government, such as ensuring all citizens are accorded due process of law, are explicitly imposed by the constitution.

Even in the absence of special courts, more informal administrative committees invariably emerge in their stead, dealing with appeals involving such areas as employment law and social security. Such committees (often called tribunals) have their own strengths: they are quicker, cheaper and more flexible – though often more secretive – than the courts of law. In Britain, most administrative cases are resolved through these tribunals.

The third approach to formal regulation of the bureaucracy is through *administrative supervision*. Peter the Great introduced this device in Russia in 1722; it is now used throughout Eastern Europe. An officer known as the procurator supervises the legality of administrative actions and can suspend bureaucratic decisions pending judicial resolution. Russia revived the role of procurator in 1992. The procurator covers principles as well as cases and so performs a broader function than an ombudsman who merely investigates citizens' allegations of maladministration arising from individual cases. The procurator can form general principles, acting as an agent of a central ruler who, as in Russia, is positioned above the bureaucracy.

Whichever approach countries adopt to the regulation of their public bureaucracy, there can be no doubting the importance of the task. The twentieth-century expansion of government created not only new rights for citizens but also fresh opportunities for public agencies to evade those rights. In a liberal state, administrative courts and tribunals make by their mere existence a worthwhile statement that public servants are indeed expected to behave in a fair and reasonable way to the public they serve. It is for such reasons that in 1982 Lord Diplock, a senior British judge, said that he regarded the development of administrative law 'as the greatest achievement of the English courts in my lifetime' (McEldowney (2003, p. 3).

Law in new democracies

New democracies are political construction sites, in which constitutional engineers seek to build a framework of law, including enhanced respect for the judiciary (Kolstø, 2000). Their task is arduous. Establishing a state based on law in a country where brute power has previously ruled the roost is inevitably a long-term assignment. Agreeing the new constitution is merely the beginning. The subsequent requirement is to ensure that an independent judiciary is available to enforce the new order and, crucially, that all political actors abide by the court's decisions.

The status of the judiciary needs to increase from its lowly position in the previous regime. The powerful must learn new limits to their behaviour and the less powerful must begin to treat the courts as a realistic form of redress. The extent to which new democracies have entrenched the constitution and judicial autonomy is at best variable, as our analysis of the Spanish-speaking and post-communist worlds will show.

Spain's transition to democracy, following the death of General Franco in 1975, is an example of a deliberate and ultimately successful attempt to build the rule of law into the country's new political architecture. As Heywood (1995, p. 103) writes,

> After nearly four decades of dictatorship under General Franco, it was to be expected that the 1978 constitution should place particular emphasis on legal accountability. A central concern of the new democracy was that it should be established as a 'state of law' in the sense of its constitutional arrangements being both legally accountable and enforceable.

Spain's constitution-makers established a new Constitutional Court with 12 members appointed for nine years by parliament, the government and the legal profession. To ensure its independence, tribunal members are debarred from holding any other public office or from playing a leading role in a political party or trade union. Even so, suspicions remained that early appointments reflected party patronage.

Although Spain's new democratic order rapidly consolidated, the judiciary initially retained its pre-democratic image as remote, inefficient and conservative. It was not until judges began investigating allegations of corruption against leading politicians in the early 1990s – thus demonstrating their practical as well as their constitutional autonomy – that their reputation began to improve.

The rule of law sought and found in Spain has proved more elusive in many post-military democracies in Latin America. Elected presidents in South America countries may be less cavalier with the constitution than their strong-armed predecessors but even so several have treated the constitution as a flexible document to be adapted to suit their own political requirements. For example, some have sought to abolish term limits so that they can stand for re-election.

Other South American constitutions have retained privileges for departing generals, thus perpetuating a sense of an institution remaining above the law. For instance, Chile's armed forces were initially granted immunity from prosecution in civilian courts, a tactic that effectively enabled former generals to escape justice for political murders committed during their tenure. In Argentina, similar legal exemptions dating from the 1980s still formed a running political sore twenty years later.

In addition to the difficulties of establishing the constitution as an effective political framework, the rule of law is held back through most of Latin America by the low standing and standards of the judiciary. Prillaman (2000) chronicles the problems: chronic inefficiency within the judicial system, the vulnerability of judges to political pressure, outdated laws and the public's lack of trust in legal remedies. These factors combine to limit the judiciary's significance in Latin American governance, holding back not just democratic consolidation but also economic advance.

In some South American countries, the rule of law remains but an aspiration. The police probably commit almost as many crimes, including murder, as they solve. Coordination between the police and judges is poor; sometimes both are bribed and threatened by drug barons. In Colombia, one in three judges received a death threat in the 1980s. Informal arbitration and indigenous justice are often more accessible than the remote legal system (Domingo and Sieder, 2001). In the absence of effective policing, the residents of shanty towns sometimes resort to lynching as a form of social control, bringing about a further devaluation of official justice.

Although moves to reform the judiciary are afoot, and are actively promoted by international organizations, the task is inevitably long-term. One legal expert estimated that reform of Chile's criminal justice system would take at least 15 years (Frühling, 1998, p. 252). An authoritarian tradition and a cultural emphasis on personal power are infertile ground on which to nurture the rule of law.

The post-communist experience with constitutions and law is again somewhat patchy. As with other aspects of democratic consolidation, Central Europe has made more progress than the successor states to the Soviet Union. In Hungary and Poland, new constitutional courts have met with considerable success. The Hungarian court has made significant judgments on such topics as capital punishment, abortion, private property and the electoral system. In Poland, the court 'has become in a short time an important part of the governmental system' (Fitzmaurice, 1998, p. 96). One factor contributing to popular acceptance of these new courts has been the adoption of a German innovation allowing citizens to petition the court directly if they believe their rights have been denied (von Beyme, 2003).

By contrast, many successor states to the Soviet Union have simply swapped one non-constitutional order for another. In many of these countries, presidents adopt the imperious style of France's King Louis XIV: 'it is legal because I wish it'. Even in Russia, 'there has been and remains a considerable gap between individual rights on paper and their realization in practice. The further one goes beyond Moscow and St Petersburg into the provinces, the enforcement gap tends to grow greater' (Sharlet, 1997, p. 134).

But we should beware of judging the constitu-

tional quality of post-communist regimes against contemporary Western standards. As Sharlet (1997, p. 134) reminds us,

> while the Founding Fathers of the American republic quickly added the Bill of Rights to their newly ratified Constitution in the late eighteenth century, a number of these rights remained essentially 'parchment rights' and did not garner nationwide respect and judicial enforcement until well into the twentieth century. Is it surprising that Russia with its thousand-year authoritarian past and long tradition of legal nihilism should be proceeding slowly in Rule of Law development? Surely it is more remarkable that Russia has made the progress it has, including in the uncharted territory of civil rights.

Law in authoritarian states

In authoritarian regimes, constitutions are feeble documents. The nature of such states is that any restraints on rule go unacknowledged; power, not law, is the political currency. It follows that the status of the judiciary, as guardian of the law, is similarly diminished.

Non-democratic rulers follow two broad strategies in limiting judicial authority. One tactic is to retain a framework of law but to influence the judges indirectly. In Indonesia, the Ministry of Justice still administers the courts and pays judges' salaries; the justices understand the implications. More crudely, unsatisfactory judges can simply be dismissed. Egypt's President Nasser adopted this strategy with vigour in 1969. He got rid of 200 in one go: the 'massacre of the judges'. In Uganda, an extreme case, the killing was real rather than metaphorical: President Amin had his Chief Justice shot dead.

A second strategy is to bypass the judicial process altogether. For instance, many non-democratic regimes use Declarations of Emergency which are exempt from judicial scrutiny. Once introduced, such 'temporary' emergencies drag on for years, even decades. Alternatively, rulers can make use of special courts that do the regime's bidding without much pretence of judicial independence. Military rulers frequently extend the scope of military courts, often meeting in secret, to include civilian troublemakers. Ordinary courts can then continue to deal with non-political cases. Even the United States proposed to use military courts to try more than 600 terrorist suspects held in Guantanamo Bay, Cuba, following the war in Afghanistan.

Communist states offered a more sophisticated downgrade of constitutions and the judiciary. Marxist theory explicitly rejected the Western idea of constitutional rule with its emphasis on limited government, individual rights and private property. What does the Western tradition amount to, asked the communists, other than an affirmation of the status quo? In communist states, legal documents were of little moment. Nothing could hinder the party's task of building socialism; the party's mission was too challenging and important to be subject to formal limits. So communist regimes were ruled by the party rather than by law, a point confirmed by the reference in the constitutions themselves to the party's leading role. Communist constitutions also stressed social and economic rights such as the right to work, in contrast to the Western emphasis on more political liberties such as freedom of speech.

Just as communist states rejected the idea of a neutral constitution, so too did they dismiss the concept of judicial independence. The judges, too, must contribute to building socialism – and protecting the party's position. Throughout the communist world, judges were selected for their party-mindedness and were expected to put this virtue to good effect in court.

Yet as with many other aspects of communist politics, this situation was beginning to alter before the 1989 revolutions. Even authoritarian regimes can discover the advantage of applying the rules consistently. When one citizen sued another, or even when one enterprise sued another, the interests of the communist party were best served by resolving the issue through law. The courts therefore observed a measure of 'socialist legality'.

China provides a contemporary example of the evolution of communist thinking about constitutions and law. Constitutional revisions have lagged behind the reformist thinking of the party's elite. References to the dictatorship of the proletariat,

and to other Marxist sacraments, have finally been removed but the supremacy of the party is still affirmed in the constitution. In that sense, power still trumps the constitution and law remains a bird in a cage (Lubman, 1999).

But the interpretation of law has become more sympathetic. In the early decades of the People's Republic, legal perspectives were dismissed as 'bourgeois rightist' thinking. There were very few laws at all, reflecting a national tradition of unregulated power; the judiciary was largely a branch of the police force. However, laws did become more precise and significant after the hiatus of the Cultural Revolution in the 1960s. In 1979, the country passed its first criminal laws; later revisions abolished the vague crime of 'counter-revolution' and established the right of defendants to seek counsel. Law could prevail to the benefit of economic development.

Reform notwithstanding, Chinese politics remains authoritarian. The courts are regarded as just one bureaucratic agency among others; many judgments are simply ignored. There is no tradition of individual rights, enforceable against the state and party. Legal institutions remain less specialized, and legal personnel less professional, than in established democracies. The death penalty is still used. Private property rights are still not secure. Above all, party officials continue to occupy a protected position above the law. Politics still comes first.

International law

We conclude this chapter with a section on international law. For three reasons, international law must now receive attention from students of comparative politics:

▸ International law helped to define the division of the world into the states which provide the unit of comparative politics. States were the only, and remain the major, subjects of international law. Through international law, states reinforced their dominant political position and it is through participation in an international legal community that statehood is formally acquired.

▶ International law forms part of national law, often without any special mechanism of incorporation. Many constitutions are explicit on this point. The German constitution, for instance, states that 'the general rules of public international law are an integral part of federal law. They shall take precedence over the laws and shall create rights and duties for the inhabitants of the federal territory.'

▶ National sovereignty notwithstanding, international laws can apply directly to individuals and their rulers. The famous example here is the Nuremberg War Crimes Tribunal in 1946. This tribunal declined to accept the defence that individuals who committed crimes against humanity were just obeying state orders. With the end of the Cold War, new international tribunals have been created.

International agreements constrain national policy-makers. Such accords set out objectives (for example reducing carbon dioxide emissions) which national governments must − or at least should − put into effect. When states fail to abide by conventions they themselves have signed, affected individuals can in principle seek a remedy through the courts, both national and international.

An example from Australia illustrates this point and also draws out some broader domestic implications of international law. After Australia's national government ratified a protocol to the International Covenant on Civil and Political Rights in 1991, Nick Toonen, a gay rights activist, lodged a complaint against Tasmania's prohibition of sexual relations between men. Tasmania remained resolute but the federal government in Canberra passed a liberalizing law, overriding provincial legislation.

Definition
International law is the system of rules which states (and other actors) regard as binding in their mutual relations. It derives from treaties, custom, accepted principles and the views of legal authorities. The term 'international law' was coined by the English philosopher Jeremy Bentham (1748–1832).

The Toonen case shows how international agreements can impinge on the balance between different levels of government within a state. Indeed, critics allege that Australia's federal government could in theory use its expanding treaty commitments to interfere in virtually any area of activity which, under the national constitution, is supposedly reserved to the states (Scott, 1997). So international law provides an indirect route through which one level of government within a country can seek to influence another.

A further bypass around the blockage of state sovereignty has been achieved by setting up international courts to try individuals directly for their alleged crimes, even if these were committed in the name of the state. Of course, the Nuremberg trials after the Second World War had established that individuals are responsible for their own acts in war. That view itself departed from the notion of treating states as the only subjects of international law.

However, in the 1990s, the International Court of Justice set up new tribunals, the first since Nuremberg, to try war crimes suspects from Rwanda and the former Yugoslavia. In 1999, for instance, a female ex-minister from Rwanda was indicted for rape by the International Criminal Tribunal on Rwanda for sexual assaults she condoned during the 1994 genocide. However, these tribunals are proving to be expensive and slow-moving. The Rwanda tribunal cost more than $550m over seven years but secured just nine convictions, including three guilty pleas, during this period. In the Yugoslav case, the trials of imprisoned Serbian leaders Slobodan Milosevic and Vojislav Seselj aided public sympathy back home, with both leaders winning election to the Serbian parliament from their prison cells in 2003. Why, asked the Serbs, should these leaders be singled out, ignoring similar atrocities committed by the other sides?

One innovation of these new tribunals has been to indict suspects who were not already in custody. This raises the prospect of international snatch squads removing people from their home country to the site of the trial, further diluting national sovereignty. However, bringing these suspects to justice has proved to be a political challenge. Such intervention can stimulate a damaging reaction in the suspect's own community. Yet the alternative is equally unpalatable. Failing to capture indicted suspects, such as Bosnian leader Radovan Karadzic and his henchman Ratko Mladic, makes the international community appear weak.

Further impetus to the development of an international judicial regime came with the establishment in 2003 of the permanent International Criminal Court (ICC). Based in the Dutch city of The Hague, the Court is charged with dealing with cases of genocide, war crimes and crimes against humanity. The emergence of this international body is significant in itself but again its practical impact remains to be seen. Already, the Court has collided with the countervailing tradition of national sovereignty. The USA has vigorously refused to accept the ICC's jurisdiction. Fearing false accusations against and malicious prosecution of its troops, the USA has sought bilateral immunity deals with countries to which it donates military aid. These agreements exempt American citizens from any arrest warrants the ICC may issue in the countries concerned, thus keeping the United States beyond the Court's ambit (Schabas, 2001).

Key reading

> **Next step:** *Stone Sweet (2000) examines constitutional politics in five European political systems.*

Shapiro and Stone Sweet (2002) is a collection on political jurisprudence, including the United States. The special issue of *Political Studies* (1996) is an excellent survey of constitutionalism; for a collection focused on the USA, see Ferejohn *et al.* (2001). Maddex (2000) surveys 100 constitutions. Von Beyme (2003) covers constitution-making in Eastern Europe. On the judiciary, Guarnieri and Perderzoli (2002), Jacob *et al.* (1996) and Tate and Vallinder (1995) are cross-national studies. For particular countries and regions, see O'Brien (1993) and Shapiro (1990) on the American Supreme Court; Solomon and Foglesong (2000) on judicial reform in post-communist Russia; Lubman (1999) on post-Mao China; and Prillaman (2000) on the judiciary in Latin America. On international law, Bull (1977) remains a good starting point.

Chapter **13**

Federal, unitary and local government

Governing always has a territorial dimension. Rulers need to extract resources from their territory while also retaining the willingness of the population to remain within the state's orbit. To achieve these ends, the modern state consists of an intricate network of organizations, typically consisting of:

▶ the central government
▶ the central government's offices in the provinces
▶ regional or provincial governments
▶ local authorities
▶ the European Union (for member states).

Governance in all established democracies comprises several levels with extensive flows of communication, money and influence between them. Multilevel governance is the term used to describe how policy-makers and experts in particular sectors (e.g. transport, education) negotiate across levels, seeking to deliver coherent policy in their specific area.

Clearly, the balance between these assorted tiers raises important questions of democratic governance. Who initiates policy? Who funds it? Who executes it? Who is accountable for it? And, in view of September 11, how well can such intricate networks respond to national emergencies?

In this chapter, we examine the two basic solutions to the territorial organization of power: federal and unitary government. We then turn to the lowest level of authority within the state, local government, before examining the patterns of subnational government found in new democracies and authoritarian regimes.

Definition
Multilevel governance emerges when several tiers of government share the task of regulating modern society. Expert networks form within particular policy sectors, cutting across tiers and often extending to relevant interest groups. Multilevel governance inheres in a federation but the term is also used in discussing unitary states, particularly in the context of the relationship between the European Union and its mainly unitary members (Hooghe and Marks, 2001). *See also* pluralism (p. 177).

Federalism

Federalism is a method for sharing sovereignty, and not just power, between governments within a single state. It is a constitutional device, presupposing a formal political agreement establishing both the levels of government and their spheres of authority. So, like the constitutions within which they are embedded, federations are always a deliberate creation. The United States gave us the first modern constitution and, as part of the settlement reflected in that document, it established the world's first and most influential federation.

In a federation, legal sovereignty is shared between the federal (or national) government and the constituent states (or provinces). Neither level can abolish the other. It is this protected position of the states, not the extent of their powers, which distinguishes federations (such as the USA and Canada) from unitary governments (such as the UK and France). Multiple levels of governance are integral to a federation whereas in a unitary system sovereignty resides solely with the centre and lower levels exist at its pleasure.

A federal constitution allocates specific functions to each tier. The centre takes charge of external relations – defence, foreign affairs and immigration – and some common domestic functions such as the currency. The functions of the states are more variable but typically include education, law enforcement and local government. Residual powers may also lie with the states, not the centre (see Box 13.1).

In nearly all federations the states have a guaranteed voice in national policy-making through an upper chamber of the assembly. In that chamber each state normally receives equal, or nearly equal, representation. The American Senate, with two senators per state, is the prototype. In unitary states, by contrast, the rationale for an upper chamber is less clear. Indeed, most legislatures in unitary states consist of only one chamber.

> **Definition**
> **Federalism** is the principle of sharing sovereignty between central and state (or provincial) governments; a **federation** is any political system that puts this idea into practice. A **confederation** is a looser link between participating countries which retain their separate statehood. A confederation does not create a new central government with a direct relationship to its citizens (Lister, 1996).

The natural federal structure is for all the states within the union to possess identical powers under the constitution. However, reflecting national circumstances, some federations are less balanced. Asymmetric federalism arises when some states within a federation are given more freedom than others. In Canada, for example, Quebec nationalists have long argued for special recognition for their French-speaking province. Asymmetric federalism is a natural response to differences in power

---

BOX 13.1
The allocation of functions in the Canadian and German federations

Type of allocation	Canada	Germany
Exclusive jurisdiction (functions allocated entirely to one level):	The national government exclusively controls 29 functions, including criminal law, the currency and defence. The provinces control 'all matters of a merely local or private nature in the province', including local government	The federal government's responsibilities include defence, citizenship, immigration and the internal market No specific powers are explicitly granted to the *Länder* but the provinces implement federal laws 'in their own right'
Concurrent jurisdiction (functions shared between levels):	Both the national and provincial governments can pass laws dealing with agriculture and immigration	Concurrent powers include criminal law and employment. A constitutional amendment in 1969/70 created a new category of joint tasks, including regional economic policy and agriculture
Residual powers (the level responsible for functions not specifically allocated by the constitution):	The national parliament can make laws for the 'peace, order and good government of Canada'	Any task not otherwise allocated remains with the *Länder*

Source for Germany: Jeffery (2003)

and culture between regions within a federation. However, the solution carries its own dangers. The risk is that a spiral of instability will develop as the less favoured states seek the privileges accorded to more autonomous provinces.

Federations must be distinguished not just from unitary states but also from confederations. In the latter, the central authority remains the junior partner; it is merely an agent of the component states. The classic instance of a confederation is the short-lived system adopted in 1781 in what is now the United States. The weak centre, embodied in the Continental Congress, could neither tax nor regulate commerce. It also lacked direct authority over the people. It was the feebleness of the Articles of Confederation that led to the drafting of a federal constitution, and to the creation of the United States proper, in 1787.

Federalism is a recognized solution to the problem of organizing the territorial distribution of power. Elazar (1996, p. 426) counts 22 federations in the world, containing some two billion people or 40 per cent of the world's population (for some examples see Table 13.1). Federalism is particularly common in large countries, whether size is measured by area or by population. Four of the world's largest states by area are federal: Australia, Brazil, Canada and the United States. In India, ten out of 25 provinces each contain more than 40 million people, providing the only realistic framework for holding together such a large and diverse democracy. Germany, the largest

European country by population, exemplifies federalism on that continent.

In theory, there are two routes to a federation: either by creating a new central authority or by transferring sovereignty from an existing national government to lower levels. Stepan (2001, p. 32) calls these methods 'coming together' and 'holding together'. In practice, coming together predominates; federalism is almost always a compact between previously separate units pursuing a common interest. The United States, for instance, emerged from a meeting of representatives of 13 American states in 1787. Similar conventions, strongly influenced by the American experience, took place in Switzerland in 1848, Canada in 1867 and Australia in 1897/98.

So far, restructuring as a federation to hold a divided country together is a rare occurrence. Belgium is the main example. First established in 1830, Belgium has been beset by divisions between its French- and Dutch-speaking regions. Constitutional revisions in 1970 and 1980 devolved more power to these separate language groups. In 1983, Belgium finally proclaimed itself a federation of three parts: French-speaking Wallonia, Dutch-speaking Flanders and Brussels, the predominantly French-speaking capital located in the Dutch-speaking part of the country (Arel, 2001). The Belgian experience does suggest that federation can be an alternative to disintegration, a lesson of value to other states confronting strong divisions of ethnicity, language, religion and culture.

Table 13.1 Some federations in established democracies

	Year established as a federation	Area (sq. km, thousands)	Population (million), 2002	Number of states within the federation
United States*	1776	9,373	290	50
Canada*	1867	9,976	32	10
Switzerland	1874	41	7	26
Brazil	1891	8,512	182	27
Australia	1901	7,687	20	6
Germany*	1949	357	82	16
India	1950	3,288	1,050	25
Belgium	1983	30	10	3

* For profiles, see p. 147 (USA), p. 232 (Canada), p. 94 (Germany).

What, then, provokes distinct peoples to set out on the journey to a federation? Motives are more often negative than positive: fear of the consequences of remaining separate overcomes the natural desire to preserve independence. Historically, the most common aspiration has been to secure the military and economic bonus accruing to large countries. More recently, however, interest in federalism has focused on its potential in enabling people with conflicting identities to continue to live together within a single state, as in Belgium.

Riker (1975, 1996) emphasizes the military factor. He argues that federations emerge when there is an external threat. The American states, for instance, joined together in 1789 partly because they felt themselves to be vulnerable in a predatory world. When large beasts are lurking in the jungle, smaller creatures must gather together for safety. Or, as the American statesman Benjamin Franklin (1706–90) put it, 'we must indeed all hang together or, most assuredly, we shall all hang separately' (Jay, 1996, p. 142).

The military case for forming new federations is currently rather weak, given the paucity of major wars in the twenty-first century. Even when a common threat such as terrorism does emerge, coordination between existing states serves the purpose more readily than sharing sovereignty through a new federation.

But it would be wrong to regard military motives as the sole reason for federation-making. The federal bargain has also been based on the economic advantages of scale. Even the Australian and American federalists felt that a common market would promote economic activity. But again, federation now seems to be a rather convoluted way of securing gains from trade. Straightforward free trade areas (FTAs) between neighbouring countries are proving to be a more popular way forward. Unlike federations, FTAs imply no risk to sovereignty.

As military and economic arguments for forming new federations have weakened, so interest in ethnic federalism has grown apace. The Belgian experience shows that federations are useful for bridging ethnic diversity within a divided society; they are a device for incorporating such differences within a single political community. People who differ by descent, language and culture can nevertheless seek the advantages of membership in a shared enterprise.

The Indian federation, for instance, has so far accommodated growing religious tensions between Hindus, Muslims, Sikhs and Christians. On a smaller scale, the Swiss federation integrates 23 cantons, two and a half languages (German and French, plus Italian) and two religions (Catholic and Protestant). Building on such experience, advocates of ethnic federalism claim that it may help to integrate ethnic groups in post-Taliban Afghanistan and post-Saddam Iraq. A Kurdish leader in Iraq expressed the spirit of ethnic federalism when, amid the jockeying for position after the American invasion in 2003, he said, 'the new constitution cannot be a constitution of the majority. It must be a constitution of the entirety' (Clover, 2003).

Federal–state relations

The relations between federal and state governments are the crux of federalism. A federal framework creates an invitation to struggle between the two levels and indeed among the states themselves. Federalism creates both competition and the means of its containment. In this section, we distinguish between two traditional views of federalism before examining some practical similarities in the workings of contemporary federations.

Dual and cooperative federalism

It is helpful to distinguish between dual and cooperative federalism. The former represents the federal spirit and remains a significant theme in American culture; the latter is an important ideal within European thinking and takes us closer to the realities of federal governance.

Reflecting the original federal principle as conceived in the United States, *dual federalism* means that the national and state governments operate independently, each tier acting autonomously in its own sphere, and linked only through the constitutional compact. In the circumstances of eighteenth-century America, such separation was a plausible objective; extensive coordination

Profile CANADA

Population: 32m.

Gross domestic product per head: $29,300.

Self-reported ethnic origin (six largest groups):

German, 2.7m
Irish, 3.8m
Scottish, 4.2m
French, 4.7m
Canadian, 11.1m
English, 6.0m

Form of government: a federal parliamentary democracy with ten provinces. Most Canadians live in Ontario or Quebec.

Legislature: the 301-seat House of Commons is the lower chamber. Most unusually for a federation, the 104 members of the Senate, the upper chamber, are appointed by the prime minister, not selected by the provinces.

Executive: the prime minister leads a cabinet whose members he selects with due regard for provincial representation. A governor-general serves as ceremonial figurehead.

Judiciary: Canada employs a dual (federal and provincial) court system, headed by a restrained Supreme Court. In 1982 the country introduced the Canadian Charter of Rights and Freedoms.

Electoral system: a plurality system with single-member districts. This produces massive swings and distortions in representation in the Commons yet electoral reform is rarely considered (see Table 9.1, p. 150).

Party system: the party system is strongly regional, with the governing Liberals dominating the key province of Ontario. The main opposition parties are currently the Parti Québécois (PQ) and the Western-based Alliance. The once-powerful Conservatives and the left-wing New Democratic Party are smaller opposition parties.

Canada is a large country with a relatively small population. Its land mass is the second largest in the world but its population is little more than a tenth of its powerful American neighbour. Most Canadians live in urban settlements in a 100-mile strip bordering the United States. Canada's economy depends heavily on the USA, a relationship reinforced by the formation of the North American Free Trade Association in 1994.

Reflecting British influence, Canada's constitution, originally set out in the British North America Act of 1867, established parliamentary government in a centralized federation. Since then, 'Canada has moved from a highly centralized political situation to one of the most decentralized federal systems in the world' (Landes, 1995, p. 101). This reflects the central issue of Canadian politics: the place within it of French-speaking Quebec. This division goes back to the country's origins. From the sixteenth century, France and then Britain colonized the territories of Canada, inhabited at that time by around ten million indigenous people. Britain finally defeated the French in 1759.

For many Francophones, Canada consists of two founding peoples – the British and French – whose status should be equal. This is taken to imply that Quebec should be more than just one among ten provinces. Since the 1960s a revived nationalist party in Quebec has sought to implement this vision. However the federal response has been to decentralize power to all provinces, not Quebec only. In Quebec itself, the PQ, elected to power in 1994, held a provincial referendum in 1995 on 'sovereignty association' for Quebec. This would have combined political sovereignty for Quebec with continued economic association with Canada. The proposal lost by the narrowest of margins. Subsequently, the issue of constitutional reform declined in intensity, with the PQ voted out of office in 2003.

Even so, the regional foundations of Canada remain central to its politics. An earthquake election in 1993 saw the national emergence not just of the PQ but also of the Western-based Reform Party (now the Canadian Alliance). The Alliance is a populist party which seeks to make members of parliament more responsive to local electorates. Thus Canada's contemporary politics are an uneasy balance between national and regional parties, and of pro- and anti-system themes. The question 'what is Canada?' remains permanently on the table, never to receive a final answer.

Yet as Williams (1995, p. 69) writes,

> despite all Canada's domestic turmoil, it is endowed with a responsive federal system. Over time this has created a good safe place to raise a family and earn a crust, the ultimate test of a state's obligations to its citizens.

Further reading: Bakvis and Skogstad (2002), Burgess (2001).

between federal and state administrations was judged to be neither necessary nor feasible.

In particular, the federal government was required to confine its activities to functions explicitly allocated to it, such as the power 'to lay and collect taxes, to pay the debts and provide for the common defence and welfare of the United States'. In the world after 9/11, 'providing for the common defence' has of course again become a pivotal and complex task, calling for cross-level collaboration. However, James Madison, one of the Founding Fathers, believed that such times would be exceptional and that in the main the states would be free to follow their own course (Hamilton, 1788a, p. 237):

> The operations of the federal government will be most extensive and important in times of war and danger; those of the State governments in times of peace and security. As the former periods will probably bear a small proportion of the latter, the State governments will here enjoy another advantage over the federal government.

Perhaps always a myth, dual federalism has long since disappeared, overwhelmed by the demands of an integrated economy and global war long before the arrival of terrorist threats. Even so, it expresses an implicit if unrealizable strand in federal thinking.

Definition

Dual federalism, as originally envisaged in the USA, meant that national and state governments retained separate spheres of action. Each level independently performed the tasks allocated to it by the constitution. **Cooperative federalism,** as practised in Germany, is based on collaboration between levels. National and state governments are expected to act as partners in following the interests of the whole.

The second approach is *cooperative federalism.* This interpretation is favoured in the main by European federations, especially Germany. While federalism in the USA is based on a contract in which the states join together to form a central government with limited functions, the European form (particularly in Germany) rests on the idea of cooperation between levels. Such solidarity expresses a shared commitment to a united society; federalism displays organic links that bind the participants together. The moral norm is solidarity and the operating principle is subsidiarity: the idea that decisions should be taken at the lowest feasible level. The central government offers overall leadership but leaves implementation to lower levels – a division rather than a separation of tasks.

Cooperative federalism lacks the theoretical simplicity of the dual model but, as a more recent form, it provides a realistic account of how federal governance proceeds in practice. It also reflects a distinctly European approach born from the desire to overcome that continent's long history of conflict. Along with proportional representation and coalition government, cooperative federalism aims to ensure social peace by awarding major interests a share in decision-making.

Consider German cooperative federalism in more detail. Imposed by the Allies in 1949 as a barrier against dictatorship, federalism represented a return to the country's strong regional roots. Federalism is reflected in the country's official title, the Federal Republic of Germany, and under the Basic Law Germany's federal character cannot be amended. Federalism quickly became an accepted part of the postwar republic (Umbach, 2002).

From its inception, German federalism was based on interdependence, not independence. All the *Länder* (states) are expected to contribute to the success of the whole; in exchange, they are entitled to be treated with respect by the centre. The federal government makes policy but the *Länder* implement it, a division of labour expressed in the constitutional requirement that 'the *Länder* shall execute federal laws as matters of their own concern'. Because the provinces are the implementing agent, they must first approve bills affecting them through parliament's upper chamber, the Bundesrat. Further, the constitution now explictly defines some 'joint tasks', such as higher education, where responsibility is shared.

These mechanisms of interdependence have been reinforced by the powerful Constitutional Court, which has encouraged the participants to show due sensitivity to the interests of other actors in the federal system.

Although German federalism remains far more organic than its American equivalent, its cooperative ethos has come under some pressure from growing economic inequalities between *Länder*, particularly since unification. The political reality is that significant competition now exists alongside the tradition of solidarity (Jeffery, 2003).

Federalism in practice

Whatever their origins or philosophy, most federations have witnessed growing interdependence between the two tiers. The German notion of joint tasks has become an administrative reality in all federations, a fact which led McDonald and McDonald (1988) to write their obituary for traditional dual federalism in the USA. The talk now is of 'intergovernmental relations' in the United States, of 'executive federalism' in Canada and of 'multilevel governance' in Europe. All such phrases point to an intermingling between tiers, implying that policy is made, funded and implemented by negotiation between levels (Simeon and Cameron, 2002).

In the game of central–state relations, the central government tended to gain influence for much of the twentieth century. Partly, this trend reflected the centre's financial muscle (see Box 13.2). The flow of money became more favourable to the centre as income tax revenues grew with the expansion of both the economy and the workforce. Income is invariably taxed mainly at national level because otherwise people and corporations could move to low-tax states. By contrast, the states must depend for their own independently raised revenue on sales and property taxes, a revenue source that is smaller and less dynamic than income tax. This shift in financial strength is clearly seen in Australia, where most of the states' revenue now comes from the federal government.

In the United States, an economic decline in the early years of the twenty-first century led to a further deterioration in the financial position of the states. Many found themselves hamstrung by the requirement of their own state constitutions to run a balanced budget. This obligation does not apply to national government, a fact the free-spending George W. Bush sought to exploit in his campaign for reelection to the White House in 2004. In the United States, as in most federations, states lack the financial flexibility available to the central government and in consequence they are more sensitive to economic trends (Braun *et al.*, 2003).

But the enhanced authority of the centre in federal systems has been more than a financial matter. More than anything, it reflects the emergence of a national economy demanding overall planning and regulation. To take just one example, when California experienced an electricity shortage in 2000, the federal government inevitably became involved as the state began to draw in power from surrounding areas. Similarly, power cuts on the Eastern seaboard three years later exposed the weaknesses of an electricity grid partly controlled by fifty separate states. Equally, national planning is needed to forestall the absurdity of highways ending at a state's borders.

BOX 13.2
Financial transfers from the federal government to states

Form of transfer	Definition
Categorical grants	For specific projects (e.g. a new hospital)
Block grants	For particular programmes (e.g. for medical care)
Revenue-sharing	General funding which places few limits on the recipient's use of funds
Equalization grants	Used in some federations (e.g. Canada and Germany) in an effort to harmonize financial conditions between the states. Can create resentment in the wealthier states.

The broader expansion of public functions has also worked to the centre's advantage. The wars and depressions of the twentieth century invariably empowered the national government. Such additional powers, once acquired, tended to be retained. And the postwar drive to complete a welfare state offering equal rights to all citizens, wherever they live, enhanced the central power still further. Of the major Western federations, only Canada has seen a long-term drift away from the centre.

The changing balance between tiers of government is reflected in decisions by constitutional courts. Generally, the courts have acceded to central initiatives, particularly when justified by national emergencies. In the rulings of the US Supreme Court, federal law prevailed over state law for most of the twentieth century. In Australia, decisions of the High Court have favoured the centre to the point where some commentators regard federalism as sustained more by political tradition than by the constitution.

However, in the 1990s a number of courts did make some efforts to restore at least some autonomy to the states. In the USA a more conservative Supreme Court used states' rights to strike down a number of congressional laws. In *United States* v. *Lopez* (1995), for example, the justices declared unconstitutional a federal law banning possession of a gun within 1,000 feet of a school. The Court ruled such matters to be a preserve of the states. Temporarily, at least, ideological fashion had moved back in favour of the states (Goodman, 2001).

Assessing federalism

What conclusions can we reach about the federal experiment? An overall assessment is particularly relevant in the twenty-first century as governments seek a way of enabling different ethnic groups to live together in the same territory.

The case for federalism is that it offers a natural and practical arrangement for organizing large states. It provides checks and balances on a territorial basis, keeps some government functions closer to the people and allows for the representation of ethnic differences. Federalism reduces overload in the national executive, preventing the over-centralized character of some unitary states such as Britain and France.

In addition, the existence of multiple provinces produces healthy competition and opportunities for experiment. As the American Supreme Court Justice Brandeis wrote in *New State Ice Co.* v. *Liebmann* (1932), 'a single courageous state may . . . try novel social and economic experiments without risk to the rest of the country'. Citizens and firms also have the luxury of choice: if they dislike governance in one state, they can always move to another.

Above all, federalism reconciles two modern imperatives: it secures the economic and military advantages of scale while retaining, indeed encouraging, cultural diversity. For such reasons, forming a federation can certainly be considered a realistic and tested option for diverse and often divided countries. As van Deth (2000, p. xv) comments, 'the rewards of federalism are evident when the alternatives of secession, oppression and war are considered'.

But a case can also be mounted against federalism. Compared to unitary government, decision-making in a federation is complicated and slow-moving. When a gunman ran amok in Tasmania in 1996, killing 35 people, federal Australia experienced some political problems before it tightened gun control uniformly across the country. By contrast, unitary Britain acted speedily when a comparable incident occurred in the same year at a primary school in Dunblane, Scotland. When the American president moved quickly to set up a new Department of Homeland Security after September 11, 2001, one of his motives was precisely to improve coordination between tiers of government in the American federation. It may well be that some of the security failings revealed on 9/11 will eventually be laid at federalism's door.

Federal policy-making is focused on compromise rather than problem-solving. Federations are at risk from what Scharpf (1988) terms the joint decision trap: the tendency for the quality – and even the number – of decisions to decline as the number of interests increases. Why, for instance, is Germany's new high-speed rail service between Frankfurt and Cologne slowed by a stop in the tiny town of Montabaur (population 13,000)?

Because otherwise there would be no stops in Rhineland-Palatinate, a province through which the line passes.

Further, federalism complicates accountability. Negotiations between levels take place away from the public gaze, bypassing the legislature and providing opportunities for politicians to pass the buck to the other level. Also, federalism distributes power by territory when the key conflicts in society are social (e.g. race and gender) rather than spatial. Federations empower neither the national majority nor the main minorities. Today, free trade areas are a simpler method of securing the economic advantages of scale.

Fundamentally, though, any final judgement of federalism must depend on taking a view of the proper balance between the concentration and diffusion of political power. Should power rest with one body to allow decisive action? If so, federalism is likely to be seen as an obstacle and impediment, as an anti-democratic device. Alternatively, should power be dispersed so as to reduce the danger of majority dictatorship? Through this lens, federalism will appear as an indispensable defence of liberty.

Unitary government

Most states are unitary, meaning that sovereignty lies exclusively with the central government. In this hierarchical arrangement, the national government possesses the theoretical authority to abolish lower levels. Subnational administrations, whether regional or local, may make policy as well as implement it but they do so by leave of the centre.

Unlike federations, a unitary framework is not always a deliberate creation; rather, such systems emerge naturally in societies with a history of rule by sovereign monarchs and emperors, such as Britain, France and Japan. Unitary structures are also the norm in smaller democracies, particularly those without strong ethnic divisions, as in Scandinavia. In Latin America, nearly all the smaller countries (but none of the largest ones) are unitary. In most unitary states, the legislature has only one chamber since there is no need for a states' house.

After the complexities of federalism, a unitary structure may seem straightforward and efficient. However, the location of sovereignty is rarely an adequate guide to political realities; unitary government is often decentralized in its operation. Indeed in the 1990s many unitary states attempted to push responsibility for more functions on to lower levels. In practice, unitary states, just like federations, involve the detailed bargaining characteristic of all multilevel governance.

We can distinguish three broad ways in which unitary states can disperse power from the centre: deconcentration, decentralization and devolution (see Box 13.3). The first of these, *deconcentration.*

BOX 13.3
Methods for distributing power away from the centre

Method	Definition	Example
Deconcentration	Central government functions are executed by staff 'in the field'	Almost 90 per cent of US federal civilian employees work away from Washington, DC
Decentralization	Central government functions are executed by subnational authorities	Local governments administer national welfare programmes in Scandinavia
Devolution	Central government grants some decision-making autonomy to new lower levels	Regional governments in France, Italy and Spain

Note: Deconcentration and decentralization occur in federal as well as unitary states.

DEBATE

A FEDERAL EUROPE?

Our understanding of federalism can be usefully tested against the challenging case of the European Union (EU). Leaving aside opinion on whether the EU ought to develop as a federation, to what extent can this singular entity already be regarded as a federation? Have those sceptics, particularly in Britain, who would prefer the EU to be merely an intergovernmental organization already been left behind?

The case for

Shared sovereignty is the core feature of federalism and by this test the Union already possesses a broadly federal character. A comparison with the USA demonstrates the point. Like the United States, the European Union has a strong legal basis in the treaties on which it is founded. In addition, plans for a formal constitution are in hand. The influential European Court of Justice, like America's Supreme Court, adjudicates disputes between levels of government. In both cases, court decisions apply directly to citizens and must be implemented by member governments. In neither the European Union nor the USA is there any provision for member states to withdraw. Further, citizens of the European Union, like those of the USA, are free to reside anywhere within the Union's territory.

As with the American national government, the Union has specific policy responsibilities, notably for the single market. Externally, the EU is represented at international bodies such as the United Nations and it maintains over 130 diplomatic missions. In short, in Europe – as in America – sovereignty is already pooled.

The case against

To describe the EU as a federation would be to exaggerate its cohesion. Again, comparisons with the American exemplar are helpful. In contrast to the USA, the EU does not possess a common currency. Sweden voted against the euro in a referendum in 2003 and neither Denmark nor the UK has even put the matter to a vote. Where the USA was designed as a federation from the start, the EU has been built on agreeing concrete policies, particularly for a single market, with a federation as a long-term aspiration. Where the American federal government now levies national taxes, the EU does not tax its citizens directly. The USA

fought a civil war to preserve its union; the EU has not faced this vital test nor, without its own military force, is it in any position to do so. As Henry Kissinger, former American Secretary of State, is reported to have said, 'When I want to speak to Europe, who do I telephone?'

In world politics, America is a dominant force; within the EU, foreign and defence policy, including control over military force, remains the preserve of member states. The United Kingdom took part in the Iraq War of 2003 but most other member states kept their troops at home. Surely we would not describe the USA as a federation if each state decided separately whether to go to war? In addition, states within the European Union – unlike American states – still possess such important markers of external sovereignty as membership of the United Nations.

Assessment

There is, in principle, no reason why all federations should share the same division of functions between levels. A unique federation is a federation still. In the eighteenth century, the USA was still described in the plural – these United States – yet no one would question that those same states had formed a federation (Forsyth, 1996). In a similar way, the EU represents a pooling of some of its members' sovereignty and consists of institutions – including a court, a parliament and a form of executive – through which sovereignty is exercised. In these respects, the Union is more than a confederation yet, as in the early decades of the United States, its members retain much of their traditional autonomy. We can conclude with Burgess (2003, p. 73) that

> there is no precedent for the creation of a multinational federation composed of 15 or more nation states, with mature, social, economic political and legal systems. In this regard the EU is a colossal and original enterprise.

Further reading: Bednar, Eskridge and Ferejohn (2001), Burgess (2000), McKay (2001a), Nicolaidis and Howse (2001).

See also: EU profile (p. 176).

is purely an administrative matter, denoting the location of many central government employees away from the capital. The case for a deconcentrated structure is that it spreads the work around, reduces costs and frees central departments to focus on policy-making. There is, after all, no reason in principle why such functions as taxation or public pensions should be administered from the capital. Indeed, field offices of central departments can benefit from local knowledge. As a French decree of 1852 pointed out, 'one can govern from afar but must be close to administer'.

The second, and politically more significant, way of dispersing power is through *decentralization*. Here, policy execution is delegated to subnational bodies such as local authorities or a range of other agencies. In Scandinavia, for instance, local governments have put into effect many welfare programmes agreed at national level. In a similar way, local government in the UK serves as the workhorse of central authority.

The third and most radical form of power dispersal is *devolution*. This occurs when the centre grants decision-making autonomy (including some legislative powers) to lower levels. In the United Kingdom, devolved assemblies were introduced in Scotland and Wales in 1999. But the contrast with federations remains. Britain remains a unitary state because these new assembles could be abolished by Westminster through normal legislation. As the English politician Enoch Powell said, 'power devolved is power retained'.

Spain is another example of a unitary state with extensive devolution. Spanish regions were created in the transition to democracy following General Franco's death in 1975. Seeking to integrate a centralist tradition with strong regional identities,

Spain's constitution-makers created a complex system in which regions could aspire to varying degrees of autonomy. The historic communities of the Basque Country and Catalonia quickly proceeded to the most autonomous level, with other regions offered the prospect of a later upgrade. The result was asymmetric devolution within the framework of what is still, in theory, a unitary state.

A distinctive trend within unitary states has been the development of at least one level of government standing between central and local authorities. France, Italy and Spain have introduced elected regional governments. The smaller Scandinavian countries took a different route, strengthening and refurbishing their traditional counties. Even a small country like New Zealand has developed 12 elected regional councils. In unitary states, the standard pattern now is to have three levels of subnational government – regional, provincial and local – as in France and Italy (Table 13.2). The result is a multilevel system that is even more intricate than the two levels of subnational authority – state and local – in a federation. Whether federal or unitary, multilevel governance has become a refrain repeated in all established democracies.

The European Union has encouraged the regional level within its member states. The European Regional Development Fund, established in 1975, stimulated regions to lobby for aid by distributing aid directly to regions, rather than through central governments. This squeeze on the centre prompted some regional nationalists to postulate a Europe of the Regions in which the EU and revived regions would exert a pincer movement on national power. The notion, somewhat exaggerated but significant in itself, was that the

---

Table 13.2 Subnational government in unitary states: some European examples

	France	Italy	The Netherlands	Norway
Regional level	22 regions	20 regions	–	–
Provincial level	96 *départements*	94 provinces	12 provinces	19 counties
Local level	36,565 communes	8,074 communes	496 municipalities	448 municipalities

Note: Figures are from the late 1990s to the early 2000s.

European Union and the regions would gradually become the leading policy-makers, outflanking central governments which would be left with less to do. In 1988, the EU further developed such aspirations by introducing a Committee of the Regions and Local Communities (CoR), a body composed of subnational authorities. However, the CoR has proved to be merely consultative. Federal Belgium apart, national executives have shown no sign of withering away in the manner originally anticipated by regional enthusiasts (Bourne, 2003).

Although regional governments can pass laws in their designated areas of competence, their main contribution has been in economic planning and infrastructure development. Such tasks are beyond the scope of small local authorities but beneath the national vision of the centre. The Spanish region of Valencia, for example, has sought to improve telecommunications, roads, railways, ports and airports. In Italy, too, regional authorities – at least outside the south – have made a notable contribution, with some left-wing parties determined to display their competence through showpiece governance.

So the evolution of regional government suggests a move away from the original demand for greater self-government toward a more administrative role, standing between other levels of government. In a system of multilevel governance, regions are indeed finding their level. As Balme (1998, p. 182) concludes of France, regional governments in Europe are becoming arenas in which policies are formed, even if they seem unlikely to become decisive actors in their own right.

Local government

Local government is universal, found in federal and unitary states alike. It is the lowest level of elected territorial organization within the state. Variously called communes, municipalities or parishes, local government is 'where the day-to-day activity of politics and government gets done' (Teune, 1995b, p. 16). For example, September 11, 2001 was certainly a global event but it was New York City that faced the most immediate consequences.

At their best, local governments express the virtues of limited scale. They can represent natural communities, remain accessible to their citizens, reinforce local identities, offer a practical education in politics, provide a recruiting ground to higher posts, serve as a first port of call for citizens and distribute resources in the light of specialist knowledge. Yet local governments also have characteristic weaknesses. They are often too small to deliver services efficiently, they lack financial autonomy and they are easily dominated by traditional elites.

Thus the perpetual problem of this level of government: how to marry local representation with efficient delivery of services. As Teune (1995a, p. 8) notes,

> there never has been a sound theoretical resolution [at local level] to the question of democracy and its necessity for familiarity, on the one hand, with the size and diversity required for prosperity, on the other.

The balance struck between intimacy and efficiency varies over time. In the 1980s, as national governments came under financial pressure, local authorities were encouraged to become more efficient and customer-led, particularly in the English-speaking world. But as the twenty-first century got under way, so signs began to emerge of a rebirth of interest in citizen involvement, stimulated by declining turnout at local elections. In New Zealand, for instance, successful managerial reforms introduced in 1989 were followed thirteen years later by the Local Government Act 2002. This law outlined a more expansive – and possibly expensive – participatory vision for the country's territorial local authorities.

The status of local government varies across countries. As a rule, the position of local government is stronger in (1) European rather than non-European democracies, (2) Northern rather than Southern Europe and (3) countries where local government can represent its community more broadly than through merely providing designated functions to local people (Box 13.4).

Consider, first, the contrast between European and New World democracies. In most of Europe, local authorities represent historic communities

---

BOX 13.4
Exploring the status of local government

Status of local government		Interpretation
Higher	*Lower*	
In European democracies	In new world democracies (e.g. Australia, USA)	In Europe, local governments often represent historic communities but in the new world, local government is more utilitarian in character
In Northern Europe (e.g. Scandinavia)	In Southern Europe (e.g. France, Italy)	Local governments administer the extensive welfare states found in Northern Europe but perform fewer functions in Southern Europe
When local governments possess general competence to represent their community	When local governments cannot act *ultra vires* ('beyond the powers')	General competence allows local authorities to take the initiative whereas *ultra vires* restricts them to designated functions

Sources: Adapted from Goldsmith (1996), John (2001) and Page and Goldsmith (1987).

---

that pre-date the emergence of strong national governments. In addition, the unitary nature of most European states allows direct links to form between powerful local administrations (especially large cities) and the centre. Reflecting this status, European constitutions normally mandate some form of local self-government. Sweden's Instrument of Government, for instance, roundly declares that Swedish democracy 'shall be realized through a representative and parliamentary polity and through local self-government'.

In the New World, by contrast, local government reveals a more pragmatic, utilitarian character. Local authorities were set up as needed to deal with 'roads, rates and rubbish'. Special boards (appointed or elected) were added to deal with specific problems such as mosquito control, harbours and land drainage. The policy style was apolitical: 'there is no Democratic or Republican way to collect garbage'. Indeed special boards were often set up precisely to be independent of party politics. Because Australia, Canada and the USA are federations, local government is the preserve of the states, often creating further diversity in organization. For instance, the USA is governed at local level by a smorgasbord of over 80,000 cities, counties, school districts, townships and special districts.

Second, the standing of local government varies within Europe, on a broad north–south axis. In the Northern countries, local authorities became important delivery vehicles for the extensive welfare states that matured after 1945. Services such as social assistance, unemployment benefit, childcare and education are funded by the state but provided locally, giving municipal authorities a significant role as the government's front office. Also, a process of amalgamation lasting until the final quarter of the twentieth century led to a large increase in populations served by local councils, notably in the United Kingdom. This expansion allowed more functions to be provided by each authority.

In Southern Europe, by contrast, welfare states are less extensive, with the Catholic Church playing a greater role in providing care, while public services such as education remain under the direct control of the central authority. In Italy, for instance, teachers are civil servants rather than employees of local councils. Also, communes in Southern Europe have remained small, especially in France (Table 13.3). Limited scale precludes an extensive administrative role except when neighbouring areas form collaborative syndicates to supply utilities such as water and energy.

Third, constitutional provisions also affect the

position of local authorities. In continental Europe, local governments often enjoy general competence: that is, the authority to make regulations in any matter of concern to the area. Germany's Basic Law, for instance, gives local communities 'the right to regulate [all local matters] under their own responsibility and within the limits of the law'.

But in other countries, including the United Kingdom, councils could traditionally only perform those tasks expressly designated by the centre; any other act would be *ultra vires* (beyond the powers). In the United States, Dillon's rule similarly restricts local governments to tasks delegated by their particular state. Some countries where *ultra vires* applies, including the United Kingdom and New Zealand, did establish a more liberal legal framework at the start of the twenty-first century but without granting the full power of general competence to local areas.

Three additional features of local government merit consideration: internal structure, functions and relationships with the centre.

Table 13.3 Average population of elected local authorities in some European democracies

Country	Average population of local authorities (lowest level)
UK	137,000
Ireland	36,100
Sweden	33,000
Netherlands	32,466
Belgium	17,384
Finland	11,206
Norway	9,000
Germany	7,900
Italy	7,036
Spain	4,997
France	1,491

Source: Updated from John (2001), table 2.1. Figures are from the late 1990s to the early 2000s, depending on country.

Structure

The structure of local government has recently attracted attention, largely in an attempt to make decision-making clearer to local electorates in an era of falling turnout. Just as political parties have sought to reverse a decline in membership by giving their supporters more say in the selection of candidates and leaders, so local governments in such countries as Italy, the Netherlands and the United Kingdom have experimented with direct election of the mayor.

There are, in fact, three broad ways of organizing local government (Box 13.5). The first and most traditional method, represented by England and Sweden, concentrates authority in a college of elected councillors. This full council often operates through powerful committees covering the main local services – housing and education, for example – with professional appointees (such as architects and educational administrators) also playing a significant role. The mayor plays a modest ceremonial role. Whatever virtues this format may have, its collegiate character presents a rather opaque picture to the electorate.

Accordingly, a second method of organization known as the mayor–council system has attracted attention. This model is based on a separation of powers between a directly elected mayor, who is the chief executive, and an elected council with legislative and budget-approving powers. This elaborate structure is used in many large American cities, notably New York, permitting a range of urban interests to be represented within the framework. The mayor and council must negotiate, if indeed they are not in conflict with each other.

The powers awarded to the mayor and council vary across localities, defining 'strong mayor' and 'weak mayor' variants of this format. Even before September 11, the perceived success of New York's Rudy Giuliani encouraged some European cities, including London, to consider introducing elected mayors as a way of reviving a demoralized council-based system. However, London's new mayor lacks the strong powers of his equivalent in New York (Sweating, 2003).

The third structure for local government, again originating in the United States, is the council–manager system. Unlike the mayor–council

---

BOX 13.5
Structures for local government

Structure	Description	Examples
Council	Elected councillors operating through committees supervise departments headed by professional officers. The mayor (if any) is largely a ceremonial post	England (pre-Local Government Act of 2000), Sweden
Mayor-council*	A mayor elected by the municipal area serves as chief executive. Councillors elected from local wards form a council with legislative and financial authority	About half of the 7,000 cities in the USA, including Chicago and New York
Council–manager	The mayor and council appoint a professional manager to run executive departments	About 3,000 American cities, including Dallas and Phoenix

* Often subdivided into strong mayor and weak mayor systems according to the mayor's executive autonomy.

Sources: Bowles (1998), Chandler (1993), Mouritzen and Svara (2002).

---

format, this arrangement seeks to depoliticize and simplify local government by separating politics from administration. This distinction is achieved by appointing a professional city manager, operating under the elected council and mayor, to administer the authority's work. This council–manager format emerged early in the twentieth century in an attempt to curb corruption; it has been widely adopted in western and south-western states in the USA. The model has corporate overtones, with the voters (shareholders) electing councillors (board of directors) to oversee the city manager (chief executive). However, the distinction between politics and administration is difficult to achieve in practice.

Functions

Leaving structure to one side, what is it that local governments do? Broadly, their tasks are two fold: to provide local public services (such as refuse collection) and to implement national welfare policies (Box 13.6). However, a static description of functions fails to reveal how the role of local government has evolved since the 1980s.

The major trend, especially prominent in the English-speaking world and Scandinavia, has been

for municipal authorities to reduce their direct provision of services by delegating tasks to private organizations, both profit-making and voluntary. In Denmark, for example, many local governments have set up 'user boards' in primary schools. These boards are given block budgets and the authority to hire and fire staff (Bogason, 1996). In

---

BOX 13.6
Typical powers of local authorities

Cemeteries	Recreation
Economic development	Refuse disposal
Environmental protection	Roads
Fire service	Social housing
Homes for the elderly	Tourism
Libraries	Water supply
Local planning	Welfare provision
Primary education	

Source: Adapted from Norton (1991), table 2.2.

a similar way, private firms located in the commercial district of some American cities have taken over much of the responsibility for funding and organizing improvements to local services such as street-cleaning.

So the local authority's role is changing from a provider to an enabler. The council does not so much provide services as ensure that they are supplied. In theory, the authority can become a smaller, coordinating body, more concerned with governance than government. More organizations become involved in local policy-making, many of them functional (for example school boards) rather than territorial (for example county councils). This shift represents an important transition in conceptions of how local governments should go about their task of serving their communities. It also represents some retreat of the service-providing style of local government found in Northern Europe to the more strategic governance in Southern Europe and the more variegated patterns of local authority in the New World.

Definition

The **enabling authority** is a term used to summarize one vision of local governance. Such an authority does not provide many services itself. Rather, its concerns are to coordinate the provision of services and to represent the community both within and beyond its territory. An enabling authority is strategic, contracting out service provision to private agencies, whether voluntary or profit-making.

Relationships with the centre

How is local government integrated into the national structure of power? This question is key to appreciating how multilevel governance operates in practice. The answer reveals contrasting notions of state authority in the established democracies.

The relationship between centre and locality usually takes one of two forms: dual or fused. In a dual approach, local government is seen as an organization separate from the centre. In a fused approach, local and central government are regarded

as comprising a single network of state authority.

Consider the *dual* system first. Here public authority is seen as separated rather than integrated; it is as if there were two spheres of authority, connected for practical reasons only. Local governments retain free-standing status, setting their own internal organization and employing staff on their own conditions of service. Employees tend to move horizontally – from one local authority to another – rather than vertically, between central and local government. Ultimate authority rests with the centre but local government employees do not regard themselves as working for the same employer as central civil servants. National politicians rarely emerge from local politics.

Traditionally, Britain was regarded as the best example of a dual system. Before the rise of the modern state, local magistrates administered their communities. This spirit of self-government survives in a perception that central and local government are distinct, if intensely interdependent, spheres. Certainly, severe centralization under Conservative administrations in the 1980s reduced local authorities to virtual servants of central government. Even so, central and local tiers still do not form a single tier of public authority. Their continuing separation contributes to the rather weak notion of the state in Britain.

Definition

A **dual** system of local government (as in Britain) maintains a formal separation of central and local government. Although the centre is sovereign, local authorities are not seen as part of a single state structure. In a **fused** system (as in France), municipalities form part of a uniform system of administration applying across the country, with a centrally appointed prefect supervising local councils.

Under a *fused* system, by contrast, central and local government combine to form a single sphere of public authority. Both levels express the leading authority of the state. In some European countries, such as Belgium and the Netherlands, the mayor is appointed by central government and is responsible to the centre for maintaining local law and order. In addition, central and local authority are fused in the office of the prefect, a central appointee who oversees the administration of a particular community and reports to the Ministry of the Interior. In theory, a prefectoral system signals central dominance by establishing a clear hierarchy running from national government through the prefect to local authorities.

France is the classic example of this fused approach. The system was established by Napoleon early in the nineteenth century and consists of 96 *départements* in France, each with its own prefect and elected assembly. The framework is uniform and rational but in practice the prefect must cooperate with local councils rather than simply oversee them. In fact, the prefect is now as much an agent of the *département* as of the centre, representing interests upwards as much as transmitting commands downwards. Although the powers of the prefect have declined, the French model remains influential. Many other countries have adopted it, including all France's ex-colonies and several post-communist states.

One effect of a fused system is the ease with which politicians can move between, or even straddle, the national and the local. France is again an interesting case. National politicians often become or remain mayor of their home town, a feature called the *cumul des mandats* (accumulation of offices). Typically, about one in two members of parliament will also be a local mayor. The *cumul* has come under attack because, after all, multiple posts beget multiple salaries. An initial reform in 1985 restricted politicians to holding no more than two major elected posts at the same time. However, even after the rules were tightened further in 2000, the most popular *cumul* – combining the office of local mayor with membership of the National Assembly – is still permitted (Stevens, 2003, p. 170).

Subnational government in new democracies

In new democracies, subnational government begins in an undernourished condition. Lacking resources, and inhibited by the legacy of central dominance, local governance is initially a matter of doing whatever can be afforded. Only as the new democracy consolidates, and economic reform brings results, do subnational governments begin to develop more weight and coherence. To the extent that a new democracy fails to consolidate, subnational government may continue in an uncertain position.

One index of democratic consolidation is precisely the development of subnational institutions with a stable relationship to the national government. In the actual transition to democracy, however, little attention is paid to regional and local levels. An outburst of local participation may herald the new order but the new activists are often inexperienced and short-lived amateurs. The real action occurs in the capital where the goal is to establish a new order of national power. Only when this primary object has been achieved can the focus turn to lower levels of governance. Establishing a uniform set of institutions beneath the national level, with clear functions, sound financing and competitive elections, tends to be a reflection as much as a dimension of democratic consolidation.

Consider post-communist states. The struggles of local government to become established demonstrate the difficult inheritance left by collapsed dictatorships. Under communism, regional party bosses, not elected councillors, had wielded power. As a result, local government was massively under-prepared for the post-communist era. 'We are starting from less than zero', complained a city official in Kiev, the capital of Ukraine, after the collapse of communist rule there. Local authorities possessed little revenue while central government had no money to spare. Often local government officers worked from buildings that were still technically owned by their former masters in the Communist Party.

Despite chronic under-resourcing, local officials had to confront the enormous welfare problems created by industrial collapse. They sought to resolve these difficulties in the context of societies which had gone without authentic local social organization for at least a generation. At local level, the organizational difficulties and human consequences of regime change became manifest. Millions of people confronted a diminished quality of life as communist welfare provision came to an abrupt halt. The policy problems were national but the human consequences were local.

In countries with a less severe history of communism (such as Hungary and Poland), subnational government has now taken root, usually drawing on the pre-communist heritage. Take Poland as an illustration. In 1999 – a full ten years after the collapse of communism – Poland reintroduced its pre-communist subnational structure, with 16 *voivodships* (regions) given responsibility for economic development within their territory. The leader of each *voivodship* was no longer appointed by the centre but was drawn from an elected council. As with other Eastern European countries, Poland's focus on the regional level was stimulated by the desire to join, and extract resources from, the European Union. Beneath the regions in Poland stand two reinvigorated levels: counties and communes. So Poland has finally moved to the three-level subnational structure familiar in the West. However, many other post-communist countries – especially those remote from the EU – are still administered in a highly centralized and authoritarian fashion, leaving little scope for coherent governance at local level.

Some of the difficulties experienced in breathing life into subnational government in post-communist states are echoed in post-military Latin America. There, a tradition of centralized personal power persists into the democratic era, holding back efforts to raise the status of elected local officials. Mexico, for instance, is a federal and substantially democratic state at national level but the political legacy of centralized control by the PRI and the traditional sway of rural landowners still prevent any sensible comparison with subnational governance in North America.

Even where federalism is more authentic, as in Brazil, excessive spending at state level has caused considerable difficulties for national governments seeking to restore their credibility with international financial institutions. Where fundamental problems arising from economic mismanagement still need to be resolved, there is a case for retaining the financial levers at national level. Argentine, for instance, suffered in negotiations with the International Monetary Fund in 2002 from excessive spending by the governor of Buenos Aires, by far the largest province in the country. It is for these reasons that Domínguez and Giraldo (1996, p. 27) question the desirability of decentralization in contemporary Latin America:

> Subnational governments can undermine the efforts of national governments to carry out economic reforms. Decentralization can also undermine democratization by reinforcing the power of local elites, their practices of clientelism and the power of their military or paramilitary allies. Decentralization may some day empower ordinary citizens to take better charge of their government, and permit a wider range of innovation at the local level, but there is still a long way to go before these promises are realized.

Subnational government in authoritarian states

In authoritarian and totalitarian regimes, the distinction between local government and local power is fundamental. The former is weak: authority flows down from the top and so bottom-up institutions of representation are subordinate. Where national power is exercised by the military or a ruling party, these institutions typically establish a parallel presence in the provinces, where their authority overrides that of formal state officials. For a humble mayor in such a situation, the main skill required is to lie low and to avoid offending the real power-holders.

But it would be wrong to conclude that authoritarian regimes are highly centralized. Rather, central rulers – just like medieval monarchs – often depend on established provincial leaders to sustain their own, sometimes tenuous, grip on power. Central–local relations therefore tend to be more personal and less structured than in an established democracy. The hold of regional strongmen on power is not embedded in local institutions; such rulers command their fiefdoms in a personal fashion, replicating the authoritarian pattern found at national level. Central and local rulers are integrated by patronage: the national ruler effectively buys the support of local bigwigs who in turn maintain their position by selectively distributing resources to their own supporters. Patronage, not institutions, binds centre and periphery.

As always, however, totalitarian regimes offered more sophisticated excuses for a centralized order. Fascism, for example, sought unqualified obedience to the state and its supreme leader. Unity in the state implied a unitary state; dividing power between multiple levels of government was dismissed as liberal folly. In Italy, Mussolini relied on centrally appointed prefects to run local areas, decreeing that the prefect represented the 'entire, undiminished power of the state'. Spain under Franco proceeded similarly, with a civil governor in each province overseeing an elaborate structure of government outposts. These were fused systems par excellence.

Given that the supreme leader could not in fact take all decisions, in practice the local representatives of the state exerted considerable influence over their own areas. They sought to become their own little dictators and they often succeeded. So in fascist regimes, as in authoritarian ones, the doctrine of central power resulted in a system where its local exercise went unchecked.

It was perhaps only some communist regimes, most notably the Soviet Union, which achieved real political centralization. In communist states, the leading role of the party in constructing a socialist utopia always took precedence over local concerns. As long as the party itself remained highly centralized, national leaders could command outlying areas through the party.

In the Soviet Union, the ability of communist leaders to command the vast territory of the country through the device of the party was an unparalleled organizational achievement. Technically, the 'Union of Soviet Socialist Republics' was a federation but in reality any attempt by a republic to exercise its constitutional right to 'freely secede from the USSR' would have been crushed by force. Centralized control exercised through the party overwhelmed federalist fiction. Although a measure of decentralization was introduced from the 1960s, Soviet federalism under communist rule was dismissed by most observers as 'false', 'façade' or 'incomplete' – a cover for what was in effect a Russian empire.

Even though many of the USSR's constituent republics became independent states in the break-up of the Soviet Union in 1991, Russia itself remains a country in which multiple nationalities continue to jostle under authoritarian rule from the centre. A brutal example is Chechnya's failed war of independence, savagely repressed by a Russian elite (and public) determined to protect its own preeminence in a multinational state. Russian federalism is no longer a façade but it still coexists uneasily with 'the dictatorship of power' (Stoliarov, 2002).

Key reading

> **Next step:** *Gagnon and Tully (2001) is a comparative study of multinational democracies, focusing on federalism and federations.*

On federalism, useful comparative studies are Stepan (2001), McKay (2001) and G. Smith (1995). Elazar (1996) provides an enthusiast's overview while Wachendorfer-Schmidt (2000) and Braun (2000) compare the performance of federal and unitary states. Burgess (2000, 2003) surveys the EU's 'federation', Bakvis and Skotsgad (2002) examine the Canadian case and Kahn (2002) looks at Russia. Loughlin (2001) reviews subnational democracy in the European Union. John (2001) and Mouritzen and Svara (2002) survey local governance; see also the special issue of the *International Political Science Review* (1998).

Chapter 14

Legislatures

Legislatures are symbols of popular representation in politics. They are not governing bodies, they do not take major decisions and usually they do not even initiate proposals for laws. Yet they are still the foundation of both liberal and democratic politics. How then does their significance arise? The importance of legislatures rests on what they stand for rather than what they do. As Olson (1994, p. 1) writes,

> legislatures join society to the legal structure of authority in the state. Legislatures are representative bodies: they reflect the sentiments and opinions of the citizens.

In potential and often in reality, legislatures are the authentic representative of the people's will. For this reason they help to mobilize consent for the system of rule. As representative democracy spreads throughout the world, so more legislatures are gaining the political weight which comes from performing the role of standing for the people.

The origin of European parliaments lies in ancient royal courts where monarchs would judge important legal cases and meet with noblemen of the realm (Marongiu, 1968). Gradually these assemblies became more settled, coming to represent the various estates – the clergy, the nobility and the towns – into which society was then divided. In the thirteenth and fourteenth centuries, kings began to consult estate leaders more consistently on issues of war, administration, commerce and taxation. Myers (1975, p. 23) describes how these early 'assemblies of estates' developed:

the leading members [of estates] might appear in the assemblies either by virtue of their office or status, or because of election. At first the composition and functions of such assemblies were very ill defined and fluid, but gradually they solidified into increasingly definite forms which, in a traditionally-minded society, came to be regarded as customary and therefore respected.

Although the initiative for calling these colloquia lay with the king, a principle of Roman law was sometimes invoked in justification. This notion was *quod omnes similter tangit, ab omnibus comprobetur* (what concerns all should be approved by all). So these early European assemblies were viewed as possessing a right to be consulted long before they became modern legislatures with the sovereign authority to pass laws.

Definition

A **legislature** is a multimember representative body which considers public issues. Its main function is to 'give assent, on behalf of a political community that extends beyond the executive authority, to binding measures of public policy' (Norton, 1990a, p. 1). The words used to denote these bodies reflect contrasting origins: 'assemblies' assemble, 'congresses' congregate, 'parliaments' talk and 'legislatures' pass laws. We use these terms interchangeably.

The history of legislatures in new republics such as the United States is more straightforward. In the USA, the Founding Fathers placed Congress at the centre of their deliberations. A leading role for the legislature was judged an essential defence against executive tyranny; the list of powers which the constitution awards to Congress is longer and more detailed than that given to the president. James Madison, an architect of the American constitution, declared that 'in republican government, the legislative power necessarily predominates' (Hamilton,

1788d, p. 265). And so, in the United States, it did. Congress remains the most influential legislature in the world.

Structure

Only two things, writes Blondel (1973), can be said with certainty about every assembly in the world: how many members and chambers it has. Both are important aspects of parliamentary structure. But a third factor, the committee system, is an increasingly significant influence on the operation and effectiveness of modern parliaments. In this section, we examine all three aspects of assembly structure.

Size

The size of an assembly, as indicated by membership of the more important lower chamber, reflects a country's population (Figure 14.1). In China, the world's most populous country, the National People's Congress has almost 3,000 members. By contrast, in the South Pacific island of Tuvalu (population 8,624), the assembly has a mere 12 members (Taagepera and Recchia, 2002).

However, with legislatures – unlike countries – size rarely indicates strength. Rather, the opposite applies: very large chambers are rendered impotent by their inability to act as a cohesive body. They are in constant danger of being taken over by more coherent actors such as political parties or even by their own committees. Ruling communist parties, as in China, preferred a large legislature precisely because of its tendency to docility.

By contrast, a very small chamber – say, under 100 – offers opportunities for all deputies to have their say in a collegial environment. A small chamber may be entirely appropriate for the small island communities in the Pacific and the Caribbean where such legislatures abound. In practice, as Figure 14.1 shows, few lower chambers are more than 500–600 in size, and this is probably a fair estimate of the maximum size for an effective body.

Number of chambers

Should a legislature have one chamber or two? If

two, what role should the second chamber play and how should its members be selected? These old questions acquired practical significance in the 1990s as a new wave of democratic constitutions moved parliaments closer to the centre of the political stage.

Unicameralism is the norm today. By 2001, 115 of the world's 178 parliaments possessed only one chamber (Russell, 2001). This proportion rose in the decades following 1945 as several smaller democracies abolished their second chamber, notably New Zealand in 1950, Denmark in 1954 and Sweden in 1970. Many smaller post-colonial and post-communist states also embraced a single chamber. Bicameral legislatures are most often found in larger countries, particularly federations where the second chamber expresses the voice of the component states (Massicotte, 2001).

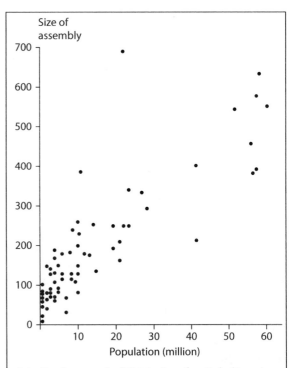

Note: Based on a sample of 70 states drawn from Derbyshire and Derbyshire (1999b), excluding countries with a population in excess of 60 million. Size of assembly is measured by the lower chamber for bicameral assemblies.

Figure 14.1 Population and assembly size

The choice between one and two chambers is not just a technical matter of institutional design. Fundamentally, the decision reflects contrasting visions of democracy. Unicameral parliaments are justified by an appeal to a majoritarian reading of popular control. The proposition is that an assembly based on direct popular election reflects the popular will and should not be obstructed by a second chamber. The radical French cleric Abbé Sièyes (1748–1836) put the point well: 'if a second chamber dissents from the first, it is mischievous; and if it agrees, it is superfluous' (Lively, 1991).

In addition to this traditional argument, modern analysts argue that a single chamber precludes the petty politicking and point-scoring which become possible as soon as two houses are created (Tsebelis and Money, 1997). A single chamber is also accountable, economical and capable, in theory, of acting with despatch.

But the defenders of bicameral parliaments reject both the majoritarian logic of Abbé Sièyes and the penny-pinching of accountants. Bicameralists stress the liberal element of democracy, arguing that the upper chamber offers checks and balances. It can defend individual and group interests against a potentially oppressive majority in the lower house. The second chamber can also serve as a house of review, revising bills (proposed laws), scrutinising constitutional amendments and delaying intemperate legislation – 'a second chamber for second thoughts'. In addition, a second house can share the workload of the lower chamber, conduct detailed committee work and assist with appointments (e.g. to the judiciary). An upper chamber provides a modern approximation to the traditional idea of a council of elders. Reflecting these points, Robert Cecil, thrice British prime minister in the nineteenth century, declared that the House of Lords 'represents the permanent, as opposed to the passing, feelings of the nation' (Russell, 2001).

Where legislatures do consist of two chambers, the question arises of the relationship between them. Usually, the lower chamber dominates. This is especially so where the form of government is parliamentary. In such a system, the government's survival depends on maintaining the assembly's support and one chamber must become the focus of such accountability. If a government were equally accountable to two houses, it might be caught in the grip of contradictory pressures, unable to command the confidence of one or other chamber. This task of sustaining or voting down the government falls naturally to the lower house, with its popular mandate. The dominance of the first chamber can also be seen in other ways. It often has special responsibility for money bills; is the forum where major proposals are initially introduced; and is entitled to override vetoes or amendments proffered by the second chamber.

In presidential systems, by contrast, the president is directly elected and his continuation in office does not depend on the legislature's confidence. This forestalls any requirement for accountability to focus on a single chamber. In these conditions, the upper chamber may acquire more significance. The American Congress is the best illustration. With its constitutional position as representative of the states, the Senate plays a full part in the country's legislative and budget-making process, with most bills ending up in a joint committee of both houses. Except for Italy, such strong second chambers are confined to federations.

A bicameral structure raises the question of how the members of the second chamber should be chosen. Some divergence with the lower house is needed if the upper chamber is not simply to mirror the party balance in the first chamber. The three main methods used for the second chamber are (Russell, 2001):

▸ direct election (used by 27 of 66 upper houses)
▸ indirect election through regional or local governments (21/66)
▸ appointment, usually by the government (16/66).

But even when election is the dominant principle, a contrast with the lower house is normally achieved. Generally, the members of the upper house are given longer tenure: typically six years compared to three to five in the lower chamber. These differences in tenure ensure that elections to the two chambers do not completely overlap, thus encouraging some variation in composition. For example, elections to the American Senate are held every two years, with only a third of the 100 seats up for election at any one time. By contrast, the entire membership of the House of Representatives must stand for reelection on an unusually short two-year cycle.

A federal structure also produces natural divergence between chambers. In federations, Canada excepted, elections to the upper chamber are organized by state, with the number of senators per state varying far less than population figures would imply. The American Senate contains two members for each of 50 states; California with a population of 35 million has the same representation as Nevada with only two million residents. In more recent federations, membership is also weighted towards the smaller states but to a lesser extent. The German Bundesrat, for instance, offers three to six seats to each *Land*, according to population. By contrast, the districts used for lower house elections are in most countries more equal in population.

Committees

The final structural feature of legislatures to consider is its internal committee system. Given the complexity of modern politics, a powerful assembly needs a well-developed committee structure if it is to develop the detailed expertise needed for real influence. Committees have become the workhorses of effective legislatures. Yet committee operations lack the profile accorded to meetings of the whole chamber. So what exactly are legislative committees? And what purposes do they serve?

Committees are small workgroups of members, created to cope with the volume of parliamentary business, particularly in the larger and busier lower

---

Table 14.1 Selection to the upper chamber in some established democracies

Country	Chamber	Members	Term (years)	Method of selection
Australia	Senate	76	6	Direct election by STV in each state[†]
Canada	Senate	104	Retire by 75	Appointed by the prime minister
France	Senate	321	9	Indirect election via *départements*[‡]
Germany	Bundesrat	69	–	Appointed by state governments
India	Council of States	245	6	Indirect election via state assemblies[+]
Italy	Senate	326	5	Direct election by a mixed member system[*]
Japan	House of Councillors	252	6	Direct election by a mixed member system
Netherlands	'First chamber' (Senate)	75	4	Elected by and from provincial councils
USA	Senate	100	6	Direct election by plurality voting in each state

Notes:
[†] STV – single transferable vote (p. 148).
[‡] units of local government (100 in total, including 4 overseas territories).
[+] except for 12 presidential nominees.
[*] elections are simultaneous with the lower house. The president can appoint 5 life members.

chamber. These workgroups traditionally took the form of standing committees (to consider bills and financial proposals) together with conference or mediation committees to reconcile differences in bills passed by the two houses of a bicameral assembly.

However, the more recent development has been the strengthening of select committees which scrutinize government administration and investigate matters of concern, drawing on external witnesses as needed (Box 14.1). The growing status of select committees reflects the increasing importance of the scrutiny function to contemporary legislatures.

A strong committee system largely defines a working (committee-oriented) as opposed to a talking (chamber-oriented) assembly. Debate in the chamber may fulfil parliament's representative role but it is in its committees that the legislature gets down to the detailed business of scrutinizing bills, overseeing government and exploring policy options. Although members are usually allocated to a committee in proportion to overall party strength in the chamber, partisanship is usually held in check.

Definition

In a **talking assembly,** such as the British House of Commons, floor debate is the central activity; it is here that major issues are addressed and reputations are won and lost. In a **working assembly,** such as the American Congress, the core activity takes place in committee rooms. There, legislators shape bills, authorize expenditure and scrutinize the executive.

The American Congress is unique in the impact of its committees. Although unmentioned in the constitution, committees rapidly became vital to Congress's work. 'Congress in session is Congress on public exhibition, whilst Congress in its committee rooms is Congress at work', wrote Woodrow Wilson (1885, p. 79). Bryce (1921, p. 68), a nineteenth-century British observer of American politics, described the House of Representatives as 'a huge panel from which committees are selected'; his comment still applies and to both chambers. Committees are uniquely well-supported, employing over 3,500 policy specialists. They decide the fate and shape of most

---

BOX 14.1
Types of parliamentary committee

Type	Function
Standing ('permanent') committee	To consider bills in detail
Select committee	▸ To scrutinize the executive, often one committee for each main government department ▸ Ad hoc committees to investigate particular matters of public interest
Conference or mediation committee	A joint committee to reconcile differences in the version of a bill passed by each chamber (bicameral legislatures only)

---

legislation. Further, each committee creates its own subcommittees: by 1994 the Senate's 20 permanent standing committees had spawned a total of 87 subcommittees.

So autonomous did these little legislatures become that they reduced the overall coherence of Congress. Their chairs became congressional lions, powerful and protective of their own territory. By the 1990s, however, party leaders were ready to fight back. They sought to rein in the committees. In the House, Republican Newt Gingrich, elected Speaker in 1995, asserted party control over appointments to committee chairs and used party task forces to drive legislation forward. But congressional committees are immensely resilient. They largely reasserted their control over bills once Gingrich's star began to wane. However, one legacy of the Republican revolution – a six-year term limit on committee chairs – may prove to be long-lasting, reducing the iron in the triangle linking committees, departments and interest groups (Evans, 2001).

Committees have less influence on legislation in party-dominated legislatures. In the British House of Commons, for instance, government bills are examined by standing committees which largely replicate party combat on the floor of the chamber. These committees, unlike those of Congress, do not challenge executive dominance in framing legislation. They are unpopular, unspecialized and under-resourced.

However, like many other legislatures the Commons has expanded its system of select committees of scrutiny. Since 1979, select committees have shadowed all the main government departments, probing government policy and monitoring its implementation. The members of a select committee can develop a shared outlook which moderates the war of the parties still waged on the floor of the House. In the context of a traditional talking assembly, Norton (1997, p. 166) suggests that Britain's select committees 'mark a remarkable advance in terms of parliamentary scrutiny'.

Where the political style is less adversarial and policy emerges through agreement, committees are a natural arena in which to seek compromise and consensus. In these circumstances, influential committees can coexist with strong parties. In the German Bundestag (lower house), party discipline is firm but the committee members have more regard for objectivity than point-scoring. Germany's second chamber, the Bundesrat – whose members are appointed by state governments – is even more committee-based. It only holds general plenary sessions once a month.

But it is Scandinavia that provides the best example of influential committees, again in combination with strong parties. Scandinavia's main governing style, sometimes called 'committee parliamentarianism', is one in which influential standing committees negotiate the policies and bills on which the whole parliament later votes. In Sweden, for instance, committees modify about one in three government proposals and nearly half these changes are substantial (Sjolin, 1993, p. 174). Many such modifications will result from discussion with relevant interest groups. So legislative committees are the vehicle for the extensive consultation which defines the character of Scandinavian policy-making.

Apart from the party system, the key to the influence of committees lies in three factors: expertise, intimacy and support.

▶ *Expertise* emerges over time from committees with specialized responsibilities and a clear field of operation. Expertise is most likely to develop in permanent committees with continuity of operation and membership.

▶ *Intimacy* emerges from small size and is reinforced by stable membership. Particularly when meetings take place in private, a small group setting can encourage cooperation and consensus, overcoming any initial hostility between members from competing parties.

▶ *Support* refers to the use of qualified staff to advise committees. Expert researchers can help busy politicians to produce well-founded recommendations.

Significantly, all three factors are present in the American Congress.

Functions

The question of the functions of legislatures raises the important issue of their role in the political system. The key roles of modern parliament are representation, deliberation and legislation. Other functions, crucial to some but not all assemblies, are authorizing expenditure and scrutinizing the executive (14.2).

Through a discussion of these functions, we will see how the significance of parliaments in established democracies extends well beyond the narrow task of simply converting bills into laws.

Representation

We have suggested that the essence of assemblies is that they 'represent' the wider society to the government. But how can we judge whether, and how well, that function is fulfilled? What features would a fully representative assembly exhibit?

One interpretation, plausible at first sight, is that a representative assembly should be a microcosm of society. The idea here is that a legislature should be society in miniature, literally 're-presenting' society in all its diversity. Such a parliament would balance men and women, rich and poor, black and white, even educated and unedu-

BOX 14.2
Functions of legislatures

Function	Comment
Representation	Most members articulate the goals of the party under whose label they were elected
Deliberation	Debating matters of moment is the classic function of Britain's House of Commons
Legislation	Most bills come from the government but the legislature still approves them and may make amendments in committee
Authorizing expenditure	Parliament's role is normally reactive, approving or rejecting a budget prepared by the government
Making governments (pp. 000–00)	In most parliamentary systems, the government emerges from the assembly and must retain its confidence
Scrutiny	Oversight of government activity and policy is growing in importance and is a task well-suited to committees

Note: In parliamentary systems, the legislature is also responsible for making and sometimes breaking governments, a key function examined separately on pp. 274–8.

cated, in the same mix as in society. How, after all, could a parliament composed entirely of middle-aged white men go about representing young black women – or vice versa? To retain the confidence of society, the argument continues, a representative assembly must reflect social diversity, standing in for society and not just acting on its behalf (Phillips, 1995).

But there is a considerable difficulty here. Achieving a legislature which mirrors society would require interfering with the normal process of election. A microcosm could only be achieved by quota, not election. Assemblies in communist states certainly achieved high levels of representation for peasants, workers and women. But this

success was at the price of strict party control over nominations and elections. Indeed, a true microcosm is best obtained by random selection, dispensing with elections altogether, as with juries in the English-speaking world. In any case, would we really want a parliament containing its due proportion of the ignorant, the inarticulate and the corrupt?

Representatives would also need to be replaced regularly, lest they become seduced by the trappings of office. Rotation is sometimes attempted by new radical parties but not usually for long. Indeed, Kay (2003) suggests that the idea of a microcosm is incoherent in itself: 'those who take part in politics are unrepresentative because, if they were representative, they would be at home watching television'. In truth, the assembly as microcosm is an impractical ideal – if it is an 'ideal' at all.

> *Definition*
> A legislature would be a **microcosm** if it formed a miniature version of society, precisely reflecting social diversity. An exact microcosm is impractical but there may still be value in ensuring that all major groups achieve some parliamentary presence (Phillips, 1995).

Representation in most assemblies operates through party. Victorious candidates owe their election to their party and they vote in parliament largely according to its commands. In New Zealand, Labour members must agree to abide by the decisions of the party caucus. In India, an extreme case, members lose their seat if they vote against their party, the theory being that they are deceiving the voters if they switch parties after their election. MPs are slowly becoming less reliable lobby fodder but they are still defined, first and foremost, by their party label.

Elsewhere, party discipline is combined with at least some independence for members. In France and Germany, for instance, party obligations must be reconciled with the constitutional requirement that members of the legislature owe allegiance to the nation and not to any group within it. In practice, party voting remains important, even if it is not enforced with the eagerness found in New Zealand and India.

Deliberation

An important function of many legislatures is to serve as a deliberative body, considering public matters of national importance. This function contrasts sharply with the microcosm and party views of representation and gives an additional perspective on what parliaments are for.

In the eighteenth and nineteenth centuries, before the rise of disciplined parties, deliberation was regarded as the central purpose of parliaments. The theory was that politicians should serve as trustees of the nation, applying exceptional knowledge and intelligence to the matters before them. Clearly, this philosophy of deliberation stands in complete opposition to the idea of representation as a microcosm.

The British conservative Edmund Burke (1729–97) gave the classic exposition of the deliberative account. Elected member of parliament for Bristol in 1774, Burke admitted in his victory speech that he knew nothing about the constituency and had played little part in the campaign. But, he continued,

> Parliament is not a congress of ambassadors from different and hostile interests; which interests each must maintain, as an agent and advocate against other agents and advocates; but Parliament is a deliberative assembly of one nation, with one interest, that of the whole; where, not local purposes, not local prejudices, ought to guide, but the general good, resulting from the general reason of the whole. You choose a member indeed; but when you have chosen him, he is not a member for Bristol, but he is a member of Parliament.

Deliberation of course continues today even if its status is no longer as exalted as in Burke's time. However, the deliberative style varies across countries and here the contrast between talking and working assemblies again proves useful.

In talking assemblies such as Britain's and New Zealand's, deliberation takes the form of debate in the chamber. In Britain, key issues eventually make their way to the floor of the House of Commons where they are debated with passion and often with flair. Floor debate sets the tone for national political discussion, forming part of a continuous election campaign. One of the achievements of the Commons is precisely its ability to combine effective deliberation, at least on vital issues, with strong partisanship.

In 'Considerations on Representative Government' (1861), the English political philosopher John Stuart Mill (1806–73) makes the case for such a talking assembly:

> I know not how a representative assembly can more usefully employ itself than in talk, when the subject of talk is the great public interests of the country, and every sentence of it represents the opinion either of some important body of persons in the nation, or of an individual in whom such body have reposed their confidence.

By contrast, in working assemblies such as the American Congress and the Scandinavian parliaments, deliberation is less theatrical. It takes the form of policy debate in the committee room. The style here is more careful and detailed; deliberative in the literal sense of a careful consideration of the alternatives.

Legislation

Most constitutions explicitly assert the legislative function of parliaments. The end of absolute executive power is affirmed by giving to parliament, and to it alone, the right to make laws. Arbitrary government is replaced by a formal procedure for law-making. This painstaking process signals the importance attached to government by rules rather than individuals. Authoritarian rulers govern by decree but in a democracy bills are scrutinized and authorised by a congress of the nation.

Yet legislation is rarely the function where 'legislatures' exert most influence. Indeed, after fifty years the European Parliament – admittedly a special case – does not even control the formal law-making process in the European Union (see '50 years of the European Parliament'). At national level, legislatures must approve bills but effective control over legislation usually rests with the government. Bills pass through the assembly without being initiated or even transformed there.

In party-dominated Australia, for instance, the

50 YEARS OF THE EUROPEAN PARLIAMENT

Although this time-line demonstrates the widening competence of the European Parliament (EP), the assembly's legislative authority remains limited. However, as the EU itself has deepened, so the parliament has become more willing to assert its expanding rights to at least be consulted on legislation, the budget and appointments.

1952 Assembly of the European Coal and Steel Community established as an instrument of scrutiny, with the right to dismiss the Commission in some circumstances. Assembly members are drawn from national legislatures.

1962 The Assembly is renamed the European Parliament.

1970 The Treaty Amending Certain Budgetary Provisions of the Treaties gives the EP more influence over the budget.

1975 The Treaty Amending Certain Financial Provisions of the Treaties gives the EP the right to propose modifications in areas where expenditure is not mandated by previous agreements.

1979 First direct elections. Average turnout 67 per cent.

1980 *Isoglucose* judgment by the European Court requires the EP to be consulted on proposed laws.

1986 The Single European Act initiates cooperation and assent procedures which give the EP more influence over legislation.

1992 The Maastricht Treaty requires members of the Commission to be approved by the EP. New co-decision procedure gives the EP some veto authority over legislation.

1997 Treaty of Amsterdam extends the co-decision procedure and formalizes the EP's right to veto the nominee for Commission president.

1999 All 20 commissioners (the Santer Commission) resign rather than face dismissal by the EP for mismanagement.

1999 Fifth direct elections to the EP. Average turnout 56 per cent.

Further reading: Judge and Earnshaw (2003), Scully (2003), Tsebelis and Garrett (1997).

government treats the legislative function of parliament with virtual contempt. On a single night in 1991 it sought to put 26 bills through the Senate between midnight and 3 a.m. In the era before New Zealand adopted proportional representation, a Prime Minister boasted that if an idea came to him while shaving, he could have it on the statute book by the evening, truly a case of slot-machine law.

In Britain, similarly, the governing party dominates law-making. Ninety-seven per cent of bills proposed by government between 1945 and 1987 became law. As Rose (1989, p. 173) said of Britain, 'laws are described as acts of Parliament but it would be more accurate if they were stamped "Made in Whitehall" '. In the party-dominated parliaments of Britain and some of its ex-colonies, the legislative function is reduced to quality control: patching up errors in bills prepared in haste by ministers and civil servants. In legislation, at least, these assemblies are reactive rather than active.

By contrast, in the parliamentary systems of continental Europe, many legislatures do play a more positive role in legislation. Coalition governments, influential committees and an elite commitment to compromise combine to deliver laws acceptable to all sides. In a few countries, this more flexible approach is reflected not just in the discussion of bills but also in their initiation. In

Switzerland, a bill may originate not just from the executive but also from members of either house of the federal assembly or from any canton.

But it is in presidential systems, including the United States, that the assembly achieves most autonomy in making law. The separation of powers and personnel inherent in a presidential regime limits executive influence in the legislature. This institutional separation is often reinforced by divided government. In the United States, one party frequently controls the White House while the other has a majority in either or both houses of Congress. In Latin America, where parties are weaker and proportional representation is the norm for congressional elections, the president's party may be no more than a minor player in the legislature.

Yet even in presidential systems the initiative in framing bills usually lies with the executive. Certainly, in the American Congress only members of the House of Representatives can formally introduce bills. But the executive can easily find a friendly representative to initiate a bill on its behalf. The political reality is that bills are developed by the administration and then transformed in Congress if indeed they do not expire in its maze of committees. 'You supply the bills and we work them over', a member of Congress said to an administration official. The executive proposes but Congress disposes, usually by saying no.

Inevitably, this pluralistic process of law-making reduces the coherence of the legislative programme. As President Kennedy said, 'It is very easy to defeat a bill in Congress. It is much more difficult to pass one' (Eigen and Siegel, 1993, p. 82). Or as Davy Crockett wrote in 1834, 'Woe betide a bill that is opposed. It is laid aside for further time, and that never comes.' The difficulty which presidential systems experience in passing laws stands in marked contrast to the tight control over the legislative programme exerted by the ruling party in the British parliamentary system.

Although the process by which a legislature transforms a bill into law naturally varies from one democracy to another, Figure 14.2 offers a general outline. The procedure is explicitly deliberative, involving several readings (debates) as the bill moves from the floor to committee and back again (Döring and Hallerberg, 2004).

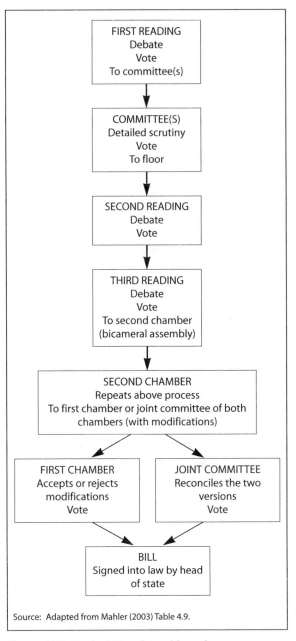

Source: Adapted from Mahler (2003) Table 4.9.

Figure 14.2 Typical steps in making a law

Bicameral legislatures face an additional problem in realizing the legislative function. What happens should the second chamber amend the bill passed by the lower house? There must be some means of resolving such discrepancies. In almost all countries, the initial step is for the amended bill to return to the lower chamber for further discussion. But if the bill continues to shuttle between houses in this way until an agreed version emerges, as in Italy's strongly bicameral legislature, the danger is that it will be delayed or never become law at all. In Italy, a bill on rape introduced in 1977 did not become law until 1995.

So most countries have developed a procedure for short-circuiting the shuttle (Box 14.3). The most common procedure is to employ a special conference committee, containing an equal number of members from each chamber, to produce an agreed bill. This compromise version must then be approved or rejected by the main chambers without further modification.

The American, French and German legislatures are among those employing conference commit-

tees. Conference committees are sometimes described as third chambers for it is here that the ultimate deals are struck and the decisive compromises made. They can be a vital arena in which political issues reach resolution.

In 2003, for example, the final shape of the German government's Agenda 2010 economic reform package was formed in and around Room 1.128 of the Bundesrat: the meeting place of the parliament's 32-member mediation committee. The people meeting there represented not just their legislative chamber but also their party and their region. In modifying the executive's proposals in a manner acceptable to the major interests in Germany, they were shaping the governance of their country.

Authorizing expenditure

This is one of the oldest functions of parliament and of the lower house in particular. The origin of European parliaments lay in the monarch's requirement for money. Since, as Spencer Walpole (1881, p. 4) wrote, 'the necessities of kings are the opportunities of peoples', assemblies were able to establish the right to raise grievances before granting supply (revenue). In Britain, this tradition continued until 1982 with 'supply days' during which the opposition could raise any issues it wished.

The power to authorize spending may be one of parliament's oldest functions but in many democracies it has become nominal. Even more than the law-making function, it forms part of the myth rather than the reality of parliamentary power. Indeed lack of real financial control is a major weakness of the modern assembly. Typically, the executive prepares the budget which is then reported to parliament but rarely modified there.

Special rules usually set out how the legislature must handle the budget. In many countries (including Britain, New Zealand and Spain) parliament cannot initiate its own expenditure proposals; it can only approve or reject spending proposed by the government. In other cases, such as Denmark and France, assembly proposals to increase expenditure must be accompanied by offsetting reductions elsewhere (Döring, 2001).

So parliamentary approval is largely after the

BOX 14.3
Resolving differences in the versions of a bill passed by each chamber

Procedure	Comment	Example
Indefinite shuttle	Amended versions continue to shuttle between chambers until agreement is reached (if ever)	Italy is the main example of this rare procedure
Lower house is decisive	The lower house decides whether to accept or reject amendments from the upper house	Czech Republic, Spain, United Kingdom
Conference or mediation committee	A joint committee of both chambers negotiates a compromise version which is then voted on by each house	Many countries, including France, Germany, Switzerland and the USA
Vote of a joint session of both chambers	The larger lower chamber exerts most weight in a joint vote	Australia, Brazil, India, Norway

Source: Adapted from Tsebelis and Money (1997), Table 2.2a, pp. 56–62.

fact, serving to confirm budget compromises worked out between government departments. In most democracies, once the budget reaches the assembly, it is a done deal. If the assembly began to unpick any part of the budget, the whole package would fall apart.

Australia is an extreme case of government control over the budget. Emy and Hughes (1991, p. 361) describe the political realities:

> there is no suggestion of the House of Representatives ever 'refusing supply' since control over the whole process of financial appropriations is firmly in the hands of the executive. Only they may propose to spend money . . . Moreover, it seems members of the House themselves lack both the knowledge of, and an interest in, the financial procedures which are, ultimately, crucial to the concept of parliamentary control.

The United States is once more the great exception. Congress remains central to the confused tangle of American budget-making. The constitution places the power of taxation specifically with the lower chamber: 'all bills for raising revenue shall originate in the House of Representatives'. Similarly, all money spent by executive departments must, under the constitution, be allocated under specific spending headings approved by members of Congress. No appropriations by Congress means no government programme. As Flammang *et al.* (1990, p. 422) write, 'without the agreement of members of Congress, no money can be doled out for foreign aid, salaries for army generals or paper clips for bureaucrats'. Given the separation of powers, the executive cannot assume that such agreement will be forthcoming.

The overall federal budget which the president is required by law to present to Congress each year is also subject to congressional review. Furthermore, in the 1970s Congress created its own Budget Office in an effort to match the skills available on the executive side. As a result, it can now deploy considerable financial expertise in analysing the president's proposals.

The result is that the annual American budget has become an elaborate game of chicken. The executive and the legislature each hopes the other side will accede to its own proposals before the money runs out and federal employees have to be sent home without pay, as briefly occurred in 1995. This rather alarming method of budget-making supports the proposition that financing the modern state, like the law-making function, is too important to be left to the assembly's many hands.

Scrutiny

The final function of legislatures is scrutiny (or oversight) of the executive. Although we are considering this role last, such activity has been growing in significance and value. Its expansion gives the lie to unqualified assertions of legislative decline.

To emphasize the scrutiny function is to accept that the executive, not the legislature, must govern. However, the assembly can restate its key role as representative of the people by acting as a watchdog over the administration. Effective monitoring can compensate for the downgrading of the assembly's legislative and expenditure functions, providing a new direction to parliament's work.

A modern assembly possesses three main instruments with which to monitor the executive:

▸ questions and interpellations (mainly used in parliamentary government)
▸ emergency debates and confidence votes (mainly used in parliamentary government)
▸ committee investigations (used in both presidential and parliamentary government).

Questions refer to direct queries of ministers. In many parliamentary systems, oral and written questions are mainstays of oversight. In Britain, for example, members of the House of Commons ask a total of over 70,000 questions a year, keeping many civil servants busy as they prepare answers for their minister. In addition, all ministers must face direct questioning in the Commons from time to time. Prime Minister's Question Time, though now reduced to once a week, remains a theatrical joust between the PM and the leader of the opposition.

In other countries, questions have lower status. French ministries often fail to answer them at all, and in the Australian House of Representatives ministers give long prepared answers to questions from their own side precisely so less time is left for opponents' queries. But in some assemblies in continental Europe, including Finland, France and Germany, the *interpellation* provides an alternative form of interrogation. An interpellation is a substantial form of question followed by a short debate and a vote on whether the government's response is deemed acceptable.

Definition

An **interpellation** is an enquiry of the government, initiated by the opposition, which is followed by a debate and usually a vote on the assembly's satisfaction with the answers given. This technique, often linked to a vote of no confidence, brought down several governments in the French Third and Fourth Republics.

Emergency debates are a further, and higher-profile, way in which the legislature can call the government to account. Normally a minimum number of members, and the Presiding Officer (Speaker), must approve a proposal for an emergency debate. Although the event normally ends with a vote – and a government win – the significance lies in the debate itself, and the fact of its calling, rather than the outcome. An emergency debate creates publicity and demands a careful response from the government.

Votes of confidence or censure motions are the ultimate test which a legislature can pose to the executive in a parliamentary system. Such motions are not so much a form of detailed scrutiny as a decision on whether the government can continue in office. Again, special rules may apply: in France and Sweden, for instance, a majority of all members (not just those voting) is required to demonstrate the legislature's loss of confidence. In other countries, however, a confidence motion is not specifically designated but is simply any vote on which the government would feel obliged to resign if defeated. In the Netherlands, this flexibility has led to rather odd motions about whether other motions should be treated as censure votes (Andeweg and Irwin, 2002, p. 130). In some countries, again including Sweden, votes of confidence can be directed against individual ministers and not just the government as a whole.

Above all, the rise of the scrutiny function has strengthened committees. Because the floor of the house is an inappropriate venue for detailed scrutiny, *committee investigations* are the key form of oversight. The American Congress is the classic case here. Exceptionally, the constitution gives Congress – rather than the executive – responsibility for such important matters as commerce, the currency, defence and taxation. Of course, Congress does not carry out these functions itself; it delegates the tasks to the bureaucracy. But because of its constitutional status, and the budgetary authority flowing from it, Congress possesses inherent powers of oversight. A British civil servant can afford to treat a parliamentary question as a minor distraction but the head of a government agency in the United States knows that next year's budget may depend on maintaining good relations with the relevant members of Congress.

The sheer extent of committee engagement in the activity of American government is remarkable. On defence issues alone, 14 committees and 43 subcommittees of Congress held hearings in 1988, creating a large and possibly excessive burden on the Pentagon. With more than 3,000 committee staffers offering support, Congress achieves a unique level of scrutiny. However even in the USA, committee oversight is limited. It can only cast light on a few corners of a vast bureaucracy; Congress often micro-manages departments rather than setting broad targets; and committees must concern themselves with finance and legislation as well as scrutiny. In America, and even more elsewhere, the government's battalions outnumber the forces available to the legislature.

Recruitment

In a democracy, by definition, virtually the entire adult population can stand for election. Legislative recruitment is the process by which this huge pool of potential members of parliament is reduced to the small number who achieve election. In parliamentary systems, government ministers are usually selected from the assembly so the legislature becomes the key channel of recruitment to political office. Its members constitute the shortlist from which national leaders are drawn.

How then does this important process of recruitment operate? Box 14.4 outlines a four-stage model of political recruitment, based on legal, social, party and electoral filters.

At the first stage, legal considerations reduce the entire population to those who are technically *eligible* to join the legislature. Many countries apply more stringent age limits for legislators than for voters. In the United States, for instance, the minimum age remains 30 for the American Senate and 25 for the House, compared to 18 for voters. Some countries also impose citizenship and residence requirements. In the USA, again, the constitution stipulates that members of Congress must be American citizens residing in the state they represent.

At the second stage, a significant social filter reduces those who are eligible to stand to those who *aspire* to do so. Here, social influences on political interest and ambition, such as being brought up in a political family, come into play.

At the third stage, a party filter reduces the aspirants to the small subset of *candidates* – those who succeed in convincing the gatekeepers that they should be nominated for an electoral district or granted a high place on a party list. Relevant factors here include personal skills such as the ability to present oneself well to the selectors as well as party rules on such issues as gender quotas.

And the fourth and final electoral filter reduces those who stand as candidates to those who win the contest and become *members* of the national parliament.

This four-stage model, taking us from the eligibles to the elected, reveals that political recruitment is a far broader process than election alone. Indeed, the voters join the game only at the end, when most winnowing out has already taken place. Over 130 million Americans were eligible to stand for president in 2000; in some states only six candidates appeared on the ballot; and only two nominees – those for the Democratic and Republican parties – stood a realistic chance of winning.

In presidential systems, of course, the separation of executive and legislature means that people cannot belong to both at the same time. Although members of the legislature can resign to join the

---

BOX 14.4
Stages of recruitment to the legislature

Segment of the population	Main influence	Example
Population		
↓	Legal rules	Age and residence requirements
Eligibles		
↓	Socialization	Growing up in a political family
Aspirants		
↓	Party gatekeepers	Gender quotas
Candidates		
↓	Elections	Popularity of government
Members of the legislature		

Source: Adapted from Norris (1996), fig. 7.1, p. 196.

---

government, and even stand for president, the assembly is generally less important as a recruiting agent to high office. In the USA, for instance, recent presidents have tended to be drawn from state governments rather than Congress: for example, Jimmy Carter, Ronald Reagan, Bill Clinton and George W. Bush. The last president to move directly from Congress to the White House was John Kennedy, in 1960. A career in Congress remains attractive in its own right; it is more than a stepping stone to higher office (Davis, 1998).

A similar point applies to the presidential systems of Latin America. There, too, joining Congress is rarely seen as a direct route to a long-term position in the national government. But the status of assemblies in South America is lower than in the USA, reducing the calibre of the members. Many legislatures are under-resourced bodies operating in the shadow of assertive presidents. In addition, constitutions commonly limit members to one or two terms of office, ensuring turnover at the cost of expertise. In Mexico, in any given legislative term about eight out of ten deputies typically have no previous experience in the Chamber of Deputies (Nacif, 2002).

Profile UNITED KINGDOM

Population: 60.1m.
GDP per head: $25,500.
Form of government: a parliamentary democracy, with an hereditary monarch playing a largely ceremonial role.
Legislature: the House of Commons (659 members) is the dominant chamber. The House of Lords, the composition and powers of which are under review, acts in a revising and restraining capacity.

Executive: the cabinet is the top decision-ratifying body; the prime minister selects and dismisses cabinet members. Most policy is formed outside the full cabinet, either in cabinet committees and surrounding discussions or in informal groups led by the prime minister.
Judiciary: based on the common law tradition. Britain's membership of the European Union and devolution to Scotland and Wales enlarged the

scope of a traditionally restrained judiciary. In 2003, the government published proposals to introduce a supreme court.
Electoral systems: national and local elections still use the plurality system. The new Scottish and Welsh parliaments, first elected in 1999, use an additional member system. The 1999 election to the European parliament used party list PR.

Britain is an established democracy whose political system has nonetheless been in transition. Traditional models portrayed Britain as a centralized, unitary state; as a two-party system; as an exemplar of parliamentary sovereignty in which ministers were held to account by the assembly; and as a political system whose uncodified constitution offered little formal protection of individual rights. Yet the accuracy of all these images has come under review, partly as a result of the election in 1997 of a modernizing Labour administration.

The centralized and even the unitary character of the United Kingdom has been put in question by creating elected assemblies for Scotland and Wales. The two-party system has been challenged by the rise of the centre-left Liberal Democrats. Parliamentary sovereignty has been dented by British membership of the European Union and a more assertive judiciary. Ministerial accountability has been complicated by the delegation of government tasks to semi-independent agencies. And individual rights now receive clearer protection from the incorporation into British law of the European Convention on Human Rights.

The new era of transition in British politics is certain to impinge on its assembly. Traditionally, Britain's parliament (the oldest in the world) mixed omnipotence and impotence in a seemingly impossible combination. Omnipotence, because parliamentary sovereignty, allied to an uncodified constitution, meant there could be no higher authority in the land. Impotence, because the governing party exercised tight control over its own backbenchers, turning parliament into an instrument rather than a wielder of power.

In the twenty-first century, parliament's position has become less certain. The tired rituals of adversary politics in the Commons have become less convincing, not least for the 260 new MPs elected in 1997 and the 99 who followed in 2001. The notion that parliament still possesses some abstract quality called 'sovereignty' still carries weight but, like many assemblies, Britain's legislature runs the risk of being left behind by international integration.

But not all developments are negative. MPs themselves have become more professional and committed. The era of the amateur MP is over. And new select committees have begun to enter the debate over policy.

To strengthen its position in an evolving political system, parliament will need to step further down the road of reform. Besides its traditional function as a talking assembly, the legislature will need to become a more effective working body. To influence a more complex decision-making process, committee reports must offer well-researched recommendations.

Yet even as the British parliament tries to broaden its repertoire, it will surely continue to do what it has always done best: acting as an arena for debating issues of central significance to the nation, its government and its leaders.

Further reading: Butler and Kavanagh (2002), Dunleavy *et al.* (2003), Searing (1994).

Where American congressmen normally seek and achieve reelection, in Latin America's legislatures many members are pursuing long-term political careers in their home province, perhaps as state governor. In a grab-and-run exercise, they use their short period in the national legislature to lobby for their home district.

> **Definition**
> **Term limits** restrict elected politicians to a set number of terms of office, or ban reelection without a break. They are commonly used in Latin America, for both legislators and presidents, in an attempt to prevent abuse of office. They are also employed in some states of the USA. Term limits enforce turnover at the risk of damage to professionalism (Carey, 1998).

One finding of research into legislative recruitment stands out: in every country the profile of parliamentarians is statistically unrepresentative of the wider society. Reflecting wider patterns of political participation, democratic assemblies remain dominated by well-educated, middle-aged white men. There are also party differences in representation. Often, representatives of right-wing parties come from business, especially finance, while educational careers provide a fruitful recruiting ground for parties of the left. In the United States, law is the most common professional background (Norris, 1995). Throughout the world, a surprising number of representatives are drawn from highly political families, suggesting that politics risks becoming, to an extent, an occupational caste.

An additional theme in the recruitment of legislators is the rise of the career politician. Where the status of the legislature is high and term limits absent, the professional politician is coming to dominate the chamber. The local farmer, the loyal trade unionist, the prominent business executive who takes up politics for a few years – all have lost ground to the professional politician for whom politics is a sole and full-time career.

What are the consequences of the rise of the career legislator? On the one hand, such members are assiduous and ambitious. They burrow away in committees, serve their constituents and influence public policy. They are not content to be mere voting machines for their party.

> **Definition**
> **Career politicians** are described by King (1981, p. 255) as:
>
> people committed to politics. They regard politics as their vocation, they seek fulfilment in politics, they see their future in politics, they would be deeply upset if circumstances forced them to retire from politics. In short, they are hooked.

On the other hand, as Berrington (1995, p. 446) comments, 'the career politician does not know when to leave well alone'. An assembly peopled by career politicians is a restless, assertive institution. It lacks the judgement of those with work experience beyond politics. A case can certainly be made that politics is inherently a broad profession and that assemblies benefit from a few colourful amateurs to offset the dark suits of the career politicians.

Of course, career politicians can only flourish in parliament when reelection prospects are good; if members are automatically removed after each election, no parliamentary career is possible. Even without term limits, electoral swings can sometimes condemn many members to defeat. In Canada, for example, MPs serve an average of just six years in post. Most members are political tourists, on vacation from other more satisfying careers. Inevitably, the esteem of the institution suffers.

> **Definition**
> The **incumbency effect** refers to the electoral bonus accruing to sitting members arising from their visibility in their district, their ability to bring home the bacon and their access to resources for their re-election campaign. The incumbency effect helps to explain the high re-election rate in most legislatures.

But such cases are exceptional. In parliaments without term limits, reelection is the norm. The success rate of incumbents in winning reelection is over 85 per cent in Germany, New Zealand and the USA. Average length of service reaches 20 years in the UK and 15 years in Japan (Table 14.2), which is certainly sufficient time to develop

Table 14.2 Average length of service in national parliaments

Years	
United Kingdom	20
Japan	15
New Zealand	12
United States (House)	12
United States (Senate)	11
Israel	11
Germany	8
Denmark	8
France	7
Canada	6

Source: Adapted from Somit (1994, p 13). Except where indicated, the figure for bicameral assemblies refers to the lower house.

a parliamentary career. Indeed, the question is whether the incumbency effect damages legislatures by limiting fresh blood. One yardstick of the political recruitment process is its ability to deliver a balanced legislature blending experience with newcomers.

Legislatures in new democracies

A transition to democracy provides new opportunities for the legislature. Since parliaments embody the idea of representation, we should expect their stature to grow in newly minted democracies. And the prestige of legislatures has undoubtedly risen in almost all new democracies, particularly when the assembly played a major role in the free for all of democratic transition.

However, parliaments remain weaker in new democracies than in established democracies. In particular, scrutiny remains a contested function, partly because rulers are reluctant to grant rights of investigation and partly because many new parliaments are only now developing well-supported committees. As Diamond (1999, p. 98) comments,

In most new democracies, legislatures lack the organisation, financial resources, information service, experienced members and staff to serve as a mature and autonomous point of deliberation in the policy process.

The political experience of new legislators drawn into the assembly by the drama of democratization was often limited and many have now left politics, to be replaced by a more professional cohort. So the revival of assemblies in post-authoritarian settings is only now beginning to gather speed, a theme we can develop by reviewing the assembly's role in transitions in Southern Europe, Latin America and Eastern Europe.

Southern Europe

In Greece, Italy, Portugal and Spain, parliaments had to recover from highly subordinate positions under right-wing dictatorships. In the Spanish transition, parliament did play a key role in developing the new democratic system because it 'was the only meeting place for the democratically-minded. At the outset of democracy, it was the place where all the advocates of renewal met' (Giol, 1990, p. 96). Yet once the new democracy consolidated, the esteem of parliament soon declined as it became dominated by disciplined parties and strong leaders.

Parliaments played a less crucial role in the other Southern European transitions and they remain weaker institutions than in Northern Europe. Pridham (1990, p. 246) notes that one feature of the new party-dominated democracies of Southern Europe is the limited expectations held of their parliaments.

Latin America

The position of legislatures in Latin America has undoubtedly strengthened in the post-military era. As presidents have become more accountable, at least in the larger and more democratic countries, so assemblies have asserted the authority which flows from the separation of powers in a presidential executive. In a previous edition, we wrote that in a more democratic era, the realistic goal facing Latin American legislatures was not to gain sovereignty but rather to find some ways of 'restraining the prince and disciplining the powerful' (Chalmers, 1990). The legislatures in Brazil and Mexico are achieving just that.

But it would be wrong to conclude that parliaments in these new democracies have achieved, or will achieve, the exalted position of Congress in the United States. In the main, Latin American constitutions do not separate powers as completely as in the USA. They give presidents greater control over the budget and some latitude to govern through decrees. Further, political tradition inclines the electorate to look to presidents rather than to multi-party legislatures for effective governance. While resources and professionalism have increased in many Latin American legislatures, their expertise and influence still lag well behind the American Congress.

Central Europe

In several Central European countries, such as Poland and Hungary, legislatures were beginning to achieve modest grievance-raising and policy-influencing powers even before the collapse of communist rule. This experience undoubtedly helped to prepare these legislatures for the post-communist era. In several ways, parliaments were in a favourable position to influence legislation and policy in the first post-communist decade. Unlike Southern Europe, political parties and interest groups remained weak, giving legislators exceptional autonomy in their work. Yet this potential was only partly realized. High turnover, limited calibre, poor support and weak internal procedures limited the assembly's ability to confront assertive but often divided executives (Ågh, 1996).

Only now, fifteen years or so after communism's downfall, are Central European assemblies beginning to settle into a more productive routine. More professional members are returning for additional terms to work in a more stable political environment. Resources have increased; indeed, legislators are now relatively well-paid in comparison to many other professions.

Paradoxically, however, the influence exerted by individual legislators is probably declining. Parties are becoming better organized, placing more constraints on their representatives. In addition, many

such countries have needed to make extensive legal changes to meet the accession requirements set by the European Union, a process in which the executive has taken the lead, working round parliament in many cases.

So the individual member is once more becoming a foot soldier rather than a free-wheeling political entrepreneur – but that is the fate of many legislators in Western Europe too. As Kopecky (2003, p. 152) concludes,

> parliaments throughout Central and Eastern Europe have begun to resemble their sister institutions in established democracies, both in their internal organization and procedures and in the external constraints normally placed upon such institutions in modern democracy.

Legislatures in authoritarian states

Since assemblies are symbols of popular representation in politics, their significance in authoritarian regimes is inherently limited. Yet legislatures are difficult to extinguish completely. In 1990 only 14 out of 164 independent states had no assembly. Of those 14, only five (traditional dynastic states in the Arabian Gulf) had no experience of assemblies at all.

Assemblies in non-democracies generally function only as shadow institutions. Sessions are often short and some members are simply appointed by the government. In Mezey's (1979) influential classification, assemblies in non-democratic systems play only a marginal or a minimal role in policy-making (Box 14.5). Members concentrate on raising grievances, pressing constituency interests and sometimes lining their own pockets. The rulers regard these activities as non-threatening; the real issues of national politics are left untouched.

Why, then, do authoritarian rulers bother with assemblies at all? Their value is fourfold:

▸ A parliament provides a fig leaf of legitimacy, both domestic and international, for the regime. The ruler can say to visiting dignitaries, 'Look! We too have an assembly, just like the British House of Commons and the American Congress!'

DEBATE
THE DECLINE OF LEGISLATURES?

The decline of parliament thesis maintains that legislatures in established democracies are losing, or have lost, power to the executive. Petersson (1989, p. 96) notes that the argument is commonly encountered: 'every description of the form of government of the modern state seems to end up with a discouraging conclusion about the actual role of parliament'. Since legislatures express popular sovereignty, the implication of the decline thesis is that democracy itself is in retreat. But is the assertion of a general loss of parliamentary authority correct?

The case for
As early as 1921, the British historian Lord Bryce (p. 370) noted that 'general causes ... have been tending to reduce the prestige and authority of legislative bodies'. He referred specifically to the growth of disciplined parties and to the increased complexity of policy-making, both of which strengthen the executive. In particular, assemblies have lost control of the legislative process. Bills pass through the assembly on their way to the statute book but their origins lie elsewhere: in the executive, the bureaucracy and interest groups.

Since then, growing interdependence between countries has posed insuperable problems for assemblies. Parliaments are creatures of the nation; they are poorly adapted to a global era. How can national parliaments grapple with a world of international trade, intergovernmental deals, complex treaties and war? To be sure, a European Parliament now exists but it remains the runt in the litter of EU institutions, lacking standard legislative powers. In today's conditions, the executive is where the action is; parliaments have become political museum-pieces.

The case against
To speak of the decline of legislatures in a global era is too simple, for three reasons:

▶ Even if parliaments no longer initiate many bills, they continue to perform such functions as representation, scrutiny and, in parliamentary systems, recruitment to government office.

▶ The alleged golden age of parliaments was as long ago as the mid-nineteenth century; there is little evidence to show that parliaments have lost further ground since 1945.

▶ In some ways assemblies are growing in importance: as arenas of debate, as intermediaries in transitions from authoritarian to democratic rule, as raisers of grievances and especially as agencies of oversight.

Moreover, where the American Congress led the way in equipping assembly members with the resources to do their jobs professionally, other legislatures are following suit. Throughout the democratic world, backbench members have become more assertive: party leaders can no longer expect educated politicians to be totally deferential. Specialized committees, and members with a driving interest in policy, are increasingly successful in contributing to political debate. Televising proceedings has raised the profile of assemblies among voters. And the transition to democracy has raised the standing of parliaments; when a new democracy consolidates, legislative professionalism eventually follows.

Assessment
The role of parliaments is changing rather than declining. The reality is that legislatures do not initiate many laws but that fact need not be mourned. Indeed, an assembly which really did settle the fate of legislation would be a dubious asset. What could be more odd, asked the English journalist Walter Bagehot (1826–77), than government by public meeting?

What modern assemblies can do, and what many are now better equipped than ever to do, is to oversee the executive. Parliaments possess a unique authority to force politicians and civil servants to account for their actions before a body which still represents the nation. They remain an essential element in the architecture of democracy.

Further reading: Norton (1998), Sjolin (1993).

BOX 14.5

A policy classification of assemblies

Type	Definition	Example
Active	Assembly makes policy autonomously	US Congress
Reactive	Assembly largely responds to, but can also influence, government policy	UK House of Commons
Marginal	Assembly is a minor partner in policy-making	Many legislatures in communist states
Minimal	Assembly is a rubber stamp under executive domination	Many African states in the era of one-party rule

Source: Adapted from Mezey (1979).

▶ The legislature can be used to incorporate moderate opponents into the regime, providing a forum for negotiating matters that do not threaten rulers' key interests.

▶ Raising constituents' grievances and lobbying for local interests provide a measure of integration between centre and periphery and between state and society. Such activity oils the political wheels without threatening those who control the machine.

▶ Even marginal and minimal assemblies provide a useful pool of potential recruits to the political elite. Behaviour in parliament provides a useful test of reliability.

In totalitarian systems, assemblies were even more marginal than in authoritarian regimes. Fascist states, in particular, had no time for parliamentary debate – or indeed for parliaments. Fascism was state-centred and opposed to parliamentary government. Decisive action, not weak debate, was the goal of a fascist regime. Power was to be concentrated in a single leader, not diluted through a separation of powers. The vital blood of national unity could not be thinned by the party divisions observed within parliament. In short, fascism condemned sovereign legislatures as the institutional expression of liberalism. For such reasons, Mussolini abolished the remnants of the Italian parliament in 1938, introducing a new if equally minimal corporate institution in its place (p. 178).

In communist states, legislatures were not treated with quite the same contempt. Indeed, communist regimes often produced statistically representative assemblies. Women and favoured groups such as industrial workers achieved greater representation than in Western legislatures. However, this feature reflected tight party control of the nomination process and the limited political significance of the legislature. In practice, a socially representative assembly has indicated an impotent institution; this is one reason why female representation initially fell after the end of communism. The short sessions of communist assemblies (typically around ten days a year) were dominated by the party, which used them to outline past successes and future targets. Standing ovations were written into the script; free debate was written out.

As communist regimes became somewhat more pluralistic in their later decades, so legislatures acquired a measure of autonomy. China illustrates this trend. In the twelve years before Mao Zedong's death in 1976, the National People's Congress (NPC) did not even meet. However, in the subsequent era of economic reform, the NPC began to flourish. A growing emphasis on the rule of law raised the status of the legislature which has also begun to express popular hostility to corruption. Many votes are no longer unanimous. Senior figures drafted into the assembly skilfully strengthened the NPC's position in Chinese politics, not by confrontation with the ruling party but by assisting the transition to a market economy and by making efforts to encourage national integration through links with subnational congresses. The number of support staff has increased, raising the Congress's professionalism (O'Brien, 1990).

However the NPC, still the world's largest legislature, remains strongly hierarchical in its internal functioning. Plenary sessions remain formal and infrequent. More than in any democracy, legislative influence operates through small subgroups of senior figures. These subgroups remain sensitive to the party's interests. As with Chinese politics generally, authority within the NPC is focused on a few senior figures, not on the institution as a whole. In short, the NPC has become part of the Chinese power network but even today its position cannot be understood through the Western notion of the separation of powers (Xia, 1999).

Key reading

Next step: *Norton (1990a) is a helpful introduction, drawing together some classic writings on legislatures.*

Olson (1994) offers a useful comparative treatment of parliaments. Bicameralism and second chambers have attracted a flurry of interest: see Tsebelis and Money (1997), Patterson and Mughan (1999), Russell (2000a) and the special issue of the *Journal of Legislative Studies* (Vol. 7, 2001). Committees are examined comparatively in Longley and Davidson (1998). Best and Cotta (2000) provide a comparative treatment of long-term changes in parliamentary careers. For studies of assemblies in specific regions see Norton (1998) on Western Europe, Morgenstern and Nacif (2002) on Latin America, Baaklini *et al.* (1999) on the Arab world and Norton and Ahmed (1999) on Asia. Judge and Earnshaw (2003) survey the European Parliament. The most intensively studied legislature remains the American Congress: Dodd and Oppenheimer (2001) is a useful collection. For comparative studies of assemblies in democratic transitions see Liebert and Cotta (1990) on Southern Europe and Kopecky (2003) on Central and Eastern Europe.

Chapter 15

The political executive

The political executive is the core of government, consisting of political leaders who form the top slice of the administration: presidents and ministers, prime ministers and cabinets. The executive is the regime's energizing force, setting priorities, making decisions and supervising their implementation. Governing without an assembly or judiciary is perfectly feasible but ruling without an executive is impossible.

The political executive, which makes policy, must be distinguished from the bureaucracy, which puts policy into effect. Unlike appointed officials, the members of the executive are chosen by political means, most often by election, and can be removed by the same method. The executive is accountable for all the activities of government; it is where the buck stops.

> **Definition**
> The **political executive** forms the top tier of government. It directs the nation's affairs, supervises the execution of policy, mobilizes support for its goals and offers crisis leadership.

The categories of democracy and authoritarian rule are defined by how the executive operates. Established democracies have succeeded in the delicate task of subjecting executive power to constitutional limits. These restrain the exercise of power and set out rules of succession to executive office. Both in theory and in practice, political leaders in liberal democracies are accountable for their conduct. In an authoritarian regime, by contrast, constitutional and electoral controls are either unacknowledged or ineffective. The scope of the executive is limited by political realities but not by the constitution.

In established democracies, executives fall into three main groups: presidential, parliamentary and semi-presidential. We examine each in turn before considering the executive in new democracies and in authoritarian states.

Presidential government

The world contains many presidents but few examples of presidential government. Any tin-pot dictator can style himself 'president' and many do so. However, the existence of a self-styled president is an inadequate sign of a presidential system.

Presidentialism proper is a form of constitutional rule in which the chief executive governs using the authority derived from direct election, with an independent legislature (Figure 15.1). Because both president and legislature are elected for a fixed term, neither can bring down the other, giving each institution some autonomy. This separation of powers is the hallmark of the presidential system and is typically reinforced by a separation of personnel. Members of the executive cannot sit in the assembly, creating further distance between the two institutions. Similarly, legislators must resign their seats if they wish to serve in the government, limiting the president's ability to buy congressional votes with the promise of jobs.

Contrasting methods of election yield a further divergence in interests: legislators depend only on the support of voters in their home district or state while the president – and the president only – is elected by national ballot.

In essence, then, presidential government divides power against itself. It sets up a requirement for the executive to negotiate with the legislature and, by this mechanism, seeks to ensure that deliberation triumphs over dictatorship. Defenders of the system argue that it captures the essence of

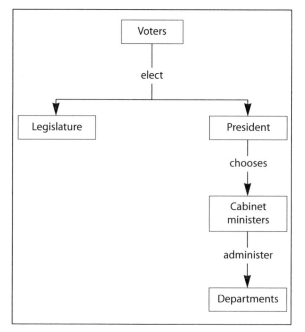

Figure 15.1 Presidential government

democracy, setting constitutional limits on executive power. However, detractors suggest that presidentialism is a conspiracy against government. The dangers of that deliberation turns into stalemate, that the democratic will is thwarted by excessive fragmentation and that the system itself becomes unstable.

Definition

Presidential government consists of three features:

▶ popular election of the president who directs the government and makes appointments to it

▶ fixed terms of offices for the president and the assembly, neither of which can bring down the other

▶ no overlap in membership between the executive and the legislature.

Presidential government predominates in the Americas. To understand the system, we must begin with the United States, where the format first emerged. We will then take Brazil as a contrast to the American case.

The United States

When the framers of the American constitution met in Philadelphia in 1787, they found that the issue of the executive created a dilemma. On the one hand, the Founding Fathers wanted to avoid anything that might prove to be a 'foetus of monarchy'. After all, the American revolution had just rid the new nation of England's George III. On the other hand, the delegates also agreed with Alexander Hamilton that a single executive was needed for 'decision, activity, secrecy and despatch'. The founders decided on the presidency, an office that could provide prompt action for a republic in which Congress was nonetheless expected to play the leading role.

But how should the president be selected? Here the delegates were less clear. One possibility was to allow the national legislature to choose the chief executive. A subcommittee of the constitutional convention did canvass this possibility, which would have led to some form of parliamentary government. But the idea that the executive should be beholden to the assembly was not yet established, even in Britain. Had it been so, the convention could well have plumped for this method of appointment.

Instead, rather late in the proceedings, the delegates settled on selecting the president through an electoral college appointed by state legislatures. Without realizing the implications, the framers had stumbled across the essential feature of presidential government: separate election of executive and legislature (Dahl, 2001).

The constitution tersely states that 'the Executive Power shall be vested in a President of the United States'. He (and so far all have been men) is chosen by popular election, operating through what has become a nominal electoral college, for a four-year term. Under a constitutional amendment of 1951, presidents are limited to two terms of office though this has not prevented several former presidents from playing an active role in public affairs (Schaller and Williams, 2003).

A vice-president serves as stand-by: a raven of death just a heartbeat away from the White House. Historically, he (and again all have been men thus far) has a one in three chance of moving on to the higher office. Presidential candidates select their own running-mate for the election and voters now express support for a vice-presidential candidate in the same way as they choose between the candidates for the senior post.

The president may only be dismissed by Congress through 'Impeachment for, and on Conviction of, Treason, Bribery, or other high Crimes and Misdemeanors'. So far, just two – including Bill Clinton in 1998 – have been impeached. Just as Congress cannot normally remove the president, neither can the president dissolve Congress and call new elections. The executive and the legislature are elected separately and survive independently until the next election.

Although the American presidency is often seen as a symbol of power, the institution was designed as part of a concerted attempt to control executive pretension. The small print of the constitution hems in the office with restrictions:

▶ The president is commander-in-chief but Congress retains the power to declare war.
▶ The president can make government appointments and sign treaties but only with Senate approval.
▶ The president 'recommends to Congress such measures as he shall judge necessary and expedient' but is offered no means to ensure his proposals are accepted.
▶ The president can veto legislation but Congress can override his objections.
▶ Congress, not the president, controls the purse strings.

President Kennedy summarized the peculiar ambivalence of the office:

The president is rightly described as a man of extraordinary powers. Yet it is also true that he must wield those powers under extraordinary limitations.

Two points flow from the president's constitutional position. First, to describe the relationship between the president and Congress as a 'separation of powers' is misleading. In reality there is a separation of institutions rather than of legislative and executive powers. President and Congress share power: each seeks to influence the other but neither is in any position to dictate. This separated system, as C. Jones (1994) calls it, is subtle, intricate and balanced. It reflects a successful attempt by the founders to build checks and balances into American government.

This tension within the system, it is important to note, continues even when one party controls both the White House and the Congress. As Mayhew observes in *Divided We Govern* (1991, p. 135), 'to suppose that an American party winning Congress and the presidency thereby wins the leeway of a British governing party is to be deluded by the election returns'. Whatever their party, members of Congress have different electoral interests from the president. They are elected without term limits from local areas for distinct terms of two years in the House and six years in the Senate (Box 15.1).

Second, in a system of shared control presidential power becomes the power to persuade (Neustadt, 1991). As President Truman said, 'the principal power that the president has is to bring people in and try to persuade them to do what they ought to do without persuasion'. In this task of persuasion, the president can take two routes, best followed simultaneously: going Washington and going public (Rose, 2000).

Going Washington involves the president in wheeling and dealing with Congress and its members, assembling majorities for his legislative proposals. Hence the saying that the president is the nation's most important lobbyist. Lyndon Johnson, a former leader of the Senate Democrats who succeeded to the presidency following President Kennedy's assassination in 1963, was a master of this strategy. Johnson was, however, less successful with the wider public, eventually deciding not to seek reelection in 1968 when the Vietnam War was at its height.

Going public means that the president exploits his unrivalled access to the mass media to influence public opinion and so persuade Washington indirectly. 'The great communicator' Ronald Reagan (President, 1981–89) adopted this approach with great success. In addition, though, Reagan ensured his senior aides kept in close touch with key members of Congress; in effect, his was a dual strategy.

BOX 15.1
Separate elections in the United States

	Electoral unit	Length of term	Limit on reelection
Presidency	A national vote, aggregated by state in an electoral college	4 years	Maximum of two terms
Senate	Direct popular vote in each of 50 states	6 years	No limits
House of Representatives	Direct popular vote in each of 435 districts	2 years	No limits

---

The paradox of the American presidency – a weak governing position amid the trappings of omnipotence – is reflected in the president's support network. To meet presidential needs for information and advice, a conglomeration of supporting bodies has evolved. Collectively known as the Executive Office of the President, these bodies provide far more direct support than is available to the prime minister in any parliamentary system.

Yet this apparatus of advice has often proved to be a weakness. Many advisers are political outsiders, appointed by the president at the start of his tenure before his eye for Washington's politics is in. Far from helping the president, advisers sometimes end up undermining his position. The Watergate scandal in the 1970s destroyed the presidency of Richard Nixon; the Iran-Contra scandal in the 1980s lay siege to the reputation of Ronald Reagan.

One problem is that the presidential system lacks a strong cabinet to offer a counterbalance to personal advisers. In the USA, the cabinet goes unmentioned in the constitution and meetings are little more than a presidential photo-opportunity. Cabinet members often experience difficulty in gaining access to the president through his thicket of advisers. For more than any prime minister, the president stands alone.

Brazil

With democracy – of an illiberal kind – now established in parts of Latin America, students of presidential government can broaden their hori-zons beyond the USA. The Latin American experience confirms that presidents often face considerable difficulty in securing legislative support for their programme, even when the constitution appears more favourable to the executive than in the United States (Mainwaring and Shugart, 1997b).

A comparison between Brazil and the USA is particularly useful. These are two large and populous former colonies though Brazil is a much poorer and far more unequal country. Both countries are federations with strongly bicameral legislatures. Brazil's political difficulties are the more recent; the military only withdrew from power in 1985 and the current constitution dates from 1988 (Martínez-Lara, 1996).

Where the American president is hemmed in with restrictions, the Brazilian constitution seems to offer the country's president an arsenal of weapons in dealing with Congress (Box 15.2). In many areas, the Brazilian president can issue decrees: provisional regulations with the force of law. These stay in effect for 60 days without parliamentary approval and can be renewed once. He can declare bills to be urgent, forcing Congress to make a prompt decision on these proposals. He – and in some areas he alone – can initiate bills in Congress. And the president proposes a budget which goes into effect, month by month, if Congress does not pass a budget itself.

Yet despite their panoply of formal powers, Brazilian presidents face the same problem as their North American colleagues: legislators who know their own mind. Indeed, Brazilian leaders experi-

BOX 15.2
Comparing presidential powers in Brazil and the USA

	Brazil	USA
Can the president issue decrees?	Yes, in many areas. Valid for 60 days, renewable once	No
Can the president initiate bills?	Yes, exclusively so in some areas	No
Can the president declare bills urgent?	Yes	No
Can the president veto legislation?	Yes, in whole and part	Yes
How can Congress override a veto?	Absolute majority in joint meeting of both houses	Two-thirds majority in each house
President's control over the budget	Stronger	Weaker
Party system	Multiparty	Two-party
Does the president's party usually possess a majority in Congress?	No	Sometimes
Party discipline in Congress	Weak	Stronger

Sources for Brazil: Ames (2002), Cox and Morgenstern (2001), Neto (2002).

ence even greater difficulty in bending Congress to their will. The explanation for this contrast lies in Brazil's fragmented multiparty system. In 2002, 19 parties were represented in the Chamber of Deputies and ten in the Senate; as usual, the president's party was in the minority in each chamber. And the interpretation for this difference rests in the electoral system. Where the American Congress is elected using the plurality method, elections to the Brazilian legislature use proportional representation with an open party list.

Furthermore, party discipline within Brazil's Congress is exceptionally weak. Deputies often switch party in mid-term; unlike the country's soccer players, they do not even wait until the end of the season before transferring their loyalties. Deputies are more concerned to obtain resources for their district than to show loyalty to their party. In Brazil, parties are not only more numerous but also less cohesive than in the USA, a contrast which complicates the Brazilian president's task.

Reflecting partisan fragmentation, Brazil's presi-

dents must attempt to build informal coalitions. This requirement takes the form of appointing ministers from a range of parties to the executive in an attempt to extract loyalty from its deputies in Congress. It is as though a Republican president in the United States confronted a hostile Congress and was able to bolster his support by appointing some Democratic congressmen to his cabinet.

In making coalitions, Brazilian presidents are assisted by a more flexible interpretation of the separation of institutions than is found in the USA:

In Brazil, ministers will occasionally resign their government positions just before an important vote in the assembly, resume their legislative seats, vote and then resign their legislative seats and resume their ministerial posts again.
(Cox and Morgenstern, 2002, p. 459)

Thus Brazil shows that presidential government does not need to be single-party government. Rather, presidents rely on a multiparty governing

DEBATE

PRESIDENTIAL GOVERNMENT FOR A NEW DEMOCRACY

In the final decades of the twentieth century, many countries emerged from military or communist rule to embrace democracy. Constitution-writers in these new regimes faced the question of whether to adopt a presidential or parliamentary form of government for the new democratic order. The drafters frequently sought advice from political scientists in established democracies. Had we been asked, should we have argued for or against presidential government for these new democracies?

The case for
A presidential system offers the stability which is the first requirement for a new regime. The president's fixed term provides continuity in the executive, avoiding the frequent collapse of governing coalitions to which parliamentary governments are prone. Winning a presidential election requires candidates to develop broad support across the country. Elected by the country at large, the president can then take a national view, rising above the squabbles between minority parties in the assembly.

A president provides a natural symbol for a new order, offering a familiar face for domestic and international audiences alike. The leader can pursue a steady course in foreign policy, free from the volatility which would arise if the executive were directly accountable to a fractious assembly. Since a presidential system necessarily involves a separation of powers, it should also encourage limited government and thereby protect liberty. Remember, finally, that the USA is the world's dominant power and has sustained presidential government for over 200 years; there is surely pragmatic good sense in following No. 1.

The case against
Presidential government is inappropriate for a new democracy because only one party can win the presidency; everyone else loses. All-or-nothing politics is unsuited to a new regime where political trust has still to develop. In addition, fixed terms of office are too inelastic; 'everything is rigid, specified, dated', wrote Bagehot (1867). The deadlock arising when executive

and legislature disagree means that the new political system may be unable to address pressing problems.

There is a danger, too, that presidents will grow too big for their boots: Latin American experience shows that they sometimes seek to amend the constitution so as to continue in office beyond their one- or two-term limit. In particular, a frustrated or ambitious president may turn into a dictator; presidential democracies are more likely to collapse than are parliamentary democracies (Cheibub, 2002). The USA remains the world's only case of stable presidential government over the long term – an exception to admire but not, it seems, to copy.

Presidential government involves betting the country on one person, thus inhibiting the development of the rule of law in new democracies. The risks are altogether too great, leading Lijphart (2000, p. 267) to regard presidentialism 'as a strongly negative feature for the future of democracy'. Prudence mandates a parliamentary system governed by a broad coalition cabinet.

Assessment
In practice, the choices made by new democracies seem to reflect history and geography more than the advice of politics professors. Central European countries such as the Czech Republic and Hungary have adopted the parliamentary form which dominates Western Europe, mindful no doubt of their decision to join the European Union. By contrast, post-military regimes in Latin American countries have drawn on their own political histories, and the presence of the USA to the north, to embrace presidential government. Only time will tell if Latin America has made the right choice.

Further reading: Andrews and Montinola (2004), Linz (1990), Lijphart (2000), Manuel and Cammisa (1999).

coalition as a technique for influencing the legislature. These coalitions are, however, more informal and unstable than the carefully crafted interparty coalitions which characterize parliamentary government in Western Europe.

So Brazilian presidents face in stern form the inherent problem of presidential government: high expectations but no guarantee that they will be able to deliver. The challenge confronting Lula da Silva, elected Brazil's president in 2002 to domestic and international acclaim, was particularly acute. He faced a demanding cocktail of popular expectations resulting from the combination of three factors: an election triumph, a cultural faith in strong leaders and a widespread belief that the state can and should resolve social problems. As leader of the left-wing Workers' Party (PT), Lula was elected on a programme of radical change. He was expected to improve the quality of life of the poor, many of whom were unaware of the practical limits of his authority.

To achieve his political objectives, Lula had to work with an independently-minded legislature in which his own PT, although relatively disciplined, won only a fifth of the seats. He had also to confront free-spending federal governors and international agencies concerned about the government's debt. In his first year in office, the president succeeded in satisfying both the poor and the International Monetary Fund, a rare combination indeed. But Brazil's fragmented political system sets many traps for incoming presidents. In Brazil, as elsewhere in Latin America, many strong men have ended their careers as weak presidents (Hagopian, 2004).

Parliamentary government

Where presidents are separate from the assembly and independently elected, the executive in parliamentary systems is organically linked to the legislature (Figure 15.2). The government emerges from the assembly and can be brought down by a vote of no confidence. By the same token the government can, in most cases, dissolve parliament and call fresh elections. If the paradox of presidentialism is executive weakness amid the appearance of strength, the puzzle of parliamentary govern-

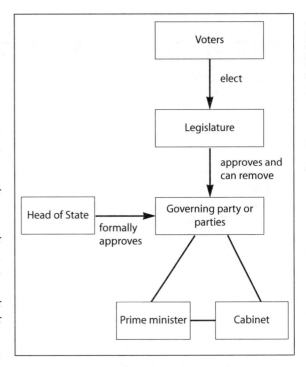

Figure 15.2 Parliamentary government

ment is to explain why effective government can still emerge from this mutual vulnerability of the assembly and the executive.

The crucial influence on the operation of parliamentary government is the party balance in parliament. Where a single party holds a majority in the assembly (as normally in Britain), government can be stable and decisive, perhaps even excessively so. But the British model of single-party majority government, based as it is on a plurality electoral system, is exceptional. Most other European countries employ proportional representation, a system which rarely results in a majority of seats for one party. The usual outcome is a coalition government.

So parliamentary government is as variable in operation as the presidential form. In effect, the parliamentary system has two variants, one based on majority government and the other on coalitions. We will examine these two forms separately before raising two broader questions about the format. How is power in parliamentary government distributed between the prime minister, cabinet and ministers? And where does the head of state fit into the scheme?

Definition

Parliamentary government has three main features:

▶ The governing parties emerge from the assembly. Government ministers are usually drawn from, and remain members of, the legislature.

▶ The head of the government (called prime minister, premier or chancellor) and the council of ministers (usually called the cabinet) can be dismissed from office through a vote of no confidence by parliament. The post of prime minister is normally separate from that of a ceremonial head of state.

▶ The executive is collegial, taking the form of a cabinet in which the prime minister is traditionally just first among equals. This plural executive contrasts with the focus in presidential government on a single chief executive.

Note: In Norway and the Netherlands, ministers are not drawn from the legislature but are accountable to it. Their system of government is still considered to be parliamentary.

Source: Adapted from Lijphart (1992).

Majority government

Britain is the classic example of parliamentary government based on a single party with a secure majority. The plurality method of election used in general elections usually delivers a working majority in the House of Commons to a single party. The leader of this party becomes prime minister (PM), selecting twenty or so parliamentary colleagues from the same party to form the cabinet. The cabinet provides the formal lynchpin of the system; it is the focus of accountability to parliament and even the strongest PM cannot govern without its support. The cabinet meets weekly, chaired by the PM. The monarch now sits above the entire political process, meeting regularly with the PM but rarely if ever intervening in political decisions.

Government accountability to the House of Commons is tight. All ministers, including the PM, must regularly defend their policies 'in the house'; the opposition will demand a vote of no confidence whenever it senses an advantage from launching an attack. However as long as the ruling party retains its majority, this accountability will not threaten the government's survival. So in Britain, the governing party spans the cabinet and the assembly. Through party discipline, the executive dominates the Commons, controlling its agenda and timetable. The cabinet is officially the top committee of state but it is also an unofficial meeting of the party's leaders. As long as senior party figures remain sensitive to the views of their backbenchers (and often even if they do not), they can control the Commons. The government does indeed emerge from its womb in the Commons but it dominates its parent from the moment of its birth.

How is this control achieved? Each party has a Whip's Office to ensure that backbenchers (ordinary MPs) vote as its leaders require. Even without the attentions of the whips, MPs will generally toe the party line if they want to become ministers themselves. In a strong party system such as Britain's, a member who shows too much independence is unlikely to win promotion. In extreme cases, MPs who are thrown out of their party for dissent are unlikely to be reelected by constituents for whom a party label is still key. In short, it is in members' own interests to show public loyalty to their party.

The importance of party to the effective operation of parliamentary government is seen even more clearly in other British-style 'Westminster' systems. In Canada, 'party discipline is conformed to even more rigidly than in the UK' (Brooks, 1996, p. 100). In Australia, a cabinet is more a meeting of the ruling party than of the government; cabinet is captured by party. So where a single party can count upon disciplined majority support in the assembly, as in these Westminster systems, parliamentary government can be decisive, perhaps excessively so.

Minority and coalition government

Most countries using parliamentary government elect their legislature by proportional representation (PR), resulting in a situation where no one party gains a majority of seats. Here the tight link between the election result and government formation weakens. In this more fragmented situation, government takes one of three forms (Müller and Strøm, 2000a):

▶ A *majority coalition* in which two or more parties with a combined majority of seats join together in government. This is the most common form of government across continental Europe; it characterizes Belgium, Finland, Germany and the Netherlands.

▶ A *minority coalition* or alliance. These are formal coalitions or informal alliances between parties which, even together, still lack a parliamentary majority. Minority coalitions have predominated in Denmark since the 1980s. They were also found in First Republic Italy (1947–92).

▶ A *single-party minority government* formed by the largest party. Single-party cabinets comprised about 30 per cent of continental European governments between 1945 and 1999 and are customary in Sweden (where the Social Democratic Party has been preeminent) and Norway.

Custom and practice provide part of the explanation for these contrasts. Once one particular type of government has emerged, this format becomes a point of reference for party leaders after the next election. But the constitution, through both its statements and its silences, is more fundamental. The constitution lays out the hurdles a new government must clear before taking office.

As indicated in Box 15.3, some constitutions demand that the legislature demonstrates majority support for the new government through a formal vote of investiture. Germany and, until 1995, Belgium are examples. This requirement for a positive vote by the assembly encourages broad coalitions.

Since 1975, Sweden has adopted a less stringent test: a vote is held but the test is negative. That is, the prime minister proposed can form a government as long as no more than half of the members of the Riksdag object (Bergman, 2000). However, in other countries the constitution is silent on the procedure for approving a new government. In these circumstances, the new government takes office, and continues in power, until it is voted down by the assembly. Denmark and Norway are examples here. These less demanding conventions facilitate the formation and survival of minority governments, sometimes with the tacit support of other parties.

How then do coalition governments emerge following an election or indeed when a government falls mid-term? What procedure do parties follow in making a coalition? Again, the answer varies. In a few countries, parties state their preferred partners during the election campaign, before the results are known. In Germany and Norway, pre-election coalition statements are an established feature, encouraged in Germany by a mixed electoral system which gives each elector two separate votes (Saalfeld, 2000). When combined with the rather small number of parties represented in the German Bundestag, these pacts simplify post-election coalition formation.

More often, the party composition of govern-

BOX 15.3

Procedure for installing a government in parliamentary systems when no party possesses a majority of seats

Installation procedure	Description	Example
Positive investiture vote	To take office, a new government must obtain majority support in parliament	Germany
Negative investiture vote	A new government takes office unless voted down by a majority in parliament	Sweden
No investiture vote	No formal parliamentary vote is required before a new government takes office	Denmark

ment is decided after the election, through intricate negotiations between the leaders of the relevant parties. While this activity is underway, the outgoing government remains as a caretaker administration, for an average period of 30 days.

Some constitutions specify a procedure which the parties follow in forming, and not merely installing, a government. This usually involves the head of state appointing the largest party, or its leader, as *formateur*. The *formateur*'s task is to form an administration through negotiation (Figure 15.3). The parties agreeing to go into coalition will detail a joint programme in a lengthy public statement. These package deals cover the policies to be pursued and the coalition's rules of conduct: for instance, how it proposes to resolve disputes. Questions of office – which party obtains which ministry and whether that party alone determines the appointment – are also negotiated if not published.

Definitions

A **minimum winning coalition (MWC)** is a government formed by the smallest number of parties (typically two to four) which together can secure a parliamentary majority.
An **oversize coalition** contains more parties than are needed for a MWC.
A **rainbow coalition** is a coalition combining several colours from the ideological spectrum, often red (left-wing) and green (environmental).
A **formateur** is a person or party charged by the head of state with starting negotiations for a coalition. The *formateur* is usually the leader of the party with most seats in parliament.

Further reading: Laver (1996).

Why do some parties end up in a governing coalition while others do not? The most common coalition contains the minimum number of parties needed to make a viable government. Party interest favours minimum winning coalitions since including additional parties in a coalition would simply dilute the number of government posts obtained by each of the participating parties.

In addition, coalitions are usually based on parties with adjacent positions on the ideological spectrum. In most Scandinavian countries, coali-

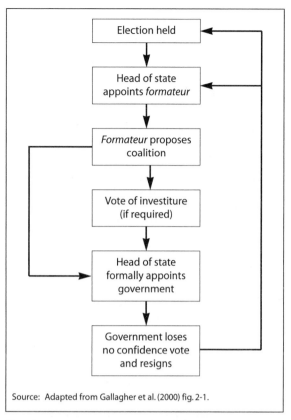

Source: Adapted from Gallagher et al. (2000) fig. 2-1.

Figure 15.3 Formateurs and coalition governments

tions draw only from parties within one of the two bloc: the bloc on the left, or the bloc on the right. Where such clearly defined blocs do not exist, the preference for policy-connected coalitions benefits pivot or swing parties in the centre which are able to jump either way. In Germany, for instance, the small liberal Free Democrat Party participated in most coalition governments between 1949 and 1998, sometimes with the more conservative Christian Democrats and sometimes with the more left-wing Social Democrats.

Occasionally, coalitions emerge which span the ideological spectrum. An influential example is the five-party rainbow coalition, ranging from the conservative National Coalition to the Left Alliance, which emerged in Finland in 1995 and was renewed in 1999 (Jungar, 2002). One reason why rainbow coalitions are unusual is that they are oversized, exceeding the minimum number of participants needed for a majority.

Coalition governments are frequently condemned as unstable, not least by English-speaking critics of proportional representation (p. 152). How valid is this charge? Certainly, in a few countries government duration has been measured in months rather than years: an average of five months for the French Fourth Republic (1945–58) and of eight months for Italian governments between 1948 and 1989. In these over-cited examples, chronic instability certainly contributed to poor governance.

But in most of contemporary Europe, coalition governments last a good deal longer, typically for around two years (Müller and Strøm, 2000b). Some coalition agreements in the Netherlands (and most in Austria and France) include a clause stating that the partners will call an election if they dissolve the coalition. This election rule, as it is called, gives the partners an incentive to soldier on. Coalitions require compromise over policy and posts but compromise can be a route to stability rather than instability.

Just as formal rules influence government formation, so too can they affect government survival. Two procedures from Germany illustrate this point. First, the constructive vote of no confidence, under which a chancellor's government can only be brought down by electing his successor with majority support, enhances government durability. And second, the chancellor cannot dissolve parliament and call new elections – or, rather, the chancellor can only request the president to dissolve the Bundestag if he has first lost a vote of confidence. More often than not, German coalitions survive the four years until the next scheduled election.

Definition

The constructive vote of no confidence requires an assembly to select a new prime minister in order to dispose of the incumbent. The purpose is to prevent legislatures from acting destructively by bringing down a government without any thought to its successor. The device comes from Germany but has also been adopted in Hungary and Israel.

In any case, a slight modification of the parties in government does not constitute a political earthquake in European countries accustomed to coalitions. When a government loses a vote of confidence mid-session and resigns, normally as a result of a defection of one of the coalition partners, the procedure for forming governments begins anew, often without troubling the voters. Indeed, in Norway the parliament cannot be dissolved during its four-year term. In some countries, many of the same characters will return to power, often to the same ministries, so that continuity is maintained. In Italy, for instance, one government was defeated only for the exact same parties to resume office when no other combination proved to be feasible. Observers accustomed to single-party government often exaggerate the instability associated with installing a new coalition.

Who governs?

Parliamentary government lacks the clear focus of the presidential system on a single chief executive. Rather, it involves a subtle, variable and evolving relationship between the prime minister, the cabinet and government ministers. For advocates of parliamentary government, collective leadership is its key strength, generating more deliberation and so resulting in fewer mistakes than occur under a presidential format. By contrast, critics allege that the emphasis on committee decision-making in parliamentary government yields second-rate compromises and frequent opportunities to pass the buck.

We can distinguish three broad patterns in the organization of top decision-making in parliamentary systems:

▶ *cabinet government:* the cabinet determines overall policy through discussion
▶ *prime ministerial government:* the PM is the dominant figure, dealing directly with individual ministers
▶ *ministerial government:* ministers operate with little direction from the PM or the cabinet.

Finland provides an exceptionally clear case of *cabinet government.* By law, the Finnish State Council is granted extensive decision-making authority. In 1988, for example, it handled 4,472 agenda items in 81 formal sessions (Nousiainen,

1994, p. 91). Both the prime minister and individual ministers are subject to constraints arising from Finland's complex, and now rainbow, coalitions. Prime ministers are little more than chairs of council meetings; individual ministers also find their hands tied by their party and its coalition agreements. The pattern is similar in the Netherlands, where a small cabinet of about 15 ministers meets about twice a week and alters about one in five of the proposals put to it (Andeweg and Irwin, 2002, p. 116).

Germany, by contrast, is an example of *prime ministerial government*, called chancellor democracy in Germany. The guiding principle here is hierarchy rather than collegiality. The Bundestag (lower house) appoints a chancellor, not a party, and accountability to the Bundestag is mainly through the chancellor. He answers to parliament; ministers answer to him. The strong position of Germany's chief executive derives from the constitution (Basic Law). This states that the 'chancellor shall determine, and be responsible for, the general policy guidelines'. So the buck stops with the Chancellor, as it does with the American president.

Prime ministerial government is more likely to emerge when the premier has the capacity to choose and dismiss ministers. In Britain, subject to some constraints of party balance, PMs form a government of their choosing from the talent available in the parliamentary party. Cabinet reshuffles and government restructurings are both within the prime minister's gift. The British cabinet now acts mainly as a ratifying body – an umpire rather than a decision-taker. In Blair's Britain, for example, cabinet meetings rarely last more than an hour; some are over in thirty minutes (Holliday, 2000, p. 89).

Ministerial government arises when ministers operate without extensive direction from either prime minister or cabinet. In Germany, the chancellor sets the guidelines but the constitution goes on to say that 'each Federal Minister shall conduct the affairs of his department autonomously and on his own responsibility'. So Germany operates ministerial government within the framework of Chancellor democracy. Ministerial government emerges when, as in Germany, department heads are appointed for their knowledge of the field and are expected to use their professional experience to shape their ministry's policy. At least until the late 1960s, the Netherlands was another example: 'a banker or economist at Finance, a lawyer at Justice, a farmer or farmer's son at Agriculture' (Andeweg and Irwin, 2002, p. 116).

Ministerial government also emerges in coalitions where parties appoint their own people to head particular ministries. In the Netherlands, the prime minister neither appoints, dismisses nor reshuffles ministers. Cabinet members serve with but certainly not under their 'leader'. In these conditions the premier's status is diminished, with ministers owing more loyalty to the party that appoints them than to the prime minister. The chief executive is neither a chief nor an executive but a skilled conciliator. Similarly, the Italian constitution enjoins collective responsibility of the Council of Ministers to parliament but this has been notably lacking. Especially in the First Republic (1947–92), interdepartmental coordination of policy was notoriously weak as factions within parties – and not just parties themselves – came to own particular ministries.

Trends in parliamentary government

In assessing the balance of power within the parliamentary executive, we must address trends in the relationship between prime minister and cabinet and in the workings of cabinet itself. In view of the fundamental differences between presidential and parliamentary government, we can immediately dismiss the popular thesis that prime ministers are becoming 'presidential' in their powers (Foley, 2000). Given the structural contrasts between the two systems, such a metaphor should be resisted.

However, the broad trend is undoubtedly for prime ministers, both in single-party and coalition governments, to acquire more weight in relation to the cabinet. This tendency reflects three factors: increasing media focus on the premier, the growing international role of the chief executive and the emerging need for policy coordination as governance becomes more complex (King, 1994a).

Two less publicized but equally significant changes have taken place in the operation of the cabinet system. First, the expansion of the cabinet has been contained at around two dozen by introducing the category of non-cabinet ministers. To belong to 'the ministry', to use a New Zealand phrase, no longer guarantees a seat round the cabinet table. In Canada, the same device of non-cabinet ministers has been used to contain a cabinet which had reached the unwieldy size of 40 by 1987.

Definition

Cabinet committees are small workgroups of the full cabinet, established to focus on specific areas such as the budget, legislation or overall strategy. In addition to these standing committees, prime ministers also set up ad hoc committees of ministers to respond to specific issues such as labour disputes or terrorist acts. Cabinet committees are much closer to the point of decision than the full cabinet.

Second, cabinet committees have emerged as key decision arenas in larger countries. These committees developed during and after wars, reflecting the volume and urgency of business, and then obtained more formal status in peacetime. New Zealand has around 12 committees, including an influential one that addresses overall strategy. In Australia, decisions made by cabinet committees can only be reopened in full cabinet with the approval of the prime minister.

So cabinet government, to the extent that it still exists, has become government by the cabinet network, with the real decisions merely confirmed in full cabinet. Indeed, even these committees now largely ratify decisions fixed up before the meeting through informal consultations usually led by the minister most directly concerned. The governing capacity of prime ministers now depends on their ability to manipulate the entire network of cabinet committees, not simply the increasingly formal meetings of the full cabinet (Dunleavy, 2003).

Heads of state and parliamentary government

One hallmark of a parliamentary system is, in Bagehot's classic analysis, the distinction between the 'efficient' and 'dignified' aspects of government (Bagehot, 1963). Where presidential systems combine the head of state and the head of government in one person, parliamentary rule separates the two roles. Efficient leadership rests with the cabinet, premier and ministers but dignified or ceremonial leadership lies with the head of state. Such worthy activity does take some pressure off prime ministers, creating more time for them to concentrate on the political aspects of their job.

The position of head of state is either inherited (a monarchy) or elected (a presidency) (Box 15.4). At least in Europe and Asia, royal heads of state remain surprisingly numerous. Half the countries of Western Europe are constitutional monarchies, including Belgium, Denmark, the Netherlands, Spain and the United Kingdom. In some former British colonies such as Canada, a governor-general acts as a stand-in for the monarch.

In a democratic era, monarchs are reluctant to enter the political arena. Yet royal influence can occasionally be significant, especially in times of transition. In the 1970s, King Juan Carlos helped to steer Spain's transition to democracy. More recently, the King of Belgium played a conciliatory role in his country's long march to federal status, leading Senelle (1996, p. 281) to claim that

> were it not for the monarchy as symbol of the cohesion of the kingdom and therefore the visible incarnation of federal loyalty, the Belgian experiment would be doomed to failure.

Monarchies aside, most presidents in parliamentary systems are elected. Sometimes the president is directly elected (e.g. Ireland); in other cases he or she is elected by parliament (e.g. Israel). Alternatively, a special electoral college is used, often comprising the national legislature plus representatives of regional or local government (e.g. Germany).

Elected presidents have a little more latitude than monarchs in addressing national issues (though far less, of course, than presidents in a presidential system). Many presidents in parliamentary systems do occasionally use their public position to nudge the political agenda towards problems receiving inadequate attention or to proposals which run counter to the national interest. For example, in 2003 the Italian President Carlo Ciampi refused to sign into law a media bill which

---

BOX 15.4
Selecting the head of state in some parliamentary democracies

Country	Head of state	Method of selection	Tenure
Austria	President	Direct popular election	6 years
Canada	British monarch*	Heredity	Life#
Germany	President	Election by a joint Bundestag and *Land* convention	5 years
India	President	Election by a college of federal and state assemblies	5 years
Sweden	Monarch	Heredity	Life#
United Kingdom	Monarch	Heredity	Life#

* Represented in Canada by a governor general appointed for five years by the monarch on a recommendation from Canada's prime minister.
# Or until abdication.

---

would have strengthened the commercial interests of the country's Prime Minister, Silvio Berlusconi. Such presidential decisions can earn respect as long as they are rare and based on an assessment of the national interest. But presidents must be careful to speak for the nation as a whole.

Semi-presidential government

Presidential and parliamentary government provide the pure models of the political executive. The semi-presidential executive draws on both formats, combining an elected president with a prime minister and cabinet accountable to parliament. So with semi-presidential government we enter more varied territory. The French political scientist Maurice Duverger (1980) provided the classic definition:

A political regime is considered semi-presidential if the constitution which established it combines three elements: (1) the president of the republic is elected by universal suffrage; (2) he possesses quite considerable powers; (3) he has opposite him, however, a prime minister and ministers who possess executive and governmental power and can stay in office only if the parliament does not show its opposition to them.

Thus, the semi-presidential executive is a hybrid, seeking to marry within the executive the national focus of an elected president with a prime minister responsive to the interests represented in the assembly (Figure 15.4). The president in such a system usually has special responsibility for foreign affairs, can appoint ministers (including the prime minister), initiate referendums, veto legislation and dissolve the assembly. In theory, the president can offer leadership on foreign affairs while the prime minister addresses the intricacies of domestic politics through parliament.

The president in a semi-presidential executive is *in* rather than *above* politics. As a two-headed system, the semi-presidential executive creates a division of authority within the executive and, for that reason, an invitation to struggle between president and prime minister.

If the United States exemplifies the presidential system, the French Fifth Republic (1958–) provides the model for the semi-presidential executive. The 1958 constitution was designed to provide stable governance in the context of a divisive war in Algeria and the legacy of the unstable Fourth Republic, which experienced 23 prime ministers in its 12-year life.

The new constitution created a presidency fit for the dominating presence of its first occupant, General Charles de Gaulle. Regarding himself as

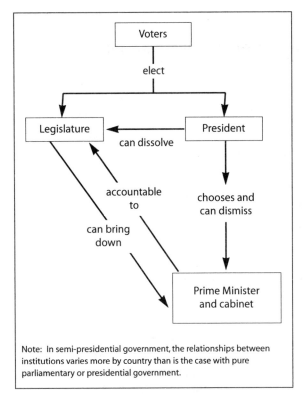

Note: In semi-presidential government, the relationships between institutions varies more by country than is the case with pure parliamentary or presidential government.

Figure 15.4 Semi-presidential government

national saviour, de Gaulle argued that 'power emanates directly from the people, which implies that the head of state, elected by the nation, is the source and holder of that power' (Knapp and Wright, 2001, p. 53). In office, de Gaulle's imperious style developed the office to – perhaps even beyond – its constitutional limits.

Definition

Semi-presidential government, sometimes called the dual executive or premier-presidentialism, combines an elected president performing political tasks with a prime minister who heads a cabinet accountable to parliament. The prime minister, usually appointed by the president, is responsible for day-to-day domestic government but the president retains an oversight role, responsibility for foreign affairs and can usually take emergency powers. The Fifth French Republic is the leading example (Shugart and Carey, 1992).

Following a constitutional amendment in 1962, the president has been directly elected, fully establishing the semi-presidential format (Elgie, 1999a). The effect of the amendment, it is argued, was to create a powerful presidency where previously there had just been a powerful president. In a further amendment in 2000, the presidential term was reduced from a renewable seven years to a renewable five years.

The constitution certainly grants the French president extensive powers. He (and as in the USA all so far have been men)

▶ is guarantor of national independence and the constitution
▶ can take emergency powers (not invoked since 1961)
▶ heads the armed forces and chairs the main defence committee
▶ negotiates treaties
▶ can call referendums (nine so far)
▶ appoints some senior judges and civil servants
▶ presides over the Council of Ministers
▶ can dissolve the assembly (but not veto legislation)
▶ formally appoints the prime minister, in practice from the party winning assembly elections.

In pursuing these roles, the president is supported by an influential personal staff in the Élysée Palace. So far, all five presidents have sought to govern in expansive style, seeking to pilot the ship of state rather than just to arbitrate conflicts emerging from below decks.

What of prime ministers in France's semi-presidential executive? Their main concern is domestic affairs, casually dismissed by de Gaulle as 'the price of milk'. Appointed by the president but accountable to parliament, the prime minister's task is rarely simple. He or she (Edith Cresson was PM 1991–92) directs the day-to-day work of the government, operating within the president's style and tone. Since the government remains accountable to parliament, much of the prime minister's work focuses on managing the National Assembly. The ability of the assembly to force the prime minister and the Council of Ministers to resign after a vote of censure provides the parliamentary component of the semi-presidential executive.

Profile FRANCE

Population: 59m.
Gross domestic product per head: $22,600.
Form of government: a unitary democratic republic, headed by an elected president. The current Fifth Republic was established in 1958.
Legislature: the lower chamber, the National Assembly, contains 577 directly elected members. The 321 members of the Senate are indirectly elected, a third at a time, through local government for a long nine-year term. The legislature is weaker than in many democracies.

Executive: France's semi-presidential executive combines a strong president, directly elected for five years, with a prime minister who leads a Council of Ministers accountable to the assembly.
Judiciary: French law is still based on the Napoleonic Codes (1804–11). The Constitutional Court has grown in significance during the Fifth Republic.
Electoral system: a two-ballot system is used for both presidential and assembly elections, with a majority vote needed for victory on the first round. The last experiment with PR was in 1986 for the National Assembly.

Party system: left–right conflict remains a principle of French politics, though parties themselves have been less stable. But the exceptional presidential election of 2002 failed to deliver the customary choice between safe candidates of the left and the right. Rather, Jacques Chirac of the centre right was reelected in a run-off with Jean-Marie Le Pen, leader of the far right Front National. On this occasion, the socialist candidate was defeated in the first round.

Just how different is modern France? The case for French exceptionalism can be stated in three words: the French Revolution. Of course, the shock waves of 1789 reverberated throughout Europe as the destruction of absolute monarchy laid the groundwork for the emergence of modern, secular nation-states. But the revolution created a distinctive ethos within France itself. Like other states built on revolution, notably the United States, France is an ideal as well as a country. But in France the ideals remained contested.

The legacy of the revolution is not just a disputed creed of liberty, equality and fraternity. It is also a widespread belief that the state can and should implement its ideas rationally, even against opposition from a diverse and sometimes antagonistic society. The result, it is claimed, is a state-centred country characterized by haughty bureaucrats, extensive regulation, limited pluralism and a mass political culture which combines dependence on the state with hostility towards it.

Yet French uniqueness certainly declined, and possibly disappeared, in the second half of the twentieth century. The country became more modern, urban and industrial, resulting in a more conventional and consolidated democracy. The country's retreat from empire left France, like Britain, as a middle-ranking power with a new base in the European Union.

France's governing architecture of a semi-presidential executive remains distinctive but it works: policies are formed, decisions are reached. Even the judiciary has acquired some weight. 'The revolutionary impulse is exhausted', concludes Hayward (1994, p. 32). France today seems to be a normal country, preoccupied with the workaday question of maintaining economic growth, full employment and sound government finances.

So contemporary France is certainly no longer a revolutionary society. But to portray France as just another democracy is perhaps to go too far. Inherited traditions still condition the way France approaches its typically European combination of a cosseted workforce, subsidized farmers and considerable but unequal affluence. Public discourse still tends to assume that the state must be capable of both creating new jobs and protecting the rights of existing workers. Dirigisme (state direction), suggests Wright (1997), has evolved rather than disappeared: the government is still prepared to intervene in the economy, albeit in a market-conforming way, when it perceives national interests at stake.

In France, sovereignty is still presented as a cardinal virtue, with the result that globalization is seen as a threat as much as an opportunity. American influences, in particular, are strongly resisted. Even if l'exception française is a myth, it is a legend which remains important to the French way of politics.

Further reading: Knapp and Wright (2001), Schain (2004), Stevens (2003).

> *Definition*
> **Cohabitation** occurs in a semi-presidential executive when president and prime minister are drawn from different political camps. This situation has occurred three times in the French Fifth Republic. Cohabitation intensifies competition between the two principals and places the president in the awkward position of leading both the nation and the opposition.

The crucial relationship in the semi-presidential executive is between the president, on the one hand, and prime minister and assembly, on the other. While the constitution may give control of foreign affairs to the president and reserve domestic policy to the prime minister, an interdependent world does not permit such pigeonholing. France's relationship with the EU, for instance, encompasses both foreign and domestic affairs, complicating the decision-making process. Before one EU summit, Germany's chancellor insisted on meeting the French president and prime minister together, to speed negotiations.

Presidents and prime ministers therefore need to work in harmony, a task made easier when the party in the Elysée Palace also has a majority in the assembly. This has been the case for most of the Fifth Republic. Indeed, the reduction of the president's term to five years was partly an attempt to coordinate presidential and parliamentary election terms, limiting the likelihood of cohabitation.

When cohabitation does occur, as it has done three times since 1986, presidential power tends to shrink. In these circumstances, prime ministers assert their constitutional duty to 'determine and direct the policy of the nation'. Crucially, though, cohabitation has not led to a crisis of the regime. The Fifth Republic has delivered the stability that its architects intended. Just as the United States copes with power divided between the White House and Congress, so the French experience confirms that the semi-presidential executive can provide stable government even when president and prime minister are drawn from different political blocs.

Semi-presidential government has held particular appeal to European countries facing international difficulties. France adopted a semi-presidential solution in 1962 following serious unrest in its Algerian colony. Finland found a semi-presidential system helpful in managing its sensitive relationship with its large Russian neighbour. And a dual executive also proved attractive to Central European states in the immediate aftermath of communism's collapse.

As international pressures recede, however, so the president's star in this format of government tends to wane. In 2000, France reduced the president's tenure from seven years to five. In the same year, Finland modified its constitution to strengthen the parliamentary element (Nousiainen, 2001). Further, some post-communist countries, such as Hungary, have moved away from semi-presidentialism into a parliamentary form. The semi-presidential executive is more than a transitional device, but the system has not threatened the preeminence of parliamentary government in Europe.

The executive in new democracies

The new democracies established in the final decades of the twentieth century have varied in their choice of presidential or parliamentary government. In general, post-military Latin America has retained presidential systems despite some serious academic prodding in the direction of parliamentary regimes (Linz, 1990). South America's continuing bias to presidential rule, confirmed by a Brazilian referendum in favour of the form in 1993, reflects a fear of social instability and violence in the absence of strong political authority. Presidential rule does not suffice to resolve the underlying tensions of unequal societies but, given the continent's strongman tradition, the presidential option is considered the safer choice.

By contrast, most post-communist democratic states in central Europe have settled on parliamentary government, following a flirtation with semi-presidential systems. In the early years of post-communism, presidential authority was considerable, particularly where the initial incumbents were endowed with the moral authority resulting from leading the revolt against communism, as with Lech Walesa in Poland and Vaclav Havel in the Czech Republic. As with General de Gaulle in France, these post-communist leaders could offer a symbol of stability in difficult times. Fitzmaurice (1998, p. 65) writes,

> There was a need for a presidency that could, in this extraordinary period of political turbulence, represent a centre of stability in shifting and often unstable parliamentary situations. There was also a need for a moral symbol in difficult times and for a respected national representative to the outside world who could be an asset on the European and world stage, especially in the battle for membership of the IMF, Council of Europe, NATO and the EU.

But as these new European democracies have stabilized, so the parliamentary dimension has gained ground. Thus Malovà and Haughton (2002) judge that

> most Central and Eastern European constitutions now have a weak head of state, even where the president is directly elected, who plays mostly a symbolic role and intervenes in politics only in explicitly defined cases to limit institutional conflicts.

Even in Poland, where the president is directly elected (Box 15.5), the new constitution of 1997 softened the president's veto powers. Millard (2003, p. 35) concludes that following these reforms Poland 'could no longer be viewed as a semi-presidential system'.

In post-communist settings, government itself – rather than the society it seeks to control – is deemed to be the danger. Such democracies have sought to contain rather than to concentrate political power but have taken the parliamentary route to this objective. They have adopted proportional representation in order to reflect social and political divisions within parliament. The coalition governments which result, though rarely as coherent or stable as those in Western Europe, do represent some sharing of political authority, at least compared to the communist era.

So, although the experience of post-communist central Europe confirms that the dividing line between semi-presidential and parliamentary government is not always clear, it also demonstrates that parliamentary government remains Europe's natural democratic form.

The executive in authoritarian states

In authoritarian states, formal executive structures – the executive, legislature and the judiciary – are less well-developed than in democracies. The top office may consist of a presidency (as in many civilian regimes) or a ruling council (as in many military regimes) but the central feature of the non-democratic executive is its lack of institutionalization. The leader seeks to focus power on himself and his supporters, not to distribute it among institutions. Jackson and Rosberg's idea of

---

BOX 15.5
Presidential powers in some new Eastern European democracies

	Directly elected?	Nominate PM and dissolve assembly?	Emergency powers?	Authority over foreign and defence policy?	Introduce bills?
Czech Republic	No	Yes	No	No	No
Hungary	No	Yes	Yes	Yes	Yes
Poland	Yes	Yes	No	Yes	Yes
Slovakia	Yes	Yes	No	No	Yes

Source: Adapted from Baylis (1996). See also White et al. (2003).

personal rule (1982), developed in the context of African politics, travels widely through the non-democratic world. Politics takes precedence over government and personalities matter more than institutions: a feast of presidents but a famine of presidential systems.

> **Definition**
> **Personal rule** is defined by Jackson and Rosberg (1982, p. 19) as 'a system of relations linking rulers not with the "public" or even with the ruled but with patrons, associates, clients, supporters and rivals who constitute the "system". The system is "structured" not by institutions but by the politicians themselves. The fact that it is ultimately dependent upon persons rather than institutions is its essential vulnerability.'

The formula of weak institutions plus strong politics is ultimately unconvincing. It results in characteristic ailments, including struggles over succession, insufficient emphasis on policy, poor governance and even a danger of regime collapse. In particular, the lack of a succession procedure (excepting hereditary monarchies) can create a conflict among potential inheritors not just after the leader's exit but also in the run-up to it. Authoritarian leaders keep their job for just as long as they can ward off their rivals. They must mount a constant threat watch and be prepared to neuter those who are becoming too strong. Politics comes before policies.

The price of defeat, furthermore, is high; politics can be a matter of life and death. When an American president leaves office, he can retire to his library to write his memoirs; yet ousted dictators risk a harsher fate. By necessity, the governing style of non-democratic rulers inclines to the ruthless.

We will use post-colonial Africa, the Middle East and post-communist countries in central Asia to illustrate these themes, before turning to the executive under totalitarian rule.

Africa

Until the era of democratization in the 1990s, post-colonial Africa illustrated the weakness of governing institutions and the importance of personal leadership. Leaders were adept at using the coercive and financial resources of the regime to reward their friends and punish their enemies. As Sandbrook (1985) wrote of Mobutu Sese Seko during his long tenure as president of Zaire:

> No potential challenger is permitted to gain a power base. Mobutu's officials know that their jobs depend solely on the president's discretion. Frequently, Mobutu fires cabinet ministers, often without explanation. Everyone is kept off balance. Everyone must vie for his patronage.

In post-colonial Africa, as in most authoritarian states, personal rule was far from absolute. Inadequately accountable in a constitutional sense, many personal rulers were highly constrained by other political actors. These included the military, leaders of ethnic groups, landowners, the business class, the bureaucracy, multinational companies and even factions in the leader's own court. To survive, leaders had to distribute the perks of office so as to maintain a viable coalition of support drawn from these groups. If they made too many false moves in the patronage game, they could find themselves replaced by a more skilful player. These domestic imperatives explain why presidents ignored the preaching of international agencies in favour of a competitive market economy. Presidents preferred to invest in their own political future rather than long-term economic development.

Middle East

In the Middle East, personal rule remains central to authoritarian rule (Bill and Springborg, 2000). In many of these oil-rich kingdoms, shahs, sheikhs and sultans continue to rule in traditional patriarchal style. 'Ruling' rather than 'governing' is the appropriate term. In Saudi Arabia, advancement within the ruling family depends not on merit but on closeness to the family's network of advisers, friends, flatterers and guards. Public and private are not sharply distinguished; each forms part of the ruler's sphere. Again, government posts are not secure but are occupied on good behaviour, as demonstrated by unswerving loyalty to the ruler's interests.

Such systems of personal rule have survived for centuries, limiting the development of strong government institutions. Leaving succession difficulties to one side, the paradox of Middle Eastern politics is that personal rule itself constitutes a stable system, providing an exception to the general theme of instability in the authoritarian executive. It remains to be seen whether September 11, 2001 has inspired America to engage with a project of liberalization and democratization in the Middle East which could seriously threaten this highly traditional order.

Central Asia

Personal rule also characterizes the post-communist states of central Asia such as Kyrgyzstan and Uzbekistan. While central Europe has moved in a democratic direction, many successor republics to the Soviet Union have seen the rise of authoritarian regimes with strong, personalized and barely accountable presidents. In these impoverished and mainly agricultural republics, where democracy has never flourished and experience of independent statehood is limited, rulers are concerned with power and voters with their daily struggle. Neither group cares greatly for structures of government.

In the central Asian republic of Uzbekistan, for example, the presidency is strongly personalized:

> power resides as much in the person of the president as in the office. The Uzbek presidency is not just a formal power position; it is also the center of an extensive informal network of regionally-based, patron–client ties. The president is, in effect, the chief patron.
>
> (Easter, 1997)

The totalitarian executive

We might expect the institutions of government to have played a central role in the totalitarian systems of fascism and communism. After all, these were political regimes par excellence, seeking to lead and transform society. But again, personal rule dominated, at least under fascism.

In fascist thinking, the personal authority of the ruler rather than the institutions of state and party provided the driving force. The state was idolized more than institutionalized and the party was exploited by Hitler and Mussolini as a device for obtaining power. Once power was achieved, state and party merged as personal vehicles of the supreme ruler. The leader defined the interests of the regime and duties owed to the dictator took priority over any obligations to state or party. In Nazi Germany, for example, the notorious SS (*Schutzstaffel*, protection units) began as a party security force but underwent a huge expansion after Hitler came to power, becoming the personal instrument of the Führer (Brooker, 2000, p. 136).

Nazi Germany, less so Mussolini's Italy, was a political, or even a revolutionary, regime in which power bases were established informally with Hitler acting as an arbiter of conflict among the barons beneath. Power was neither contained in institutions nor exercised through bureaucratic rules; had it been, the Führer's personal ascendancy would have been threatened.

The situation differed substantially in communist states. Here, certainly, power was more regularized. However, the party was the driving force, offering political direction to the state. Of course, most communist states did have a clear structure of government. This resembled the parliamentary form (Figure 15.5). A presidium (equivalent to a cabinet) was headed by a chairperson (prime minister). This presidium was, in turn, an inner steering body of a larger Council of Ministers which was itself formally 'elected' by the parliament. An honorific post of state president also existed.

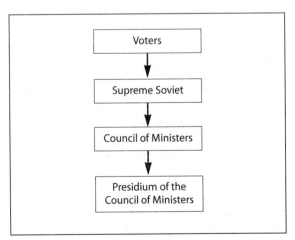

Figure 15.5 Typical executive structure in communist states

But in practice the ruling communist party dominated the formal institutions of the state; the key post was general secretary of the party, not chairman of the presidium. The party secretary often confirmed his supremacy by taking a state post, whether prime minister or president. However, power remained rooted in the party; if the top leader lost his position as party secretary, he was politically doomed.

China offers a partial exception to this picture of the communist executive. Chinese politics has always been more fluid and personal than in other communist states; some past leaders have not occupied any formal positions at all, whether in the party or the government. As is customary in communist countries, the state is led by the party. But the party itself is divided into factions based on personality and patronage more than policy. It is these factions within the party which provide the glue of politics, binding the actors together in a predictable but non-institutionalized way.

In China's factional environment, the top figure requires cunning and patronage to prosper. Indeed, China confirms that even this massive communist state can be ruled in a highly personal way. As Saich (2004, p. 83) observes,

> Personal power and relations with powerful individuals are decisive throughout the Chinese political system. While this may decline as reforms become more insitutionalized, most Chinese recognize that the best way to survive and flourish is to develop personal relationships (*guanxi*) with a powerful political patron.

Authoritarian rule and despotism

The personal basis of rule in many non-democratic regimes poses an important question: are such states are always likely to degenerate into despotism and even barbarism? Are the murderous excesses of twentieth-century dictators an inherent risk of failing to subject power to constitutional limits?

Certainly, some communist states fell victim to brutal tyranny, despite – or because of? – the strong organization provided by the communist party. The Soviet Union under Joseph Stalin was an extreme but important example. After Lenin's death in 1924, Stalin slowly acquired ascendancy over the party. He methodically picked off the other party leaders, becoming undisputed ruler of the Soviet Union by 1929 and remaining so until his death in 1953. Having risen to power through the party, he eventually reshaped it into one of his personal instruments, alongside the political police and the state bureaucracy.

Stalin's methods were fierce indeed:

> In the Great Terror of 1937–38, the political police arrested some five million people, executed over 800,000 of them and incarcerated most of the remainder in prisons or labour camps. Among the victims were a large majority of the party's Central Committee and more than half the delegates to the most recent Party Congress. The Terror destroyed the party as an independent political entity; it was now officially described as a party of Lenin-Stalin followers.
>
> (Brooker, 2000, p. 138)

One-man rule and extreme leadership cults were features of many other communist states. Examples include Mao Zedong in China, Castro in Cuba, Ho Chi Minh in Vietnam, Tito in Yugoslavia, Ceaucescu in Romania and Kim Il Sung in North Korea. And such cults of personality were often linked with extreme brutality, albeit rarely on the scale of Stalin's Russia.

But not all totalitarian, and still less all authoritarian, regimes descended into barbarity. After all, Stalin drew not just on communist ideology and party organization but also on Russia's highly autocratic history. Elsewhere, communist rule was less severe. In Eastern Europe, rulers in late communism sought to soften the harshness of Soviet domination. Some national leaders were anonymous party functionaries. Janos Kadar, the harmless leader of Hungary between 1958 and 1988, rode the tramcar to work each day, unrecognized by his people. The communist experience suggests that personal despotism is far from an inevitable consequence of authoritarian rule.

In any case, many non-communist authoritarian rulers have lacked the means of social control needed to indulge in Stalinist terror. The experience of black Africa and the Middle East is that personal rule is usually far from despotic. It can be a balanced and stable, if rarely progressive, form of governance.

Key reading

> **Next step:** *Lijphart (1992) remains an excellent collection on parliamentary and presidential government.*

Much recent work on executive institutions has focused on presidential government (including Latin America): for instance, Linz and Valenzuela (1994), Mainwaring and Shugart (1997b) and Shugart and Carey (1992). On semi-presidential government, the original source is Duverger (1980); Elgie (1999b) provides a more recent perspective. On the American presidency, see Rose (2000) and the classic study by Neustadt (1991). Comparative but contrasting studies of parliamentary government include Laver and Shepsle (1994) and Müller and Strøm (2000a). For comparative studies of prime ministers see Wright *et al.* (2000); Rose (2001) examines the British prime minister in an interdependent world. The executive in postcommunist Europe is covered in White *et al.* (2003). On personal rule, Jackson and Rosberg (1982) is the classic analysis, using African examples; Bill and Springborg (2000) examine the Middle East. Brooker (1995) assesses twentieth-century dictatorships.

The bureaucracy

The bureaucracy is the state's engine room. It consists of permanent salaried officials employed by the state to advise on, and carry out, the policies of the political executive. The bureaucracy is indispensable to modern government yet, lacking the legitimacy of election, it has always aroused controversy. The central strands of this debate are responsiveness and efficiency. On responsiveness, the question is: how can civil servants be made accountable to the politicians they notionally serve? And on effectiveness, the issue is: how in the absence of a competitive market can we ensure that the bureaucracy does its job with efficiency and economy? This theme of value for money became particularly prominent in the era of lean government in the 1990s.

Delimiting the bureaucracy raises tricky issues of definition. Reflecting the complexity of modern government, public employees have a range of employment relationships with the state (Figure 16.1). The broadest term is the *public sector,* also called the public service or public administration.

This covers all employees whose salary comes directly or indirectly from the public purse. However, the public sector includes several areas not normally counted as part of the civil service, such as teachers and the armed forces. *Civil servants* proper are usually defined as employees who are

▶ paid directly by the national exchequer
▶ subject to the state's conditions of service (including access to its pension scheme)
▶ engaged in shaping or more commonly implementing government decisions.

Just to complicate matters, a few countries such as Germany do extend civil service status to teachers, even though this group works at one remove from the government.

Definition
Bureaucracy is, literally, rule by officials. The word 'bureau' comes from the Old French term *burel,* meaning the cloth used to cover a writing desk or bureau. The second half of the word comes from the Greek *kratos,* meaning rule, just as in democracy. Today, the bureaucracy refers to the salaried officials who conduct the detailed business of public administration, advising on and applying policy decisions.

The number of civil servants with a direct *policy-advising role,* the group of special political interest, is no more than a few thousand. This is because most civil servants work in the field, applying policy away from the decision-making centre. Traditionally, the 'mandarins' (to use the old Chinese term for high-level bureaucrats) formed a special grade in the civil service, often filled by able graduates recruited straight from university. However, some countries have now introduced more flexible practices at this highest level, making more use of short-term contracts and open recruit-

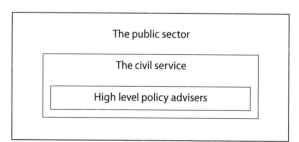

Figure 16.1 Delimiting the bureaucracy

ment. Examples include the Senior Executive Services established in the United States (1978), Australia (1984) and New Zealand (1988).

While the word 'bureaucracy' is often used descriptively as a synonym for the civil service, it is also employed in a more abstract way as a model for organizing public administration. The analysis of bureaucracy presented by the German sociologist Max Weber (1864–1920) is preeminent here; it is an important model to examine. Weber conceived of bureaucracy as a structured hierarchy in which salaried officials reached rational decisions by applying explicit rules to the facts before them. Specifically, Weber's model contains the following features:

▶ Bureaucracy involves a carefully defined division of tasks.
▶ Authority is impersonal, vested in the rules that govern official business. Decisions are reached by methodically applying rules to particular cases; private motives are irrelevant.
▶ People are recruited to serve in the bureaucracy based on proven or at least potential competence.
▶ Officials who perform their duties competently have secure jobs and salaries. Competent officials can expect promotion according to seniority or merit.
▶ The bureaucracy is a disciplined hierarchy in which officials are subject to the authority of their superior.

Weber's central claim was that bureaucracy made administration more efficient and rational; he believed that it was the means by which modern industrial efficiency could be brought to bear on civil affairs. To quote Weber himself:

the fully developed bureaucratic apparatus compares with other organizations exactly as does the machine with non-mechanical modes of production. Precision, speed, clarity, knowledge of files, continuity, discretion, unity, strict subordination, reduction of friction and of material and personal costs – these are raised to the optimum in the strictly bureaucratic administration.

(Gerth and Mills, 1948)

For Weber, the ideal bureaucracy was a fine piece of administrative machinery. But like many modern devices, bureaucracy brought the risk of dominating its supposed masters. Weber's contribution was therefore to pose the question of the relationship between bureaucracy and democracy, a concern that inspired much discussion in the twentieth century.

Evolution

To appreciate why Weber considered modern bureaucracy so efficient, we must consider what preceded it. As with other aspects of government, the precursors varied between Europe and the New World. In Europe, clerical servants were originally agents of the royal household, serving under the personal instruction of the ruling monarch (Raadschelders and Rutgers, 1996). Many features of modern bureaucracies – regular salaries, pensions, open recruitment – arose from a successful attempt to overcome this idea of public employment as personal service to the monarch. Indeed, the evolution of royal households into twentieth-century Weberian bureaucracies was a massive transformation, intimately linked to the rise of the modern state itself. It was a transition from patriarchy to bureaucracy, a story of the depersonalization of administration as the royal household was slowly converted into public service (Hyden, 1997, p. 243). Today, we take the features of bureaucratic organization for granted but for Weber the form was strikingly new, a modern phenomenon to be both admired and feared.

In the New World, however, civil service development was more pragmatic. Lacking the long state tradition of West Europe, public administration was initially considered a routine application of political directives. In the United States, the original philosophy was that almost every citizen was qualified for almost every public job; indeed, a professional civil service was considered somewhat undemocratic (Christensen and Peters, 1999, p. 100). This populist theory conveniently underpinned the spoils system, a term deriving from the phrase 'to the victor, the spoils'. Spoils meant that successful candidates, including newly-elected presidents, were expected to distribute government jobs to those with the foresight to support the winning candidate. The spoils system continued at least until 1883 when the Pendleton Act created a Civil Service Commission to recruit and regulate federal employees. So where a merit-based bureaucracy had emerged in Europe in reaction to monarchy, in the USA a professional administration supplanted spoils.

In the twentieth century, bureaucracies reached their zenith. The depression and two world wars vastly increased government intervention in society. The welfare state, completed in Europe in the decades following the Second World War, required a massive Weberian bureaucracy to distribute grants, allowances and pensions in accordance with complex eligibility conditions set by politicians. By 1980, public employment accounted for almost a third of the total workforce in Britain and Scandinavia, though much of the expansion had occurred at local level.

However, the final quarter of the twentieth century witnessed declining faith in government and, more to the point, deteriorating public finances. Seizing on this fiscal crisis, right-wing politicians such as Ronald Reagan and Margaret Thatcher called for, and to an extent delivered, not just a reduced role for the state but also a changing style of bureaucratic operation away from strict Weberian guidelines. As a result, the contemporary emphasis is on management, results and efficiency. At the start of the twenty-first century, modern civil servants therefore face conflicting expectations. At one and the same time, they are expected to show flexibility but also to abide by rules; to deliver results but also to work within set procedures; and to act decisively while also consulting widely.

Recruitment

Recruitment to bureaucracies has evolved in tandem with the development of the civil service itself. The shift from patrimonial to Weberian bureaucracies was a transition from recruitment by personal links with the ruler to open selection on merit. Jobs became available, at least in theory, to the whole population. Even though these reforms occurred in most democracies as long ago as the

late nineteenth century, recruitment to the civil service remains an important theme. Selection methods and employee profiles are scrutinized more carefully than in the private sector. Further, what counts as 'merit' still varies between countries, revealing subtle contrasts in conceptions of a civil servant's role.

Britain exemplifies a unified (or generalist) tradition. Indeed, it pushes the cult of the amateur to extremes. Administration is seen as the art of judgement, born of intelligence and honed by experience. Specialist knowledge should be sought by bureaucrats but then treated with scepticism; experts should be on tap but not on top. Recruiters look for general ability, not technical expertise. All-round ability should enable successful candidates to acquire or at least interpret whatever technical knowledge is needed; the key requirement is not knowledge but the ability to learn. For the same reason, a good administrator should be able to serve in a variety of departments and will be more rounded for doing so.

Definition

In a **unified** (or **generalist**) bureaucracy, recruitment is to the civil service as a whole, not to a specific job within it. Administrative work is conceived as requiring intelligence, education and appropriate personal skills but not technical knowledge. By contrast, a **departmental** (or **specialist**) approach recruits people with technical backgrounds to a specific department or job. Unified bureaucracies are career-based while departmental civil services are job-based.

An alternative method of pursuing the unified approach is to recruit to a *corps* (body) of civil servants rather than to a specific job in a ministry. The French civil service, for example, recruits civil service through competitive examinations to such bodies as the Diplomatic Corps or the Finance Inspectorate. Certainly, these *corps* offer their own specialized post-entry training but the seemingly technical basis of this induction is rather misleading. Although civil service recruitment is in theory to a specific *corps*, it is in reality as much to an elite which encompasses both public and private realms. Even within the civil service over a third of *corps* members are working away from their home *corps* at any one time. At its highest levels, the French bureaucracy is clearly generalist albeit with *corps* that provide more of a bow to specialized training than is offered in Britain.

Some unified civil services stress one particular form of technical expertise: law. In many European countries with a codified law tradition, a legal training is common among higher bureaucrats. Germany is a good illustration. Over 60 per cent of top German civil servants are lawyers, compared to just 20 per cent in the United States. The German model has influenced other countries, notably Japan, where the recruitment base is narrower still. Most of those who pass through the 'dragon gate' examination for recruitment to high-level positions in the Japanese civil service are graduates of just one department: Tokyo University's law school. Where law is less central to politics, however, the dominance of legal training has declined as other degrees, such as economics, have achieved recognition. For instance since 1945, the percentage of law graduates among civil servants working in Norway's central ministries has fallen from a half to a fifth (Christensen and Egeberg, 1997).

Definition

The theory of **representative bureaucracy** claims that a civil service recruited from all sections of society will produce policies that are responsive to the public and, in that sense, democratic (Meier, 1993, p. 1). **Passive representation** exists when the demographic profile of the bureaucracy matches that of the population. **Active representation** occurs when civil servants take the same decisions as would be made by the represented – that is, the public.

In a departmental (specialist) system, recruiters follow a different philosophy from Britain's generalist approach or the French *corps*. They look for specialist experts for individual departments, with more movement in and out of the civil service at a variety of levels. The Finance Ministry will recruit economists and the Department of Health will employ staff with medical training. Recruitment is to particular posts, not to an elite civil service or a *corps*. This emphasis on a specific job is common in countries with a weak state in which the admin-

istration lacks the status produced by centuries of service to pre-democratic rulers. The United States, New Zealand and the Netherlands are examples. In the Netherlands, each department sets its own recruitment standards, normally requiring training or expertise in its own area. Once appointed, mobility within the civil service is limited; staff who remain in public service usually stay in the same department for their entire career (Andeweg and Irwin, 2002, p. 176). The notion of recruiting talented young graduates to an elite, unified civil service is weak or non-existent.

Organization

Here we examine the detailed organization of central government activity, looking at how the cogs of the administrative machine are arranged. Although structures – and labels – vary by country, the key distinction is between three kinds of organization (Box 16.1). The first and most important unit is the department (sometimes called ministry) where policy is made. In nearly all countries, a dozen or so established departments form the stable core of central government, covering such areas as finance, defence and foreign affairs. A second unit comprises the divisions, sections or bureaus into which departments are divided. These are the operating units of government – the powerhouses where expertise resides and in which detailed policy is both formed and applied (to complicate matters, these divisions are sometimes called 'departments' in countries where the larger unit is termed a 'ministry'). For example, departments of transport have sections covering road, rail and air travel. And the third unit is the non-departmental body operating at one or more removes from ministries. These semi-detached organizations combine public funding with operational autonomy; they are growing in number and significance.

Departments and divisions

Government departments (or ministries) form the centrepiece of modern bureaucracies. Here we find the bodies pursuing the traditional tasks of gov-

BOX 16.1

The organization of government: departments, divisions and agencies

Government department or ministry
An administrative unit over which a minister exercises direct management control. Usually structured as a formal hierarchy and often established by statute.

Division, section or bureau
An operating unit of a department, responsible to the minister but often with considerable independence in practice (especially in the USA, where many such divisions are called 'agencies').

Non-departmental public body
Operates at one or more removes from the government, in an attempt to provide management flexibility and political independence. Sometimes called 'quangos', a term of American origin that originally meant 'a quasi non-governmental organization' but which is often now taken to mean a 'quasi-governmental organization'.

ernment: for example, finance, defence and foreign affairs. The United States has 15 departments, each headed by a Secretary of State appointed by the president. The Netherlands has 13; Canada, always prone to political inflation, has over twenty. New Zealand leads the field with around forty departments, though a single minister may take charge of several departments.

Most countries follow a similar sequence in introducing departments. The first to be established are those performing the core functions of the state: finance, law and order, defence and foreign affairs. These ministries are often as ancient as the state itself. In the United States, for instance (see Figure 16.2), the Department of State and the Treasury each date from 1789. At a later stage countries add extra ministries to deal with new functions. Initially these are usually agriculture (1862 in the USA) and commerce and labour (1903 and 1913), followed later in the twentieth century by welfare departments dealing with social security, education, health and housing.

Reflecting Weber's principles, departments are usually organized in a clear hierarchy. A single minister sits at the pinnacle of the organization albeit often supported in large departments by junior ministers with responsibilities for specific divisions. A senior civil servant, often called the Secretary, is responsible for administration and for forming the crucial bridge between political and bureaucratic levels (in Japan this person is called the vice-minister, reflecting the high status of top bureaucrats there). Table 16.1 shows the elaborate structure of the German Economics Ministry, a fine illustration of Weber's quasi-military chain of command.

Departments are typically arranged into several divisions, each responsible for an aspect of

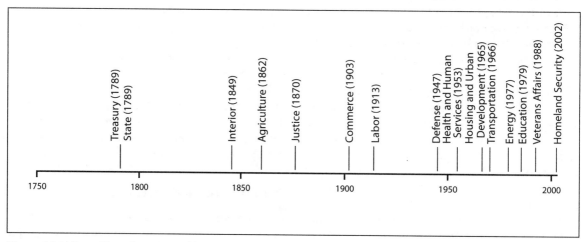

Figure 16.2 Founding of current cabinet level departments in the USA

DEBATE

A REPRESENTATIVE BUREAUCRACY?

The social background of senior civil servants is invariably unrepresentative of the general population. In the Western world, the typical high-level civil servant is a male graduate, from an urban background and from a middle- or upper-class family that was itself active in public affairs (Aberbach *et al.*, 1981, p. 80). These findings have disturbed advocates of a 'representative bureaucracy'. This term was introduced by Kingsley (1944), an American scholar who claimed that the middle-class composition of Britain's civil service exploded the myth of its supposedly neutral bureaucracy. By implication, the same argument could be applied to other countries. But should we be concerned about the social skew of public servants? And, if so, should recruitment on merit be modified by positive discrimination in favour of under-represented groups such as ethnic minorities and women?

The case for

Three arguments support the thesis that a bureaucracy should reflect the social profile of the population:

▶ Civil servants whose work involves direct contact with specific groups will be better at the job if they also belong to that category. A shared language is the most obvious example but the point can perhaps be extended to ethnicity and gender.

▶ A civil service balanced between particular groups, such as religions or regions, may encourage stability in divided societies such as Northern Ireland.

▶ Democracy is said to involve government by, and not just for, the people. A representative civil service, involving participation by all major groups in society, will enhance the acceptability of decisions. Positive discrimination in favour of under-represented groups is the only effective solution to the problem. But it will only be needed for a short period because, once a representative bureaucracy is established, it will maintain itself naturally as minorities notice the role models in post and become more likely to apply for jobs themselves.

The case against

The principle of recruitment on merit is fundamental to public administration and should not be abandoned in favour of social engineering. The public interest is best served by selecting the best people for the job, irrespective of their background. The correct solution to under-representation is not positive discrimination but improving the qualifications of the excluded minorities. In any case, positive discrimination creates two problems of its own. First, those denied jobs because they belong to the 'wrong' social category are naturally resentful. Second, those who are accepted just because they come from the 'right' social background are placed in an awkward position. In any case, it is far from clear that the narrow social background of senior civil servants does produce the prejudice against the left that Kingsley claimed to detect. Norwegian studies show that the attitudes of civil servants depend more on their post, level and department than on their social or educational background: 'where you stand depends on where you sit' (Laegreid and Olsen, 1978). And where civil servants are allowed to pursue political careers, they frequently join parties of the left. In France, a third of the senior public servants elected to the French National Assembly in 1978 were members of the Socialist Party. Generally, the dominant ideology among top bureaucrats seems to be centrist, not conservative (Aberbach *et al.*, 1981). Broadening the social base of recruits would not, in practice, change bureaucratic decisions.

Assessment

The arguments for a representative public service did lead to affirmative action programmes in some countries, notably the United States, in the 1970s and 1980s. Considerable efforts were made to ensure that the staff profile matched that of the wider population. Canadian governments, concerned since the 1960s to improve recruitment from French-speakers, also extended their recruitment efforts. However, such schemes never achieved the same popularity in Europe, perhaps because they would have involved accepting the inadequacy of the constitutional requirement of neutrality imposed on some civil services there. Even in North America, attitudes were ambivalent, reflecting a tension between social engineering and merit-based recruitment. In any event, affirmative action schemes lost momentum in the more conservative 1990s.

Further reading: Birch (1972), Kingsley (1944), Meier (1993), van der Meer and Roborgh (1996).

Table 16.1 The structure of Germany's Ministry of Economics and Labour

Position	Number of positions	Service level
The minister	1	–
Parliamentary state secretaries	3	–
Administrative state secretaries	3	Political officials
Department heads	11	Political officials
Subdepartment heads	34	Higher service
Section heads	150	Higher service
Section assistants	460	Higher service
Caseworkers	615	Elevated service
Clerical/secretarial	822	Intermediate service
Messengers etc.	288	Lower-level service

Note: In Germany, 'political officials' are tenured civil servants who must be transferred to another job of suitable status if not retained by their minister.

Source: Conradt (2001), Table 8.1, updated from the department's website at http://www.bmwi.de.

the organization's work. Thus an Education Department might have separate divisions for primary, secondary and higher education – and, in practice, for many other aspects of its work. Divisions are the operating units of departments, the sections within which the work gets done. They are the workhorses of government, the store of its experience and, in practice, the site where many important decisions are reached. In short, divisions within ministries are the engine-rooms of government.

In many democracies, such divisions or bureaus acquire added importance because they are partially autonomous from their parent department. The extreme example is the USA, whose bureaucracy is the great exception to the principle of hierarchy in departments. Even in their formal structure, American departments are more like multinational corporations, containing many divisions jostling within a single shell. The departments are merely the wrapping round a collection of disparate divisions and it is these bureaus which form the main operating units of the federal government. For example, within the Department of Health and Human Services it is divisions such as the Centers for Medicare and Medicaid Services which administer specific federal welfare schemes. Reporting formally to the president, bureau chiefs spend much of their time ensuring their operational independence from the White House. Congress, not the president, creates and funds bureaus. And what Congress gives it can (and occasionally does) take away. The autonomy of bureaus within American departments is a major and often underestimated reason why American presidents experience such difficulty in imposing their will on Washington's complex political process.

The contrast between America's fragmented bureaucracy and the German system of hierarchical departments could hardly be more extreme. Even in Germany, however, it would be wrong to suppose that working practices correspond exactly to the organization chart implied in Table 16.1, with its Weberian image of information moving smoothly up and down the administrative pyramid. In practice, the 2,000 divisions ('sections') of the German federal ministries possess a concentration of expertise that enables them to block or at least circumvent changes proposed from on high. In most other democracies, too, divisions within departments possess their own ethos derived from long experience with their area. This 'house view' can breed a natural cynicism towards the latest political initiative and the top minister may need to circumvent divisional resistance by seeking advice from political advisers.

Non-departmental public bodies

The defining feature of non-departmental public bodies is that in theory they operate at one remove from government departments, with a formal relationship of at least semi-independence. Such institutions occupy an ambivalent position, created and funded by the government, but in contrast to divisions within a department they are free from day-to-day ministerial control. Once appointed by the government, the members of such bodies are expected to operate with considerable autonomy.

In the United States, where such agencies are prominent, leading examples include the Central Intelligence Agency (CIA), the Environmental Protection Agency (EPA) and the National Aeronautics and Space Administration (NASA).

Scandinavian countries, notably Sweden, have also long relied on non-departmental bodies to implement policy set by the ministry. In Sweden, government departments are small and ministers exercise no authority over the implementation of policy. Rather, a network of independent and relatively autonomous central boards and agencies – the Social Welfare Board, the National Labour Market Board, the National Pensions Board, etc. – executes policy directives (Arter, 1999, p. 154).

Non-departmental public bodies are established for a range of reasons. These include: to provide protection from political influence, to operate with more flexibility than would be acceptable for a division of a ministry, to acknowledge the professional status of staff employed in them or simply as a response to short-term pressure to 'do something' about a problem. Throughout the democratic world, non-departmental bodies are growing in number, complicating not just the academic task of mapping government but also the practical job of ensuring that the government as a whole acts in a coherent manner. Indeed, modern governance cannot be understood without delving deeper into the undergrowth of these organizations.

The classification of non-departmental bodies in Box 16.2 distinguishes between state-owned enterprises, other agencies operating separately from departments and non-statutory bodies created by departments for specific, often short-term, reasons. In many established democracies in the English-speaking world, the balance between these formats changed considerably in and after the 1980s. Specifically, privatization finished off many state-owned enterprises while demand for agencies to provide services (including regulation) increased. As a result, the shape of the public sector underwent considerable alteration.

A *state-owned enterprise* (SOE) is – or perhaps we should say 'was' – a government corporation established by law to sell goods and services, with no private shareholders. Examples include Canada's Crown Corporations, the US Postal Service and Britain's nationalized industries. Although such bodies were supposed to operate at arm's length from government, political interference often led to overstaffing and underinvestment. In Britain, most government corporations

---

BOX 16.2
Types of non-departmental public body

Type	Definition	Examples
State-owned enterprise (SOE)	A government corporation established by statute to trade goods or services	Most countries: mail service New Zealand: Coal Corporation of NZ USA: Amtrak (a passenger rail network)
Other statutory agencies	Statutory bodies operating separately from (and sometimes independently of) government departments. Most agencies *either* supply a public service directly *or* regulate an aspect of society	Sweden: Social Welfare Board USA: Federal Election Commission UK: Food Standards Agency
Non-statutory organization	Bodies set up by departments to offer specialized services or advice	Such bodies are often temporary (e.g. advisory committees on mad cow disease). In many countries, stable examples include scientific research councils and bodies for distributing public funds to the arts

were sold back to the private sector during
Conservative rule between 1979 and 1997, a
policy that has now been copied by other countries. Indeed, the SOEs that remain in public
hands in Britain, such as the Post Office, face
growing competition in international markets
from private companies advantaged by their
freedom to raise money from the market for
investment.

Yet far from the privatization earthquake
destroying the role of the state in the economy, it
has simply reshaped the landscape of regulation.
Ownership and control have given way to supervision. Today, the most important non-departmental bodies are not government corporations
but *agencies*. These are public organizations operating separately from departments and charged
(normally by statute) either with delivering public
services or with regulating an aspect of social life
where a public interest is held to be at stake.
Services provided by agencies include intelligence-
gathering, management of public buildings and
the provision of driving licences. According to the
school of new public management (p. 301), specialist agencies, operating in a businesslike manner
free from detailed political interference, should be
more efficient at supplying services than a division
of a government department.

The other form of agency is the regulatory body.
Examples include bodies to regulate natural
monopolies (e.g. water supply), adoption, broadcasting, elections, food standards and nuclear
energy. Regulatory agencies are increasing in
nearly all established democracies, partly to
balance risks which cannot be well-judged by the
private sector. For example, weighing the benefits
of introducing a new drug against the danger of
side effects is perhaps a task for public-minded
experts rather than for self-interested drug companies or even busy politicians (Boyne, 2003).
Britain now has well over 100 regulatory bodies,
employing over 20,000 people and costing around
£1 billion ($1.5 billion) per year. The media entre-
preneur Rupert Murdoch even claims that regulation represents socialism's comeback trail; his view
is that 'socialism is alive and well, and living in
regulatory agencies'.

The hope, at least partly reflected in reality, is
that regulatory agencies will act as a buffer

between the government and the regulated
bodies, reducing the excessive intervention which
held back many government corporations.
However, the danger is that such agencies will
come to serve the interests of those they supervise. Regulatory capture has been widely
observed, not least with state utility commissions
in the United States (Wilson, 1989). Even if regulators avoid capture, they will still want to perpetuate their own existence, a bias which leads
them to over-value the need for public regulation.

> **Definition**
> **Regulatory capture** arises when public agencies
> created to regulate a particular industry come to
> serve the interests of those they supervise.

Reflecting their importance, government corporations and agencies are usually established by a
specific statute (i.e. law). However, ministers also
set up (and occasionally dissolve) non-statutory
organizations to offer advice or provide an executive function in specialized areas of activity.
Whether a particular function is handled by a
statutory or non-statutory body varies by country
but non-statutory examples might include scientific advisory panels, research funding committees,
arts councils and training boards. Although much
of their work is routine, non-statutory bodies still
attract recurring if sometimes unjust criticism. In
contrast to bodies established under law, they
report to the sponsoring minister, not to the
assembly. Membership tends to be seen as political
patronage and accountability is regarded as
opaque and intermittent. Criticism is especially
sharp in countries such as Britain where the myth
of parliamentary sovereignty still conditions political discourse. But even in Britain many non-
statutory bodies survived a crusading cull
launched by Mrs Thatcher in the 1980s. Even if
many non-statutory bodies do outlast their usefulness, the device seems to be indispensable in providing ministers with a flow of information and
advice on specialized topics. Charting the non-
departmental public bodies in any established
democracy confirms the complexity of contemporary governance and gives the lie to any simple
claims of a diminished role for the state.

Accountability

How should civil servants be rendered accountable for their actions? Given its detailed knowledge, its permanence, its scale and its control of policy implementation, the bureaucracy is bound to be more than a mechanical conduit for political directives. Senior public employees – department secretaries, heads of divisions, chairs of non-departmental public bodies – are invariably in a position to influence policy. The 'problem' of controlling bureaucratic 'power' in a democracy was a particular concern of Weber's (Gerth and Mills, 1948, pp. 232–5). He identified the danger of public 'servants' coming to dominate their elected 'masters'. Indeed, Weber argued that

> under normal conditions, the power position of a fully developed bureaucracy is always overwhelming. The 'political master' finds himself in the position of the 'dilettante' who stands opposite the 'expert,' facing the trained official who stands within the management of administration.

As Weber himself realized, his model of civil servants reporting to a single minister in a self-contained department provided inadequate accountability in practice. Today, more emphasis is placed on a looser but also more flexible view of accountability. High-level civil servants are increasingly subject to 'multiple accountabilities' – for example, to the prime minister and the finance ministry and to agreements with other organizations (international and domestic) as well as to the ministers in their own department. Polidano (1998, p. 35) argues that in a complex environment, where most policy-making involves coordination between several organizations, 'bureaucrats can be prevented from complying with ministerial directions, however legitimate those directions may be. Multiple accountabilities are an inescapable part of the reality of government'. For such reasons, many analysts now accept that senior administrators should learn and indeed be taught 'political craft' – the ability to see policy options in a wider political context (Goetz, 1997).

So the issue today is not so much preventing bureaucrats from influencing policy as ensuring some measure of accountability for the decisions which public servants help to shape. Box 16.3 distinguishes two main forms of accountability: internal controls within the civil service (including direction by the minister) and the increasing range of accountabilities to external bodies such as the legislature and the judiciary. We discuss each type separately.

Internal controls

The traditional form of bureaucratic accountability is, of course, to the minister in charge of the department. Ministers direct; public servants execute. Although no longer sufficient, hierarchical control by a minister remains an essential part of bureaucratic accountability. However, in practice, the capacity of ministers to exert such control is conditioned by two other factors: the reach of political appointments into the bureaucracy and the use ministers make of personal advisers.

In theory, the greater the number of political appointments to a department, the easier it is to ensure political accountability. Recognizing that senior bureaucrats should possess political craft, many established democracies now tend to staff important ministries with politically loyal and sympathetic civil servants. This practice, long

---

BOX 16.3
Forms of bureaucratic accountability

Internal controls

Ministerial direction
Formal regulation
Competition between departments
Professional standards

External scrutiny by

Legislature and judiciary
Ombudsmen
Interest groups and the mass media

Sources: Polidano (1998), Stone (1995).

familiar in Germany and Finland, is spreading to other Western democracies. Increasingly, politicians want civil servants who are, in Mrs Thatcher's famous phrase, 'one of us'. As Page and Wright (1999, p. 278) write,

> there is a common trend among administrative systems which stress the norm of civil service neutrality to appoint, either as civil servants or advisers, people in whom one has trust. Increasing political influence in senior appointments suggests the possibility that membership of a 'neutral' civil service is decreasing as a guide to trust among political elites.

Yet it is far from clear that in practice ministerial control does increase with the number of political appointments. In the United States, an incoming president appoints around 3,000 people, a task which itself becomes an administrative distraction for a new president. Ministers who want to get things done might be well-advised to trust their civil servants rather than to seek ever-closer political control.

Political accountability of the bureaucracy can also be aided by providing ministers with personal advisory staff. Because such gurus are not part of the department's permanent staff, they can act as their minister's eyes and ears, reporting back on issues which might otherwise be lost in the official hierarchy. The Executive Office of the President and the White House Office of the American presidency are the fullest expression of this approach. These offices form a counter-bureaucracy within the political system and one that is more likely to be ideologically or politically driven than the formal bureaucracy. Again, however, this sword has two edges. Political advisers may help to assert political control but they create their own problems of accountability. Advisers are neither elected nor vetted by Congress. The danger is that they are too dependent on their patron, preferring to offer blandishments and flattery rather than home truths.

A preferable system, perhaps, is the French *cabinet* (not to be confused with the cabinets which form the apex of the government in parliamentary systems). A French *cabinet* is a group of about 15 to 20 people who form the minister's personal advisory staff and work directly under his or her control. *Cabinets* provide the minister with ideas and help in liaising with the department, other ministries, the party and the constituency. However, most *cabinet* members come from the civil service and return to it after a few years with their minister. Thus the French system offers a method of securing political advisers who are more than mere yes-men.

In addition to formal control by their minister, public officials are subject to increasing scrutiny by an army of regulators within government: the 'waste watchers, quality police and sleaze busters' as Hood *et al.* (1999) term them. Auditors inspect the books, standard-setters check performance, funders assess the outcomes achieved and assorted inspectors monitor everything from employment trends to recycling rates. Contemporary ideology may preach a bonfire of regulations but modern practice is an overdose of inspection, sometimes breeding cynicism among officials and occasionally distracting from the main business at hand. To illustrate the growth of oversight, Hood *et al.* (1999, p. 42) project ten regulating bodies for each UK government department by the end of the twenty-first century should the rate of regulatory expansion observed in the final quarter of the twentieth century continue unchecked.

A more informal, but perhaps more effective, internal device for regulating the bureaucracy is competition between departments. Spending ministries must compete against each other for money, with the finance ministry acting as umpire and cashier. In addition, established democracies rely on the professional standards of civil servants, particularly in bureaucracies with a strong technical emphasis. In Norway and Sweden, for instance, many civil servants work in specialist directorates covering areas such as engineering, medicine and railways. These directorates give expression to professional expertise and are at least partially independent of ministries. In these small Scandinavian countries, trust between politicians and bureaucrats remains high and the system usually functions smoothly. In the main, senior civil servants respond to political signals without explicit direction – a nice result but not easily replicated elsewhere (Christensen and Peters, 1999).

External scrutiny

External scrutiny is an expanding form of accountability for public servants. Traditionally, bureaucrats could easily escape both political and public scrutiny when, as in Britain, ministers alone were considered responsible to parliament for the actions of their officials. Civil servants could and did hide under their minister's skirts. Fortunately, perhaps, the British stress on the anonymity of higher civil servants was never matched in other liberal democracies. In the United States, bureaucrats are more forthcoming in their congressional appearances. But even in secretive Britain the rise of legislative committees of scrutiny has added a new dimension to bureaucratic accountability. Slowly and shyly, and not before time, public officials are becoming willing to account in public for their work.

Definition

An **ombudsman** is a public official appointed by the legislature to investigate allegations of maladministration in the public sector. These watchdogs originated in Scandinavia but they have been emulated elsewhere though often with more restricted jurisdiction and resources.

As with other areas of politics, the judiciary is also growing in importance as an arena in which the bureaucracy can be called to account. Judges are increasingly willing to use administrative law as a device for influencing bureaucratic procedures (p. 221). A more recent addition to the mechanisms of external scrutiny is the ombudsman. This watchdog was first introduced in Sweden and then emulated in New Zealand, followed later by other European countries. Assigned to investigate complaints of maladministration, ombudsmen must have strong powers of investigation if they are to succeed. So far, governments outside Scandinavia have proved reluctant to grant this facility. Finally, interest groups and the mass media also provide increasing external checks on bureaucratic bungling. A vigorous mass media can also act as a selective check on the bureaucracy: regular television programmes, for example, now specialize in exposing public scandal and bureaucratic ineptitude. However, oversight tends to be selective and, in the case of the media, short-term. Exposés rarely lead to structural reform; the specific case may be resolved but the complacency of the bureaucracy often continues.

New public management

'Government is not the solution to the problem; government is the problem.' This famous declaration by Ronald Reagan is one inspiration behind the new public management (NPM), a creed which swept through the Anglo-American world of public administration in the final decades of the twentieth century. NPM represents a powerful critique of Weber's ideas about bureaucracy. It has attracted many specialists who do not share the ideological perspective of Ronald Reagan, it is spoken of warmly by international bodies such as the Oganization for Economic Cooperation and Development and it has led to radical change in the public sectors of Australia, Canada, the United Kingdom and especially New Zealand.

The best way to approach NPM is to consider Osborne and Gaebler's *Reinventing Government* (1992), an exuberant statement of the new approach. Subtitled 'How the Entrepreneurial Spirit is Transforming the Public Sector', this American best-seller outlined ten principles which government agencies should adopt to enhance their effectiveness (Box 16.4). Where Weber's model of bureaucracy was based on ideas of efficiency drawn from the Prussian army, Osborne and Gaebler are inspired by the freewheeling world of American business.

The authors cite with enthusiasm several examples of public sector organizations which have followed their tips. One is the California parks department that allowed managers to spend their budget on whatever they needed, without seeking approval for individual items of expenditure. Another is the public convention centre which formed a joint venture with private firms to bring in well-known entertainment acts, with each side sharing both the risk and the profit. The underlying theme in such anecdotes is the gains achievable by giving public servants the flexibility to manage by results (that is, 'managerialism'). And the significance of this, in turn, is the break it rep-

---

BOX 16.4

Steer, don't row! Osborne and Gaebler's ten principles for improving the effectiveness of government agencies

- Promote competition between service providers.
- Empower citizens by pushing control out of the bureaucracy into the community.
- Measure performance, focusing not on inputs but on outcomes.
- Be driven by goals, not rules and regulations.
- Redefine clients as customers and offer them choices – between schools, between training programmes, between housing options.
- Prevent problems before they emerge, rather than offering services afterwards.
- Earn money rather than simply spend it.
- Decentralize authority and embrace participatory management.
- Prefer market mechanisms to bureaucratic ones.
- Catalyse all sectors – public, private and voluntary – into solving community problems.

Source: Adapted from Osborne and Gaebler (1992).

---

resents with Weber's view that the job of a bureaucrat is simply to apply fixed rules to cases. For its supporters, NPM is public administration for the twenty-first century; Weber's model is dismissed as history. Public administration has been displaced by public management.

While Osborne and Gaebler provide a convert's handbook, Hood (1996, p. 271) offers a more dispassionate and comparative perspective (Box 16.5). Hood shows that NPM has penetrated furthest in Anglo-American countries and Scandinavia, where the public sector is most amenable to political control. By contrast, countries with a strong state and high-prestige bureaucracy, for example Germany, Japan and Spain, have made little progress in implementing the new philosophy. In these countries, senior civil servants continue to guard the public interest; their task is to apply codified law to specific cases. Given such traditions, the managerial ethos of economy, efficiency and effectiveness will not easily prosper. A particular problem is that the status and duties of

civil servants are entrenched in extensive legal codes, making radical change impossible without legislation.

Within the Anglo-American countries, New Zealand proved to be a testing-ground for NPM. In the 1980s and 1990s, successive governments – first Labour and then National – revolutionized the structure, management and role of the public sector. A remarkable coalition (perhaps even conspiracy) of economic theorists in the Treasury, senior politicians from both major parties and business leaders came together to ram through unpopular but far from ineffective reforms. One particular feature of the 'New Zealand model' is its massive use of contracts (Boston *et al.*, 1995). This goes far beyond the standard fare of using private firms to supply local services such as garbage collection. It extends to engaging private suppliers in sensitive areas such as debt collection. By such means, the Department of Transport reduced its direct employees from around 5,000 staff in 1986 to fewer than fifty in the mid-1990s, an astonishing transformation. In addition, contracts are widely used *within* New Zealand's public sector to govern the relationships between purchasers (for example the Transport Department) and providers (for example Transit New Zealand, responsible for roading, and the Civil Aviation Authority, charged with air safety and security). 'Contractualism' within the public sector is an

---

BOX 16.5

Components of new public management

- Managers are given more discretion but are held responsible for results.
- Explicit targets are set and used to assess results.
- Resources are allocated according to results.
- Departments are 'unbundled' into more independent operating units.
- More work is contracted out to the private sector.
- More flexibility is allowed in recruiting and retaining staff.
- Costs are cut in an effort to achieve more with less.

Source: Adapted from Hood (1996).

---

additional step, and a more direct challenge to Weber's model, than simply contracting out services to the private sector.

What lessons can be learned from New Zealand's ambitious innovations in public administration? Mulgan (1997, p. 146) offers a balanced assessment. He concludes that

> the recent reorganization of the public service has led to greater clarity of government functions and to increased efficiencies in the provision of certain services to the public. At the same time, it has been expensive in the amount of resources consumed by the reform process itself and also in the added problems of coordination caused by the greatly increased number of individual public agencies.

The rise of NPM and the contract culture is one reason why the accountability of public officials has become more complex. When something goes wrong with a service provided by an agency operating under contract to government, who should take the blame: the supplier or the department? In Britain, parliament has traditionally held ministers to account for all the actions carried out in their name. As *The Times* wrote in 1977, 'the constitutional position is both crystal clear and entirely sufficient. Officials propose. Ministers dispose. Officials execute.' Yet by 1994 most British civil servants were working in one of about 100 semi-independent agencies (O'Toole and Chapman, 1995). In theory, the minister sets the policy and the agency carries it out. But when a political storm blows up – when convicts escape from prison or the Child Support Agency pursues absent fathers too zealously – it is still ministers who are hauled before parliament. Knowing this, ministers are inclined to interfere with operational matters, thus contradicting the original purpose of the reform. Agency managers discover that they are not free to manage after all, with damage to morale.

The complexities of accountability in a reformed civil service lead some critics to suggest that 'a huge hole now exists in the operation of British democracy' (Campbell and Wilson, 1995, p. 287). Public servants are becoming more responsive downwards, to their users, and also more open to scrutiny from alternative political authorities, such as parliamentary committees. Probably these developments represent a change in accountability rather than a decline. Control is melting away from the minister's office to a diffuse set of agencies and their clients. Weber's hierarchy of control based on direct provision by departments is giving way to a looser network based on persuasion rather than order-giving. Governance is replacing government. For previously centralized countries, notably Britain and New Zealand, the political implications of NPM are profound. Members of parliament wedded to the idea of ministerial accountability to the assembly are not pleased to discover that their cherished myth of sovereignty has shrivelled under pressure from the complex realities of modern policy-making.

Bureaucracy in new democracies

A common legacy of an authoritarian regime is an over-powerful, unaccountable and corrupt bureaucracy. Overcoming this difficult inheritance by establishing the supremacy of elected over bureaucratic authority is an important component of democratic consolidation. In particular, the task is to move the bureaucracy away from the highly political mode of operation under the old order towards a more professional Weberian model, where appointments are based on merit and corruption is contained. Only when these challenging long-term goals have been achieved does it make sense to contemplate applying the fads and fashions of new public management to the public sector. A bureaucracy based on 'old-fashioned' Weberian ideas remains a sensible and even demanding aspiration for a new democracy even as it comes to be seen as inadequate for a consolidated democracy (Verheijen, 1998).

Spain's transition to democracy illustrates the difficulties of bringing a post-authoritarian bureaucracy to heel. Under the old regime dominated by General Franco, 'the bureaucracy had been a central linchpin of the highly centralized, backward-looking dictatorship and was accordingly well-represented within the power elite' (Heywood, 1995, p. 130). Especially in the dictatorship's early years, the dominant test of appointment as a public official was loyalty to the regime. In operation the bureaucracy remained overstaffed and corrupt – albeit with some modernization as Franco's rule began to soften before the general's death in 1975. Even after the old order collapsed, administrative restructuring remained a low priority amid the drama of democratic transition. It was not until the crushing electoral victory of the Socialists in 1982 that major reforms of a now demoralized service were attempted. The Socialists initiated such obvious changes as preventing the same person from occupying more than one public post; they sought also to reduce the significance of *cuerpos* (corps of officials) by focusing recruitment on specific jobs in particular ministries. But these changes met with only partial success. They were followed by further reforms later in the 1980s aimed at inducing a more managerial and less legalistic outlook among public servants. Yet again the outcome was mixed. As late as 1992, Socialist Prime Minister Felipe Gonzalez could describe the continuing inertia of the public service as the greatest frustration of his premiership. Continuing public distrust of state offices is one of the few weaknesses in Spain's generally successful transition to democracy. The Spanish experience reveals in particular that adapting an authoritarian bureaucracy to a democratic environment is a long-term task.

The difficulties of establishing an efficient public administration are even greater in post-communist countries. After all, the collapse of communism was not just the end of a dictatorship; it was also the disintegration of an all-pervasive, over-extended and over-politicized bureaucracy. Initially, regime change led to administrative chaos. For example, many civil servants only received their salary on an irregular basis, forcing them to find ways of supplementing their income. A common response was to exploit the massive bank of formal regulations inherited from the communist era. An official stamp, for example to authorize a new business, remained a valuable commodity. One result of post-communism, suggests Crawford (1996, p. 105), was simply that the price of bribes went up. And a distinctive feature of post-communist societies was, of course, the vast inheritance of public ownership. Bureaucrats found that they could manipulate privatization or exploit the monopoly position of

newly privatized companies for their own benefit. So *post*-communist bureaucracies remained in a *pre*-Weberian stage – they did not operate by the consistent application of formal regulations. As with the royal households of premodern Europe, a public job was valued as an opportunity to tax as much as a source of a regular salary. Ironically, public officials found themselves perfectly positioned to exploit the transition to a 'market economy'.

> *Definition*
> **Civil Service Acts** specify procedures for recruiting, training, promoting, paying and dismissing bureaucrats. In post-communist states, such laws affirm bureaucratic professionalism against a backdrop of communist party control.

Some post-communist states, particularly the Czech Republic, Hungary, Poland and Slovenia, have now made considerable progress in overcoming these problems. In 1992, for instance, Hungary became the first country in Central and Eastern Europe to introduce a Civil Service Act (Baka, 1998). Such legislation is a sensitive issue throughout the post-communist world because it breaks with the communist practice of political control of appointments. Civil service laws are part of an attempt to strengthen the distinction between political and administrative roles, pushing the bureaucracy in a Weberian direction. However, in the least democratic post-communist countries, such battles have often been lost. In Bulgaria, for instance, 'the civil service has traditionally been considered to be a tool of a particular political party rather than a servant of society as a whole. The civil service is perceived not only as a tool to govern but also as a weapon against the political opponent' (Nikolova, 1998). Only a dreamer, suggests Stainov (1993), could imagine 'a picture where, when a government [in Bulgaria] is changed, the civil servant remains firmly in his place without caring too much about the political subject in power'.

Bureaucracy in authoritarian states

The bureaucracy, like the military, is usually a more powerful force in non-democratic regimes

Profile **JAPAN**

Population: 127m.
Gross domestic product per head: $28,700.
Form of government: unitary parliamentary state with a ceremonial emperor.
Legislature ('Diet'): the 480 members of the House of Representatives are elected for a four-year term. The smaller upper house, the House of Councillors, is less significant.
Executive: an orthodox parliamentary executive, with a cabinet and prime minister accountable to the Diet.

Senior bureaucrats play a major role in policy-making.
Judiciary: the 15-member Supreme Court possesses the power of judicial review under the 1946 constitution but has proved to be unassertive.
Electoral system: under the additional member system introduced in 1996, 300 members of the lower house are elected in single-member constituencies while the other 200 are elected by proportional representation. Although the new system was designed to reduce corruption and increase policy

debate, turnout in 1996 fell seven points to 60 per cent.
Party system: postwar Japanese politics has been dominated by the conservative Liberal Democratic Party (LDP). It monopolized power from its formation in 1955 until 1993 and has participated in coalition rule since 1994. In 2003, the LDP won 244 seats, with major opposition coming from the reformist Democratic Party of Japan (177 seats).

Contained in a series of islands the size of Montana, and lacking all major natural resources, Japan's 127m people have built the second largest economy in the world. From the ashes of defeat in the Second World War, Japan by the early 1990s had become the world's largest creditor nation and donor of economic aid. How was this transformation achieved?

Specific historical factors were part of the answer. After the war, American aid, an undervalued yen, cheap oil and the procurement boom caused by the Korean War all contributed to economic recovery. Yet Japan took remarkable advantage of these favourable circumstances, focusing its initial efforts on heavy industry but eventually becoming the world's leading producer and exporter of sophisticated industrial and consumer goods.

'Japan, Inc.' was a popular (and populist) explanation of the country's success. According to this interpretation, the ethnically homogenous Japanese were driven not just by memories of wartime hunger but also by a shared desire to catch up with the West. A more sophisticated explanation was institutional. Although the country's postwar constitution was an American-imposed liberal democracy, in practice the political system was dominated by business. This enabled long-term investment to proceed by repressing any popular demands for rapid increases in domestic consumption, creating the Japanese paradox of 'a rich country with poor people'.

The Japanese civil service is accorded high status, attracts able recruits through open competition and motivates them with the thought of plum post-retirement jobs in the private sector. As Johnson (1987, p. 68) writes, senior bureaucrats form part of 'the economic general staff, which is itself legitimated by its meritocratic character'. The bureaucracy certainly played a major role in postwar reconstruction. It was intertwined with the dominant Liberal Democratic Party (conservative in all but name) and big business. These groups formed a ruling elite though one that is now declining in coherence.

The professional economic bureaucracy, and in particular the Ministry of International Trade and Industry (MITI), was a key force behind Japan's success. As postwar reconstruction began, MITI targeted specific growth industries such as cameras which were shielded from overseas competition until they became competitive. MITI operated mainly through persuasion, thus reducing the risk of major mistakes.

In the 1990s, Japan's economy suffered prolonged asset deflation and even the once-dominant LDP was forced into coalition. State-led deflation painted the bureaucracy in a harsher light than did state-led growth. Corruption scandals made large companies wary of hiring retired bureaucrats. But in the earlier postwar decades, Japan was a preeminent example of how a small, meritocratic bureaucracy, operating largely on the basis of persuasion, can guide economic development within a predominantly market economy.

Further reading: Johnson (1987), Koh (1989), Rosenbluth and Thies (2000).

than it is in democracies. By definition, institutions of representation – elections, competitive parties and freely organized interest groups – are weak in authoritarian regimes, leaving more room for agencies of the state to prosper. A dictator can dispense with elections or even with legislatures but he cannot rule without bureaucrats to implement his will. But the bureaucracy can be more than a dictator's service agency, not least in developing countries. Often in conjunction with the military, it can itself become a leading political force, claiming that its technical expertise and ability to resist popular pressures is the only route to long-term economic development. This claim may have initial merit but eventually bureaucracies in non-democratic regimes are prone to become bloated, over-politicized and inefficient, acting as a drag on rather than a stimulus to further progress. In the long run, bureaucratic regimes, like military governments, become part of the problem rather than the solution.

The bureaucracy has undoubtedly played a positive role in most authoritarian regimes that have experienced rapid economic growth. In the 1950s and 1960s, for instance, the bureaucracy helped to foster economic modernization in several Middle East regimes. In conjunction with the military and a strong national leader such as Abdul Nasser (President of Egypt, 1956–70), modernizing bureaucracies were able to initiate state-sponsored development even against the opposition of conservative landowners. In similar vein, O'Donnell (1973) coined the term 'bureaucratic authoritarianism' to describe Latin American countries such as Brazil and Argentina in which bureaucratic technocrats, protected by a repressive military government, imposed a more modern economy against opposition from some social groups. Many of the high-performing economies of East Asia, such as Indonesia and Malaysia, provide more recent examples of the contribution the bureaucracy can make to development in authoritarian settings.

But instances of the bureaucracy instigating successful modernization are the exception rather than the rule. More often, the bureaucracy has tended to inhibit rather than encourage economic development. The experience of sub-Saharan Africa following independence provides a more sobering and representative assessment of the role of bureaucracy in non-democratic regimes. After colonial rulers departed, authoritarian leaders used their control over public appointments as a political reward, overwhelming the delicate distinction between politics and administration. Their cavalier approach to public appointments was compounded by chronic unemployment which led to excess labour, especially among the newly educated, being absorbed into the administration as a way of buying off trouble. The result was uncontrolled expansion of the civil service; by the early 1990s, public employment accounted for most non-agricultural employment in Africa (Smith, 1996, p. 221). Once appointed, public employees found that ties of kinship meant that they were duty-bound to use their privileged positions to reward their families and ethnic group, producing further expansion of the civil service. The result was a fat bureaucracy incapable of acting as an effective instrument for development. Rather, the expanding administrative 'class' extracted resources from society for its own benefit, in that sense continuing rather than replacing the colonial model. Only towards the end of the twentieth century, under pressure from international agencies, were attempts made to rein in the public sector through an emphasis on building administrative capacity (Turner and Hulme, 1997, p. 90).

> *Definition*
> **Administrative capacity** refers to the bureaucracy's ability to address social problems through effective management and implementation of public policy.

Even where bureaucratic-led development has succeeded, the formula often outlasts its usefulness. As several East Asian states began to discover at the end of the twentieth century, public administrators are more effective at building an industrial economy than at continuing to manage it once it becomes mature and open to international competition. In Indonesia, for example, the Asian financial crisis of the late 1990s exposed the extent to which investment patterns had been distorted by 'crony capitalism', with access to capital depending on official contacts rather than the anticipated rate of return.

The position of the bureaucracy in totalitarian systems in some ways echoes its role in authoritarian regimes. But one key difference marks out administration in the communist world in particular: its sheer scale. The size of the bureaucracy under communism flowed from the totalitarian character of its guiding ideology. To achieve its theoretical mission of building a new society, the party had to control all aspects of development, both economic and social, through the state. Most obviously, the private sector disappeared and the economy became an aspect of state administration. In the extreme case of the Soviet Union virtually every farm, factory and shop formed part of the bureaucracy. The shop assistant, the butcher, the electrician – all were employees of the Union of Soviet Socialist Republics. This required one army of administrators to do the work and another to provide coordination. The Soviet Union became the most bureaucratic state the world had ever seen.

Definition
The **nomenclatura** (Russian for a list of names) was a panel of trusted people from which ruling communist parties appointed to posts in the bureaucracy.

In addition, communist bureaucracies were intensely political, with the ruling party penetrating deeply into the administration. Indeed, the essence of communist rule lay in combining bureaucratic and political rule in one gigantic system. The party regarded the bureaucracy as both indispensable and potentially unreliable – as a force which through its control of implementation might one day dominate its political masters (Lewin, 1997). Hence, the party sought to dominate the bureaucracy in the same way that it controlled the armed forces: by controlling all major appointments. It achieved this goal through the *nomenklatura*, a mechanism that provided a powerful incentive for the ambitious to gain and retain a sound reputation within the party. The *nomenklatura* system continues to this day in China, where the list is now said to contain over eight million names (Manion, 2000, p. 434).

Fascist regimes provide both similarities and contrasts with the communist approach to bureau-

cracy. Like communist states, fascism was an ideology of mobilization, seeking to place the entire resources of the society at the service of an expansionist state. Although in Germany Hitler sought 'war in peacetime', unlike communist leaders Hitler was not interested in how the administration should achieve his demanding objectives. Instead, the 'leadership of men' was regarded as superior to sterile rules and bureaucratic procedures. Hitler applauded the personal form of rule practised in Germany's annexed territories, where local commanders wielded complete power. The Führer himself was a poor administrator, preferring highly informal decision-making when indeed he could be persuaded to take decisions at all. As Mommsen (1997, p. 75) writes, 'the Nazi dictatorship did not so much expand governmental prerogatives through bureaucratic means as progressively undermine hitherto effective public institutions through arbitrary use of power'. Caplan (1988, pp. 322–3) argues that under Hitler the 'subversion of the civil service was piecemeal and *ad hoc*, the effect of incompetence, impatience and neglect rather than the pursuit of a clear alternative'. The profoundly non-bureaucratic character of Nazi rule – described by Caplan as 'government without administration' – contrasts deeply with communist practice.

Key reading

Next step: Peters (2000) is a clear and comparative introduction to bureaucracy.

Heady (1996) is an alternative to Peters, while Page (1992) is a comparative study adopting a Weberian approach. Bekke *et al.* (1996) is a lively edited collection. Osborne and Gaebler (1992) is an enthusiast's account of new public management. Verheijen and Coombes (1998) assess NPM's impact in Europe, both East and West, while Minogue *et al.* (1999) focus more on developing countries. For bureaucracy in particular countries and regions, see Chandler (2000) for a range of consolidated democracies, Fesler and Kettl (1996) for the United States, Campbell and Wilson (1995) for Britain viewed comparatively, Boston (1995) for New Zealand and Page and

Wright (1999) for Europe. For Japan, Johnson (1987) is an influential interpretation. Kershaw and Lewin (1997) contains useful chapters on bureaucracy in the contrasting dictatorships of Stalin and Hitler. With an emphasis on the relationship between administration and development, Turner and Hulme (1997) portray the role of bureaucracy in authoritarian regimes.

The policy process

The task of policy analysis is to understand what governments do, how they do it and what difference it makes (Dye, 2001). Where orthodox political science examines the organization of the political factory, policy analysis examines the products emerging from it. So the focus is on the content, instruments, impact and evaluation of public policy. The prime emphasis is downstream, on the implementation and results of policy, rather than upstream, on the origins of policy in its institutional sources. Policy analysis is concerned with improving the quality and efficacy of public policy, giving the subject a distinctly practical air. Policy analysts want to know whether and why a policy is working and how else it might be pursued.

> *Definition*
> A **policy** is a broader notion than a decision. At a minimum, a policy covers a bundle of decisions. More generally, it reflects an intention to decide in a particular way in the future. According to Colebatch (1998), policies are expected to show coherence (policy as strategy), hierarchy (policy as instructions to staff) and instrumentality (policy as purpose). In fact, many policies are little more than aspiration (policy as window-dressing).

Stages of the policy process

In approaching the study of public policy, it is helpful to distinguish the five stages of the policy process shown in Figure 17.1. These divisions are more analytical than chronological, meaning that in the real world they often overlap. It is, of course, possible to find examples of policy that do closely follow the sequence shown in the figure. An oft-cited example is Britain's Clean Air Act 1956, a successful attempt to use smoke abatement to eliminate unhealthy winter smogs in London. An issue emerged, a solution was proposed and the problem duly went away (Sanderson, 1961). Although no contemporary policy analyst would regard this example as typical of the rather uncertain nature of most policy, a brief review of the stages approach will nonetheless help to introduce the distinct focus of the approach.

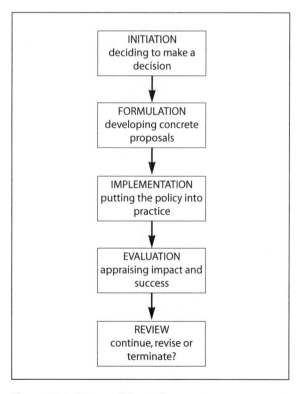

Figure 17.1 Stages of the policy process

Initiation

Why did governments expand welfare policy for the first three decades after 1945 and then reduce it thereafter? Why did many Western governments take companies into public ownership after the war and then start selling them back to the private sector in the 1980s and 1990s? These are questions about policy initiation – about the decision to make (or, almost as important, to change) policy in a particular area. As these examples illustrate, the policy agenda often shows considerable similarity across countries. This resemblance reflects some mixture of shared problems, international competition and explicit lesson-drawing across countries.

Control over policy initiation would be an accomplished form of power. At least within democracies, however, the agenda cannot be controlled by a single group. Rather, policy proposals emerge from what Kingdon (1984) calls the 'policy primeval soup' in uncertain and unpredictable ways. Whether particular issues and solutions are extracted from the soup depends on the opening of policy windows (such as the opportunities for innovation created by the election of a new government). These openings soon close: the cycle of attention to a particular issue is short, and both political debate and the public mood continue to evolve. So Kingdon suggests that policy entrepreneurs are not confined to social movements (see p. 130). A similar role needs to be performed in orthodox policy-making in order to ensure that a given proposal is put forward when its moment arrives.

Beyond the political process itself, we can identify three general influences on policy initiation: science, technology and the media. *Science* is clearly one factor driving policy agendas. The current concern with global warming, for instance, began primarily with scientific assessments of its future implications. Rather unusually, the science forewarned us that a problem was on its way.

However, we should note that governments commission as well as consume science. Ministers' power over the production of knowledge can help them to keep uncomfortable issues off the policy agenda. The British government, for instance, was unduly slow in commissioning research into mad cow disease which swept through the country's herds (and into the brains of a few of its people) in the 1990s. In this case, manipulation of the research process proved fatal. Thus scientific research cannot be seen as wholly external to politics.

Second, the application of science – that is, *technology* – also influences policy initiation. Governments have an incentive to encourage new technology: it stimulates economic competitiveness and its prompt introduction allows a country to steal a march on other states. But many new technologies involve regulation. Designs for nuclear power stations must be assessed for safety; frequencies for mobile telephones must be allocated; new drugs must be examined for side effects; and the effects of allowing genetically altered plants, fish and animals into the environment must be considered. In all these cases technological innovation forces policy initiation from government. The danger is that governments will approve those 'advances' which offer clear short-term gain at the cost of wider long-term risk. Nuclear energy is arguably an example.

Third, the ability of the *media* to highlight issues means they are also a significant, if sometimes overstated, influence on policy initiation. A single and perhaps unusual incident is often taken up by one media outlet and then, through pack journalism, amplified by other channels until politicians are forced to respond to what has suddenly become a serious social problem. Common topics of such media-induced moral panics include asylum seekers, crime waves, drug crazes, food scares, gang wars, infectious diseases, mad dogs, teenage hooligans and welfare scroungers (Henshel, 1990). These balloons of concern often collapse as quickly as they are inflated; only in a few cases are the media turning their searchlight on a problem where public policy does indeed need to be initiated.

Formulation

Once a decision has been taken to address a specific problem, policy must be formulated. Deciding *to* decide is one thing; deciding *what* to decide is much more difficult. The coalition which formed behind the vague idea that something must be done soon dissolves when it comes to concrete proposals producing losers as well as winners. Formulating precise legislative and administrative proposals in response to diffuse support for action is a task requiring good political craft.

In analysing policy formulation, analysts have developed two models: the rational or synoptic model associated with Simon (1983) and the incremental model developed by Lindblom (1979). These accounts form an important part of the policy analysis tradition and we will consider them in more detail.

The key contrast between the two models is this. The rational model views policy as emerging from a systematic search for the most efficient means of achieving defined goals. By contrast, the incremental model sees policy as resulting from a compromise between actors who have goals which are ill-defined or even contradictory (Box 17.1). Put differently, where the rational model seeks the best policy in theory, an incremental framework seeks out a practical policy acceptable to all the interests involved.

An example will clarify this contrast. Suppose we are in charge of education and we have decided to initiate a policy to improve students' perfor-

mance. If we were to adopt a rational approach, we would first specify the outcomes sought, such as the proportion of students achieving a given level of qualifications. Then we would consider the most efficient means of maximizing that goal: should we invest in new schools, improved facilities, more teachers or some combination thereof?

An incremental approach, however, starts from a different point. Here we would begin (and end) with regular consultation with all the organized interests: teacher unions, parents' associations, educational researchers. We would hope that from these discussions a consensus would emerge on how extra resources should be spent. The long-term goals of this expenditure might not be measured or even specified but we would assume that a policy acceptable to all is unlikely to be disastrous. Such an approach is policy-making by evolution, not revolution; an 'increment' is literally a small change to an existing sequence.

Of these two approaches, the rational model is clearly more demanding, requiring detailed analysis rather than careful politics. Specifically, it requires policy-makers to:

- rank all their values
- formulate specific options
- check all the results of choosing each option against each value
- select the alternative that achieves most values.

BOX 17.1
Rational and incremental models of policy-making

Rational model	Incremental model
Goals are set before means are considered	Goals and means are considered together
A good policy is the most appropriate to achieve explicit goals	A good policy is one on which all main actors can agree
Analysis is comprehensive; all effects of all options are addressed	Analysis is selective; the object is acceptable policy, not the best policy
Theory is heavily used	Comparison with similar problems is heavily used

Sources: Adapted from Lindblom (1959, p. 81) and Parsons (1995, p. 285).

> **Definition**
> **Cost–benefit analysis** involves giving a monetary value (positive or negative) to every consequence of choosing each option and then selecting the option with the highest net benefit. Thus, the efficiency gain from adding a new runway to an airport can be netted off against the additional noise pollution for local residents. The technique is transparent but time-consuming.

This is an unrealistic counsel of perfection. It requires policy-makers to foresee the unforeseeable and measure the unmeasurable. Even so, techniques such as cost–benefit analysis (CBA) have developed in an attempt to implement aspects of the rational model (Boardman *et al.*, 2000). Seeking to analyse the costs and benefits associated with each possible decision does have strengths, particularly when one from a small set of options needs to be chosen.

CBA brings submerged assumptions to the surface and can benefit those interests which would otherwise lack political clout. It contributes to transparent policy-making by forcing decision-makers to account for policies where costs exceed benefits. In other words CBA can help to keep policy-makers honest. For such reasons, CBA is now formally applied to any regulatory proposal in the USA expected to have an impact on the economy exceeding $100m.

However, CBA, and with it the rational model of policy formulation, also has weaknesses. It underplays soft factors such as fairness and the quality of life. It is also cumbersome and expensive and in the real political world its conclusions are often sidestepped. Just as the 'rational' model is not always more rational than an incremental approach, so too a CBA of CBA would not always yield positive results.

The incremental model was developed by Lindblom (1959) as part of a reaction against the rational model. Lindblom's starting point is that policy is continually remade in a series of minor adjustments, rather than as a result of a single, comprehensive plan. Incrementalism represents what Lindblom calls the science of muddling through. This approach may not lead to achieving grand objectives but, by taking one step at a time, it does at least avoid making huge mistakes. In incremental policy-making, what matters is not that those involved should agree on objectives but that agreement should be reached on the desirability of following a particular policy, even when objectives differ. Hence policy emerges from, rather than precedes, negotiation with interested groups.

A broadly comparable view of policy-making emerges from Kingdon's rather alarmingly titled garbage can model of decision-making (1984). The garbage can model imagines that issues and policy-makers mix at random within an organization, just as different forms of trash blend haphazardly in a garbage can. In a university, for instance, a committee containing one group of staff may happen to address one aspect of a particular problem, with some implications possibly picked up later by a completely separate group within the institution. Policy-making is partial, fluid, chaotic and incomplete, exhibiting no more rationality than is found in the arrangement of waste in a dustbin (Cohen *et al.*, 1972).

Although Kingdon was mainly concerned with decision-making within organizations, his perspective also has relevance to the political system as a whole. Clearly, his model suggests that real policy-making is far removed from the rigours of rationality. At best, some problems will be partly addressed some of the time (Bendor *et al.*, 2001).

As Lindblom (1977, 1990) himself came to recognize, incremental policy formulation deals with existing problems rather than with avoiding future ones. It is politically safe but unadventurous; public policy becomes remedial rather than innovative. But the threat of ecological disaster, for instance, has arisen precisely from human failure to consider the long-term, cumulative impact of industry upon the environment. So neither incrementalism nor decision-making via the garbage can will provide an adequate response to complex global issues. The trick is to find ways of dealing with such problems which do not fall victim to the shortcoming of the rational model, namely demanding more of policy-makers than they can possibly deliver.

Implementation

After a policy has been set, it must be put into effect. An obvious point, of course, except that much political science stopped at the point where government reached a decision, ignoring the myriad difficulties which arise in policy execution. Probably the main achievement of policy analysis has been to direct attention to these problems of implementation.

Even today, putting the policy into practice is sometimes still regarded as a technical matter of administration. Turning a blind eye to implementation issues can be politically convenient for ministers but is always dangerous and can be damaging. For example, the British government's failure to prevent mad cow disease from crossing the species barrier to humans in the late 1980s is a classic instance of implementation failure. Official committees instructed abattoirs to remove infective material (such as the spinal cord) from slaughtered cows but initially took no special steps to ensure these regulations were carried out carefully. As a result of incompetence in slaughterhouses, the disease agent continued to enter the human food chain.

Again reflecting the standard conventions of political science, the traditional view of implementation adopted a top-down approach (Hogwood and Gunn, 1984). The question posed was the classical problem of bureaucracy: how to ensure political direction of unruly public servants. Elected ministers had to be able to secure compliance from departments and agencies already committed to pet projects of their own. Without vigilance from on high, sound policies would be hijacked by lower-level officials obsessed with existing procedures, thus diluting the impact of new initiatives.

Definition

A **top-down** approach conceives the task of policy implementation as ensuring that policy execution delivers the outputs and outcomes specified by the policy-makers. By contrast, a **bottom-up** approach considers that the role of those who execute policy in reshaping broad objectives to fit local and changing circumstances should be both recognized and welcomed.

But this top-down approach to implementation focuses excessively on control and compliance issues. Like the rational model of policy-making from which it springs, it may be an unrealistic and even counterproductive approach. The plausible suggestion emerging from a bottom-up perspective is that policy-makers should seek to engage rather than control those who translate policy into practice. Writers in this tradition, such as Hill and Hupe (2002), ask: what if circumstances have changed since the policy was formulated? And what if the policy itself is poorly designed?

Many policy analysts now suggest that objectives are more likely to be met if those who execute policy are given flexibility over its application and therefore its content. At street level (the point where policy is delivered), policy emerges from interaction between local bureaucrats and affected groups. Here at the sharp end, goals can often be best achieved by adapting them to local conditions. If the policy is left unmodified, its fate will be that of the mighty dragon in the Chinese proverb: no match for the neighbourhood snake.

For instance, education, health care and policing must surely differ between the rural countryside and multicultural areas in the inner city. Further, local implementers will often be the only people with full knowledge of how policies interact, and sometimes contradict, each other. They will also know the significant actors in the locality and will be able to seek their support. When the American politician Tip O'Neill said, 'all politics is local', he could well have had policy implementation in mind.

So a bottom-up approach reflects an incremental view of policy-making in which implementation is seen as policy-making by other means. This approach reflects the contemporary emphasis on governance, with its stress on the many stakeholders involved in the policy process.

Evaluation

Just as policy analysis has increased awareness of the importance of implementing policy, so too has it sharpened our focus on evaluation. The job of policy evaluation is to work out whether a policy has achieved its goals. Like the recipe for rabbit stew which begins 'first catch your rabbit', this neatly sidesteps initial difficulties. As we have seen, the motives behind a policy are often multiple, unclear and even contradictory. This 'mushiness of goals', to use Fesler and Kettl's phrase (1996, p. 287), means that policy-makers' intent is often a poor benchmark for evaluation. Given that most policy is made incrementally, identifying precise targets is a difficult task.

The question of evaluation was often ignored not just in traditional political analysis but also by governments themselves. Sweden is a typical example. In the postwar decades, a succession of Social Democratic governments concentrated on building a universal welfare state without even conceiving of a need to evaluate the effectiveness with which services were delivered by an expanding bureaucracy. In France and Germany, and other continental countries where bureaucratic tasks are interpreted as the legalistic application of rules to cases, the issue of policy evaluation still barely surfaces.

Yet without some evaluation of policy, governments will fail to learn the lessons of experience. In the United States, Jimmy Carter (President, 1977–81) did insist that at least 1 per cent of the funds allocated to any project should be devoted to evaluation. The vast number of reports required did not noticeably improve policy effectiveness. It was not until a wave of public sector reform in the 1990s that evaluation began to return to the fore. To take the USA again, the Government Performance and Results Act 1993 now requires each agency to perform an annual programme evaluation which is then intended to be used by the government to revise plans and budgets. Similarly, the Labour government elected in Britain in 1997 claimed a new pragmatic concern with evidence-based policy: what matters is what works (Sanderson, 2002). In some other democracies, too, public officials began to think, often for the first time, about whether policies were achieving their goals and at what cost.

Definition
Policy outputs are what government does; **policy outcomes** are what government achieves. Outcomes are the activity; outcomes are the effects, both intended and unforeseen. Outputs are measured easily enough: so many new prisons built or a specified increase in the state pension. Outcomes are harder to ascertain: a reduction in recidivism or in the number of elderly people living in poverty.

Evaluation studies distinguish between outputs (what government does) and outcomes (what government achieves, including unintended consequences). The link between the two is often tenuous. In 1966, for example, the US government published the results of the Coleman Report, a massive sociological study of American secondary schools. This renowned study found that outputs such as teachers' salaries and educational expenditure had little effect on the ultimate outcome of education: namely, children's learning. The main influence on pupils' educational success was the family background of the child and its

peers, not public spending. Children from a lower-class background were likely to underperform even if they were placed in a well-resourced school. The Coleman Report illustrates a point familiar to most policy-makers: outcomes resist change, even when resources are devoted to altering them.

Just as policy implementation in accordance with the top-down model is an unrealistic goal, so judging policy effectiveness against specific objectives is an implausibly scientific approach to evaluation. A more bottom-up, incremental view is that evaluation should simply gather in the opinions of all the stakeholders affected by the policy, yielding a qualitative narrative rather than a barrage of implausibly precise statistics. As Parsons (1995, p. 567) describes this approach,

> evaluation has to be predicated on wide and full collaboration of all programme stakeholders: agents (funders, implementers); beneficiaries (target groups, potential adopters); and those who are excluded ('victims').

In such a naturalistic evaluation, the varying objectives of different interests are welcomed. They are not dismissed as a barrier to objective scrutiny of policy. This is a more bottom-up – indeed incremental – approach because the stakeholders might agree on the success of a policy even though they judge it against different standards.

Review

Once a policy has been evaluated, or even if it has not, the three possibilities are: to continue, to revise or to terminate. Most policies, or at least the functions associated with them, continue with only minor revisions. Once a role for government is established, it tends to continue. But the agency charged with performing the function does change over time. In the United States, for instance, 426 separate agencies were established between 1946 and 1997 but a majority of these had been terminated by the end of the period. The agent of change was usually an alteration in the partisan colour of the administration (Lewis, 2002). So the observation that there is nothing so permanent as a temporary government organization appears to be wide of the mark. Functions continue but the agencies performing them can change.

Yet even if agency termination is surprisingly common, the intriguing question remains: why is policy termination so rare? Why does government as a whole seemingly prefer to adopt new functions than to drop old ones? Bardach (1976) suggests five reasons for the difficulties of policy termination:

▶ Policies are designed to last a long time.
▶ Policy termination brings conflicts which leave too much blood on the floor.
▶ No one wants to admit the policy was a bad idea.
▶ Policy termination may affect other programmes and interests.
▶ Politics rewards innovation rather than tidy housekeeping.

Public policy in established democracies

While policy can be usefully analysed into its component parts, it is also helpful to take a broader view. In this section, we seek to chart the major shifts in the policy agenda of Western states, transformations which reflect evolving conceptions of the state itself yet which, like other aspects of policy analysis, remain understated in descriptions of government institutions.

Broadly, we can divide the history of public policy in what are now the established democracies into three phases: the nightwatchman or liberal state of the nineteenth century and earlier, the welfare state of the later twentieth century and the emerging regulatory state of the twenty-first century (Box 17.2). Such a scheme fits the experience of Northern European states, including the UK, with fair accuracy. However, the history of the USA, which never developed a welfare state but which was one of the first democracies to introduce independent regulatory agencies, is exceptional once more.

The nightwatchman state

The nightwatchman state was a minimal operation, concentrating on maintaining law and order, protecting private property and extracting suffi-

---

BOX 17.2
The changing agenda of the Western state

Type of state	Domestic agenda	Period
Nightwatchman state	Maintains law and order and protects private property	Nineteenth century and earlier
Welfare state	Provides minimum welfare to all citizens	Second half of twentieth century, particularly in Western Europe
Regulatory state	Sets rules and standards	Final decades of the twentieth century and later

---

cient resources to allow rulers to pursue their foreign policy. The state apparatus remained poorly developed, with a limited bureaucracy and local administration largely the responsibility of provincial notables. The nightwatchman role was an early form taken by the post-feudal but pre-democratic state in much of Europe, notably the United Kingdom, up to the nineteenth century; it reflected a liberal philosophy of non-intervention.

The nightwatchman metaphor comes from John Locke (1632–1704), an English philosopher who laid the early foundations of liberal thinking. Locke considered the sole function of government to be that of protecting natural, God-given rights to life, liberty and property. In Locke's view, citizens should merely be provided with order, protection and the means of enforcing contracts.

In the United States, a country built to a liberal design, Thomas Jefferson (1743–1826) expressed the nightwatchman conception when he wrote: 'that government is best which governs least'. The nightwatchman state had no interest in public welfare: 'the drunkard in the gutter is just where he ought to be', commented the American sociologist William Sumner (1840–1910).

In America and beyond, this liberal philosophy of clear but limited individual rights reflected the struggle for religious toleration. However, limiting the state to a night watchman role also proved highly congenial to the emerging business class. Indeed, the free-market doctrine of laissez faire ('to allow to do') was perhaps the most significant element in the nightwatchman construct. As Opello and Rosow (1999, p. 97) comment,

The liberal state, then, is in one respect a minimal state; that is, it is deliberately structured not to be itself a threat to the 'natural right' of property ownership, which is the ultimate justification for the dominant position of the bourgeoisie within the state.

The welfare state

The welfare state, which reached its zenith in Western and especially Northern Europe in the 1960s and 1970s, was clearly based on a more expansive and positive view of the state's role. However, the culmination of the welfare state in the postwar decades reflected a long evolution. Even as industrialization proceeded in the nineteenth century, the nightwatchman state had been drawn into a measure of economic and environmental regulation. In Britain, for example, the Factory Act 1833 had created a framework for inspecting factories while the Factory Act 1847 limited the working day to a maximum of ten hours.

However, the real origins of collective welfare provision lay in Germany before the First World War. Under the rule of Otto von Bismarck (German Chancellor, 1871–90), Germany had pioneered social insurance schemes which shared risks such as accident and illness, at least for industrial workers. Building on this innovative German model, the period from the 1920s saw the gradual extension of collective welfare in most democracies to more areas of life (e.g. pensions and family allowances) and to more groups in the population (e.g. rural people and dependants of industrial workers). By the 1970s, coverage for the main aspects of welfare extended to virtually the entire population in most democracies (Table 17.1).

By then, European democracies had become 'welfare states' in a triple sense. First, the state took

---

Table 17.1 Introduction of social insurance to some democracies

	Industrial accident	Health	Pensions	Unemployment benefit	Family allowances
Australia	1902	1945	1909	1945	1941
Austria	1887	1888	1927	1920	**1921**
Canada	1930	1971	1927	1940	1944
Denmark	1898	1892	1891	1907	1952
Finland	1895	1963	1937	1917	1948
France	1898	1898	1895	**1905**	1932
Germany	**1871**	**1883**	**1889**	1927	1954
Netherlands	1901	1929	1913	1916	1940
New Zealand	1900	1938	1898	1938	1926
Norway	1894	1909	1936	1906	1946
Sweden	1901	1891	1913	1934	1947

* Innovator in **bold**.

Source: Adapted from Pierson (1998), table 4.1.

a prime role in ensuring the provision of a minimum standard of welfare to all its citizens, supplanting the ad hoc provision through churches and charities in the nightwatchman state. Second, providing welfare became the main function of public administration, consuming the lion's share of both taxpayers' revenue and officials' time. Third, welfare rights became an expression of social citizenship, a notion which sought to extend the scope of democracy itself.

The concept of social citizenship was developed by the British sociologist T. H. Marshall (1893–1981). In an influential account written in the aftermath of war, Marshall (1950, pp. 16–19) defined social citizenship as covering 'the whole range from the right to a modicum of economic welfare and security to the right to share to the full in the social heritage and to live the life of a civilized being according to the standards prevailing in society'. Influenced by such considerations, several democracies – for instance, France – began to embed a statement of welfare rights in their constitution.

This development of social citizenship contrasts sharply with the nightwatchman state in which those who received public welfare through the poor laws were denied the vote. Where the nightwatchman state gave priority to liberty, the welfare state was premised on equality.

Of course, democracies continued to vary both in their levels of welfare support and in the ideological support offered. Several factors help to account for variations in the share of national product devoted to public welfare:

▸ Wealthier countries spend a higher proportion of national income, and not just a higher amount, on welfare (Wilensky, 1984).
▸ Unitary states (such as Britain) tend to be higher spenders than federations (such as Canada). Unitary status permits national welfare schemes to be set up and administered, often through local government.
▸ Welfare spending is higher in countries where parties of the left predominate (e.g. the Social Democrats in Sweden).
▸ Countries such as Austria in which Catholic parties are a major governing force also tend to be generous providers. Catholic traditions favour social support, particularly when administered through the church.
▸ Low spenders include countries where collective provision is still seen as 'state welfare' rather than a 'welfare state'. The USA is still seen as an example of this 'residual' or 'liberal' welfare state despite an expansion of government responsibility in the New Deal (1933–39), and heavy contemporary support for the elderly (Esping-Andersen, 1990).

Definitions

In a public **pay-as-you-go** pension scheme, the pensions of retirees are paid directly by contributions from current workers. This system, which forms an important plank of pensions provision in much of continental Europe, becomes unsustainable as the population ages and the **dependency ratio** (the number of pensioners divided by the number of contributors) deteriorates. The state will need to take corrective action.

By contrast, in a **funded pension** system, usually operated through private or occupational pension providers, individual contributions are invested on behalf of the individual so that a pot of capital accumulates from which a retirement income can be drawn. Funded pensions should require little call on the public purse. Funded pensions predominate in, for example, the Netherlands, the United Kingdom and the USA.

The 1980s witnessed the first real setbacks for the welfare state. The underlying problem was financial: as the average age of the population increased, so the total cost of pensions, medical care and support services went up – and was projected to continue growing well into the twenty-first century. At the same time the working population, which shoulders the burden of support for the elderly, declined in number. Financial projections looked particularly bleak in those countries, such as Germany, which combined a greying population with a pay-as-you-go pensions scheme. But even in the USA projections of future welfare spending were daunting. Given the expanding cost of its Social Security and Medicare schemes, one journalist was even moved to describe the American government as 'a giant insurance company with a small defence affiliate' (i.e. its military forces) (Plender, 2003).

International economic pressures also impinged on thinking about welfare. If the cost of one country's welfare system was higher than all the rest, the international competitiveness of its economy might be endangered. Pierson (1998) suggests that the move to a more open international economy at least 'curtailed opportunities for the further development of national welfare states'. Certainly the oil crises of the 1970s, marking a transition to slower growth in the established democracies, were a catalyst to rethinking first the feasibility and then the desirability of state-provided welfare from cradle to grave.

Such problems led to some retrenchment of the welfare state in the 1980s and 1990s. Benefits were marginally reduced, eligibility rules were tightened, charges were introduced for services such as medical treatment, few new commitments were taken on and the state made an effort to revive the old caring agencies, such as charities and the church.

But the welfare state experienced a correction rather than a crisis. On the whole, taxpayers' revolts did not materialize and the basic structures of the welfare state remained in place. In practice, the generous welfare states found in Scandinavia did not seem to suffer a dramatic loss of economic competitiveness. At least in the Nordic world, Kuhnle (2000, p. 226) argues that welfare provision helped to maintain political legitimacy through difficult times:

> the Nordic experience in the 1990s shows that the universal and comprehensive welfare state can be a vital shock absorber which stabilizes the economy so that the economy can recuperate fast and well.

So Marshall's notion of social citizenship may be touted less often in the twenty-first century but both its cash value and its public popularity remain substantial (Esping-Andersen, 2002).

The regulatory state

Although the crisis of the welfare state may have been overplayed, the final decades of the twentieth century did witness a fundamental shift in the agenda and focus of public policy in many established democracies, especially in Europe. In social welfare, service delivery was increasingly contracted out to private agencies; in the economy, public industries were privatized (Feigenbaum *et al.*, 2003).

Since one motive here was to render economies more competitive, this transition is sometimes discussed as a move from a welfare state to a competition state (Cerny, 1990). But it is not clear that the frontiers of the state have been decisively modified; indeed, newly privatized monopolies must be regulated and public oversight has become more intense in such sectors as education, the environment, employment, scientific research and consumer protection. Indeed, smart regulation – allocating radio frequencies to mobile telephony, encouraging broadband internet use, developing digital television – can enhance growth in advanced economies.

For want of a happier term we will describe this shift in the policy approach as a transition to a regulatory state (Box 17.2). Such a state uses rules, standards and other public statements as major policy instruments, rather than relying on direct provision of goods and services. More than in most democracies, regulation has always been a leading mode of governance in the USA; the notion of a regulatory state suggests that American practice is now diffusing to other established democracies in Europe and elsewhere.

The most striking evidence for the retreat of the state from direct provision comes from the influential policy of privatization followed by Britain's Conservative government under Mrs Thatcher in the 1980s. The speed and thoroughness with which the United Kingdom government 'sold off the family silver' (to quote the disapproving words of former Conservative prime minister Harold Macmillan) attracted international interest (Table 17.2). Just as nationalization had been seen by the postwar Labour government as a way of introducing public control and rational planning to key industrial sectors, so privatization reflected an ideologically charged desire to 'roll back the frontiers of the state'.

The key point, though, was that creating private monopolies – as with telephones, gas and electricity – required the creation of new offices of regulation at least until competition became established. As

Table 17.2 Case-by-case privatization in the United Kingdom, 1980s

Year	Company privatized	Proceeds (£ million)
1981	British Aerospace	149
1981	Cable & Wireless*	224
1982	Britoil	549
1983	BP*	565
1984	Enterprise Oil	392
1984	Jaguar Cars	294
1984	British Telecom*	3,916
1985	British Aerospace	551
1986	British Gas	5,434
1987	British Airways	900
1987	Rolls Royce	1,362
1987	British Airports Authority	1,281
1988	British Steel Corporation	2,482
1989	Water Authorities	5,240

* Privatized in stages: only the first tranche is shown.

Note: Only privatizations yielding over £100m are shown. Electricity distribution was privatized in 1990 and electricity generation the following year.

Source: Adapted from Prosser and Moran (1994), table 3.2.

Majone (1996, p. 2) notes, 'in Britain and elsewhere, the privatization of the public utilities has been followed by price regulation . . . the last fifteen years have been a period less of deregulation than of intense regulatory reform'. The outcome is as much a regulatory state as a rolled-back state.

In analysing the rise of the regulatory state in Britain, Moran (2003) identifies three major dimensions. These are:

▶ regulation of privatized industries where competition remains weak (e.g. water supply)
▶ external supervision of previously self-regulating institutions such as universities and financial markets
▶ social regulation in such areas as equal opportunities, health and safety and food standards.

This new style of governance through regulation does, however, bring forth new problems. Perhaps the most important of these is the issue of democratic legitimacy. Most new regulatory bodies operate not as divisions of ministries but as agencies operating at one remove from the centres of political – and therefore democratic – power. Similar attempts to depoliticize regulation can be observed in the independence given to central banks to set interest rates, as now applies in both Britain and the eurozone. In the European Union, also, the capacity of the unelected Commission to issue enforceable regulations represents its major lever of influence.

Majone (1996) suggests two reasons in defence of this trend away from political control, even though it runs counter to orthodox democratic thinking. First, autonomous agencies can adopt more consistent, credible and long-term policies than is feasible for elected politicians who remain subject to short-term pressures from the voters. If an unelected central bank can control inflation more effectively than an elected government, the argument goes, surely the bank should be given the job?

Second, delegating political authority to specialized professional regulators is most appropriate for issues that are technical (e.g. telecommunications) rather than redistributive (e.g. taxation) in nature. The level of taxation is a political question for which there is no technical answer but there may well be a single best way of regulating mobile telephony. Clearly, as the regulatory state matures, so we may expect more discussion about its uncertain relationship with traditional ideas of democracy.

Public policy in new democracies

'Rebuilding the ship at sea' is an apt metaphor for the problems confronting new democracies in general and post-communist democracies in particular (Elster *et al.*, 1998). The policy challenge is precisely to design new institutions that restructure the role of the state in society. In established democracies, institutions process new policies; in new democracies, the policy is to develop new institutions.

On the one hand, the state must reduce its involvement in some sectors, notably the economy, to allow room for a more competitive private sector to develop. On the other hand, the state must develop new modes of regulation: for example, overseeing the functioning of markets, giving independent authority to the judiciary and creating an efficient and professional bureaucracy. Thus the state in most new democracies must alter its entire shape, thinning out in some areas but building up in others.

The scope of the policy changes needed to consolidate a new democracy is far greater than that involved in the transition from welfare to regulatory states in established democracies. Further, the difficulties are increased in the aftermath of transition by the threatening combination of unrealistic expectations and economic decline. If there is one lesson to be learnt from the policy experience of third-wave democracies, it is that freshly elected governments – and especially their army of Western advisers – vastly understated the size, complexity and likely duration of the task of recasting the state's relationship with society.

Post-communist states provide the most dramatic examples of the policy transformation required of new democracies. When the communist order collapsed, an entire method of organizing society went with it; far from springing a leak, the communist boat sank. The task facing new leaders was to transform societies fuelled by power into societies based on rules, a project that still continues.

Take the economy as an example. Under communism, the state owned most major enterprises, with a central plan offering coordination. Large enterprises also served as welfare providers, producing what Elster *et al.* (1998, p. 204) describe as a 'tight coupling' between the workplace and social provision:

> Firms provided crèches, holiday homes, housing, health services, training and other welfare facilities for their staff. Continuous and lifelong participation in the production process was the proviso of collectivist protection.

This elaborate, inefficient but functioning network could not be quickly replaced by market mechanisms. Partly as a result of the post-communist experience, it is now clear that market economies must be constructed; the task is far more complicated than merely allowing the command economy to fade away. A successful *private* economy, as in the established democracies, is in fact an intricate *public* and even political achievement. It requires entrepreneurs to show initiative, capital markets to provide resources for investment, consumers to spend money, courts to resolve disputes, bureaucrats to keep their fingers out of the pie and a government to act as an umpire rather than a player (see Box 17.3).

Initially, few of these conditions were met in any post-communist state. The legal challenge of establishing property rights, as well as tax, competition and bankruptcy laws, was considerable. In addition, state-owned enterprises had no experience of marketing their products. To understand the transformation required, Schmieding (1993, p. 236) invites us to imagine

> the problems that would befall a Western market economy if all firms discovered one morning that their entire staff for sales, advertising, finance and legal matters had gone off on a three-year holiday to Mars – together with all the lawyers, judges, bankers and public administrators.

A comparison of post-communist privatization policy with that of the established democracies demonstrates the difficulties. In Britain, privatization of state-owned corporations had proceeded on a case-by-case basis, with a sophisticated financial sector available to underwrite the issue (that is, to buy any shares left unsold) and to offer advice on pricing and marketing. Public monopolies were sold into an established private sector, with sweeteners offered to small investors who were only too pleased to take advantage.

By contrast, in post-communist states, the object was not to sell into the private sector but to create a private sector by, in effect, disposing of an entire economy. Further, individual enterprises were often in poor condition and any commercial banks lacked both the sophistication and the access to capital available in London's financial district.

Difficulties abounded. What if the original owners of the enterprise, whose property had originally been confiscated by the communists, demanded restitution? What about the enterprises'

BOX 17.3
Building market institutions in post-communist societies

Dimension	Description
Privatization	Creating privately-owned companies
Corporate governance	Ensuring these companies are professionally managed, thus encouring external investment
Capital markets	Developing banks and investment companies with capital to invest and the skill to invest it wisely
Regulatory policy	Establishing a stable framework of regulation e.g. patent and copy-right law, competition policy
Judiciary	Ensuring that judges have the training, resources and autonomy to apply rules in a consistent way, resisting bribes and political pressure
Government	Facilitating an arms-length relationship between companies and government

Definition

Mass privatization refers to attempts by post-communist governments to sell off many state-owned enterprises at the same time, often by providing the public with low-cost vouchers exchangeable for shares. By contrast, established democracies (notably Britain) practised **case-by-case privatization** in which public corporations were sold one at a time.

welfare obligations? Why should investors trust governments to deliver on their promises? And, most important, who had money to buy?

In practice, post-communist states adopted a range of strategies in restructuring their economies. Several Eastern European countries such as Hungary and Czechoslovakia could draw on economic liberalization which had preceded communism's fall. Throughout the post-communist world, many enterprises were acquired by existing managers ('spontaneous privatization'), whether by design, default or theft. Occasionally, organizations were sold to overseas companies, a method of bringing in foreign expertise and capital which nonetheless risked domestic unpopularity. Or, in many cases, strategic parts of the economy were simply left in public hands with the expectation that performance would improve as market disciplines emerged, permitting a case-by-case solution later in the reform cycle.

Interestingly, many post-communist countries (excluding Hungary) also attempted mass or voucher privatization at the early stage. Here, coupons which could be exchanged for shares in privatized enterprises were offered to the public at little or no cost. Alternatively, vouchers were placed with investment companies that stood between the investing citizen and the enterprise. Mass privatization succeeded in disposing of many enterprises at once, using a standard charter for each enterprise, and contributed to public education about investment; it achieved far more – and far faster – than the better-known case-by-case method pioneered in Britain. Given the turbulence of early post-communism, mass privatization can be viewed as a significant policy achievement.

But mass privatization led to mass disappointment since many of the enterprises turned out to be duds; the citizens of Eastern Europe gained fewer rewards than did Mrs Thatcher's army of small shareholders in the UK. Also, vouchers tended to fragment control over enterprises at a time when a few powerful shareholders might have been able to force through much-needed restructuring; Hungary's emphasis on 'real owners' rather than voucher ownership was understandable. In retrospect, the voucher method was simply one step along a winding road to a functioning market economy. Lieberman *et al.* (1996, p. 9) offer an overall assessment:

Mass privatization achieved a great deal by creating a critical mass of private companies on which other reforms could build. But considerable effort would be needed to complete the privatization process, largely through case-by-case privatization of large strategic enterprises.

Although post-communist states require most rebuilding, the nature of the task is fundamentally similar in other new democracies with a strong state tradition. In authoritarian Latin America, for example, the state had not replaced the capitalist sector but had nurtured powerful corporations (and industrialists), producing a requirement for the new democracy to engineer privatization and deregulation, and to open up protected companies to domestic and international competition.

Lijphart and Waisman (1996a) note the main similarities between privatization in Eastern Europe and Latin America. In both regions,

▶ The transition occurred as a result of an economic as well as political crisis of the old regime, including in the case of Argentina, hyperinflation and massive capital flight.
▶ The transition was carried out by the state itself, allowing the old elite to recycle itself as the new bourgeoisie.
▶ Privatization was contested, with opposition centred on those whose wealth was threatened by liberalization.

When we turn to new democracies in the smaller states of Africa and Latin America, we find that the problems of institution-building are even greater. The policy agenda here is about strengthening the capacity of *both* the public sector and the private sectors; the emphasis in established or post-communist democracies on rebalancing the relationship between public and private is a dubious prescription for new democracies in poor countries where capacity of any kind is limited.

It is certainly true that the state has been a dominant economic and political force in these smaller countries, sometimes crowding out the private sector. But the solution is not so much less government but a different kind of government, embedded in rule-following institutions rather than personal rule. Similarly, there is little point in adopting Western ideas of new public management within the bureaucracy; rather, the purpose should be to build up an orthodox civil service that applies rules consistently and economically. Developing the market also requires enhancing the public infrastructure of transport, communication and education.

In Africa, however, fragmentary attempts at capacity-building have so far produced only meagre results. Governments often lack the ability to implement their policies throughout the territory. They lack numbers on the ground and must often rely on traditional local leaders who are therefore able to veto the implementation of the reform agenda. A state that barely exists cannot be expected to engage in serious and effective policy-making and implementation. It is of course true, as Chazan *et al.* note (1999, p. 344), that the underlying problems of the African continent extend well beyond politics; the difficulties include poor soil, an arid climate, tropical diseases, Aids and a labour surplus. As a result, even in a world that is more democratic than ever before, millions of people continue to live lives of extreme poverty and degradation. If solutions are to be had, the comparative study of politics should help to find them.

Public policy in authoritarian states

Studying public policy in non-democratic regimes confirms the importance of distinguishing between different types of authoritarian government. At one extreme, many communist states attempted a type of planning virtually without precedent in history; every communist state formulated clearer national goals and targets than any democracy. The result was an often decisive and generally ruthless commitment to a single goal, notably industrialization. At the other extreme, many military and personal rulers show immense concern about their own prosperity but none at all for their country's, leading to a policy shortage.

If there is a general theme to the policy process in non-democracies (including even communist states), it is this subservience of policy to politics. In the more competitive world in which authoritarian rulers now find themselves, such weaknesses are increasingly exposed, adding to pressures for democratic reform. In this section, we will review the communist experience before turning to the policy process in contemporary authoritarian regimes.

Communist states differed enormously from established democracies in their policy goals and means. For one thing, the ruling party articulated clear objectives for society; for another, the state sought to implement these goals though detailed planning. Yet planning eventually yielded economic stagnation and thus contributed to the collapse of communism in Eastern Europe and the Soviet Union. But why did planning fail? To answer these questions, we must first look at how planning worked.

The Soviet Union is the clearest example because it ran the most planned economy on earth. The Soviet Union was the land of The Plan. Gosplan, the State Planning Committee, drew up annual five-year plans which were given the status of law once they had received political approval. Implementation was the responsibility of ministries which controlled individual enterprises through a complex administrative network. Detailed planning was forced by a command economy. A factory could not buy its components on the market when there was no market. Instead arrangements had to be made for another factory to manufacture the parts and deliver them on time – and that factory in turn had to be supplied with raw materials.

The flaw became obvious. For anything to go right everything had to go right – so inevitably something went wrong! Because the right components did not arrive at the right time, all sorts of informal and often illegal deals had to be fixed up to ensure that the arbitrary production quota was met. Further, the system was dominated by planners and producers, rather than customers. Targets were based on quantity, not quality. As a result, goods were shoddy when they were produced at all. Local managers were not empowered to use initiative, even though they were well-aware of what needed to be done.

The endemic weaknesses of an over-centralized economy led to a black market. Shortages encouraged corrupt swaps among individuals with access to resources: good cuts of meat in exchange for cigarettes, train tickets for university places. Those with little to offer, notably old people, just waited in line – for an average of three hours a day in the Soviet Union.

So was the planned economy an unmitigated disaster? Not completely. Notably in the USSR, it did prove successful at building the foundations of industrial development, albeit at a horrifying human price. Heavy industry was the great success of the planned economy, both in communist states which were undergoing industrialization for the first time and in those which were rebuilding after 1945.

This success derived from the philosophy of the big push. The resources needed to meet the goal would be allocated to the priority area, whatever the impact on other sectors. The objective of the big push took precedence and other consequences (including a degraded environment in the case of industrialization) were ignored. Objectives determined budgets rather than vice versa.

The big push was a deliberately blinkered approach which ignored the overall view but often succeeded in achieving its specific targets. For instance, Stalin's drive to industrialize Russia transformed a society of peasants into a world industrial power within a generation. Later, China and Cuba applied the big push to their own societies, again with spectacular results. The targets were often economic, such as steel production, but sometimes extended to social objectives such as adequate housing and health care.

Where, then, does the collapse of state planning leave the remaining 'communist' states, notably China? The PRC's rulers have certainly reduced the importance of central planning yet they can hardly be said to have created the conditions for a market economy. Massive, and massively inefficient, state-owned enterprises still pervade the economy, soaking up labour and serving as an indirect welfare state. The expansion of the non-state sector has stimulated continued growth but party contacts still determine access to economic opportunities. To most eyes, the system is inherently corrupt; it is certainly technically inefficient in that political criteria distort economic decisions, leading to a huge misallocation of capital. Yet this idiosyncratic model is still delivering growth in what remains a poor country. As long as economic growth continues, China's nominally communist rulers may succeed in resolving the political tensions induced by corruption and increasing inequality. Yet judging by the experience of communism in Eastern Europe and the Soviet Union, that same growth will eventually deliver a demand for more fundamental political reform.

Some non-communist authoritarian regimes have also led economic development, notably in East Asian states such as Malaysia and Singapore (see Japan profile, p. 305). But policy stagnation is a more familiar pattern under authoritarian rule. Policy inertia often results from a lack of motivation among the ruling elite. Often, the key task for non-elected rulers is to play off domestic political forces against each other so as to ensure the ruler's own continuation in office, an art developed to its highest level by the cautious ruling families of the Middle East. Or the ruler may want to enrich himself, his family and his ethnic group, a task hardly conducive to orderly policy development. More commonly, patronage is the main political currency; the age-old game of building up and paying down political debts again works against coherent policy, transparently applied. As Chazan *et al.* (1999, p. 171) note in their discussion of Africa,

> patriarchal rule has tended to be conservative: it propped up the existing order and did little to promote change. It required the exertion of a great deal of energy just to maintain control.

Finally, rulers may simply lack the ability to make coherent policy. This weakness was common enough among military governments. The generals may seize power in an honest attempt to eliminate corruption and improve policy-making but they soon discover that governance is more complicated than they had imagined. Eventually, they slink back to their lair, with little achieved.

Key reading

> **Next step:** *Stone (2001) introduces policy analysis from a political perspective.*

John (1998) and Parsons (1995) are alternatives to Stone while Fischer (2003) adopts a critical but accessible approach. Colebatch (1998) discusses the policy concept while Sabatier (1999) reviews theories of the policy process. On implementation, the classic American study by Pressman and Wildavsky (1973) can be supplemented by Hill and Hupe (2002). Rose (2004) is a comparative study of lesson-drawing in public policy. Pierson (1998, 2000) and Esping-Andersen (2002) are excellent sources on the welfare state, while Majone (1996) is outstanding on regulation. Elster *et al.* (1998) cover institutional design in post-communist societies, while Lijphart and Waisman (1996b) draw comparisons with Latin America. On privatization, see Wright (1994) for Western Europe and Lieberman *et al.* (1997) for Eastern Europe.

Appendix: list of boxes

References

To search these references by chapter, go to http://www.palgrave.com/politics/hague

A

Aberbach, J. *et al.* (1981) *Bureaucrats and Politicians* (Cambridge, MA: Harvard University Press).

Adams, F. (2003) *Deepening Democracy: Global Governance and Political Reform in Latin America* (New York: Praeger).

Addison, J. and Schnabel, C. (eds) (2003) *International Handbook of Trade Unions* (Cheltenham and Northampton, MA: Edward Elgar).

Ágh, A. (1996) 'Democratic Parliamentarism in Hungary: The First Parliament (1990–94) and the Entry of the Second Parliament', in *The New Parliaments of Central and Eastern Europe,* ed. D. Olson and P. Norton (London: Frank Cass) pp. 16–39.

Ágh, A. (1998) *The Politics of Central Europe* (London and Thousand Oaks, CA: Sage).

Agüero, F. and Stark, J. (eds) (1998) *Fault Lines of Democracy in Post-Transition Latin America* (Coral Gables, FL: University of Miami).

Almond, G. and Bingham Powell, G. (2000) *Comparative Politics Today: A World View,* 7th edn (New York: HarperCollins).

Almond, G. and Verba, S. (1963) *The Civic Culture* (Princeton, NJ: Princeton University Press).

Almond, G. and Verba, S. (eds) (1980) *The Civic Culture Revisited* (Princeton, NJ: Princeton University Press).

Altunisik, M. and Kavli, Ö. (2003) *Turkey* (London and New York: Routledge).

Ames, B. (2002) 'Party Discipline in the Chamber of Deputies', in *Legislative Politics in Latin America,* ed. S. Morgenstern and B. Nacif (Cambridge and New York: Cambridge University Press) pp. 185–221.

Anderson, B. (1991) *Imagined Communities: Reflections on the Origins and Spread of Nationalism,* revised edn (London and New York: Verso).

Anderson, B. (1998) *The Spectre of Comparisons: Nationalism, South-East Asia and the World* (London and New York: Verso).

Anderson, C. and Ward, D. (1996) 'Barometer Elections in Comparative Perspective', *European Journal of Political Research* (15) 447–60.

Anderson, M. (1997) Frontiers: Territory and State Formation in the Modern World (Cambridge: Polity).

Anderson, P. (1974) Lineages of the Absolutist State (London: NLB).

Andeweg, R. and Irwin, G. (1993) *Dutch Government and Politics* (Basingstoke: Macmillan).

Andeweg, R. and Irwin, G. (2002) *Governance and Politics of the Netherlands* (Basingstoke and New York: Palgrave).

Andrews, J. and Momtinola, G. (2004) 'Veto Players and the Rule of Law in Emerging Democracies', *Comparative Political Studies* (37) 55–87.

Arblaster, A. (2002) *Democracy,* 3rd edn (Buckingham and Philadelphia, PA: Open University Press).

Arel, D. (2001) 'Political Stability in Multinational Democracies: Comparing Language Dynamics in Brussels, Montreal and Barcelona', in *Multinational Democracies,* ed. A.-G. Gagnon and J. Tully (Cambridge and New York: Cambridge University Press) pp. 65–89.

Arendt, H. [1951] (1966 edn) *The Origins of Totalitarianism* (New York: Harcourt Brace).

Arendt, H. (1958) *The Human Condition* (Chicago, IL: University of Chicago Press).

Arendt, H. (1970) *On Violence* (London: Penguin).

Argun B. (2003) Turkey in Germany: The Transitional Sphere of Deutschkei (London and New York: Routledge).

Aristotle (1962 edn) *The Politics,* trans. T. Sinclair (Harmondsworth and Baltimore, MD: Penguin).

Arter, D. (1999) *Scandinavian Politics Today* (Manchester: Manchester University Press, and New York: St Martin's Press).

Asher, H. (1988b) *Polling and the Public: What Every Citizen Should Know* (Washington, DC: Congressional Quarterly, Inc.).

B

Baaklini, A., Denoeux, G. and Springborg, R. (1999) *Legislative Politics in the Arab World: The Resurgence of Democratic Institutions* (Boulder, CO and London: Lynne Rienner).

Baer, M. (1993) 'Mexico's Second Revolution: Pathways to Liberalization', in *Political and Economic Liberalization in Mexico: At a Critical Juncture?,* ed. R. Roett (Boulder, CO and London: Lynne Rienner) pp. 51–68.

Bagehot, W. [1867] (1963 edn) *The English Constitution* (London: Fontana).

Baka, A. (1998) 'The Framework for Public Management in Hungary', in *Innovations in Public Management: Perspectives from East and West Europe,* ed. T. Verheijen and D. Coombes (Cheltenham and Northampton, MA: Edward Elgar) pp. 128–42.

Baker, B. (2002) Taking the Law into Their Own Hands: Lawless Law Enforcers in Africa (Aldershot and Burlington, VT: Ashgate).

Bakvis, H. and Skogstad, G. (eds) (2002) *Canadian Federalism: Performance, Effectiveness and Legitimacy* (Don Mills, Ontario and Oxford: Oxford University Press).

Balme, R. (1998) 'The French Region as a Space for Public Policy', in *Regions in Europe,* ed. P. Le Galès and C. Lequesne (London and New York: Routledge) pp. 181–98.

Barber, J. (1992) *The Pulse of Politics: Electing Presidents in the Media Age* (New Brunswick, NY and London: Transaction Books).

Bardach, E. (1976) 'Policy Termination as a Political Process', *Policy Sciences* (7) 123–31.

Barry, B. (1988) *Sociologists, Economists, and Democracy* (Chicago, IL: University of Chicago Press).

Bartolini, S. and Mair, P. (1990) *Identity, Competition and Electoral Availability: The Stabilization of European Electorates 1885–1985* (Cambridge and New York: Cambridge University Press).

Batt, J. (2003) 'Defining Central and Eastern Europe' in Developments in Central and East European Politics 3, ed. S. White S., J. Batt and P. Lewis (Basingstoke: Palgrave Macmillan) pp. 3–22.

Bauböck, R. (1994) Transnational Citizenship (Cheltenham and Northampton, MA: Edward Elgar).

Bayart, J.-F. (1993) The State in Africa: The Politics of the Belly (Harlow and New York: Longman).

Bayley, S. (1998) Labour Camp: The Failure of Style over Substance (London: Batsford).

Baylis, T. (1996) 'Presidents versus Prime Ministers: Shaping Executive Authority in Eastern Europe', World Politics (48) 297–322.

Beattie, A. (2003) 'Decoding the Fed: The Art of Reading Between the Lines', Financial Times, 27 June.

Bednar, J., Eskridge, W. and Ferejohn, J. (2001) 'A Political Theory of Federalism', in Constitutional Culture and Democratic Rule, ed. J. Ferejohn, J. Rakove and J. Riley (Cambridge and New York: Cambridge University Press) pp. 223–70.

Bekke, H., Perry, J. and Toonen, T. (1996) Civil Service Systems in Comparative Perspective (Bloomington, IN: Indiana University Press).

Bell, D. et al. (eds) (1995) Towards Illiberal Democracy in Pacific Asia (London: Macmillan).

Bell, J. (1991) 'Administrative Law', in The Blackwell Encyclopaedia of Political Science, ed. V. Bogdanor (Oxford and Cambridge, MA: Blackwell) pp. 9–12.

Bendor, J., Moe, T. and Shotts, K. (2001) 'Recycling the Garbage Can: An Assessment of the Research Program', American Political Science Review (95) 169–90.

Bennett, W. Lance and Entman, R. (eds) (2001) Mediated Politics: Communication in the Future of Democracy (Cambridge and New York: Cambridge University Press).

Bentley, A. (1908) The Process of Government (Chicago, IL: University of Chicago Press).

Bentley, T., Jupp, B. and Stedman Jones, D. (2000) Getting to Grips with Depoliticization (London: Demos) at http://www.demos.co.uk.

Berger, S. (2002) 'Social Partnership 1880–1989: The Deep Historical Roots of Diverse Strategies' in Policy Concertation and Social Partnership in Western Europe: Lessons for the 21st Century, ed. S. Berger and H. Compston (New York and Oxford: Berghahn) pp. 335–52.

Berger, S. and Compston, H. (eds) (2002) Policy Concertation and Social Partnership in Western Europe: Lessons for the 21st Century (New York and Oxford: Berghahn).

Berglund, S. (1990) 'Finland in a Comparative Perspective', in Finnish Democracy, ed. J. Sunberg and S. Berglund (Jyväskylä: Finnish Political Science Association) pp. 11–25.

Bergman, T. (2000) 'Sweden: When Minority Cabinets Are the Rule and Majority Coalitions the Exception', in Coalition Governments in Western Europe, ed. W. Müller and K. Strøm (Oxford and New York: Oxford University Press) pp. 192–230.

Berrington, H. (1995) 'Political Ethics: The Nolan Report', Government and Opposition (30) 429–51.

Best, H. and Cotta, M. (2000) Parliamentary Representatives in Europe, 1848–2000 (Oxford and New York: Oxford University Press).

Bevir, M. and Rhodes, R. (2002) 'Interpretive Theory', in Theory and Methods in Political Science, 2nd edn, ed. D. Marsh and G. Stoker (Basingstoke and New York: Palgrave Macmillan) pp. 131–52.

Bill, J. and Springborg, R. (2000) Politics in the Middle East, 4th edn (New York: Longman).

Birch, A. (1972) Representation (London: Pall Mall).

Blais, A. and Massicote, L. (2002) 'Electoral Systems', in Comparing Democracies 2: New Challenges in the Study of Elections and Voting, ed. L. LeDuc, R. Niemi and P. Norris (Thousand Oaks, CA and London: Sage) pp. 40–69.

Blais, A., Massicotte, L. and Dobrzynska, A. (1997) 'Direct Presidential Elections: A World Summary', Electoral Studies (16) 441–55.

Block, F. (1977) 'The Ruling Class Does Not Rule', Socialist Revolution (3) 6–28.

Blom-Hansen, J. (2000) 'Still Corporatism in Scandinavia: A Survey of Recent Empirical Findings', Scandinavian Political Studies (23) 157–81.

Blondel, J. (1973) Comparative Legislatures (Englewood Cliffs, NJ: Prentice-Hall).

Blondel, J. (1993) 'Consensus Politics and Multiparty Systems', paper presented at the Conference on Consensual Policymaking and Multiparty Politics, Australian National University, 1993.

Boardman, A. et al. (2000) Cost–Benefit Analysis: Concepts and Practice, 2nd edn (Englewood Cliffs, NJ: Prentice-Hall).

Bodin, J. [1576] (1962 edn) The Six Books of a Commonweal, ed. K. McRae (Cambridge, MA: Harvard University Press).

Bogason, P. (1996) 'The Fragmentation of Local Government in Scandinavia', European Journal of Political Research (30) 65–86.

Bogdanor, V. (ed.) (1991) The Blackwell Encyclopaedia of Political Science (Oxford and Cambridge, MA: Blackwell).

Boli, J. and Thomas, G. (eds) (1999) Constructing World Culture: International Non-Governmental Organizations since 1875 (Stanford, CA: Stanford University Press).

Bork, R. (2003) Coercing Virtue: The Worldwide Rule of Judges (Washington, DC: American Enterprise Institute).

Borón, A. (1998) 'Faulty Democracies? A Reflection on the Capitalist "Fault Lines"', in Fault Lines of Democracy in Post-Transition Latin America, ed. F. Agüero and J. Stark (Coral Gables, FL: University of Miami) pp. 41–66.

Boston, J. (1995a) 'Inherently Governmental Functions and the Limits to Contracting Out', in The State Under Contract, ed. J. Boston (Wellington: Bridget Williams) pp. 78–111.

Boston, J. (ed.) (1995b) The State Under Contract (Wellington: Bridget Williams).

Boston, J. et al. (eds) (1995) Reshaping the State: New Zealand's Bureaucratic Revolution (Oxford and New York: Oxford University Press).

Boulding, K. (1989) Three Faces of Power (Thousand Oaks, CA and London: Sage).

Bourgault, L. (1995) Mass Media in Sub-Saharan Africa (Bloomington, IN: Indiana University Press).

Bourne, A. (2003) 'Regional Europe', in European Union Politics, ed. M. Cini (Oxford and New York: Oxford University Press) pp. 278–93.

Bowler, S. and Donovan, T. (2002) 'Democracy, Institutions and Attitudes about Citizen Influence on Government', British Journal of Political Science (32) 371–90.

Bowler, S. and Farrell, D. (eds) (1992) Electoral Strategies and Political Marketing (London: Macmillan).

Bowler, S., Donovan, T. and Tolbert, C. (eds) (1998) Citizens as Legislators: Direct Democracy in the United States (Columbus, OH: Ohio State University Press).

Bowles, N. (1998) Government and Politics of the United States, 2nd edn (Basingstoke: Macmillan).

Boyne, R. (2003) Risk (Milton Keynes: Open University Press).

Bratton, M. (1997) 'Deciphering Africa's Divergent Transitions', Political Science Quarterly (112) 67–93.

Bratton, M. (1998) 'Second Elections in Africa', Journal of Democracy (9) 51–66.

Bratton, M. and van de Walle, N. (1997) Democratic Experiments in

Africa: Regime Transitions in Comparative Perspective (Cambridge and New York: Cambridge University Press).

Braun, D. (ed.) (2000) *Public Policy and Federalism* (Aldershot and Burlington, VT: Ashgate).

Braun, D. *et al.* (2003) *Fiscal Policies in Federal States* (Aldershot and Burlington, VT: Ashgate).

Breslin, S. *et al.* (eds) (2002) *New Regionlaism in the Global Political Economy: Theories and Cases* (London and NY: Routledge).

Breuilly, J. (1993) *Nationalism and the State,* 2nd edn (New York: St Martin's Press).

Brewer, P., Aday, S. and Gross, K. (2003) 'Rallies All Round: The Dynamics of System Support', in *Framing Terrorism: The News Media, the Government and the Public,* ed. P. Norris, M. Kern and M. Just (London and NY: Routledge) pp. 229–54.

Bromley, C. and Curtice, J. (2002) 'Where Have All the Voters Gone?', in *British Social Attitudes: the 19th Report,* ed. A. Park et al. (London and Thousand Oaks, CA: Sage) pp. 118–32.

Brooker, P. (1995) *Twentieth-Century Dictatorships: The Ideological One-Party States* (Basingstoke: Macmillan).

Brooker, P. (2000) *Non-Democratic Regimes: Theory, Government and Politics* (Basingstoke: Macmillan, and New York: St Martin's Press).

Brooks, S. (1996) *Canadian Democracy: An Introduction,* 2nd edn (Toronto and Oxford: Oxford University Press).

Broughton, D. (1995) *Public Opinion Polling and Politics in Britain* (Hemel Hempstead: Harvester Wheatsheaf).

Broughton, D. (2002) 'Participation and Voting', in *Developments in West European Politics 2,* ed. P. Heywood, E. Jones and M. Rhodes (Basingstoke and New York: Palgrave) pp. 94–114.

Brown, A. (ed.) (2001) *Contemporary Russian Politics: A Reader* (Oxford and New York: Oxford University Press).

Brown, L. (1984) *International Politics and the Middle East: Old Rules, Dangerous Games* (Princeton, NJ and London: Princeton University Press).

Bryce, J. (1921) *Modern Democracies,* Vol. 2 (New York: Macmillan).

Brzezinski, Z. (1997) 'The New Challenge to Human Rights', *Journal of Democracy* (8) 3–8.

Brzezinski Z. (2002) 'Confronting Anti-American Grievances', *New York Times,* 1 September.

Buckley, M. and Fawn, R. (eds) (2003) *Global Responses to Terrorism: 9/11, Afghanistan and Beyond* (London and New York: Routledge).

Budge, I. (1996) *The New Challenge of Direct Democracy* (Cambridge: Polity).

Bull, H. (1977) *The Anarchical Society: A Study of Order in World Politics* (Basingstoke: Macmillan).

Burgess, M. (2000) *Federalism and European Union: The Building of Europe, 1950–2000* (London and New York: Routledge).

Burgess, M. (2001) 'Competing National Visions: Canada–Quebec Relations in a Comparative Perspective', in *Multinational Democracies,* ed. A.-G. Gagnon and J. Tully (Cambridge and New York: Cambridge University Press) pp. 257–74.

Burgess, M. (2003) 'Federalism and Federation', in *European Union Politics,* ed. M. Cini (Oxford and New York: Oxford University Press) pp. 65–79.

Burgess, M. and Gagnon, A.-G. (eds) (1993) *Comparative Federalism and Federation: Competing Traditions and Future Directions* (Hemel Hempstead: Harvester Wheatsheaf).

Burke, E. [1774] (1975 edn) 'Speech to the Electors of Bristol' in *Edmund Burke on Government, Politics and Society,* ed. B. Hill (London: Fontana) pp. 156–8.

Burnham, W. (1982) 'The Constitution, Capitalism and the Need for Rationalized Regulation', in *How Capitalistic Is the Constitution?* ed. R. Goldwyn and W. Schambra (Washington, DC: American Enterprise Institute) pp. 72–87.

Burns, N. *et al.* (2001) *The Private Roots of Public Action: Gender, Equality and Political Participation* (Cambridge, MA: Harvard University Press).

Butler, A. (2004) *Contemporary South Africa* (Basingstoke and New York: Palgrave).

Butler, D. (1989) *British General Elections Since 1945* (Oxford and Cambridge, MA: Blackwell). [new ed?]

Butler, D. and Kavanagh D. (2002) *The British General Election of 2001* (Basingstoke and New York: Palgrave).

C

Camp, R. (2002) *Politics in Mexico: The Democratic Transformation,* 4th edn (Oxford and New York: Oxford University Press).

Campbell, A., Converse, P., Miller, A. *et al.* (1960) *The American Voter* (New York: Wiley).

Campbell, C. and Wilson, G. (1995) *The End of Whitehall: Death of a Paradigm?* (Oxford and Cambridge, MA: Blackwell).

Canel, E. (1992) 'Democratization and the Decline of Urban Social Movements in Uruguay: A Political Institutional Account', in *The Making of Social Movements in Latin America: Identity, Strategy and Democracy,* ed. A. Escobar and S. Alvarez (Boulder, CO and Oxford: Westview) pp. 276–90.

Caplan, J. (1988) *Government Without Administration: State and Civil Service in Weimar and Nazi Germany* (Oxford: Clarendon Press).

Carey, J. (1998) *Term Limits and Legislative Representation* (Cambridge and New York: Cambridge University Press).

Carothers, T. (2002) 'The End of the Transition Paradigm', *Journal of Democracy* (13) 5–21.

Carty, H. (2002) 'Canada's Nineteenth Century Parties at the Millennium', in *Political Parties in Advanced Industrial Democracies,* ed. P. Webb, D. Farrell and I. Holliday (Oxford and New York: Oxford University Press) pp. 345–78.

Case, W. (1996) 'Can the "Halfway House" Stand? Semidemocracy and Elite Theory in Three Southeast Asian Countries', *Comparative Politics* (28) 437–64.

Centeno, M. and Silva, R (1998) 'Introduction', in *The Politics of Expertise in Latin America,* ed. M. Centeno and P. Silva (Basingstoke: Macmillan, and New York: St Martin's Press) pp. 1–12.

Cerny, P. (1990) *The Changing Architecture of Politics* (Thousand Oaks, CA and London: Sage).

Chalmers, D. (1990) *Dilemmas of Latin American Democratization: Dealing with International Forces,* Papers on Latin America, No. 18 (New York: Columbia University Institute of Latin American and Iberian Studies).

Chandler, J. (1993) *Local Government in Liberal Democracies: An Introductory Survey* (London and New York: Routledge).

Chandler, J. (ed.) (2000) *Comparative Public Administration* (London and New York: Routledge).

Chatterjee, D. and Scheid, D. (eds) (2003) *Ethics and Foreign Intervention* (Cambridge and New York: Cambridge University Press).

Chazan, N. *et al.* (1999) *Politics and Society in Contemporary Africa,* 3rd edn (Boulder, CO: Lynne Rienner).

Chebabi, H. and Linz, J. (eds) (1998) *Sultanistic Regimes* (Baltimore, MD and London: Johns Hopkins University Press).

Cheibub, J. (2002) 'Minority Governments, Deadlock Situations and the Survival of Presidential Democracies', *Comparative Political Studies* (35) 284–312.

Christensen, T. and Egeberg, M. (eds) (1997) *Forvaltnings-kunnskap* (Oslo: Aschehoug Tano).

Christensen, T. and Guy Peters, B. (1999) *Structure, Culture and Governance: A Comparison of Norway and the United States* (Lanham, MD and Oxford: Rowman & Littlefeld).

Cigler, C. and Loomis, B. (eds) (2002) *Interest Group Politics,* 6th edn (Washington: Congressional Quarterly Press).

Clark S. (1995) *State and Status: The Rise of the State and Aristocratic Power in Western Europe* (Montreal and Kingston: McGill-Queen's University Press).

Close, D. (ed.) (1995) *Legislatures and the New Democracies in Latin America* (Boulder, CO and London: Lynne Rienner).

Clover, C. (2003) 'Iraqi Jigsaw Confronts Makers of Constitution', *Financial Times*, 29 September, p. 8.

Cohen, M., March, J. and Olsen, J. (1972) 'A Garbage Can Model of Organizational Choice', *Administrative Science Quarterly* (17) 1–25.

Colebatch, H. (1998) *Policy* (Buckingham: Open University Press).

Collier, D. (1991) 'The Comparative Method: Two Decades of Change', in *Comparative Dynamics: Global Research Perspectives,* ed. D. Rustow and K. Erickson (New York: HarperCollins) pp. 7–31.

Conover, P. and Searing, D. (1994) 'Democratic Citizenship and the Study of Political Socialization', in *Developing Democracy: Essays in Honour of J. F. P. Blondel,* ed. I. Budge and D. McKay (Thousand Oaks, CA and London: Sage) pp. 24–55.

Conradt, D. (2001) *The German Polity,* 7th edn (New York: Longman).

Constable, P. (2001) 'Pakistan's Predicament', *Journal of Democracy* (12) 15–29.

Conway, M. (2001) 'Political Participation in American Elections: Who Decides What?', in *America's Choice 2000,* ed. W. Crotty (Boulder, CO: Westview) pp. 79–94.

Cornelius, W. and Weldon, J. (2004) 'Politics in Mexico', in *Comparative Politics Today: A World View,* 8th edn, ed. G. Almond *et al.* (New York and London: Pearson Longman) pp. 466–519.

Cotta, M. (2000) 'Defining Party and Government', in *The Nature of Party Government: A Comparative European Perspective,* ed. J. Blondel and M. Cotta (Basingstoke: Macmillan) pp. 56–95.

Cottey, A. et al. (eds) (2003) *Democratic Control of the Military in Post-Communist Europe* (Basingstoke: Palgrave).

Cox, G. and Morgenstern, S. (2002) 'Latin America's Reactive Assemblies and Proactive Presidents', in *Legislative Politics in Latin America,* ed. S. Morgenstern and B. Nacif (Cambridge and New York: Cambridge University Press) pp. 446–68.

Craske, M. (2001) 'Another Mexican Earthquake: An Assessment of the 2 July 2000 Elections', *Government and Opposition* (36) 27–47.

Crawford, K. (1996) *East Central European Politics Today* (Manchester: Manchester University Press and New York: St Martin's Press).

Crawford, N. (2003) *Argument and Change in World Politics: Ethics, Decolonization and Humanitarian Intervention* (Cambridge and New York: Cambridge University Press).

Crick, B. (2000) *In Defence of Politics,* 5th edn (Harmondsworth: Penguin).

Crockett, D. [1834] (1987 edn) *A Narrative of the Life of David Crockett of the State of Tennessee*, intro. J. Shackford and S. Folmsbee (Knoxville, TN: University of Tennessee Press).

Cronin, T. (1989) *Direct Democracy: The Politics of Initiative, Referendum and Recall* (Cambridge, MA and London: Harvard University Press).

Crothers L. and Lockhart C. (eds) (2000) Culture and Politics: A Reader (Basingstoke: Palgrave Macmillan).

Crouch, H. (1996) *Government and Society in Malaysia* (Cornell, NY: Cornell University Press).

Curran, J. and Seaton, J. (2003) *Power Without Responsibility: The Press and Broadcasting in Britain,* 6th edn (London and New York: Methuen).

Cutler, L. (1980) 'To Form a Government', *Foreign Affairs* (59) 126–43.

D

Dahl, R. (1957) 'The Concept of Power', *Behavioral Science* (2) 201–15.

Dahl, R. (1961) *Who Governs? Democracy and Power in an American City* (New Haven, CT and London: Yale University Press).

Dahl, R. (1989) *Democracy and its Critics* (New Haven, CT and London: Yale University Press).

Dahl, R. (1993) 'Pluralism', in *The Oxford Companion to Politics of the World,* ed. J. Krieger (New York and Oxford: Oxford University Press) pp. 704–7.

Dahl, R. (1998) *On Democracy* (New Haven, CT and London: Yale University Press).

Dahl, R. (1999) 'Can International Organizations Be Democratic?', in *Democracy's Edges,* ed. I. Shapiro and C. Hacker-Cordon (New Haven, CT and London: Yale University Press) pp. 19–36.

Dahl, R. (2000) 'A Democratic Paradox?', *Scandinavian Political Studies* (23) 246–51.

Dahl, R. (2001) *How Democratic is the American Constitution?* (New Haven, CT and London: Yale University Press).

Dahl, R., Shapiro, I. and Cheibub, J. (eds) (2003) *The Democracy Sourcebook* (Cambridge, MA: MIT Press).

Dalton, R. (1994) *The Green Rainbow: Environmental Groups in Western Europe* (New Haven, CT and London: Yale University Press).

Dalton, R. (2002) 'Political Cleavages, Issues and Electoral Change', in *Comparing Democracies 2: New Challenges in the Study of Elections and Voting,* ed. L. LeDuc, R. Niemi and P. Norris (London and Thousand Oaks, CA: Sage) pp. 189–209.

Dalton, R. and Wattenberg, M. (2000) *Politics Without Partisans: Political Change in Advanced Industrial Democracies* (Oxford and New York: Oxford University Press).

Dalton, R., McAllister, I. and Wattenberg, M. (2000) 'The Consequences of Partisan Dealignment', in *Parties Without Partisans,* ed. R. Dalton and M. Wattenberg (Oxford and New York: Oxford University Press) pp. 37–63.

Davies, J. (1962) 'Toward a Theory of Revolution', *American Sociological Review* (27) 5–18.

Davies, N. (1996) *Europe: A History* (Oxford and New York: Oxford University Press).

Davis, J. (1998) *Leadership Selection in Six Western Democracies* (Westport, CT: Greenwood).

Day, S. and Shaw, J. (2002) 'European Union Electoral Rights and the Political Participation of Migrants in Host Polities', *International Journal of Population Geography* (8) 183–99.

de Burea, G. and Wieler, J. (eds) (2002) *The European Court of Justice* (Oxford and New York: Oxford University Press).

de Swaan, A. (1973) *Coalition Theories and Cabinet Formation* (Amsterdam: Elsevier).

de Tocqueville, A. [1835] (1966 edn) *Democracy in America* (New York: Vintage Books). Also available on-line at the American Studies website at the University of Virginia: http://xroads. virginia.edu.

de Tocqueville, A. [1856] (1954 edn) *The Ancien Regime and the Revolution in France* (London: Fontana).

Deegan, H. (2001) *The Politics of the New South Africa: Apartheid and After* (Harlow and New York: Longman).

Dehousse, R. (1998) *The European Court of Justice* (London: Macmillan).

della Porta, D., Kriesi, H. and Rucht, D. (eds) (1999) *Social Movements in a Globalizing World* (London: Macmillan and New York: St Martin's Press).

Denemark, D. (2002) 'Choosing MMP in New Zealand: Explaining the 1993 Electoral Reform', in *Mixed-Member Electoral Systems: The Best of Both Worlds*, ed. M. Shugart and M. Wattenberg (Oxford and New York: Oxford University Press) pp. 70–95.

Derbyshire, J. and Derbyshire, I. (1999a) *Encyclopedia of World Political Systems* (London and Armonk, NY: M.E. Sharpe).

Derbyshire, J. and Derbyshire, I. (1999b) *Political Systems of the World* (Oxford: Helicon).

Diamond, L. (1992) 'Economic Development and Democracy Reconsidered', in *Reexamining Democracy: Essays in Honor of Seymour Martin Lipset*, ed. G. Marks and L. Diamond (Thousand Oaks, CA and London: Sage) pp. 93–131.

Diamond, L. (1997) 'Democracy in the Americas', *Annals of the American Academy of Political and Social Sciences* (550) 12–41.

Diamond, L. (1999) *Developing Democracy: Toward Consolidation* (Baltimore, MD and London: Johns Hopkins University Press).

Diamond, L. and Lipset, S. (1995) 'Legitimacy', in *The Encyclopaedia of Democracy*, ed. S. Lipset (London and New York: Routledge) pp. 747–51.

Diamond, L. and Plattner, M. (eds) (1996) *The Global Resurgence of Democracy*, 2nd edn (Baltimore, MD and London: John Hopkins University Press).

Diamond, L. and Plattner, M. (eds) (2001) *The Global Divergence of Democracies* (Baltimore, MD: Johns Hopkins University Press).

Diamond, L. and Plattner, M. (eds) (2002) *Democracy after Communism* (Baltimore, MD and London: Johns Hopkins University Press).

Diamond, L., Linz, J. and Lipset, S. (1995) 'Introduction: What Makes For Democracy?', in *Politics in Developing Countries: Comparing Experiences with Democracy*, ed. L. Diamond, J. Linz and S. Lipset (Boulder, CO and London: Lynne Rienner) pp. 1–33.

Diamond, L., Plattner, M. and Brumberg, D. (eds) (2003) *Islam and Democracy in the Middle East* (Baltimore, MD and London: Johns Hopkins University Press).

Dicey, A. [1885] (1959 edn) *Introduction to the Study of the Law of the Constitution*, 10th edn (London: Macmillan).

Diehl, P. (2001) *The Politics of Global Governance: International Organizations in an Interdependent World* (Boulder, CO and London: Lynne Rienner).

Dittmer, L. and Gore, L. (2001) 'China Builds a Market Culture', *East Asia* (19) 1–50.

Dodd, L. and Oppenheimer, B. (eds) (2001) *Congress Reconsidered*, 7th edn (Washington, DC: Congressional Quarterly Press).

Dogan, M. and Kazancigil, A. (eds) (1994) *Comparing Nations:*

Concepts, Strategies, Substance (Cambridge, MA and Oxford: Blackwell).

Dogan, M. and Pelassy, G. (1990) *How to Compare Nations* (Chatham, NJ: Chatham House).

Doherty, B. *et al.* (2003) 'Explaining the Fuel Protests', *British Journal of Politics and International Relations* (5) 1–23.

Domingo, P. and Sieder, R. (2001) 'Conclusions', in *Rule of Law in Latin America: The International Promotion of Judicial Reform*, ed. P. Domingo and R. Sieder (London: Institute of Latin American Studies, University of London) pp. 142–64.

Domínguez, J. and Giraldo, J. (1996) 'Parties, Institutions and Market Reforms in Constructing Democracies', in *Constructing Democratic Governance: Mexico, Central America and the Caribbean in the 1990s*, ed. J. Domínguez and A. Lowenthal (Baltimore, MD and London: Johns Hopkins University Press) pp. 3–41.

Donovan, M. (1995) 'The Politics of Electoral Reform in Italy', *International Political Science Review* (16) 47–64.

Dooley, B. and Baron, S. (eds) (2001) *The Politics of Information in Early Modern Europe* (London and New York: Longman).

Döring, H. (2001) 'Parliamentary Agenda Control and Legislative Outcomes in Western Europe', *Legislative Studies Quarterly* (26) 145–65.

Döring, H. and Hallerberg, M. (eds) (2004) *Patterns of Parliamentary Behaviour: Passage of Legislation Across Western Europe* (Aldershot and Burlington, VT: Ashgate).

Dorussen, H. and Taylor, M. (eds) (2002) *Economic Voting* (London and New York: Routledge).

Downs, A. (1957) *An Economic Theory of Democracy* (New York: Harper).

Downs, G., Roche, D. and Baroom, P. (1996) 'Is the Good News about Compliance Good News about Cooperation?', *International Organization* (50) 379–406.

Drake, P. and Jaksic, I. (eds) (1989) *The Struggle for Democracy in Chile* (Lincoln, NE and London: University of Nebraska Press).

Duchacek, I. (1973) *Power Maps: The Comparative Politics of Constitutions* (Santa Barbara, CA: ABC Clio).

Duchacek, I. (1991) 'Constitutions/Constitutionalism', in *The Blackwell Encyclopaedia of Political Science*, ed. V. Bogdanor (Oxford and Cambridge, MA: Blackwell) pp. 142–4.

Dunleavy, P. (2003) 'Analysing Political Power', in *Developments in British Politics 7*, ed. P. Dunleavy *et al.* (Basingstoke and New York: Palgrave Macmillan) pp. 338–59.

Dunleavy, P. *et al.* (eds) (2003) *Developments in British Politics 7* (Basingstoke and New York: Palgrave Macmillan).

Duverger, M. [1954] (1970 edn) *Political Parties* (London: Methuen).

Duverger, M. (1980) 'A New Political System Model: Semi-Presidential Government', *European Journal of Political Research* (8) 165–87.

Dye, T. (2001) *Understanding Public Policy*, 10th edn (Englewood Cliffs, NJ: Prentice-Hall).

Dyson, K. (1980) *The State Tradition in Western Europe: A Study of an Idea and Institution* (Oxford: Martin Robertson).

E

Easter, G. (1997) 'Preference for Presidentialism: Postcommunist Regime Change in Russia and the NIS', *World Politics* (49) 184–211.

Easton, D. (1965a) *A Framework for Political Analysis* (Englewood Cliffs, NJ: Prentice-Hall).

Easton, D. (1965b) *A Systems Analysis of Political Life* (New York: Wiley).

Eberle, J. (1990) 'Understanding the Revolutions in Eastern Europe', in *Spring in Winter: The 1989 Revolutions*, ed. G. Prins (Manchester: Manchester University Press) pp. 193–209.

Eckstein, H. (1998a) 'Congruence Theory Explained', in *Can Democracy Take Root in Post-Soviet Russia? Explorations in State–Society Relations*, ed. H. Eckstein *et al.* (Lanham, MD and Oxford: Rowman & Littlefield) pp. 3–33.

Eckstein, H. (1998b) 'Russia and the Conditions of Democracy', in *Can Democracy Take Root in Post-Soviet Russia? Explorations in State–Society Relations*, ed. H. Eckstein *et al.* (Lanham, MD and Oxford: Rowman & Littlefield) pp. 349–81.

Eckstein, H. *et al.* (eds) (1998) *Can Democracy Take Root in Post-Soviet Russia? Explorations in State–Society Relations* (Lanham, MD and Oxford: Rowman & Littlefield).

Edelman, M. (1964) *The Symbolic Uses of Politics* (Urbana, IL: University of Illinois Press).

Edelman, M. (1995) 'Israel', in *The Global Expansion of Judicial Power*, ed. C. Tate and T. Vallinder (New York and London: New York University Press) pp. 403–16.

Eigen, L. and Siegel, J. (1993) *The Macmillan Dictionary of Political Quotations* (New York: Macmillan).

Eising, R. (2003) 'Interest Groups and the European Union' in *European Union Politics*, ed. M. Cini (Oxford and New York: Oxford University Press) pp. 192–204.

Eising, R. and Cini, M. (2002) 'Disintegration or Reconfiguration? Organized Interests in Western Europe', in *Developments in West European Politics 2*, ed. P. Heywood, E. Jones and M. Rhodes (Basingstoke and New York: Palgrave) pp. 168–83.

Elazar, D. (1996) 'From Statism to Federalism: A Paradigm Shift', *International Political Science Review* (17) 417–30.

Elazar, D. (1998) *Constitutionalizing Globalization: The Postmodern Revival of Confederal Arrangements* (Lanham, MD and Oxford: Rowman & Littlefield).

Eley, G. and Suny, R. (1996) 'From the Moment of Social History to the Work of Cultural Representation', in *Becoming National: A Reader*, ed. G. Eley and R. Suny (Oxford and New York: Oxford University Press) pp. 3–37.

Elgie, R. (1995) *Political Leadership in Liberal Democracies* (Basingstoke: Macmillan).

Elgie, R. (1999a) 'France', in *Semi-Presidentialism in Europe*, ed. R. Elgie (Oxford and New York: Oxford University Press) pp. 1–21.

Elgie, R. (ed.) (1999b) *Semi-Presidentialism in Europe* (Oxford and New York: Oxford University Press).

Elgie, R. (2003) *Political Institutions in Contemporary France* (Oxford and New York: Oxford University Press).

Elster, J., Offe, C. and Preuss, U. (1998) *Institutional Design in Post-Communist Societies: Rebuilding the Ship at Sea* (Cambridge and New York: Cambridge University Press).

Emy, M. and Hughes, O. (1991) *Australian Politics: Realities in Conflict* (South Melbourne: Macmillan).

Englebert, D., Tarango, S. and Carter, M. (2002) 'Dismemberment and Suffocation: A Contribution to the Debate on African Boundaries', *Comparative Political Studies* (35) 1093–1118.

Englebert, P. (2002) *State Legitimacy and Development in Africa* (Boulder, CO and London: Lynne Rienner).

Entman, R. (1993) 'Framing: Toward Clarification of a Fractured Paradigm', *Journal of Communications* (43) 51–8.

Eriksen, E. (1990) 'Towards the Post-Corporate State?', *Scandinavian Political Studies* (13) 345–64.

Esping-Andersen, G. (1990) *The Three Worlds of Welfare Capitalism* (Oxford: Polity).

Esping-Andersen, G. (1996a) 'After the Golden Age? Welfare State Dilemmas in a Global Economy', in *Welfare States in Transition: National Adaptations in Global Economies*, ed. G. Esping-Andersen (Thousand Oaks, CA and London: Sage) pp. 1–31.

Esping-Andersen, G. (ed.) (1996b) *Welfare States in Transition: National Adaptations in Global Economies* (Thousand Oaks, CA and London: Sage).

Esping-Andersen, G. (ed.) (2002) *Why We Need a Welfare State* (Oxford and New York: Oxford University Press).

Eulau, H. (1963) *The Behavioral Persuasion in Politics* (New York: Random House).

Evans, C. (2001) 'Committees, Leaders and Message Politics', in *Congress Reconsidered*, 7th edn, ed. L. Dodd and B. Oppenheimer (Washington, DC: Congressional Quarterly Press) pp. 82–97.

Evans, J. (2003) *Voters and Voting: An Introduction* (London and Thousand Oaks, CA: Sage).

Evans, P., Rueschemeyer, D. and Skocpol, T. (eds) (1985) *Bringing The State Back In* (Cambridge and New York: Cambridge University Press).

Fairbanks, C. (2001) 'Ten Years After the Soviet Breakup: Disillusionment in the Caucasus and Central Asia', *Journal of Democracy* (2001) 49–56.

Farnen, R. and Meloen, J. (eds) (2000) *Democracy, Authoritarianism and Education* (Basingstoke: Palgrave).

Farrell, D. (2001) *Electoral Systems: A Comparative Introduction* (London and New York: Palgrave).

Farrell, D. and Schmitt-Beck, R. (eds) (2002) *Do Political Campaigns Matter? Campaign Effects in Elections and Referendums* (London and New York: Routledge).

Feigenbaum, H., Henig, J. and Hamnett, C. (2003) *Shrinking the State: The Political Underpinnings of Privatization* (Cambridge and New York: Cambridge University Press).

Feldman, N. (2000) *After Jihad: America and the Struggle for Islamic Democracy* (New York: Farrar, Straus and Giroux).

Feldman, O. (1993) *Politics and the News Media in Japan* (Ann Arbor, MI: University of Michigan Press).

Fensmith, J. (2001) 'The Political and Social Implications of China's Accession to the World Trade Organization', *China Quarterly* (167) 573–91.

Ferejohn, J. Rakove, J. and Riley, J. (eds) (2001) *Constitutional Culture and Democratic Rule* (Cambridge and New York: Cambridge University Press).

Fernando J. and Heston A. (1997) 'NGOs between States, Markets and Civil Society' *Annals of the American Academy of Political and Social Sciences* (554) 8–19.

Fesler, J. and Kettl, D. (1996) *The Politics of the Administrative Process*, 2nd edn (Chatham, NJ: Chatham House).

Figgis, J. (1960) *Political Thought from Gerson to Grotius, 1414–1625* (New York: Harper Torchbooks).

Finer, S. [1962] (1988 edn) *The Man on Horseback: The Role of the Military in Politics* (Boulder, CO: Westview).

Finer S. (1975) 'State- and Nation-building in Europe: The Role of the Military', in *The Formation of National States in Western Europe*, ed. C. Tilly (Princeton, NJ: Princeton University Press) pp. 84–163.

Finer, S. (1997) *The History of Government from the Earliest Times*, 3 vols (Oxford and New York: Oxford University Press).

Finley, M. (1985) *Democracy Ancient and Modern* (London: Hogarth Press).

Fiorina, M. (1981) *Retrospective Voting in American National Elections* (New Haven, CT: Yale University Press).

Fischer, F. (2003) *Reframing Public Policy: Discursive Practice and Deliberative Practices* (Oxford and New York: Oxford University Press).

Fishkin, J. (1991) *Democracy and Deliberation: New Directions for Democratic Reform* (New Haven, CT and London: Yale University Press).

Fitzmaurice, J. (1998) *Politics and Government in the Visegrad Countries: Poland, Hungary, the Czech Republic and Slovakia* (London: Macmillan and New York: St Martin's Press).

Flammang, J. *et al.* (1990) *American Politics in a Changing World* (Pacific Grove, CA: Brooks/Cole).

Flora, P. and Heidenheimer, A. (eds) (1981) *The Development of Welfare States in Europe and America* (New York: Transaction).

Foley, M. (1999) 'In Kiev They Fine a Journalist $1m and Cut Off All the Phones', *The Times,* April 2 1999, p. 45.

Foran, J. (ed.) (1997) *Theorizing Revolutions* (London and New York: Routledge).

Forsyth, M. (1989) *Federalism and Nationalism* (Leicester: Leicester University Press).

Forsyth, M. (1996) 'The Political Theory of Federalism: The Relevance of Classical Approaches', in *Federalizing Europe: The Costs, Benefits and Preconditions of Federal Political Systems*, ed. J. Hesse and V. Wright (Oxford and New York: Oxford University Press) pp. 47–64.

Fortescue, J. (1714) *On the Governance of the Kingdom of England* (London: Bowyer).

Foucault, M. (1977) *Discipline and Punish: The Birth of the Prison*, trans. A. Sheridan (New York: Pantheon).

Frank, A. (1969) *Capitalism and Underdevelopment in Latin America* (New York: Monthly Review Press).

Franklin, M. (1992) 'The Decline of Cleavage Politics', in *Electoral Change: Responses to Evolving Social and Attitudinal Structures in Western Countries,* ed. M. Franklin, T. Mackie and H. Valen (Cambridge and New York: Cambridge University Press) pp. 383–405.

Franklin, M. (1996) 'Electoral Participation', in *Elections and Voting in Global Perspective,* ed. L. LeDuc, R. Niemi and P. Norris (Thousand Oaks, CA and London: Sage) pp. 216–35.

Franklin, M. (2002) 'The Dynamics of Electoral Participation' in *Comparing Democracies 2*, ed. L. LeDuc, R. Niemi and P. Norris (London and Thousand Oaks, CA) pp. 148–68.

Franklin, M., Mackie, T., Valen, H. *et al.* (eds) (1992) *Electoral Change: Responses to Evolving Social and Attitudinal Structures in Western Countries* (Cambridge and New York: Cambridge University Press).

Fransmyr, T. *et al.* (eds) *The Quantifying Spirit in the Eighteenth Century* (Berkeley, CA: University of California Press).

Fried, R. (1990) *Nightmare in Red: The McCarthy Era in Perspective* (New York and Oxford: Oxford University Press).

Friedrich, C. (1937) *Constitutional Government and Politics* (New York: Harper).

Friedrich, C. and Brzezinski, Z. (1965) *Totalitarian Dictatorship and Autocracy* (New York: Praeger).

Frühling, H. (1998) 'Judicial Reform and Democratization in Latin America', in *Fault Lines of Democracy in Post-Transition Latin America,* ed. F. Agüero and J. Stark (Coral Gables, FL: University of Miami) pp. 237–62.

G

Gagnon, A.-G. and Tully, J. (eds) (2001) *Multinational Democracies* (Cambridge and New York: Cambridge University Press).

Gallagher, M. *et al.* (2000) *Representative Government in Modern Europe*, 3rd edn (New York and London: McGraw-Hill).

Gallagher, M. and Uleri, P. (eds) (1996) *The Referendum Experience in Europe* (Basingstoke: Macmillan).

Gamble A. (2003) 'Remaking the Constitution' in *Developments in British Politics 7*, ed. P. Dunleavy *et al.* (Basingstoke and New York: Palgrave Macmillan) pp. 18–38.

Gamble, A. and Payne, A. (eds) (1996a) *Regionalism and World Order* (Basingstoke: Macmillan).

Gamble, A. and Payne, A. (1996b) 'The New Regionalism', in *Regionalism and World Order,* ed. A. Gamble and A. Payne (Basingstoke: Macmillan) pp. 247–64.

Gardner, J. (2000) *About Common Cause.* Common Cause home page, available at http://www.commoncause.org/about/fact.htm .

Gavin, N. and Sanders, D. (2003) 'The Press and its Influence on British Political Attitudes under New Labour', *Political Studies* (51) 573–91.

Gay, P. du (2000) *In Praise of Bureaucracy: Weber, Organization, Ethics* (London and Thousand Oaks, CA: Sage).

Geertz, C. [1973] (1993 edn) 'Thick Description: Toward an Interpretative Theory of Culture', in *Interpretation of Cultures,* ed. C. Geertz (London: Fontana) pp. 1–33.

Gellner, E. (1983) *Nations and Nationalism* (Oxford and Cambridge, MA: Blackwell).

Gerth, H. and Mills, C. Wright (1948) *From Max Weber* (London: Routledge & Kegan Paul).

Gill, G. (2000) *The Dynamics of Democratization: Elites, Civil Society and the Transition Process* (Basingstoke: Macmillan, and New York: St Martin's Press).

Gill, G. and Markwick, R. (2000) *Russia's Stillborn Democracy: From Gorbachev to Yeltsin* (Oxford and New York: Oxford University Press).

Gills, B., Rocamora, J. and Wilson, R. (eds) (1993) *Low Intensity Democracy: Political Power in the New World Order* (Boulder, CO and London: Pluto).

Ginsberg, B. (1982) *The Consequences of Consent* (Reading, MA: Addison Wesley).

Ginsberg, B. (1986) *The Captive Public: How Mass Opinion Promotes State Power* (New York: Basic Books).

Giol, J. (1990) 'By Consociationalism to a Majoritarian Parliamentary System: The Rise and Decline of the Spanish Cortes', in *Parliament and Democratic Consolidation in Southern Europe,* ed. U. Liebert and M. Cotta (London: Pinter) pp. 92–131.

Glaser, D. (2001) *Politics and Society in South Africa* (London and Thousand Oaks, CA: Sage).

Gleason, A. (1995) *Totalitarianism: The Inner History of the Cold War* (New York: Oxford University Press).

Glynn, C. *et al.* (1998) *Public Opinion* (Boulder, CO and Oxford: Westview Press).

Goban-Klas, T. and Sasinka-Klas, T. (1992) 'From Closed to Open Communication Systems', in *Democracy and Civil Society in Eastern Europe,* ed. P. Lewis (London: Macmillan and New York: St Martin's Press) pp. 76–90.

Goetz, K. (2003) 'Government at the Centre', in *Developments in German Politics 3*, ed. S. Padgett, W. Paterson and G. Smith (Basingstoke: Palgrave Macmillan) pp. 17–37.

Goetz, K. (1997) 'Acquiring Political Craft: Training Grounds for Top Officials in the German Core Executive', *Public Administration* (75) 753–75.

Goldsmith, M. (1996) 'Normative Theories of Local Government: A European Survey', in *Rethinking Local Democracy,* ed. D. King and G. Stoker (Basingstoke and New York: Macmillan).

Goldstone, J. (1991) 'An Analytical Framework', in *Revolutions of* the Late Twentieth Century, ed. J. Goldstone, T. Gurr and F. Moshiri (Boulder, CO and Oxford: Westview) pp. 37–51.

Gomm, R. and Hammersley, M. (eds) (2000) *Case Study Method: Key Issues, Key Texts* (Thousand Oaks, CA and London: Sage).

Gong, T. (2002) 'Dangerous Collusion: Corruption as a Collective Venture in Contemporary China', *Communist and Postsocialist Studies* (35) 85–103.

Goodman, F. (2001) 'The Supreme Court's Federalism: Real or Imagined?', *Annals of the American Academy of Political and Social Science* (574) 9–23.

Graber, D. (1997) *Mass Media and American Politics,* 5th edn (Washington, DC: CQ Press).

Green, D. (2002a) 'Constructivist Comparative Politics: Foundations and Framework', in *Constructivism and Comparative Politics,* ed. D. Green (Armonk, NY and London: M.E. Sharpe) pp. 3–59.

Green, D. (ed.) (2002b) *Constructivism and Comparative Politics* (Armonk, NY and London: M.E. Sharpe).

Green, D. and Shapiro, I. (1994) *Pathologies of Rational Choice Theories* (New Haven, CT and London: Yale University Press).

Green, J. (1994) *Dictionary of Cynical Quotations* (London: Cassell).

Greenbaum, T. (1998) *Handbook for Focus Group Research,* 2nd edn (Thousand Oaks, CA and London: Sage).

Greenwood, J. (2003) *Interest Representation in the European Union* (Basingstoke and New York: Palgrave Macmillan).

Griffin, R. (ed.) (2004) *Fascism as a Totalitarian Movement* (London: Frank Cass).

Griffith, J. (1997) *The Politics of the Judiciary,* 4th edn (London: Fontana).

Griffiths, I. (1995) *The African Inheritance* (London and New York: Routledge).

Grugel, J. (2002) *Democratization: A Critical Introduction* (Basingstoke: Palgrave Macmillan).

Guarnieri, C. and Pederzoli, P. (2002) *The Power of Judges: A Comparative Study of Courts and Democracy,* trans. C. Thomas (Oxford and New York: Oxford University Press).

Guéhenno, J.-M. (1995) *The End of the Nation-State* (Minneapolis, MN and London: University of Minnesota Press).

Guibernau M. (1999) *Nations Without States: Political Communities in a Global Age* (Cambridge and Malden, MA: Polity).

Gunther, R. and Mughan, A. (eds) (2000) *Democracy and the Media: A Comparative Perspective* (Cambridge and New York: Cambridge University Press).

Gunther, R., Montero, J. and Linz, J. (eds) (2002) *Political Parties: Old Concepts and New Challenges* (Oxford and New York: Oxford University Press).

Gurr, T. (1980) *Why Men Rebel* (Princeton, NJ: Princeton University Press).

H

Habermas, J. (1978) *Knowledge and Human Interests,* 2nd edn, trans. J. Shapiro (London: Heinemann Education).

Hadenius, A. (ed.) (1997) *Democracy's Victory and Crisis* (New York and Cambridge: Cambridge University Press).

Hagopian, F. (1998) 'Democracy and Political Representation in Latin America in the 1990s: Pause, Reorganization or Decline?', in *Fault Lines of Democracy in Post-Transition Latin America,* ed. F. Agüero and J. Stark (Coral Gables, FL: University of Miami) pp. 99–144.

Hagopian, F. (2004) 'Brazil' in *Comparative Politics Today: A World View,* 8th ed., ed. G. Almond et al. (New York and London: Pearson Longman) pp. 520–79.

Hall, B. and Biersteker, T. (2002) (eds) *The Emergence of Private Authority in Global Governance* (Cambridge and New York: Cambridge University Press).

Hall, P. and Ikenberry, G. (1989) *The State* (Milton Keynes: Open University Press).

Halliday, F. (1999) *Revolution and World Politics: The Rise and Fall of the Sixth Great Power* (Basingstoke: Macmillan).

Hamilton, A. [1788a] (1970 edn) *The Federalist,* No. 51, intro W. Brock (London: Dent and New York: Dutton) pp. 263–7.

Hamilton, A. [1788a] (1970 edn) *The Federalist,* No. 70, intro W. Brock (London: Dent and New York: Dutton) pp. 357–63.

Hamilton, A. [1788b] (1970 edn) *The Federalist,* No. 84, intro W. Brock (London: Dent and New York: Dutton) pp. 436–45.

Hamilton, A. [1788c] (1970 edn) *The Federalist,* No. 45, intro W. Brock (London: Dent and New York: Dutton) pp. 233–8.

Handelman, H. (1997) *Mexican Politics: The Dynamics of Change* (New York: St. Martin's Press).

Hansen, M. (1991) *The Athenian Democracy in the Age of Demosthenes* (Oxford and Cambridge, MA: Blackwell).

Harding, N. (ed.) (1984) *The State in Socialist Society* (London: Macmillan).

Hare, T. (1873) *The Election of Representatives* (London: Longmans).

Harriss, J. (1995) 'A Time of Troubles: Problems of Humanitarian Intervention in the 1990s', in *The Politics of Humanitarian Intervention,* ed. J. Harriss (London and New York: Pinter) pp. 1–15.

Harrop, M., and Miller, W. (1987) *Elections and Voters: A Comparative Introduction* (Basingstoke: Macmillan).

Haugaard, M. (ed.) (2002b) *Power: A Reader* (Manchester and New York: Manchester University Press).

Hay, C. (2002) *Political Analysis: A Critical Introduction* (Basingstoke and New York: Palgrave).

Hayek, F. (1960) *The Constitution of Liberty* (Chicago, IL: University of Chicago Press).

Haynes, J. (1998) *Religion in Global Politics* (Harlow and New York: Addison Wesley Longman).

Haynes, J. (2001) *Democracy in the Developing World: Africa, Asia, Latin America and the Middle East* (Cambridge: Polity).

Haynes, J. (2003) 'Comparative Politics and "Globalization"', *European Political Science* (2) 17–26.

Hayward, J. (1994) 'Ideological Change: The Exhaustion of the Revolutionary Impulse', in *Developments in French Politics,* ed. P. Hall, J. Hayward and H. Machin (Basingstoke: Macmillan) pp. 15–32.

Hazan, R. (1997a) 'The 1996 Election in Israel: Adopting Party Primaries', *Electoral Studies* (16) 95–102.

Hazan, R. (1997b) 'Legislative-Executive Relations in an Era of Accelerated Reform: Reshaping Government in Israel', *Legislative Studies Quarterly* (22) 329–50.

Hazan, R. (2002) 'Candidate Selection', in *Comparing Democracies 2: New Challenges in the Study of Elections and Voting,* ed. L. LeDuc, R. Niemi and P. Norris (London and Thousand Oaks, CA: Sage) pp. 108–26.

Heady, F. (1996) *Public Administration: A Comparative Perspective,* 5th edn (New York: Marcel Dekker).

Heater, D. (1999) *What Is Citizenship?* (Cambridge: Polity and Malden, MA: Blackwell).

Hechter, M. (2000) *Containing Nationalism* (Oxford and New York: Oxford University Press).

Heclo, H. (1974) *Modern Social Policies in Britain and Sweden* (New Haven, CT and London: Yale University Press).

Heclo, H. (1978) 'Issue Networks and the Executive Establishment', in *The New American Political System,* ed. A.

King (Washington, DC: American Enterprise Institute) pp. 87–124.

Held, D. (1996) *Models of Democracy*, 2nd edn (Cambridge: Polity).

Helms, D. (ed.) (2000) *Institutions and Institutional Change in the Federal Republic of Germany* (Basingstoke: Palgrave).

Henry, N. (2004) *Public Administration and Public Affairs*, 9th edn (Upper Saddle River, NJ: Pearson).

Henshel, R. (1990) *Thinking About Social Problems* (New York: Harcourt Brace Jovanovich).

Herbst, J. (2001) 'Political Liberalization in Africa after 10 Years,' *Comparative Politics* (33) 357–75.

Herbst, S. (1998) *Reading Public Opinion: How Political Actors View The Political Process* (Chicago and London: University of Chicago Press).

Hesse, J. and Wright, V. (eds) (1996) *Federalizing Europe? The Costs, Benefits and Preconditions of Federal Political Systems* (Oxford and New York: Oxford University Press).

Hettne, B. (ed.) (1999) *Globalism and the New Regionalism* (Basingstoke: Macmillan).

Heywood, P. (1995) *The Government and Politics of Spain* (Basingstoke: Macmillan).

Hilderband, M. (2002) 'Capacity Building', in *Handbook on Development Policy and Management*, ed. C. Kirkpatrick, R. Clarke and C. Polidano (Aldershot and Brookfield, VT: Edward Elgar) pp. 323–32.

Hill, L. (2002) 'On the Rightness of Compelling Citizens to "Vote": The Australian Case', *Political Studies* (50) 80–101.

Hill, M. and Hupe, P. (2002) *Implementing Public Policy: Governance in Theory and Practice* (London and Thousand Oaks, CA: Sage).

Hinsley, F. (1986) *Sovereignty* (Cambridge and New York: Cambridge University Press).

Hirschl, R. (2002) 'The Political Origins of Judicial Empowerment through Constitutionalization: Lessons from Israel's Constitutional Review', *Comparative Politics* (33) 315–35.

Hirst, P. and Thompson, G. (1999) *Globalization in Question: The International Economy and the Possibilities of Governance*, 2nd edn (Oxford and Cambridge, MA: Blackwell).

Hobbes, T. [1651] (1968 edn) *Leviathan*, ed. M. Oakeshott (Toronto: Crowell-Collier).

Hoffman, J. (1998) *Sovereignty* (Buckingham: Open University Press).

Hoffman, S. (1995) 'The Politics and Ethics of Military Intervention', *Survival* (37) 29–51.

Hogwood, B. and Gunn, L. (1984) *Policy Analysis for the Real World* (Oxford: Oxford University Press).

Holland, K. (1991) 'Introduction', in *Judicial Activism in Comparative Perspective*, ed. K. Holland (Basingstoke: Macmillan) pp. 1–11.

Holliday, I. (2000) 'Executives and Administrations', in *Developments in British Politics 6*, ed. P. Dunleavy *et al.* (Basingstoke: Macmillan and New York: St Martin's Press) pp. 88–107.

Hollifield, J. and Jillson, C. (2000) 'The Democratic Transformation: Lessons and Prospects in Pathways to Democracy', in *The Political Economy of Democratic Transitions*, ed. J. Hollifield and C. Jillson (London and New York: Routledge) pp. 3–20.

Holman, M. and Wallis, W. (2000) 'In Office But Out of Power', *Financial Times Survey of Nigeria*, 30 March, p. 1.

Holmstrom, B. (1995) 'Sweden', in *The Global Expansion of Judicial Power*, ed. C. Tate and T. Vallinder (New York and London: New York University Press) pp. 345–68.

Holzgrefe, J. and Keohane, R. (eds) (2003) *Humanitarian Intervention: Ethical, Legal and Political Dilemmas* (Cambridge and New York: Cambridge University Press).

Hood, C. (1996) 'Exploring Variations in Public Management Reform in the 1990s', in *Civil Service Systems in Comparative Perspective*, ed. H. Bekke, J. Perry and T. Toonen (Bloomington, IN: Indiana University Press) pp. 268–87.

Hood, C. *et al.* (1999) *Regulation Inside Government: Waste-Watchers, Quality Police and Sleaze-Busters* (Oxford and New York: Oxford University Press).

Hooghe, L. and Marks, G. (2001) *Multilevel Governance and European Integration* (Lanham, MD: Rowman & Littlefield).

Horowitz, D. (1977) *The Courts and Social Policy* (Washington, DC: Brookings).

Hosli, M., van Deemen, A. and Widgrén, M. (eds) (2002) *Institutional Challenges in the European Union* (London and New York: Routledge).

Howe, H. (2001) *Ambiguous Order: Military Forces in African States* (Boulder, CO and London: Lynne Rienner).

Hrebenar, R. and Scott, R. (1997) *Interest Group Politics in America*, 3rd edn (Englewood Cliffs, NJ: Prentice-Hall).

Huntington, S. (1991) *The Third Wave: Democratization in the Late Twentieth Century* (Norman, OK and London: University of Oklahoma Press).

Huntington, S. (1993) 'Clash of Civilizations', *Foreign Affairs* (72) 22–49.

Huntington, S. (1996) *The Clash of Civilizations and the Making of World Order* (New York: Simon & Schuster).

Hurrell, A. (1995) 'Explaining the Resurgence of Regionalism in World Politics', *Review of International Studies* (21) 331–58.

Huth, P. and Allee, T. (2003) *The Democratic Peace and Territorial Conflict in the Twentieth Century* (Cambridge and New York: Cambridge University Press).

Hyden, G. (1997) 'Democratization and Administration', in *Democracy's Victory and Crisis*, ed. A. Hadenius (Cambridge and New York: Cambridge University Press) pp. 242–62.

I

Ibarra, P. (2003) *Social Movements and Democracy* (London: Palgrave Macmillan).

Ignazi, P. (1992) 'The Silent Counter-Revolution: Hypotheses on the Emergence of Extreme Right-Wing Parties in Europe', *European Journal of Political Research* (22) 3–35.

Ignazi, P. (2003) *Extreme Right Parties in Western Europe* (Oxford and New York: Oxford University Press).

Illner, M. (1998) 'Local Democratization: The Czech Republic after 1989', in *Participation and Democracy: Comparisons and Interpretations*, ed. D. Rueschmeyer, M. Rueschmeyer and B. Wittrock (Armonk, NY and London: M.E. Sharpe) pp. 51–82.

Inglehart, R. (1971) 'The Silent Revolution in Europe: Intergenerational Change in Post-Industrial Societies', *American Political Science Review* (65) 991–1017.

Inglehart, R. (1990) *Culture Shift in Advanced Industrial Society* (Princeton, NJ: Princeton University Press).

Inglehart, R. (1997) *Modernization and Postmodernization: Cultural, Economic and Social Change in 43 Societies* (Princeton, NJ and London: Princeton University Press).

Inglehart, R. (1999) 'Postmodernization Erodes Respect for Authority, but Increases Support for Democracy', in *Critical Citizens: Global Support for Democratic Governance*, ed. P. Norris (Oxford and New York: Oxford University Press) pp. 236–56.

Inoguchi, T. (2002) 'Broadening the Basis of Political Capital in Japan', in *Democracies in Flux: The Evolution of Social Capital in Contemporary Society*, ed. R. Putnam (Oxford and New York: Oxford University Press) pp. 359–92.

Inter-Parliamentary Union (2000) *Women in National Parliaments*, IPU home page at: http://www.ipu.org/wmn-e/world.htm.

International Organization for Migration (IOM) (2003) *Annual Report* (Geneva: IOM).

J

Jackson, J. (1996) 'Political Methodology: An Overview', in *A New Handbook of Political Science*, ed. R. Goodin and H. Klingemann (Oxford and New York: Oxford University Press) pp. 714–48.

Jackson, J. (1998) *The World Trade Organization* (Herndon, VA and London: Cassell).

Jackson, P. and Nexon, D. (2002) 'Globalization, The Comparative Method, and Comparing Constructions', in *Constructivism and Comparative Politics*, ed. D. Green (Armonk, NY and London: M.E. Sharpe) pp. 88–120.

Jackson, R. and Rosberg, C. (1982) *Personal Rule in Black Africa: Prince, Autocrat, Prophet, Tyrant* (Berkeley, CA: University of California Press).

Jacob, H. *et al.* (1996) *Courts, Law and Politics in Comparative Perspective* (New Haven, CT and London: Yale University Press).

Jasiewicz, K. (2003) 'Elections and Voting Behaviour', in *Developments in Central and East European Politics 3*, ed. S. White, J. Batt and P. Lewis (Basingstoke and New York: Palgrave Macmillan) pp. 173–89.

Jay, A. (1996) *The Oxford Dictionary of Political Quotations* (Oxford and New York: Oxford University Press).

Jayanntha, D. (1991) *Electoral Allegiance in Sri Lanka* (Cambridge and New York: Cambridge University Press).

Jeffery, C. (2003) 'Federalism and Territorial Politics' in *Developments in German Politics 3*, ed. S. Padgett, W. Paterson and G. Smith (Basingstoke: Palgrave Macmillan) pp. 38–59.

Jenkins, J. (1983) 'The Transformation of a Constituency into a Movement: Farmworker Organizing in California', in *Social Movements of the Sixties and Seventies*, ed. J. Freeman (London and New York: Longman) pp. 52–70.

John, P. (1998) *Analysing Public Policy* (London and New York: Continuum).

John, P. (2001) *Local Governance in Western Europe* (London and Thousand Oaks, CA: Sage).

Johnson, C. (1987) *Japan: Who Governs? The Rise of the Developmental State* (New York and London: Norton).

Johnson, J. (2001) 'Path Contingency in Postcommunist Transformations', *Comparative Politics* (33) 253–74.

Jones, C. (1994) *The Presidency in a Separated System* (Washington, DC: Brookings Institution).

Jones, M. (1995a) 'A Guide to the Electoral Systems of the Americas', *Electoral Studies* (14) 5–21.

Jones, M. (1995b) *Electoral Laws and the Survival of Presidential Democracies* (Notre Dame, IN: University of Notre Dame Press).

Joyce, P. (2002) *The Politics of Protest: Extra-Parliamentary Politics in Britain since 1970* (London: Palgrave Macmillan).

Judge, D. and Earnshaw, D. (2003) *The European Parliament* (Basingstoke and New York: Palgrave Macmillan).

Jungar, A.-C. (2002) 'A Case of a Surplus Majority Government: The Finnish Rainbow Coalition', *Scandinavian Political Studies* (25) 57–83.

K

Kahn, J. (2002) *Federalism, Democratization and the Rule of Law in Russia* (Oxford and New York: Oxford University Press).

Karatnycky, A. (2002) 'Muslim Countries and the Democracy Gap', *Journal of Democracy* (13) 99–112.

Karvonen, L. and Kuhnle, S. (eds) (2001) *Party Systems and Voter Alignments Revisited* (London and New York: Routledge).

Katz, R. (1997) *Democracy and Elections* (Oxford and New York: Oxford University Press).

Katz, R. (2002) 'Reforming the Italian Electoral Law, 1993', in *Mixed-Member Electoral Systems: The Best of Both Worlds*, ed. M. Shugart and M. Wattenberg (Oxford and New York: Oxford University Press) pp. 96–122.

Katz, R. and Mair, P. (1995) 'Changing Models of Party Organization and Party Democracy: The Emergence of the Cartel Party', *Party Politics* (1) 5–28.

Katzenstein, J. (1984) *Corporatism and Change: Austria, Switzerland and the Politics of Industry* (Ithaca, NY: Cornell University Press).

Kay, J. (2003) 'Too Many Polls Are Apt to Harm a Democracy', *Financial Times*, 14 August.

Kelsen, H. (1942) 'Judicial Review of Legislation: A Comparative Study of the Austrian and the American Constitution', *Journal of Politics* (4) 183–200.

Keman, H. (ed.) (1993) *Comparative Politics: New Directions in Theory and Method* (Amsterdam: VU University Press).

Kennedy, P. (1993) *Preparing for the Twenty-First Century* (London: HarperCollins).

Kennedy, P. (1994) *Preparing for the Twenty First Century* (London: Fontana).

Kennedy, P. and Roudometof, V. (eds) (2002) *Communities Across Borders: New Immigrants and Transnational Cultures* (London and New York: Routledge).

Kershaw, I. (2001) *Hitler, 1936–1945: Nemesis* (London: Penguin).

Kershaw, I. (2000) *The Nazi Dictatorship: Problems and Perspectives of Interpretation*, 4th edn (London: Arnold).

Kershaw, I. and Lewin, M. (eds) (1997) *Stalinism and Nazism: Dictatorships in Comparison* (Cambridge and New York: Cambridge University Press).

Khong, Y. (1992) *Analogies at War: Korea, Munich, Dien Bien Phu and the Vietnam Decisions of 1965* (Princeton, NJ: Princeton University Press).

Kieh, G. and Agbese, P. (eds) (2003) *The Military and Politics in Africa: From Intervention to Democratic Control* (Aldershot and Burlington, VT: Ashgate).

Kieh G. and Ogaba P. (eds) (2003) *The Military and Politics in Africa: From Intervention to Democratic Control* (Aldershot: Ashgate).

King, A. (1981) 'The Rise of the Career Politician in Britain – and its Consequences', *British Journal of Political Science* (11) 249–85.

King, A. (1994a) 'Ministerial Autonomy in Britain', in *Cabinet Ministers and Parliamentary Government*, ed. M. Laver and K. Shepsle (Cambridge and New York: Cambridge University Press) pp. 203–25.

King, A. (1994b) '"Chief Executives" in Western Europe', in *Developing Democracy: Comparative Research in Honour of J. F. P. Blondel*, ed. I. Budge and D. McKay (Thousand Oaks, CA and London: Sage) pp. 150–64.

King, A. (ed.) (2002) *Leaders' Personalities and the Outcomes of Democratic Elections* (Oxford and New York: Oxford University Press).

King, G., Keohane, R. and Verba S. (1994) *Designing Social Inquiry: Scientific Inference in Qualitative Research* (Princeton, NJ: Princeton University Press).

Kingdon, J. (1984) *Agendas, Alternatives and Public Policy* (Boston, MA: Little, Brown).

Kingsley, J. (1944) *Representative Bureaucracy* (Yellow Springs, OH: Antioch).

Kircheimer, O. (1966) 'The Transformation of the Western European Party Systems', in *Political Parties and Political Development*, ed. J. LaPalombara and M. Weiner (Princeton, NJ: Princeton University Press) pp. 177–200.

Kitschelt, H. *et al.* (1999) *Postcommunist Party Systems: Competition, Representation and Inter-Party Competition* (Cambridge and New York: Cambridge University Press).

Klapper, J. (1960) *The Effects of Mass Communication* (New York and London: Free Press).

Knapp, A. and Wright, V. (2001) *The Government and Politics of France*, 4th edn (London and New York: Routledge).

Knutsen, O. (1990) 'Materialist and Postmaterialist Values and Structures in the Nordic Countries', *Comparative Politics* (23) 85–101.

Knutsen, O. (2001) 'Social Class, Sector Employment and Gender as Party Cleavages in the Scandinavian Countries: A Comparative Longitudinal Study, 1970–95', *Scandinavian Political Studies* (24) 311–50.

Kobach, K. (1997) 'Direct Democracy and Swiss Isolationism', *West European Politics* (20) 185–211.

Koh, B. (1989) *Japan's Administrative Elite* (Berkeley, CA: University of California Press).

Kolstø, P. (2000) *Political Construction Sites: Nation-Building in Russia and the Post-Soviet States* (Boulder, CO: Westview Press).

Koopmans, R. (1999) 'Globalization or Still National Politics? A Comparison of Protests Against the Gulf War in Germany, France and the Netherlands', in *Social Movements in a Globalizing World*, ed. D. della Porta, H. Kriesi and D. Rucht (London: Macmillan and New York: St Martin's Press) pp. 57–70.

Kopecky, P. (1995) 'Developing Party Organizations in East-Central Europe: What Type of Party is Likely to Emerge?', *Party Politics* (1) 515–34.

Kopecky, P. (2003) 'Structures of Representation: The New Parliaments of Central and Eastern Europe', in *Developments in Central and East European Politics 3*, ed. S. White, J. Batt and P. Lewis (Basingstoke and New York: Palgrave Macmillan) pp. 133–52.

Kornhauser, W. (1959) *The Politics of Mass Society* (Glencoe, IL: Free Press).

Kostadinova, T. (2002) 'Do Mixed Electoral Systems Matter? A Cross-National Comparison of Their Effects in Eastern Europe', *Electoral Studies* (21) 23–34.

Kostiner, J. and Teitelbaum, J. (2000) 'State Formation and the Saudi Monarchy', in *Middle East Monarchies: The Challenge of Modernity*, ed. J. Kostiner (Boulder, CO and London: Lynne Rienner) .

Krasner, S. (1999) *Sovereignty: Organized Hypocrisy* (Princeton, NJ and Chichester: Princeton University Press).

Krasner, S. (ed.) (2001) *Problematic Sovereignty: Contested Rules and Political Possibilities* (New York and Chichester: Columbia University Press).

Krauthammer, C. (1990) 'In Praise of Low Voter Turnout', *Time*, 21 May, p. 88.

Kudrle, R. and Marmor, T. (1981) 'The Development of Welfare States in North America' in *The Development of Welfare States in Europe and America,* ed. P. Flora and A. Heidenheimer (New Brunswick, NJ and London: Transaction) pp. 187–236.

Kuhn, T. [1970] (1996 edn) *The Structure of Scientific Revolutions*, 3rd edn (Chicago, IL: University of Chicago Press).

Kuhnle, S. (2000) 'The Scandinavian Welfare State in the 1990s: Challenged but Viable', *West European Politics* (23) 209–28.

Kvavik, R. (1976) *Interest Groups in Norwegian Politics* (Oslo, Bergen and Tromsø: Universitetforlaget).

L

Lachmann, R. (1997) 'Agents of Revolution: Elite Conflicts and Mass Mobilization from the Medici to the Yemen', in *Theorizing Revolutions,* ed. J. Foran (London and New York: Routledge) pp. 73–101.

Laegreid, P. and Olsen, J. (1978) *Byråkrati og Beslutninger* (Bergen: Norwegian University Press).

Landes, R. (1995) *The Canadian Polity: A Comparative Introduction* (Scarborough, Ontario: Prentice-Hall Canada).

Landman, T. (2003) *Issues and Methods in Comparative Politics: An Introduction*, 2nd edn (London and New York: Routledge).

Lane, J.-E. and Ersson, S. (2002) *Culture and Politics: A Comparative Approach* (Aldershot and Burlington, VT: Ashgate).

LaPalombara, J. (1974) *Politics Within Nations* (Englewood Cliffs, NJ: Prentice-Hall).

Latouche, S. (1996) *The Westernization of the World* (Cambridge and Cambridge, MA: Polity).

Laver, M. (1983) *Invitation to Politics* (Oxford: Martin Robertson).

Laver, M. and Shepsle, K. (eds) (1994) *Cabinet Ministers and Parliamentary Government* (Cambridge and New York: Cambridge University Press).

Lazarsfeld, P. and Merton, R. [1948] (1996 edn) 'Mass Communication, Popular Taste and Organized Social Action', in *Media Studies: A Reader*, ed. P. Marris and S. Thornham (Edinburgh: Edinburgh University Press) pp. 14–24.

Lechner, F. and Boli, J. (eds) (2003) *The Globalization Reader* (Oxford and Cambridge, MA: Blackwell).

LeDuc, L. (2002) 'Referendums and Initiatives: The Politics of Direct Democracy', in *Comparing Democracies 2: New Challenges in the Study of Elections and Voting*, ed. L. LeDuc, R. Niemi and P. Norris (London and Thousand Oaks, CA: Sage) pp. 70–87.

LeDuc, L., Niemi, R. and Norris, P. (2002a) 'Comparing Democratic Elections', in *Comparing Democracies 2: New Challenges in the Study of Elections and Voting*, ed. L. LeDuc, R. Niemi and P. Norris (Thousand Oaks, CA and London: Sage) pp. 1–39.

LeDuc, L., Niemi, R. and Norris, P. (eds) (2002b) *Comparing Democracies 2: New Challenges in the Study of Elections and Voting* (Thousand Oaks, CA and London: Sage).

Lenin, V. [1902] (1963 edn) *What Is To Be Done?* (Oxford: Clarendon Press).

Lesch, A. (2003) 'Politics in Egypt', in *Comparative Politics Today: A World View*, 8th edn, ed. G. Almond *et al.* (New York: Longman) pp. 581–632.

Levitsky, S. (2000) 'The "Normalization" of Argentine Politics', *Journal of Democracy* (11) 56–69.

Levy, D. and Bruhn, K. (2001) *Mexico: The Struggle for Democratic Development* (Berkeley, CA: University of California Press).

Lewin, M. (1997) 'Bureaucracy and the Stalinist State', in *Stalinism and Nazism: Dictatorships in Comparison*, ed. I.

Kershaw and M. Lewin (Cambridge and New York: Cambridge University Press) pp. 53–74.

Lewis, B. (2003) *The Crisis of Islam: Holy War and Unholy Terror* (London: Weidenfeld & Nicolson).

Lewis, B. (2002) *What Went Wrong? Western Impact and Middle Eastern Response* (London: Weidenfeld & Nicolson).

Lewis, D. (2002) 'The Politics of Agency Termination: Confronting the Myth of Agency Termination', *Journal of Politics* (64) 89–1207.

Lewis, P. (ed.) (1996a) *Party Structure and Organization in East-Central Europe* (Aldershot and Brookfield, VT: Edward Elgar).

Lewis, P. (1996b) 'Introduction and Theoretical Overview', in *Party Structure and Organization in East-Central Europe,* ed. P. Lewis (Aldershot and Brookfield, VT: Edward Elgar) pp. 1–19.

Lewis, P. (2000) *Political Parties in Postcommunist Eastern Europe* (London and New York: Routledge).

Lewis, P. (2003) 'Political Parties', in *Developments in Central and East European Politics 3,* ed. S. White, J. Batt and P. Lewis (Basingstoke and New York: Palgrave Macmillan) pp. 153–72.

Liddle, R. (1996) 'A Useful Fiction: Democratic Legitimation in New Order Indonesia', in *The Politics of Elections in Southeast Asia,* ed. R. Taylor (Cambridge and New York: Cambridge University Press) pp. 34–60.

Lieberman, I., Nestor, S. and Desai, R. (eds) (1997) *Between State and Market: Mass Privatization in Transition Economies* (Washington, DC: World Bank).

Liebert, U. and Cotta, M. (eds) (1990) *Parliament and Democratic Consolidation in Southern Europe* (London: Pinter).

Lijphart, A. (1971) 'Comparative Politics and the Comparative Method', *American Political Science Review* (65) 682–93.

Lijphart, A. (1977) *Democracy in Plural Societies: A Comparative Exploration* (Berkeley, CA: University of California Press).

Lijphart, A. (1984) *Democracies: Patterns of Majoritarian and Consensual Government in Twenty One Countries* (New Haven, CT and London: Yale University Press).

Lijphart, A. (ed.) (1992) *Parliamentary versus Presidential Government* (Oxford and New York: Oxford University Press).

Lijphart, A. (1994) *Electoral Systems and Party Systems* (New Haven, CT and London: Yale University Press).

Lijphart, A. (1997) 'Unequal Participation: Democracy's Unresolved Dilemma', *American Political Science Review* (91) 1–14.

Lijphart, A. (1999) *Patterns of Democracy: Government Forms and Performance in Thirty Six Countries* (New Haven, CT and London: Yale University Press).

Lijphart, A. (2000) 'The Future of Democracy: Reasons for Pessimism but also Some Optimism', *Scandinavian Political Studies* (23) 265–72.

Lijphart, A. and Crepaz, M. (1991) 'Corporatism and Consensus Democracy in Eighteen Countries: Conceptual and Empirical Linkages', *British Journal of Political Science* (21) 235–46.

Lijphart, A. and Waisman, C. (1996a) 'The Design of Democracies and Markets: Generalizing Across Regions', in *Institutional Design in New Democracies: Eastern Europe and Latin America,* ed. A. Lijphart and C. Waisman (Boulder, CO and Oxford: Westview) pp. 235–48.

Lijphart, A. and Waisman, C. (eds) (1996b) *Institutional Design in New Democracies: Eastern Europe and Latin America* (Boulder, CO and Oxford: Westview).

Lindblom, C. (1959) 'The Science of Muddling Through', *Public Administration* (19) 78–88.

Lindblom, C. (1977) *Politics and Markets* (New York: Basic Books).

Lindblom, C. (1979) 'Still Muddling, Not Yet Through', *Public Administration Review* (39) 517–26.

Lindblom, C. (1990) *Inquiry and Change: The Troubled Attempt to Understand and Shape Society* (New Haven, CT and London: Yale University Press).

Linz, J. (1970) 'An Authoritarian Regime: The Case of Spain', in *Mass Politics: Studies in Political Sociology,* ed. E. Allard and S. Rokkan (New York: Free Press and London: Collier-Macmillan) pp. 251–83.

Linz, J. [1975] (2000 edn) *Totalitarian and Authoritarian Regimes* (Boulder, CO and London: Lynne Rienner).

Linz, J. (1978) 'Crisis, Breakdown and Re-equilibration', in *The Breakdown of Democratic Regimes,* ed. J. Linz and A. Stepan (Baltimore, MD and London: Johns Hopkins University Press) pp. 1–124.

Linz, J. (1990) 'The Perils of Presidentialism', *Journal of Democracy* (1) 51–69.

Linz, J. and Stepan, A. (1996) *Problems of Democratic Transition and Consolidation: Southern Europe, South America and Postcommunist Europe* (Baltimore, MD and London: Johns Hopkins University Press).

Linz, J. and Stepan, A. (eds) (1978) *The Breakdown of Democratic Regimes* (Baltimore, MD and London: Johns Hopkins University Press).

Linz, J. and Valenzuela, A. (eds) (1994) *The Failure of Presidential Democracy* (Baltimore, MD: Johns Hopkins University Press).

Lippman, W. (1922) *Public Opinion* (London: Allen & Unwin).

Lipset, S. [1960] (1983 edn) *Political Man* (New York: Basic Books).

Lipset, S. (1990) *Continental Divide: The Values and Institutions of the United States and Canada* (London and New York: Routledge).

Lipset, S. and Rokkan, S. (1967) 'Cleavage Structures, Party Systems and Voter Alignments', in *Party Systems and Voter Alignments,* ed. S. Lipset and S. Rokkan (New York and London: Free Press) pp. 1–65.

Lister, F. (1996) *The European Union, the United Nations and the Revival of Confederal Governance* (Westport, CT: Greenwood Press).

Lively, J. (1991) 'Sieyès, Emmanuel Joseph' in *The Blackwell Encyclopaedia of Political Thought,* ed. D. Miller (Oxford and Cambridge, MA: Blackwell) pp. 475–6.

Locke, J. [1690] (1965 edn) *Two Treatises of Government* (New York: New American Library).

Longley, L. and Davidson, R. (eds) (1998) *The New Roles of Parliamentary Committees* (London: Frank Cass).

Loughlin, J. (2001) *Subnational Democracy in the European Union: Challenges and Opportunities* (Oxford and New York: Oxford University Press).

Lowi, T. (1969) *The End of Liberalism* (New York: Norton).

Lowndes, V. (2002) 'Institutionalism', in *Theory and Methods in Political Science,* 2nd edn, ed. D. Marsh and G. Stoker (Basingstoke and New York: Palgrave Macmillan) pp. 90–108.

Lubbers, M., Gijsberts, M. and Scheepers, P. (2002) 'Extreme Right-wing Voting in Western Europe', *European Journal of Political Research* (41) 345–78.

Lubman, S. (1999) *Bird in a Cage: Legal Reform in China after Mao* (Princeton, NJ: Princeton University Press).

Luce, E. and Sevastopulo, D. (2003) 'Mother India Calls In Her Asset-Rich but Far-Flung Offspring', *Financial Times,* 18 January, p. 7.

Luckham, R. and White, G. (1996b) 'Democratizing the South', in *Democratization in the South: The Jagged Wave,* ed. R.

Luckham and G. White (Manchester and New York: Manchester University Press) pp. 1–10.

Lukes, S. (1974) *Power: A Radical View* (London: Macmillan).

Lukes, S. (ed.) (1986) *Power* (Oxford and Cambridge, MA: Basil Blackwell).

Luong, P. and Weinthal, E. (2001) 'Prelude to the Resource Curse: Explaining Oil and Gas Development Strategies in the Soviet Successor States', *Comparative Political Studies* (34) 367–99.

Lutz, J. and Lutz, B. (2004) *Global Terrorism* (London and New York: Routledge).

Lyon, D. (2003) *Surveillance after September 11* (Cambridge and Cambridge, MA: Polity).

M

Mackenzie, W. (1958) *Free Elections* (London: Allen & Unwin).

Maddex, R. (2000) *Constitutions of the World*, 2nd edn (Washington, DC and London: CQ Press).

Madeley, J. (ed.) (2003) *Religion and Politics* (Aldershot and Burlington, VT: Ashgate).

Madison J. [1781] (1970 edn) 'The Federalist, No. 10' in A. Hamilton, J. Madison and J. Jay, *The Federalist or, The New Constitution* (London: Dent and New York: Dutton). First pub. in the *New York Packet*, November 23.

Magyar, K. (1992) 'Military Intervention and Withdrawal in Africa: Problems and Perspectives', in *From Military to Civilian Rule*, ed. C. Danopoulos (London and New York: Routledge) pp. 230–48.

Mahler, G. (2003) *Comparative Politics: An Institutional and Cross-National Approach*, 4th edn (Upper Suddle River, NJ: Pearson).

Maier, K. (2002) *This House Has Fallen: Nigeria in Crisis* (London and New York: Penguin).

Mainwaring, S. (1992) 'Presidentialism in Latin America', in *Parliamentary versus Presidential Government*, ed. A. Lijphart (Oxford and New York: Oxford University Press) pp. 111–17.

Mainwaring, S. (1997) 'Multipartism, Robust Federalism and Presidentialism in Brazil', in *Presidentialism and Democracy in Latin America*, ed. S. Mainwaring and M. Shugart (Cambridge and New York: Cambridge University Press) pp. 55–109.

Mainwaring, S. and Scully, T. (eds) (1995) *Building Democratic Institutions: Party Systems in Latin America* (Stanford, CA: Stanford University Press).

Mainwaring, S. and Shugart, M. (1997a) 'Juan Linz, Presidentialism and Democracy: A Critical Appraisal', *Comparative Politics* (29) 449–72.

Mainwaring, S. and Shugart, M. (eds) (1997b) *Presidentialism and Democracy in Latin America* (Cambridge and New York: Cambridge University Press).

Mair, P. (1994) 'Party Organizations: From Civil Society to the State', in *How Parties Organize: Change and Adaptation in Party Organizations in Western Democracies*, ed. R. Katz and P. Mair (Thousand Oaks, CA and London: Sage).

Mair, P. (1996) 'Comparative Politics: An Overview', in *A New Handbook of Political Science*, ed. R. Goodin and H. Klingemann (Oxford and New York: Oxford University Press) pp. 309–35.

Mair, P. (ed.) (1990) *The West European Party System* (Oxford and New York: Oxford University Press).

Mair, P. (2001) 'The Freezing Hypothesis: An Evaluation', in *Party Systems and Voter Alignments Revisited*, ed. L. Karvonen and S. Kuhnle (London and New York: Routledge) pp. 27–44.

Mair, P. and van Biezen, I. (2001) 'Party Membership in Europe, 1980–2000', *Party Politics* (7) 5–22.

Majone, G. (1996) *Regulating Europe* (London and New York: Routledge).

Malovà, D. and Haughton, T. (2002) 'Making Institutions in Central and Eastern Europe, and the Impact of Europe', *West European Politics* (25) 101–20.

Mamdani, M. (2001) *When Victims Become Killers: Colonialism, Nativism and Genocide in Rwanda* (Princeton, NJ: Princeton University Press).

Mandaville, P. (2003) *Transnational Muslim Politics: Reimagining the Umma* (London and New York: Routledge).

Manion, M. (2000) 'Politics in China', in *Comparative Politics Today: A World View*, 7th edn, ed. G. Almond *et al.* (New York: Longman) pp. 419–62.

Manion, M. (2004) 'Politics in China', in *Comparative Politics Today: A World View*, 8th edn, ed. G. Almond *et al.* (New York and London: Pearson Longman) pp. 418–65.

Mann, M. (1986) *The Sources of Social Power, Volume 1: A History of Power from the Beginning to AD 1780* (Cambridge and New York: Cambridge University Press).

Mann, M. (1997) 'The Contradictions of Continuous Revolution', in *Stalinism and Nazism: Dictatorships in Comparison*, ed. I. Kershaw and M. Lewin (Cambridge and New York: Cambridge University Press) pp. 135–57.

Mann, T. and Orren, G. (eds) (1992) *Media Polls in American Politics* (Washington, DC: Brookings Institution).

Manuel, P. and Cammisa, A. (1999) *Checks and Balances? How a Parliamentary System Could Change American Politics* (Boulder, CO: Westview Press).

Manza, J., Cook, F. and Page, B. (2002) *Navigating Public Opinion: Polls, Policy and the Future of American Democracy* (Oxford and New York: Oxford University Press).

March, D. and Olsen, J. (1984) 'The New Institutionalism: Organizational Factors in Political Life', *American Political Science Review* (78) 778–49.

March, J. and Olsen, J. (1996) 'Institutional Perspectives on Political Institutions' *Governance* (9) 247–64.

Marks, G. and Diamond, L. (eds) (1992) *Reexamining Democracy: Essays in Honour of Seymour Martin Lipset* (Thousand Oaks, CA and London: Sage).

Marongiu, A. (1968) *Medieval Parliaments: A Comparative Study* (London: Eyre & Spottiswoode).

Marshall, T. [1950] (1991 edn) *Citizenship and Social Class and Other Essays* (London: Pluto Press).

Martínez-Lara, J. (1996) *Building Democracy in Brazil: The Politics of Constitutional Change, 1985–95* (Basingstoke: Macmillan and New York: St Martin's Press).

Marvin, C. (1988) *When Old Technologies Were New: Thinking about Communications in the Late Nineteenth Century* (Oxford and New York: Oxford University Press).

Mark, K. and Engels, F. [1848] (1967 edn) *The Communist Manifesto*, intro. G. Stedman Jones (Harmondsworth: Penguin).

Massicotte, L. (2001) 'Legislative Unicameralism: A Global Survey and a Few Case Studies', *Journal of Legislative Studies* (7) 68–83.

Matthews, T. (1989) 'Interest Groups', in *Politics in Australia*, ed. R. Smith and L. Watson (Sydney: Allen & Unwin) pp. 211–27.

May, R. (2000) 'The Limits of Democracy in Commonwealth Africa', *Commonwealth & Comparative Politics* (38) 171–80.

Mayall, J. (1996) *The New Interventionism, 1993–1994: United Nations Experience in Cambodia, Former Yugoslavia and Somalia* (Cambridge and New York: Cambridge University Press).

Mayhew, D. (1991) *Divided We Govern: Party Control, Lawmaking and Investigations, 1946–1990* (New Haven, CT and London: Yale University Press).

Mazey, S. and Richardson, J. (eds) (1998) *Interest Intermediation in the EU* (London and New York: Routledge).

Mazey, S. and Richardson, J. (2001) 'Interest Groups and EU Policy-Making: Organizational Logic and Venue Shopping', in *European Union: Power and Policy-Making*, 2nd edn, ed. J. Richardson (London and New York) pp. 217–38.

Mazmanian, D. and Sabatier, P. (1989) *Implementation and Public Policy* (Lanham, MD and London: University Press of America).

McAllister, I. and Studlar, D. (2002) 'Electoral Systems and Women's Representation: A Long-Term Perspective', *Representation* (39) 3–14.

McCargo, D. (2002) *Media and Politics in Pacific Asia* (London and New York: Routledge).

McChesney, R. (1999) *Rich Media, Poor Democracies* (Urbana, IL: University of Illinois Press).

McCreery, D. (2002) 'State and Society in Nineteenth Century Goiás', in *Studies in the Formation of the Nation State in Latin America*, ed. J. Dunkerley (London: Institute of Latin American Studies) pp. 133–60.

McDonald, F. and McDonald, E. (1988) 'Federalism in America: An Obituary', in *Requiem: Variations on Eighteenth Century Themes* ed. E. McDonald and F. MacDonald (University of Kansas Press) pp. 195–206.

McEldowney, J. (2003) 'Administrative Law' in *The Concise Oxford Dictionary of Politics*, 2nd edn, ed. I. McLean and A. Macmillan (Oxford and New York: Oxford University Press) p. 3.

McKay, D. (1997) *American Politics and Society*, 4th edn (Oxford and Cambridge, MA: Blackwell).

McKay, D. (2001a) *Designing Europe: Comparative Lessons From the European Experience* (Oxford and New York: Oxford University Press).

McKay, D. (2001b) *American Politics and Society*, 5th edn (Oxford and Cambridge, MA: Blackwell).

McKenzie, R. (1955) *British Political Parties* (London: Heinemann).

Meadows, D. (1994) 'If the World Were a Village of One Thousand People', in *Futures by Design: The Practice of Ecological Planning*, ed. D. Aberley (Gabriola Island, British Columbia: New Society).

Meier, K. (1993) 'Representative Bureaucracy: A Theoretical and Empirical Exposition', *Research in Public Administration* (2) 1–35.

Melleuish, G. 'The State in World History: Perspectives and Problems' (2002) *Australian Journal of Politics and History* (48) 322–35.

Mendelsohn, M. and Parkin, A. (eds) (2001) *Referendum Democracy: Citizens, Elites and Deliberation in Referendum Campaigns* (Basingstoke: Palgrave).

Meny, Y. and Knapp, A. (1998) *Government and Politics in Western Europe: Britain, France, Italy, West Germany*, 3rd edn (Oxford and New York: Oxford University Press).

Mernissi, F. (1993) *Islam and Democracy: Fear of the Modern World* (London: Virago).

Meyer, A. (1983) 'Cultural Revolutions: The Uses of the Concept of Culture in Comparative Communist Studies', *Studies in Comparative Communism* (16) 1–8.

Mezey, M. (1979) *Comparative Legislatures* (Durham, NC: Duke University Press).

Michels, R. [1911] (1915 edn) *Political Parties* (New York: Dover Publications).

Migdal, J. (2001) *State in Society: Studying how States and Societies Transform and Constitute One Another* (Cambridge and New York: Cambridge University Press).

Milbrath, L. and Goel, M. (1977) *Political Participation: How and Why Do People Get Involved in Politics?*, 2nd edn (Chicago, IL: Rand McNally).

Mill, J. [1861] (1991 edn) 'Considerations on Representative Government', in *Collected Works of John Stuart Mill*, Vol. 19, ed. J. O'Grady and B. Robson (Toronto: University of Toronto Press and London: Routledge) pp. 371–577.

Mill, J. S. [1861] (1972 edn) *Considerations on Representative Government*, ed. H. Acton (London: Dent).

Millard, F. (2003) 'Poland', in *Developments in Central and East European Politics 3*, ed. S. White, J. Batt and P. Lewis (Basingstoke: Palgrave Macmillan) pp. 23–40.

Miller, D. (1991) 'Politics', in *Blackwell Encyclopaedia of Political Thought*, ed. V. Bogdanor (Oxford and Cambridge, MA: Blackwell) pp. 390–1.

Miller, W. (1995) 'Quantitative Methods', in *Theory and Methods in Political Science*, ed. D. Marsh and G. Stoker (Basingstoke and New York: Macmillan) pp. 154–72.

Mills, C. Wright (1956) *The Power Elite* (New York and Oxford: Oxford University Press).

Milton, A. (2000) *The Rational Politician: Exploiting the Media in New Democracies* (Aldershot: Ashgate).

Minkenberg, M. (2001) 'The Radical Right in Public Office: Agenda-setting and Policy Effects', *West European Politics* (24) 1–21.

Minogue, M., Polidano, C. and Hulne, D. (eds) (1999) *Beyond the New Public Management: Changing Ideas and Practices in Governance* (Cheltenham and Northampton, MA: Edward Elgar).

Mishra, S. (1994) 'Party Organization and Policy Making in a Changing Environment: The Indian National Congress', in *How Political Parties Work: Perspectives from Within*, ed. K. Lawson (Westport, CT: Praeger) pp. 153–79.

Moe, T. (1980) *The Organization of Interests* (Chicago, IL: University of Chicago Press).

Mommsen, H. (1997) 'Cumulative Radicalization and Progressive Self-Destruction as Structural Determinants of the Nazi Dictatorship', in *Stalinism and Nazism: Dictatorships in Comparison*, ed. I. Kershaw and M. Lewin *et al.* (Cambridge and New York: Cambridge University Press) pp. 75–87.

Momoh, A. and Adejumobi, S. (2002) *The National Question in Nigeria: Comparative Perspectives* (Aldershot: Ashgate).

Montesquieu, C.-L. (1949) *The Spirit of the Laws*, ed. F. Neumann (New York: Hafner). [1748] (1949 edn).

Moran, M. (2003) *The British Regulatory State: High Modernism and Hyper-Innovation* (Oxford and New York: Oxford University Press).

Morgenstern, S. and Nacif, B. (eds) (2002) *Legislative Politics in Latin America* (Cambridge and New York: Cambridge University Press).

Morgenthau, H. (1966) 'The Purpose of Political Science', in *A Design for Political Science: Scope, Objectives and Methods*, ed. J. Charlesworth (Philadelphia, PA: American Academy of Political and Social Science) pp. 63–79.

Morlino, L. (1995) 'Italy's Civic Divide', *Journal of Democracy* (6) 173–7.

Morton, F. (1995) 'The Living Constitution', in *Introductory Readings in Canadian Government and Politics*, ed. R. Wagenberg (Mississauga, Ontario: Copp Clark) pp. 41–72.

Motyl, A. (2002) 'Imagined Communities, Rational Choices, Invented Ethnies', *Comparative Politics* (34) 233–50.

Mouritzen, P. and Svara, J. (2002) *Leadership at the Apex: Politicians and Administrators in Western Local Governments* (Pittsburgh, PA: University of Pittsburgh Press).

Mughan, A. (2000) *Media and the Presidentialization of Parliamentary Elections* (Basingstoke: Palgrave).

Mulgan, R. (1997) *Politics in New Zealand,* 2nd edn (Auckland: Auckland University Press).

Mulgan, R. (2003) *Holding Power to Account: Accountability in Modern Democracies* (Basingstoke: Palgrave Macmillan).

Müller, W. and Strøm, K. (1999a) 'Party Behaviour and Representative Democracy', in *Policy, Office or Votes? How Political Parties in Western Europe Make Hard Decisions,* ed. W. Müller and K. Strøm (Cambridge and New York: Cambridge University Press) pp. 279–310.

Müller, W. and Strøm, K. (1999b) *Policy, Office, or Votes? How Political Parties in Western Europe Make Hard Decisions* (Cambridge and New York: Cambridge University Press).

Müller, W. and Strøm, K. (eds) (2000a) *Coalition Governments in Western Europe* (Oxford and New York: Oxford University Press).

Müller, W. and Strøm, K. (2000b) 'Coalition Governance in Western Europe', in *Coalition Governments in Western Europe,* ed. W. Müller and K. Strøm (Oxford and New York: Oxford University Press) pp. 559–92.

Müller-Rommel, F. and Poguntke, T. (eds) (2002) *Green Parties in National Governments* (London: Frank Cass).

Munro, W. (1925) *The Governments of Europe* (New York: Macmillan).

Myers, A. (1975) *Parliaments and Estates in Europe to 1789* (London: Thames & Hudson).

Myers, D. and O'Connor, R. (1998) 'Support for Coups in Democratic Political Culture', in *Comparative Politics* (30) 193–212.

N

Nacif, B. (2002) 'Understanding Party Discipline in the Mexican Chamber of Deputies: The Centralized Party Model', in *Legislative Politics in Latin America,* ed. S. Morgenstern and B. Nacif (Cambridge and New York: Cambridge University Press) pp. 254–86.

Nadeau, R., Niemi, R. and Yoshinaka, A. (2002) 'A Cross-National Analysis of Economic Voting: Taking Account of the Political Context across Time and Nations', *Electoral Studies* (21) 403–23.

Neto, O. (2002) 'Presidential Cabinets, Electoral Cycles and Coalition Discipline in Brazil', in *Legislative Politics in Latin America,* ed. S. Morgenstern and B. Nacif (Cambridge and New York: Cambridge University Press) pp. 48–78.

Neustadt, R. (1991) *Presidential Power and the Modern Presidents* (New York: Free Press).

Neustadt, R. (2001) 'The Weakening White House', *British Journal of Political Science* (31) 1–11.

Newell, J. and Bull, M. (2002) 'Italian Politics After the 2002 General Election: Plus ça change, plus c'est la même chose', *Parliamentary Affairs* (55) 626–42.

Newton, K. (1999) 'Social and Political Trust in Established Democracies', in *Critical Citizens: Global Support for Democratic Governance,* ed. P. Norris (Oxford and New York: Oxford University Press) pp. 169–87.

Niblock, T. (2003) *Saudi Arabia* (London and New York: Routledge).

Nicolaidis, K. and Howse, R. (eds) (2001) *The Federal Vision: Legitimacy and Levels of Governance in the United States and the European Union* (Oxford and New York: Oxford University Press).

Nikolova, K. (1998) 'The Framework for Public Management Reform in Bulgaria: A View From the Inside', in *Innovations in Public Management: Perspectives from East and West Europe,* ed. T. Verheijen and D. Coombes *et al.* (Cheltenham and Northampton, MA: Edward Elgar) pp. 59–102.

Norden, D. (1996) *Military Rebellion in Argentina: Between Coups and Consolidation* (Lincoln, NE and London: University of Nebraska Press).

Norpoth, H. (1996) 'The Economy', in *Elections and Voting in Global Perspective,* ed. L. LeDuc, R. Niemi and P. Norris (Thousand Oaks, CA and London: Sage) pp. 299–318.

Norris, P. (1995) *Comparative Models of Political Recruitment* (Bordeaux: ECPR Workshop on Political Recruitment).

Norris, P. (1996) 'Legislative Recruitment', in *Elections and Voting in Global Perspective,* ed. R. Niemi and P. Norris (Thousand Oaks, CA and London: Sage) pp. 184–215.

Norris, P. (1999a) 'The Growth of Critical Citizens and Its Consequences', in *Critical Citizens: Global Support for Democratic Governance,* ed. P. Norris (Oxford and New York: Oxford University Press) pp. 257–72.

Norris, P. (1999b) 'Who Surfs Cafe Europa? Virtual Democracy in the USA and Western Europe', paper presented at the American Political Science Association Annual Meeting, Atlanta, GA, 1–5 September.

Norris, P. (ed.) (1999c) *Critical Citizens: Global Support for Democratic Governance* (Oxford and New York: Oxford University Press).

Norris, P. (2000) *A Virtuous Circle: Political Communication in Postindustrial Societies* (Cambridge and New York: Cambridge University Press).

Norris, P. (2002) *Democratic Phoenix: Reinventing Political Activism* (Cambridge and New York: Cambridge University Press) http://www.pippanorris.com.

Norris, P. (2004) *Electoral Engineering: Voting Rules and Political Behaviour* (Cambridge and New York: Cambridge University Press).

Norris, P., Kern, M. and Just, M. (eds) (2003) *Framing Terrorism: The News Media, the Government and the Public* (London and New York: Routledge).

Norton, A. (1991) 'Western European Local Government in Comparative Perspective', in *Local Government in Europe: Trends and Developments,* ed. R. Batley and G. Stoker (Basingstoke: Macmillan) pp. 21–40.

Norton, P. (1990a) *Legislatures* (Oxford and New York: Oxford University Press).

Norton, P. (1990b) *Parliaments in Western Europe* (London: Frank Cass).

Norton, P. (1997) 'Parliamentary Oversight', in *Developments in British Politics 5,* ed. P. Dunleavy *et al.* (Basingstoke: Macmillan, and New York: St Martin's) pp. 155–76.

Norton, P. (ed.) (1998) *Parliaments and Governments in Western Europe* (London and Portland, OR: Frank Cass).

Norton, P. (2001) *The British Polity,* 4th edn (Harlow and New York: Longman).

Norton, P. and Ahmed, N. (eds) (1999) *Parliaments in Asia* (London and Portland, OR: Frank Cass).

Nousiainen, J. (1994) 'Finland: Ministerial Autonomy, Constitutional Collectivism and Party Oligarchy', in *Cabinet Ministers and Parliamentary Government,* ed. M. Laver and K. Shepsle (Cambridge and New York: Cambridge University Press) pp. 88–105.

Nousiainen, (2001) 'From Semi-Presidentialism to Parliamentary

Government: Political and Constitutional Developments in Finland', *Scandinavian Political Studies* (24) 95–109.

Nugent, N. (2002) *The Government and Politics of the European Union,* 5th edn (Basingstoke and New York: Palgrave Macmillan).

Nurmi, H. and Nurmi, L. (2002) 'The 2000 Presidential Election in Finland', *Electoral Studies* (21) 473–9.

Nye, J. (1990) *Bound to Lead: the Changing Nature of America's Power* (New York: Basic Books).

Nye, J., Zelikow, P. and King, D. (eds) (1997) *Why People Don't Trust Government* (Cambridge, MA: Harvard University Press).

Nye, N. (2002) *The Paradox of American Power: Why the World's Only Superpower Can't Go It Alone* (Oxford and New York: Oxford University Press).

O

O'Brien, D. (1993) *Storm Center: The Supreme Court in American Politics* (New York: Norton).

O'Brien, K. (1990) *Reform Without Liberalization: China's National People's Congress and the Politics of Institutional Change* (Cambridge and New York: Cambridge University Press).

O'Donnell, G. (1973) *Modernization and Bureaucratic Authoritarianism: Studies in South American Politics* (Berkeley, CA: California University Press).

O'Donnell, G. (1994) 'Delegative Democracy', *Journal of Democracy* (5) 55–69.

O'Donnell, G. (1996) 'Delegative Democracy', in *The Global Resurgence of Democracy,* 2nd edn, ed. L. Diamond and M. Plattner (Baltimore, MD and London: Johns Hopkins University Press) pp. 94–110.

O'Donnell, G. and Schmitter, P. (1986a) 'Tentative Conclusions about Uncertain Democracies', in *Transitions from Authoritarian Rule: Prospects for Democracy,* ed. G. O'Donnell, P. Schmitter and L. Whitehead (Baltimore, MD and London: Johns Hopkins University Press) pp. 1–65.

O'Donnell, G. and Schmitter, P. (1986b) *Transitions from Authoritarian Rule: Tentative Conclusions from Uncertain Democracies* (Berkeley and Los Angeles, CA: University of California Press).

O'Donnell, G., Schmitter, P. and Whitehead, L. (eds) (1986) *Transitions from Authoritarian Rule* (Baltimore, MD and London: Johns Hopkins University Press).

O'Sullivan, N. (1986) *Fascism* (London: Dent).

O'Toole, B. and Chapman, R. (1995) 'Parliamentary Accountability', in *Next Steps: Improving Management in Government?,* ed. B. O'Toole and G. Jordan (Aldershot and Brookfield, VT: Dartmouth) pp. 118–41.

Oksenberg, M. (2001) 'The Issue of Sovereignty in the Asian Historical Context', in *Problematic Sovereignty: Contested Rules and Political Possibilities,* ed. S. Krasner (New York and Chichester: Columbia University Press) pp. 83–104.

Olson, D. (1994) *Legislative Institutions: A Comparative View* (New York: M.E. Sharpe).

Olson, M. (1968) *The Logic of Collective Action: Public Goods and the Theory of Groups* (New York: Schocken Books).

Olson, M. (1982) *The Rise and Decline of Nations* (New Haven, CT and London: Yale University Press).

Olson, M. (2000) *Power and Prosperity: Outgrowing Communist and Capitalist Dictatorships* (New York: Basic Books).

Ong, W. (1982) *Orality and Literacy: The Technologizing of the Word* (London and New York: Methuen).

Opello, W. and Rosow, S. (1999) *The Nation-State and Global Order: A Historical Introduction to Contemporary Politics* (Boulder, CO and London: Lynne Rienner).

Osborne, D. and Gaebler, T. (1992) *Reinventing Government: How the Entrepreneurial Spirit Is Transforming the Public Sector* (New York and London: Penguin).

Osiander, A. (2001) 'Sovereignty, International Relations and the Westphalian Myth', *International Organization* (55) 251–89.

Ostrogorski, M. (1902) *Democracy and the Organisation of Political Parties* (London: Macmillan).

Owen, J. (2002) 'The Foreign Imposition of Domestic Institutions' *International Organization* (50) 375–409.

Owen, R. (1993) 'The Practice of Electoral Democracy in the Arab East and North Africa: Some Lessons from Nearly a Century's Experience' in *Rules and Rights in the Middle East,* ed. E. Goldberg *et al.* (Seattle, WA: University of Washington Press) pp. 17–40.

Owen, R. (2002) *State, Power and Politics in the Middle East,* 2nd edn (London and New York: Routledge).

P

Padgett, S. (2000) *Organizing Democracy in Eastern Germany: Interest Groups in Post-Communist Society* (Cambridge and New York: Cambridge University Press).

Page, E. (1992) *Political Authority and Bureaucratic Power: A Comparative Analysis,* 2nd edn (Hemel Hempstead: Harvester Wheatsheaf).

Page, E. and Goldsmith, M. (1987) *Central and Local Government Relations* (London and Thousand Oaks, CA: Sage).

Page, E. and Wright, V. (eds) (1999) *Bureaucratic Elites in Western European States: A Comparative Analysis of Top Officials* (Oxford and New York: Oxford University Press).

Paine, T. [1791/2] (1984 edn) *Rights of Man* (Harmondsworth: Penguin).

Palan R. (2002) 'Tax Havens and the Commercialization of State Sovereignty' *International Organization* (56) 151–76.

Panebianco, A. (1988) *Political Parties: Organization and Power* (Cambridge and New York: Cambridge University Press).

Parkinson, J. (2001) 'Who Knows Best? The Creation of the Citizen-Initiated Referendum in New Zealand', *Government & Opposition* (36) 403–421.

Parry, G., Moyser, G. and Day, N. (1992) *Political Participation and Democracy in Britain* (Cambridge and New York: Cambridge University Press).

Parsons, T. (1967) 'On the Concept of Political Power', in *Sociological Theory and Modern Society,* ed. T. Parsons (New York and London: Free Press) pp. 286–99.

Parsons, W. (1995) *Public Policy: An Introduction to the Theory and Practice of Policy Analysis* (Brookfield, VT and Aldershot: Edward Elgar).

Partridge, H. (1998) *Italian Politics Today* (Manchester: Manchester University Press).

Patterson, S. and Mughan, A. (eds) (1999) *Senates: Bicameralism in the Contemporary World* (Columbus, OH: Ohio State University Press).

Paul, T. (ed.) (2004) *The Nation-State in Question* (Princeton, NJ: Princeton University Press).

Pennings, P., Keman, H. and Kleinnijenhuis, J. (1999) *Doing Research in Political Science: An Introduction to Comparative Methods and Statistics* (Thousand Oaks, CA and London: Sage).

Peregudov, S. (2001) 'The Oligarchical Model of Russian Capitalism', in *Contemporary Russian Politics: A Reader,* ed. A.

Brown (Oxford and New York: Oxford University Press) pp. 259–68.

Peretti T. (2001) *In Defence of a Political Court* (Princeton, NJ: Princeton University Press).

Perlmutter, A. (1981) *Modern Authoritarianism* (New Haven, CT: Yale University Press).

Perlmutter, A. (1997) *Making the World Safe for Democracy: A Century of Wilsonianism and its Totalitarian Challenges* (Chapel Hill, NC: University of North Carolina Press).

Peters, B. Guy (1998) *Comparative Politics: Theory and Methods* (London: Macmillan and New York University Press).

Peters, B. Guy (1999) *Institutional Theory in Political Science: The 'New Institutionalism'* (London and New York: Pinter).

Peters, B. Guy (2000) *The Politics of Bureaucracy*, 5th edn (White Plains, New York: Longman).

Petersson, O. (1989) *Maktens Natverk* (Stockholm: Carlssons).

Petracca, M. (1992) 'The Rediscovery of Interest Group Politics', in *The Politics of Interests: Interest Groups Transformed*, ed. M. Petracca (Boulder, CO and Oxford: Westview) pp. 3–31.

Petro, N. (1995) *The Rebirth of Russian Democracy: An Interpretation of Political Culture* (Cambridge, MA and London: Harvard University Press).

Pharr, S. and Putnam, R. (eds) (2000) *Disaffected Democracies: What's Troubling The Trilateral Countries?* (Princeton, NJ: Princeton University Press).

Phillips, A. (1995) *The Politics of Presence* (Oxford and New York: Oxford University Press).

Pierre, J. and Peters, B. Guy (2000) *Governance, Politics and the State* (Basingstoke: Macmillan and New York: St Martin's Press).

Pierson, C. (1998) *Beyond the Welfare State? The New Political Economy of Welfare*, 2nd edn (University Park: Pennsylvania State University Press and Cambridge: Polity).

Pierson, C. (ed.) (2000) *The New Politics of the Welfare State* (Oxford and New York: Oxford University Press).

Pinkney, R. (1990) *Right-Wing Military Government* (London: Pinter).

Pion-Berlin, D. (ed.) (2001) *Civil–Military Relations in Latin America* (Chapel Hill, NL: University of North Carolina Press).

Plender, J. (2003) 'Wheezing Through the Fiscal Fog', *Financial Times*, 4 April, p. 17.

Poggi, G. (1978) *The Development of the Modern State: A Sociological Introduction* (London: Hutchinson).

Poggi, G. (1990) *The State: Its Nature, Development and Prospects* (Cambridge and Cambridge, MA: Polity).

Poggi, G. (2001) *Forms of Power* (Oxford and Cambridge, MA: Blackwell).

Polidano, C. (1998) 'Why Bureaucrats Can't Always Do What Ministers Want: Multiple Accountabilities in Westminster Democracies', *Public Policy and Administration* (13) 35–50.

Pomper, G. *et al.* (2001) *The Election of 2000: Reports and Interpretations* (Chatham, NJ: Chatham House).

Power, T. (1998) 'The Pen Is Mightier than the Congress: Presidential Decree Power in Brazil' in *Executive Decree Authority*, ed. J. Carey and M. Shugart (Cambridge and New York: Cambridge University Press) pp. 197–232.

Pressman, J. and Wildavsky, A. (1973) *Implementation* (Berkeley, CA: University of California Press).

Pridham, G. (1990) 'Political Parties and Consolidation in Southern Europe: Empirical and Theoretical Perspectives', in *Parliament and Democratic Consolidation in Southern Europe*, ed. U. Liebert and M. Cotta (London: Pinter) pp. 225–48.

Pridham, G. (ed.) (1995) *Transitions to Democracy* (Brookfield, VT and Aldershot: Dartmouth).

Prillaman, W. (2000) *The Judiciary and Democratic Decay in Latin America: Declining Confidence in the Rule of Law* (Westport, CT: Praeger).

Prosser, T. and Moran, M. (1994) 'Privatization and Regulatory Change: The Case of Great Britain', in *Privatization and Regulatory Change in Europe*, ed. M. Moran and T. Prosser (Buckingham and Bristol, PA: Open University Press) pp. 35–49.

Prunier, G. (1997) *The Rwanda Crisis: History of a Genocide* (London: Hurst).

Przeworski, A. (1991) *Democracy and the Market: Political and Economic Reforms in Eastern Europe and Latin America* (Cambridge and New York: Cambridge University Press).

Przeworski, A. (1995) 'The Role of Theory in Comparative Politics', *World Politics* (48) 16–21.

Przeworski, A. and Teune, H. (1970) *The Logic of Comparative Inquiry* (New York: Wiley).

Przeworski, A. *et al.* (2000) *Democracy and Development* (Cambridge and New York: Cambridge University Press).

Putnam, R. (1976) *The Comparative Study of Political Elites* (Englewood Cliffs, NJ: Prentice Hall).

Putnam, R. (1993) *Making Democracy Work: Civic Traditions in Modern Italy* (Princeton, NJ: Princeton University Press).

Putnam, R. (1995) 'Bowling Alone: America's Declining Social Capital', *Journal of Democracy* (6) 65–78.

Putnam, R. (2000) *Bowling Alone: The Collapse and Revival of American Community* (New York: Simon & Schuster).

Putnam, R. (2001) 'Civic Engagement in Contemporary America', *Government and Opposition* (30) 135–56.

Putnam, R. (ed.) (2002) *Democracies in Flux: The Evolution of Social Capital in Contemporary Society* (Oxford and New York: Oxford University Press).

Putnam, R., Pharr, S. and Dalton, R. (2000) 'What's Troubling the Trilateral Countries?', in *Disaffected Democracies: What's Troubling the Trilateral Countries?* ed. S. Pharr and R. Putnam (Princeton, NJ: Princeton University Press) pp. 3–30.

Putzel, J. (1997) 'Why Has Democratization Been a Weaker Impulse in Indonesia and Malaysia than in the Philippines?', in *Democratization*, ed. D. Potter *et al.* (Cambridge: Polity) pp. 240–68.

Pye, L. (1985) *Asian Power and Politics: The Cultural Dimensions of Authority* (Cambridge, MA: Harvard University Press).

Pye, L. (1995) 'Political Culture', in *The Encyclopaedia of Democracy*, ed. S. Lipset (London and New York: Routledge) pp. 965–9.

Q

Qualter, T. (1991) 'Public Opinion', in *The Blackwell Encyclopaedia of Political Science*, ed. V. Bogdanor (Oxford and Cambridge, MA: Blackwell) p. 511.

R

Raadschelders, J. and Rutgers, M. (1996) 'The Evolution of Civil Service Systems', in *Civil Service Systems in Comparative Perspective*, ed. H. Bekke, J. Perry and T. Toonen (Bloomington, IN: Indiana University Press) pp. 67–99.

Ragin, C. (1994a) 'Introduction to Qualitative Comparative Analysis', in *The Comparative Political Economy of the Welfare State*, ed. T. Janoski and A. Hicks (New York and Cambridge: Cambridge University Press) pp. 299–319.

Ragin, C. (1994b) *Constructing Social Research* (Thousand Oaks, CA and London: Sage).

Ragin, C., Berg-Schlosser, D. and de Meur, G. (1996) 'Political Methodology: Qualitative Methods', in *A New Handbook of Political Science*, ed. R. Goodin and H. Klingemann (Oxford and New York: Oxford University Press) pp. 749–68.

Ramseyer, J. and Rasmusen, E. (2001) 'Why Are Japanese Judges so Conservative in Politically Charged Cases?', *American Political Science Review* (95) 331–44.

Ranney, A. (2004) 'Politics in the United States', in *Comparative Politics Today: A World View*, 8th ed., ed. G. Almond *et al.* (New York and London: Pearson Longman) pp. 742–86.

Reed, S. and Thies, M. (2002) 'The Causes of Electoral Reform in Japan', in *Mixed-Member Electoral Systems: The Best of Both Worlds*, ed. M. Shugart and M. Wattenberg (Oxford and New York: Oxford University Press) pp. 152–172.

Remington, T. (2004) 'Politics in Russia', in *Comparative Politics Today: A World View*, 8th edn, ed. G. Almond *et al.* (New York and London: Pearson Longman) pp. 366–417.

Remmer, K. (1989) *Military Rule in Latin America* (Boston, MA: Unwin Hyman).

Rhodes, R. (1994) 'State-building Without a Bureaucracy: The Case of the United Kingdom', *in Developing Democracy: Essays in Honour of J. F. P. Blondel*, ed. I. Budge and D. McKay (Thousand Oaks, CA and London: Sage) pp. 165–88.

Rhodes, R. (1995) 'The Institutional Approach', in *Theory and Methods in Political Science*, ed. D. Marsh and G. Stoker (Basingstoke: Macmillan) pp. 42–57.

Rhodes, R. (1996) 'The New Governance: Governing without Government', *Political Studies* (44) 652–67.

Rich, R. (2001) 'Bringing Democracy into International Law', *Journal of Democracy* (12) 20–34.

Ridley, F. (1975) *The Study of Government: Political Science and Administration* (London: Allen & Unwin).

Riesman, D. (1950) *The Lonely Crowd* (New Haven, CT: Yale University Press).

Riker, W. (1962) *The Theory of Political Coalitions* (New Haven, CT and London: Yale University Press).

Riker, W. (1975) 'Federalism', in *The Handbook of Political Science*, Vol. 5, ed. F. Greenstein and N. Polsby (Reading, MA: Addison-Wesley) pp. 93–172.

Riker, W. (1996) 'European Federalism: The Lessons of Past Experience', in *Federalizing Europe? The Costs, Benefits and Preconditions of Federal Political Systems*, ed. J. Hesse and V. Wright (Oxford and New York: Oxford University Press) pp. 9–24.

Ripley, R. and Franklin, G. (1991) *Congress, the Bureaucracy and Public Policy*, 5th edn (Homewood IL: The Dorsey Press).

Roberts, G. (2002) 'The Politics of Legislative Membership in the Federal Republic of Germany', *Government & Opposition* (37) 231–49.

Robinson, M. and White, G. (eds) (1998) *The Democratic Developmental State: Political and Institutional Design* (Oxford and New York: Oxford University Press).

Rogers, E. (1971) *Communication of Innovation: A Cross-cultural Approach* (New York: Free Press).

Rokkan, S. (1970) *Citizens, Elections, Parties* (New York: McKay).

Rose, R. (1989) *Politics in England: Change and Persistence* (Basingstoke: Macmillan).

Rose, R. (1991) 'Comparing Forms of Comparative Analysis', *Political Studies* (39) 446–62.

Rose, R. (2000) *The Post-Modern President*, 2nd edn (Chatham, NJ: Chatham House).

Rose, R. (2001) *The Prime Minister in a Shrinking World* (Cambridge: Polity).

Rose, R. (2004) *Learning Lessons in Comparative Public Policy* (London and New York: Routledge).

Rose, R. and Munro, N. (2002) *Elections Without Order: Russia's Challenge to Vladimir Putin* (Cambridge and New York: Cambridge University Press).

Rose, R. and Shin, D. (2001) 'Democratization Backwards: The Problem of Third-Wave Democracies', in *British Journal of Political Science* (31) 331–54.

Rosenau, J. (1992) 'Governance, Order and Change in World Politics', in *Governance without Government: Order and Change in World Politics*, ed. J. Rosenau and E.-O. Czempiel (Cambridge and New York: Cambridge University Press) pp. 3–6.

Rosenbluth, F. and Thies, M. (2000) 'Politics in Japan', in *Comparative Politics Today: A World View*, 7th edn, ed. G. Almond *et al.* (New York: Longman) pp. 327–72.

Rothstein, B. (2002) 'Sweden: Social Capital in the Social Democratic State', in *Democracies in Flux: The Evolution of Social Capital in Contemporary Society*, ed. R. Putnam (Oxford and New York: Oxford University Press) pp. 289–332.

Rousseau, D. (1994) 'The Constitutional Judge: Master or Slave of the Constitution?', in *Constitutionalism, Identity, Difference and Legitimacy: Theoretical Perspectives*, ed. M. Rosenfeld (Durham, NC and London: Duke University Press) pp. 261–83.

Roy, O. (1994) *The Failure of Political Islam* (London: I.B. Taurus).

Rudd, C. and Hayward, J. (2001) 'Coverage of Post-war Election Campaigns: The *Otago Daily Times*', paper presented at the New Zealand Political Studies Conference, Massey University, December 2001.

Rueschmeyer, D., Rueschmeyer, M. and Wittrock, B. (eds) (1998) *Participation and Democracy: Comparisons and Interpretations* (Armonk, New York and London: M.E. Sharpe).

Rummel, R. (1997) *Death by Government* (New Brunswick, NJ and London: Transaction Books).

Russell, M. (2000a) *Reforming the House of Lords: Lessons from Overseas* (Oxford and New York: Oxford University Press).

Russell, M. (2000b) 'A "More Democratic and Representative" Upper House? Some International Comparisons', *Representation* (37) 131–8.

Russell, M. (2001) 'What Are Second Chambers For?', *Parliamentary Affairs* (54) 442–58.

S

Saalfeld, T. (2000) 'Germany: Stable Parties, Chancellor Democracy and the Art of Informal Settlement', in *Coalition Governments in Western Europe*, ed. W. Müller and K. Strøm (Oxford and New York: Oxford University Press) pp. 32–85.

Sabatier, P. (1999) *Theories of the Policy Process* (Boulder, CO: Westview).

Sabatier, P. and Jenkins-Smith, H. (1993) *Policy Change and Learning: An Advocacy Coalition Approach* (Boulder, CO: Westview).

Saich, A. (2004) *Governance and Politics of China*, 2nd edn (Basingstoke and New York: Palgrave).

Saikal, A. (2003) *Islam and the West: Conflict or Cooperation?* (Basingstoke and New York: Palgrave Macmillan).

Sait, E. (1938) *Political Institutions: A Preface* (New York: Appleton-Century).

Sakwa, R. (2000) 'Russia's Permanent Uninterrupted Elections of 1999–2000', *Journal of Communist and Transition Studies*, (16) 85–112.

Sandbrook R. (1985) *The politics of Africa's Economic Stagnation* (Cambrige and New York: Cambridge University Press).

Sanderson, I. (2002) 'Evaluation, Policy Learning and Evidence-Based Policy Making', *Public Administration* (80) 1–22.

Sanderson, J. (1961) 'The National Smoke Abatement Society and the Clean Air Act (1956)', *Political Studies* (9) 236–53.

Sartori, G. (1976) *Parties and Party Systems: A Framework for Analysis* (Cambridge and New York: Cambridge University Press).

Sartori, G. (1993) 'Totalitarianism: Model Mania and Learning from Error', *Journal of Theoretical Politics* (5) 5–22.

Sartori, G. (1994) *Comparative Constitutional Engineering: An Inquiry into Structures, Incentives and Outcomes* (Basingstoke: Macmillan).

Sassen, S. (ed.) (2002) *Global Networks, Linked Cities* (London and New York: Routledge).

Scarrow, H. (1969) *Comparative Political Analysis* (New York: Harper & Row).

Scarrow, S. (2002a) 'Party Decline in the Parties State? The Changing Environment of German Politics', in *Political Parties in Advanced Industrial Democracies*, ed. P. Webb, D. Farrell and I. Holliday (Oxford and New York: Oxford University Press) pp. 77–106.

Scarrow. S. (2002b) 'Germany: The Mixed-Member System as a Political Compromise', in *Mixed-Member Electoral Systems: The Best of Both Worlds*, ed. M. Shugart and M. Wattenberg (Oxford and New York: Oxford University Press) pp. 55–69.

Schabas, W. (2001) *An Introduction to the International Criminal Court* (Cambridge and New York: Cambridge University Press).

Schain, M. (2004) 'Politics in France', in *Comparative Politics Today: A World View*, 8th edn, ed. G. Almond *et al.* (New York and London: Pearson Longman) pp. 206–59.

Schaller, T. and Williams, T. (2003) 'The Contemporary Presidency: Postpresidential Influence in the Postmodern Era', *Presidential Studies Quarterly* (33) 188–200.

Scharpf, F. (1988) 'The Joint Decision Trap: Lessons From German Federalism and European Integration', *Public Administration* (66) 239–78.

Schattschneider, E. (1942) *Party Government* (New York: Farrar & Reinhart).

Schatzberg, M. (2001) *Political Legitimacy in Middle Africa: Father, Family, Food* (Bloomington, IN: Indiana University Press).

Schirazi, A. (1998) *The Constitution of Iran: Politics and the State in the Islamic Republic* (London: L.-B. Taurus).

Schmidt, M. (2003) *Political Institutions in the Federal Republic of Germany* (Oxford and New York: Oxford University Press).

Schmieding, H. (1993) *Europe after Maastricht* (London: Institute of Economic Affairs).

Schmieding, H. (1998) 'From Plan to Market: On the Nature of the Transformation Crisis', *Weltwirtschaftliches Archiv* (129) 216–53.

Schmitter, P. and Lehmbruch, G. (eds) (1979) *Trends Towards Corporatist Intermediation* (Thousand Oaks, CA and London: Sage).

Schöpflin, G. and Hosking, G. (eds) (1997) *Myths and Nationhood* (London: Hurst).

Schubert, G. (1972) 'Judicial Process and Behaviour During the Sixties', *Political Science* (5) 6–15.

Schumpeter, J. (1943) *Capitalism, Socialism and Democracy* (London: Allen & Unwin).

Scott, S. (1997) 'Australia and International Institutions', in *New Developments in Australian Politics*, ed. B. Galligan, I.

McAllister and J. Ravenhill (South Melbourne: Macmillan) pp. 271–90.

Scully, R. (2003) 'The European Parliament', in *European Union Politics*, ed. M. Cini (Oxford and New York: Oxford University Press) pp. 166–78.

Searing, D. (1994) *Westminster's World: Understanding Political Roles* (Cambridge, MA and London: Harvard University Press).

Selden, M. (1995) *China in Revolution: The Yenan Way Revisited* (Armonk, New York: M.E. Sharpe).

Senelle, R. (1996) 'The Reform of the Belgian State', in *Federalizing Europe? The Costs, Benefits and Preconditions of Federal Political Systems*, ed. J. Hesse and V. Wright (Oxford and New York: Oxford University Press) pp. 266–324.

Shanks, C., Jackobson, H. and Kaplan, J. (1996) 'Inertia and Change in the Constellation of Intergovernmental Organizations', *International Organization* (50) 593–627.

Shapiro, M. [1964] (2002 edn) 'Political Jurisprudence', in *On Law, Politics and Judicialization*, ed. M. Shapiro and A. Stone Sweet (Oxford and New York: Oxford Univeristy Press) pp. 19–54.

Shapiro, M. (1990) 'The Supreme Court from Early Burger to Early Rehnquist' in *The New American Political System,* 2nd edn, ed. A. King (Washington: American Enterprise Institute) pp. 47–86.

Shapiro, M. and Stone, A. (1994) 'The New Constitutional Politics of Europe', *Comparative Political Studies* (26) 397–420.

Shapiro, M. and Stone Sweet, A. (2002) *On Law, Politics and Judicialization* (Oxford and New York: Oxford University Press).

Sharlet, R. (1997) 'The Progress of Human Rights', in *Developments in Russian Politics 4*, ed. S. White, A. Pravda and Z. Gitelman (Basingstoke: Macmillan) pp. 129–48.

Shively, W. (2002) *Power and Choice: An Introduction to Political Science,* 8th edn (New York and London: McGraw-Hill).

Shugart, M. and Carey, J. (1992) *Presidents and Assemblies: Constitutional Design and Electoral Dynamics* (Cambridge and New York: Cambridge University Press).

Shugart, M. and Wattenberg, M. (eds) (2000) *Mixed-Member Electoral Systems: The Best of Both Worlds* (Oxford and New York: Oxford University Press).

Silva, P. (ed.) (2001) *The Soldier and the State in South America* (London: Palgrave).

Simeon, R. and Cameron, D. (2002) 'Intergovernmental Relations and Democracy: An Oxymoron If Ever There Was One', in *Canadian Federalism: Performance, Effectiveness and Legitimacy*, ed. H. Bakvis and G. Skogstad (Don Mills, Ontario and Oxford: Oxford University Press) pp. 278–95.

Simon, H. (1983) *Reason in Human Affairs* (Oxford and Cambridge, MA: Blackwell).

Sjolin, M. (1993) *Coalition Politics and Parliamentary Power* (Lund: Lund University Press).

Skinner, Q. (1978) *The Foundations of Modern Political Thought,* Vol. 1 (Cambridge and New York: Cambridge University Press).

Sklair, L. (2003) *The Transnational Capitalist Class* (Oxford and Cambridge, MA: Blackwell).

Skocpol, T. (1979) *States and Social Revolutions: A Comparative Analysis of France, Russia and China* (Cambridge and New York: Cambridge University Press).

Slaughter, A. (1997) 'The Real New World Order', *Foreign Affairs* (76) pp. 183–94.

Smith, A. (1998) *Nationalism and Modernism: A Critical Survey of*

Recent Theories of Nations and Nationalism (London and New York: Routledge).

Smith, B. (1996) *Understanding Third World Politics* (London: Macmillan).

Smith, G. (1989) *Politics in Western Europe*, 5th edn (Aldershot: Gower).

Smith, G. (1995) *Federalism: The Multiethnic Challenge* (Harlow and New York: Longman).

Smith, M. (1995) *Pressure Politics* (Manchester: Baseline Books).

Smooha, S. (2002) 'The Model of Ethnic Democracy', *Nations and Nationalism* (8) 475–503.

Soley, L. (1998) *Free Radio: Electronic Civil Disobedience* (Boulder, CO and Oxford: Westview).

Solomon, P. and Foglesong, T. (2000) *Courts and Transition in Russia: The Challenge of Judicial Reform* (Boulder, CO and Oxford: Westview).

Somit, A. (1994) '. . . And Where We Came Out', in *The Victorious Incumbent: A Threat to Democracy?*, ed. A. Somit *et al.* (Aldershot and Brookfield, VT: Dartmouth) pp. 11–18.

Sørensen, G. (1997a) 'An Analysis of Contemporary Statehood: Consequences for Conflict and Cooperation', *Review of International Studies* (23) 253–70.

Sørensen, G. (1997b) *Democracy and Democratization*, 2nd edn (Boulder, CO and Oxford: Westview).

Sørensen, G. (2004) *The Transformation of the State: Beyond the Myth of Retreat* (Basingstoke and New York: Palgrave Macmillan).

Spruyt, H. (1994) *The Sovereign State and Its Competitors* (Princeton, NJ: Princeton University Press).

Stainov, P. (1993) *Durzhava i Chinovnichestvo* (Sofia: Slavianska Beseda).

Steen, A. (1995) *Change of Regime and Political Recruitment: The Parliamentary Elites in the Baltic States* (Bordeaux: ECPR Workshop on Political Recruitment).

Steinmo, S. (2003) 'The Evolution of Policy Ideas: Tax Policy in the Twentieth Century', *British Journal of Politics and International Relations* (5) 206–36.

Stepan, A. (2001) *Arguing Comparative Politics* (Oxford and New York: Oxford University Press).

Stevens, A. (2003) *Government and Politics of France* 3rd edn (Basingstoke and New York: Palgrave Macmillan).

Stoliarov, M. (2002) *Federalism and the Dictatorship of Power in Russia* (London and New York: Routledge).

Stone, B. (1995) 'Administrative Accountability in the "Westminster" Democracies: Towards a New Conceptual Framework', *Governance* (8) 505–26.

Stone, D. (2001) *Policy Paradox: The Art of Political Decision Making*, rev. edn (New York: Norton).

Stone Sweet, A. (2000) *Governing with Judges: Constitutional Politics in Europe* (Oxford and New York: Oxford University Press).

Stone Sweet, A. (2002) 'Constitutional Courts and Parliamentary Democracy', *West European Politics* (25) 77–110.

Stouffer, S. (1966) *Communism, Conformity and Civil Liberties* (New York: Wiley).

Strange, S. (1994) *States and Markets* (London and New York: Pinter).

Strayer, J. (1965) *Feudalism* (Princeton, NJ: Princeton University Press).

Street, J. (2001) *Mass Media, Politics and Democracy* (Basingstoke and New York: Palgrave).

Strom, K. (1990) *Minority Government and Majority Rule* (Cambridge and New York: Cambridge University Press).

Stubbs, R. and Underhill, R. (eds) (1999) *Political Economy and the Changing Global Order*, 2nd edn (Basingstoke: Macmillan).

Sundberg, J. (2002) 'The Scandinavian Party Model at the Crossroads', in *Political Parties in Advanced Industrial Democracies*, ed. P. Webb, D. Farrell and I. Holliday (Oxford and New York: Oxford University Press) pp. 181–216.

Sunstein, C. (2001) *Republic.com* (Princeton, NJ: Princeton University Press)

Sweating, D. (2003) 'How Strong Is the Mayor of London?', *Policy and Politics* (31) 465–78

T

Taagepera, R. and Recchia, S. (2002) 'The Size of Second Chambers and European Assemblies', *European Journal of Political Research* (41) 165–85.

Tálos, E. and Kittel B. (2002) }Austria in the 1990s: The Routine of Social Partnership in Question?' in *Policy Concertation and Social Partnership: Lessons for the 21st Century*, ed. S. Berger and H. Compston (New York and Oxford: Berghahn) pp. 35–50.

Taras, R. (2003) 'Executive Leadership: Presidents and Governments', in *Developments in Central and East European Politics 3*, ed. S. White S., J. Batt and P. Lewis (Basingstoke: Palgrave Macmillan) pp. 115–31.

Tarrow, S. (1998) *Power in Movement: Social Movements and Contentious Politics*, 2nd edn (Cambridge and New York: Cambridge University Press).

Tate, C. and Vallinder, T. (eds) (1995) *The Global Expansion of Judicial Power* (New York and London: New York University Press).

Taylor, C. (1993) *Reconciling the Solitudes: Essays on Canadian Federalism and Nationalism* (Montreal and Kingston: McGill-Queen's University Press).

Telhami, S. (2001) 'The Road to Palestinian Sovereignty: Problematic Structures or Conventional Obstacles?', in *Problematic Sovereignty: Contested Rules and Political Possibilities*, ed. S. Krasner (New York and Chichester: Columbia University Press) pp. 301–22.

Tetlock, P. and Belkin, A. (1996) *Counterfactual Thought Experiments in World Politics* (Princeton, NJ and London: Princeton University Press).

Teune, H. (1995a) 'Preface', *Annals of the American Academy of Political and Social Sciences* (540) 8–10.

Teune, H. (1995b) 'Local Government and Democratic Political Development', *Annals of the American Academy of Political and Social Sciences* (540) 11–23.

Thatcher M. (1988) *Speech to the College of Europe* (London: Margaret Thatcher Foundation). http://www.margaret thatcher.org.

Thatcher, M. and Stone Sweet, A. (2002) 'Theory and Practice of Delegation to Non-Majoritarian Institutions', *West European Politics* (25) 1–22.

Thomas, B. (2003) 'What the Poor Watch on TV', *Prospect* (January) 46–51.

Thomas, C. (1997) 'Globalization and the South', in *Globalization and the South*, ed. C. Thomas and P. Wilkin (Basingstoke: Macmillan) pp. 1–17.

Thomas, C. (ed.) (2001) *Political Parties and Interest Groups: Shaping Democratic Goverance* (Boulder CO and London: Lynne Rienner).

Thompson M. (2001) 'Whatever Happened to "Asian Values"?', *Journal of Democracy* (12) 154–65.

Tilly, C. (1975) 'Reflections on the History of European State-Making', in *The Formation of National States in Western Europe*, ed. C. Tilly (Princeton, NJ: Princeton University Press) pp. 3–83.

Tilly, C. (1997) 'Means and Ends of Comparison in Macrosociology', *Comparative Social Research* (16) 43–53.

Tismaneanu, V. (ed.) (1995) *Political Culture and Civil Society in Russia and the New States of Eurasia* (New York: M.E. Sharpe).

Tivey, L. (ed.) (1981) *The Nation-State: The Formation of Modern Politics* (London: Martin Robertson).

Tracey, M. (1998) *The Decline and Fall of Public Service Broadcasting* (New York and Oxford: Oxford University Press).

Trotsky, L. [1932/3] (1965 edn) *The History of the Russian Revolution*, Vol. 1, trans. M. Eastman (London: Gollancz) p. 216.

Tsebelis, G. and Garrett, G. (1997) 'Agenda Setting, Vetoes and the European Union's Co-Decision Procedure', *Journal of Legislative Studies* (3) 74–92.

Tsebelis, G. and Money, J. (1997) *Bicameralism* (Cambridge and New York: Cambridge University Press).

Turner, F. (1995) 'Reassessing Political Culture', in *Latin America in Comparative Perspective: New Approaches to Methods and Analysis*, ed. P. Smith (Boulder, CO and Oxford: Westview) pp. 195–224.

Turner, M. and Hulme, D. (1997) *Governance, Administration and Development* (London: Macmillan).

U

Ulam, A. (1974) *The Russian Political System* (New York: Random House).

Uleri, P. (2002) 'On Referendum Voting in Italy: Yes, No or Non-Vote? How Italian Parties Learned to Control Referendums', *European Journal of Political Research* (41) 863–883.

Umbach, M. (ed.) (2002) *German Federalism: Past, Present, Future* (Basingstoke: Macmillan).

UNHCR (United nations High Commission for Human Rights) (1966) *United Nations Covenant on Civil and Political Rights* (http://www.unhcr.ch).

US Congress (2002) *Report of the Joint Enquiry into the Terrorist Attacks of September 11, 2001* (Washington, DC: US Congress) http://usinfo.state.gov/topical/pol/terror.

V

van Biezen, I. (2003) *Political Parties in New Democracies: Party Organization in Southern and East–Central Europe* (Basingstoke and New York: Palgrave Macmillan).

van Creveld, M. (1999) *The Rise and Decline of the State* (Cambridge and New York: Cambridge University Press).

van der Meer, F., and Roborgh, R. (1996) 'Civil Servants and Representativeness', in *Civil Service Systems in Comparative Perspective*, ed. H. Bekke, J. Perry and T. Toonen (Bloomington, IN: Indiana University Press) pp. 119–33.

van Deth, J. (2000) 'Interesting but Irrelevant: Social Capital and the Salience of Politics in Western Europe', *European Journal of Political Research* (37) 115–147.

van Eijk, R. (1997) 'The United Nations and the Reconstruction of Collapsed States', *African Journal of International and Comparative Law* (9) 543–72.

Vanhanen, T. (1997) *Prospects of Democracy: A Study of 172 Countries* (London and New York: Routledge).

Vatikiotis, M. (1995) *Political Change in Southeast Asia: Trimming the Banyan Tree* (London and New York: Routledge).

Verba, S. (1987) *Elites and the Idea of Equality: A Comparison of Japan, Sweden and the United States* (Cambridge, MA and London: Harvard University Press).

Verba, S., Scholzman, K. and Brady, H. (1995) *Voice and Equality: Civic Voluntarism in American Politics* (Cambridge, MA and London: Harvard University Press).

Vereshchetin, V. (1996) 'New Constitutions and the Old Problem of Relationship between International Law and National Law', *European Journal of International Law* (7) 29–41.

Verheijen, T. (1998) 'NPM Reforms and Other Western Reform Strategies', in *Innovations in Public Management: Perspectives from East and West Europe*, ed. T. Verheijen and D. Coombes (Cheltenham and Northampton, MA: Edward Elgar) pp. 407–17.

Verheijen, T. and Coombes, D. (eds) (1998) *Innovations in Public Management: Perspectives from East and West Europe* (Cheltenham and Northampton, MA: Edward Elgar).

von Beyme, K. (2003) 'Constitutional Engineering in Central and Eastern Europe', in *Developments in Central and East European Politics 3*, ed. S. White, J. Batt and P. Lewis (Basingstoke and New York: Palgrave Macmillan) pp. 190–210.

W

Wachendorfer-Schmidt, U. (ed.) (2000) *Federalism and Political Performance* (London and New York: Routledge).

Wahlke, J. *et al.* (1962) *The Legislative System* (New York: Wiley).

Walpole, S. (1881) *The Electorate and the Legislature* (London: Macmillan).

Wang, X. (2002) 'The Postcommunist Personality: The Spectre of China's Market Reforms', *The China Journal* (47) 1–17.

Ware, A. (2002) *The Direct Primary in the United States: Party Institutionalization and Transformation in the American North* (Cambridge and New York: Cambridge University Press).

Warwick, P. (1994) *Government Survival in Parliamentary Democracies* (Cambridge and New York: Cambridge University Press).

Waters, M. (2000) *Globalization*, 2nd edn (London and New York: Routledge).

Watt, E. (1982) *Authority* (London: Croom Helm).

Wattenberg, M. (2000) 'The Decline of Party Mobilization', in *Parties Without Partisans*, ed. R. Dalton and M. Wattenberg (Oxford and New York: Oxford University Press) pp. 64–76.

Weaver, R. and Rockman, B. (eds) (1993) *Do Institutions Matter? Government Capabilities in the United States and Abroad* (Washington: The Brookings Institution).

Webb, P., Farrell, D. and Holliday, I. (eds) (2002) *Political Parties in Advanced Industrial Democracies* (Oxford and New York: Oxford University Press).

Weber, M. [1923] (1946 edn) 'The Social Psychology of the World Religions' in *From Max Weber: Essays in Sociology*, ed. and trans. H. Gerth and C. Wright Mills (Oxford and New York: Oxford University Press) pp. 267–301.

Weber, M. [1922] (1957 edn) *The Theory of Economic and Social Organization* (Berkeley, CA: University of California Press).

Weber, M. [1918] (1990 edn) 'The Advent of Plebiscitarian Democracy', in *The West European Party System*, ed. P. Mair (Oxford and New York: Oxford University Press) pp. 31–7. First pub. 1918.

Weiler, J. (1994) 'A Quiet Revolution: The European Court of Justice and its Interlocutors', *Comparative Political Studies* (26) 510–34.

Weiss, T. and Gordenker, C. (1996) 'Pluralizing Global Governance', in *Nongovernmental Organizations, the United Nations and Global Governance*, ed. T. Weiss and C. Gordenker (Boulder, CO and London: Lynne Rienner) pp. 17–50.

Weissberg, R. (1998) *Political Tolerance: Balancing Community and Diversity* (Thousand Oaks, CA and London: Sage).

Weissberg, R. (2002) *Polling, Policy and Public Opinion: The Case Against Heeding 'The Voice of the People'* (London and New York: Palgrave Macmillan).

Werbner, R. and Ranger, T. (eds) (1996) *Postcolonial Identities in Africa* (London and Atlantic Highlands, NJ: Zed Books).

Wheare, K. (1951) *Modern Constitutions* (London and New York: Oxford University Press).

Wheare, K. (1963) *Federal Government*, 4th edn (Oxford and New York: Oxford University Press).

Wheare, K. (1968) *Legislatures* (Oxford: Oxford University Press).

Wheeler, N. (2002) *Saving Strangers: Humanitarian Intervention in International Society* (Oxford and New York: Oxford University Press).

White, S., Batt, J. and Lewis, P. (eds) (2003) *Developments in Central and East European Politics 3* (Basingstoke: Palgrave Macmillan).

Whittaker, D. (2004) *Terrorists and Terrorism in the Contemporary World* (London and New York: Routledge).

Wiarda, H. (ed.) (2004) *Comparative Politics: Critical Concepts in Political Science*, six vols. (London and New York: Routledge).

Wilensky, H. (1984) *The Welfare State and Equality* (Berkeley, CA: University of California Press).

Williams, C. (1995) 'A Requiem for Canada?', in *Federalism: The Multiethnic Challenge*, ed. G. Smith (Harlow: Longman) pp. 31–72.

Williams, R. (1962) *Communications* (Harmondsworth and New York: Penguin).

Williams, R. (1989) *Television: Technology and Cultural Form*, 2nd edn (London and New York: Routledge).

Wilson, G. (2003) *Business and Politics: A Comparative Introduction*, 3rd edn (Basingstoke: Macmillan).

Wilson, G. (1990b) *Interest Groups* (Oxford and Cambridge, MA: Blackwell).

Wilson, J. (1989) *Bureaucracy: What Government Agencies Do and How They Do It* (New York: Basic Books).

Wilson, J. and Dilulio, J. (2004) *American Government: Institutions and Policies*, 9th edn (Boston, MA: Houghton Mifflin).

Wilson, W. (1885) *Congressional Government* (Boston, MA: Houghton Mifflin).

Wiseman, J. (1985) 'Introduction' in *Democracy and Political Change in Sub-Saharan Africa*, ed. J. Wiseman (London and New York: Routledge) pp. 1–10.

Wiseman, J. (1996) *The New Struggle for Democracy in Africa* (Aldershot and Brookfield, VT: Avebury).

Wolinetz, S. (ed.) (1997) *Political Parties* (Aldershot and Brookfield, VT: Ashgate).

Wong, D. (2002) 'Ready for Debate and Democracy' *Financial Times Survey of Singapore*, April 12, p. 7.

World Bank (1997) *World Development Report: The State in a Changing World* (Oxford and New York: Oxford University Press).

Wright, V. (ed.) (1994) *Privatization in Western Europe: Pressures, Problems and Paradoxes* (London and New York: Pinter).

Wright, V. (1997) 'La Fin du Dirigisme?', *Modern and Contemporary France* (5) 151–5.

Wright, V., Guy Peters, B. and Rhodes, R. (eds) (2000) *Administering the Summit: Administration of the Core Executive in Developed Countries* (Basingstoke: Macmillan).

Wuthnow, R. (2002) 'The United States: Bridging the Privileged and the Marginalized?', in *Democracies in Flux: The Evolution of Social Capital in Contemporary Society*, ed. R. Putnam (Oxford and New York: Oxford University Press) pp. 59–102.

X, Y, Z

Xia, M. (1999) 'China's National People's Congress: Institutional Transformation in the Process of Regime Transition (1978–98)', in *Parliaments in Asia*, ed. P. Norton and N. Ahmed (London and Portland, OR: Frank Cass) pp. 103–30.

Yayla, A. (2002) 'Islam or Democracy', in *Islam, Civil Society and Market Economy*, ed. A. Yayla (Ankara: Liberte) pp. 1–18.

Yin, R. (2002) *Case Study Research: Design and Methods*, 3rd edn (Thousand Oaks, CA and London: Sage).

Young, L. and Cross, W. (2002) 'The Rise of Plebiscitary Democracy in Canadian Political Parties', *Party Politics* (8) 673–99.

Zaslavsky, K. and Brym, J. (1978) 'The Functions of Elections in the USSR', *Soviet Studies* (30) 362–71.

Zassoursky, I. (2003) *Media and Power in Post-Soviet Russia* (armonk, NY: M.E. Sharpe).

Zilliacus, K. (2001) '"New Politics" in Finland: The Greens and the Left Wing in the 1990s', *West European Politics* (24) 27–54.

Zirakzadeh, C. (1997) *Social Movements in Politics: A Comparative Study* (London and New York: Longman).

Index